ELVIS

DAY BY DAY

Also by Peter Guralnick

CARELESS LOVE:
The Unmaking of Elvis Presley

LAST TRAIN TO MEMPHIS:
The Rise of Elvis Presley

SEARCHING FOR ROBERT JOHNSON

SWEET SOUL MUSIC:
Rhythm and Blues and the Southern Dream of Freedom

NIGHTHAWK BLUES

LOST HIGHWAY:
Journeys and Arrivals of American Musicians

FEEL LIKE GOING HOME:
Portraits in Blues and Rock 'n' Roll

Also by Ernst Jorgensen

ELVIS PRESLEY:
A Life in Music

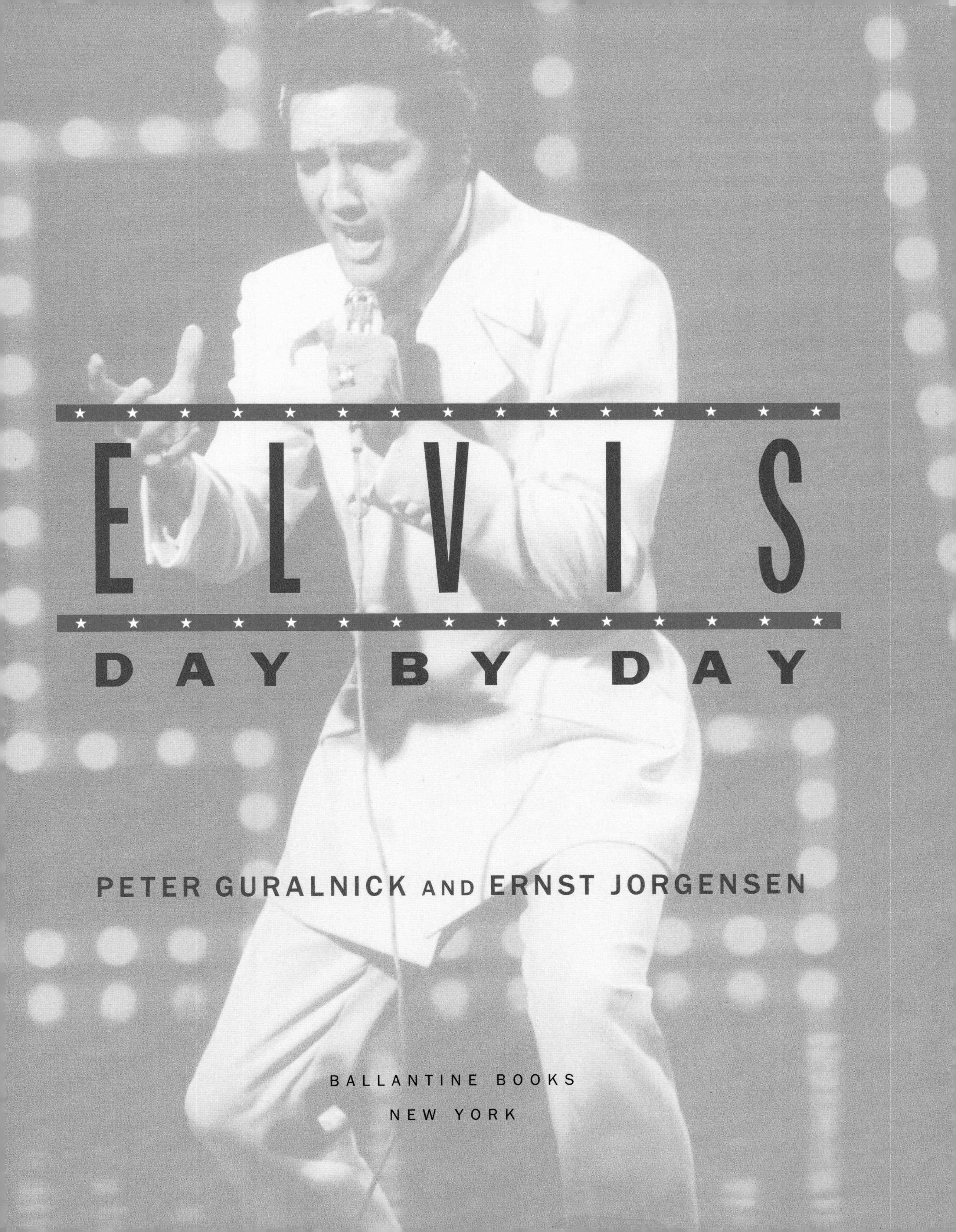

ELVIS

DAY BY DAY

PETER GURALNICK AND ERNST JORGENSEN

BALLANTINE BOOKS

NEW YORK

A Ballantine Book
Published by The Ballantine Publishing Group

http://www.randomhouse.com/BB/

Library of Congress Cataloging-in-Publication Data

Guralnick, Peter.

   Elvis day by day / Peter Guralnick and Ernst Jorgensen.—1st ed.
     p. cm.
   ISBN 0-345-42089-6 (bhc : alk. paper)
   1. Presley, Elvis, 1935–1977 Chronology. 2. Rock musicians—
United States Biography.   I. Jorgensen, Ernst.
ML420.P96G86 1999
782.42166'092—dc21
[B]   99-24340
                                         CIP

Text design by H Roberts Design

Manufactured in the United States of America

First Edition: October 1999

10 9 8 7 6 5 4 3 2 1

INTRODUCTION

This book had at least three principal sources of inspiration.

It started, of course, with the research that I conducted while writing my biography of Elvis Presley and the closely allied work of Ernst Jorgensen in developing his definitive Elvis sessionography.

One of the first obstacles that we both encountered was trying to sort out the stories. Often some of the most vividly detailed recollections by unimpeachable eyewitnesses were impossible to place in chronological context simply because: who was watching the clock? And yet it *mattered* when events took place, it was of crucial consequence whether one event occurred before another, for without that knowledge, on the most basic level, there could be no understanding of cause and effect.

For that reason alone, I learned early on, my first obligation was to go back to primary sources, if only to try to establish a chain of evidence that might conceivably lead to objective truth. Ernst and I tested out our theories on each other, challenged each other's logic and sanity, and very quickly adopted a single double-edged rule: scorn no source, however humble, but—conversely—trust no source implicitly without first testing its assumptions. Just as an archaeologist carefully studies and preserves layers of debris left in turn by successive generations, we tried to sift through not just the evidence but the provenance of the evidence to determine as accurately as possible *just what happened here.*

Our big breakthrough—at least in terms of this book—came with our introduction to the Grace-land archives in 1996. Obviously Ernst and I had access to a wide variety of sources prior to this date, but we could never have imagined the wealth of hitherto unexamined documentation that awaited us on our first joint archival venture. When we initially encountered this material, it lay virtually untouched, much as it had been left when Elvis' father, Vernon, died in 1979, and as it had been received from Colonel Parker's Madison, Tennessee, offices, when the Elvis Presley Estate purchased Elvis' manager's collection of photographs, artifacts, posters, products, contracts, and correspondence in 1990, transporting thirty-five tons of material in two eighteen-wheelers, two large moving vans, and a host of smaller vans and vehicles. What we confronted on our first visit was almost unimaginable: carefully preserved, lovingly filed, but completely unsorted in rusted file cabinets and colorful pink, red, and green trunks that could have served as magician's props. It presented a challenge that Ernst, my wife Alexandra, and I were scarcely about to shrink from—but, on the other hand, I'm not sure that Ernst and I could have maintained what little equilibrium we were still holding on to had it not been for Alexandra's steadily realistic perspective and the quiet encouragement of Graceland's chief archivist, Greg Howell.

I said there were three basic sources of inspiration for this book. One was the persistent drive to establish a timeline on both Ernst's and my part. Another was to pool our resources in a more formal way than extended transatlantic debate. The third, however, was in many ways the most compelling: to have fun with the material that we found. I don't know if the reader can fully imagine the excitement we all felt when Alexandra discovered Vernon Presley's touching postcards from prison anxiously seeking news of his three-year-old boy. To be presented by Greg with photographs of Colonel Parker as a young man in Holland, serving in the Sixty-Fourth Regiment of the U.S. Coast Guard Artillery in Honolulu, putting on a New Year's Eve show with Dick Powell and Ruby Keeler in Tampa in the mid-1930s; to have a single ticket for a previously undocumented 1955 show in Dermott, Arkansas, flutter out of a miscellaneous file; to at last be able to understand and date the origins of Elvis' unsuccessful try-out for *Arthur Godfrey's Talent Scouts* and the sur-prisingly tangled plot behind his eventual television debut on the Dorsey brothers' *Stage Show*—these are the kinds of discoveries you want to share in the same spirit with which they were received. We look upon this book, then, as a kind of treasure trove of moments, the patchwork of a life, informed with a wealth of illu-minating illustrations and facts both well and little known, all placed as close as we could possibly get, *at this time,* to proper chronological sequence—we had to believe it wasn't just us, that this was was some-thing that could appeal to Elvis fan, student of American popular culture, and casual reader alike.

Obviously, even a book of this sort involves any number of choices and discriminations, so we are by no means pretending either to omniscience or to the one unassailable truth—if, indeed, such a thing exists. We wanted to tell a story that could be used as a starting point for any understanding of Elvis' life, a kind of biographical exoskeleton that was broad enough to allow various thematic threads to emerge and detailed enough to provide a context to understand the many scrambled (and sometimes innocently thesis-driven) accounts that have been carried from volume to volume, in many cases in the absence of actual knowledge.

Our methodology was simple, even if the road it took (and continues to take) was bumpy more often than not. Almost every entry in this book is based on a contemporaneous document or documents, in many cases augmented by eyewitness accounts. If a group of people is listed as having traveled with Elvis, it is because we have seen airline tickets or hotel bills. If a time is given for a recording session, it is because we have had access to the paperwork for that session. If Elvis is said to have visited a particular place, purchased a particular item, performed in a little Texas town on a given date, signed a specific contract, sent or received a letter or telegram, it is because documentary evidence of this event exists. And where we do not have that documentation but what we believe to be compelling anecdotal evidence exists, we have tried to indicate likelihood as opposed to fact by the language of the entry, in the hope that keen-eyed readers may verify or refute our hypothesis.

There is no question, though, that documents require interpretation, too (just because a train or airline ticket exists, for example, does not always mean that it is used, and receipts only begin to tell a story), and we are resigned by now to the idea that we are not infallible, that we are providing neither the first nor the last word on the subject. The first word, of course, belongs to the many indispensable sources that we have relied upon: newspaper archives; helpful local librarians; Lee Cotten's pioneering research (his two-volume account of "Elvis on Tour" in the '50s and '70s, *Did Elvis Sing in Your Hometown?*, remains authoritative); the astonishing, primary-source research on Elvis' early success carried out from Sweden by Brian Petersen (*The Atomic Powered Singer*) and Holland by Ger Rijff (*Long Lonely Highway*, among many others); Donna Lewis' meticulously observed diaries (published in two volumes so far as "*Hurry Home, Elvis*"); Stein Erik Skar's *Elvis: The Concert Years, 1969–1977*; Joe Tunzi's indefatigable photographic and discographical research (*Elvis Sessions II*, among others)—if we were to list every one of our individual sources, the source notes would be as long as this book! Jim Cole of the Mississippi Valley Collection at the University of Memphis proved an enormous help, as did Sam Gill at the Academy of Motion Picture Arts and Sciences Margaret Herrick Library, where the Hal Wallis papers are housed.

In the end, however, two men are responsible for the continued survival of much of the information contained in this book, and it is they who should be recognized as keepers of the historical record. I'm not sure either one of them would have fully embraced the title, and yet the character of each is absolutely consistent with the notion of careful preservation and attention to detail. Colonel Tom Parker, Elvis' manager of twenty-two years and one of the most colorful figures ever to set foot in what he liked to describe as "the wonderful world of show business," and Elvis' father, Vernon Presley, a man of humble means and (like the Dutch-born "Colonel") limited education, showed a spirit of scrupulous, almost academic dedication to the task of maintaining these records, and without their efforts much of this history would simply not exist.

Well, it has been a great adventure for us all, not just for Ernst and Alexandra and me but, I think, for Greg Howell and his entire staff (Carol Drake, Carrie Stetler, Angie Marchese, Phoebe Neal, Sheila James, Michele Desrosiers, and LaVonne Gaw), who threw themselves wholeheartedly and unstintingly into the project. Discovering the informal home tape recordings that Elvis had made at various points in his life (including a brief glimpse of Elvis' parents, Vernon and Gladys, singing religious songs, which certainly went to show one thing: Elvis got his talent from his father) was just one of the many ancillary benefits that stemmed from a frequently messy but never less than mesmerizing plunge into a past that has so often been all but buried in a blur of myth and repetition. Obviously we couldn't put everything in, and I'm sure we haven't gotten everything right, despite what has seemed at times like an increasingly irresistible obsession with our obsession. It's an ongoing process, which others are bound to carry on. But we hope we have provided some of the tools to do so—for hobbyists and historians alike. And we hope we have provided a portrait, in words and in pictures, of the trajectory of a life, the life of one of the century's major cultural forces, around whom controversy will continue to swirl (as it does around every significant historical figure, for whom each generation must find its own truth) but whose voice will unquestionably continue to be heard.

Peter Guralnick

If you have any corrections, suggestions, additions, documentation, or early concert dates to add, please contact us at www.elvis-presley.com, and we will do our best to incorporate all pertinent amended information in future editions of this book.

ELVIS

DAY BY DAY

1 9 3 5 - 1 9 5 3

April 25, 1912

Gladys Love Smith is born in Pontotoc County, Mississippi.

April 10, 1916

Vernon Elvis Presley is born in Fulton, Mississippi.

June 17, 1933

Vernon and Gladys, both now living in East Tupelo with relatives, are married by the circuit clerk of Pontotoc County. After their marriage, Gladys continues working at the Tupelo Garment Center, while Vernon works on a dairy farm owned by Orville Bean, who subsequently loans the couple $180 to build a house. The arrangement allows Vernon to pay rent on the house until he has repaid the loan and can assume ownership.

January 8, 1935

In the house that Vernon has built with the help of his father and brothers (the new home is located next to that of his parents, Jessie and Minnie Mae, on Old Saltillo Road in East Tupelo), Gladys, attended by Dr. William R. Hunt, gives birth to twin boys. The first, Jesse Garon, is delivered stillborn at 4:00 A.M. and will be buried the next day in an unmarked grave in the Priceville Cemetery, near Tupelo. The second, named Elvis Aron Presley (Aron evidently is intended to rhyme

with Garon, with each pronounced with a hard "a"), is born at 4:35 A.M.

January 7, 1936

Jessie Presley's brother, Noah, a store owner and school bus driver, becomes mayor of East Tupelo, and under his guidance great civic improvements are made within the small community.

April 5, 1936

A devastating tornado sweeps through Tupelo, killing 235 and injuring another 350. In Presley family lore it will always be remembered how Vernon and Gladys took refuge in Jessie and Minnie Mae's home, with Gladys holding her baby tight.

1937

Sometime during this year Gladys' uncle, Gains Mansell, becomes the preacher at the newly built First

Elvis, Gladys,
and Vernon,
c. 1937

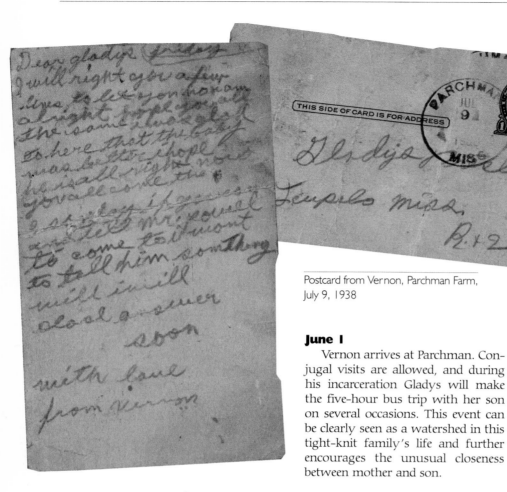

Postcard from Vernon, Parchman Farm, July 9, 1938

Assembly of God Church, just around the corner from the Presleys' home. It is here that Gladys later recalls a two-year-old Elvis slipping off her lap, climbing up on the platform, and trying to sing with the choir.

November 16

Vernon, Gladys' brother Travis Smith, and a third man named Lether Gable are charged with "uttering a forged instrument." They have evidently altered a four-dollar check from Orville Bean in payment for a hog. None of the three men can come up with the $500 bail, and all remain confined in the Lee County jail.

1938

May 25

Vernon and Travis are sentenced to three years in the Mississippi State Penitentiary at Parchman.

June 1

Vernon arrives at Parchman. Conjugal visits are allowed, and during his incarceration Gladys will make the five-hour bus trip with her son on several occasions. This event can be clearly seen as a watershed in this tight-knit family's life and further encourages the unusual closeness between mother and son.

1939

February 6

Vernon is released from prison with a six-month suspension of his sentence, granted on condition of his continued good behavior. This leniency is the result of a "petition of the citizens of Lee County and on a letter from Mr. O. S. Bean, the party on whom the checks were forged." The document is signed by Governor Hugh White.

May 3

During Vernon's incarceration, Gladys has been unable to maintain the repayment schedule on their home, and she and Elvis have been forced to move in with relatives in East Tupelo. Upon Vernon's release, the first work that we know him to obtain is with the Federal Works Project Agency (WPA), an employment program created by the New Deal. He is assigned to the Sanitation Project in Lee County (Tupelo). For 140 hours' work per month he receives $30.10.

July 29

By summer, Vernon is reclassified as a skilled carpenter on the Sanitation Project, with pay upgraded to $52 per month.

August 5

Governor White grants Vernon an additional ninety-day suspension "for good behavior while out on former suspension."

November 3

Vernon is granted an indefinite suspension of his sentence.

November 30

The local bank repossesses a car that Vernon has purchased with a loan and threatens to sue if he does not pay the $72.58 still owed after repossession. Vernon will finally pay off the note in full on June 4, 1943.

1940

August 25

Vernon continues to work on the Lee County Sanitation Project as a carpenter and also as a cement finisher.

October 31

Vernon pays the Mississippi Road and Bridge Privilege Tax of $11 on a 1930 Chevrolet truck (license plate 49129) with a six-horsepower engine and a market value of $50. In later years Elvis will remember the family listening to the Grand Ole Opry every Saturday night on a radio powered by the battery of one or another of the family's vehicles.

November 6

The Presleys are now living in a rented house at 510½ Maple Street in

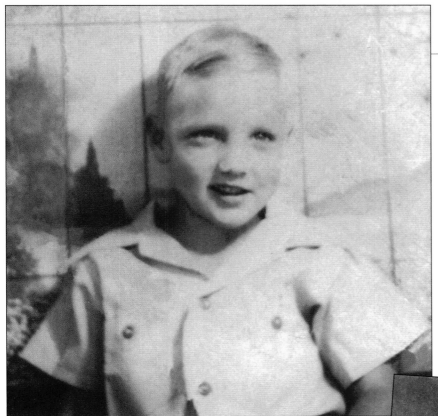

Elvis, c. 1939

per hour. In addition to a regular eight-hour day five days a week, each week he receives overtime pay of $15 to $18. With rent of $8 a week on the Maple Street house, the family is at last able to breathe a financial sigh of relief.

November 22

Vernon finds work as a carpenter for the S&W Construction Company in Como, Mississippi, helping to build an internment camp for prisoners of war. Como is more than fifty miles west of Tupelo. Salary remains $1 per hour and $1.50 for overtime.

Elvis, Vernon, and Gladys, c. 1941

East Tupelo. The Federal Works Project Agency notifies Vernon by mail that effective 5:00 P.M. on this date he will be released from his job "in accordance with statutory requirement prohibiting continuous employment for more than 18 months." Vernon will requalify for employment on December 10.

1941

February 15

Vernon purchases a 1932 Chevrolet coupe from a Mr. E. Sheffield for $65. He will make $5 payments until a total of $85 (including interest) is paid on July 26, 1941. And Vernon saves, carefully folded, the receipt for each $5 payment.

Fall

Elvis enters first grade at the East Tupelo Consolidated School on Lake Street.

1942

January 24

For an unknown period of time Vernon has been working at the S&W Construction Company in Sardis, Mississippi, some fifty miles west of Tupelo, but on this day he quits, citing illness.

August 1

To support his family, Vernon has moved temporarily to Ozark, Alabama, located in the far southeastern corner of the state, more than 300 miles from Tupelo, to work for J. A. Jones Construction Co., at its Ozark Triangular Division Camp. He receives $44.05 for the week ending August 1, with an additional $5 for five hours of work the following week.

August 8

Vernon finds work closer to home in Aberdeen, Mississippi, just thirty miles south of Tupelo, at the Fergerson Oman Gulf Ordnance plant, as a carpenter at $1

December 7

Vernon is discharged from work in Como because of a reduction in the workforce.

December 12

Vernon begins work for the Dunn Construction Company in Millington, Tennessee, just outside of Memphis, where he receives $1.25 an hour and lives in company barracks, returning to Tupelo every weekend. He continues to pay his dues to the carpenters union.

1943

February 14

Vernon gets his last paycheck from the Millington job.

March 6

Vernon borrows $25 from the People's Bank and Trust in Tupelo, paying off a total of $27, with interest, on June 2, 1943.

March 10

Vernon is now working at the Pepsi Cola Bottling Company in Tupelo but quits on April 29. The paymaster notes on his last pay slip: "Gone to shipyard."

May 16

The whole family moves to the Mississippi Gulf Coast with Vernon's cousin Sales and Sales' wife, Annie, where Vernon and Sales go to work at the Moss Point Shipyard near Pascagoula. There he receives $1.20 per hour and $1.80 overtime until he quits on June 20 and the Presleys all return to Tupelo, homesick for family and friends.

June 31

Vernon goes back to work for the Dunn Construction Company near Memphis for just one week before finding employment as a driver for L. P. McCarty and Sons, a local grocer.

Vernon Presley's "Optional U.S. Income and Victory Tax" is filed at the end of this year, with the form neatly typed and the name spelled "Pressley,"

as many others in the family are accustomed to do. The declaration lists $539.60 in income from L. P. McCarty and Sons; $352.50 from Moss Point Shipyard; $89.50 from the Pepsi Cola Bottling Co.; and $251.28 from the Dunn Construction Co. in Millington, Tennessee. Total income comes to $1,232.88, with total taxes of $12.56.

1944

Paycheck stubs indicate Vernon's continued employment at L. P. McCarty and Sons and the family's continued enjoyment of relative prosperity.

During this same time period, a thirty-five-year-old animal officer for the Tampa Humane Society and sometime promoter of shows in the Tampa area is in the process of making a decision to move to Nashville to become country singer Eddy Arnold's full-time manager. Unbeknownst to any of his show-business acquaintances, Thomas A. Parker was born Andreas ("Dries") Cornelis van Kuijk in Breda, Holland, entering this country illegally in 1929 and then enlisting in the U.S. Army. Parker was stationed in Hawaii for roughly two years before mustering out and briefly joining the Johnny J. Jones and Royal American carnivals, then marrying and settling down in Tampa, where the carnival people wintered and where he drifted into show business.

1945

August 18

Vernon purchases a new four-room house on Berry Street in East

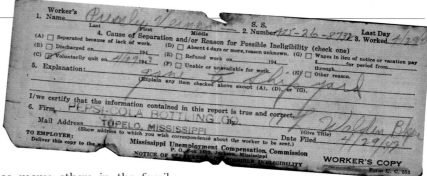

Vernon's pay slip, April 29, 1943

Tupelo from Orville Bean, the man who sent him to prison. The price is $2,000 with a down payment of $200, and Vernon agrees to monthly installments of $30 plus 6 percent interest.

October 3

It is Children's Day at the annual Mississippi-Alabama Fair and Dairy Show at the Fairgrounds in the middle of town. All of the local schools are let out, and there are prizes to be awarded in the talent contest, from a $25 war bond for first prize down to $2.50 worth of rides. Elvis' fifth-grade teacher, Mrs. Oleta Grimes, a neighbor of the Presleys and the daughter of Orville Bean, has entered Elvis in the talent show after hearing him sing in the morning prayer program at school. He performs Red Foley's country weeper "Old Shep," about a boy and his dog, as he stands on a chair and sings without accompaniment. By his own recollection, he wins fifth place but gets a whipping the same day from his mother, probably for going on one of the more "dangerous" rides.

1946

January 7

A small tornado rips through Tupelo at 5:00 A.M., causing little damage but stirring up memories of the tornado of 1936 and frightening Gladys and Elvis, who hide in a storm cellar.

January 8

On Elvis' eleventh birthday, his parents buy him a guitar at the Tupelo

A very young Andreas Cornelis
van Kuijk, c. 1926–27

Andreas Cornelis van Kuijk,
64th Regiment of the
Coast Guard Artillery,
Fort Shafter, Honolulu

Tom Parker (third from right), Tampa, Florida, December 31, 1934

Hardware Store. As Gladys Presley later tells the story, Elvis wanted a bicycle, but she was put off both by the cost and by her fears that he might get hurt.

Elvis applies himself to learning the guitar all through the year, getting pointers from his uncle Johnny Smith and the new Assembly of God pastor, Frank Smith, who with other East Tupeloans, both children and adults, regularly travels to town to attend the WELO Jamboree, a Saturday-afternoon amateur show broadcast from the Tupelo courthouse. There Elvis gets encouragement from local star Mississippi Slim (Carvel Lee Ausborn),

whose own Saturday noontime show serves as a lead-in to the Jamboree and whose music falls somewhere between Jimmie Rodgers' and Ernest Tubb's.

May 21
Vernon borrows $12 from Tower Loan Brokers in Tupelo.

July 18
With war work having come to an end, Vernon is unable to make payments on the Berry Street house and is forced to deed it over to a friend, Aaron Kennedy. The Presley

family moves from the little hamlet of East Tupelo into town, first to Commerce Street, then to Mulberry Alley, a small lane running beside the Fairgrounds, just opposite the town's black neighborhood, "Shake Rag."

August 5
Vernon takes out a loan of $10 from the People's Bank and Trust.

September
Elvis enters the sixth grade at Milam Junior High School in Tupelo. He is remembered by his classmates as a loner who doesn't fit in. A few of those

classmates, however, also recall his passion for music, from the hymns he has learned in church to the music he hears on the street to hillbilly tunes from the Grand Ole Opry to the Sister Rosetta Tharpe records he hears on WELO.

December 17

Vernon borrows $12 from Tower Loans.

1947

February

Vernon has repairs done on the family car, a 1936 Chevrolet, both this month and again in April, at the Hale Brothers Garage in Tupelo.

September

By the time that Elvis enters the seventh grade, the family is living at 1010 North Green Street in Tupelo, a house designated for whites only in a respectable "colored" neighborhood, just down the street from the Elks Club and the vacant lot that is the site of a popular annual gospel revival.

November

The family purchases from W. H. Baker Furniture in Tupelo one mattress and spring, eight pairs of pillows, one linoleum rug, and a heater, for a total of $77.50, with a down payment of $17.30. Monthly payments are made on these items plus an oil stove purchased on February 14, 1948, until September 24, 1951, three years after the family has moved to Memphis. At this time $22.76 is still due, and remains due until October 17, 1959, when a letter from Mr. J. David Baker to Elvis' accountant elicits the outstanding amount.

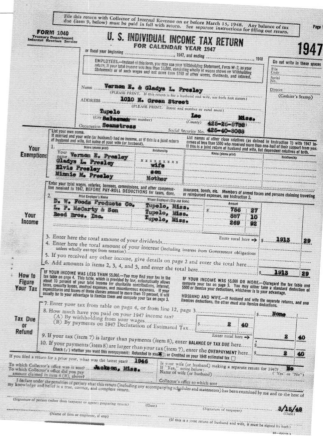

Income tax return, 1947

Seventh grade, Milam Junior High, 1947–48

Sixth-grade class picture, 1946–47 (Elvis is at far right, second row from back)

It is during his seventh-grade year that Elvis starts to take his guitar to school every day, playing for his gener-ally indifferent classmates in the basement during recess and lunch hour.

Sometime during this year, Elvis' grandfather, Jessie Presley, leaves his wife, Minnie Mae, and subsequently files for divorce. Minnie Mae moves in with Vernon and Gladys and Elvis, whom she adores.

U.S. Individual Income tax for 1947 for Vernon E. and Gladys L. Presley, 110 North Green St., Tupelo, Lee County, Mississippi. Occupations listed are salesman and seamstress; dependents are Elvis Presley, son, and Minnie M. Presley, mother. Income: $756.27 from D. W. Food Products and Co.; $887.10 from L. P. McCarty and Sons; and $269.92 from Reed Bros. Inc. (where Gladys works as a seamstress), for a total income of $1,913.29 and a tax of $2.40.

1948

January

The Presley family buys a Philco Radio Phonograph. They also pay their monthly bill of $9 at the Carr-Myers Dairy for sixty quarts of buttermilk.

February 13

Elvis gets a Tupelo Public Library card made out to "Elvis Aron Presley, age 13," and signed by Gladys Presley.

April 1

Vernon buys a life insurance policy for ten months from Tower Loan Brokers that will pay $120.

April 15

Vernon borrows $120, to be repaid in twenty monthly install-ments of $6 each.

May 3

Vernon borrows $63, which is repaid in twelve semimonthly install-ments of $5.30 each.

August 18

Vernon borrows $200, which is repaid in weekly installments of $10.

September

Elvis enters the eighth grade at the Milam School. When some of the "rougher-type" boys cut his guitar strings early in the school year, his classmates take up a collection to buy him another set of strings.

September 4

Elvis fills in the blank lines of his parents' folded marriage certificate with this date and his own name and that of "Magdline" (Magdalene) Mor-gan, a girl his age whom he knows from the First Assembly of God church. He writes in September 11 as the date of their marriage, something at which Morgan expresses great surprise when she learns of it almost fifty years later. "It was just a very sweet relationship," she says of their closeness. "At that time, if you just held hands, it was very serious. And we did hold hands a lot."

October 19

Vernon takes out a loan for $200, to be repaid in twenty weekly install-ments of $10 each.

November 6

The Presley family pack their 1937 Plymouth with all their belongings and move to Memphis, where they take up residence in a rooming house at 370 Washington Street for $11 a week. Sometime after their arrival, Vernon gets a job at the Precision Tool Company on Kansas Street in South Memphis, where Gladys' brothers Travis and Johnny are working.

November 8

Elvis Aaron (with two as) Presley is enrolled in the eighth grade at Humes High School. (There have been sugges-tions that he was first enrolled at the Christine School for a brief period—but so far no concrete evidence has turned up to support this.) Vernon later recalls that shortly after walking Elvis to school on his first day, the boy reappeared at home "so nervous he was bug-eyed." His first year at school he is present 165 days, absent fifteen, and never tardy. He receives an A in language; B's in spelling, history, and phys ed; and C's in arithmetic, music, and science.

Sixth-grade report card

During this same time period, Tom Parker has become one of the top managers in the country music field, with his sole client, Eddy Arnold, enjoying five number-one hits in 1948 alone. Parker persuades Arnold at this point to quit the Grand Ole Opry for more lucrative show-business opportunities, including—in the next year—television exposure, a Las Vegas booking, and motion pictures. Parker himself receives an honorary colonel's commission in October from Louisiana governor Jimmie Davis, a noted country singer in his own right, and henceforth will employ the title, first as a kind of joke, later as if it were his legitimate due.

1949

January 8

Vernon gives Elvis a paperback book of cartoons by George Price with the inscription: "May your birthday be sprinkled through 'n through with joy and love and good times too. Daddy." The book traveled with him to Germany and was left behind in his rented house at 14 Goethestrasse.

April 29

Not long after the family's arrival in Memphis, Vernon left Precision Tool and went to work at United Paint Company in North Memphis, closer to home. For the week of April 29, he is paid $37.62 for forty-five hours' work. On the same day he pays an $11.28 bill at Williams Grocery, 116 Poplar Avenue.

May 5

Vernon's pay with overtime comes to $51.88, and the next day he pays his $12.11 bill at Williams Grocery.

May 14

The family is still living at 370 Washington Street but is about to move to another rooming house on nearby Poplar Avenue.

June 17

As a follow-up to Vernon's application for public housing, Jane Richard-son, a home service adviser for the Memphis Housing Authority, visits Gladys and Elvis in the Presley family's rented room at 572 Poplar while Vernon is at work. She notes that they share a bathroom with other residents and cook on a hot plate. They pay $9.50 a week in rent. Miss Richardson's report indicates that their application has merit and that they could use housing, preferably near Mr. Presley's work. The son, she notes, is a "nice boy," and both Mrs. Presley and the boy seem "very nice and deserving." Vernon's salary is listed as $40.38 per week at $.85 per hour.

September

Elvis enters his ninth-grade year at Humes. He will receive mostly B's, with some C's. By the time Elvis completes his senior year he will be getting all C's.

September 20

The family is accepted into the Memphis Housing Authority's Lauderdale Courts, just around the corner from where they presently live. They will pay $35 a month for a two-bedroom, first-floor apartment at 185 Winchester Street.

October 15

The *Memphis Housing Appeal*, the Housing Authority's newspaper, lists the Presleys as one of seventeen new families who have recently moved into the Courts.

Quietly, without going out of his way to call attention to himself, Elvis starts to make new friends, playing guitar with a group of older boys under the leafy trees of Market Mall, the path that bisects the neatly kept housing development. He remains in the background for the most part, singing the gospel numbers and popular ballads that he loves and learning all that he can from these more experienced teenage musicians.

1950

January

Sam Phillips opens the Memphis Recording Service at 706 Union Avenue, ten minutes' walk from the Hotel Peabody downtown, where he and his assistant, Marion Keisker, work for WREC, Memphis' most prestigious radio station. (Among other things, Phillips engineers the big-band broadcasts on a network hookup from the Peabody Skyway every Saturday night.) About his new venture Phillips, a native of Florence, Alabama, lets it be known that his purpose is to record "Negro artists of the South who [want] to make a record [and have] no place to go," and he begins with such soon-to-be-legendary figures as B. B. King, Joe Hill Louis, and (the following year) Howlin' Wolf.

June

Sam Phillips meets with DJ Dewey Phillips (no relation), whose *Red, Hot, and Blue*, a mélange of "boogies, blues, and spirituals," is the hottest thing on Memphis radio, attracting a huge black and white audience (particularly white teenagers) with its idiosyncratic style. Sam Phillips recognizes a kindred spirit in Dewey, and while the partnership that they form later this summer, known as "The Phillips" label, doesn't last more than a month or two, they remain the closest of ideological allies.

September

Elvis enters his tenth-grade year, enrolling in ROTC, in which he receives a grade of C for the first term and B for the second. Except for an A in English and an F in typing, his grades are C's and B's.

Elvis Aron Presley is issued a Social Security card, number 409-52-2002.

Social Security card, 1950

During the fall he begins work as an usher at the Loew's State movie theater on South Main Street.

1951

June

Elvis gets a summer job at Precision Tool, where Gladys' brother Travis Smith continues to work. In 1953 Elvis will report on his state employment application that he worked for three months during the summer at $27 per week, operating a spindle drill press in the manufacture of rocket shells.

September

Elvis enters his junior year. He receives C's and is reported tardy three times. During this year at school, friends and teachers notice a change in Elvis, as he begins to gain self-confidence, attempts to grow sideburns, and grooms his hair meticulously (some would say obsessively) with Rose Oil hair tonic and Vaseline. His clothes, too, become more flamboyant, and without calling attention to himself in any other way, he becomes a kind of visual focal point. His attempt to join the football team would seem to have been thwarted by his appearance, his size, and his mother's opposition.

With friends from the Courts, *(left to right)* Farley Guy, Elvis, Paul Dougher, and Buzzy Forbess *(courtesy of Ger Rijff)*

With cousin Gene Smith, c. 1951–52

November

Gladys begins work as a nurse's aide at St. Joseph's Hospital within sight of the Courts at a salary of $4 a day. She has worked at Britling's Cafeteria downtown in the past, but this is the best job she has ever had, and she is very proud of it.

At some point during the year Elvis takes the test for his driver's license on his uncle Travis' 1940 Buick.

1952

February

Gladys is forced to quit her job at St. Joseph's because, with her salary figured in, the family is earning too much money to qualify for public housing. Vernon explains to the Housing Authority that he has hurt his back and been out of work for a while and that the family is "trying to pay ourselves out of debt. Bills are pressing and don't want to be sued." As a result, the Presleys are permitted to sign a new lease at $43 per month.

April

Elvis returns to work at Loew's State but is fired five weeks later after an altercation with another usher.

Summer

Most likely in June Vernon buys a 1941 Lincoln, which will come to be considered Elvis' car. "My daddy was something wonderful to me," Elvis says four years later of his father's purchase.

August

Elvis applies for a job at Upholsterers Specialties Company, giving his birth date on the application as January 8, 1934, in order to qualify for the position as an eighteen-year-old. He works for approximately one month, receiving total pay of $109.

September

Elvis finds work at MARL Metal Products, furniture manufacturers, on the 3:00 P.M. to 11:00 P.M. shift, using hand tools and an electric screw drill on the job.

Elvis enters his junior year at Humes, and teachers soon report to his parents that he frequently falls asleep in class. The result, according to Gladys, is that "we made him quit, and I went [back] to work at St. Joseph's."

SPECIAL INFORMATION

EMPLOYMENT COUNSELING STATEMENT

Speech defect

Biology Club

Wants factory work at once — must help father work off financial obligations.

Owns an automobile.

Making assumptions & choices. Took tests Fair clues. GATB scores indicate applicant mechanically inclined, but should avoid line work with fingers. Plan appl. not too interested in machinist appr. But thought might like industrial maint. & repair. 8-3-53 Expressed desire for a job where he could keep clean. 4-6-54 Re evaluation by Appl. Thinks machinist appr. job would be fine. Really wants to "speak big talk."

LEISURE TIME ACTIVITIES

Sing, playing ball, writing on Ear going to movies

COMMENTS

Rather flashily dressed — "playboy" type denied by fact has worked hard past 3 summers. Wants a job dealing with people.

INTERVIEWER *Miss M. Harris*

A	B	C	D	E	F	G	H	I	J	1	2	3	4	5	6	7	8	9

PRINT LAST NAME — FIRST — MIDDLE
Presley   Elvis   Aron

5. SOC. SEC. NO. *409 52 7002*

462 Alabama   STATE
TELEPHONE NO. *37-4185*

TITLES / CODES
Multiple Spindle
Drill Press 6-78.081
All Round Mech Rep. 4 -x2.100
Public Contact 1-x5.

SKILLS, KNOWLEDGE, ABILITIES   DATES
614   5-6-53
7-1-53
8-3-53
6-4-54

8. DATE OF BIRTH   7. ☐MARRIED ☐DIVORCED   8. HEIGHT   9. WEIGHT   10. ☑WHITE
Jan. 8 1935   ☑SINGLE ☐SEPARATED   *5 11*   *150*   ☐NEGRO ☐OTHER
☐WIDOWER

11. VETERAN, ENTER YOUR LAST MILITARY SERVICE   SERIAL NO.
ENTRY ON ACTIVE SERVICE / RELEASE FROM ACTIVE SERVICE

Pub Contact   mchnt   6-29-54
1-x5, 4-x2.4
TEST RESULTS

12. IF NEEDED FOR WORK   TOOLS ☑YES ☐NO   AUTOMOBILE ☑YES ☐NO
DO YOU HAVE   LICENSE ☑YES ☐NO   TRUCK ☐YES ☐NO

13. IF UNION MEMBER, GIVE NUMBER, NAME AND AFFILIATION OF LOCAL

14. CIRCLE HIGHEST YEAR OF EDUCATION COMPLETED AND GIVE DEGREES RECEIVED
TRADE SCHOOL / HIGH SCHOOL / COLLEGE   DEGREES
2 3 4 5 6 7 8   1 2 3 ④   1 2 3 4 5 6 7

3-26-53
GATB # 9,11,13,15,16,19,
G V N S P Q K F M
'28 '04 '02 '33 '15 '28 '01   '70 '08

NAME SCHOOL AND LIST COURSES OR TRAINING (INCLUDING MILITARY) WHICH PREPARED YOU FOR WORK. GIVE LENGTH AND DATES ENDED.
Humes HS   5 53
Speech 2 yrs.
Woodshop 3 yrs.
ROTC 2 yrs.
Science 2 yrs.

WILLING TO MOVE CITY ☐YES ☑NO
WILLING TO LIVE AT WORK ☐YES ☑NO

TENNESSEE
DEPARTMENT OF EMPLOYMENT SECURITY

APPLICATION CARD

FORM ES-511 (6/22/48)

IMPORTANT CIVILIAN AND MILITARY EXPERIENCE

DESCRIBE YOUR LONGEST AND MOST IMPORTANT JOBS. BEGIN WITH YOUR MOST RECENT JOB.
UNDER 19, 24, 29, 34 & 39 BELOW, NAME JOB AND DESCRIBE EXACTLY WHAT YOU DID AND HOW YOU DID IT)

15. NAME EMPLOYER OR BRANCH OF MILITARY SERVICE   *Precision Tool,*
16. ADDRESS   *Memphis*
17. EMPLOYER'S BUSINESS
18. LENGTH OF JOB *6½ mos* / DATE ENDED *3-19-54* / PAY *$1.55*
19. *Laborer: Operated drill press, and hand drill. also reamer in making of shells. also inspected shells using gages.   L.O.O.*

20. NAME EMPLOYER OR BRANCH OF MILITARY SERVICE
21. ADDRESS
22. EMPLOYER'S BUSINESS
23. LENGTH OF JOB / DATE ENDED / PAY
24.

25. NAME EMPLOYER OR BRANCH OF MILITARY SERVICE
26. ADDRESS   29.
27. EMPLOYER'S BUSINESS
28. LENGTH OF JOB / DATE ENDED / PAY

30. NAME EMPLOYER OR BRANCH OF MILITARY SERVICE
31. ADDRESS   34.
32. EMPLOYER'S BUSINESS
33. LENGTH OF JOB / DATE ENDED / PAY

35. NAME EMPLOYER OR BRANCH OF MILITARY SERVICE
36. ADDRESS   39.
37. EMPLOYER'S BUSINESS
38. LENGTH OF JOB / DATE ENDED / PAY

SUMMARY OF OTHER WORK EXPERIENCE

Furniture Assembler: Worked with elect. screw driver & hand tools 3 months summer '52. Saw & still understd. t. 3-53, Precision Tool, on Opr. Multiple Spindle Drill Press in mfg. of rocket shells (steel) 3 mos 1951

CALLED	REFERRED	EMPLOYER OR AGENCY	JOB TITLE OR PURPOSE	DUR.	PAY	RESULTS	REMARKS
7-1-53	7-1-53	M.B. Parker Co	Assembler	Temp	$40h	AT	to 9-29-53 Job Compl.
	8-5-53	Sears Roebuck	Salaried interview				
	8-6-53	Ashwin Upholst	Delivery boy	R	$25	NH	
	8-6-53	Kroger				NH	
	4-20-54	Crown Elect Co	Truck Delivery	A	$42	H	

Employment application

November 17

The Presleys receive an eviction notice from the Memphis Housing Authority, ordering them to vacate as of February 28 because, with a combined income of $4,133, they are far above the family ceiling for housing assistance.

On the family's 1952 tax return Gladys declares an income of $555.70 from St. Joseph's Hospital and Vernon $2,781.18 from United Paint. Vernon's mother, Minnie Mae, is declared a live-in dependent, and Gladys' retarded brother, Tracy Smith, is listed as a resident ten days a month. This copy of the form, which is filled out in pencil, does not include any income for Elvis.

1953

January 7

The Presleys leave Lauderdale Courts, moving to 698 Saffarans Street, opposite Humes, where they will remain for less than three months.

January 19

Elvis registers for the selective service.

March 26

Elvis visits the Tennessee State Employment Security office, listing his address as 462 Alabama (just across from Lauderdale Courts), where the

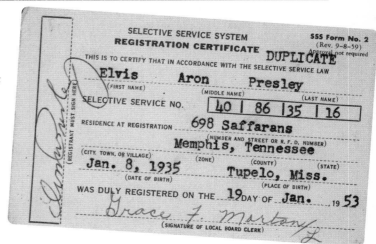

Selective Service card

Minstrel Show program (*courtesy of John Heath*)

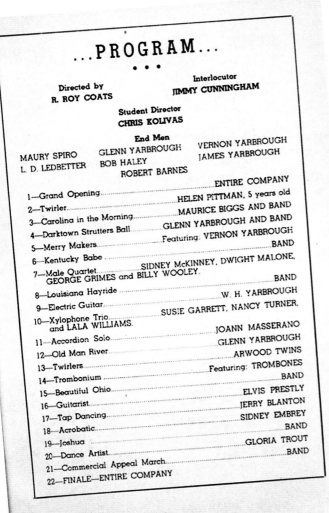

family has moved to an apartment in a large Victorian home at a rent of $50 a month. Elvis fills out the application carefully in pencil, noting under "leisure time activities": "Sings, playing ball, working on car, going to movies" and indicating that he would like to work as a machinist. At the end of the application form, the interviewer notes that his appearance as a "rather flashily dressed 'playboy' type [is] denied by fact has worked hard past three summers, wants a job dealing with people."

April 6

On a second visit to the employment office Elvis states that he has reevaluated his professional ambitions and wants to operate "big lathes."

April 9

The Humes High School band presents its annual Minstrel Show at 8:00 P.M. in the auditorium, with Elvis the sixteenth-listed act on the bill, as "Guitarist . . . Elvis Prestly." Both Elvis and his classmates date this as the begin-

With cousin Gene Smith, September 1953

ning of his rise to fame. According to Elvis: "I wasn't popular in school. I wasn't dating anybody. . . . And then they entered me in this talent show, and I came out and did my [first number], 'Till I Waltz Again With You,' by Teresa Brewer. . . . It was amazing how popular I became after that."

June 1

The Prisonaires, a quartet whom Sam Phillips has discovered in the Tennessee State Penitentiary, are transported to the Memphis Recording Service under armed guard (paid for by Phillips) to record for Phillips' recently formed Sun label. The story in the *Memphis Press-Scimitar* the following month is headlined "Prison Singers May Find Fame with Record They Made in Memphis"—and indeed they do, with an original composition, "Just Walkin' in the Rain," which Johnnie Ray will later record.

June 3

At 8:00 P.M., in a ceremony at Ellis Auditorium, Elvis Presley receives his high school diploma, the first member of his immediate family to do so. The diploma will always occupy an honored place in the family home.

The 1953 Humes High *Herald*'s senior class prophecy reads: "We are reminded at this time to not forget to invite you all out to the 'Silver Horse' on Onion [sic] Ave to hear the singing hillbillies of the road. Elvis Presley, Albert Teague, Doris Wilburn, and Mary Ann Propst are doing a bit of picking and singing out that-away."

July 1

Elvis goes to the Tennessee Employment Security office once again, saying that he must help his father "work off financial obligation and that he owns his own automobile." He is sent to M. B. Parker Company for a temporary job that pays $.90 per hour, $36 per week. Elvis works as an assembler until July 29, when the job runs out.

Summer

Perhaps inspired by the lengthy article that appears in the *Press-Scimitar* on July 15 on the subject of the Prisonaires, the Memphis Recording Service, and its proprietor, Sam Phillips, Elvis goes to the studio at 706 Union Avenue to make a two-sided acetate at his own expense. He sings the popular ballad "My Happiness" and the Ink Spots' "That's When Your Heartaches Begin," accompanied uncertainly by his own guitar, and does all that he can to attract the attention of Phillips and his assistant, Marion Keisker. He tells them that the record is a present for his mother.

August 3

Once again back at the Tennessee Employment Security Office, Elvis expresses interest in obtaining a job where he can "keep clean" and is sent out for several interviews.

August 5

Elvis interviews for a job at Sears Roebuck but is not hired.

August 6

Elvis applies for a job as a delivery boy but is not hired. Elvis applies for a job at Kroger's grocery store but is not hired.

August 21

Colonel Tom Parker, whose managerial skills have by now become legendary in Nashville, is let go by his single client, number-one-selling country artist Eddy Arnold. Arnold's letter comes out of the blue, leaving Parker both emotionally shaken and at professional loose ends, though a relatively amicable financial settlement leaves him with some of Arnold's bookings.

September 21

Elvis has by now returned to work at Precision Tool as a sander and manufacturer of shelves as well as the operator of a hand drill and drill press. His pay is $1.55 per hour. He will remain at this job until March 19, 1954.

1 9 5 4

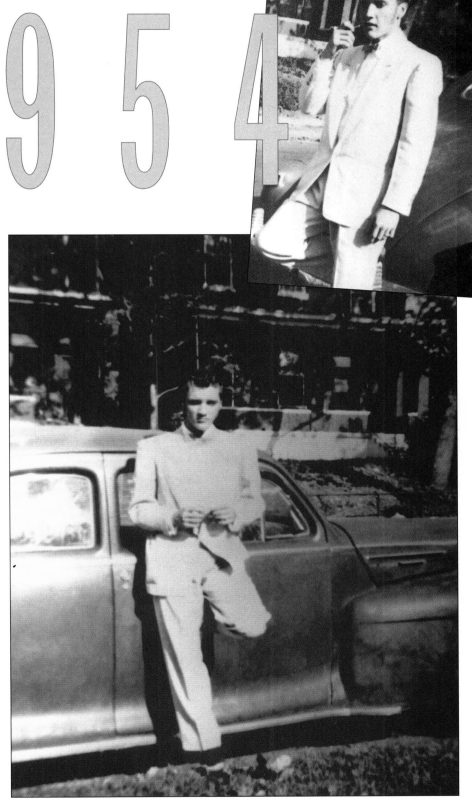

JANUARY

Elvis pays for a second acetate at the Memphis Recording Service, cutting two country numbers, "I'll Never Stand in Your Way" and "It Wouldn't Be the Same Without You." Once again he engages the interest of Marion Keisker and Sam Phillips, but once again there are no direct results.

Elvis and his cousin Gene Smith start to attend the First Assembly of God Church in South Memphis. The Presleys have not attended any one church regularly since their arrival in Memphis, but Elvis and his cousin are looking for ways to meet girls. Perhaps the most prominent members of the Assembly of God congregation are the Blackwood Brothers quartet, one of the leading gospel groups in the country. Cecil Blackwood, a nephew of founding member James Blackwood, lives with his new wife in Lauderdale Courts and has recently started a kind of apprentice quartet called the Songfellows.

24 Sunday

Fourteen-year-old Dixie Locke, a sophomore at South Side High, notices Elvis at a church function and, making sure that he overhears, makes plans with a girlfriend to go roller-skating Saturday night.

Outside 462 Alabama with the family's Lincoln, c. 1953–54. *(Top)* Note pipe, extra-long sideburns, and permanent wave.

c. 1953–54. Note that the barely grown-in sideburns have been darkened on this print, which was used as one of Elvis' earliest publicity shots. Scotty Moore believes it was taken when Elvis was in high school or shortly after.

30 Saturday

Elvis, dressed in a black outfit with a bolero jacket, appears at the Rainbow Rollerdrome, where he "bumps into" Dixie, speaking to her for the first time. He drives her home in his 1941 Lincoln.

31 Sunday

Elvis calls up Dixie, and they go to the movies.

FEBRUARY

16 Tuesday

Barely two weeks after their first meeting, Elvis brings Dixie home to meet his parents.

26 Friday

Elvis and Dixie attend the All-Night Gospel Singing at Ellis Auditorium together for the first time. Elvis, Vernon, and Gladys are regulars at this monthly event, an all-star gospel show put on by the Blackwood Brothers. The Blackwoods are Gladys' favorite group, but Elvis prefers the more charismatic Statesmen, whose flamboyant bass singer, Jim Wetherington ("Big Chief"), and virtuosic lead singer, Jake Hess, he particularly admires.

Elvis and Dixie will see each other virtually every day throughout the spring and summer, going to double features two or three times a week, attending DJ Bob Neal's *High Noon Round-Up* at the WMPS studio on the corner of Union and Main (the Blackwood Brothers appear regularly), frequenting K's Drive-In, and pursuing Elvis' passion for blues and rhythm and blues at Charlie's Record Shop on North Main, where Elvis has gotten the proprietor to put his first acetate on the jukebox. On Sundays Elvis and Dixie and other members of their Sunday school class sneak off from the Assembly of God service to hear the preaching and singing at Reverend W. Herbert Brewster's "colored" church on East Trigg, just a few blocks away. Brewster, a noted gospel songwriter and civil rights activist, is a stirring orator, perhaps best known today for Mahalia Jackson's version of his "Move On Up a Little Higher" and Clara Ward's "How I Got Over."

MARCH

05 Friday

Elvis and Dixie attend the annual Minstrel Show at Humes.

06 Saturday

Elvis Presley files his first federal income tax return. His job classification is checked off as "semi-skilled," and his return shows income of $129.74 from M. B. Parker and $786.59 from Precision Tool, with no deductions or exemptions.

19 Friday

Elvis leaves Precision Tool, where he is not particularly happy with either the work or the razzing he is forced to put up with because of the length of his hair.

Pay slip from Precision Tool

Elvis' first income tax return

In the warmer weather, Elvis and Dixie often go to Riverside Park, where Elvis plays his guitar and sings for Dixie and their friends. Sometime during the spring Elvis tries out for the Songfellows, the junior Blackwood group, and is crushed when according to his recollection, he is told that he "can't sing"—though other members of the group later insist that they meant he couldn't sing *harmony*.

MAY

08 Saturday

Elvis and Dixie attend the annual Memphis Cotton Carnival, where Elvis runs into Ronald Smith, a friend they both know from Dixie's South Memphis neighborhood. Smith, with whom Elvis has played in public on a couple of occasions (the highlight was a Lodge banquet), is a regular in twenty-one-year-old Eddie Bond's band. Ronald tells Elvis there is an opening in the band for a vocalist and he should come try out at the Hi-Hat.

09 Sunday

Elvis and Dixie attend the Oral Roberts Crusade.

15 Saturday

Elvis and Dixie go to the Hi-Hat on South Third. Elvis is wearing his bolero jacket with a pink shirt and accompanies himself on the guitar, singing two songs. The tryout does not get him a job, and in later years Elvis will dramatize the rejection by saying that Eddie Bond told him to go back to driving a truck.

APRIL

02 Friday

With Dixie, Elvis returns to Humes for another talent show.

17 Saturday

A *Billboard* article headlined "Teenagers Going for 'Music With a Beat'" explores the increasing fascination with rhythm and blues among white teenagers, as well as the inviting commercial possibilities for record companies and record retailers. "The teen-age tide has swept down the old barriers which kept this music restricted at a segment of the population," the New York–based trade weekly declares, merely hinting at the social implications.

18 Sunday

Dixie has Easter dinner with Elvis' family.

20 Tuesday

Elvis begins work at Crown Electric, where he starts out driving a truck at $1 an hour, delivering supplies to building sites. He is hoping for the chance to train to be an electrician.

With Dixie Locke, spring 1954

HEAR THEM

RECENTLY RE-ORGANIZED

BLACKWOOD BROS. GOSPEL QUARTET

AT ELLIS AUDITORIUM AUG. 27

—IN—

Sunday School Sing

9:40 A. M. AUGUST 29, 1954

First Assembly of God

1084 E. McLEMORE

(1,000 FREE SEATS)

• your choice of a Blackwood record FREE for bringing 3 visitors

(OVER)

Blackwood Brothers' shows, August 1954
(card saved by Gladys Presley)

17 Monday

By unanimous vote the Supreme Court overturns the "separate but equal" doctrine of school segregation in *Brown v. Board of Education of Topeka*. Separating Negro children from others "solely because of their race," writes Chief Justice Earl Warren, "generates a feeling of inferiority . . . that may affect their hearts and minds in a way unlikely ever to be undone."

JUNE

26 Saturday

Elvis has still not given up hope of recording for Sun Records and continues to stop by the Memphis Recording Service with that in mind. Today, seemingly, his prayers are answered, as Marion Keisker, Sam Phillips' assistant, keeps after Phillips to have "the boy with the sideburns" come in and try out a new song Sam has gotten from Nashville song publisher Red Wortham. Elvis is at the studio practically before Keisker hangs up the phone and tries all afternoon to record "Without You," a somewhat cloyingly sweet ballad, but fails to come up with a successful version of the song.

First management contract, July 12, 1954

29 Tuesday

R. W. Blackwood and bass singer Bill Lyles, members of the Blackwood Brothers quartet, are killed in a plane crash in Alabama. When the group decides some weeks later to carry on, bass singer J. D. Sumner will join them.

JULY

02 Friday

The funeral for the two Blackwood Brothers singers is held at Ellis Auditorium, drawing a huge crowd that includes Elvis and Dixie and his parents.

03 Saturday

Dixie leaves for a vacation in Florida with her family.

After supper, Scotty Moore, a local guitar player who has secured a recording deal with Sam Phillips for his own band, the Starlite Wranglers,

---

PERSONAL MANAGEMENT CONTRACT ENTERED
INTO BETWEEN W. S. MOORE III AND
ELVIS PRESLEY

WHEREAS, W. S. Moore, III, is a band leader and a booking agent, and Elvis Presley, a minor, age 19 years, is a singer of reputation and renown, and possesses bright promises of large success, it is the desire of both parties to enter into this personal management contract for the best interests of both parties.

This contract is joined in and approved by the Father and Mother of Elvis Presley, *Vernon Presley* and *Mrs Vernon Presley* Presley.

IT IS AGREED that W. S. Moore, III, will take over the complete management of the professional affairs of the said Elvis Presley, book him professionally for all appearances that can be secured for him, and to promote him, generally, in his professional endeavors. The said W. S. Moore, III, is to receive, as his compensation for his services, ten (10%) percent of all earnings from engagements, appearances, and bookings made by him for Elvis Presley.

IT IS UNDERSTOOD AND AGREED that this is an exclusive contract and the said Elvis Presley agrees not to sign any other contract pertaining to his professional work nor make any appearances at any time for any other person or manager or booking agent, for a period of one (1) year.

Now, we, *Vernon Presley* and *Mrs Vernon Presley* father and mother of Elvis Presley, join in this contract for and in his behalf, confirm and approve all of its terms and his execution of same and our signatures are affixed thereto.

The said W. S. Moore, III, agrees to give his best efforts to the promotion and success of the said Elvis Presley professionally.

SIGNED AND EXECUTED on this 12th day of July 1954.

W. S. Moore
W. S. Moore, III

Elvis Presley
Elvis Presley

Vernon Presley
Father of Elvis Presley

Gladys Presley
Mother of Elvis Presley

in person
THE SENSATIONAL
RADIO-RECORDING
STAR

Slim
WHITMAN

with Billy Walker, Ellis Presley and many others
Tonight On: Big Show—8:00 P.M.
Adv. reserved seats today at Walgreen's. Main and Union,
$1.00. Tonight at Shell, $1.25 reserved; kids, 75c; general admission $1.00.

OVERTON PARK SHELL

Overton Park show, July 30, 1954

Slim Whitman Show
July 30, 8:00 P. M.
Overton Park Shell
Reserved - Advance $1.00 - At Door $1.25 - Kid .75
Section____CR____ Row__Q__

Ticket for show *(courtesy of John Heath)*

calls Elvis' home, identifying himself as a scout for Sun. Elvis is at the movies, but his mother goes to fetch him, and when Elvis calls back, Scotty explains that he has gotten his name from Sam Phillips and wonders if he would be interested in an audition.

04 Sunday

Elvis shows up at Scotty's apartment on Belz Avenue, near the

Goodyear plant, and runs through nearly every song he knows. Starlite Wrangler bass player Bill Black, whose bass-playing brother, Johnny, Elvis is acquainted with from the Courts, also shows up, but neither Scotty nor Bill is particularly impressed. Still, in talking with Sam Phillips later that evening, Scotty agrees that maybe it would be worth another try in the studio with the boy.

05 Monday

The unlikely trio reports to Sun after work, attempting one ballad after another without sparking Phillips' interest. Then, during a break in what has been technically termed a "rehearsal session," with everyone feeling pretty discouraged, Elvis launches without warning into blues singer Arthur "Big Boy" Crudup's "That's All Right." The other musicians quickly fall into line, and Sam Phillips finally hears what he has been

waiting for all along. They do several takes of "That's All Right," and while Scotty and Bill remain skeptical, Phillips is convinced that all they need at this point is a second side to make up Elvis Presley's first single.

06 Tuesday

Elvis, Scotty, and Bill are back in the studio trying to cut that second side, but once again they are stymied by Elvis' almost exclusive predilection for ballads. It should be noted that this and the following dates are estimates, based on anecdotal evidence and the most likely juxtaposition of events. There is simply no verifiable certainty as to when "Blue Moon of Kentucky" (the B-side of the single) was actually recorded or when Dewey Phillips first played Elvis on the air.

07 Wednesday

After a third brief and unsuccessful session, Sam plays an acetate of "That's All Right" alone for DJ Dewey Phillips, who flips over the song and vows to play it on his show the following evening.

08 Thursday

Sam brings Dewey two one-sided acetates of the song at the WHBQ studio in the Hotel Chisca downtown. Gladys and Vernon listen to Dewey's evening show in anticipation of hearing their son on the radio, but Elvis goes to the movies a few blocks away. When Dewey plays the acetate, the switchboards light up and he continues to play the song

---

July Record Release

First single: "That's All Right"/"Blue Moon of Kentucky" (Sun 209) comes out in mid-July (the exact release date is not known) and hits all over town with scattered initial sales in Mississippi, Arkansas, and as far as New Orleans. By October the *Memphis Commercial Appeal* will report that the record has sold 6,300 copies in Memphis alone.

over and over again, calling the Presley home to try to get Elvis down to the studio. Gladys and Vernon go up and down the aisles at the Suzore #2, finally locating Elvis and sending him down to the radio station. When a nervous Elvis finally appears, Dewey makes casual conversation with him, not informing him until afterward that they have been on the air.

09 Friday

While the exact date of the session that produced the B-side for Elvis' first record is not known, the urgent need for a second side is reemphasized by the sensation that Dewey's show has created. Once again, almost by accident, Elvis, Scotty, and Bill improvise a free-wheeling, up-tempo, backbeat-laden version of a familiar song, in this case Bill Monroe's bluegrass classic in waltz time, "Blue Moon of Kentucky."

12 Monday

Scotty Moore becomes both manager and booking agent for the new group. His contract with Elvis begins: "WHEREAS W.S. Moore, III, is a band leader and a booking agent, and Elvis Presley, a minor, age 19 years, is a singer of reputation and renown, and possesses bright promises of large success, it is the desire of both parties to enter into this personal management contract for the best interests of both parties." Elvis and his parents sign the document, and the group agrees to split all earnings, 50 percent to Elvis, 25 percent each to Scotty and Bill.

17 Saturday

★ Bon Air, Memphis

Sam Phillips takes Elvis to the Bon Air Club, where the Starlite Wranglers have a regular booking. Elvis, Scotty, and Bill perform the two songs that are to be the new single, the only two songs they know well enough to play in front of an audience.

18 Sunday

Late in the evening, the Locke family returns from their Florida vacation, and while driving into Memphis Dixie hears "Blue Moon of Kentucky" on the car radio.

24 Saturday

Elvis plays with the Starlite Wranglers again at the Bon Air, but Dixie cannot attend because she is underage.

26 Monday

Sam Phillips persuades Bob Neal, the WMPS disc jockey whose noontime hillbilly and gospel show Elvis has frequently attended, to add the young singer to his upcoming "hillbilly hoedown," a package show starring Louisiana Hayride performers Slim Whitman and Billy Walker, to be held this Friday at Memphis' Overton Park Shell.

On this same day Elvis Aron Presley signs a formal contract with Sun Records, which must be countersigned once again by his parents. It is for a minimum of eight sides over a period of two years, with the contract renewable at the record company's option for a second period of two years. The royalty rate is 3 percent of the wholesale price.

27 Tuesday

Marion Keisker takes Elvis to a lunch-hour interview with Edwin Howard at the *Memphis Press-Scimitar* to promote both the record and his upcoming live appearance at the Overton Park show.

28 Wednesday

The *Press-Scimitar* story refers to Elvis as "equally popular on popular, folk and race record programs." Ads have already appeared in the paper promoting the Overton Park show, with one advertising "Ellis Presley," another leaving the name out altogether. Friday's ad, however, partially paid for by Sam Phillips, will call prominent attention to "ELVIS PRESLEY, new Memphis Star Who Sings 'Blue Moon of Kentucky' and 'That's All Right Mama.'"

Elvis receives his weekly paycheck of $46 from Crown Electric, representing forty hours at $1 an hour and four hours of overtime.

30 Friday

★ Overton Park Shell, Memphis

Elvis once again performs his two released songs, with Sam Phillips, Dixie, and his parents in attendance. He is evidently so nervous that, without even being aware of it, he says later, his legs begin to shake. On the other hand, this is the hallmark of his idol, Big Chief's, performing style, and the crowd goes wild for Elvis, just as they always do for the Statesmen's bass singer. Elvis, Scotty, and Bill encore with "Blue Moon of Kentucky," and Elvis responds by shaking some more.

31 Saturday

★ Bon Air, Memphis

Elvis plays the Bon Air again, forgetting his jacket at the club. This gives Dixie the opportunity to see where he has been playing when they go back to pick it up.

AUGUST

01 Sunday

Elvis makes a brief radio appearance with Scotty and Bill in the evening on radio station KWEM in West Memphis, Arkansas, with Dixie and Scotty's wife Bobbie accompanying them.

04 Wednesday

Elvis' weekly paycheck from Crown Electric totals $42.51. He, Scotty, and Bill will continue working their regular jobs until sometime in mid-October.

07 Saturday

Billboard reviews Sun 209 in its "Spotlight" section under the heading "Talent." In a break with standard editorial policy, editor Paul Ackerman champions the new sound, calling Presley "a potent new chanter who can sock over a tune for either the country or the r & b markets. . . . A strong new talent."

At the Eagle's Nest, summer or early fall 1954
(note that Elvis is not playing the
Martin D-18 guitar that he acquired sometime
during this period)

★ *The Eagle's Nest, Memphis*

Splitting off permanently from the Starlite Wranglers, Elvis, Scotty, and Bill alone are booked into the Eagle's Nest, the nightclub over the changing room at the Clearpool complex. The house band is a western swing ensemble led by influential Memphis DJ Sleepy-Eyed John (Lepley) and including at one time or another future Stax Records founder Jim Stewart and future Sun producer Jack Clement.

18 Wednesday

Billboard's regional Country and Western chart for Memphis shows Elvis, Scotty, and Bill at #3 with "Blue Moon of Kentucky."

19 Thursday

Equally inspired by black balladeer Billy Eckstine, country yodeler Slim Whitman, and r & b "bird group" the Orioles, Elvis records several takes of the Rodgers and Hart standard "Blue Moon" at the Sun studio. These will remain unreleased by Sun.

27 Friday

★ *The Eagle's Nest, Memphis*

At this point, Elvis, Scotty, and Bill become a regular attraction at the Eagle's Nest, with solid weekend bookings for the next three months.

28 Saturday

"Blue Moon of Kentucky" enters *Billboard*'s Country and Western chart for the Mid-South region.

Dewey Phillips celebrates his fifth anniversary on the air with a rhythm-and-blues package show at the Hippodrome, with performances at 7:00 P.M. for whites and 10:00 P.M. for "colored." The show stars Roy Hamilton, the Drifters, Faye Adams, LaVern Baker, the Spaniels, the Counts, and Big Maybelle, and while it is by no means certain that Elvis attends, it seems likely both from anecdotal accounts and from the very strong influence that Hamilton, the Drifters, and LaVern Baker in particular exert on him over the years.

SEPTEMBER

08 Wednesday

Advertisements for the opening of a new shopping center in Memphis highlight an appearance by the "newest Memphis hit in the recording business . . . Elvis Presley" in front of Katz Drug Store the following night between 9:00 and 10:00 P.M.

09 Thursday

★ *Katz Drug Store, Lamar and Airways, Memphis*

Elvis' appearance draws a huge crowd of teenagers and is MCed by former Humes classmate George Klein, who spent the summer working as a DJ at a small Arkansas station and has been a "gofer" for Dewey Phillips for much of the past year.

10 Friday

★ *The Eagle's Nest, Memphis*

11 Saturday

★ *The Eagle's Nest, Memphis*

Elvis returns to the Sun studio over the weekend to record several tunes, including Dean Martin's "I Don't Care If the Sun Don't Shine" and Roy Brown's "Good Rockin' Tonight."

17 Friday

Sometime during this period Elvis very likely played *Bethel Springs, Tennessee*, not far from Jackson. By Carl Perkins' account, this took place at the high school gym, where his appearance had "an electric effect" on the small audience, "particularly the girls." Perkins asked Elvis after the

---

September Record Release

Single: "Good Rockin' Tonight"/"I Don't Care If the Sun Don't Shine" (Sun 210). Elvis' second Sun single is released at the end of September. While it is an immediate hit in the Memphis area and "Good Rockin' Tonight" becomes a favorite on Elvis' live shows, the new single never matches the success of the first.

---

show whether he thought Sun might be interested in someone else who sang in a similar style, and while Elvis professed ignorance of Sam Phillips' inclinations, it was this event that led to Perkins' first visit to Sun in October.

18 Saturday

★ *The Eagle's Nest, Memphis*

24 Friday

★ *The Eagle's Nest, Memphis*

25 Saturday

★ *The Eagle's Nest, Memphis*

Sometime after making his first record Elvis trades in his beat-up old guitar at O.K. Houck Piano Company, a music store on Union Avenue, for a 1942 Martin D-18 costing $175. Some months later, he recalls to *Memphis Press-Scimitar* reporter Bob Johnson how the music store proprietor gave him $8 for his old guitar and then promptly threw it in the trash. "Shucks, it still played good," Elvis remarks sorrowfully to Johnson. Elvis has his name spelled out in metal letters attached at an angle to the guitar body just below the strings. A photograph taken at Memphis State on November 8 shows him with this new guitar, but very likely he bought it prior to his October 2 appearance on the Grand Ole Opry. Sometime after the first of the year, the letters spelling out his name appear parallel to the strings on what is presumably the same D-18.

OCTOBER

01 Friday

★ *The Eagle's Nest, Memphis*

02 Saturday

★ *The Grand Ole Opry, Ryman Auditorium, Nashville, Tennessee*

From the moment that Elvis first hits the regional *Billboard* charts at the end of August, Sam Phillips has been trying to set up an Opry appearance, which he is finally able to arrange through the good offices of Opry manager Bill Denny. Elvis sings "Blue Moon of Kentucky" on

With Buzzy Forbess (*left*) and Farley Guy, fall of 1954, on the Third Street side of the Courts (according to a third friend, Paul Dougher, Elvis was just back from a Louisiana Hayride appearance)

the Hank Snow portion of the show and receives a polite, but not vociferously enthusiastic, reception. He, Scotty, and Bill meet Bill Monroe, who has nothing but praise for their treatment of his song. After the Opry, Elvis appears briefly on Ernest Tubb's *Midnight Jamboree* radio show, broadcast live from Tubb's record shop just down the street from the Ryman. Whether out of insecurity or just a natural desire to curry favor with one of the country music giants he has grown up listening to, Elvis blurts out to Tubb that his real ambition is to sing country music. The "Texas Troubadour's" characteristically thoughtful response is that Elvis should go on doing what has obviously gotten him off to a good start until he's had enough success to do what he wants to do.

06 Wednesday
★ *The Eagle's Nest*, Memphis

13 Wednesday
★ *The Eagle's Nest*, Memphis

14 Thursday
The *Memphis Commercial Appeal* reports that "our homegrown hillbilly singer is continuing his swift, steady stride toward national prominence in the rural rhythm field."

15 Friday
★ *The Eagle's Nest*, Memphis
After the show, Sam Phillips, Elvis, Scotty, and Bill set off on a seven-hour drive to Shreveport, Louisiana, where Sam has arranged a tryout on the Louisiana Hayride, a kind of upstart cousin of the Opry's that has jump-started the careers of Hank Williams, Webb Pierce, Slim Whitman, and Faron Young, among others. Upon arrival, they check into the Captain Shreve Hotel, before setting forth on various promotional tasks of the day.

16 Saturday
★ *Louisiana Hayride, Municipal Auditorium, Shreveport, Louisiana*
"Just a few weeks ago," declares announcer Frank Page, "a young man from Memphis, Tennessee, recorded a song on the Sun label, and in just a matter of a few weeks that record has skyrocketed up the charts." Over the course of the evening Elvis, Scotty, and Bill perform both sides of their first single twice, with Scotty even contributing a brief instrumental to

warm, demonstrative applause. After it is over, Sam Phillips knows that Elvis is really on his way, not because he has fully worked out a performing style but because he has proved he can "stand on his own."

A brief note in *Billboard* announces that Bob Neal "is planning fall tours with Elvis Presley [and country acts] the Louvin Brothers and J. E. and Maxine Brown" which he will book and MC. At Scotty's urging Neal has agreed to help set up shows in the Memphis area and the Mississippi-Arkansas region, within reach of the strong radio signal of his early-morning and noon shows.

20 Wednesday
The *Press-Scimitar* notes that Elvis is now a regular on the Louisiana Hayride. In fact, Elvis' contract with the Hayride has not yet been finalized.

23 Saturday
Billboard announces that "Presley, with his gui-

Weekend shows in Memphis, October 30–31, 1954

tar and bassman, Scotty and Bill, made an appearance recently at Texas Bill Strength's Nitery (The Silver Slipper Club on Highway 42) in Atlanta." No further evidence of this Atlanta gig has been found, which leads one to wonder if it may not have taken place in Memphis, where Strength, a brand-new DJ on KWEM who had only recently moved to the area, has just started performing and booking gigs.

29 Friday
★ *The Eagle's Nest, Memphis*
Bob Neal brings Oscar Davis to the club on either this or the following night. Davis, a flamboyant vaudeville, carnival, and country music promoter a little down on his luck, is working at this time as an advance man for Colonel Tom Parker on an Eddy Arnold show booked into Memphis' Ellis Auditorium for this weekend. Parker has continued to book Arnold in certain markets after his managerial split with the country music star the previous year.

30 Saturday
★ *The Eagle's Nest, Memphis*

31 Sunday
Bob Neal brings Elvis backstage at Ellis to meet Oscar Davis, who tells the young singer how impressed he was with his performance at the Eagle's Nest. Elvis also meets the Jordanaires, Eddy Arnold's smooth backup singers, who have a solo spot on the show as well. With what they take to be youthful naïveté, he tells them he hopes he will be able to have them sing on his records someday.

NOVEMBER

06 Saturday
★ *Louisiana Hayride, Municipal Auditorium, Shreveport*
With only two singles out, the trio is forced to rely on cover versions to expand their show. Tonight they

With Memphis State dean R. M. Robison and Mayor Frank Tobey holding Elvis' new Martin D-18 guitar, November 8, 1954 *(courtesy of Ger Rijff)*

include the Clovers' "Fool, Fool, Fool," Roy Hamilton's "I'm Gonna Sit Right Down and Cry," and the blues and hillbilly standard "Sittin' On Top Of The World." The advertisement for this week's show lists Elvis fourth out of fourteen acts, behind Slim Whitman, Jim Reeves, and Jim Ed and Maxine Brown.

Elvis' parents, Vernon and Gladys, travel to Shreveport to sign his new Hayride contract, since he is still underage. The standard contract runs for one year, requiring a performance every Saturday night, with only five annual absences excused. Elvis will receive $18 per show, Scotty and Bill $12 apiece.

Billboard announces that Colonel Tom Parker will be booking all personal appearances by current number-one country star Hank Snow from now on, and as of January 1 will take over Snow's management, including radio, television, film, and record commitments. In addition, Parker and Snow will share a booking agency and management partnership under the joint umbrella of Hank

Snow Enterprises and Jamboree Attractions.

08 Monday
★ *Memphis State University, Memphis*
Most likely on this date Elvis makes a solo appearance (without Scotty and Bill) for a Student Government Association blood drive. Just how momentous an event this is on campus can be judged by the fact that when Elvis' picture (taken with the Memphis mayor and college dean) appears in *The DeSoto*, the MSU yearbook, the singer is not even identified.

At some point, probably during the early part of the month, Elvis plays a not-very-successful engagement at the high school in *Nettleton, Arkansas*, put on by Bob Neal.

13 Saturday
★ *Louisiana Hayride, Municipal Auditorium, Shreveport*

17 Wednesday
★ *The Eagle's Nest, Memphis*
Elvis appears on a double bill with Jimmy and Johnny, a Hayride act managed by Hayride bass player and talent coordinator Tillman Franks. Franks and influential Houston DJ Biff Collie show up at the club, on their way to the third annual country music Disc Jockey Convention in Nashville. Impressed by what he has seen, Collie books Elvis into a show that he hosts, the Houston Hoedown, for $150 the following week.

19 Friday
★ *The Lake Cliff Club, Lake Cliff, Louisiana (outside Shreveport)*
Elvis, Scotty, and Bill appear in place of popular regulars Hoot and

Curley, and are greeted not only with a misspelling of Elvis' name ("Pressley") but by a generally disgruntled crowd.

20 Saturday
★ *Louisiana Hayride, Municipal Auditorium, Shreveport*

24 Wednesday
★ *Municipal Auditorium, Texarkana, Arkansas*

According to *Cash Box*, December 11, Elvis appears on a bill here with Johnny Horton and Tibby Edwards.

25 Thursday
★ *Paladium Club, Houston, Texas*

It is unclear whether this was the first Houston date that Biff Collie booked, or if Elvis played the Houston Hoedown at another location earlier in the week. In any case, the ad for the Paladium Club on Friday indicates that Elvis will be held over for two more nights "by popular demand."

26 Friday
★ *Paladium Club, Houston*

Elvis sends a telegram to his parents: "HI BABIES, HERE'S THE MONEY TO PAY THE BILLS. DON'T TELL NO ONE HOW MUCH I SENT I WILL SEND MORE NEXT WEEK. THERE IS A CARD IN THE MAIL. LOVE ELVIS."

27 Saturday
★ *Paladium Club, Houston*

28 Sunday

Elvis had been booked for two shows in Memphis with Opry star Kitty Wells and, once again, Jimmy and Johnny. The show is hosted by prominent Memphis DJs Bob Neal and Sleepy-Eyed John, but Elvis is unable to get back from Houston in time.

DECEMBER

02 Thursday
★ *Catholic Club, Helena, Arkansas*

Elvis appears with fellow Hayride stars Jim Ed and Maxine Brown, with Bob Neal acting as MC.

04 Saturday
★ *Louisiana Hayride, Municipal Auditorium, Shreveport*

08 Wednesday

Most likely either this week or next, Elvis has his next Sun session, at which he records "Milkcow Blues Boogie" and "You're a Heartbreaker."

10 Friday
★ *The Eagle's Nest, Memphis*

This is Elvis' last performance at the Eagle's Nest.

11 Saturday
★ *Louisiana Hayride, Municipal Auditorium, Shreveport*

Billboard reports that "the hottest piece of merchandise on the . . . Louisiana Hayride at the moment is Elvis Presley, the youngster with the hillbilly blues beat."

13 Monday

Having seen a listing for Jamboree Attractions in *Billboard*, Scotty Moore writes to Colonel Parker's associate, Tom Diskin, at Jamboree's Chicago office, about booking the group. "I am the personal manager of Elvis Presley, a Sun recording star who has two current hit records," Scotty says by way of introduction. "If you do not do booking I would appreciate any information you can give me in regard to someone who does. . . ."

14–17 Tuesday–Friday

At some point during this time, most likely before Christmas, Elvis makes his first appearance in Gladewater, Texas, at a show put on at the Mint Club by Tom Perryman, a local DJ, who will continue to book Elvis in the northeast Texas area well into the following year. Because newspaper ads either do not exist or simply have not been found, his earliest appearances in this region have yet to be precisely dated.

18 Saturday
★ *Louisiana Hayride, Municipal Auditorium, Shreveport*

Elvis includes Otis Williams and the Charms' "Hearts of Stone" and Joe Turner's "Shake, Rattle and Roll," two current r&b hits, along with his more familiar repertoire.

23–24 Thursday–Friday

In a 1966 interview Elvis recalls being stopped for speeding on his way home from Shreveport. "I thought, 'Here goes my Christmas money for a traffic ticket.' But the

Telegram home from Houston, November 26, 1954

With Scotty Moore, Bill Black, and unknown steel player in early photographs taken at the Mint Club, Gladewater, Texas, found with Gladys' papers and marked December 1954

officer let us go with a warning. . . . After the officer left, the three of us got out of the car and counted our money by the car headlights. The money was mostly in dollar bills. Man, that was the most money I ever had in my pockets at one time! I blew the whole bundle the next day for Christmas presents."

25 Saturday
Christmas on Alabama Street.

28 Tuesday
★ *Cook's Hoedown Club, Houston*
Elvis "That's All Right" Presley returns to Houston for a "Yule Tide

Elvis, Scotty, and Bill, promotional photograph, late 1954 or early 1955 (note Scotty and Bill still wearing Starlite Wranglers shirts)

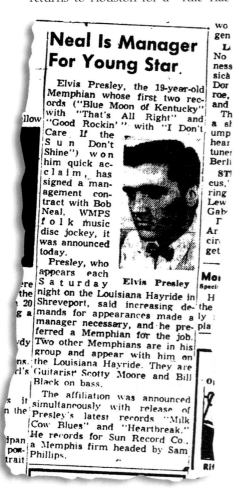

Neal Is Manager For Young Star

Elvis Presley, the 19-year-old Memphian whose first two records ("Blue Moon of Kentucky" with "That's All Right" and "Good Rockin'" with "I Don't Care If the Sun Don't Shine") won him quick acclaim, has signed a management contract with Bob Neal, WMPS folk music disc jockey, it was announced today.

Presley, who appears each Saturday night on the Louisiana Hayride in Shreveport, said increasing demands for appearances made a manager necessary, and he preferred a Memphian for the job. Two other Memphians are in his group and appear with him on the Louisiana Hayride. They are Guitarist Scotty Moore and Bill Black on bass.

The affiliation was announced simultaneously with release of Presley's latest records "Milk Cow Blues" and "Heartbreak." He records for Sun Record Co., a Memphis firm headed by Sam Phillips.

Memphis Press-Scimitar,
December 29, 1954

Jamboree," topping a Hayride bill that is being promoted once again by Biff Collie. Elvis may well have played other Texas and Arkansas dates over the next three days, including the Red River Arsenal, near Texarkana.

29 Wednesday
The *Memphis Press-Scimitar* reports that "Elvis Presley, the 19-year-old Memphian whose first two records . . . won him quick acclaim, has signed a management contract with Bob Neal, WMPS folk music disc jockey, it was announced yesterday." Starting in the new year Neal will book dates within his own listening area on an exclusive basis as well as setting up engagements through the Hayride network in such far-flung new territory as west Texas and eastern New Mexico. A variant of the "spiky-haired" photograph from Elvis' original July 27 interview at the *Press-Scimitar* is used to accompany this story, which also announces the simultaneous release of Elvis' third Sun single.

Sometime in late December or early January, Elvis purchases what will

December Record Release

Single: "Milkcow Blues Boogie"/"You're a Heartbreaker." (Sun 215, released December 28). According to the *Billboard* review on January 29, 1955, the A-side "continues to impress" while "'You're a Heartbreaker' is a slick country-style reading." The record follows the same pattern that Sam Phillips has already established with the two earlier singles, combining a blues-influenced number with an up-tempo country treatment. It differs from the previous releases in that the country number here is an original, solicited by Sam Phillips from Covington, Tennessee, theater owner Jack Sallee, who came into Sun to record promo spots for his theater.

become the band's first official automobile. With Bob Neal's help, he buys a used, tan-colored, 1951 Cosmopolitan Lincoln, putting a rack on top for the bass, with "Elvis Presley—Sun Records" painted on the side. It replaces Scotty's wife Bobbie's 1954 Chevrolet Bel Air.

1 9 5 5

A fan's view, Gilmer, Texas, January 26, 1955

JANUARY

01 Saturday

★ *Grand Prize Saturday Night Jamboree, Eagles Hall, Houston, Texas*

On a bill that includes both seventeen-year-old Tommy Sands, who began his recording career four years earlier under the guidance of Colonel Parker and Tom Diskin, and George Jones, among others, the show is hosted for radio broadcast by Biff Collie.

Elvis' new managerial contract with Bob Neal goes into effect on this date, with a smiling picture of Elvis, Neal, and Sam Phillips that commemorates the occasion appearing in various periodicals and fan magazines over the next couple of months.

02 Sunday

A note in *Billboard* indicates that Elvis may have remained and performed in the Houston area through Tuesday, January 4.

05 Wednesday

★ *City Auditorium, San Angelo, Texas*

"Alvis Presley" tops the bill at a show in this 1,855-seat auditorium, where hundreds of teenaged girls rush the stage for autographs. Hayride artists Billy Walker and Jimmy and Johnny and country comic Peach Seed Jones complete the lineup.

**Big Stage Show
5 Big Stars
ALVIS PRESLEY
(That's Alright)**

★ ★ ★

**BILLY WALKER
(Thank You For Calling)**

★ ★ ★

**PEACH SEED JONES
(If You Don't Someone Else Will)**

★ ★ ★

CITY AUDITORIUM

**SAN ANGELO
Wednesday, Jan. 5th
8:00 P.M.
Adults $1.00 Children 50¢**

San Angelo, Texas

Showtimes for all tour dates throughout the book are presumed to be one performance at normal evening hours (or, at a club, a number of sets) unless otherwise specified.

06 Thursday

★ *Fair Park, Lubbock, Texas*

This *may* be the date of a much-remembered show by Elvis, Billy Walker, and Jimmy and Johnny, at which future country star (and sometime bass player with Buddy Holly) Waylon Jennings recalls having met the young "hillbilly cat." In Jennings' recollection, Elvis declared that his next record would be "Tweedlee Dee," by rhythm-and-blues star LaVern Baker, which is just picking up steam, hitting the rhythm-and-blues charts on January 15, 1955.

With Bob Neal *(left)* and Sam Phillips at the signing of management contract with Neal

With Maxine Brown (found with Gladys' papers and marked as Gilmer, Texas). Date unknown.

On this same date, or else upon his return to Lubbock on February 13, Elvis records his version of two r & b hits, "Fool, Fool, Fool" by the Clovers, and "Shake, Rattle and Roll" by Big Joe Turner, at local radio station KDAV, as a promotion for the evening's show.

07 Friday

★ *High School Auditorium, Midland, Texas*

Elvis appears with other top Louisiana Hayride stars before a crowd of more than 1,600.

08 Saturday

★ *Louisiana Hayride, Municipal Auditorium, Shreveport*

Elvis is introduced as the "Memphis Flash" and described to the radio audience by announcer Frank Page as wearing crocodile-skin shoes with pink socks. He performs "That's All Right," "Hearts of Stone," "Blue Moon of Kentucky," and "Fool, Fool, Fool." The bill includes rising country star Johnny Horton, known as "The Singing Fisherman," who will have a huge pop hit four years later with "The Battle of New Orleans."

11 Tuesday

★ *High School Gym, New Boston, Texas*

This is the most likely date for a show that Elvis definitely played. From this appearance till the end of the month, Elvis' band is augmented by piano player Leon Post and steel guitarist Sonny Trammell, members of the Hayride's staff band. The show is hosted by Texarkana, Arkansas, DJ Uncle Dudley (Ernest Hackworth), and it is most likely Hackworth's report of the crowd's reaction to the young "hillbilly cat" that prompts Colonel Tom Parker and Tom Diskin's first interest in Elvis.

12 Wednesday

★ *City Auditorium, Clarksdale, Mississippi*

This marks the known beginning of two weeks of touring with Jim Ed and Maxine Brown. Bob Neal has booked the tour and appears as MC at all the shows. The Browns are a highly polished brother-and-sister country act and in many locations attract a majority of the crowd.

13 Thursday

★ *Catholic Club, Helena, Arkansas*

In a strange coincidence of timing, Tom Diskin's Chicago office replies to Scotty Moore's December 13 letter soliciting Chicago dates. There are "few outlets for hillbilly entertainers" in the Chicago area, Scotty is informed in a stock letter of rejection, which has obviously been composed without any knowledge of the New Boston show.

14 Friday

★ *Futrell High School Gym, Marianna, Arkansas*

Although no advertisements for this engagement have been found, there is persuasive evidence that Elvis did play here on a Friday in early 1955, the day after playing Helena.

15 Saturday

★ *Louisiana Hayride, Municipal Auditorium, Shreveport*

Elvis sports a rust-colored suit, black-dotted purple tie, and pink socks

January 27, 1955

Mr. George Ferguson
WLS ARTIST BUREAU
1230 W. Washington
Chicago, Illinois

Dear George:

Just to say hello and let you in on a few things.

We have a new boy that is absolutely going to be one of the biggest things in the business in a very short time. His name is ELVIS PRESLEY. Currently he is on the Louisiana Hayride and on a small label Sun records. He gets the girls excited the way Frank Sinatra used to do it. And he's as good looking as all heck. I really know that you'd get terrific reaction on the TV show with this boy. He's a hot box office attraction and everybody is trying to get him for repeat dates where he has appeared.

Also let us know when you can use EDDIE HILL.

Take good care of yourself and give my regards to Earl.

Sincerely,

Tom Diskin
HANK SNOW-JAMBOREE ATTRACTIONS

TD/st

Did I tell you about June Carter? Doing great as a comedian. If you have an open date let me know and I'll see what we can do on price. She gets as good reaction as Minnie on the shows.

Tom Diskin on Colonel Parker's new find

and performs "Hearts of Stone," "That's All Right," and "Tweedlee Dee."

Colonel Tom Parker and Tom Diskin arrive in Shreveport and register at the Captain Shreve Hotel. This is almost certainly the first time either of them has seen Elvis Presley perform, and the Colonel takes steps to forge a link with Bob Neal after the show.

17 Monday
★ *Junior College Auditorium, Booneville, Mississippi (sponsored by the Kiwanis Club)*
The *Booneville Banner* carries a front-page story declaring that "the fastest rising country music star in the nation will be performing in his own top-notch manner." Elvis visits

local radio station WBIP for an interview with DJ Lynn McDowell to support airplay of his records.

Bob Neal writes to Ed McLemore of the Big "D" Jamboree to let him know that Colonel Parker will be doing bookings for him and Elvis, "just like MCA or William Morris or any other agency." According to Neal, Parker is attempting to get a booking at "one of the big resort hotels in Nevada" and is "negotiating a deal that is terrific, to say the least."

18 Tuesday
★ *Alcorn County Courthouse, Corinth, Mississippi (sponsored by the Jaycees)*

19 Wednesday
★ *Community Center, Sheffield, Alabama (sponsored by the Jaycees)*
The local paper reports that Elvis' appearance on this Louisiana Hayride package show is one of the most successful dates ever at the center.

20 Thursday
★ *Leachville High School Gym, Leachville, Arkansas (sponsored by the senior class)*

21 Friday
★ *National Guard Armory, Sikeston, Missouri*

22 Saturday
★ *Louisiana Hayride, Municipal Auditorium, Shreveport*
Elvis performs "Money Honey," "I Don't Care If the Sun Don't Shine," "Blue Moon of Kentucky," and "That's All Right."

Colonel Parker informs Bob Neal by letter that he has booked Elvis on the Hank Snow Tour from February 14 to 18, sending both a contract and a check made out to Elvis Presley for $425, a 50 percent advance on what he can expect to earn for the tour.

24 Monday
★ *Humble Oil Company Camp, Hawkins, Texas*
This week's shows, and others in the oil fields area of east Texas, are presented by Gladewater disc jockey Tom Perryman.

25 Tuesday
★ *Mayfair Building, Tyler, Texas*

26 Wednesday
★ *REA (Rural Electric Administration) Building, Gilmer, Texas*

27 Thursday
★ *Reo Palm Isle Club, Longview, Texas*
At this time the Colonel and Tom Diskin begin spreading Elvis' name throughout their world of show-business acquaintances. Diskin writes to a booking agent in Chicago looking for a TV spot for a "new boy" who he

believes will be one of the "biggest things in the business." He goes on to explain that Elvis gets the girls as excited as Frank Sinatra used to, as well as being "as good looking as all heck."

28 Friday

★ *High School, Gaston, Texas*

29 Saturday

★ *Louisiana Hayride, Shreveport*

By Scotty Moore's meticulous accounting, Elvis, Scotty, and Bill have grossed $2,083.63 from their last month of touring. Half goes to Elvis, 25 percent each to Scotty and Bill, after expenses have been paid.

FEBRUARY

01 Tuesday

★ *High School, Randolph, Mississippi*
Elvis begins a week of Bob Neal bookings, appearing with local singer Bud Deckelman of "Daydreamin'" fame.

02 Wednesday

★ *High School, Augusta, Arkansas (sponsored by the senior class)*
The newspaper ad for the show pictures Elvis, Scotty, and Bill ("The Blue Moon Boys") still dressed in their western shirts. This photograph will continue to be used for some months

Elvis, Scotty, and Bill with Sam Phillips at the Sun Studio, c. February 3, 1955

in newspapers throughout the South, though Scotty and Bill have by now stopped wearing the cowboy-styled outfits that are a carryover from their Starlite Wrangler days.

03 Thursday

Most likely, Elvis, Scotty, and Bill take time to work on new songs in the studio during this week. On February 5 a posed photograph appears in the *Memphis Press-Scimitar* showing the three of them at Sun, with Sam Phillips at the console. During this time they record "Baby Let's Play House," which will be the A-side of their next single, along with still-unreleased (and undiscovered as of 1999) versions of Ray Charles' "I Got a Woman" and "Trying to Get to You." After the session Stan Kesler, a steel guitarist who works primarily on Sun's hillbilly sides, goes home and writes what will become the B-side, "I'm Left, You're Right, She's Gone," based on the melody of the Campbell's Soup commercial.

During this week the trio also appear at school programs at Messick High School and Messick Junior High to help Sonny Neal, Bob's son, in his campaign for the student council.

04 Friday

★ *Jesuit High School, New Orleans, Louisiana*
Elvis appears with Ann Raye, daughter of Biloxi promoter Yankie Barhanovich. He is late for an appearance at radio station WWEZ to promote the show.

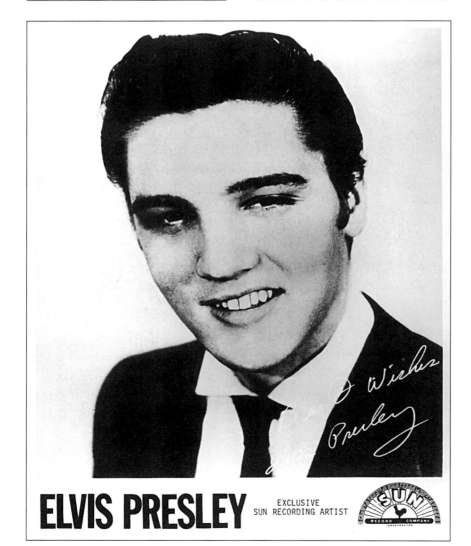

ELVIS PRESLEY   EXCLUSIVE SUN RECORDING ARTIST

Publicity photograph, January 1955

05 Saturday

★ *Louisiana Hayride, Municipal Auditorium, Shreveport*

Wearing pink pants and tie with a charcoal jacket, Elvis performs "That's All Right," "Blue Moon of Kentucky," "Tweedlee Dee," and "Money Honey."

A four-column story in the *Memphis Press-Scimitar* announces, "Through the Patience of Sam Phillips Suddenly Singing Elvis Presley Zooms into Recording Stardom," noting that "a white man's voice singing Negro rhythms with a rural flavor [has] changed life overnight for Elvis Presley."

Colonel Parker sends Elvis a second check for $550 as a deposit for additional dates on the upcoming Hank Snow tour.

06 Sunday

★ *Ellis Auditorium, Memphis, at 3:00 and 8:00 P.M.*

For all of his local eminence, Elvis is listed down on the bill, below such established stars as Hayride graduate Faron Young, Ferlin Huskey, and "Beautiful Gospel Singer" Martha Carson, whose signature tune, "Satisfied," is one of Elvis' favorites.

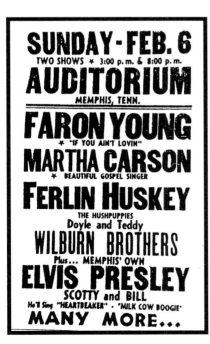

Ellis Auditorium show

Onstage with Dewey Phillips, Ellis Auditorium, February 6, 1955

Between shows Bob Neal arranges a meeting between Sun Records president Sam Phillips and Colonel Tom Parker and Tom Diskin at Palumbo's Restaurant across the street from the auditorium. The ostensible purpose of the meeting is to discuss the future of the young performer in whom they are all so interested. Neal is very much encouraged by the Colonel's enthusiasm, but the meeting does not go well, as Parker explains to Sam Phillips that Elvis is going nowhere on a small-time label like Sun and that he has already made overtures to RCA to buy the contract. Phillips does not react well to this piece of information, and Parker silently revises his plan without ever retreating.

07 Monday

★ *Ripley High School Gym, Ripley, Mississippi (sponsored by the senior class)*

10 Thursday

★ *High School, Alpine, Texas (to benefit the Future Farmers of America)*

Harry Kalcheim, an agent with the powerful William Morris Talent Agency office in New York, writes to Colonel Parker that he has mislaid the

RADIO CORPORATION OF AMERICA
830 FIFTH AVENUE
NEW YORK 20, N.Y.

RCA VICTOR
RECORD DIVISION

RCA VICTOR

February 15th, 1955

Mr. Tom Diskin,
Box 417,
Madison, Tenn.

Dear Tom:

I received your note of February 10th, just as I am
about to leave for California.

Thanks very much for all the promotional work you are
doing on the various RCA Victor artists you have on
tour. I am glad to see you are working closely with
Chick Crumpacker and I am sure there will be mutual
benefits from the Association.

I did receive the Tommy Sands tape, probably the same
one you had, and I have listened to and returned it to
him. I did not think we could make use of the tape for
Tommy Sands releases but there is a possibility that
we could record Tommy on some of the Rhythm and Blues
type Country and Western music. The last I heard from
the Colonel seemed quite favorable toward our signing
Elvis Presley so naturally your comments with respect
to Presley were a little surprising.

Please let me have some reply to my inquiry with respect
to the future recording plans of Jimmie Rodgers Snow.
I think we must try some gimmicks with this young fellow
and would like to know whether or not I can plan combination recordings with him.

Best regards,

STEPHEN H. SHOLES
Artist & Repertoire Dept.

HOK

RCA Pioneered and Developed Compatible Color Television
RCA VICTOR RECORDS

Feb. 10, 1955

Mr. Stephen H. Sholes
RCA Victor Divisions
630 Fifth Avenue
New York, New York

Dear Steve:

I talked to Chick Crumpacker today and we are working
closely with him not only in promoting your artists but
in doing a little good will for the label. We've been
running into kicks about not getting records etc. and
I've been explaing the problems involved etc. We've been
doing nothing but interviews with Jimmie and getting very
favorable reaction from the dj's not only as to his records
but to his personality. I told Chick that anything or
anyway that we can help him we'll be glad to do so.

The thought occured to me that since Elvis Presley is
pretty securely tied up it might be possible to come out
with something in that vien by Tommy. He said that he
had sent you a sample tape. I'd appreciate knowing your
thoughts on this.

We'll be doing some promotion on Anita Carter's new record
in that she will be with us on five dates with the Carter
Sisters.

I should be back in the office (Madison office) by
Febaruary 26th. Be sure and give my best to all the girls
and your wffe.

Sincerely,

Tom Diskin

Tom Diskin to Steve Sholes, February 10, 1955,
with Steve Sholes' February 15 reply

promotion and get the schedule for his first appearance this evening on the already-in-progess Hank Snow Jamboree tour.

★ North Junior High School Auditorium, Roswell, at 7:30 and 9:30 P.M. (sponsored by the Fire Department)

15 Tuesday
★ Fairpark Auditorium, Abilene, Texas, at 7:00 and 9:00 P.M.
Elvis "and his Bop Band" are advertised below headliner Hank Snow and popular hillbilly comedian the Duke of Paducah, with Charlene Arthur and Jimmie Rodgers Snow completing the lineup.

On February 10, Colonel Parker has had Tom Diskin inform Steve Sholes, RCA's head of A & R in the company's country-and-western division (A & R stands for "artists and repertoire" and encompasses everything to do with recording, from

picture of Presley that Parker has sent him but agrees that he sounds promising with "a very special type of voice."

11 Friday
★ Sports Arena, Carlsbad, New Mexico, at 4:00 P.M.
★ Hobbs, New Mexico, in the evening

12 Saturday
★ Legion Hut, Carlsbad, New Mexico
Cash Box reports that Bob Neal, Elvis' new manager, has opened a booking office at 160 Union Avenue in Memphis.

13 Sunday
★ Fair Park Coliseum, Lubbock, Texas, at 4:00 P.M.
"Elvis Presley, The Be-Bop Western

Star of the Louisiana Hayride, returns to Lubbock" reads the advertisement, with "Big 'D' [Dallas] Jamboree" regular Charlene Arthur and Jimmie Rodgers Snow, Hank Snow's nineteen-year-old son and an RCA recording artist in his own right. This is the first booking that Neal has obtained directly through Colonel Parker, and the group receives $350 for their matinee performance. A young Buddy Holly appears at the bottom of this bill as half of the country-and-western duo Buddy and Bob.

14 Monday
Tom Parker has instructed Elvis to meet Tom Diskin at Roswell, New Mexico's, "leading hotel" no later than 3:00 P.M. in order to do radio

renting the studio to finding the songs to producing the session) that Elvis Presley "is pretty securely tied up" at Sun while simultaneously trying to convince Sholes to sign Tommy Sands instead. Sholes replies on this date that "the last I heard from the Colonel seemed quite favorable toward our signing Elvis Presley so naturally your comments with respect to Presley were a little surprising." His letter does not indicate that he feels Tommy Sands is a suitable replacement.

16 Wednesday

★ *Odessa Senior High School Field House, Odessa, Texas, at 7:30 and 9:30 P.M. (sponsored by the Voting Home Owners Club)*

The shows in Odessa attract more than 4,000 people, including local singer Roy Orbison, who later comments, "His energy was incredible, his instinct was just amazing." It is swiftly becoming apparent that any other act has trouble following him.

17 Thursday

★ *City Auditorium, San Angelo, Texas, at 7:30 and 9:30 P.M.*

18 Friday

★ *West Monroe High School Auditorium, Monroe, Louisiana, at 7:30 and 9:30 P.M.*
The end of the Hank Snow tour.

19 Saturday

★ *Louisiana Hayride, Municipal Auditorium, Shreveport*

20 Sunday

★ *Robinson Auditorium, Little Rock, Arkansas, at 3:00 and 8:15 P.M.*

Elvis begins another Jamboree Attractions tour, this one billed as a "WSM Grand Ole Opry" show and headlined as an Extra Added Attraction by the Duke of Paducah and country music legends Mother Maybelle (Carter) and her daughters, the Carter Sisters. As a specially advertised feature attraction, however, with billing throughout the tour as big as the Duke of Paducah's (the tickets for Little Rock actually advertise "The Elvis Presley

Show"), Elvis, Scotty, and Bill receive $350 for these two shows instead of their usual $200 per day.

21 Monday

★ *City Auditorium, Camden, Arkansas*

22 Tuesday

★ *City Hall, Hope, Arkansas*

23 Wednesday

★ *High School Auditorium, Pine Bluff, Arkansas, at 7:30 and 9:30 P.M.*

Seeking bookings for Elvis all over the country, the Colonel contacts A. V. "Bam" Bamford, an influential promoter who first gained prominence in Nashville by booking Hank Williams in the early fifties, now located in California. Parker informs Bamford that Elvis is "a great artist but will need lots of buildup before he's a good investment."

24 Thursday

★ *South Side Elementary School, Bastrop, Louisiana, at 7:30 and 9:30 P.M.*

The last show of this second Jamboree Attractions tour. This package has proven far less of a draw than the Hank Snow show, and Jamboree Attractions loses money on the tour.

25 Friday

Elvis, Scotty, and Bill drive to Cleveland with Bob Neal to play their first date outside the South. They make stops at various radio stations along the way, in hopes of getting subsequent airplay.

Colonel Parker writes to Harry Kalcheim at the William Morris Agency office in New York, once again soliciting Kalcheim's opinion of "this ELVIS PRESLEY BOY" at the end of his letter. The Colonel adds his own opinion that Elvis can succeed if he is "exploited properly." It should be noted here that, as a master promoter, the Colonel saw proper "exploitation" as his calling card, with no element of opprobrium attached.

26 Saturday

★ *Hillbilly Jamboree, Circle Theater,*

Cleveland, Ohio, at 7:30 and 10:30 P.M.

Hosted by WERE disc jockey Tommy Edwards, the weekly show attracts country music fans living in the city, including a number who have first been exposed to Elvis' records through Edwards' broadcasts (Sun distribution does not effectively reach as far as Cleveland). After the show, Elvis meets top WERE jock Bill Randle, who has just returned from his nationally syndicated Saturday-afternoon CBS show in New York. Randle suggests to Bob Neal that he has "a big artist on his way" and gives Neal the name of a contact for *Arthur Godfrey's Talent Scouts*, which Randle thinks would be the perfect vehicle for national exposure.

When the group totals up its income at the end of February, earnings have doubled to over $4,000. Bookings will peak the following month, bringing in over $5,000, then return to approximately $1,000 a week through September. Out of this sum, the band pays for its own expenses (gas and automobile maintenance, hotel bills, booking and promotion commissions) before making the agreed-upon 50-25-25 split.

MARCH

During the early part of March, Elvis returns to Sun and records "I'm Left, You're Right, She's Gone" both as a slow blues and in the up-tempo country form in which it was written. The faster version incorporates drums, which are played by Memphis teenager Jimmie Lott, the first non–Blue Moon boy to play on an Elvis Presley record.

02 Wednesday

★ *U.S. Armory, Newport, Arkansas, at 8:00 P.M.*
★ *Porky's Rooftop Club, Newport, Arkansas, at 10:00 P.M.*

These and all of Elvis' other performances during the month will be booked by Bob Neal, who continues to push the Colonel for another Hank Snow tour.

04 Friday

★ *High School, De Kalb, Texas (unconfirmed)*

05 Saturday

★ *Louisiana Hayride, Municipal Auditorium, Shreveport*

07 Monday

★ *City Auditorium, Paris, Tennessee*
Elvis, Scotty, and Bill are now the headliners on a show made up for the most part of lesser-known artists like Betty Amos, Onie Wheeler, and Jimmy Work.

William Morris agent Harry Kalcheim telegrams Colonel Parker to inquire if Elvis can audition for *Arthur Godfrey's Talent Scouts*, the same show that Bill Randle has recommended so enthusiastically just a short time before. Parker replies blusteringly that he is willing to pay for the trip to New York only if Neal and Elvis agree to give the Colonel the right to represent Elvis on "any bookings that may arise [from] the appearance."

08 Tuesday

★ *Catholic Club, Helena, Arkansas*

09 Wednesday

★ *Armory, Poplar Bluff, Missouri*
In a letter to his associate, Tom Diskin, the Colonel complains once again that they can't waste time and money on Presley without being assured of exclusive control on certain dates and places. He does not want Neal or any other promoter benefiting from the effort and expense he puts into opening up new territory for the young singer.

10 Thursday

★ *City Auditorium, Clarksdale, Mississippi*
Harry Kalcheim cables the Colonel that he has set up the Godfrey audition for March 23, and should Elvis win first place, he will appear on Godfrey's morning TV show for the following three weeks.

11 Friday

★ *Jimmie Thompson's Arena, Alexandria, Louisiana*

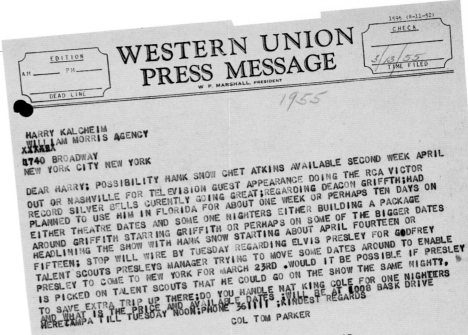

Colonel Parker to Harry Kalcheim re the Arthur Godfrey show

12 Saturday

★ *Louisiana Hayride, Municipal Auditorium, Shreveport*

14 Monday

The Colonel agrees to pay for the trip to the Arthur Godfrey show after securing Neal's promise to protect the Colonel's interest in any bookings that may arise from the tryout.

15 Tuesday

Elvis signs an amended one-year agreement with Bob Neal from which Neal will receive a 15 percent management fee.

16 Wednesday

★ *Ruffin Theater, Covington, Tennessee*
Most likely this is the date on which Elvis plays a "small time Grand Ole Opry"–type show, promoted by theater owner Jack Sallee ("You're a Heartbreaker") and the local radio station. It seems likely that he returns to the area to play the Tipton County Fair later in the year.

Sometime in March, Bill Black wrecks the Lincoln under a hay truck in Arkansas. Elvis borrows the family car from Jim Ed and Maxine Brown for a brief Texas tour that may have included dates not yet identified.

17 Thursday

★ *Dessau Hall, Austin, Texas*

19 Saturday

★ *Grand Prize Jamboree, Eagles Hall, Houston, Texas*
Elvis "Pressley" tops a bill that includes both Hoot Gibson, the western movie star, and Tommy Sands, with Biff Collie once again master of ceremonies. Live recordings of "Good Rockin' Tonight," "Baby Let's Play House," "Blue Moon of Kentucky," "I Got a Woman," and "That's All Right" have surfaced on various bootlegs over the years.

23 Wednesday

In what is almost certainly Elvis' first airplane flight, he travels to New York City with Scotty, Bill, and Bob Neal. The Arthur Godfrey audition

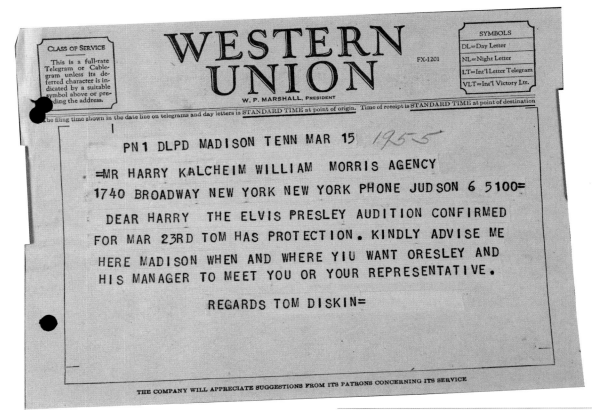

ELVIS PRESLEY SHOW

MARCH 25 7:30 P.M.

DERMOTT HIGH SCHOOL

CHILDREN 50¢

This is one of the earliest known tickets found to date for a show headlined by Elvis

takes place at 2:30 P.M. on the four-teenth floor at 501 Madison Avenue. The Talent Scouts show no interest whatsoever.

25 Friday
★ *Dermott High School, Dermott, Arkansas*

26 Saturday
★ *Louisiana Hayride, Municipal Auditorium, Shreveport*

28 Monday
★ *Big Creek High School Gym, Big Creek, Mississippi (sponsored by the senior class)*

29 Tuesday
★ *High School, Tocopola, Mississippi (sponsored by the junior class)*
The Colonel voices his concern to Bob Neal once again about Sun Records. It is very difficult, he says, to interest promoters outside of the small range of Sun's distribution in the young singer. He asks Neal to find out from Sam Phillips where the records are selling so that he can seek out promoters in those areas.

30 Wednesday
★ *El Dorado High School Auditorium, El Dorado, Arkansas*

31 Thursday
★ *Reo Palm Isle, Longview, Texas*

APRIL

01 Friday
Ector County Auditorium, Odessa, Texas (sponsored by the Voting Home Owners Club)
Elvis, Scotty, and Bill, plus Hayride piano player Floyd Cramer and "a local boy on drums," draw 850 paid admissions "for a rockin' and rollin' dance for teenagers," according to Odessa record shop owner Cecil Holifield in the June 4 edition of *Billboard*.

02 Saturday
★ *Louisiana Hayride, from the City Auditorium, Houston, Texas*
Elvis appears on a Hayride remote broadcast with Slim Whitman, Hoot and Curley, Johnny Horton, Tibby Edwards, Floyd Cramer, and others. He performs "Little Mama," "That's All Right,"

Tom Diskin to Harry Kalcheim, re Godfrey show, March 15, 1955

"You're a Heartbreaker," and "Shake, Rattle and Roll." *Billboard* reports on June 4 that 2,000 people were turned away from this performance and that Elvis and Slim Whitman both tore the house down.

03 Sunday

Elvis is stopped for speeding outside of Shreveport in the 1954 four-door pink-and-white Cadillac that he has bought since Bill wrecked the Lincoln. He posts $25 bond and is notified to appear for arraignment on Tuesday, April 5.

04 Monday

Bob Neal reports to the Colonel that he is unable to fulfill the Colonel's request that he find out where Elvis' records are selling. Meanwhile, the Colonel and Tom Diskin continue to try to drum up interest in Elvis from promoters throughout the South.

07 Thursday

★ *Court House, Corinth, Mississippi, at 2:30 and 8:00 P.M.*
Presenting "that Country Music Star" Elvis Presley.

08 Friday

★ *B&B Club, Gobler, Missouri*

09 Saturday

★ *Louisiana Hayride, Municipal Auditorium, Shreveport*
Elvis performs "That's All Right," "I Got a Woman," and "Blue Moon of Kentucky" on a show that also includes Johnny Horton, Hoot and Curley, and Jim Reeves.

13 Wednesday

★ *High School, Breckenridge, Texas*
Elvis sings "That's All Right," "I Don't Care If the Sun Don't Shine," "Tweedlee Dee," and ends with "Blue Moon of Kentucky." The paper reports that many of the young women "swooned with his every appearance on stage." It is also noted that more than one man is overheard saying: "I'd like to meet him out behind the bar," or "I'd better not see any girlfriend of mine going up after an autograph from that singer."

14 Thursday

Elvis leaves Breckenridge in the morning behind the wheel of his pink-and-white Cadillac, sporting pink slacks and an orchid-colored shirt.

★ *Owl Park, Gainesville, Texas*
Largely unknown in Gainesville, Elvis draws only a handful of people. He appears shaken by the small turnout but promises that he will return and make up for it. He never does.

15 Friday

★ *High School, Stamford, Texas*

16 Saturday

★ *The Big "D" Jamboree, Sportatorium, Dallas, Texas*
Elvis tops a bill that includes rising country star Sonny James, veteran Hayride performer Hank Locklin, Charlene Arthur, and many others. Tickets are $.60 for adults, $.30 for children. Like the Grand Ole Opry and the Louisiana Hayride, Ed McLemore's Big "D" Jamboree in Dallas is a live Saturday-night show broadcast over a prominent local radio station with a strong signal. It serves as an important vehicle to expose Elvis to listeners across Texas, and Bob Neal arranges for four appearances on the show, despite the fact that Elvis will have to pay a substantial penalty for missed Hayride shows. At this time Neal also commits Elvis to do two Beaumont, Texas, shows in June with the same promoter.

20 Wednesday

★ *American Legion Hut, Grenada, Mississippi*

23 Saturday

★ *Louisiana Hayride, from Heart O' Texas Arena, Waco, Texas*
Another remote, with Hayride regulars Slim Whitman, Jim Reeves, Jim Ed and Maxine Brown, and Jimmy "C" Newman, among others. *Billboard* reports that the show draws 5,000 people, one of the largest crowds ever seen in this venue. "Making it great with the Cen[tral] Texans were Elvis Pressley [sic] and J. E. and Maxine Brown."

24 Sunday

★ *Magnolia Gardens, Houston, Texas, in the afternoon*

★ *Cook's Hoedown Club, Houston, Texas, in the evening*
There is good circumstantial evidence to suggest that Elvis played both these clubs on this date, but no confirming advertisements or paperwork have been found.

25 Monday

★ *M-B Corral, Wichita Falls, Texas*

★ *High School, Seymour, Texas*

DANCE
WEDNESDAY,
April 27 8:30—12:00

IN PERSON

Elvis PRESLEY
SCOTTY and BILL

"That's All Right, Mama"
"Blue Moon of Kentucky"
"Good Rockin Tonite"
"Heartbreaker"

FUN! MUSIC! JOKES!

Plus TNT's Newest Recording Artist, CHUCK LEE, the Hill Billy Crooner, and GENE KAY

Along with the Walking A Ranch Hands.

Come One, Come All
Admission: $1.50

American Legion Hall
Hobbs, N. M.

Hobbs, New Mexico

With Dixie, Bessie Wolverton, and Gene Smith at Dixie's junior prom, May 6, 1955

MAY

01 Sunday
★ *Municipal Auditorium, New Orleans, Louisiana, at 2:00, 5:00, and 8:00 P.M.*

Elvis begins a new three-week tour as a "Special Added Attraction" on Hank Snow's All Star Jamboree, with Faron Young, the Wilburn Brothers, Mother Maybelle and the Carter Sisters, the Davis Sisters (Davis Sister Skeeter will go on to have a successful solo career), Jimmie Rodgers Snow, and Onie Wheeler. This tour will take Elvis into new territory as he travels to Florida and the Southeast, requiring the Colonel to work hard to get his recordings in the hands of local DJs and promoters.

02 Monday
★ *High School, Baton Rouge, Louisiana, at 7:00 and 9:00 P.M.*

For one night the Jamboree splits into two units, with Elvis joining a group headlined by Faron Young, and Hank Snow playing Jennings, Louisiana.

03 Tuesday
The tour reunites in Mobile, Alabama, where Elvis and the others participate in radio interviews.

04 Wednesday
★ *Ladd Stadium, Mobile, Alabama*

05 Thursday
★ *Ladd Stadium, Mobile, Alabama*

A pack of girls chases Elvis across the football field.

06 Friday
The show, including Scotty and Bill but not Elvis, plays Birmingham, Alabama. Elvis returns to Memphis to attend Dixie Locke's junior prom, where he double-dates with his

---

Elvis begins a five-day tour with artists from TNT Records, the San Antonio label that is sponsoring the show. The M-B Corral poster proclaims "Elvis 'That's All Right Mama' Prestley" as the headliner. As each artist finishes his performance, he leaves for Seymour, Texas, an hour away, where a second gig has been booked. Elvis doesn't arrive in Seymour until after midnight, because he runs out of gas (and money) along the way. In addition to TNT's Chuck Lee and Gene Kay, Capitol recording artist Dub Dickerson ("Mama Laid the Law Down, Boy") is on the bill. According to Doug Dixon, one of the "hardcore Elvis fans" who remained, when Elvis finally took the stage in Seymour, he was wearing "a fire-engine red sport coat, bow tie, white shirt and blue trousers . . . about two sizes too large so he could make his moves without ripping something. . . . For a long moment he stood there with half-closed eyelids, not saying a word. Scotty stepped up behind Elvis and pretended to wind him up," as if he were a windup toy. With that, "Elvis suddenly grabbed his guitar . . . and the show was on."

26 Tuesday
★ *City Auditorium, Big Spring, Texas*

The ad promises "LOTS OF CLEAN FUN AND HEAPS OF MUSIC."

27 Wednesday
★ *American Legion Hall, Hobbs, New Mexico*

29 Friday
★ *The Cotton Club, Lubbock, Texas*

30 Saturday
★ *Louisiana Hayride, from the Gladewater, Texas, High School*

Elvis' performance of "Tweedlee Dee" is recorded at this remote broadcast.

April Record Release

Single: "Baby Let's Play House"/"I'm Left, You're Right, She's Gone" (Sun 217). April 10, 1955, is generally cited as the release date for Elvis' fourth single. *Cash Box* reviews the single in May, saying: "The polished style of 'I'm Left, You're Right, She's Gone' comes over in true fashion on an intriguing and forceful item with a solid beat." About "Baby Let's Play House" the reviewer opines, "[This] is a real different, fast-paced piece on which Presley sparkles."

cousin Gene Smith and Bessie Wolverton, one of Dixie's best friends.

07 Saturday

★ *Peabody Auditorium, Daytona Beach, Florida*

Colonel Parker is back in home territory in Florida. A resident of Tampa for almost fifteen years, Parker began promoting shows in the mid-1930s and is well known to local promoters and DJs. Jacksonville schoolteacher and sometime songwriter Mae Boren Axton, who has done promotion work for the Colonel in the past, works as a publicist on at least some of these dates.

08 Sunday

★ *Fort Homer Hesterly Armory, Tampa, Florida, at 2:30 and 8:15 P.M.*

09 Monday

★ *City Auditorium, Fort Myers, Florida*

10 Tuesday

★ *Southeastern Pavilion, Ocala, Florida*

11 Wednesday

★ *Auditorium, Orlando, Florida, at 7:30 and 9:30 P.M.*

In Faron Young's recollection, the audience calls for Elvis when Hank Snow takes the stage. The announcer tries to restore order by telling the crowd that Elvis is out back signing autographs, and the auditorium empties.

12 Thursday

★ *The new baseball park (eventually named the Gator Bowl), Jacksonville, Florida*

13 Friday

★ *The new baseball park, Jacksonville, Florida*

At the conclusion of his performance, Elvis announces to a good portion of the audience of 14,000: "Girls, I'll see you backstage." The response is a full-scale riot, with fans pursuing Elvis into the dressing room and tearing off his clothes and shoes. In the opinion of the Colonel's advance man, Oscar Davis, this was the point at which Colonel Parker

was irrevocably sold on the growth potential of Elvis Presley.

14 Saturday

★ *Shrine Auditorium, New Bern, North Carolina, at 7:00 and 9:00 P.M.*

15 Sunday

★ *Auditorium, Norfolk, Virginia, at 3:00 and 8:00 P.M.*

16 Monday

★ *Mosque Theater, Richmond, Virginia*

RCA field representative Brad McCuen (responsible for east Tennessee, Virginia, and the Carolinas) and country-and-western promotion manager Chick Crumpacker are in the audience to check out some of their acts. Crumpacker remembers being bowled over. "What really got the listeners was his energy and *the way he sang the songs.* The effect was galvanic." Subsequently Crumpacker makes a point of taking all of Elvis' records back to New York to give to his boss, Steve Sholes, who, unbeknownst to him, is already well aware of the new act.

17 Tuesday

★ *City Auditorium, Asheville, North Carolina, at 7:00 and 9:00 P.M.*

18 Wednesday

★ *American Legion Auditorium, Roanoke, Virginia, at 7:00 and 9:00 P.M.*

19 Thursday

★ *Memorial Auditorium, Raleigh, North Carolina*

This is Elvis' last show on the tour.

20 Friday

The show plays Chattanooga, Tennessee, but Elvis does not appear. He may have played at the Municipal Auditorium in Texarkana, Arkansas, on this night.

21 Saturday

★ *Louisiana Hayride, Municipal Auditorium, Shreveport*

Jacksonville, Florida

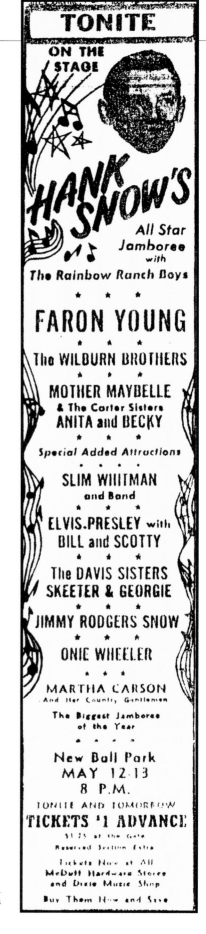

With Jimmie Rodgers Snow in the parade at the Jimmie Rodgers Festival, Meridian, Mississippi. Note that a little-known Elvis Presley attracts no attention from the crowd. *(from the Southern Folklife Collection, Southern Historical Collection, Wilson Library, The University of North Carolina at Chapel Hill)*

22 Sunday

★ *Magnolia Gardens, Houston, Texas*

Elvis plays this outdoor venue in the afternoon and very likely appears at Cook's Hoedown, a Houston club, in the evening.

25 Wednesday

★ *American Legion Hall, Meridian, Mississippi*

Elvis attends the third annual Jimmie Rodgers Memorial Celebration honoring the universally acknowledged "Father of Country Music" in his hometown. An afternoon barbecue attracts 10,000 people with Ernest Tubb, Hank Snow, and many other current country-and-western stars in attendance, while the evening's shows are divided among five different venues in town. "Music will be provided by Elvis Pressley and his orchestra" at the American Legion hall, according to the *Meridian Star*. The September issue of *Country Song Roundup* reports that Elvis was called

back for encore after encore, performing "Baby Let's Play House," "I'm Left, You're Right, She's Gone," "Milkcow Blues Boogie," and "You're a Heartbreaker," among others.

26 Thursday

★ *Junior College Stadium, Meridian, Mississippi*

The Jimmie Rodgers celebration continues with a noontime parade that attracts a crowd of 60,000. All the performers ride in the parade, including Elvis, and he subsequently does a show at the Junior College Stadium. Some of the other celebrities on hand are Louisiana's ex–"singing governor," Jimmie Davis, Tennessee governor Frank Clement, Red Foley, Slim Whitman, Webb Pierce, and Faron Young. Also present are RCA promotion manager Chick Crumpacker and Grelun Landon, a representative of country-and-western song publisher Hill and Range, who initiates discussions with

Elvis about a song folio, a kind of promotional publicity bio with pictures built around the sheet music for some of Elvis' songs.

On this same day Colonel Parker writes a long letter to Bob Neal outlining all that he has done for Presley and offering to work more closely with Neal in promoting the career of the young singer. "If ever you wish to tie in with me closely and let me carry the ball," he declares in somewhat disingenuous fashion, "I will be happy to sit down with both of you and try to work it out."

28 Saturday

★ *The Big "D" Jamboree, Sportatorium, Dallas*

29 Sunday

★ *North Side Coliseum, Fort Worth, at 4:00 P.M.*

★ *Sportatorium, Dallas, at 8:00 P.M.*

30 Monday

Bob Neal books this week's tour with Ferlin Huskey, the Carlisles, and Martha Carson. According to a notice in *Billboard*, the tour is scheduled to open tonight at the *Fair Park Auditorium in Abilene, Texas*, but no notices for that show have been found.

31 Tuesday

★ *High School Auditorium, Midland, Texas, at 7:30 P.M.*

★ *High School Field House, Odessa, Texas, at 8:30 P.M. (sponsored by the Voting Home Owners Club)*

J U N E

Sometime roughly within the past month, the Presleys have moved out of their apartment on Alabama into a rented single-family brick home at 2414 Lamar.

01 Wednesday

★ *High School Auditorium, Guymon, Oklahoma*

02 Thursday

★ *City Auditorium, Amarillo, Texas*

03 Friday

★ *Johnson-Connelley Pontiac Showroom, Lubbock, Texas*

★ *Fair Park Coliseum, Lubbock, Texas, at 8:00 P.M.*

Fourteen-year-old Mac Davis attends the car-dealer show and is knocked out by Elvis' performance. Elvis will later record such Davis compositions as "Memories," "In the Ghetto," and "Don't Cry Daddy."

04 Saturday

★ *Louisiana Hayride, Municipal Auditorium, Shreveport*

Cecil Holifield reports in *Billboard* that his record shops in Midland and Odessa, Texas, show sales on Presley's four singles that "beat any individual artist in our eight years in the record business."

05 Sunday

★ *Hope Fair Park, Hope, Arkansas*

Elvis' 1954 pink Cadillac after fire, June 5, 1955

After the show Elvis sets off for Texarkana with a girl from that town, while Scotty and Bill ride with other friends. About halfway to Texarkana, in Fulton, Arkansas, Elvis' pink-and-white Cadillac catches on fire and burns. Elvis' mother, Gladys, will always recall how she was awakened out of a sound sleep at home by the feeling that something was wrong. Others recall Elvis sitting by the side of the road, looking desolate as he watched his dreams go up in smoke. From Texarkana Scotty returns to Memphis to get the new pink-and-white Ford Crown Victoria that Elvis has recently purchased for his parents, while Elvis and Bill fly on to Texas.

08 Wednesday

★ *Auditorium, Sweetwater, Texas*

MGM Records telegrams Sam Phillips to inquire if Elvis' contract is for sale. Both Phillips and Bob Neal begin at this time to receive unsolicited offers from other major record labels as well.

09 Thursday

Either tonight or Tuesday, June 7, is the most likely date of an appearance in *Andrews, Texas*, booked in conjunction with the Breckenridge appearance on the tenth.

10 Friday

★ *American Legion Hall, Breckenridge, Texas*

11 Saturday

★ *Louisiana Hayride, Shreveport*

14 Tuesday

★ *Bruce High School Gym, Bruce, Mississippi (sponsored by the senior class)*

Elvis appears tonight and tomorrow night with Onie Wheeler and the Miller Sisters, a recently signed Sun act. Elvis is paid $450, one quarter of the admissions, and the remaining profit helps the class of 1956 travel to Washington, D.C.

Colonel Parker writes to Tom Diskin concerning his feelings about Bob Neal's inability to handle Elvis and book him properly. He stresses that it will take patience and skill to build up Elvis' popularity before sending him into new territory. "Let's go slow," he concludes, "and watch Neal on Elvis."

Parker writes to Neal on the same day, suggesting that perhaps with great salesmanship he can get Elvis a Las Vegas booking, but that since he is still an unknown performer he will have to really "prove his worth" once he gets there.

15 Wednesday

★ *Belden High School Gym, Belden, Mississippi*

DJ Bobby Ritter recalls that in order to get into the building without being mobbed, Elvis has to crawl through a back window, ripping the seat of his pants, which have to be held together with a safety pin during his performance.

17 Friday
★ *Roundup Hall, High School Gym, Stamford, Texas*

Bob Neal travels to see the Colonel at his headquarters in Madison, Tennessee, where the two men arrive at the basis of the understanding that the Colonel has been seeking all along. Neal will remain Elvis' manager, but from July 24 all booking and long-term planning will be handled by the Colonel's office, including a concerted effort to move the singer off Sun Records and onto a major label.

18 Saturday
★ *The Big "D" Jamboree, Sportatorium, Dallas, Texas*

19 Sunday
★ *Magnolia Gardens, Houston, Texas*

20 Monday
★ *City Auditorium, Beaumont, Texas, at 7:00 and 9:00 P.M. (presented by the Beaumont Police Department)*

Over two days Elvis appears in five shows, organized by Ed McLemore, to benefit the Beaumont Police.

From Beaumont Bob Neal wires the Colonel that he has been unsuccessful so far in his efforts to convince Elvis of the wisdom of leaving Sun, and he feels the Colonel should speak to him.

21 Tuesday
★ *City Auditorium, Beaumont, Texas, at 2:30, 7:00, and 9:00 P.M.*

The 2,400-seat auditorium has been filled for all five shows.

From Beaumont, Bob Neal wires the Colonel once again to inform him that Elvis continues to be ambivalent on the matter of leaving Sun. Neal thinks it would be best to wait until he is home before pursuing the matter any further. On the same day the Colonel informs Steve Sholes at RCA of his new business arrangement

with Neal and Presley, and invites Sholes to make a bid to acquire the singer.

22 Wednesday
Billboard lists a date in *Vernon, Texas,* on this night, though no supporting documentation has been found.

23 Thursday
★ *McMahon Memorial Auditorium, Lawton, Oklahoma, at 8:00 P.M.*

★ *Southern Club, Lawton, at 11:00 P.M.*

Elvis arrives in his parents' 1955 Crown Victoria, Bill's bass strapped to the roof. He headlines a bill with "8 big stars," including Leon Payne, the blind composer of "I Love You Because," and TNT Records' Chuck Lee, for both tonight's and tomorrow night's shows.

24 Friday
★ *Altus, Oklahoma*

25 Saturday
★ *Louisiana Hayride, Municipal Auditorium, Shreveport*

26 Sunday
★ *Slavonian Lodge, Biloxi, Mississippi*
Elvis, Scotty, and Bill open the new air-conditioned club to a sellout crowd.

27 Monday
★ *Airman's Club, Keesler Air Force Base, outside Biloxi*

Local girl June Juanico attends with a friend who saw the Slavonian Lodge performance and has told June that Elvis Presley is "the most gorgeous man I've ever seen in my life." Elvis picks June out of the crowd and spends the rest of the evening with her.

28 Tuesday
★ *Airman's Club, Keesler Air Force Base*

The group receives $600 for its three nights in the Biloxi area. All shows are booked by Yankie Barhanovich, whom Elvis met in Feb-

ruary when he shared the bill with Barhanovich's daughter, Ann Raye, in New Orleans. Ann recalls Elvis' mother, Gladys, being at Keesler to see at least one of the shows.

29 Wednesday
★ *Curtis Gordon's Radio Ranch, Mobile, Alabama*

Elvis, Scotty, and Bill appear with Curtis Gordon's Radio Ranch Boys for two nights.

30 Thursday
★ *Curtis Gordon's Radio Ranch, Mobile*

JULY

01 Friday
★ *Plaquemine Casino Club, Baton Rouge, Louisiana*

02 Saturday
★ *Louisiana Hayride, Municipal Auditorium, Shreveport*
Cash Box announces that Elvis Presley has been voted number one "Up-and-Coming Male Vocalist" by country music disc jockeys.

03 Sunday
★ *Hoedown Club, Corpus Christi, Texas, from 4:00 to 8:00 P.M.*

04 Monday
★ *Hodges Park, De Leon, Texas*

★ *Recreation Hall, Stephenville, Texas*
Elvis participates at these two all-day events approximately twenty miles apart, the first a family picnic put on by gospel promoter W. D. Nowlin, the second an indoor "jamboree" with pretty much the same lineup. Influenced by the presence of two of his favorite gospel quartets, the Statesmen and the Blackwood Brothers, Elvis sings nothing but gospel music in De Leon, getting a very poor reception, but does his regular show both in Stephenville and in Brownwood later that evening.

★ *Memorial Hall, Brownwood Texas, at 8:00 P.M..*

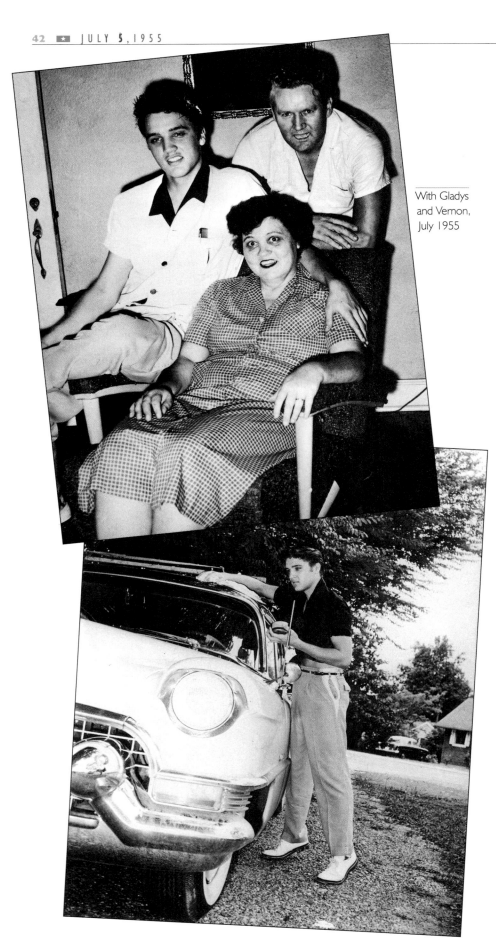

With Gladys and Vernon, July 1955

This is a regularly scheduled dance that Elvis plays with local star Slim Willet (composer of the standard "Don't Let the Stars Get in Your Eyes," a #1 country hit for him in 1952) and the Farren Twins, both of whom were also on the show in Stephenville.

05 Tuesday

Elvis returns to Memphis for a two-week vacation. During this week his next-door neighbor, fifteen-year-old Jackson Baker, recalls hearing Elvis rehearse the song "Mystery Train," and then, after recording it, listen to the acetate over and over again.

07 Thursday

Scotty Moore trades his Gibson ES 295 guitar for a Gibson L5 at O.K. Houck Piano Company. The new guitar will go with the custom-built Echosonic amplifier he purchased for $495 in May, which he is currently paying off in installments.

It is most likely at around this same time that Elvis, too, purchases a new guitar, a Martin D-28, which will be seen in pictures taken in Tampa on July 31. The new guitar has a tooled leather cover which, in addition to its decorative qualities, prevents the back of the instrument from being scratched during performances by Elvis' belt buckle.

Elvis also buys a pink 1955 Cadillac Fleetwood Sixty with a black top to replace the Cadillac that has burned. A removable wooden roof rack is used for the band's instruments.

11 Monday

Elvis successfully records three new songs at Sun. They are: "I Forgot to Remember to Forget," an original composition written for him once again by Stan Kesler; Little Junior Parker's "Mystery Train," which Sam Phillips originally produced on Parker in 1953; and a number by the Washington, D.C., r & b group the Eagles, "Trying to Get to You." Memphis drummer Johnny Bernero plays on

Waxing his new 1955 pink-and-black Cadillac, summer 1955

Fort Homer Hesterly Armory, Tampa, Florida, with his new Martin D-28

Backstage on the Florida tour, probably Tampa

Elvis headlines a two-day package featuring seventeen-year-old country singer Wanda Jackson, Bud Deckelman, and others on a show that promises "FUN! MUSIC! JOKES!" In the course of the engagement Elvis converts Jackson to the rockabilly cause, of which she becomes one of the most prominent, and convincing, female progenitors.

The Colonel by now is gearing up for full representation, instructing Tom Diskin not to mail the Presley "poop sheet" all over the country at once but instead to send batches to one geographic area at a time. This will mean that resulting bookings will not be spaced so far apart. "Let's not plug Sun records for this time," he adjures Diskin. "Sun is doing nothing for us."

21 Thursday
★ *Silver Moon Club, Newport, Arkansas*

22 Friday
In a conference call, Colonel Parker, Bob Neal, Hank Snow, and Tom Diskin continue the discussion about moving Presley to a major label as well as booking him on a proposed Hank Snow weekly television show. At this point Parker and Snow (in partnership as Hank Snow Attractions, producers of the Jamboree Attractions tours), agree to put up $10,000 in cash to buy Elvis' release from Sun Records. In exchange they would expect a 2 percent share of Elvis' record royalties, calculating that he will receive a standard 5 percent and will presumably be satisfied with the 3 percent that he has been getting from Sun all along.

On this same day, in a clearly related development, RCA makes an offer of "either a flat $12,000 toward settlement and delivery of Presley to RCA," or a $5,000 nonrefundable bonus to Presley plus $20,000 recoupable from future record royalties. The offer includes the guarantee of an appearance on network television within sixty days of signing and

all but "Mystery Train," and the first two songs will become the next single.

16 Saturday
★ *Louisiana Hayride, Municipal Auditorium, Shreveport*
"Baby Let's Play House" enters *Cash Box*'s Country and Western chart at #15, marking Elvis' debut on the national charts.

20 Wednesday
★ *Cape Arena Building, Cape Girardeau, Missouri*

can be presumed to be in response to terms demanded by the Colonel.

23 Saturday

★ Big "D" Jamboree, Sportatorium, Dallas, Texas

24 Sunday

As of this date, Elvis Presley will be exclusively represented by Colonel Parker/Hank Snow Attractions, though he continues to be managed by Bob Neal.

25 Monday

★ New City Auditorium, Fort Myers, Florida

Popular hillbilly comic "Deacon" Andy Griffith, who will star in the 1957 Elia Kazan film *A Face in the Crowd* (which chronicles the rise of a performer very much like Elvis Presley), before going on to greater television fame, headlines a show with Grand Ole Opry stars. At the bottom of the bill, boldface letters announce: "EXTRA EXTRA By Popular Demand ELVIS PRESLEY with Scotty and Bill." This is the start of a seven-day tour, the first under the new regime. Once again Mae Boren Axton works as a publicist and interviews Elvis at the beginning of the tour.

26 Tuesday

★ Municipal Auditorium, Orlando, Florida

27 Wednesday

★ Municipal Auditorium, Orlando

28 Thursday

★ The new baseball stadium, Jacksonville, Florida

Again, there is a near riot when Elvis performs.

29 Friday

★ The new baseball stadium, Jacksonville

30 Saturday

★ Peabody Auditorium, Daytona Beach, Florida, at 7:30 and 9:30 P.M.

31 Sunday

★ Fort Homer Hesterly Armory, Tampa, Florida, at 2:15 and 8:15 P.M.

At the Colonel's behest, well-known celebrity photographer Popsie (William S. Randolph) takes a series of action shots, including the tonsil-revealing portrait that is used for the cover of Elvis' first album the following year.

AUGUST

01 Monday

★ Fairgrounds, Tupelo, Mississippi

Webb Pierce is the headliner on this new four-day tour set up by Bob Neal in June and featuring Wanda Jackson, Bud Deckelman, the Miller Sisters, and others. Also included is Charlie Feathers, a twenty-three-year-old incipient rockabilly recording for Sun subsidiary Flip. This is Elvis' first performance in Tupelo since his appearance at age ten in the singing competition at these same fairgrounds, and it is held before a crowd of about 3,000.

Backstage at the Overton Park Shell, August 5, 1955

02 Tuesday

★ Community Center, Sheffield, Alabama, at 7:00 and 9:30 P.M.

Elvis steals the show from headliner Webb Pierce, with Sun newcomer Johnny Cash added to the bill.

Tom Diskin writes Colonel Parker that Bob Neal is still trying to get Elvis to commit himself to a switch to a major label and hopes to have him "pinned down" soon.

03 Wednesday

★ Robinson Auditorium, Little Rock, Arkansas

04 Thursday

★ Municipal Auditorium, Camden, Arkansas, at 7:00 and 9:30 P.M.

Colonel Parker is furious when he learns for the first time of the Hill and Range song folio originally discussed in Meridian. He sees this as one more example of Bob Neal's lack of foresight.

05 Friday

★ Overton Park Shell, Memphis

Bob Neal's eighth annual Country Music Jamboree, prominently featuring Elvis Presley, includes Webb Pierce, Sonny James, and Johnny Cash, drawing an audience of over 4,000 to the open-air amphitheater where Elvis began his professional career.

06 Saturday

★ River Stadium, Batesville, Arkansas

Elvis' appearance at this "12th Annual White River Carnival" elicits an indignant letter from local promoter Ed Lyon, who writes to the Colonel that Elvis was guilty of unprofessional behavior, told off-color jokes, and "stormed off stage" after singing just four songs, thereby "ruin[ing]" the show. Lyon demands an "adjustment," and the Colonel swiftly complies with a refund of $50, writing Bob Neal a scathing letter on August 22 about the

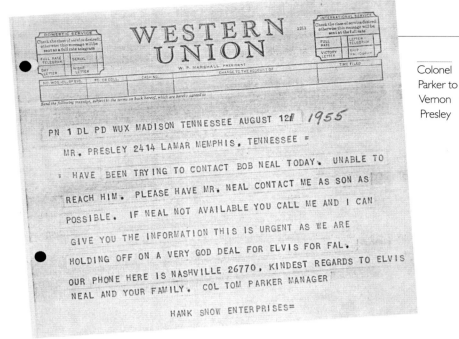

WESTERN UNION

PN 1 DL PD WUX MADISON TENNESSEE AUGUST 12# 1955

MR. PRESLEY 2414 LAMAR MEMPHIS, TENNESSEE =

= HAVE BEEN TRYING TO CONTACT BOB NEAL TODAY. UNABLE TO REACH HIM. PLEASE HAVE MR. NEAL CONTACT ME AS SON AS POSSIBLE. IF NEAL NOT AVAILABLE YOU CALL ME AND I CAN GIVE YOU THE INFORMATION THIS IS URGENT AS WE ARE HOLDING OFF ON A VERY GOD DEAL FOR ELVIS FOR FAL. OUR PHONE HERE IS NASHVILLE 26770, KINDEST REGARDS TO ELVIS NEAL AND YOUR FAMILY. COL TOM PARKER MANAGER

HANK SNOW ENTERPRISES=

necessity of establishing professional standards. Elvis is "young, inexperienced, and it takes a lot more than a couple of hot records in a certain territory to become a big-name artist," the Colonel lectures Neal, whom he blames both implicitly and explicitly for this foul-up in the education of a young artist.

07 Sunday
★ *Magnolia Gardens, Houston (afternoon show)*

★ *Cook's Hoedown, Houston*

08 Monday
★ *Mayfair Building, Tyler, Texas*

Elvis begins a weeklong Tom Perryman tour with Jim Ed and Maxine Brown. Hayride drummer D. J. Fontana, who has played with the group occasionally both in Shreveport and on Hayride tours, joins Elvis for the first time on a regular basis, but unlike Scotty and Bill he is not a percentage participant but a salaried member of the band.

09 Tuesday
★ *Rodeo Arena, Henderson, Texas*

10 Wednesday
★ *Baseball Park, Gladewater, Texas*

11 Thursday
★ *Reo Palm Isle, Longview, Texas*

12 Friday
★ *Driller Park, Kilgore, Texas*

"This cat came out," recalled future country star Bob Luman in later years, "[he was] wearing red pants and a green coat with pink shirt and socks, and he had this sneer on his face and stood behind the mike for about five minutes, I'll bet, before he made a move." Then the girls started screaming, and Luman, a high school student at the time, felt cold chills run up his back, as he knew his life's course was set.

Meanwhile, the Colonel, frustrated by what he sees as Bob Neal's incompetence and not above capitalizing on it, writes directly to Vernon Presley, because, he explains, he has been unable to reach Neal and wants Vernon to know right away that he has a "very good deal" pending.

13 Saturday
★ *Louisiana Hayride, Municipal Auditorium, Shreveport*

14 Sunday
Elvis attends Jim Ed and Maxine Brown's parents' twenty-fifth wedding anniversary party in Gladewater, Texas. A photograph of the group includes 1955 Humes High School graduate Red West, who has been going out with the group occasionally throughout the year, and Elvis' sometime accompanists, piano player

Floyd Cramer and steel guitarist Jimmy Day.

15 Monday
Elvis attends a meeting in Memphis with the Colonel, Bob Neal, and Vernon Presley, at which a new contract is signed that names Colonel Parker as "special advisor," with control of virtually every aspect of the operation.

Meanwhile, the Colonel's pal, booking agent A. V. "Bam" Bamford, remains dubious about Elvis' future, conceding in a letter to the Colonel that he may be "hotter than a firecracker," but reminding Parker that this is true only in certain areas. Bamford says he will consider booking Elvis into new territories if he can pair those bookings with ones in established towns. He mentions that KXLA, the only country-and-western station in L.A., doesn't play Presley at all.

17 Wednesday
In a letter to Julian Aberbach of Hill and Range, the Colonel explains that he now has a three-year representation deal with Elvis and Vernon and is close to making a deal with a major label. Through reliable sources he has learned that Elvis' 1955 record sales are a little more than 100,000 copies. This letter appears to be a follow-up to an earlier request by the Colonel for financial support from the Aberbachs in purchasing Elvis' contract from Sun—which may in turn have been a follow-up to his expressed outrage about the folio.

20 Saturday
★ *Louisiana Hayride, Municipal Auditorium, Shreveport*
Live recordings of "Baby Let's Play House," "Maybellene," and "That's All Right" are available from this date.

21 Sunday
Sometime during the summer Elvis appears in *Mount Pleasant, Texas*, at the American Legion Hall, very likely on this date, or a week later.

Mimosa Room on Lake Gladewater, Gladewater, Texas, August 14, 1955 *(clockwise around the table from bottom left)* Floyd Brown and Birdie Brown celebrating their twenty-fifth wedding anniversary, Norma Brown, Jim Ed Brown, Scotty Moore, Bill Black, D. J. Fontana, Floyd Cramer, Red West, Tom Paul, Jimmy Day, Elvis, Billie Perryman, Tom Perryman, Vicki Perryman, Marilyn Perryman, Maxine Brown, and Bonnie Brown *(courtesy of Tom Perryman)*

22 Monday
★ *Spudder Park, Wichita Falls, Texas*
Elvis begins a weeklong tour with Hayride artists Johnny Horton and Betty Amos. While in Wichita Falls Elvis visits DJ/promoter/bandleader Bill Mack's newborn daughter in the hospital.

23 Tuesday
★ *Bryan, Texas*

24 Wednesday
★ *Davy Crocket High School Football Stadium, Conroe, Texas*
A stage is created on the football field by parking two flatbed trucks side by side. Elvis trips and hits his head as he bounds up the makeshift steps but goes right on with his performance.

August Record Release

Single: "I Forgot to Remember to Forget" /"Mystery Train" (Sun 223). Elvis' fifth and last Sun single is released sometime in August, the by-now-classic mix of country and blues. It premieres on *Cash Box*'s regional charts in Ocala, Florida; Memphis; and Gladewater, Texas, where local DJs play both sides of the record.

25 Thursday
★ *The Sportcenter, Austin, Texas*

26 Friday
★ *Baseball Park, Gonzales, Texas*

27 Saturday
★ *Louisiana Hayride, Municipal Auditorium, Shreveport*

SEPTEMBER

01 Thursday
★ *Pontchartrain Beach Amusement Park, New Orleans*
"The Fireball Star of Records and

Mr. Bob Neal
Radio Station WMPS
Memphis, Tennessee

Dear Bob:

It was nice talking to you on the phone yesterday. It is regrettable that the Batesville situation was goofed up. I know there are always two sides to every story, but after talking to Mr. Lyon on the telephone and getting the story from the DUKE OF PADUCAH, somehow ELVIS must either have been sick or upset, as he surely was not himself. May I suggest that if you can see your way clear a refund of at least $50 to the Batesville people--which you can handle direct or I will handle for you, as it is very important for ELVIS PRESLEY to maintain the best relationship with sponsors. One bad sponsor can undo full years of work just from bad publicity alone.

You must definitely set up a new deal with ELVIS where he goes on the stage as a singer, stays on the stage as a singer, and comes off like a singer. There is always enough comedy on any of my shows that they don't have to do comedy. To be exact, I just can't have any more comedy on ELVIS PRESLEY'S part of the program. If I had received on gripe, or two or three, I would understand that you can't please all of the people all of the time, but from all sources--my connections, friends, people I work with, customers--the complaints have been dominant in all situations and I think we are very fortunate to be able to nip this before it is too late. ELVIS has great talents and he does not have to resort to smutty comedy to sell his attractions. When we ask for more money for ELVIS we definitely must give better production or we should sell him as a comic, and you know how much we can get for him doing that.

Colonel Parker to Bob Neal re professional standards

the famous Louisiana Hayride" is featured on this Hillbilly Jamboree honoring local DJ Red Smith, together with a 1955 "Miss Hillbilly Dumplin'" competition, in front of a crowd of 20,000 people.

02 Friday

Fifteen miles south of Texarkana, Arkansas, Scotty Moore drives the pink-and-black Cadillac Fleetwood into an oncoming vehicle that is in the process of passing a pickup truck. Scotty recalls the Cadillac as requiring approximately $1,000 worth of repairs.

★ *Arkansas Municipal Auditorium, Texarkana, Arkansas*

Elvis is late to the show because of the accident, so local high school student Carl "Cheesie" Nelson entertains the audience until he shows up. Also on the show are Johnny Cash and Charlene Arthur.

At some point early in September, new addition D. J. Fontana becomes

---

Mr. Bob Neal   Page Two.

I think the most important thing is that he needs guidance. He is young, inexperienced, and it takes a lot more than a couple of hot records in a certain territory to become a big name artist, level-headed, courteous, and carry the responsibility that goes with being a star as ELVIS wants to be. There is no way we can play this down--even if we tried--as we would only be fooling ourselves and would be out of business in no time. My reputation is more important than my friendship and belief in the talents that ELVIS has. He can cash in on this to the fullest, but he must contribute all the qualities that I know he has or can have if he makes up his mind to do so. You, as his manager, carry the biggest part of this responsibility. I don't know whether you have ever thought about it that way. They don't say this ELVIS PRESLEY, the first thing they say is who is his manager to let it go on--then they say who books him here, and it all falls back on our shoulders. You know that I am only quoting the things I've heard--I was not there--but the complaints are overwhelmingly the same, so there must be something that happened.

Inclosed are two copies of the first letters received from Mr. Lyon. There are more forthcoming, and we will pass them on to you. I have straightened out this situation pretty well, and next year I will have the show again and will make up for it by being there in person to see that things go right as much as possible.

We will advise you in a day or so regarding September 11, 12, 13, 14, and 15. I may pick up the 13th, 14, and 15th, on my own to keep them working. Please rush a complete set of all records to my office as we are out. I suggest a box of each at least, or more.

I am sure you know how to handle this situation, and impress upon ELVIS the importance if he plans to stay in show business. It is important for him to be on time as per contracts, just as much as he is looking for the money when he finishes playing--even more so the buyer is looking for the talent to be on time and do the job he is paying for. I know that if I had not collected the money in Batesville in advance they would not have paid us for part of the show without a gripe. You must be firm, Bob--this is not something to play with. I have some clients that would cancel him out even while he was on the stage if they thought it would hurt their business, and definitely would not pay for something that they didn't bargain for. There is a time to play for ELVIS but he must not do it too close to his working agreement.

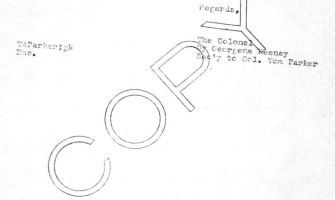

Mr. Bob Neal
                                                    Page Three.

I don't know of any stronger words than to say it is a lot easier to undo all the good things you and I have done, and ELVIS will be just a floating memory no matter who handles him, because he has to please the masses and also the people that invest in him.

Get back to me with your thoughts and also let me know in plenty of time whenever you want me to move in on the record situation and the Logan set-up. The New Orleans deal for ELVIS could be tremendously important for his career, as with two performances there he has not created the following that I thought would be his. I know it is there--this is his opportunity to wake them up.

Regards,

The Colonel
By Georgene Keeney
Sec'y to Col. Tom Parker

TAParker:gk
Enc.

ill and will miss well over a month before rejoining the group.

03 Saturday

★ *The Big "D" Jamboree, Sportatorium, Dallas*

★ *The Round-Up Club, Dallas (later in the evening)*

05 Monday

★ *St. Francis County Fair and Livestock Show Jamboree, Smith Stadium, Forrest City, Arkansas*

Elvis is the headliner on a new five-day tour featuring Johnny Cash, Bud Deckelman, Floyd Cramer, and Eddie Bond. It was Bond for whom Elvis unsuccessfully auditioned at the Hi-Hat on May 15, 1954.

A local musician, Ollie Warren, a high school student at the time, recalls meeting Gladys Presley at this show as she sat in the Crown Victoria parked behind the flatbed trailer on which Elvis was performing.

06 Tuesday

★ *High School Gym, Bono, Arkansas*

After returning to Memphis for the night, the band travels to Bono eighty miles to the northwest, where attendance is so great that the floor gives way in the middle of the show, but fortunately no one is injured.

Jimmy Day remembers Elvis showing off a newly purchased yellow 1954 Cadillac Eldorado convertible at this date.

07 Wednesday

★ *National Guard Armory, Sikeston, Missouri*

08 Thursday

★ *City Auditorium, Clarksdale, Mississippi*

Bob Neal complains to the Colonel that Elvis' fee is too low and receives a scathing telegram in return. The Colonel informs Neal in no uncertain terms that he can either accept the older man's expertise or go his own way. It might be possible, he lectures Neal, to get $500 for certain scattered dates, but it is impossible to get this sum every night of a two-week tour. The Colonel

Colonel Parker to Tom Diskin

is paying Elvis $250 in locations that he has already played and can be counted on to draw a crowd, and $175 for shows in new territory. "I would like to have a telegram from you immediately," the Colonel concludes, "which way do you want it to go: your way, the way Elvis wants it, or the way I have set it up? It is immaterial to me."

09 Friday

★ *McComb High School Auditorium, McComb, Mississippi*

10 Saturday

★ *Louisiana Hayride, Municipal Auditorium, Shreveport*

The Colonel writes Tom Diskin to tell him to remind Elvis how difficult it

is to get enough dates to make up a good tour. In a second letter the Colonel tells his lieutenant to be sure to "talk to Presley alone, take him to lunch or get him in your room," so as to convey two linked ideas: first, that the Colonel is doing more for Elvis than he would for anyone else, unless he was being paid "big dough"; and second, that while "we are going ahead with great plans . . . if we are to be checked every time, we better work out a finish."

11 Sunday

★ *City Auditorium, Norfolk, Virginia, at 3:00 and 8:00 P.M.*

Elvis joins the Hank Snow Jamboree for two days, this time as coheadliner. Other performers include country star Cowboy Copas and popular gospel-based brother act the Louvin Brothers.

12 Monday
★ *City Auditorium, Norfolk, Virginia*

13 Tuesday
★ *Shrine Auditorium, New Bern, North Carolina*

The tour goes on without Hank Snow.

In order to be certain that Elvis and the band are fully covered (and Sun Records does not suffer any undue liability exposure), Sam Phillips takes out an insurance policy on the yellow '54 Eldorado that Elvis purchased earlier in the month. Phillips lists himself as "named insured" and 2414 Lamar (the Presley residence) as the principal place of garaging, though within a matter of weeks the Presleys will move around the corner, to 1414 Getwell, where they will pay $85 a month in rent.

14 Wednesday
★ *Fleming Stadium, Wilson, North Carolina*

15 Thursday
★ *American Legion Auditorium, Roanoke, Virginia*

Although all decisions with respect to Elvis' career must by contract go through the Colonel's office, Bob Neal negotiates a new one-year contract with the Hayride, at $200 a performance, a raise of over 1000 percent. Vernon signs the agreement, which goes into effect November 11, 1955, and carries a penalty of $400 for each missed performance beyond the one every two months allowed. One can only surmise that this represents one last attempt by Neal to assert his independence and that it is endorsed by Vernon out of an ingrained hunger for financial security and an almost desperate uncertainty about the future.

16 Friday
★ *City Auditorium, Asheville, North Carolina*

17 Saturday
★ *High School Auditorium, Thomasville, North Carolina*

The bickering between Colonel Parker and Bob Neal continues. After being pushed mercilessly by the Colonel, Neal pulls out of their joint arrangement, terming his withdrawal a "pleasant parting." The Colonel immediately sends copies of the correspondence to Elvis, expressing the hope that they will be able to work together again in future and concluding somewhat disingenuously, "Sincerely, Your Pal, The Colonel."

18 Sunday
★ *WRVA Theater, Richmond, Virginia, at 2:30 and 8:30 P.M.*

19 Monday
★ *WRVA Theater, Richmond*

20 Tuesday
★ *Danville Fairgrounds, Danville, Virginia*

21 Wednesday
★ *Memorial Auditorium, Raleigh, North Carolina*

22 Thursday
★ *Civic Auditorium, Kingsport, Tennessee*
The end of the tour.

23 Friday
Back home in Memphis, Elvis attends an All-Night Singing put on by the Blackwood Brothers at Ellis Auditorium. When James Blackwood discovers that Elvis has purchased his own ticket to get in, he sends his apologies along with a refund check.

24 Saturday
★ *Louisiana Hayride, Municipal Auditorium, Shreveport*
The newspaper advertisement now lists Elvis at the top of the bill.

26 Monday
★ *Junior High School Gym, Gilmer, Texas*
Elvis begins another tour booked by Bob Neal in familiar territory. It is

possible that Elvis played *Houlka, Mississippi*, during this week.

28 Wednesday
★ *B&B Club, Gobler, Missouri*

29 Thursday
Elvis may have appeared at the ★ *Aubrey, Arkansas, High School* with the Louvin Brothers on a show MCed by Bob Neal.

30 Friday
Actor James Dean is killed, and Bonnie Brown (Jim Ed and Maxine's sister, who sometimes performed with her siblings) recalls Elvis crying in a Gladewater hotel when he heard the news.

The group's gross income for September is $3,300, with Elvis still getting only 50 percent of the net, and Scotty and Bill 25 percent—after the new drummer has been paid. This is the last month that this arrangement will remain in effect. At the Colonel's instigation, as of October 1 Scotty and Bill are put on a fixed salary of $200 a week when they are working, with a retainer of $100 when they are not.

OCTOBER

01 Saturday
★ *Louisiana Hayride, Municipal Auditorium, Shreveport*

03 Monday
★ *G. Rolle White Coliseum, College Station, Texas*
The beginning of a four-day tour with other Hayride acts.

04 Tuesday
★ *Boys Club Gymnasium, Paris, Texas (sponsored by the Optimist Club)*

05 Wednesday
★ *City Auditorium, Greenville, Texas*

06 Thursday
★ *Southwest Texas State University, San Marcos, Texas (afternoon)*

★ *Skyline Club, Austin, Texas (evening)*

07 Friday

With no Friday-night booking, Elvis and promoter Tillman Franks take a bus to Houston to see "Western Swing" king Bob Wills at Cook's Hoedown Club. According to Franks, neither Elvis nor Wills is particularly impressed with the other.

08 Saturday

★ *Louisiana Hayride, Municipal Auditorium, Shreveport*

09 Sunday

★ *Cherry Springs Dance Hall, Cherryspring, Texas*

The first show in a weeklong tour with Johnny Cash, Wanda Jackson, and fledgling country star Porter Wagoner.

10 Monday

★ *Memorial Hall, Brownwood, Texas (sponsored by the Brownwood Volunteer Fire Department)*

11 Tuesday

★ *Fair Park Auditorium, Abilene, Texas, at 7:00 and 9:15 P.M.*

12 Wednesday

★ *Midland High School Auditorium, Midland, Texas*

13 Thursday

★ *Municipal Auditorium, Amarillo, Texas*

The advertisement refers to Elvis as "the king of western bop," but notes that "his wardrobe runs to the 'cool cat' type of dress rather than western apparel."

14 Friday

★ *High School Field House, Odessa, Texas*

15 Saturday

★ *Fair Park Auditorium, Lubbock, Texas*

★ *Cotton Club, Lubbock (later in the evening)*

16 Sunday

★ *Municipal Auditorium, Oklahoma City, Oklahoma, at 3:30 and 8:00 P.M.*

For one night Elvis joins yet another Hank Snow tour, this one costarring Bill Haley, whose "Rock Around the Clock" is in its fifth month at the top of the charts. The phenomenal success of Haley's 1954 record, re-released when the song was used over the credits of the hit film *The Blackboard Jungle*, in some ways certifies the success of the new music and validates its name once and for all as "rock 'n' roll." In subsequent weeks *Billboard* will note the clever strategy of "Col Tom Parker of Jamboree Attractions, one of the nation's major bookers and promoters of country & western talent, [who] instituted a new policy when he presented a combination of popular and country & western music on a recent one-nighter tour." It might further be noted that Haley and Elvis are advertised on the top half of the poster, above Hank Snow.

17 Monday

★ *Memorial Stadium, El Dorado, Arkansas*

Elvis, Scotty, and Bill appear after a "Big Free Hillbilly Amateur Show."

19 Wednesday

★ *Circle Theater, Cleveland, Ohio, at 7:30 and 10:00 P.M.*

Elvis returns to Cleveland as an "extra added attraction" on a show headlined by Grand Ole Opry stars Roy Acuff and Kitty Wells.

20 Thursday

★ *Brooklyn High School Auditorium, Cleveland, at 1:30 P.M.*

This is a show put together by Cleveland DJ Bill Randle, who, in his October 22 column in the *Cleveland Press*, describes the film to be made from it, a Universal picture in which Randle will be "supported by Pat Boone, the Four Lads, Bill Haley and his Comets, and the phenomenal Elvis Presley. Called 'Top Jock' [or "A Day in the Life of a Famous Disc Jockey"], the film will run about 15 minutes when it hits your movie house." It never did, and it never has—

though the show by all accounts sounds fabulous. Whether it was the Colonel or union problems that blocked its release, in subsequent years the footage has never been located, though some stills survive.

★ *St. Michael's Hall, Cleveland, at 8:00 P.M.*

Hosted once again by Bill Randle, this show climaxed, according to Randle's later recollection, when Elvis broke the strings on his guitar and then smashed the guitar on the floor. "It was mass hysteria," recounted the DJ. "We needed police to get him out of the hall."

In what will turn out to be the penultimate act of the long struggle of wills between Bob Neal and Colonel Parker, Gladys and Vernon Presley sign a telegram provided by Tom Diskin granting the Colonel "sole and exclusive" representation of their son with respect to "all negotiations" for a new recording contract. Diskin's accompanying message seeks to reassure the Presleys that they are in the "most competent hands."

21 Friday

★ *Missouri Theater, St. Louis, Missouri, at 7:00 and 9:30 P.M.*

The Grand Ole Opry tour with Roy Acuff and Kitty Wells continues for three more days.

22 Saturday

★ *Missouri Theater, St. Louis, at 7:00 and 9:30 P.M.*

23 Sunday

★ *Missouri Theater, St. Louis, at 2:00, 5:00, and 8:00 P.M.*

Elvis is scheduled to open the 2:00 P.M. show but arrives late, saying that he was searching for his wallet. As a result of his tardiness, he is not permitted to perform and, with the Colonel's approval, is docked $125 pay.

24 Monday

★ *Silver Moon Club, Newport, Arkansas*

Cleveland, October 19–20, 1955
(note Elvis' conscious emulation of Bill Haley
right down to a red jacket and hairstyle
similar to Haley's)

With Bill Haley, Cleveland,
October 20, 1955

Tom Diskin to Vernon and Gladys

Elvis is booked with local rockabilly Sonny Burgess, who will start recording for Sun himself the following year. The newspaper advertisement promises: "If you like GOOD Western Music (and who doesn't) You'll enjoy Elvis Presley and the Moonlighters singing and playing your favorite western tunes." Show time is "9 til ?"

Colonel Parker telegrams Sam Phillips from the Warwick Hotel in New York to inform him that he has been authorized by Elvis' parents to handle all negotiations for the sale of Elvis' Sun Records contract. Putting the horse somewhat after the cart, Parker asks Phillips to name his price.

WESTERN UNION

NL OCT 20 1955

MR & MRS VERNON PRESLEY   (COPY.)

2124 LAMAR ST PHONE 484921 MEMPHIS TENN

DEAR MR & MRS PRESLEY FOLLOWING IS THE COPY FOR THE WIRE AUTHORIZING COL PARKER TO NEGOTIATE A RECORD CONTRACT ON BEHALF OF ELVIS. "DEAR COL PARKER, WE HERBY AUTHORIZE YOU TO ACT AS OUR SOLE AND EXCLUSIVE REPRESENTATIVE IN ALL NEGOTIATIONS PERTAINING TO THE RECORDING CONTRACT OF ELVIS PRESLEY THIS AUTHORIZATION TO INCLUDE THE SETTLEMENT FOR THE PRESENT CONTRACT WITH SUN RECORDS AND FULL AUTHORITY TO NEGOTIATE A NEW RECORDING CONTRACT WITH A MOAJOR RECORDING FIRM NO OTHER PERSON OR PERSONS ARE AUTHORIZED TO REPRESENT ELVIS PRESLEY IN ANY RECORDING CONTRACT NEGOTIATIONS OTHER THAN COL PARKER AND WE WILL BE BOUND BY YOUR DECISSION AS WE FEEL THAT YOU WILL BE FOR THE BEST INTEREST OF ELVIS PRESLEY SIGNED MR & MRS VERNON PRESLEY AS GUARDIANS FOR ELVIS PRESEEY". SEND THIS WIRE TO COL PARKER CARE THE HOLIDAY MOTEL ROUTE 3 MECHANICSBURG PA, COLONEL IS NOT ONLY INTERESTED IN GETTING ELVIS ON MAJOR LABEL BUT WANTS TO GET THE BEST, POSSIBLE DEAL FOR HIM NOW AND FOR THE FUTURE YOU CAN BE ASSURED THAT YOU ARE PUTTING THIS IN MOST CONFIDENT HANDS KINDEST REGARDS

TOM DISKIS

WESTERN UNION

STRAIGHT WIRE

Mr. Sam Phillips   10/24/55   COL. TOM PARKER
SUN RECORDS   BOX 417
706 Union Ave.,   MADISON, TENN.
Memphis, Tennessee

IMPORTANT. TO BE DELIVERED = NOT PHONED.

Dear Sam:

Elvis Presley and his parents Mr. & Mrs. Presley have requested and authorized me to handle all negotiations on an exclusive basis towards affecting a settlement of the Elvis Presley recording contract with you and the Sun Record Company. If interested will you please advise me your best flat price for a complete dissolution and release free and clear of the talents and recording services of ELVIS PRESLEY and also to include

WESTERN UNION

Oct 24 1955

Page two - Sam Phillips wire

the masters of all Elvis Presley recordings now held by your firm and your associates if any. It is of course understood that you will allowed to service your distributors and dealers with the releases that are currently on sale and for a reasonable period of time. Advise me here at the Warwick Hotel in New York City, by wire today as I will have to leave here in the morning, kindest regards,
Colonel Tom Parker

25 Tuesday

On this date, Elvis most likely appeared at the *Armory, Houston, Mississippi.*

26 Wednesday

★ *Vigor High School, Mobile, Alabama,* at 10:00 A.M.

After thirty minutes the school principal stops the show when Elvis tells an off-color joke about "milking through the fence."

★ *Greater Gulf States Fair, Prichard, Alabama,* at 3:30 and 7:30 P.M.

27 Thursday

★ *National Guard Armory, Jackson, Alabama*

Bob Neal learns for the first time (from Sam Phillips and the Presleys virtually simultaneously) that the Colonel is in the midst of selling Elvis' contract and writes to Parker, demanding a meeting to straighten things out.

Colonel Parker to Sam Phillips

Silver Moon Club, Newport, Arkansas

28 Friday

★ *Curtis Gordon's Ranch Club,*
Mobile, Alabama

Bill Bullock, manager of the single records division of RCA Records, wires Colonel Parker in Madison, Tennessee, that $25,000 is as high as RCA can go for the acquisition of Presley's contract. This is a reiteration of what Steve Sholes has written to Parker the day before.

29 Saturday

★ *Louisiana Hayride, Municipal*
Auditorium, Shreveport

Colonel Parker drives to Memphis to meet with Sam Phillips and hammer out the terms of an option agreement. It will take effect on October 31 and give Parker until November 15 to put down a nonrefundable deposit of $5,000 against the $35,000 purchase price for Elvis' recording contract.

Harry Kalcheim of William Morris suggests to the Colonel that Elvis would make a good subject for a Hollywood short, but Parker remains unimpressed by Kalcheim's New York vision, informing him that he is in the middle of making a deal.

30 Sunday

Elvis returns to his new home on Getwell.

During the week Elvis goes into the Sun studio one last time to record a B-side for "Trying to Get to You." There appears to be some mix-up in communications, because the session breaks off in the middle after several attempts at "When It Rains It Really Pours," a Billy "the Kid" Emerson blues, and drummer Johnny Bernero comes away with the clear impression that this is because Elvis' contract is about to be sold.

NOVEMBER

05 Saturday

★ *Louisiana Hayride, Municipal*
Auditorium, Shreveport

The latest single, "I Forgot to Remember to Forget"/"Mystery Train," appears on three of *Billboard*'s national charts, representing country music sales, jukebox, and radio play.

06 Sunday

★ *Biloxi Community House, Biloxi,*
Mississippi, at 2:00 and 8:00 P.M.
(to benefit the Daily Herald *Doll &*
Toy Fund)

07 Monday

★ *Keesler Air Force Base, outside,*
Biloxi, Mississippi

08 Tuesday

★ *Keesler Air Force Base*

10 Thursday

Elvis attends the fourth annual Country Music Disc Jockey Convention in Nashville, where he tells everyone he meets of his imminent switch to RCA, although the Colonel has yet to finalize the deal. In his room at the Andrew Jackson Hotel, Mae Boren Axton plays him a demo of a new song she has written with Tommy Durden called "Heartbreak Hotel."

11 Friday

After a second day of meeting DJs at the convention, Elvis flies home to Memphis.

12 Saturday

★ *Carthage Milling Company,*
Carthage, Texas, at 2:00 P.M.

Elvis appears at the opening of the new mill with other Hayride performers.

★ *Louisiana Hayride, Municipal*
Auditorium, Shreveport

Billboard's Annual Disc Jockey Poll names Elvis the "Most Promising C&W Artist."

13 Sunday

★ *Ellis Auditorium, Memphis, at 3:00*
and 8:00 P.M.

This "Western Swing Jamboree," dedicated to departing KWEM DJ Texas Bill Strength, who is bound for Minneapolis, and featuring Texas-born, Princeton-educated, star of western swing and honky tonk Hank Thompson, top country act Carl Smith, Charlene Arthur, and Sun artist Carl Perkins (just a few weeks away from recording his first hit, "Blue Suede Shoes"), marks the beginning of a six-day tour.

14 Monday

★ *Forrest City High School*
Auditorium, Forrest City, Arkansas,
at 7:00 and 9:15 P.M.

Undoubtedly in response to Harry Kalcheim's suggestion of two weeks before, and despite the fact that the deal with RCA has yet to come together, the Colonel informs the William Morris agent that he would be "interested in making a picture with this boy. However, we must be very careful to expose him in a manner befitting his personality, which is something like the James Dean situation." Two days later he will elaborate further, wondering if Warner Brothers may have shelved plans for any James Dean pictures for which his boy might be suited. "Believe me," he informs Kalcheim, "if you ever follow one of my hunches, follow up on this one and you won't go wrong." He adds that he already has three tentative coast-to-coast television appearances for Elvis—which would appear, on the evidence, to have been tentative indeed.

15 Tuesday

★ *Community Center, Sheffield,*
Alabama, at 7:00 and 9:30 P.M.

Colonel Parker finally wears down RCA after a barrage of phone calls and telegrams. On the last day of the option Bill Bullock agrees to Sam

Phillips' price of $35,000, an unheard-of amount, and Parker sends Phillips the $5,000 earnest via airmail, special delivery. Several days later he receives a refund from RCA, but he will always point to the fact that it was *his* money that secured Presley's contract, his money that was at risk.

16 Wednesday

★ *Camden City Auditorium, Camden, Arkansas,* at 7:00 and 9:15 P.M.

17 Thursday

★ *Arkansas Municipal Auditorium, Texarkana, Arkansas,* at 7:00 and 9:15 P.M.

Johnny Cash joins the show for this performance and is amazed to see Elvis take time to carefully hand-wash his car after driving it through the rain and mud on his way to Texarkana.

18 Friday

★ *Reo Palm Isle, Longview, Texas*

19 Saturday

★ *Louisiana Hayride, remote broadcast from the Gladewater, Texas, high school*

Elvis performs "Baby Let's Play House," "That's All Right," and Bill Haley's "Rock Around the Clock."

20 Sunday

Elvis flies back to Memphis.

21 Monday

RCA executives Steve Sholes and Coleman Tily, along with song publisher Hill and Range's lawyer Ben Starr, Hank Snow, Tom Diskin, and the Colonel, all converge on the tiny Sun studio, where the sale of Elvis' contract and all of his Sun masters is formally executed and signed by Tily for RCA, Phillips for Sun, Elvis, Vernon, the Colonel, and Bob Neal, with Gladys Presley proudly looking on. Elvis' contract with RCA of the same date calls for a minimum of eight sides per year, two one-year options, and a 5 percent royalty, with the purchase price of the contract recoupable from one half of that royalty and a $5,000 nonrecoupable bonus going to the artist. Back in the Colonel's room at the Hotel Peabody,

At the RCA contract signing, Sun Studio, November 21, 1955, with *(left to right)* Colonel Parker, Gladys, Elvis, Vernon, RCA attorney Coleman Tily, and Bob Neal

a further sum of $1,000 is conveyed from Hill and Range, with whom a contract has been worked out to handle song publishing via a 50-50 partnership with Elvis. Elvis and Vernon sign for receipt of $4,500, with the Colonel taking his 25 percent commission on the full $6,000.

22 Tuesday

Telegram from Elvis Presley to Colonel Parker:

Dear Colonel, Words can never tell you how my folks and I appreciate what you did for me. I've always known and now my folks are assured that you are the best, most wonderful person I could ever hope to work with. Believe me when I say I will stick with you through thick and thin and do everything I can to uphold your faith in me. Again, I say thanks and I love you like a father. Elvis Presley

The Colonel writes to Harry Kalcheim at William Morris that he now has things tied up in such a way that "I can expect 100% protection and cooperation." He wants Kalcheim to work out a deal for a short motion picture with both Elvis and Hank Snow, still his nominal partner.

23 Wednesday

Kalcheim pitches Presley to NBC-TV, describing him as a young singer along the lines of former teen idol Johnnie Ray.

Meanwhile, Elvis has gone shopping in Memphis, where he spends over $600 at Ed's Camera Shop.

24 Thursday

Kalcheim pressures Parker to have Elvis play dates in New York and New Jersey in order to increase his exposure. The Colonel, for his part, adamantly ignores the suggestions of a man he feels is missing the point, resisting the pressure to pursue any other tactics but his own.

25 Friday

★ *Woodrow Wilson High School, Port Arthur, Texas*

This is Elvis' first performance after signing his RCA contract. The group is paid $350.

26 Saturday

★ *Louisiana Hayride, Municipal Auditorium, Shreveport*

The Colonel writes to Neal, who will remain Elvis' personal manager by contract for another four months, to be sure that Elvis reports to all his shows on time. He advises Neal once again to remind Elvis to cut out the

Publicity photograph with Eddy Arnold at RCA Records studio in New York, December 1, 1955

comedy during the shows and make sure the band does as well.

28 Monday

Back home in Memphis, Elvis spends $61.29 at Wells Clothing Store.

29 Tuesday

★ *The Mosque Theater, Richmond, Virginia, Philip Morris Employees Night*

Elvis appears at this company show with the Hank Snow All Star Jamboree.

30 Wednesday

Elvis and the Colonel fly to New York, where they register at the Hotel Victoria on Fifty-first Street.

DECEMBER

01 Thursday

In New York Elvis and the Colonel meet with RCA executives, including president Larry Kanaga and publicity director Anne Fulchino. A photo shoot has been arranged and pictures of Elvis and the Colonel, Elvis and Steve Sholes, and Elvis and fellow RCA artist Eddy Arnold, who happens to be in New York for a session, are taken in RCA's Twenty-fourth Street studio, along with posed action shots that will be used on the back of Elvis' first album.

02 Friday

★ *Sports Arena, Atlanta, Georgia*

Elvis appears before a small crowd and is paid $300.

03 Saturday

★ *State Coliseum, Montgomery, Alabama*

Talent Contest Final, followed by a show that includes Roy Acuff, Kitty Wells, and others. Elvis is paid $400.

Billboard announces that Elvis, "one of the most sought-after warblers this year, signed two big-time contracts," one with RCA and one with Hill and Range, the music publishing company under which newly formed BMI company Elvis Presley Music will operate. The story points out that RCA plans to push Elvis' "platters in all three fields—pop, r.&b., and c.&w. However, RCA . . . plans to cut the warbler with the same backing—electric guitar, bass fiddle, drums and Presley himself on rhythm guitar—featured on his previous Sun waxings."

04 Sunday

★ *Lyric Theater, Indianapolis, Indiana*

The start of a four-day booking with the Hank Snow show that includes country comedian Rod Brasfield and the Carter family and advertises Elvis as an "extra added" attraction.

05 Monday

★ *Lyric Theater, Indianapolis*

While in Indianapolis, Elvis and Anita Carter take a tour of the RCA manufacturing plant.

06 Tuesday

★ *Lyric Theater, Indianapolis*

07 Wednesday

★ *Lyric Theater, Indianapolis*

Elvis and the group get $1,000 for the four shows.

Tom Diskin reports to the Colonel from Indianapolis that Elvis has done better and better, getting the kids "all hopped up" each night—but he still needs to work on pacing his act.

08 Thursday

★ *Rialto Theater, Louisville, Kentucky*

Elvis appears with Hank Snow on another show for Philip Morris Company employees.

09 Friday

★ *High School, Swifton, Arkansas*
Elvis appears with Johnny Cash.

★ *B&I Club, Swifton, Arkansas (later in the evening)*

December Record Release

Singles: RCA re-releases Elvis' latest Sun single, "I Forgot to Remember to Forget"/"Mystery Train," on December 2, while it is still high on the national country-and-western charts.

On December 20, RCA re-releases the four earlier Sun singles: "That's All Right"/"Blue Moon of Kentucky," "Good Rockin' Tonight"/"I Don't Care If the Sun Don't Shine," "Milkcow Blues Boogie"/"You're a Heartbreaker," and "Baby Let's Play House"/"I'm Left, You're Right, She's Gone."

In B&I Club owner Bob King's recollection, Elvis sings "Heartbreak Hotel" and declares, "It's gonna be my first hit."

10 Saturday

★ *Louisiana Hayride, Municipal Auditorium, Shreveport*

12 Monday

★ *National Guard Armory, Amory, Mississippi*

Elvis appears with Johnny Cash and Carl Perkins on a show in Amory either this night or the next.

13 Tuesday

Harry Kalcheim is furious when he learns that Colonel Parker has booked Elvis for four consecutive weeks in January on CBS's Saturday-night variety show, Jimmy and Tommy Dorsey's *Stage Show*, through another agent, Steve Yates.

14 Wednesday

As a follow-up to the *Stage Show* booking, CBS requests a list of Elvis' songs, from which a selection will be made with input from the show's producer at the dress rehearsal. Elvis is to be paid $1,250 for each appearance, with an option for two more weeks at $1,500 each.

15 Thursday

★ *Catholic Club, Helena, Arkansas*

All five hundred tickets for this show with Carl Perkins are sold two days in advance.

16 Friday

The Colonel responds unrepentantly to Harry Kalcheim, reprimanding him for failing to work hard enough to get Elvis on television. He lectures the agent that it is not enough just to send out letters and sit and wait for a reply. An agent must pitch his artist "full force." If he himself were simply to depend on people calling him back, the Colonel concludes, "I would have to start selling candy apples again. Nuff said."

Dec 16, 1955

Mr Harry Kalcheim
William Morris Agency
1740 Broadway
New York City New York.

Dear Harry;

Have just returned from my advance promotion tour for my date in St Louis Jan 1st 1956 at Kiel Auditorium,I also have received the contracts from Sid Epstein from Chicago on the Moline dates for EDDY ARNOLD. I am meeting EDDY Today to have everything in order for Sid. Plane tickets have also been secured for EDDY for this date.Jan 28th and 29th .I was Right I notice on the letter to Sid that this is the same party that I have been workin with for close to Six Months on this date,I guess he thought he could save money bypassing me,however its all cleared up and the dates are set

Now regarding your note on ELVIS PRESLEY . Knowing you as I do I will be very frank;Some-one is giving you a bum steer regarding Bob Neal advising the producer to get in touch with Steve Yates,a letter from Bob Neal is on its way advising me that no One called him if they had he would have advised them to contact me here,Bob Neal does not advise any-one to contact any agency but myself First so we do not run into any snags. Steve Yates called me with an offer for the Gleason show One shot,and the price he gave me was way out of line so I told him what I wanted for PRESLEY and he got it I called you up right after this and asked you why your man had not worked on this setup since Yates called me as the producer had called him but not on advise of Bob Neal,this producer knew that Yates handles Country and Western Talent so he called Steve. Only after we had already been talking and confirmed the 4 dates did the producer called Yates and asked him what William Morris had to do with it,since your man called this producer but from what I gather only after I had spoken to you asking you why your man missed out on this, Harry you know as well as I do offering a new artist is one thing but selling One is another,I cant go for a pitch that my artist has been submitted and then wait till you hear from some-one that wants him that way you can write One hundred letters and just sit and wait till some-one comes up with a deal. So till I get up there lets just leave everything as is,and I am not exclusive with any-one for the time being,for we surely will have to clearup a few details or we will always be in hot water and have misunderstandings. I dont think that this artist was pitched full force for the reaction that I got on my own deals have been very good and so far we got nothing from William Morris,Steve Yates did a good job with this deal and some-one just did not get on the ball in time to nail this down If I waited for some-one to call me with deals all the time,I would have to start selling candy apples again.Nuff said,I just spoke to you and you know my feelings towards you and William Morris but I cant let my friendship keep my artist from working. so lets all dig-in and keep things rolling. I think this will work out for the best of all of us . But I do hope that your man will at least dig in a little more often and tell every-one so they will know who they should call. My best to you and the Family.

Your Pal

The Colonel .

Colonel Parker to Harry Kalcheim

17 Saturday

★ *Louisiana Hayride, Municipal Auditorium, Shreveport*

Elvis performs six songs, including Tennessee Ernie Ford's huge hit on Merle Travis' parable of the coal mines, "Sixteen Tons"; the Platters' doo-wop classic "Only You"; and Little Richard's debut (and definitive) rocker, "Tutti Frutti." The crowd does not want to let him leave the stage.

The Colonel sends Bob Neal the *Stage Show* contract for Elvis to sign, pointing out that there must be no "ad libs or gestures" on the show other than those the producer recommends.

19 Monday

Elvis goes shopping in Memphis, spending $39.04 at Harry Levitch's jewelry store in the Peabody and $50 at Lansky Brothers on Beale, around the corner. Later in the week he spends $691.28 at Ed's Camera Shop.

In the evening Elvis attends a Memphis charity show at Ellis Auditorium that features an all-star wrestling program.

RCA VICTOR RECORD BULLETIN

BIGGEST C&W RECORD NEWS OF THE YEAR!

In Elvis Presley we've acquired the most dynamic and sought-after new artist in country music today, one who's topped the "most promising" category in every trade and consumer poll held during 1955!

Promotion is being spearheaded with disc jockey records to the entire Pop and C&W "A" lists, an initial coverage of more than 4,000 destinations!

Page ads will appear this week in Billboard and Cash Box, reprints about 10 days later. The issues will carry full publicity on Presley's joining the label.

It's imperative that you follow up this all-market approach to every station receiving Pop or Country service. Use the trade articles to sell your dealers and one stops across the board!

The tunes: I FORGOT TO REMEMBER TO FORGET and MYSTERY TRAIN. The number: 20/47-6357. The name: ELVIS PRESLEY, one that will be your guarantee of sensational plus-sales in the months to come!

#55C-489
11/28/55

John Y. Burgess, Jr., Manager
Sales and Promotion
Single Record Department

RCA VICTOR RECORD BULLETIN

NEW KIND OF HIT RE-RUN!

Following the excellent reaction to our first Elvis Presley release, I FORGOT TO REMEMBER and MYSTERY TRAIN, we are immediately making available four other Presley releases from Sun label. They are . . .

THAT'S ALL RIGHT	
BLUE MOON OF KENTUCKY	20-6380
	47-6380
GOOD ROCKIN' TONIGHT	
I DON'T CARE IF THE SUN DON'T SHINE	20-6381
	47-6381
MILKCOW BLUES BOOGIE	
YOU'RE A HEARTBREAKER	20-6382
	47-6382
BABY, LET'S PLAY HOUSE	
I'M LEFT, YOU'RE RIGHT, SHE'S GONE	20-6383
	47-6383

Remember, these top performances by the "Most talked-about new record personality" had only spotty distribution on Sun. With the current excitement about Presley you should be able to pick up plenty of plus-business - if you stock and sell these sides.

Use the Hit Re-run Order Form to order, and don't underestimate on quantity! If Elvis Presley has any performance or sales history in your territory, you have the promise of sure turnover on these four bonus hits!

#55C-495
12/19/55

John Y. Burgess, Jr.
Manager, Sales & Promotion
Singles Record Department

RCA Victor record bulletins
(saved by Gladys Presley)

22 Thursday

A & R head Steve Sholes sends Elvis demonstration records of ten songs he would like him to consider for his first RCA recording session, scheduled for January in Nashville. Elvis will eventually record two, "I'm Counting on You" and "I Was the One," both ballads.

24 Saturday

Elvis remains at home over Christmas. He does not appear on the Louisiana Hayride show this week.

31 Saturday

★ *Louisiana Hayride, Municipal Auditorium, Shreveport*

On his 1955 income tax return Elvis reports a total income of $25,240.15.

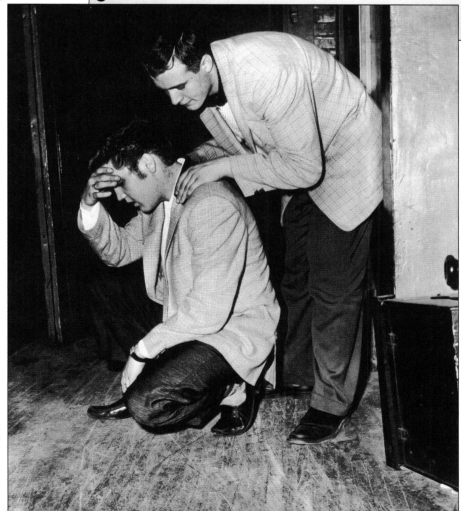

Backstage, St. Paul, Minnesota, May 13, 1956
(courtesy of Joe Tunzi)

Rehearsing for the first *Stage Show* appearance, January 28, 1956

1956

JANUARY

01 Sunday

★ *Kiel Auditorium, St. Louis, Missouri, at 3:00 and 8:00 P.M.*

Elvis flies from Shreveport with Red West to play a Grand Ole Opry package headlined by Hank Snow and featuring Webb Pierce.

02 Monday

Elvis and Red return to Memphis to begin a five-day tour with Johnny Cash, up-and-coming Hayride star David Houston, and others.

★ *High School, Charleston, Mississippi*

Here Elvis is billed as "The King of Western Bop."

03 Tuesday

★ *Von Theater, Booneville, Mississippi, at 6:00 and 8:00 P.M.*

Elvis is advertised as "The Folk Music Fireball" and is described by the local paper as having "a natural sense of rhythm along with a unique voice quality benefited from his childhood surroundings in which country music and Negro blues were everyday music to him."

04 Wednesday

★ *Community Center, Jonesboro, Arkansas (sponsored by the Delta Beta Sigma Sorority)*

06 Friday

★ *High School, Randolph, Mississippi*

07 Saturday

★ *Louisiana Hayride, Municipal Auditorium, Shreveport*

Elvis and Red West fly in to Shreveport for a bill that includes George Jones.

08 Sunday

Elvis and Red fly back to Memphis, arriving in the early-morning hours. Elvis is asleep when the Colonel telephones to wish him a happy twenty-first birthday.

Elvis insures the pink-and-black '55 Cadillac Fleetwood and a '56 Plymouth station wagon, most likely used by Vernon and Gladys. The '54 Cadillac Eldorado remains insured in Sam Phillips' name.

09 Monday

RCA's Steve Sholes is in Nashville to prepare for Elvis' first RCA recording session.

10 Tuesday

Elvis arrives at the RCA studio at 1525 McGavock Street, a building the record company shares with the Methodist TV, Radio and Film Commission. Working from 2:00 to 10:00 P.M., he records his first sides for his new label. Chet Atkins, the virtuoso country guitarist who is both an RCA recording artist and its Nashville studio chief, plays on the session, and pianist Floyd Cramer, who has worked with Elvis on Hayride shows and only recently arrived in Nashville himself, helps augment the small-group sound, which is anchored for the first time on record by drummer D. J. Fontana. Florida songwriter Mae Axton's original composition "Heartbreak Hotel" and Ray Charles' r & b classic "I Got a Woman," which Elvis has been singing since it came out a year ago, are both recorded, along with the Drifters' "Money Honey"—but everyone agrees that they are not getting the sound that they are aiming at: the crude echo effect of the McGavock studio is nothing like the unique combination of room ambience and technical legerdemain that Sam Phillips has achieved at Sun, and there is a good deal of disappointment in the booth.

11 Wednesday

The recording session continues from 4:00 to 7:00 P.M. Both Steve Sholes–supplied ballads are recorded, with the addition of gospel singers Ben and Brock Speer and Gordon Stoker of the Jordanaires (whom Elvis had met in Memphis on the Eddy Arnold show) on backup vocals.

13 Friday

Elvis spends $3 at Poplar Tunes, a record shop near his home.

★ *Humes High School, Memphis*

Elvis makes an unscheduled appearance at the school and performs for about ten minutes at a Father's Night show.

14 Saturday

★ *Louisiana Hayride, Municipal Auditorium, Shreveport*

Elvis sings "Baby Let's Play House," "I Got a Woman," "Only You," "Tutti Frutti," and "That's All Right."

Perhaps motivated by the Colonel's pep talk, William Morris agents begin contacting Hollywood executives to let them know that they should not miss Elvis Presley in his upcoming television debut.

15 Sunday

★ *Municipal Auditorium, San Antonio, Texas, at 3:00 and 8:00 P.M.*

On this six-day Hank Snow tour, Elvis, billed as "RCA Victor's newest singing sensation," plays his last dates as a supporting act. Box office gross for the day is $6,800. Elvis will receive $1,800 for the entire tour.

While in San Antonio, Elvis visits D. J. Fontana's aunt and uncle at their restaurant. He misses a cocktail party held by the RCA field representative in his honor, upsetting both Bob Neal and the Colonel, each of whom reminds him of his professional obligations.

16 Monday

★ *Municipal Auditorium, Galveston, Texas*

17 Tuesday

★ *City Auditorium, Beaumont, Texas, at 7:00 and 9:00 P.M.*

Worried about adverse reaction within the company to "Heartbreak Hotel," Sholes makes plans for an LP (a twelve-cut Long Playing Record, recorded at 33⅓ rpm) and an EP (a four- or five-cut Extended Play, 45 rpm) in case the first RCA single is a flop. To

---

January Record Release

Single: "Heartbreak Hotel" (#1)/"I Was the One" (#23) (shipped January 27). Just seventeen days after it is recorded, RCA puts out its first official Elvis Presley record. The eerie, rhythm-and-blues–based A-side sounds like nothing Elvis has done before, and like nothing else on the charts at this time. *Billboard* describes it as "a strong blues item wrapped up in his usual powerful style and a great beat." In spite of Elvis' extensive television exposure, however, it takes some time for the record to register, only adding to the general sense of confusion and panic at RCA. On March 3 "Heartbreak Hotel" finally enters the charts at #68, reaching #1 seven weeks later, where it will remain for the next eight weeks. By April "Heartbreak Hotel" has sold a million copies.

---

that end he sifts through the unreleased Sun material, looking for the strongest cuts. By letter he informs Elvis that "Heartbreak Hotel" will go on sale around January 30, and he forwards six new demos for a fast-approaching session that is now being planned for New York. Of the six, Elvis will record only "One-Sided Love Affair."

18 Wednesday

★ *Coliseum, Austin, Texas*

19 Thursday

★ *Memorial Auditorium, Wichita Falls, Texas, at 7:00 and 9:00 P.M.*

20 Friday

★ *North Side Coliseum, Fort Worth, Texas*

21 Saturday

★ *Louisiana Hayride, Municipal Auditorium, Shreveport*

Bob Neal informs the Colonel that because of his new radio job he will have to "bow out" of participation in the upcoming February tour. This marks the end of his official association with Elvis Presley. The Colonel is now in full control of all aspects of Elvis' career.

22 Sunday

Elvis and Red West fly from Shreveport to Memphis.

23 Monday

At home in Memphis, Elvis, Scotty, Bill, and D.J. rehearse for their upcoming appearance on *Stage Show.*

25 Wednesday

At 11:42 A.M., Elvis and the Colonel fly first-class from Nashville to New York City, paying $107.69 per ticket. They stay at the Warwick Hotel on Fifty-second Street, near Sixth Avenue, and have dinner at the nearby Hickory House Restaurant. From his hotel room, Elvis makes many telephone calls home, as he always does when he is on the road.

27 Friday

Scotty, Bill, and D.J. arrive in New York by car from Memphis.

A Note on RCA Record Releases and Chart Positions There are no official release dates for RCA Victor records. The company's policy was to try to get the record into all stores across the country at approximately the same time. Record releases are, therefore, listed at the end of the month in which they occurred, and when it is known, the date shipping began is also indicated. The number in parentheses following the title indicates the record or song's highest placement on *Billboard*'s Top 100 or Hot 100 charts for popular music. EPs are listed on the basis of the highest position that any of the songs on the EP may have achieved on these same charts. (EPs appear on the singles charts until September of 1957, when they get a chart of their own, returning once again to singles status in 1961.) Chart positions are based on a combination of sales, jukebox, and airplay, hence the concept of the double-sided hit and the somewhat arbitrary distinction between a two-sided hit like "Don't Be Cruel" (#1) and "Hound Dog" (#2), which is more a matter of historical record than absolute truth. Sales figures represent U.S. sales only, unless otherwise indicated.

28 Saturday

Morning rehearsals for *Stage Show* are held at the Nola Studios located between Fifty-first and Fifty-second Streets. *Stage Show* is produced by Jackie Gleason and hosted by Jimmy and Tommy Dorsey, out of whose celebrated band Frank Sinatra emerged at the height of the swing era. The show is broadcast from the CBS Studio between Fifty-third and Fifty-fourth Streets at 8:00 P.M. Because of the weather, and because Elvis is virtually unknown in New York City, attendance is sparse. Cleveland DJ Bill Randle introduces the young singer, and Elvis performs "Shake, Rattle and Roll" (in the middle of which he segues into another Big Joe Turner number, "Flip, Flop and Fly") and "I Got a Woman." He does not perform "Heartbreak Hotel."

★ *Stage Show, CBS Studio, at 8:00 P.M.*

30 Monday

Between 11:00 A.M. and 6:00 P.M., Elvis records four songs at RCA's New York studio at 155 East Twenty-fourth Street, including a cover version of Carl Perkins' current hit for Sun, "Blue Suede Shoes." Steve Sholes wants this recording available in case "Heartbreak Hotel" fails, but he has promised Sam Phillips that he will not steal Perkins' success by putting the record out as a single. Sholes' anxiety reflects the continuing fears of higher-ups that they may have made a mistake in signing Elvis. There are no backing vocalists on this session, and New York–based piano player Shorty Long, who is currently featured in the Broadway musical *The Most Happy Fella*, is the only addition to the regular group.

31 Tuesday

During the second day's session, which begins at noon and runs for only three hours, Elvis records an additional two songs and is interviewed by Fred Danzig, a young New York reporter.

01 Wednesday

Colonel Parker flies back to Nashville, leaving RCA in charge of Elvis for his second television appearance and one additional day of recording in New York.

After a few hours' sleep Elvis is driven to Trenton, New Jersey, for a radio interview with WAAT DJ Don Larkin, later attending a press reception in his honor at the Hickory House. Asked about his reaction to his success, he says, "It scares me. You know, it just scares me."

02 Thursday

Stage Show exercises its option for two additional shows, but the Colonel is unable to get Elvis out of his Saturday-night commitment to the Louisiana Hayride again until March 17 and 24.

03 Friday

Elvis records "Shake, Rattle and Roll" and "Lawdy, Miss Clawdy," another r & b standard, at RCA's New York studio between 10:30 A.M. and 1:30 P.M.

04 Saturday

★ *Stage Show, CBS Studio, at 8:00 P.M.*
Elvis makes his second *Stage Show* appearance, performing "Tutti Frutti" and "Baby Let's Play House," but evidently he still is not permitted to sing "Heartbreak Hotel." After the show, at the Dorsey brothers' invitation, Elvis goes to Roseland, a popular dance club in midtown Manhattan.

Steve Sholes writes to the Colonel to report that Elvis has "conducted himself very well." He describes Elvis mixing with the press at the Hickory House reception earlier in the week and making a good impression on all.

05 Sunday

★ *Mosque Theater, Richmond, Virginia, at 2:30 and 8:30 P.M.*
Elvis begins a broken three-week tour headlining over such well-known country acts as Justin Tubb, the Louvin Brothers, and the Carter Sisters.

06 Monday

★ *National Theater, Greensboro, North Carolina, at 2:30, 4:30, 7:00, and 9:00 P.M.*
According to the box office report, the audience of 2,900 includes 249 "Colored."

After witnessing both of Elvis' television performances and the show in Richmond, William Morris agent Harry Kalcheim writes the Colonel to suggest that on television it would be better if Elvis' singing stood out more from the contributions of the other musicians. "As a matter of suggestion in Elvis' act," he writes in reference to the Richmond package show, "he should avoid too much clowning as it detracts from his singing. . . . After sitting through two hours of singing and clowning, when the star of the show, Elvis Presley, comes on, they really want to hear Elvis go to town instead of the clowning, which gets a little repetitious even though some of it is funny. Was pleasantly amazed at the reaction. One has to see this to understand and appreciate what he does to an audience."

07 Tuesday

★ *Center Theater, High Point, North Carolina, at 2:30, 4:30, 7:00, and 9:00 P.M.*

08 Wednesday

★ *Ambassador Theater, Raleigh, North Carolina, at 2:30, 4:30, 7:00, and 9:00 P.M.*

09 Thursday

★ *Carolina Theater, Spartanburg, South Carolina, at 3:15, 5:15, 7:15, and 9:15 P.M.*

10 Friday

★ *Carolina Theater, Charlotte, North Carolina, at 2:30, 4:30, 7:00, and 9:00 P.M.*
The Charlotte News reports a total of 6,000 people at the four shows, with

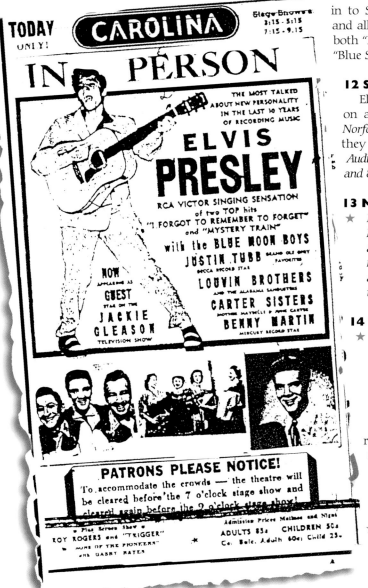

TODAY ONLY!

CAROLINA

Stage Shows
3:15 - 5:15
7:15 - 9:15

IN PERSON

THE MOST TALKED
ABOUT NEW PERSONALITY
IN THE LAST 10 YEARS
OF RECORDING MUSIC

ELVIS
PRESLEY

RCA VICTOR SINGING SENSATION
of two TOP hits
"I FORGOT TO REMEMBER TO FORGET"
and "MYSTERY TRAIN"

with the BLUE MOON BOYS

JUSTIN TUBB GRAND OLE OPRY
FAVORITE

NOW
APPEARING AS
GUEST
STAR ON THE
JACKIE
GLEASON
TELEVISION SHOW

LOUVIN BROTHERS
AND THE ALABAMA SUNBONNETS

CARTER SISTERS
MOTHER MAYBELLE & ANITA CARTER

BENNY MARTIN
MERCURY RECORD STAR

PATRONS PLEASE NOTICE!
To accommodate the crowds — the theatre will
be cleared before the 7 o'clock stage show and
cleared again before the 9 o'clock stage show!

Plus Screen Show •
ROY ROGERS and "TRIGGER"
KING OF THE COWBOYS
and GABBY HAYES

Admission Prices Matinee and Night
ADULTS 85¢   CHILDREN 50¢
Col. Sale. Adult 60¢; Child 25¢

Spartanburg, South Carolina, February 9, 1956

more than a thousand turned away. Elvis, declares the newspaper, sings in the "style of Johnnie Ray with a little of [the almost equally extroverted] Frankie Laine thrown in."

11 Saturday
★ *Stage Show, CBS Studio, New York City, at 8:00 P.M.*
For his third appearance CBS gives

in to Steve Sholes' pressure and allows Elvis to perform both "Heartbreak Hotel" and "Blue Suede Shoes."

12 Sunday
Elvis and the band leave on a 7:30 A.M. flight for *Norfolk, Virginia,* where they play the *Monticello Auditorium, at 2:00, 5:00, and 8:00 P.M.*

13 Monday
★ *Paramount Theater, Newport News, Virginia, at 4:30, 7:00, and 9:00 P.M. (with a fourth show added at 11:00 P.M., due to the overflow crowds)*

14 Tuesday
★ *Charles L. Coon High School, Wilson, North Carolina, at 7:00 and 9:00 P.M. (with a third show added at 11:00 P.M.)*
The other performers refuse to play the last show, until the Colonel promises them extra pay.

15 Wednesday
★ *Walter Williams High School Auditorium, Burlington, North Carolina*

16 Thursday
★ *Carolina Theater, Winston-Salem, North Carolina, at 4:30, 7:00, and 9:00 P.M.*
The local paper reports, "He slouches; he scratches; he mugs; he bumps; he grinds. . . . The frenzy, the hysteria, the wild and wonderful shrieks of sheer joy, these were reserved for the remarkable young man with the long hair, the pearly teeth, the stylish slouch, the incredible conceit: Elvis Presley."

Harry Kalcheim writes the Colonel, asking if he should try to set up a Las Vegas engagement.

17 Friday
Elvis and the band leave Winston-Salem at 5:50 A.M. on a flight to New York City.

18 Saturday
★ *Stage Show, CBS Studio, New York City, at 8:00 P.M.*
For Elvis' fourth appearance he repeats Little Richard's "Tutti Frutti" and "I Was the One," the B-side of his new single, a ballad of which he is particularly proud.

At 11:45 P.M. Elvis and the band fly to Tampa, Florida.

For each of the *Stage Show* appearances, the band has rented its equipment in New York, while Red West and Elvis' cousin, Gene Smith, transport the instruments to the next live gig, towing a small pink trailer built by Vernon behind the '55 Cadillac. A bill from Carroll Musical Instrument Service in New York City includes the cost of repairs to the bass, whose neck and back have been broken off.

19 Sunday
★ *Fort Homer Hesterly Armory, Tampa, Florida, at 2:00, 5:00, and 8:00 P.M.*
Elvis is billed as "Country Music's Mr. Rhythm." The poster advises: "Come early for best seats."

The Colonel wires Bill Bullock from the road to report on the phenomenal success they are experiencing. "I'm using the old circus style promotion," he declares, "and it's paying off. No gimmicks and giveaways. Just plain old advertising. It's coming, it's here, and now it's gone."

20 Monday
★ *Palms Theater, West Palm Beach, Florida, at 2:00, 5:00, 7:00, and 9:00 P.M.*
Steve Sholes writes the Colonel that the new record is doing very well but that he is anxious to get Elvis back in the studio, since he needs a B-side for the next single and additional material for a second album.

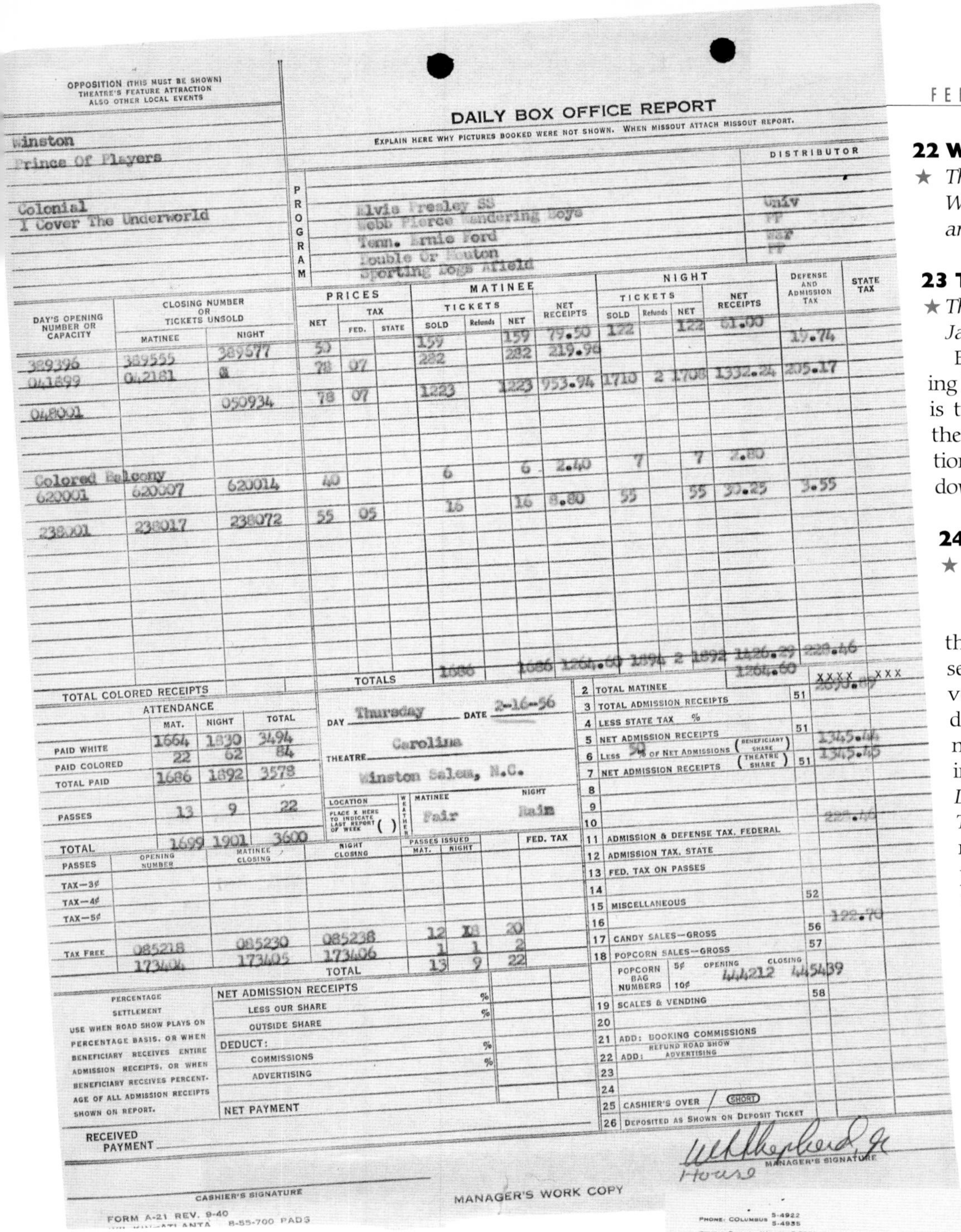

OPPOSITION (THIS MUST BE SHOWN) THEATRE'S FEATURE ATTRACTION ALSO OTHER LOCAL EVENTS

Winston
Prince Of Players

Colonial
I Cover The Underworld

DAILY BOX OFFICE REPORT

EXPLAIN HERE WHY PICTURES BOOKED WERE NOT SHOWN. WHEN MISSOUT ATTACH MISSOUT REPORT.

PROGRAM	DISTRIBUTOR
Elvis Presley SS	Univ
Webb Pierce Wandering Boys	PP
Tenn. Ernie Ford	WBF
Double Or Nouton	PP
Sporting Dogs Afield	

DAY'S OPENING NUMBER OR CAPACITY	CLOSING NUMBER OR TICKETS UNSOLD MATINEE	NIGHT	PRICES NET	TAX FED.	TAX STATE	MATINEE TICKETS SOLD	Refunds	NET	NET RECEIPTS	NIGHT TICKETS SOLD	Refunds	NET	NET RECEIPTS	DEFENSE AND ADMISSION TAX	STATE TAX
										122		122	61.00		
		389577	50			159		159	79.50					19.74	
389396	389555		78	07		282		282	219.96						
041899	042181	&												205.17	
						1223		1223	953.94	1710	2	1708	1332.24		
048001		050934	78	07											
										7		7	2.80		
Colored Balcony						6		6	2.40						
620001	620007	620014	40							55		55	30.25	3.55	
						16		16	8.80						
238001	238017	238072	55	05											
TOTALS						1686		1686	1264.60	1894	2	1892	1426.29	228.46	
													1264.60		

TOTAL COLORED RECEIPTS

ATTENDANCE	MAT.	NIGHT	TOTAL
PAID WHITE	1664	1830	3494
PAID COLORED	22	62	84
TOTAL PAID	1686	1892	3578
PASSES	13	9	22
TOTAL	1699	1901	3600

DAY Thursday DATE 2-16-56

THEATRE Carolina
Winston Salem, N.C.

LOCATION PLACE X HERE TO INDICATE LAST REPORT OF WEEK ( )

WEATHER MATINEE Fair NIGHT Rain

PASSES	OPENING NUMBER	MATINEE CLOSING	NIGHT CLOSING	PASSES ISSUED MAT.	NIGHT		FED. TAX
TAX—3¢							
TAX—4¢							
TAX—5¢							
TAX FREE	085218	085230	085238	12	8	20	
	173404	173405	173406	1	1	2	
			TOTAL	13	9	22	

XXXX XXX
2690.89
2 TOTAL MATINEE 51
3 TOTAL ADMISSION RECEIPTS
4 LESS STATE TAX %
5 NET ADMISSION RECEIPTS 51 1345.44
6 LESS 50% OF NET ADMISSIONS (BENEFICIARY SHARE) (THEATRE SHARE) 1345.45
7 NET ADMISSION RECEIPTS 51
8
9
10 228.46
11 ADMISSION & DEFENSE TAX, FEDERAL
12 ADMISSION TAX, STATE
13 FED. TAX ON PASSES
14 52
15 MISCELLANEOUS
16 122.70
17 CANDY SALES—GROSS 56
18 POPCORN SALES—GROSS 57
POPCORN BAG NUMBERS 5¢ OPENING 444212 CLOSING 445439
10¢
58
19 SCALES & VENDING
20
21 ADD: BOOKING COMMISSIONS
22 ADD: REFUND ROAD SHOW ADVERTISING
23
24
25 CASHIER'S OVER / (SHORT)
26 DEPOSITED AS SHOWN ON DEPOSIT TICKET

PERCENTAGE SETTLEMENT
USE WHEN ROAD SHOW PLAYS ON PERCENTAGE BASIS, OR WHEN BENEFICIARY RECEIVES ENTIRE ADMISSION RECEIPTS, OR WHEN BENEFICIARY RECEIVES PERCENTAGE OF ALL ADMISSION RECEIPTS SHOWN ON REPORT.

NET ADMISSION RECEIPTS %
LESS OUR SHARE %
OUTSIDE SHARE
DEDUCT: %
COMMISSIONS %
ADVERTISING
NET PAYMENT

RECEIVED PAYMENT

W H Shepherd, Jr.
House
MANAGER'S SIGNATURE

CASHIER'S SIGNATURE

MANAGER'S WORK COPY

FORM A-21 REV. 9-40
8-55-700 PADS

Box office report, Carolina Theater, Winston-Salem, North Carolina

21 Tuesday

★ *Florida Theater, Sarasota, Florida, at 2:15, 4:30, 7:35, and 9:45 P.M.*

The *Sarasota Herald Tribune* calls Elvis "the most talked-about new personality in the last 10 years of recorded music," reporting that between his first two shows at this Sarasota movie theater Elvis put his feet up and watched the western that was on the regular bill.

22 Wednesday

★ *The City Auditorium, Waycross, Georgia, at 7:00 and 9:00 P.M.*

23 Thursday

★ *The new baseball park, Jacksonville, Florida*

Elvis collapses in the parking lot after the first show and is taken to a hospital, where the doctor diagnoses exhaustion and tells him to slow down.

24 Friday

★ *The new baseball park, Jacksonville, Florida*

Harry Kalcheim confirms that a screen test has been set up with Hal Wallis, a veteran independent producer affiliated with Paramount, whose films include *Casablanca, Yankee Doodle Dandy,* and *The Rose Tattoo.* Elvis will receive one round-trip fare and $50 per day living expenses while in Los Angeles from March 26-28.

25 Saturday

★ *Louisiana Hayride, Municipal Auditorium, Shreveport*

Elvis performs "Heartbreak Hotel" for the first time on the Hayride. In

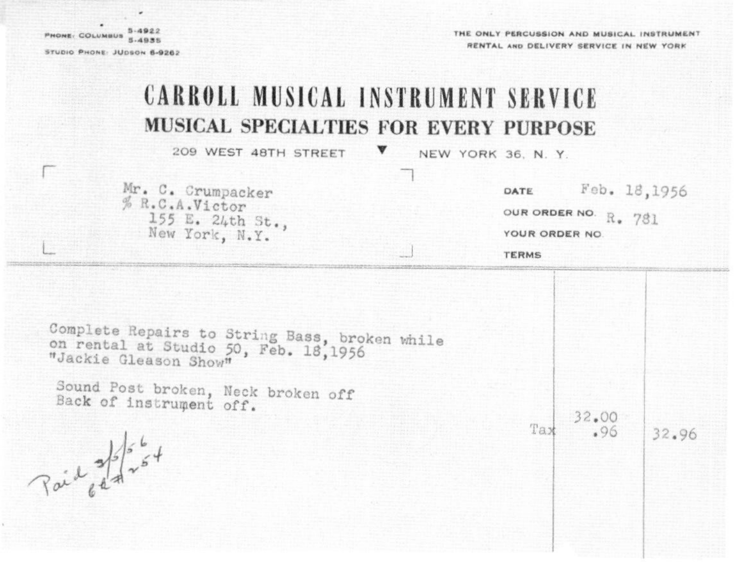

PHONE: COLUMBUS 5-4922 5-4935
STUDIO PHONE: JUDSON 6-9262

THE ONLY PERCUSSION AND MUSICAL INSTRUMENT RENTAL AND DELIVERY SERVICE IN NEW YORK

CARROLL MUSICAL INSTRUMENT SERVICE
MUSICAL SPECIALTIES FOR EVERY PURPOSE
209 WEST 48TH STREET ▼ NEW YORK 36, N. Y.

Mr. C. Crumpacker
% R.C.A.Victor
155 E. 24th St.,
New York, N.Y.

DATE Feb. 18,1956
OUR ORDER NO. R. 781
YOUR ORDER NO.
TERMS

Complete Repairs to String Bass, broken while on rental at Studio 50, Feb. 18,1956 "Jackie Gleason Show"

Sound Post broken, Neck broken off Back of instrument off.

32.00
Tax .96 32.96

Paid 3/5/56
ck #254

Repair bill for string bass rented for the February 18, 1956, *Stage Show*

Scotty Moore's recollection, the auditorium explodes as it never has before.

Billboard records Elvis' first national number-one hit, as "I Forgot to Remember to Forget" reaches the top position after twenty-four weeks on the country-and-western charts.

26 Sunday

★ *City Auditorium, Pensacola, Florida, at 2:00, 5:00, and 8:00 P.M.*
The tour's total net receipts come to $22,623.02 after all taxes and expenses have been paid. Elvis' share comes to $6,759.85.

28 Tuesday

Back in Memphis, another driver runs into Elvis in his Eldorado convertible in a downtown parking garage.

In another vehicular note, Elvis has the upholstery replaced in his '55 Cadillac as well as getting some paint work done. This may well be when the black roof is painted white, and it is almost surely not long after this that Elvis presents the refurbished pink-and-white Cadillac to his mother, who will always proudly point to it as "her" car, though she does not drive. By summer, photographs show the band with what appears to be an all-pink 1954 Cadillac limousine with a bolted-on metal roof rack, which they will use for just a few months before graduating to a black 1957 Cadillac limousine. Gladys Presley's pink-and-white Cadillac is currently on display at Graceland.

MARCH

01 Thursday

Elvis appears in Memphis traffic court as a witness to the garage accident two days earlier. The woman who drove the other car is charged with reckless driving.

02 Friday

Elvis is stopped for speeding on Riverside Drive in Memphis. Later, between 5:00 and 6:00 P.M., he signs autographs at the Bob Neal Record Shop, where you can "Always Find 50 Top Pops! 25 Top R & R!"

The Colonel informs his attorney that Bob Neal no longer has any business association with Elvis and that a recent unpleasantness with Hank Snow has been resolved in the following manner. All bookings for Snow, the Colonel writes of his former business partner, an integral player in all of the Colonel's dealings with Elvis over the past thirteen months, including the sale of the Sun contract, will continue to come through Parker's Madison office, but both his management contract and booking agency partnership with Snow have been dissolved. Snow, Parker declares, "has nothing to do with anything I am doing at present or going to do in the future." This is a development that clearly comes as a surprise to Hank Snow, who expected to reap great financial rewards from his and Colonel Parker's mutual involvement in Elvis' career. It continues to be a subject of controversy and recrimination over the next forty years—but for whatever reason Snow never finds any satisfactory legal recourse.

03 Saturday

Before flying to Shreveport with his cousin, Gene Smith, Elvis writes a check for $500 toward the purchase of a house for himself and his parents at 1034 Audubon Drive, a well-to-do suburban neighborhood east of downtown Memphis.

Billboard magazine announces "A WINNAH! Presley Hot as a $1 Pistol," with six hit singles in RCA's top twenty-five best-sellers, consisting of "Heartbreak Hotel" and the five Sun Records re-releases. "Heartbreak Hotel" debuts at #68 on the pop chart, #9 country and western.

★ *Louisiana Hayride, Municipal Auditorium, Shreveport*

04 Sunday

Elvis and Gene Smith fly home to Memphis.

05 Monday

Elvis and Gene fly to Nashville, returning to Memphis in the evening. This may well have been to reaffirm the new exclusive contractual arrangement with the Colonel, with both Bob Neal and Hank Snow now officially out of the picture.

07 Wednesday

Bill Bullock writes to the Colonel to express concern that Elvis' record sales are lagging in some areas of the country. He wants Parker to take Elvis off the country-and-western circuit and book him on pop shows in the north and on the West Coast, where potential sales are the greatest.

William Morris agent Harry Kalcheim forwards the script of *The Rainmaker*, which is to be used for Elvis' screen test, mentioning the possibility of a fifteen-minute radio series for Elvis as well. The Colonel passes the script along to Elvis with the stern adjuration that he study it well but keep it to himself, not share it with anyone or leave it lying around. "You can show it to your parents but don't show it to anyone else because this is a private matter. . . . DO NOT DISCUSS THIS MATTER WITH ANYONE—NOT THE BOYS IN THE BAND, THE PEOPLE AT THE HAYRIDE, ANYONE, BECAUSE THIS IS PRIVATE."

08 Thursday

Elvis receives another speeding ticket in Memphis.

09 Friday

Elvis spends $103 at Lansky Brothers Clothing Store.

★ *Chickasaw Ballroom, Chisca Hotel, Memphis*
Elvis appears with Sy Rose's Band in a "red hot and blue dance session" hosted by Dewey Phillips. Sy Rose is future Memphis music lawyer and Charlie Rich manager Seymour Rosenberg.

10 Saturday

★ *Louisiana Hayride, Municipal Auditorium, Shreveport*

With fans (saved by Gladys and marked March 1956)

12 Monday

At 8:44 A.M. Vernon Elvis Presley, Gladys L. Presley, and Elvis Aron (sic) Presley sign papers to complete the purchase of their new home for $29,500 from Welsh Plywood Corporation.

13 Tuesday

Elvis appears at the Traffic Violations Bureau in Memphis to pay his March 8 speeding ticket.

14 Wednesday

★ *Fox Theater, Atlanta, Georgia, at 4:30, 7:18, and 10:06 P.M.*

Elvis arrives at the theater for an 11:30 A.M. dress rehearsal for shows that alternate with scheduled screenings of *The Square Jungle*, starring Tony Curtis.

The Colonel complains to Harry Kalcheim that he can't even consider Saturday dates in Brooklyn or Los Angeles because he can get Elvis free from the Louisiana Hayride only once every sixty days. He has been working hard to get Elvis out of this contract, he says. "This stupid deal was made last fall against my advice, so we are stuck with it."

15 Thursday

★ *Fox Theater, Atlanta, Georgia, at 4:30, 7:18, and 10:06 P.M.*

Elvis is paid $1,831.54, representing 50 percent of the net proceeds, for the two-day engagement.

16 Friday

Elvis and the band fly to New York City from Atlanta, arriving at 4:03 P.M.

17 Saturday

Rehearsals are held at the Nola Studio at 12:30 P.M., after which Elvis goes to the CBS Studio at 4:00 P.M.

★ *Stage Show, CBS Studio, at 8:00 P.M.*

With "Heartbreak Hotel" now storming up the national charts, Elvis is allowed to make his own song selection and includes both the new single and "Blue Suede Shoes."

18 Sunday

Elvis and the band fly from New York City to Charleston, South Carolina, arriving at 11:03 A.M.

★ *County Hall, Charleston, South Carolina, at 3:30 and 8:15 P.M.*

19 Monday

After attending an interview

Saturday afternoon, Harry Kalcheim writes to the Colonel, cautioning him to be sure that Elvis takes his appointments with the press seriously and (since "we know that reporters like to inflate the importance of the artist when talking to them, so that they can secure information which most of them use in a caustic way") learn how to duck personal questions in a graceful manner. Kalcheim adds that he has urged Elvis to open the next *Stage Show* with "Blue Suede Shoes."

★ *Township Auditorium, Columbia, South Carolina*

20 Tuesday
★ *Bell Municipal Auditorium, Augusta, Georgia*
While Elvis is on tour, his parents move into the new house on Audubon Drive.

21 Wednesday
★ *YMCA Arena, Lexington, Kentucky*
Elvis, sick with the flu, is attended by a physician before the show. He tells reporters his success "appears to be a dream to me. I hope I can continue to please the public."

The Colonel repeatedly turns down offers to play the northeast and Canada, impatiently explaining to Harry Kalcheim that he is not interested in placing Elvis on anyone else's show. It will be the Elvis Presley

Hollywood Knickerbocker Hotel bill, March 25–28, 1956

Show, with the Colonel in sole charge and making sure that Elvis is presented properly.

Carl Perkins and his band have a terrible automobile accident on their way to perform "Blue Suede Shoes" on *The Perry Como Show* in New York. Perkins and two of his brothers, who play in the band, are badly injured. The Colonel wires flowers in Elvis' name to the Delaware hospital to which they are brought.

22 Thursday
★ *Mosque Theater, Richmond, Virginia, at 7:00 and 9:00 P.M.*

23 Friday
★ *SS Mount Vernon, Washington, D.C.*
Elvis is the featured attraction on the Country Music Cruise promoted by well-known country DJ and promoter Connie B. Gay.

24 Saturday
A snowstorm delays Elvis' and the band's arrival in New York, where they stay once again at the Warwick Hotel.

Jeweler Benny Kaplan delivers a $185 EP initial ring in a fourteen-carat gold setting with white diamonds that Elvis very likely purchased the previous week.

New York jeweler's bill for "EP" initial ring

★ *Stage Show, CBS Studio, at 8:00 P.M.*
Contrary to Harry Kalcheim's advice, and probably out of his refusal to capitalize on Carl Perkins' bad luck, Elvis chooses not to perform "Blue Suede Shoes," and instead showcases the Drifters' "Money Honey" with his big hit "Heartbreak Hotel."

25 Sunday

Elvis flies from New York to Los Angeles for his Hollywood screen test and is picked up at the airport by the Colonel, Tom Diskin, and a young William Morris agent, Leonard Hirshan, who recalls Elvis getting off the plane with a camera around his neck like any other tourist.

March Record Releases

EP: *Elvis Presley* (#24) (shipped March 23). Elvis' first extended-play record features the Carl Perkins hit "Blue Suede Shoes" which peaks at #24 on the singles chart, selling an unprecedented (for an EP) 400,000 copies.
Double EP: *Elvis Presley* (shipped March 23). This double EP (a short-lived category, generally—as here—made up of eight songs) also features "Blue Suede Shoes," and, as with the single EP, all tracks are taken from Elvis' first long-playing album. Without reaching the charts, it sells 150,000 copies.
LP: *Elvis Presley* (#1) (shipped March 23). Like the EPs, Elvis' first LP is simply titled with his name. All three records feature the same basic artwork, employing a photograph taken at the July 1955 Tampa, Florida, show that has been furnished by Colonel Parker. The album combines seven tracks recorded by RCA with five unreleased Sun cuts. As per the Colonel's philosophy of controlled availability and trickle-down economics, the single, "Heartbreak Hotel," is not on the LP, but its success provides the impetus to launch the album, which replaces Harry Belafonte's eponymous RCA LP, *Belafonte*, at the top of the charts. *Elvis Presley* remains at #1 for ten weeks, with sales of 300,000 copies in its initial chart run, as it becomes RCA's biggest-selling pop album to date.

Elvis' band drives back to Memphis, stopping to visit Carl Perkins in his Dover, Delaware, hospital room with a get-well message from Elvis. Perkins' "Blue Suede Shoes" is currently battling "Heartbreak Hotel" for supremacy on *Billboard*'s pop, country, and r & b charts.

26 Monday

Elvis' screen test for Hal Wallis at Paramount Studios lasts three days and is overseen by inventive director Frank Tashlin, who will make *The Girl Can't Help It* later in the year. Elvis performs two scenes from *The Rainmaker*, which is scheduled to start shooting in June with Burt Lancaster and Katharine Hepburn in the starring roles. Elvis also lip-synchs and gyrates to his recording of "Blue Suede Shoes." Of his dramatic performance, screenwriter Allen Weiss later wrote that he came across "like the lead in a high school play." With the music added, however, "the transformation was incredible . . . electricity bounced off the walls of the sound stage, [it was] like an earthquake in progress, only without the implicit threat."

Elvis' formal agreement with Colonel Parker is ratified as of this date in the form of a letter signed by Elvis and "agreed to" by Col. Thomas A. Parker which stipulates that Parker shall now act as "sole and exclusive Advisor, Personal Representative, and Manager in any and all fields of public and private entertainment."

27 Tuesday

Vernon buys a new TV, drapes, and other items for the Audubon Drive house.

28 Wednesday

Elvis flies from Los Angeles to Dallas to Memphis.

31 Saturday

★ *Louisiana Hayride, Municipal Auditorium, Shreveport*
This is Elvis' last appearance on a regularly scheduled Hayride show.

APRIL

01 Sunday

Elvis, Gene Smith, and the band fly from Shreveport to San Diego, where Elvis will appear on Milton Berle's popular television variety show.

02 Monday

The Colonel sends a cashier's check for $10,000 to the Louisiana Hayride in exchange for Elvis' release from his contract. The cash payment is further sweetened by Elvis' agreement to appear on a special Hayride charity show in December.

In Hollywood Hal Wallis offers a contract for one motion picture with options for six more. Negotiations are finalized on April 25, with Elvis signing a deal that will pay $15,000 for his first movie, $20,000 for the second, $25,000 for the third, and so on up to $100,000 for the seventh picture. The Colonel reserves the right to make one picture each year with another studio, though that picture can be preempted by Wallis for a comparable fee. In the end two films will be made under this contract, *Loving You* and *King Creole*, both of which will pay considerably more than the agreed-upon salary. In October 1958 the contract will be completely rewritten.

03 Tuesday

★ *Milton Berle Show, USS Hancock, San Diego, California*
Elvis is paid $3,000 for his appearance on the show, which is broadcast from the deck of an aircraft carrier.

04 Wednesday

★ *Arena, San Diego, California*

05 Thursday

★ *Arena, San Diego*
Elvis receives $15,000 for his two nights in San Diego.

06 Friday

In the evening Elvis flies to Las Vegas for a one-night holiday at the New Frontier Hotel, with which the

Colonel has begun discussions about a booking. It is his first trip to the show business mecca, and he is entranced.

07 Saturday

Elvis flies to Denver to begin a new tour booked by A .V. Bamford.

08 Sunday

★ *Coliseum, Denver, Colorado, at 3:00 and 8:00 P.M.*

Elvis begins a tour featuring Faron Young and Jimmy and Johnny.

09 Monday

Elvis and the band fly to Wichita Falls, Texas.

★ *Municipal Auditorium, Wichita Falls, Texas, at 7:00 and 9:00 P.M.*

In a radio interview Elvis announces somewhat prematurely, but with great enthusiasm, that his first motion picture will be *The Rainmaker.*

10 Tuesday

★ *Fair Park Auditorium, Lubbock, Texas, at 8:00 P.M., plus an added show at 9:45 P.M.*

Elvis' 1954 Cadillac has been driven to Lubbock for use on the tour. Vernon makes out an application for automobile liability insurance naming Elvis Presley, a "professional singer," as his employer. On the form Vernon lists a 1956 Plymouth station wagon owned by him and a 1954 Cadillac convertible and 1955 Cadillac Fleetwood owned by Elvis. It is estimated that the two Cadillacs will be driven 100,000 miles in the next year, divided between Scotty Moore (30,000 miles), Bill Black, D. J. Fontana, and Bobby (Red) West (20,000 each), and Elvis (the remainder).

11 Wednesday

★ *Coliseum, El Paso, Texas*

Elvis calls Bob Johnson at the *Press-Scimitar* in Memphis to thank him for his recent stories.

While in El Paso Elvis' car (which has 32,581 miles on the odometer) is serviced at the Lone Star Motor Co. He pays $58 for replacement of the left rear window glass, new wiper blades, a new outside rearview mirror and radio aerial, and the installation of a clothes hanger. The lube and oil order is crossed out with the notation, "No time."

Variety reports that "Heartbreak Hotel" has sold one million copies,

---

Jamboree Attractions
PERSONAL APPEARANCE CONTRACT

3/14/56

AGREEMENT entered into this ____ 14 ____ day of ____ March 1956 ____, 1956

between JAMBOREE ATTRACTIONS and Mr A.V. Bamford Of North Hollywood California

hereinafter called the EMPLOYER.

1. The EMPLOYER hereby warrants that he is the EMPLOYER herein at the present time and for the duration of this contract and enters into this contract with JAMBOREE ATTRACTIONS for the presentation of ELVIS PRESLEY WITH THE BLUE MOON BOYS. ONE HUNDRED PERCENT TOP BILLING IN ALL ADVERTISING RADIO NEWSPAPER, ADVERTISING PAPER, TELEVISION SPOTS. STARRING ELVIS PRESLEY. DENVER TWO SHOWS, LUBBOCK ONE SHOW, ELPASO ONE SHOW, ALBUQURQUE TWO SHOWS AMARILLO TWO SHOWS. RATES WILL REMAIN THE SAME IF ONLY ONE SHOW IS GIVEN IN EACH PLAYDATE. IF EXTRA SHOW IS REQUIRED OTHER THAN THE SCHEDULE RATE AT HALF PRICE

For a period of _____ days commencing SUNDAY APRIL EIGHT AT DENVER COLORADO 1953 TUESDAY APRIL TENTH LUBBOCK TEXAS

Performance to be presented at APRIL ELEVENTH EL PASO, TEXAS, TWELVE ALBUQUERQUE N.M. APRIL THIRTEEN AMARILLO TEXAS. TOTAL FIVE DATES. NO PERSONAL APPEARANCES OTHER THAN LISTED ABOVE CAN BE SCHEDULED. No other talent is to appear on this show date other than those listed above. JAMBOREE ATTRACTIONS reserves the right to substitute talent of equal value other than the stars of the show. In the case of sickness of the star such star to be replaced with a star of equal value. NO APPEARANCE AT ANY NIGHT CLUBS ANYTIME.

2. In consideration of the above the EMPLOYER agrees to pay to JAMBOREE ATTRACTIONS Compensation as follows FOR APRIL EIGHT THIRTY FIVE HUNDRED DOLLARS TWO SHOWS. APRIL 10-11 12-13 th SEVENTY FIVE HUNDRED DOLLARS FLAT RATE FOR THE FOUR DATES. TOTAL SELLING PRICE ELEVEN THOUSAND DOLLARS FLAT RATE.

A deposit of _____ PAYABLE IN FULL IN ADVANCE PAYMENT RECEIVED WITH CONTRACT and the balance of _____ payable in cash on date of the show and prior to the performance. Show is to be paid rain or shine. All deposit checks to be made payable to JAMBOREE ATTRACTIONS. Advertising material to be sent after deposit check has cleared. ELVIS PRESLEY TO BE PRESENTED AT CLOSE OF THE PERFORMANCE.

3. The EMPLOYER agrees to furnish suitable auditorium, hall, or theater, sound system, stage hands, ticket takers and pay for same. EMPLOYER agrees to pay all advertising, radio, and newspaper costs and all city, state, federal, and county taxes and licenses if any. FIFTEEN PERCENT TO HOWARD ATTRACTIONS BOOKING.

4. It is understood that JAMBOREE ATTRACTION SHOWS will have the free privilege to sell its souvenirs, novelties, songbooks and photos at all shows. ELVIS PRESLEY SHOW

5. If compensation is based upon a percentage of receipts the following conditions apply: A representative of JAMBOREE ATTRACTIONS shall have free access to the box office and may inspect and audit the records of the EMPLOYER covering the sale of tickets, receipts, disbursements, etc., for such performance and shall have the right to have a representative in the box office at all times and to collect and examine the tickets of admission.

6. Admission prices must be approved by both parties. AS PER SHOW SCHEDULE.

7. It is mutually agreed by both parties that if either party to this agreement should be unable to carry out the terms of this agreement by reason of accident or death, strikes, or any acts of Providence then and in that event neither shall be held liable upon this agreement. TRANSPORATION TO BE PROVIDED FROM DENVER TO LUBBOC

8. It is understood that the EMPLOYER is in good standing with the American Federation of Musicians local in TEXAS. community.

9. Special terms COL TOM PARKER TO RECEIVE FIFTY PERCENT OF THE GROSS SALES OF FOLIOS SOLD BY MR A.V. BAMFORD OR ITS REPRESENTATIVE AFTER DEDUCTION OF FOLIO COST AND PERCENTAGE IF ANY AT AUDITORIUMS.

IN WITNESS WHEREOF, we have signed this agreement in the day and the year first written above.

A.V. BAMFORD.
_____
Name of EMPLOYER

11605 Dilling Street
_____
Address of EMPLOYER

North Hollywood, California
_____
City and State

Poplar 3-9309
_____
Phone

EMPLOYER

FOR ELVIS PRESLEY BY COLONEL TOM PARKER

JAMBOREE ATTRACTIONS-Agent
BOX 417, Madison, Tennessee

Jamboree Attractions contract for April 1956 tour

day recording session set up at the last minute by Steve Sholes is plagued with problems. First the pilot loses his way and has to land in El Dorado, Arkansas, to refuel. Then one of the engines cuts out because the plane has not been switched over to its full tank. "Man, I don't know if I'll ever fly again," Elvis announces when he arrives in Nashville.

14 Saturday

Whether because of the flight problems they have encountered, or simply because Elvis is fatigued from his constant touring, the session at RCA's Nashville studio does not go well. Just one song is recorded in three hours, before the session ends at noon. The ballad that is cut, "I Want You, I Need You, I Love You," with vocal backup by the same mismatched trio used on the first Nashville session, will

With Brock Speer, Nashville recording session, April 14, 1956 *(courtesy of Joe Tunzi)*

thus becoming Elvis' first gold record.

12 Thursday

★ *Armory, Albuquerque, New Mexico, at 7:00 and 9:00 P.M.*

Lionel Crane, of the *London Daily Mirror*, is on the scene and reports that Elvis wore a plum-colored jacket with black trousers as two armed guards escorted him to the stage. He is greeted with a "scream that I thought would split the roof." Afterward, in the dressing room, when asked about the reception, Elvis declares, "It makes me want to cry. How does all this happen to me?" He then shows off his horseshoe diamond ring and boasts that he owns forty suits and twenty-seven pairs of shoes.

13 Friday

★ *Municipal Auditorium, Amarillo, Texas, at 7:00 and 9:00 P.M.*

This marks the beginning of a two-day break in a tour that will stick in Scotty Moore's memory as the time the crowd noise became so loud the musicians could no longer hear the music. "We were the only band in history that was directed by an ass. It was like being in a sea of sound."

Elvis' booking at the New Frontier in Las Vegas is confirmed, and the Colonel suggests he be billed as "America's Only Atomic Powered Singer."

The chartered flight that Elvis and the band take to Nashville for a one-

Elvis enters the chartered plane that will take him and the band from Nashville to Memphis, April 14, 1956 *(courtesy of Joe Tunzi)*

become the A-side of Elvis' second RCA single, but after spending $1,000 to fly the group in, Steve Sholes is upset and frustrated and subsequently complains to the Colonel that material is urgently needed for a second album.

While at the studio Elvis is presented with a gold record for "Heartbreak Hotel," with the event duly recorded by photographer Don Cravens.

Immediately after the session Elvis and the band take a bumpy flight to Memphis on the same chartered plane. In the evening Elvis stops by Dewey Phillips' *Red, Hot and Blue* radio show on the mezzanine floor of the Hotel Chisca.

15 Sunday

Elvis, the band, and Gene Smith fly—by commercial carrier this time—to San Antonio, Texas.

★ *Municipal Auditorium, San Antonio, Texas, at 3:00 and 8:00 P.M.*
According to the *San Antonio Light*, Elvis amuses himself between shows by playing "Silent Night" and "Harbor Lights" on the organ. Later, when the reporter asks a fan why she likes the singer, the response is, "Because he looks so mean."

16 Monday

★ *Memorial Coliseum, Corpus Christi, Texas*
Immediately following the show, the building manager outlaws rock 'n' roll at the Coliseum, after a number of fans and their parents complain that the performance was "vulgar." Some days later, Tom Diskin explains to the Colonel that it was another act on the bill that was guilty of the offending behavior.

17 Tuesday

Elvis and Gene Smith fly to Waco, Texas, while the band drives.

At the New Frontier, Las Vegas

★ *Heart O' Texas Coliseum, Waco*
Elvis drives out on the field and up to the stage in his Cadillac. Later he tells a local reporter that his fame "happened so fast, I'm scared. You know, I could go out like a light, just like I came on."

18 Wednesday

Elvis and Gene Smith fly to Tulsa, Oklahoma.

★ *Fairgrounds Pavilion, Tulsa, at 7:00 and 9:00 P.M.*

19 Thursday

★ *Municipal Auditorium, Oklahoma City, at 7:30 and 9:30 P.M.*
The *Daily Oklahoman* reports that Elvis' response to critics of his music is that "it's a healthy thing. You don't have to be doped up to do it."

20 Friday

★ *North Side Coliseum, Fort Worth, Texas, at 7:00 and 9:30 P.M.*
The local press receives complaints from angry mothers, one of whom calls Presley "vulgar and immoral."

Colonel Parker is in Las Vegas preparing for Elvis' opening when Harry Kalcheim informs him that Elvis has been booked to appear on Milton Berle's June 5 show for $5,000.

21 Saturday

★ *Municipal Auditorium, Houston, Texas, at 7:30 and 9:30 P.M.*
"Don't go milking a cow on a rainy day," Elvis remarks at the conclusion of the show. "If there's lightning, you may be left holding the bag." Harry Kalcheim would not be pleased.

These shows mark the end of a two-week tour in which Elvis has earned $21,679.04 for twenty-three shows.

22 Sunday

Elvis flies from Houston to Las Vegas, Nevada.

23 Monday

★ *Venus Room, New Frontier Hotel, Las Vegas, at 8:00 P.M. and midnight*

Elvis opens a two-week engagement in front of a more jaded, older audience. In 1959 Elvis will recall, "After that first night I went outside and just walked around in the dark. It was awful. . . . I wasn't getting across to the audience." At the same time he falls in love with Las Vegas and is thrilled to meet such show-business legends as Johnnie Ray, an emotive singer with whom he has often been compared, and Liberace, a favorite of his mother's, whose flamboyant style makes its mark on Elvis as well. He catches a number of other shows, including that of Freddie Bell and the Bellboys, whose novelty performance of Big Mama Thornton's rhythm-and-blues hit, "Hound Dog," impresses him as a potential showstopper.

28 Saturday

"Heartbreak Hotel" hits the #1 spot on the pop charts.

The Colonel arranges for Elvis to play a special matinee show for

---

April Record Release

EP: *Heartbreak Hotel* (#76) (shipped April 20). Encouraged by the success of the first EP, RCA releases a second and is quickly rewarded with more than 300,000 sales. That "Money Honey" alone reaches the charts—and then only at the lowest rungs—is probably due to the fact that "Heartbreak Hotel," the single, has run its course on radio and the charts reflect both sales and radio play.

In Las Vegas

teenagers, who for one dollar not only get to see Elvis but are served one soft drink.

The William Morris Agency continues to pressure the Colonel to book Elvis in the North; the Colonel responds that he would be interested only if he were to receive a guarantee of $50,000 against a percentage for two weeks' worth of work, and that he and Elvis require approval of all the other acts on the bill.

30 Monday

Life magazine runs a story titled "Howling Hillbilly Success."

In the month of April Elvis earns $15,000 for his Las Vegas engagement, $37,121.45 from touring, and $25,000 in RCA royalties. After paying a commission to the William Morris Agency for the Las Vegas booking, and paying out band salaries, travel and hotel expenses, and a 25 percent management fee on all earnings to Colonel Parker, Elvis takes home a total of $37,110.63.

MAY

02 Wednesday

Variety reviews the Las Vegas show and concludes "for teenagers he's a whiz; for the average Vegas spender, he's a fizz."

04 Friday

A long story in the *Memphis Press-Scimitar* by Bob Johnson quotes Elvis as saying: "I like Crosby, Como, Sinatra, all the big ones. They had to be good to get there. I've always been kind of partial to Dean Martin. I like the Four Lads [the group he'd met in

October at the filming of the Bill Randle feature in Cleveland]." More than anything else, however, he wants "the folks back home to think right of me. Just because I managed to do a little something, I don't want anyone back home to think I got the big head."

05 Saturday

Elvis' first LP, *Elvis Presley*, reaches #1 on *Billboard*'s albums chart, where it remains for ten weeks out of its total of forty-eight weeks on the chart.

06 Sunday

During his final show at the New Frontier Hotel Elvis introduces "Blue Suede Shoes" with typical off-the-wall "barnyard" humor: "This song here is called 'Get out of the stables, Grandma, you're too old to be horsing around.'"

08 Tuesday

Back in Memphis Elvis stops by the newspaper office and announces, "Man, I really like Vegas. I'm going back there the first chance I get." This Memphis visit is his first extended stay at his new Audubon Drive home.

10 Thursday

Elvis stops by to see Dewey during his broadcast.

12 Saturday

Elvis flies to Minneapolis, where he and the band stay in different hotels, an arrangement that begins to occur with greater and greater frequency at this time.

13 Sunday

★ *Auditorium, St. Paul, Minnesota, at 3:00 P.M.*

From this point on, virtually all of Elvis' personal appearances are variety shows produced by the Colonel, on which no other performer who might be considered a rival (as opposed to dancers, jugglers, and Irish tenors) appears. Despite pressure from both RCA and William Morris, the Colonel insists upon this format both as a guarantee that Elvis will stand alone and as a way of presenting Elvis as a mainstream per-former, not just another "rock 'n' roller" to be tagged with the same "juvenile delinquent" line that the press is applying increasingly to every aspect of the new music. These acts are supplied by Chicago talent agent Al Dvorin, a longtime associate of Tom Diskin, who helps set up the following date in LaCrosse and remains with the show off and on for the next twenty-one years.

★ *Auditorium, Minneapolis, at 8 P.M.*

14 Monday

★ *Mary B. Sawyer Auditorium, LaCrosse, Wisconsin, at 7:00 and 9:30 P.M.*

Reports of this performance cause the editor of the local newspaper to complain to FBI director J. Edgar Hoover that from what he's heard Elvis' act consists of "sexual self-gratification on stage."

Both *Time* and *Newsweek* run stories describing Elvis' phenomenal rise, beginning what amounts to his first exposure to the glare of national (as opposed to trade or regional) publicity.

15 Tuesday

★ *Ellis Auditorium, Memphis*

Bob Neal's Cotton Pickin' Jamboree is part of the twenty-second annual Cotton Carnival, with Elvis headlining over Hank Snow and the Jordanaires. Before Elvis performs, Bob Neal announces that he will be playing another show in Memphis, on July 4, for the benefit of local charities. "A wild roar of approval was evidence that Elvis will have plenty of company" for that show, reports the *Memphis Press-Scimitar*, but that is nothing compared to the reception he gets when he appears on stage. He wears black pants, a white shirt, and a kelly-green jacket, sings "Heartbreak Motel," and introduces Little Richard's "Long Tall Sally" as a beautiful song "recorded by a friend of mine. . . . I never met him, but here's the song." He closes with the number that has become his showstopper since Las Vegas, "Hound Dog."

16 Wednesday

★ *Robinson Memorial Auditorium, Little Rock, Arkansas, at 7:00 and 9:30 P.M.*

Asked by local DJ Ray Green to name his favorite song, Elvis picks "I Was the One" from his first RCA session.

17 Thursday

With Gene Smith and Tom Diskin, Elvis flies to Springfield, Missouri, while the band drives to the show in Elvis' '54 Cadillac.

★ *Shrine Mosque, Springfield, Missouri*

18 Friday

★ *Forum, Wichita, Kansas, at 7:00 and 9:30 P.M.*

19 Saturday

★ *University of Nebraska Coliseum, Lincoln, Nebraska*

Elvis wears a yellow sports coat with black stripes, a blue iridescent shirt with a kimono collar, and black pegged trousers. Asked if rock 'n' roll is a bad influence on teenagers, Elvis tells the reporter, "I don't even smoke or drink, and I started singing as a gospel singer and come from a Christian home."

20 Sunday

★ *Civic Auditorium, Omaha, Nebraska, at 3:00 and 8:00 P.M.*

21 Monday

Elvis steps off the plane in Topeka wearing nothing above the waist but a loose-fitting, two-button, shantung suit coat.

★ *Municipal Auditorium, Topeka, Kansas*

22 Tuesday

★ *Veterans Memorial Auditorium, Des Moines, Iowa*

23 Wednesday

★ *Municipal Auditorium, Sioux City, Iowa*

24 Thursday

Elvis, Gene Smith, and Tom Diskin fly to the next gig while the band drives.

While the group is out on this trip, the O.K. Houck Piano Company obtains a Fender Bassman amplifier for Bill Black at a cost of $355.50.

★ *Municipal Auditorium Arena, Kansas City, Missouri*

After a riot in which D.J.'s drums and Bill's stand-up bass are smashed and D.J. is thrown into the orchestra pit, the headline in the paper the next day reports, "Elvis Presley Flees to Car After 20 Minutes on Stage." He flies out of Kansas City at 4:35 A.M. for Detroit.

25 Friday
★ *Fox Theater, Detroit, Michigan, at 4:00, 7:00, and 9:45 P.M.*

26 Saturday
★ *Veterans Memorial Auditorium, Columbus, Ohio, at 7:00 and 10:00 P.M.*

27 Sunday
★ *University of Dayton Fieldhouse, Dayton, Ohio, at 2:00 and 8:00 P.M.*

28 Monday
Elvis and Gene Smith fly home to Memphis.

29 Tuesday
Elvis stops by his ex-girlfriend Dixie Locke's house as she returns from a dress rehearsal for her high

---

May Record Release

Single: "I Want You, I Need You, I Love You" (#3)/"My Baby Left Me" (#31) (shipped May 4). Opinions at RCA differ over which song should be the A-side prior to release. In the end the ballad ("I Want You, I Need You, I Love You") is chosen over the Arthur Crudup blues, which is very similar in approach to Elvis' original version of Crudup's "That's All Right." While the single fails to match the sales figures of "Heartbreak Hotel," the A-side's success helps make Elvis' dream of becoming a ballad singer a reality. Sales total 1.3 million.

---

school graduation and takes her for a ride on his motorcycle.

30 Wednesday
Elvis attends the Humes and South Side High School graduations at Ellis Auditorium.

JUNE

01 Friday
Elvis makes a surprise visit to the Overton Park Shell in Memphis, where old friends Johnny Cash and Carl Perkins and new Sun artists Roy Orbison and Warren Smith are performing.

02 Saturday
Elvis and Gene Smith fly to Oakland, California, arriving at 4:00 A.M. and catching up with the band, who have driven to the Coast. On their way out Scotty, Bill, and D.J. hear "Be Bop A Lula" on the radio and think at first that Elvis has recorded without them. They are relieved to discover that the record is by newcomer Gene Vincent, clearly schooled in the Presley style.

03 Sunday
★ *Auditorium Arena, Oakland, California, at 3:00 and 8:00 P.M.*

Elvis tells the *Oakland Tribune* why he doesn't like to stand still. "I get nervous. If the police and my managers would let me, I'd get mobbed all the time. It makes you feel good. I would feel worse if they didn't swoon over me." He goes on to cite Colonel Parker's perspicacity, saying, "My income taxes are really high. But I've [got] a manager who can get the most out of a deal. He drains them."

04 Monday
Elvis and Gene Smith fly to Los Angeles for rehearsals for Elvis' second appearance on *The Milton Berle Show.*

05 Tuesday
★ *The Milton Berle Show, NBC Studio, Los Angeles, at 8:00 P.M.*

Elvis appears with "sultry" twenty-

one-year-old actress Debra Paget, Arnold Stang, and Irish McCalla, the leopard-skin-clad star of the television show *Sheena, Queen of the Jungle.* Berle presents Elvis with a *Billboard* award for reaching number one on retail, disc jockey, and jukebox charts on both the pop and country-and-western charts with "Heartbreak Hotel," as Elvis performs both his new single, "I Want You, I Need You, I Love You," and a worked-up version of "Hound Dog," complete with all the bumps and grinds of a stripper to the exaggerated half-time ending he has perfected.

06 Wednesday
★ *Arena, San Diego, California*

Almost overnight, newspapers across the country are filled with outraged reaction to Elvis' "obscene performance." Most follow the lead of *New York Times* critic Jack Gould, who writes that "Mr Presley has no discernible singing ability." Three days later, Jack O'Brian of the *Journal American* decries "a display of primitive physical movement difficult to describe in terms suitable to a family newspaper," and Ben Gross of the *Daily News* suggests that popular music "has reached its lowest depths in the 'grunt and groin' antics of one Elvis Presley."

07 Thursday
★ *Municipal Auditorium, Long Beach, California*

Harry Kalcheim tells the Colonel that everyone in the William Morris office is worried because Elvis looked tense and overtired on the Berle show. He also suggests that the young performer might consider doing less shaking during his performance.

08 Friday
★ *Shrine Auditorium, Los Angeles*

09 Saturday
Elvis' '54 Cadillac convertible has 47,798 miles on the odometer when he has the car checked and the outside mirror replaced in Phoenix, Arizona.

★ *State Fairgrounds Grandstand, Phoenix, Arizona*

Milton Berle Show rehearsal with Scotty Moore, June 4, 1956 *(courtesy of Michael Ochs Archives/Venice, California)*

10 Sunday

★ *Rodeo Grounds, Tucson, Arizona*

11 Monday

Elvis flies home to Memphis for the funeral of his cousin Lee Edward Smith, Gene and Junior's brother, who has drowned.

Among the crowd of fans outside his Audubon Drive house, Elvis finds June Juanico, the girl he met just one year ago in Biloxi, Mississippi. He will spend much of the week showing her around Memphis.

Meanwhile, in Hollywood the negative publicity over *The Milton Berle Show* appearance causes Hal Wallis to express some concern to his partner, Joe Hazen. But, he concludes, he would still sign Presley, even if he were unknown, because of the fine quality of his screen test.

12 Tuesday

Elvis flies to Houston with June Juanico, whose ticket is issued in the name of Miss June Prichard in order to protect her from the scrutiny of the press. (Prichard may have been chosen because Elvis had tried to call her on October 26, 1955, from Prichard, Alabama, soon after they first met.) They are traveling to pick up the new convertible that he has ordered, a 1956 ivory-colored Cadillac Eldorado Biarritz.

Harry Kalcheim reports to the Colonel that there is a great deal of British interest in Elvis playing the Palladium in London.

13 Wednesday

Elvis and June have breakfast at the restaurant of the Colonel's old friend Bill Williams on South Main Street, where Elvis is surrounded by "swooning" Rainbow Girls, in town for an annual gathering. He tells reporters he is "engaged to only one—my career."

Variety television show host Steve Allen announces that he has received strong pressure to cancel Elvis' July 1 appearance on his show. If he does appear, Allen says, Elvis Presley "will

Audubon Drive, summer 1956

not be allowed any of his offensive tactics."

16 Saturday

Elvis shows up on local TV host Wink Martindale's *Dance Party* to promote his July 4 charity show at Russwood Park in Memphis. Elvis says that the door prize will be his diamond initial ring.

Elvis visits a café near the Strand movie theater on Main Street, where he poses for pictures with a young woman named Robbie Moore. On August 27 her attorney will threaten to bring a lawsuit against him for invasion of privacy when the photograph appears in a magazine-format bio, *Elvis Presley Speaks!* The suit will be settled out of court for $5,500.

With June Juanico, June 1956

20 Wednesday

The African-American newspaper *Memphis World* reports that the previous evening Elvis "crack[ed] Memphis segregation laws by attending the Fairgrounds Memphis amusement park on East Parkway, during what is designated as 'colored night.'" Whether or not this actually happened, it says something about the way in which Elvis was viewed in Memphis' black community at the time.

With motorcycle cap, summer 1956

Larry Kanaga, vice president of RCA, writes to the Colonel to reassure him that the negative press Elvis has received is of little consequence because of Elvis' great talent and the Colonel's keen business sense.

21 Thursday

Accompanied to Atlanta in his new Cadillac Biarritz by his cousins Gene and Junior Smith, Elvis has the oil changed, with 2,185 miles registered on the odometer.

22 Friday

★ *Paramount Theater, Atlanta, Georgia, at 2:00, 5:50, and 8:00 P.M.*

The Jordanaires, whom Elvis has long admired both as an independent act and as a gospel-based backup quartet, join the Elvis Presley show. Elvis had first expressed his wish to have them sing behind him at the Eddy Arnold show in Memphis in the fall of

1954 and subsequently voiced his displeasure when Chet Atkins failed to get the group to back him on his Nashville sessions, using Gordon Stoker alone from the quartet, along with Ben and Brock Speer of the Speer Family. Henceforth Elvis will have his wish.

Stage instructions for Elvis' show read: "Pull all white lights. Presley works all in color . . . . Presley act has no encore. When he leaves stage, immediately close curtains. Also, be sure and lower set mike at center, for Presley uses portable mike only."

23 Saturday
★ *Paramount Theater, Atlanta, Georgia, at 12:35, 3:15, 5:30, and 8:30 P.M.*

24 Sunday
★ *Paramount Theater, Atlanta, at 2:00, 5:50, and 8:30 P.M.*

25 Monday
★ *Sports Arena, Savannah, Georgia, at 7:00 and 9:30 P.M.*

Elvis tells local reporters, "I can't believe that music could cause anybody to do anything wrong. And what I'm doing is nothing but music."

26 Tuesday
★ *Coliseum, Charlotte, North Carolina*

In another interview Elvis discusses his Berle appearance once again. He doesn't see that his performance was any sexier than that of Debra Paget, who wore a "tight thing with feathers on the behind where they wiggle

June Record Release

EP: *Elvis Presley* (shipped June 8). Yet another EP with the generic title *Elvis Presley*, this one features two previously unreleased numbers recorded by RCA and originally intended for the second album, Big Joe Turner's "Shake, Rattle and Roll" and Lloyd Price's "Lawdy, Miss Clawdy." Two tracks from the first album not on the previous EPs are also included.

the most [and who] bumped and pooshed out all over the place." Of his music, which is his main concern, he declares passionately: "The colored folks been singing it and playing it just like I'm doin' now, man, for more years than I know. They played it like that in the shanties and in their juke joints, and nobody paid it no mind 'til I goosed it up. I got it from them. Down in Tupelo, Mississippi, I used to hear old Arthur Crudup bang his box the way I do now, and I said if I ever got to the place where I could feel all old Arthur felt, I'd be a music man like nobody ever saw."

27 Wednesday
★ *Bell Auditorium, Augusta, Georgia*

28 Thursday
★ *College Park, Charleston, South Carolina*

Headlines across the country the following day announce that Elvis "Bites Hand of [Charleston] Girl Reporter." The story reveals that, while being interviewed, he flirtatiously nibbled the reporter's fingers.

29 Friday
Elvis and his party take a chartered plane to Charlotte, North Carolina, where they catch a Delta flight to New York City. At the morning rehearsal for *The Steve Allen Show*, Elvis is fitted for a tux before taking the train to Richmond, Virginia. It is at this rehearsal that photographer Al Wertheimer, who photographed Elvis on the fifth Dorsey show at RCA publicity director Anne Fulchino's invitation, hooks up with him once again and begins a series of pictures that will eloquently chronicle the next week of his life.

30 Saturday
★ *Mosque Theater, Richmond, Virginia, at 5:00 and 8:00 P.M.*

Immediately after the show Elvis climbs aboard the Richmond, Fredericksburg, and Potomac Railroad train, returning to New York in Car 20, Roomette #7.

Elvis receives $9,328 for this June 23–30 tour.

JULY

01 Sunday
★ *The Steve Allen Show, Hudson Theater, New York City, at 8:00 P.M.*

Elvis opens with "I Want You, I Need You, I Love You," backed by the Jordanaires, then performs his yet-to-be-recorded showstopper, "Hound Dog," to a nervous basset hound, while wearing the tuxedo that Steve Allen had presented him with. Later he appears in a comedy skit titled "Range Round-Up" with Andy Griffith, Imogene Coca, and Allen. His pay for the night is $5,000.

At some point during the day Steve Sholes takes the opportunity to play some demos for Elvis, among which are a ballad, "Any Way You Want Me," and a rocker, "Too Much," which he will go on to record.

At 11:30 P.M. Elvis appears live on the popular television interview show *Hy Gardner Calling!* Asked if he has learned anything from his critics, he responds, "No, I haven't. I don't feel like I'm doing anything wrong." Discussing his effect on teenagers, Elvis reiterates what he has been saying all along. "I don't see how any type of music would have any bad influence on people when it's only music. . . . I mean, how would rock 'n' roll music make anyone rebel against their parents?" It is his sleepy-eyed, almost doped-up appearance, though, almost certainly a conscious evocation of James Dean, that leaves the most lasting impression.

02 Monday
Elvis reports to the RCA studio at 2:00 P.M., where he records three songs, "Hound Dog," "Don't Be Cruel," and "Any Way You Want Me," over the next seven hours. This is the first time that Elvis takes over full leadership of a session, and he insists on completing each song to his own satisfaction, continuing with "Hound Dog" (thirty-one takes) and "Don't Be Cruel" (twenty-eight)

Audubon Drive, summer 1956, with *(left to right)* Arthur Hooton, Gladys, Vernon, Elvis, and Red West behind Junior Smith

well past the point that nominal producer Steve Sholes would have quit. "Don't Be Cruel," by r & b songwriter Otis Blackwell, is the first song brought directly to Elvis by Hill and Range representative Freddy Bienstock, who will henceforth be designated as the song publisher's (and his cousins Jean and Julian Aberbach's) special emissary to the singer. Elvis' band is augmented by pianist Shorty Long and the Jordanaires. While the session is going on, fans outside the studio hold up signs for "The Real Elvis," as opposed to the homogenized Elvis who had appeared on Steve Allen the night before.

In related developments, Colonel Parker tells RCA vice president and general manager Larry Kanaga during the day that "Hound Dog" may become such a big hit that RCA will have to change its corporate symbol from the "Victor Dog" to the "Hound Dog." Meanwhile, the William Morris Agency informs Universal International Films, which is planning to distribute the Bill Randle short *A Day in the Life of a Famous DJ*, that they are not authorized to include Elvis' performance "unless and until he receives proper payment for his appearance in it. In the light of Mr. Presley's present wide public appeal it is our belief and Colonel Parker's that proper payment for such an appearance is at least $50,000."

03 Tuesday

Elvis runs into Gene Vincent at Pennsylvania Station in New York City and congratulates him on the success of "Be Bop A Lula," then boards the 11:30 A.M. train for Memphis, a twenty-seven-hour ride.

04 Wednesday

Upon arriving in Memphis, Elvis disembarks at a small signal stop called White Station and walks home to Audubon Drive, arriving just as the new swimming pool is being filled. He spends the afternoon with his family and a Memphis girlfriend, Barbara Hearn, for whom he plays acetates of "Don't Be Cruel" and "Any Way You Want Me."

At June Juanico's house, Biloxi, Mississippi, summer 1956

★ *Russwood Park, Memphis*

During the show Elvis tells cheering hometown fans, "You know those people in New York are not going to change me none. I'm gonna show you what the real Elvis is like tonight."

05 Thursday

Elvis begins the first real vacation that he has had since gaining national recognition.

07 Saturday

Elvis drives down to Tupelo for the day.

09 Monday

Elvis shows up unexpectedly at June Juanico's house in Biloxi, along with Red West, Gene and Junior Smith, and Arthur Hooton, a friend whose mother once worked with Gladys at Britling's

Cafeteria. The entire party registers at the Sun 'N' Sand Hotel Court.

10 Tuesday

Elvis' presence in Biloxi fuels escalating rumors (which will continue throughout the summer) that he is engaged to June. After hearing this rumor articulated on a New Orleans radio station, he and June drive to New Orleans with the rest of the gang to try to dispel it, then visit the Pontchartrain Beach Amusement Park before heading back to Biloxi. The following morning, June is awakened by a phone call from a *New Orleans Item* reporter. "Did I kiss him goodnight? What do you think?" she says. "He's wonderful!"

11 Wednesday

Elvis spends much of the next three weeks in Biloxi, moving initially

into a villa at the Gulf Hills Dude Ranch resort, then into a private home nearby, after his car is scratched and covered with messages by fans in the Sun 'N' Sand parking lot.

12 Thursday

Elvis, June, and the guys go deep-sea fishing on the *Aunt Jennie* with June's mother, May, and her boyfriend, Eddie Bellman. They have so much fun that Elvis calls his parents and invites them to come down and join him.

In New York Ed Sullivan, who had previously declared that he wouldn't touch Elvis Presley with a ten-foot pole, announces that he has booked Elvis on his variety show, one of the highest-rated shows on television. The Colonel insists to Harry Kalcheim that Elvis must retain complete control of the presentation of his songs and adds that mail is running ten to one against any restriction of Elvis' movements.

13 Friday

Vernon and Gladys arrive in Biloxi, and Gladys reports to Elvis that the Sun 'N' Sand parking lot is filled with fans who think he has returned to the hotel, not realizing that the pink-and-white Cadillac is hers. The following day Elvis takes his parents deep-sea fishing as Eddie Bellman takes home movies.

16 Monday

Elvis and June show Elvis' parents New Orleans, after which the older Presleys return to Memphis.

17 Tuesday

John Lardner, writing in *Newsweek*, excoriates Steve Allen for his attempt to "civilize" Elvis Presley.

While in Biloxi, Elvis spends his evenings at various nightclubs. Tonight he sees Brother Dave Gardner, a southern version of the hipster comedian Lord Buckley.

20 Friday

On his way back to Memphis, Elvis is mobbed by fans at a stop in Hattiesburg, Mississippi.

21 Saturday

Elvis trades in his yellow 1954 Cadillac for a lavender 1956 Lincoln Premiere.

25 Wednesday

The Colonel, hearing that Dewey Phillips has sprained his ankle at Elvis' pool, suggests that Vernon check into the family's liability insurance coverage and advises him to keep changing their phone number to avoid unwanted calls.

26 Thursday

The Colonel solidifies the deal he has been working on with merchandiser Hank Saperstein over the summer for the exclusive right to exploit and commercially promote the image of Elvis Presley on different articles of merchandise, from lipstick to lockets, from pedal pushers to portable typewriters. Elvis and the Colonel will receive $35,000 against 45 percent of licensing fees and royalties. Saperstein is photographed with Elvis on the set of *Love Me Tender* in August or September with an assortment of the merchandise.

27 Friday

Elvis attends a Blackwood Brothers All-Night Singing, joining the group to sing "Jesus Filled My Every Need" and "You'll Never Walk Alone." Later he takes in the movie *Somebody Up There Likes Me*, starring Paul Newman as boxer Rocky Graziano.

July Record Release

Single: "Don't Be Cruel" (#1)/"Hound Dog" (#2) (shipped July 13). The success of "Heartbreak Hotel" does not even begin to prepare RCA for the response to Elvis' third single. In just a few weeks "Hound Dog" shoots to #2 and sells more than one million copies before being overturned by the chart-topping performance of "Don't Be Cruel." At year's end, sales figures on the double-sided smash approach four million copies.

---

29 Sunday

In the evening Elvis heads back to Biloxi, making another stop in Hattiesburg, this time for a speeding ticket. Unable to return to the private home he has rented, Elvis occupies both sides of a two-family villa at the Gulf Hills resort, and once again his parents make a visit.

AUGUST

01 Wednesday

Elvis does a promotional appearance for Eddie Bellman at the downtown clothing store whose shoe department Bellman and a friend own. In appreciation, Bellman, his friend Lew Sonnier, and storeowner Dave Rosenblum present Elvis with a Winchester shotgun, which he takes skeet shooting.

02 Thursday

Elvis leaves for Miami in his new Lincoln.

03 Friday

★ *Olympic Theater, Miami, Florida, at 3:30, 7:00, and 9:00 P.M.*

June arrives with a friend to join Elvis on tour, and her appearance is immediately noted by the press. "Right now, he's married to his career," she tells the *Miami News* in a backstage interview, but this does not begin to assuage the Colonel, who is beside himself about this new speculation regarding Elvis' "morals."

04 Saturday

Elvis trades in the new lavender Lincoln, already defaced by fans' messages, for an even more upscale white 1956 Lincoln Continental Mark II. He is allowed $3,515 for the old car against the $10,688 price of the new one. The Colonel pays for the car on August 14, deducting its cost from Elvis' earnings at the end of the tour.

★ *Olympic Theater, Miami, at 1:30, 3:30, 7:00, and 9:00 P.M.*

05 Sunday

★ *Fort Homer Hesterly Armory, Tampa, Florida, at 3:30 and 8:15 P.M.*

06 Monday

★ *Polk Theater, Lakeland, Florida, at 3:30, 7:00, and 9:00 P.M.*

Backstage Elvis responds angrily to *Tampa Tribune* reporter Paul Wilder, an old pal of the Colonel from his Tampa days, when Wilder reads him a scathing review of his Miami performance. "Sir, those kids that come here and pay their money to see this show come to have a good time," Elvis declares. "I don't see that [the reviewer] should call those people idiots—because they're somebody's kids. They're somebody's decent kids."

Ed Sullivan is hospitalized after a bad automobile accident that will prevent him from hosting Elvis' first appearance on his show in September.

07 Tuesday

★ *Florida Theater, St. Petersburg, Florida, at 3:30, 7:00, and 9:00 P.M.*

Paul Wilder quotes Elvis as saying: "I never was a lady killer in high school. I had my share of dates, but that's all."

08 Wednesday

★ *Municipal Auditorium, Orlando, Florida, at 8:00 and 10:15 P.M.*

09 Thursday

★ *Peabody Auditorium, Daytona Beach, Florida, at 8:00 P.M., with a 10:15 show added by demand*

Elvis Presley Speaks!, a magazine-format pictorial biography written by *Memphis Press-Scimitar* reporter Bob Johnson, chronicles Elvis' rise with accuracy and occasional eloquence, selling out of its first printing almost immediately.

10 Friday

★ *Florida Theater, Jacksonville, Florida, at 3:30, 7:00, and 9:00 P.M.*

Judge Marion Gooding warns Elvis in chambers after the first show that he must tone down his act. Elvis tells reporters, "I can't figure out what I'm doing wrong. I know my

Unknown 1956 performance

able script ready, and perhaps also to allow someone else to test the waters, Hal Wallis has waived his right to produce Elvis' first picture, thus allowing him to appear in *The Reno Brothers*, which will begin shooting later in the month. Elvis will receive $100,000 and costar billing. Fox has an option for two additional films at $150,000 and $200,000. (The two films that are eventually shot are 1960's *Flaming Star* and *Wild in the Country*.)

14 Tuesday

Back in Memphis Elvis is spotted at a service station in his new Lincoln, and Red West gets into a fight while he is with Elvis at the Fairgrounds. This causes Elvis' father, Vernon, to

mother approves of what I'm doing." But he modifies the show nonetheless, wiggling his little finger suggestively with a gesture that replaces some of his less restrained body movements and at the same time still drives the audience wild.

11 Saturday

★ *Florida Theater, Jacksonville, at 3:30, 7:00, and 9:00 P.M.*

12 Sunday

★ *Municipal Auditorium, New Orleans, Louisiana, at 4:00 and 8:15 P.M.*

The tour ends with an uninhibited performance and Elvis' being awarded the key to the city. The Colonel has guaranteed Elvis $500 a performance or $2,000 a day, whichever is greater, and Elvis receives a total of $20,000, plus a $7,500 commission on souvenir sales for the ten-day tour.

Harry Kalcheim telegrams the Colonel that he has rejected Dean Martin's offer of $30,000 for an October television appearance.

13 Monday

William Morris Agency president Abe Lastfogel telegrams the Colonel from Hollywood that a movie deal with 20th Century Fox has been set. Because he does not yet have a suit-

Rehearsal, Jacksonville, Florida, August 10, 1956

On the set of *Love Me Tender*

On the set of *Love Me Tender* with *(left to right)* Scotty Moore, Elvis, Neal Matthews, Richard Egan, Bill Black, D.J. Fontana, Gordon Stoker, Hoyt Hawkins, and Hugh Jarrett

decide that Red should not accompany Elvis to Hollywood—which causes Red in turn to join the Marines.

16 Thursday

Elvis leaves Memphis on an American Airlines flight for Los Angeles, and Tom Diskin duly informs the Colonel by telegram that "The Cat" has arrived and is ready to go. Elvis reports to 20th Century Fox for pre-production meetings for his first film, to be produced by *Rebel Without a Cause* producer David Weisbart and directed by veteran Robert Webb.

18 Saturday

Ed Braslaff photographs Elvis at the Knickerbocker Hotel, where he is staying. Elvis, Gene, and Junior Smith reportedly spend $750 at the Long Beach Amusement Park.

20 Monday

Elvis reports to the Fox lot for pre-production, where he is assigned to Dressing Room 6. Elvis soon meets actor Nick Adams, a close friend of *Rebel Without a Cause* star, the late James Dean.

22 Wednesday

Principal photography for *The Reno Brothers* begins.

Elvis gives an interview on the set, to be released as a special 45 rpm disc inserted into the magazine *Teen Parade* and titled "The Truth About Me."

24 Friday

Soundtrack recording of the three songs to be included in *The Reno Brothers* begins on the Fox soundstage and runs from 1:00 to 6:00 P.M. Scotty, Bill, and D.J. have driven to Hollywood,

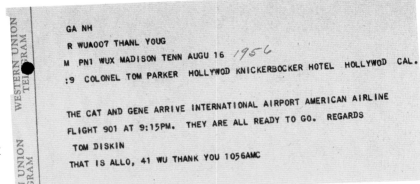

WESTERN UNION TELEGRAM

GA NH
R WUA007 THANL YOUG
M PN1 WUX MADISON TENN AUGU 16 *1956*
:9 COLONEL TOM PARKER HOLLYWOD KNICKERBOCKER HOTEL HOLLYWOD CAL.

THE CAT AND GENE ARRIVE INTERNATIONAL AIRPORT AMERICAN AIRLINE FLIGHT 901 AT 9:15PM. THEY ARE ALL READY TO GO. REGARDS
TOM DISKIN
THAT IS ALLO, 41 WU THANK YOU 1056AMC

Tom Diskin to Colonel Parker

Behind the plough, on location, *Love Me Tender*

August Record Releases

EP: *The Real Elvis* (shipped August 17). RCA puts both sides of the new single "Don't Be Cruel" and "Hound Dog" on this EP before the singles have peaked on the charts. Four hundred thousand copies of the EP will sell, but the record never charts because all radio airplay, a key element in determining chart position, is assigned to the single.
Single: "Blue Suede Shoes"/"Tutti Frutti"
Single: "I Got a Woman"/"I'm Counting on You"
Single: "I'll Never Let You Go"/"I'm Gonna Sit Right Down and Cry"
Single: "I Love You Because"/"Trying to Get to You"
Single: "Just Because"/"Blue Moon" (#55)
Single: "Money Honey"/"One-Sided Love Affair"
Single: "Shake, Rattle and Roll"/"Lawdy, Miss Clawdy"
(All singles shipped August 31)
In an industry first, RCA releases seven singles simultaneously, six of them from the first LP, the seventh ("Shake, Rattle and Roll"/"Lawdy, Miss Clawdy") from the EP issued in June. Only the eerie "Blue Moon" (one of the first sides recorded for Sun) charts, but combined sales total 1.6 million copies.

with Elvis' encouragement, in hopes of appearing in the movie as well as cutting an RCA session. Upon their rejection by the musical director (they are told they are not "hillbilly" enough), Elvis finds himself working with studio musicians in an uncomfortable situation, though the Colonel has arranged for him to receive cowriting credit and for all songs to be assigned to his publishing company. In the end, recording does not go badly, and he particularly likes one of the songs, "Love Me Tender," a reworking of the Civil War ballad "Aura Lee." "People think all I can do is belt," Elvis tells reporter Army Archerd, for whom he performs the new song. "I used to sing nothing but ballads before I went professional. I love ballads." But he vows that he will work with his band hereafter.

31 Friday
Elvis calls Memphis DJ Dewey Phillips at home. He quips that making movies is hard work—he's spent the entire day plowing behind a team of mules.

SEPTEMBER

01 Saturday
Elvis reports to Radio Recorders, an independent studio on Santa Monica Boulevard, for the RCA recording session that Steve Sholes has been so desperate for. He immediately feels comfortable both with the room and with the man in charge of the room, engineer Thorne Nogar. Elvis works from 1:00 to 8:00 P.M., recording material both for his second album and for a new single. No piano player has been hired, so all piano parts are taken by either Elvis or Jordanaire Gordon Stoker.

02 Sunday
Recording continues from 1:00 to 11:00 P.M. at Radio Recorders.

03 Monday
Recording at Radio Recorders from 2:00 to 8:30 P.M.

04 Tuesday
Additional music for Elvis' new film, whose title has now officially become *Love Me Tender*, is recorded at the 20th Century Fox soundstage.

05 Wednesday
Elvis continues soundtrack work at Fox, recording vocals for a new song, "Let Me," and an additional verse for "Poor Boy," one of the three songs originally slotted for the picture.

09 Sunday
★ *The Ed Sullivan Show*, CBS Studios, *Los Angeles*
Because of Sullivan's automobile accident in August, Elvis' first appearance on the show is hosted by actor Charles Laughton in New York City, where the show originates. Over 80 percent of the national viewing audience watch Elvis' live performance of "Don't Be Cruel," "Love Me Tender," "Ready Teddy," and two verses of "Hound Dog."

10 Monday
Elvis continues filming of *Love Me Tender*. In the evening Elvis has a date with the young actress Natalie Wood, a close friend of Nick Adams, with whom she appeared with James Dean in *Rebel Without a Cause*.

Sometime during the making of the picture Elvis moves from the Knicker-

With cast members William Campbell, James Drury, and Mildred Dunnock, on location, *Love Me Tender*

23 Sunday

Using the name of Clint Reno, the character he is playing in *Love Me Tender*, Elvis flies to Memphis, accompanied by Nick Adams and Gene Smith. In advance of his arrival, Tom Diskin telegrams the Memphis press that no pictures are to be taken at the Presley home. "I am sure you can appreciate the need for this action nor would you want to impose on their friendship." In the evening, Elvis is spotted at the Memphis Fairgrounds with Nick.

24 Monday

Elvis takes Nick to visit Mildred Scrivener, his senior-class homeroom teacher at Humes High School, and gives $900 to the school for new uniforms for its ROTC (officer training) program.

25 Tuesday

Steve Sholes reports to Elvis and the Colonel that RCA has received 918,230 orders for the still-unreleased

bocker Hotel to the more posh Beverly Wilshire Hotel, where the Colonel now stays when he is in town.

12 Wednesday

The police chief of San Diego, California, announces that if Elvis ever returns to his city and performs in the way that he did in the spring he will be jailed for disorderly conduct.

21 Friday

Elvis concludes filming of *Love Me Tender*.

As a result of RCA's unprecedented release policy, whereby every song on the first LP has now been put out both in single and EP form, there is an amendment to the recording agreement. By a letter of this date RCA confirms that it does not have permission to release any of the recordings from the most recent session as singles without the express written consent of Colonel Parker.

With the Jordanaires at the September 1956 recording sessions: *(left to right)* Gordon Stoker, Hoyt Hawkins, Neal Matthews, and Hugh Jarrett

Tupelo, September 26, 1956

Backstage interview, Tupelo

September Record Releases

EP: *Any Way You Want Me* (#74) (shipped September 21). The title track, the B-side of the upcoming single ("Love Me Tender," scheduled to be released the following week), is programmed with three Sun Records singles, of which one ("I Don't Care If the Sun Don't Shine") will chart. The EP will sell more than 100,000 copies.

Single: "Love Me Tender" (#1)/"Any Way You Want Me" (#27) (shipped September 28). The release of this new single is timed to follow Elvis' performance of the song on *The Ed Sullivan Show* and to precede the movie's opening by six weeks. By Christmas the record will have sold more than 2.5 million copies.

single of "Love Me Tender," and that Benny Goodman's daughter is a big fan. RCA telegrams Elvis with official congratulations for an industry first when additional orders make the single a gold record before it is even released.

26 Wednesday

Elvis drives to Tupelo with his parents, Nick Adams, and Memphis girlfriend Barbara Hearn for a hometown appearance at the Mississippi-Alabama Fair and Dairy Show, where he first performed at the age of ten. Governor J. P. Coleman certifies Elvis "America's number one entertainer in the field of popular music" and our "own native son." A fourteen-year-old Wynette Pugh (Tammy Wynette) watches from the front row as Elvis performs, wearing a blue velvet shirt made for him by Natalie Wood's dressmaker. The show is filmed by Fox Movietone News, but faulty audio makes it virtually a silent (if very kinetic) picture.

29 Saturday

Elvis and Nick return to the Memphis Fairgrounds for the Mid–South Fair, with Elvis taking the stage for a brief bow with Irish tenor (and Jack Benny comedy regular) Dennis Day.

30 Sunday

Elvis, Gene Smith, and Nick Adams fly to Los Angeles, where Elvis and Gene check into the Beverly Wilshire Hotel.

OCTOBER

01 Monday

Elvis records an extra verse of "Love Me Tender" on the Fox soundstage for use over the final credits of the movie. Backing vocals and strings are subsequently overdubbed.

03 Wednesday

The Colonel negotiates a new five-year contract with RCA, which he and Elvis will sign on October 18. Elvis will receive an immediate non-refundable advance of $135,000 against a 5 percent royalty, as well as a guaranteed $1,000 weekly payment for the term of the contract, also against royalties. He is required to make at least ten appearances either in person or on radio or television to promote his recordings.

08 Monday

With all postproduction work completed, Elvis is released from the film.

09 Tuesday

Elvis pays $150 to have plastic inserts for his upper anterior teeth made by a Beverly Hills dentist.

11 Thursday

Elvis, Nick Adams, and Gene Smith arrive in Dallas, Texas, by train, to begin a brief, four-day tour promoted by "Bam" Bamford.

★ *Cotton Bowl, Dallas, Texas*

Elvis enters in an open convertible, which takes him to a stage set up at the fifty-yard line before a crowd of 26,500. Drummer D. J. Fontana later says of the thousands of flashbulbs going off: "It looked like war out there." The show grosses $29,955.84 with Elvis receiving $17,973.50 on a guarantee of $15,000 against 60 percent of the gross after federal taxes.

12 Friday

★ *Heart O' Texas Coliseum, Waco, Texas*

13 Saturday

★ *Coliseum, Houston, Texas, at 4:00 and 9:00 P.M.*

According to a *Houston Post* report, the Colonel's advance man, Oscar Davis, appeals to the crowd to sit down before the show begins. "Just remember," he declares, "it might be your child that gets trampled."

14 Sunday

★ *Bexar County Coliseum, San Antonio, Texas, at 3:00 and 8:00 P.M.*

15 Monday

Elvis and Gene Smith fly from San Antonio to Memphis.

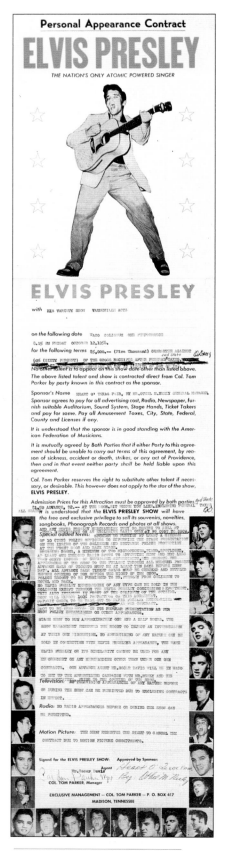

Contract for appearance, Waco, Texas

Second *Ed Sullivan Show*

16 Tuesday

Elvis is having dinner with Dewey Phillips and Barbara Hearn at the State Café when he breaks his two dental inserts.

18 Thursday

Elvis stops for gas at a Gulf station in downtown Memphis, when his car is surrounded by a mob of fans. The attendant, Edd Hopper, asks him to move along, and an altercation erupts, with Hopper pulling a knife and a third man entering the fray. Elvis gives the 6'3" Hopper a black eye, and all three men are booked on charges of assault and battery and disorderly conduct.

19 Friday

All charges against Elvis are dismissed, while the two station attendants are fined for their involvement in the Thursday incident.

June Juanico arrives from Biloxi for a visit.

21 Sunday

Because of the constant crush of fans, Elvis and June stay in the house much of the time, but on this evening they venture out to see the newsreel footage of the Tupelo concert at a local theater. Fans spot the band's black limousine and vandalize it for souvenirs. The next day's paper

With Natalie Wood and Nick Adams, Memphis, October 31, 1956

incorrectly names Barbara Hearn as Elvis' date.

22 Monday

In the evening Elvis rehearses at home with the band and the Jordanaires for an upcoming second appearance on *The Ed Sullivan Show.*

23 Tuesday

Nick Adams arrives for a visit.

24 Wednesday

Before leaving for New York, Elvis attends a special screening of a rough cut of *Love Me Tender* with June and his parents. Everyone thinks it's wonderful, but Elvis is dissatisfied with his performance.

Variety declares "Elvis a Millionaire in 1 Year," based on the trade paper's projections of income from movies, records, song publishing, merchandising, and personal appearances.

25 Thursday

Elvis flies first class to New York City with Gene Smith, Nick Adams, and Bitsy Mott, Marie (Mrs. Colonel) Parker's brother, who has been supervising security and acting as road manager from time to time in recent months. Meanwhile, the band travels north in Gladys' Cadillac Fleetwood, which loses a wheel bearing in Pennsylvania.

26 Friday

After arriving in New York City,

Elvis rehearses with the Jordanaires, and the Colonel concludes a deal permitting RCA to use the Presley name and likeness to promote an RCA record player called the "Victrola phonogram."

28 Sunday

Dewey Phillips and Cliff Gleaves, a new acquaintance whom Elvis has met through George Klein, fly in from Memphis at Elvis' expense.

While Elvis attends a rehearsal for the show, the Colonel hands out "Elvis for President" buttons at the unveiling of a forty-foot cutout of Elvis on top of the Times Square Paramount Theater marquee announcing the upcoming premiere of *Love Me Tender.*

Elvis readily handles a press conference in a "polite, personable, quick-witted and charming" manner, responding to reporters' questions about his influence on teenagers in supremely diplomatic fashion. "My Bible tells me that what he sows he will also reap, and if I'm sowing evil and wickedness it will catch up with me," Elvis declares. "If I did think I was bad for people, I would go back to driving a truck, and I really mean this."

Elvis gets inoculated with the new Salk polio vaccine as part of a public service announcement for the March of Dimes.

★ *Maxine Elliot Theater, West Thirty-ninth Street, at 8:00 P.M.*
Elvis sings "Don't Be Cruel," "Love Me," "Love Me Tender," and "Hound Dog" on his second appearance on *The Ed Sullivan Show.*

29 Monday

A new ending for *Love Me Tender* is filmed at the Junco Studio on East Sixty-ninth Street. Even though his character dies in the movie, the new scene has a "ghostly" image hovering over the mourners walking away from the grave and recapitulating the title tune as the family grieves. It appears as if Elvis' hair (its natural color throughout the rest of the movie) may be dyed black in this scene.

30 Tuesday

Elvis has sold over ten million singles, a figure representing about two-thirds of RCA's singles sales for the year.

Elvis and his friends return to Memphis by train.

31 Wednesday

Natalie Wood flies to Memphis for a visit. In the evening Elvis and Nick Adams take her down to the Hotel Chisca to meet Dewey Phillips.

October Record Releases

EP: *Elvis Vol. 1* (#6) (shipped October 19). This EP accompanies the release of Elvis' second album and contains four of the same songs. The lead song, "Love Me," written by "Hound Dog" composers Jerry Leiber and Mike Stoller, is strong enough to climb to #6 on the singles chart at the same time that "Love Me Tender" replaces "Don't Be Cruel" at the top spot. One million copies of the EP will be sold by Christmas.

LP: *Elvis* (#1) (shipped October 19). Amazingly, in the midst of all this marketing flurry, Elvis' second album outsells his first by almost 200,000 copies, reaching half a million in sales.

With Colonel Parker and Ed Sullivan backstage

NOVEMBER

01 Thursday

Elvis buys a new Harley-Davidson motorcycle and takes Natalie Wood for a ride, accompanied by Nick Adams on the old Harley and a police escort.

03 Saturday

Natalie Wood and Nick Adams return to Los Angeles. Sometime during the fall Nick Adams' mother visits Elvis and his family on Audubon Drive.

05 Monday

Elvis makes a surprise appearance at a police-sponsored "Beginner Driving Range," part of a new driver-education program.

Elvis asks Cliff Gleaves to move into his Audubon Drive home as a combination friend and "gofer," who can help make things easier for Elvis and his parents. Cliff agrees, as long as he can keep his "free-agent" status. At around the same time Elvis meets Lamar Fike, a three-hundred-pound émigré from Texas who has been hanging around with George Klein trying to break into radio.

08 Thursday

Elvis' automobile insurance policy shows that as of this date among the vehicles he owns are one 1956 Messerschmitt (a three-wheeled German minicar); two Harley-Davidsons; one 1956 Lincoln Continental; one 1956 Cadillac Eldorado; and one 1950 Chevrolet one-ton truck, in which he likes to drive anonymously around town.

Elvis takes a train to Las Vegas with Bitsy Mott and Gene Smith.

09 Friday

Vernon wires Elvis $1,000 in cash at the New Frontier, where he is staying. Over the next ten days Elvis will take in most of the shows in town and date a dancer named Dottie Harmony. He makes four trips to see Billy Ward and His Dominoes, because he is so taken by lead singer Jackie Wilson's version of "Don't Be Cruel."

10 Saturday

Elvis pays $91.95 in cash at Jack Garns Men's Shop for two pairs of slacks and two jackets.

12 Monday

Elvis rents a Cadillac from Hertz for $139.

15 Thursday

Elvis attends Liberace's late show at the Clover Room of the Riviera Hotel and fools around for photographers during a visit backstage.

Love Me Tender opens at the Paramount theater in New York City, where 1,500 fans begin lining up the night before under the forty-foot cutout of Elvis. Reviews are generally critical, if not condescending. The Colonel's one piece of advice to theater operators is to be sure to empty the house after every matinee showing.

16 Friday

Gladys Music is registered with ASCAP (the American Society of Composers, Authors and Publishers), so that Elvis can have a song-publishing company with each of the two major songwriting societies (Elvis Presley Music is a BMI [Broadcast Music Incorporated] company). Some songwriters are signed up with one society, some with the other, and although BMI, which was formed in 1940 to fill the void left by ASCAP with respect to vernacular ("race," hillbilly, folk) music, represents the preponderance of country and rhythm-and-blues songwriters, this gives Elvis and Hill and Range, originally a BMI company exclusively, both greater business leverage and wider song selection.

20 Tuesday

Back in Memphis, Elvis and Nick Adams are spotted riding motorcycles before attending a private midnight showing of *Love Me Tender* at the Loew's State Theater, prior to the scheduled Wednesday opening. Gladys Presley cries when the character her son plays in the picture dies.

21 Wednesday

Love Me Tender is released nationwide in 575 prints, a record number for 20th Century Fox. In Memphis it breaks all records, and *Variety* will report its first-week earnings of $540,000 as second only to the Rock Hudson–Elizabeth Taylor–James Dean film, *Giant*, that week.

22 Thursday

★ *Sports Arena, Toledo, Ohio, at 2:30 and 8:00 P.M.*

After the second show Elvis is accosted at the Commodore Perry Hotel by a jealous young man whose estranged wife carries Elvis' picture in her pocketbook. According to police, Elvis holds his own in the fight, and the young man is arrested.

23 Friday

★ *Arena, Cleveland, Ohio*

24 Saturday

★ *Hobart Arena, Troy, Ohio, at 3:00 and 8:00 P.M.*

25 Sunday

★ *Jefferson County Armory, Louisville, Kentucky, at 2:00 and 8:00 P.M.*

Elvis' grandfather, Jessie, who

November Record Release

EP: *Love Me Tender* (#35) (shipped November 21). Rounding off a year that has seen the release of seven EPs to date, one double EP, two albums, and eleven singles, RCA releases the *Love Me Tender* soundtrack on an extended-play 45. It includes the title cut as well as the three other fabricated folk songs that appear in the picture, only one ("We're Gonna Move," based on a rousing gospel number) the genuine article. "Poor Boy," with accordion accompaniment, charts and the record will eventually sell more than 600,000 copies.

"Million Dollar Quartet": Jerry Lee Lewis, Carl Perkins, Elvis, Johnny Cash. Sun studio, Memphis, December 4, 1956

works at the Louisville Pepsi Cola bottling plant, attends the show, and later Elvis visits him at his home.

26 Monday

Elvis drives back to Memphis, stopping at the Colonel's Madison headquarters for a visit.

28 Wednesday

Elvis drops by the Loew's State for a matinee performance of *Love Me Tender*.

30 Friday

Elvis attends the E. H. Crump Memorial Football Game, a Memphis charity event to benefit the blind.

DECEMBER

03 Monday

Elvis buys a new 1957 two-door, hardtop Eldorado Cadillac Seville for $8,400.

In a letter to the Colonel, Steve Sholes acknowledges Elvis' desire to do his future recording at Radio Recorders in Hollywood.

04 Tuesday

Accompanied by Marilyn Evans, a showgirl he met in Las Vegas, Elvis stops by the Sun recording studio in the middle of a Carl Perkins recording session and stays to jam with Carl and Sun's newest artist, Jerry Lee Lewis, who is playing piano on the session. Elvis takes over the piano seat as Sam Phillips keeps the tape running. The resulting recordings will become known as the "Million Dollar Quartet" session (Johnny Cash is present for the picture-taking ceremony only). While the group sings some country and rock 'n' roll, it is ragged gospel harmonies which predominate, along with Elvis' animated impression of the unnamed "colored" singer (Jackie Wilson) who has so captivated him in Las Vegas with his version of "Don't Be Cruel." "He tried so hard," Elvis tells a disbelieving audience of fellow singers and hangers-on, "till he got much better,

boy, much better than that record of mine. Man, he was cutting out. I was under the table when he got through singing."

06 Thursday

At 8:00 P.M. Elvis returns to the Loew's State for another viewing of *Love Me Tender*.

07 Friday

Elvis gets his hair cut at Jim's Barber Shop on South Main.

In the evening Elvis and George Klein attend radio station WDIA's Goodwill Revue, a charity event that takes place twice a year. WDIA, the first radio station in the country to feature all-Negro talent, is known as "The Mother Station of the Negroes" and presents an array of gospel music, rhythm and blues, and comedic talent at these events. This year the show features Ray Charles, B. B. King, the Moonglows, and DJ Rufus Thomas, among others, and Elvis' brief emergence from behind the curtain causes the audience to go wild. In succeeding weeks the black press will for the most part picture Elvis as a hero for his public embrace of the Negro cause, although WDIA personality Nat D. Williams wonders in his column in the *Pittsburgh Courier*, "How come cullud girls would take on so over a Memphis white boy . . . when they hardly let out a squeak over B. B. King?"

11 Tuesday

Elvis runs out of gas downtown in his new Seville and is mobbed by fans.

Louisiana governor Earl K. Long promotes Elvis to the same rank as his manager, giving him the honorary commission of a Louisiana colonel.

12 Wednesday

Elvis donates toys to a Marine drive for underprivileged children, stops by the police station for a visit, and goes to see *Storm of the Nile* at the downtown Malco Theater.

13 Thursday

Hal Kanter, screenwriter-director for Elvis' upcoming film for Hal Wal-

lis at Paramount, comes to town to meet the young singer, with the idea of adding flavor to his script. His plan is to accompany Elvis to the specially arranged Louisiana Hayride benefit show on the fifteenth, which was stipulated as part of the April buyout agreement.

Hill and Range and Paramount, working together, have already come up with much of the soundtrack for the picture, currently titled *Lonesome Cowboy*, including four numbers by "Hound Dog" composers Jerry Leiber and Mike Stoller. Hill and Range representative Freddy Bienstock is also in Memphis to help Elvis with song selection.

14 Friday

Elvis and director Hal Kanter drive to Shreveport with the Colonel's brother-in-law, Bitsy Mott, and Gene and Junior Smith, stopping off at the Trio restaurant in Pine Bluff, Arkansas, where they have dinner with Jim Ed and Maxine Brown. According to the Pine Bluff newspaper, "The singer was not recognized until about ten o'clock, when a crowd began to grow. When one teenager admired his sport shirt, Elvis good-naturedly traded shirts with him." Elvis and his party do not leave till after midnight, arriving in Shreveport at five in the morning, where they register at the Captain Shreve Hotel.

15 Saturday

★ *Louisiana Hayride, Hirsch Youth Center, Louisiana Fairgrounds, Shreveport*

The crowd's hysterical reaction to Elvis' only public appearance in December provides the basis for a number of touches that Hal Kanter adds to his finished screenplay, the story of the rise of a young singer who very much resembles—Elvis Presley.

24 Monday

Elvis goes Christmas shopping at Lamar Airways Center with his Christmas houseguest, Dottie Harmony, the showgirl he dated in Las Vegas.

25 Tuesday

Christmas is celebrated in the Audubon Drive house.

At some point around this time, very likely during the Christmas season, Elvis buys a new tape recorder, and home recordings exist of Vernon and Gladys belting out a crude but enthusiastic "If We Never Meet Again" and "I'll Fly Away," Elvis, Arthur Hooton, and Marine private-on-leave Red West singing "When the Saints Go Marching In," and Elvis shooting pool.

27 Thursday

Elvis plays touch football at the Dave Wells Community Center in Memphis with friends, including Red West.

31 Monday

Elvis is scheduled to appear on Dewey Phillips' new TV show, *Phillips' Pop Shop*, between 3:30 and 4:30 P.M.

Elvis' U.S. income tax return shows earnings of $282,349.66 in 1956.

December Record Release

EP: *Elvis Vol. 2* (#47). A second EP from Elvis' second album, released just one month before, evidently put out on the theory that not only are teenagers indiscriminately voracious for Elvis Presley "product" but not every teenager has a record player that can play LPs. With "So Glad You're Mine" as the lead track, this EP sells 400,000 copies, and one of the first songs Elvis learned, "Old Shep," reaches #47.

1957

With Colonel Parker on the set of *Loving You*

JANUARY

04 Friday

Elvis drives his Cadillac Eldorado to the Kennedy Veterans Hospital in Memphis for a pre-induction physical that will determine his draft status. He is accompanied by Cliff Gleaves and Dottie Harmony. Later in the day, Dottie flies back to Los Angeles and Elvis takes the train to New York City for his third Ed Sullivan appearance.

06 Sunday

★ *The Ed Sullivan Show, Maxine Elliot Theater, West Thirty-ninth Street, at 8:00 P.M.*

Elvis wears the same velvet shirt he wore in Tupelo, with a gold lamé vest given to him as a Christmas present by Barbara Hearn. His performance of "Don't Be Cruel" deliberately suggests the manner of Jackie Wilson's rendition of the song in Las Vegas in November. At the network's request he sings "Peace in the Valley," a gospel song written by black gospel composer Thomas A. Dorsey, which has become a classic in both the black and white traditions. Not coincidentally, during his secular performances Elvis is shot only from the waist up. Ed Sullivan thanks Elvis at the conclusion of the show, telling the audience that "this is a real decent, fine boy. . . . We want to say that we've never had a

pleasanter experience with a big name than we've had with you."

After the show, Elvis takes the midnight train back to Memphis.

08 Tuesday

Elvis celebrates his twenty-second birthday at home with his parents.

The Memphis Draft Board announces at a press conference that Elvis Presley will be classified 1A, meaning he will most likely be drafted within the next six to eight months.

While he is home, Elvis stops by to see Dixie Locke, who has recently married.

10 Thursday

Elvis, Gene Smith, Cliff Gleaves, and Bitsy Mott leave by train for Los Angeles, where they check into the Beverly Wilshire Hotel upon arrival. Elvis is scheduled to record for RCA over the weekend before starting work on the soundtrack for his new Paramount picture.

12 Saturday

Elvis embarks upon his first session in four months, at Radio Recorders. RCA has been anxious for some time to get new material for both a single and a gospel EP, but

Elvis has been unwilling to record in Nashville. He works from noon to 7:00 P.M., completing five songs, including "Don't Be Cruel," songwriter Otis Blackwell's latest, "All Shook Up," and the pop inspirational number "I Believe."

13 Sunday

Elvis continues recording at Radio Recorders from noon to 11:00 P.M. Among the songs recorded is "Peace in the Valley," which Elvis performed on the Sullivan show, and another Thomas A. Dorsey favorite, "Take My Hand, Precious Lord."

14 Monday

Elvis reports to the Paramount makeup department to have his hair dyed black, then to the wardrobe department. The script, originally called *Lonesome Cowboy*, is about to be retitled *Loving You*, after the Leiber-Stoller song.

15 Tuesday

Soundtrack recording for the new picture begins on Paramount's scoring stage at 10:00 A.M., ending at 5:05 P.M. The Jordanaires, Scotty, Bill, and D.J. have all been hired, just as Elvis promised they would be after his disappointing experience with *Love Me Tender*. The band is augmented by two well-known Los Angeles musicians frequently used on Paramount sessions, Hilmer "Tiny" Timbrell on guitar and Dudley Brooks on piano. Both will be regulars on Elvis' Hollywood sessions well into the sixties.

16 Wednesday

Sessions continue at Paramount from 9:00 A.M. to 3:30 P.M., though Elvis is clearly uncomfortable working on the giant soundstage and recording goes slowly. New York songwriter Ben Weisman is present, presumably in hopes of seeing that his song, "Got a Lot O' Livin' to Do," will be included in the soundtrack. He may well be unaware that it has already been recorded by RCA on January 12.

17 Thursday

Vernon ships Elvis his Cadillac Eldorado Seville by train.

Although he continues to put in long hours on the soundstage (from 9:00 A.M. to 6:00 P.M. on this particular day), Elvis complains frequently of the impersonality of such a large, unfriendly space.

18 Friday

Elvis spends an even longer day, from 9:00 A.M. to 11:25 P.M., on the soundstage.

19 Saturday

Elvis returns to Radio Recorders to work on material for RCA, completing the gospel EP and three additional album tracks.

21 Monday

At Paramount, Elvis works on both a fast and a slow version of "Loving You." After eleven hours, he has still not achieved a satisfactory take.

22 Tuesday

Elvis starts at 8:00 A.M. on the soundstage, working for three hours before he reports for filming.

Hal Wallis announces at around this time that Elvis' second Paramount picture will be *Sing, You Sinners*, based on an Oscar Saul script and set in New Orleans.

23 Wednesday

The Colonel puts pressure on Wallis to upgrade Elvis' boilerplate contract, finally succeeding in convincing him to pay Elvis a $50,000 bonus on top of his agreed-upon $15,000 salary for *Loving You.*

27 Sunday

Gladys is admitted to Baptist Hospital for tests that will delay a planned trip with her husband to visit their son in Hollywood.

FEBRUARY

01 Friday

Steve Sholes informs the Colonel that neither recorded version of "Loving You" is strong enough for single release. Eventually Elvis will record three more versions of the song before it is judged to be satisfactory.

08 Friday

Gladys is released from Baptist Hospital.

Hal Wallis informs Colonel Parker that the picture has officially been retitled *Loving You.*

11 Monday

Elvis films the "tavern" scene, in which envious local thugs pick a fight with singer Deke Rivers, who, like his real-life counterpart, definitely appeals to their girlfriends.

12 Tuesday

In Memphis Vernon and Gladys board a 7:30 P.M. train bound for Los Angeles with their friends, Carl and Willy Nichols. Carl is the contractor and housepainter who has done much of the remodeling work at Audubon, including the installation of the swimming pool.

13 Wednesday

Hal Wallis shows his grasp of realpolitik, agreeing to let Elvis finish up soundtrack recording at Radio Recorders. Studio rehearsals begin almost immediately with the band.

14 Thursday

Elvis re-records both fast and slow versions of "Loving You" at Radio Recorders.

RCA informs Elvis that it is exercising its option to extend the term of his contract, currently due to expire on October 15, 1961, until October 15, 1966.

21–22 Thursday–Friday

Gladys and Vernon Presley visit Elvis on the set and appear as extras in the scene where Elvis performs "Loving You" and "Got a Lot O' Livin' to Do" in front of an audience. They can be seen quite plainly sitting on the aisle, with Gladys clapping enthusiastically to the beat. It is said that Elvis was never able to watch the film again after his mother's death.

23 Saturday

Steve Sholes sets up a session at Radio Recorders for Elvis to cut "Loving You" yet again—this time as an RCA single—but Elvis instead turns his attention to other material during the 10:00 A.M. to 6:30 P.M. session. "I Beg of You" and "One Night" both come out of this session, with each a potential candidate for single release.

January Record Releases

Single: "Too Much" (#2)/"Playing For Keeps" (#34) (shipped January 4). Though the single does not reach the #1 spot, sales are two million copies.

EP: *Strictly Elvis* (shipped January 25). This is the third EP to include material from the second album, and it chalks up another 200,000 in sales, although it does not chart.

On the set
of *Loving You*

24 Sunday

Elvis finally nails the version of "Loving You" that will appear on record. He also keeps his promise to Sam Phillips to record "When It Rains It Really Pours," a song they had tried unsuccessfully to complete at Sun. With the conclusion of this session, Sholes has seven finished masters from two days of work.

25 Monday

Colonel Parker announces that he has completed a deal with MGM for Elvis' third film, scheduled to begin in May and tentatively titled *The Rock*. He claims it is "the biggest deal ever made in Hollywood," though its specifics do not altogether bear out his claim (Elvis will receive $250,000 plus 50 percent of the net profits). Still, it is a very good deal and puts Hal Wallis on notice.

Louis Armstrong is quoted in today's *Memphis Press-Scimitar* as saying: "I'm definitely gonna do a record with him. You'd be surprised what we could do together. You ask me if I think he's good. How many Cadillacs was it he bought? That boy's no fool."

26 Tuesday

Through an attorney, the Colonel warns 20th Century Fox that the adaptation they are planning of the recently broadcast television drama "The Singing Idol" (starring Tommy Sands) is ill-advised, because the two principal characters, closely based on Elvis and the Colonel, are portrayed in a manner "most disparaging and damaging to their characters and careers." It's hard to say how seriously the Colonel takes this, since he appears to have been instrumental in getting Tommy Sands the starring role.

27 Wednesday

Shooting for *Loving You* moves to the Jessup Ranch north of Hollywood for much of this week.

Elvis' telegram to Private Hershel Nixon

TELEGRAM RECEIVED BY TELEPHONE

PFC HERSCHEL NIXON

XXXXXXXXXXXN NAVAL AIR TECHNICAL TRAINING CENTER

I READ IN THE PAPER THAT YOU WANTED AN APOLOGY AND I AM WILLING TO GIVE YOU AN APOLOGY IN FACT I THINK WE OWE EACH OTHER ONE. THE WHOLE THING IS KIND OF UNCALLED FOR. I'M SORRY THAT IT HAPPENED BUT HEAVEN KNOWS IT WAS ALL WAS STRICTLY UNCALLED FOR. I WOULD LIKE TO STRAIGHTEN OUT ANOTHER RUMOR THAT STARTED OUT THERE A FEW MONTHS AGO. SOMEBODY STARTED THE RUMOR THAT I DIDN'T LIKE MARINES OR SAILORS AND IT WAS FOR A WHILE THAT EVERY XX TIME I GOT OUT THERE WAS SOME

1957 MAR 25 PM 8 15
MILLINGTON TENN

1034 AUDUBON DRIVE

TELEGRAM RECEIVED BY TELEPHONE

MARINE OR SAILOR THAT TRIED TO CAUSE TROUBLE WITH ME. AND ALSO SOMEBODY STARTED A RUMOR IN MEXICO THAT I DIDN'T LIKE MEXICANS AND A LOT OF THE MEXICANS GOT MAD AT ME AND THEN HERE IN MEMPHIS THE RUMOR GOT OUT THAT XXXX I DIDN'T LIKE COLORED PEOPLE AND GOD KNOWS THAT I HAVE NEVER SAID THAT I DIDN+T LIKE ANYBODY. ITS JUST THAT RUMORS LIKE THAT GET STARTED AND THERE IS NOTHING I CAN DO ABOUT IT. THE MARINES AND THE NAVY AND THE ARMY AND THE AIR FORCE PROTECT OUR COUNTRY AND THEY HAVE BEEN AROUND FOR A LONG TIME PROTECTING US SO WHO AM I TO SAY THAT I DON'T LIKE ANYBODY BECAUSE GOD CREATED EVERYBODY EQUAL AND I WOULD NEVER SAY THAT I DIDN+T

LIKE ANYBODY. I'M NOT SAYING THIS BECAUSE I AM AFRAID FOR HEAVEN KNOWS I AM NOT IN THE LEAST BIT AFRAID BUT I JUST DON'T WANT ANYBODY THINKING I SAID THINGS LIKE THAT WHEN I NEVER EVEN THOUGHT ABOUT IT. I GOT A LUCKY BREAK IN LIFE AND I AM VERY THANKFUL FOR IT BUT THERE ARE FEW PEOPLE WHO WANT TO TAKE SHOTS AT ME. THE MAJORITY OF THE PEOPLE ALL OVER THE WORLD ARE VERY NICE BUT THERE FEW WHO WANT TO PROVE SOMETHING. I HAVE TALKED WAY OUT OF TROUBLE SO MANY TIMES THAT I COULDN'T EN COUNT THEM NOT BECAUSE I WAS AFRAID BUT JUST AUSE I WAS ALWAYS THE TYPE OF PERSON THAT I

TELEGRAM RECEIVED BY TELEPHONE

NEVER DID BELIEVE IN FIGHTING AND ALL THAT KIND OF XXXXXXX STUFF UNLESS I THOUGHT IT WAS ABSOLUTELY NECESSARY. AND ABOUT THE INSTANCE THE OTHER NIGHT AND ABOUT THE GUN. THE GUN IS A HOLLYWOOD PROP GUN AND I BROUGHT IT HOME BECAUSE A LOT OF PEOPLE ASK ME ABOUT HOW MOVIES ARE MADE AND ABOUT THE GUNS AND SO ON. I HAD ABOUT SIX OF THOSE GUNS WITH ME AND I WAS JUST SHOWING THEM TO SOME PEOPLE AND YOU CALLED ME OVER THERE. MANY TIMES THERE HAVE BEEN PEOPLE WHO CAME UP TO ME AND STICK OUT THEIR HANDS TO SHAKE HANDS WITH ME AND THEY HIT ME OR I HAVE HAD GUYS TO COME UP AND ASK FOR AUTOGRAPHS AND HIT ME AND THEN TAKE OFF FOR NO REASON AT ALL. I HAD NEVER LAID

MARCH

10 Sunday

RCA A & R director Steve Sholes continues to push Elvis to record. One would presume that this reflects the prevailing RCA view that Elvis Presley is little more than a passing fad. Despite the saturation release schedule of the past year, the Colonel continues to resist this point of view with every fiber of his managerial being. "Overexposure is like a sunburn," he tells Steve Sholes in yet another attempt at education by indirection. "It can hurt."

At the conclusion of filming, the Colonel throws a party on the *Loving You* set, setting up a booth where he gives away all manner of Elvis promotional material and raffles off an RCA Victrola under a banner declaring: "Elvis and the Colonel Thank You."

16 Saturday

Shortly after their return from Hollywood, Vernon and Gladys Presley start looking for a bigger (and more secluded) home, somewhere they can escape the constant fan invasion of Audubon Drive. In no time they find a mansion on the outskirts of Memphis, on Highway 51 South just before it enters Mississippi. The house, completed in 1941, is set well back from the road, "in a grove of towering oaks," on almost fourteen acres of land. It is called Graceland, after the great-aunt of the woman who built it, and the elder Presleys call Elvis in Hollywood to announce that they think they have found the ideal new home.

17 Sunday

Elvis leaves Los Angeles by train for Memphis.

18 Monday

Elvis telegrams June Juanico to meet his train during a brief layover in New Orleans, and it is there that she informs him that she is engaged to be married.

Elvis arrives in Memphis at 11:35 P.M.

19 Tuesday

As soon as he has seen Graceland, Elvis makes a $1,000 deposit toward its purchase for himself and his parents.

22 Friday

In an incident in downtown Memphis, across from the Hotel Chisca, from which Dewey Phillips broadcasts his show, Elvis is accused of pulling a gun on Private Hershel Nixon, a nineteen-year-old Marine, who claims that Elvis insulted his wife.

A headline in the *Memphis Press-Scimitar* announces: "Elvis to Appear at Tupelo Fair: No Charge!" According to fair spokesman Ike Savery, the fair initially offered Colonel Parker a guarantee of $10,000 for a return appearance at the Mississippi-Alabama Fair in September, but the Colonel turned them down. Elvis wanted no money beyond expenses, the Colonel said; the rest should go toward a youth center in the place that Elvis grew up, an idea, the Colonel said, that Elvis has had for some time.

23 Saturday

Elvis attends an all-night gospel singing at Ellis Auditorium.

25 Monday

Elvis sends a rambling six-page telegram of explanation and apology to Private Nixon that seems to go far beyond anything to do with the specific incident and offers up a kind of discursive guide to the social, personal, and political philosophy that will govern Elvis all his life.

Elvis and his parents finalize their purchase of Graceland for $102,500. They receive $55,000 from the realty company for their home on Audubon Drive, pay $10,000 in cash, and obtain a twenty-five-year mortgage for the remaining amount. Registration of the purchase is filed on March 28 and recorded the following day.

Within a matter of days, Elvis has hired George Golden, a local interior decorator, who has just completed the "space age" renovation of Sam Phillips' new ultramodern ranch house. Golden, who has several flatbed trucks traveling around Memphis complete with miniature rooms to advertise his wares, will soon brighten up the conventional decor with bold colors and futuristic touches.

Elvis meets with Judge Boushe in chambers and the incident with Private Nixon is settled without legal action.

27 Wednesday

Elvis leaves for Chicago with Gene Smith and Arthur Hooton. For the first time Humes classmate and Memphis DJ George Klein travels with the group.

28 Thursday

A press conference is held at the Saddle and Sirloin Club at the Stockyards Inn in Chicago.

★ *International Amphitheater, Chicago*
Elvis wears a $2,500 gold-leaf suit that the Colonel has had made up by Nudie Cohen, a Brooklyn émigré famous for the extravagance of the sequined suits he designs for country music stars like Hank Snow and Ferlin Huskey. The show grosses $32,000 from a crowd of 12,000.

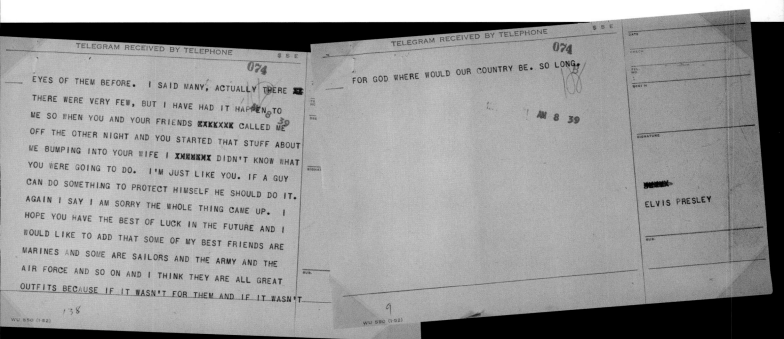

Performing in the gold suit, March–April 1957
(courtesy of Joe Tunzi)

Backstage in the gold suit
(courtesy of Robin Rosaaen)

29 Friday
★ *Kiel Auditorium, St. Louis, Missouri*
Elvis once again wears the gold suit, but after tonight will seldom wear the trousers again. He is embarrassed by what he considers the clownishness, not the coolness of the look, and the Colonel has asked him not to drop to his knees anymore, because the gold is flaking off and gold is expensive. Elvis will wear black pants for most of the rest of the tour, which once again features traditional vaudeville acts supplied by Chicago booker and bandleader Al Dvorin and is being promoted by Detroit-born entrepreneur Lee Gordon.

30 Saturday
★ *Memorial Coliseum, Fort Wayne, Indiana*

31 Sunday
★ *Olympia Stadium, Detroit, Michigan, at 2:00 and 8:00 P.M.*
The local paper reports, "Hysterical Shrieks Greet Elvis in his Gold Jacket and Shoes," noting that "the trouble with going to see Elvis Presley is that you're liable to get killed."

March Record Release

Single: "All Shook Up" (#1)/"That's When Your Heartaches Begin" (#58) (shipped March 22). "All Shook Up" remains at #1 for eight weeks, selling close to 2.5 million copies. The B-side is a heartfelt version of the same Ink Spots number that Elvis paid four dollars to record when he first entered the Sun recording studio in 1953.

A PRIL

01 Monday
★ *Memorial Auditorium, Buffalo, New York*
Elvis appears in gold jacket, black pants, and "gold slippers with rhinestones on the tassels."

02 Tuesday
★ *Maple Leaf Gardens, Toronto, Canada, at 6:00 and 8:00 P.M.*
Elvis wears the full gold suit, accompanying himself on piano when he sings "Blueberry Hill" a chart-topping hit for Fats Domino, the New Orleans rhythm-and-blues singer whom Elvis idolizes.

03 Wednesday
Elvis takes the 8:00 A.M. train to Ottawa, Canada.
★ *Ottawa Auditorium, Ottawa, at 4:40 and 8:00 P.M.*
After the show Elvis tells reporters, "It's a very uncertain business. The end may come in a lot less time than a few years." The *Ottawa Citizen* reports on the actions of a local girls' school at the Notre Dame Convent, which suspends eight Elvis fans for attending the concert.

At some point in the tour, advance man Oscar Davis approaches the Jordanaires and the band about becoming their manager. With Elvis now making hundreds of thousands of dollars, he argues, it is not right for the band to still be on the same pay scale as they were in October of 1955, getting $200 a week on the road, $100 when they are off. "He offered us a better deal than what the Colonel offered us," recalled Jordanaire Gordon Stoker, but in the end "we more or less didn't trust him."

04 Thursday
The Montreal booking in suburban Verdun is canceled because of a combination of civic concern and pressure from local Catholic officials.

05 Friday
★ *Sports Arena, Philadelphia, Pennsylvania, at 7:00 and 9:00 P.M.*
Elvis appears in a half-filled 6,500-seat arena after first facing hostile questions from a group of high school newspaper reporters.

06 Saturday
★ *Sports Arena, Philadelphia, at 2:30 and 8:00 P.M.*
Villanova students throw eggs at Elvis during the evening show, hitting the guitar he has laid down on the stage.

08 Monday
Elvis returns home to Audubon Drive.

In Hollywood MGM executives decide that Elvis' next film will be titled *Jailhouse Kid*.

09 Tuesday
Elvis and Dewey Phillips drop by Sam Phillips' house late in the evening, and Sam wakes up his young sons, Knox and Jerry. Knox in later years will recall watching the way Elvis played pool and trying to imitate the catlike way he slunk around the table and just defined everything there was to know about "cool."

13 Saturday
Elvis is the first contributor to Coffee Day for Crippled Children, a Memphis fund-raiser.

15 Monday
Elvis visits his new estate, posing for photographs with a fan while sitting on a tractor he has just purchased for work around the grounds.

16 Tuesday
William Morris agent Harry Kalcheim writes the Colonel to congratulate him on the "unheard-of" box-office figures from the recent tour and "the wonderful organization you have with Elvis. . . . Because of the fact that he is not shown too often on TV, there is great curiosity about him so that when he does appear he is sure to attract."

19 Friday
Hollywood starlet Yvonne Lime arrives in Memphis for a visit. Elvis takes her out to see Graceland, currently in the midst of renovation, and the two pose for a series of photographs in front of the house.

20 Saturday
Elvis and Yvonne attend a party at Sam Phillips' home in East Memphis with Dewey and Dot Phillips. The night ends with an early-morning breakfast and spirituals sung out by the pool.

21 Sunday

On Easter Sunday, Elvis attends church for the first time in a long time, with Yvonne Lime. After the service he tells the Assembly of God pastor, the Reverend Hamill, "I am the most miserable young man you have ever seen. I have got more money than I can ever spend. I have thousands of fans out there, and I have a lot of people who call themselves my friends, but I am miserable."

22 Monday

The new iron gates with a special guitar motif, manufactured by the Veterans Ornamental Iron Works of Phoenix, Arizona, at a cost of $1,300, are delivered to Graceland by a local firm and installed with their electronic equipment for $1,752.

26 Friday

Elvis is photographed standing proudly in front of the gates at the foot of the Graceland drive wearing a yellow jacket, brown trousers, red socks and belt, and white-green-and-blue shoes decorated with guitar-shaped figures.

27 Saturday

Elvis boards a train for Los Angeles. Freddy Bienstock is part of the group and plays Elvis demos of the songs that Hill and Range has commissioned for the new movie on the ride out to the coast.

28 Sunday

Elvis arrives in Los Angeles, checking into the penthouse apartment and the presidential suite of the Beverly Wilshire Hotel with Gene and

At the Graceland gates soon after their installation in April 1957

Junior Smith, George Klein, Arthur Hooton, and Bitsy Mott. The band remains at the downtown Knickerbocker Hotel.

29 Monday

Bill Bullock tries to persuade the Colonel to allow Elvis, as RCA Victor's leading artist, to introduce the company's "Galaxy of Stars" television special, scheduled for June 15 broadcast. The Colonel, however, holds the line.

30 Tuesday

Elvis works on soundtrack recordings at Radio Recorders from 10:00 A.M. to 6:10 P.M. It is at this session that he first meets Jerry Leiber and Mike Stoller, the twenty-four-year-old cowriters of "Hound Dog" and "Love Me." Up to this point, self-styled hipsters Leiber and Stoller have

considered Elvis little more than a poseur (they have nothing but scorn for his version of "Hound Dog"), but after observing him at work and talking to him a little about rhythm

With Mike Stoller and Jerry Leiber at MGM, spring 1957

April Record Release

EP: *Peace in the Valley* (#39 on singles chart). There is no question of Elvis' emotional involvement with the material on this four-track gospel EP, and it bears fruit both in sales (more than 400,000 copies) and in the public's evolving view of Elvis as more than just another rock 'n' roll rebel.

and blues, they are impressed both with his knowledge of and shared passion for the music that has inspired them. By the time the day is over, and Elvis has laid down a highly convincing version of their title song, Leiber and Stoller are effectively coproducers of the session, the first time Elvis has had any real outside creative input since leaving Sun.

MAY

01 Wednesday

MGM soundtrack sessions are scheduled to continue at Radio Recorders all day, but Elvis walks out shortly after lunch when the MGM executive-in-charge attempts to cut off a gospel jam with the Jordanaires. This is Elvis' way of relaxing, and he has no intention of surrendering either belief or control to what he considers a clock-watching, bureaucratic way of doing things. As he says again and again over the years, music is a feel, and he will do anything he can to achieve that feel.

02 Thursday

There is no session.

03 Friday

Soundtrack recording resumes and goes on from 9:00 A.M. to 6:25 P.M. Today it is Bill Black's turn to walk out, when he is unable to manage the introduction to "Baby I Don't Care" on his new Fender electric bass. Following his departure, Elvis picks up the instrument and plays the part himself, overdubbing his vocal on the instrumental track the following week.

06 Monday

Elvis reports to the MGM studio to meet with producer Pandro Berman, director Richard Thorpe, and Loving You costar Dolores Hart. He is assigned Clark Gable's dressing room, and the week is spent in costume fittings, makeup tests, and dance rehearsals with choreographer Alex Romero.

08 Wednesday

Elvis reports to the MGM sound-

Jailhouse Rock

stage for a one-hour session to record vocals for "Baby I Don't Care," followed by script rehearsals.

09 Thursday

Elvis returns to Radio Recorders from 1:00 to 4:15 P.M., completing work on the *Jailhouse Rock* soundtrack.

10 Friday

Elvis rehearses the fight sequence that lands his character, Vince Everett, in jail.

11 Saturday

Elvis visits the Topanga Canyon home of Russ Tamblyn, the young dancing star of *Seven Brides for Seven Brothers* and a friend of Nick Adams.

12 Sunday

Elvis has a date with Anne Neyland, who has a minor part in the film.

13 Monday

Principal photography begins on the jailhouse dance sequence.

14 Tuesday

While working on the dance sequence Elvis aspirates a cap from one of his teeth.

The Colonel writes to Elvis that he has "been bombarded, befuddled, befogged, bewildered and snowed under" with RCA requests for Elvis to appear on their NBC spectacular. "They have told me everything under the sun how good this would be for you for exposure [and have] come up with pretty good offers several times, but I turned them all down with respect to our motion picture for reasons I know are best for us. I told them that our next TV show for any sponsor we do would be $50,000, as I want to do one or two TV shows this year, and with a set-up like we would blast the whole country with. . . . They say we will never get it from no one. Well, maybe we won't [but] at least you will not be overexposed like some of the top stars that are now working for nothing as they are worn out on TV." He is writing so that Elvis will "know what is going on. Please indicate by marking yess [sic] if you think you should work cheaper, or nuts if you think I should keep snowing for the $50,000. I will guide myself either way you want to go.

"Yess, if you want to cut the price

"Nuts if we battle to go on getting top money"

15 Wednesday

Elvis has the aspirated cap removed from his lung and is visited in the hospital by Anne Neyland.

16 Thursday

Elvis is released from the hospital on the same day that Gladys and Vernon move into Graceland.

Columnist Joe Hyams quotes Elvis in the *New York Herald-Tribune* today as saying, "I can't get it into my head that I'm property. People tell me you can't do this or that, but I don't listen to them. I do what I want. I can't change, and I won't change." He goes on to say that "Colonel Parker is more or less like a daddy when I'm away from my own folks." On the other hand, the Colonel "doesn't meddle in my affairs . . . and never butts into record sessions."

17 Friday

Elvis writes to the staff of the Cedars of Lebanon Hospital: "Dear Friends, I want you to know how very much I appreciate your very wonderful treatment while I was there. When I went in I was all shook up but I left loving you.

"Thanks a million. My best to all. Sincerely, Elvis Presley."

18 Saturday

Lamar Fike, having read that Elvis is in the hospital, drives straight from Texas, where he has been visiting his mother, and shows up unexpectedly at the Beverly Wilshire Hotel, where he soon becomes a full-fledged member of the group.

20 Monday

Elvis is back on the set.

21 Tuesday

Elvis has a 7:00 A.M. makeup call for the fitting of the "butch cut" wig that he will wear in the prison scenes.

22 Wednesday

Tom Diskin reports to the Colonel that Elvis wants Leiber and Stoller's "Treat Me Nice" as the B-side to the songwriting team's title track, "Jailhouse Rock."

27 Monday

Scotty, Bill, and D.J. report to the set at 10:00 A.M. for a rehearsal of their parts.

28 Tuesday

Elvis' first grand piano is purchased for Graceland, a used white Knabe bought from Jack Marshall Pianos-Organs in Memphis for $795.

From January through May 1957, Elvis' income comes to $135,000 from live performance, $52,000 in royalties from RCA, $85,500 from publishing, $96,875 from motion pictures, and $16,000 from radio and television, for a total of $385,375.

JUNE

01 Saturday

June Juanico gets married in Biloxi.

On one of these weekend afternoons Robert Mitchum stops by the Beverly Wilshire to try to persuade Elvis to play his son in Mitchum's upcoming production, *Thunder Road.*

03 Monday

Elvis films his scene in the prison coal yard.

With butch-cut wig in *Jailhouse Rock*

06 Thursday

The Colonel turns down a South American tour for Elvis.

Toward the end of filming Dewey Phillips comes out for a visit, staying in Elvis' Beverly Wilshire suite. He proves an embarrassment both at MGM (where he declares, upon being introduced to Yul Brynner, "You're a short little mother, aren't you?") and in public, where he not infrequently calls attention to himself as "Dewey Phillips, Memphis, Tennessee," and proves it. Immediately after his return to Memphis he plays a purloined acetate of Elvis' unreleased single "Teddy Bear" on the air, causing a serious rift in his relationship with his onetime protégé.

11 Tuesday

The Colonel reiterates to Steve Sholes his belief that Elvis should release no more than four singles a year.

12 Wednesday

Elvis ships a wallaby that he has received as a gift from Australia to the Memphis Zoo.

14 Friday

The final scenes of *Jailhouse Rock* are filmed.

17 Monday

Elvis completes still photography for *Jailhouse Rock*.

The Colonel raises the theoretical price for a single television appearance by Elvis to $75,000.

18 Tuesday

A kidney-shaped swimming pool has been installed at Graceland at a cost of $8,481.35 by Paddock of California.

Jumping with Jennifer Holden, publicity shot from *Jailhouse Rock*

19 Wednesday

Mike Stoller sends Elvis lead sheets and demos for two new songs, "Don't," which he will record, and "I'm a Hog for You," which later becomes a hit for the Coasters.

20 Thursday

Elvis reports to the studio at 10:00 A.M. for looping.

25 Tuesday

With all of his duties completed, Elvis boards a train for Memphis.

26 Wednesday

An impatient Elvis gets off the train in Lafayette, Louisiana, rents a car, and drives the rest of the way to Memphis with Cliff Gleaves. This will be his first night in his new home.

Jailhouse Rock

On the set of *Jailhouse Rock* with Mike Stoller at the piano, Elvis, Scotty Moore, Judy Tyler, Bill Black, costar Mickey Shaughnessy, and D.J. Fontana

June Record Releases

Single: "Teddy Bear" (#1)/"Loving You" (#28) (shipped June 11). Another single, another # 1 hit, another million-plus-seller.

EP: *Loving You* (#4 on EP chart) (shipped June 26). This EP contains four songs that will appear on Elvis' forthcoming LP. One of them, "Mean Woman Blues," becomes a big radio hit, which contributes to the EP's high chart position.

28 Friday

Elvis appears briefly on stage with Danny Thomas at Thomas' Shower of Stars to benefit St. Jude's Hospital at Russwood Park in Memphis. The show includes movie stars Jane Russell and Susan Hayward, country singer Ferlin Huskey, pop singer Roberta Sherwood, and comedian Lou Costello.

At Danny Thomas' Shower of Stars, Memphis, with Lou Costello and Jane Russell

JULY

04 Thursday

After hearing of the death of his *Jailhouse Rock* costar, Judy Tyler, in an automobile accident, a distraught Elvis shows up at George Klein's house early in the morning.

07 Sunday

Klein introduces Elvis to Anita Wood, a nineteen-year-old beauty contest winner, singer, and aspiring actress, whom Elvis has spotted on Wink Martindale's Memphis TV show, *Top Ten Dance Party*.

08 Monday

George, Lamar, and Cliff all tag along on Elvis' first date with Anita, riding in the backseat as they drive by the Strand to view the giant cutout of Elvis that the theater has displayed for the premiere of *Loving You* the following night. They subsequently go to Chenault's drive-in restaurant for hamburgers.

10 Wednesday

After skipping the premiere, Elvis takes his parents and Anita to a private midnight screening.

13 Saturday

Anita Wood has dinner at Graceland with Elvis and his parents.

24 Wednesday

The Colonel informs Steve Sholes that Elvis wants to recut some of the numbers from the *Jailhouse Rock* soundtrack for record release. In addition, he very much wants to take another stab at "One Night," the r & b hit by Smiley Lewis, which he also recorded at the February sessions.

25 Thursday

The Colonel turns down a television appearance on Dean Martin's show in October, which will not meet his price of $75,000.

27 Saturday

Elvis has the 1956 Cadillac Eldorado that he picked up in Houston with June Juanico customized with flared rear fender skirts, white taillight bullets on the rear fenders, and a purple paint job. The new interior is a matching purple and white with "EP" and guitars on the floor mats. This car is currently on display at Graceland.

30 Tuesday

Loving You opens nationwide. The picture will appear on *Variety*'s National Box Office Survey for four weeks, peaking at #7.

Sometime during the month George Klein introduces Elvis to Alan Fortas, a former All-City tackle at Memphis' Central High School who has dropped out of college and gone to work at his father's junkyard. For-

Publicity shot with Judy Tyler

July Record Releases

LP: *Loving You* (#1) (shipped July 1). Like each of his earlier albums, Elvis' third, which combines movie songs with a handful of tracks from the January and February sessions, shoots straight to the top of the charts. Sales of 350,000 equal that of the first album, but the figure is probably less than it might have been due to the immense success of the single and the two EPs (the second not yet released), which split up all of the movie songs.

EP: *Loving You* (#1 on EP chart) (shipped July 19). This second EP from the picture is released just two weeks after the album and, with the title track featured, eventually goes gold.

tas quickly becomes a regular member of the gang. During this same time period Klein brings r & b singer and songwriter Ivory Joe Hunter out to Graceland. Elvis loves Hunter's 1950 hit "I Almost Lost My Mind" and recorded Hunter's "I Need You So" at his February sessions. When Hunter plays him a new composition, "My Wish Came True," Elvis promises to cut it at his next session. He does—but the song will not be released until 1959.

AUGUST

01 Thursday

A rumor has been circulating in the black community for some time that Elvis has declared, "The only thing Negroes can do for me is buy my records and shine my shoes." After determining that "tracing the rumored racial slur was like running a gopher to earth," *Jet* magazine, a leading African-American periodical, dispatched reporter Louie Robinson to the set of *Jailhouse Rock* to confront the singer himself. "I never said anything like that," Elvis protests in what amounts to an extremely rare on-set interview with anyone but one of the Colonel's chosen columnists. "People who know me," he tells Robinson, "know I wouldn't have said that." The reporter goes on to interview a number of black folk who do know Elvis, from Dr. W. A. Zuber, a Negro physician in Tupelo, to rhythm-and-blues singer Ivory Joe Hunter, pointing out that Elvis never even visited any of the places where he is supposed to have made the remark. "To Elvis," Robinson concludes in the August issue of the national magazine, "people are people, regardless of race, color, or creed."

The Colonel turns down an appearance in Great Britain.

07 Wednesday

Actress Venetia Stevenson arrives from Hollywood for a visit.

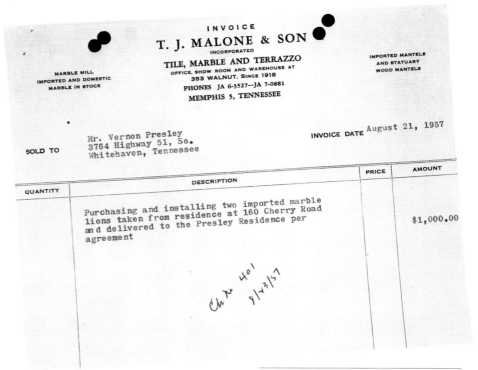

Invoice for lions beside Graceland's front steps

08 Thursday

Elvis takes Venetia, Lamar Fike, George Klein, Cliff Gleaves, and others to the Memphis Fairgrounds and then to a private midnight showing of *Loving You* at the Strand.

14 Wednesday

James Savery calls to inform Elvis how plans for the Elvis Presley Youth Center behind his birthplace in East Tupelo are progressing. This is to be financed in large part by his upcoming benefit performance at this year's Mississippi-Alabama Fair.

15 Thursday

Elvis asks Steve Sholes to hire soprano Millie Kirkham, who often works with the Jordanaires, for his next session. He has admired her backup work on Ferlin Huskey's "Gone," and on a new Jimmy "C" Newman single in particular.

21 Wednesday

Elvis purchases two stone lions from a residence at 160 Cherry Road in Memphis and has them installed on either side of the steps leading up to Graceland's front door at a cost of $1,000.

22 Thursday

Anita Wood wins the Mid-South Hollywood Star Hunt competition. She will go on to the finals in New Orleans, where she wins the grand prize of a small role in an independent Hollywood film.

27 Tuesday

Anita says goodbye to Elvis at the railroad station as he departs for the West Coast with George Klein, Lamar Fike, and Cliff Gleaves on an 11:00 P.M. train.

29 Thursday

Elvis arrives in Spokane, Washington, at 11:20 P.M. for the beginning of a tour, which will once again be managed by Al Dvorin and promoted by Lee Gordon.

30 Friday

★ *Memorial Stadium, Spokane, Washington*

Wearing black slacks, a black shirt, and shiny bow-topped black dress shoes with his gold jacket, Elvis enters the stadium in a Cadillac through lines of police guards. He performs eighteen songs on the second half of a show that includes a juggler, tap dancers, acrobats, and comedians. It attracts a crowd of 12,500.

31 Saturday
★ Empire Stadium, Vancouver, British Columbia

Twice the show has to be stopped, as the audience surrounds the stage and the Colonel, who has bitterly protested the lax Canadian security arrangements for a crowd of 26,500, pulls Elvis offstage and cautions him to tone down his act. Not surprisingly, Elvis is impervious to suggestion, and tension continues to rise until in the end, as George Klein recalls, "the last thing we saw was the stage being turned over."

In a press conference before the show Elvis tells reporters that his first love was "old colored spirituals." He goes on to say, probably with very little exaggeration, "I know practically every religious song that's ever been written."

August Record Release

EP: *Just For You* (#2 on the EP charts) (shipped August 21). The three songs from the *Loving You* album that did not appear on the two previous EPs are coupled with an unreleased Faron Young composition, "Is It So Strange."

SEPTEMBER

01 Sunday
★ Lincoln Bowl, Tacoma, Washington, at 2:00 P.M.

★ Sick's Stadium, Seattle, Washington, at 8:00 P.M.

Elvis rides into Sick's Stadium at 10:00 P.M., putting on a thirty-minute show in front of 15,000 fans. In addition to his hits, he sings "Fool's Hall of Fame," a new Sun release by Rudi Richardson that he says will be his next single but which in fact he never records.

02 Monday
★ Multnomah Stadium, Portland, Oregon

In an interview before the show, Elvis tells reporters, "There's nothing more important than love and marriage. I do think that marriage would hurt my career now, though." Elvis is able to complete a forty-minute show only after near-riot conditions are quelled by the police.

03 Tuesday
Elvis takes a train at 4:45 P.M. from Portland to Los Angeles, where he checks into the Beverly Wilshire Hotel.

05 Thursday
At Radio Recorders Elvis begins the Christmas album that Steve Sholes has been urging on him while also recording three songs for single release, including a studio version of "Treat Me Nice," the Leiber-Stoller number he has already recorded for the *Jailhouse Rock* soundtrack. The regular Hollywood session band is joined by Millie Kirkham and the Jordanaires from noon to 8:00 P.M.

06 Friday
Elvis reports to Radio Recorders at noon, where he continues working on Christmas numbers. The session concludes at 8:00 P.M. with the new Leiber and Stoller tune, "Don't."

Colonel Parker has asked Hal Wallis for $100,000 for Elvis' second Paramount picture, to match the $100,000 Elvis received from 20th Century Fox for *Love Me Tender*. By November Wallis capitulates to the Colonel's unrelenting siege, agreeing to pay Elvis $30,000 in expenses and a $50,000 bonus in addition to his contractual $20,000 salary.

07 Saturday
In the midst of another noon-to-eight session, with the Christmas album still short one song, Jerry Leiber and Mike Stoller retreat to the mix room to write a bluesy new double entendre, "Santa Claus Is Back in Town," which is right up Elvis' alley.

Scotty, Bill, and D.J. have been promised time at the end of the session to record some instrumentals that

they plan to put out under the group name The King's Men. Elvis has even indicated that he may join them as a sideman on piano, but when Tom Diskin announces that time has run out, Elvis does not speak up for them, and hurt feelings lead to dark mutterings, which in turn lead to a determination to take action. Back at the hotel, Scotty and Bill compose a letter of resignation that expresses some of their long-held feelings of resentment. D.J. declines to go along with them, and for the next month there are expressions of bitterness on both sides.

Anita Wood arrives this same evening to play the movie role she has won in the Mid-South Hollywood Star Hunt.

08 Sunday
After breakfast at the Beverly Wilshire, Anita visits Radio Recorders to listen to the songs Elvis has been recording over the last few days. They then take in four movies at theaters around town ("*3:10 to Yuma* was the best," says Anita), while making plans to screen *Jailhouse Rock* at MGM the following day.

09 Monday
Anita and Elvis board a train for Memphis.

10 Tuesday
Colonel Parker strikes a new deal with RCA, whereby he and Elvis will receive payment for all photographs of Elvis used on record sleeves to be split 75 percent to Elvis and 25 percent to the Colonel. It is agreed that RCA will pay $10,000 for photos for the upcoming gatefold-sleeve Christmas album, and another $6,000 for the EP. This deal will remain the model for all arrangements for album art in years to come.

11 Wednesday
Elvis leaves the train in Houston, driving the rest of the way to Memphis, where he arrives at 10:00 P.M.

12 Thursday
Elvis calls Scotty to discuss his and

Backstage, Tupelo Fair, with Anita Wood

Bill's resignations and to ask what it will take to bring them back. Scotty, deeply in debt, asks for a $50-per-week raise and a flat payment of $10,000.

13 Friday

Scotty is quoted in the *Memphis Press-Scimitar* as saying that Elvis "promised us that the more he made the more we would make. But it hasn't worked out that way."

14 Saturday

Elvis responds to Scotty's statement by publicly wishing Scotty and Bill good luck. "If you had come to me," he says in an open letter in the *Press-Scimitar*, "we would have worked things out. But you went to the papers and tried to make me look bad. . . . All I can say to you is 'good luck.'"

17 Tuesday

Elvis visits Dewey Phillips at WHBQ,

seeing him for the first time since Dewey's trip to Hollywood and the subsequent furor, public and private, over his premature airing of "Teddy Bear."

18 Wednesday

Hank "Sugarfoot" Garland, a twenty-six-year-old guitar virtuoso working as a session player in Nashville, signs on as Elvis' new guitar player and Vernon Presley sends

Scotty and Bill their final salary checks, indicating acceptance of their resignations as of September 21.

19 Thursday

The Colonel brings Steve Sholes up to date on the situation with Scotty and Bill. In his belated reply two weeks later, Sholes expresses the hope that Elvis will not take the two musicians back since in his view they only hold up the sessions.

20 Friday

Elvis appears on Memphis television station WKNO to promote traffic safety and driver education.

23 Monday

RCA hires Leiber and Stoller as independent producers to work both with Elvis Presley and with other artists.

26 Thursday

Elvis and his friends spend the evening at the Fairgrounds, attracting a large crowd.

27 Friday

Elvis drives to Tupelo with Anita and his parents, along with Cliff Gleaves, George Klein, Lamar Fike, and Alan Fortas. The local paper refers to him as "the best ambassador any town could have" and urges all townspeople to give him a warm welcome.

★ *Fairgrounds, Tupelo*

In a show to benefit the planned Elvis Presley Youth Center, Elvis performs before a crowd of 12,000 under

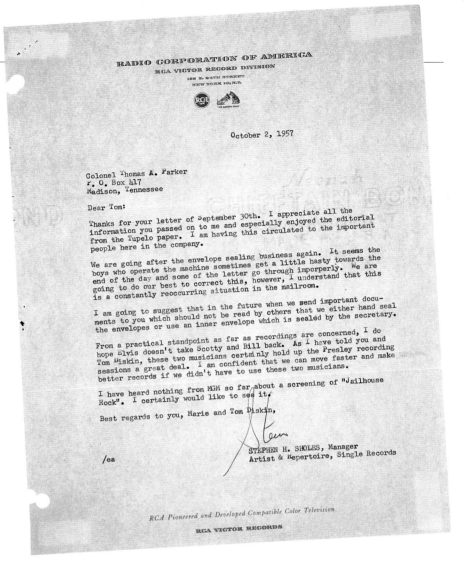

Steve Sholes to Colonel Parker in the aftermath of Scotty and Bill's resignation

a banner announcing *Jailhouse Rock.* He is accompanied by Hank Garland, D. J. Fontana, and Chuck Wiggington, a friend of D.J.'s from Dallas, on bass.

OCTOBER

01 Tuesday

Elvis appears on a WMCT radio and TV fund-raising event in Memphis but does not sing. He tells the audience that his next picture will begin shooting on October 30.

02 Wednesday

With his parents, Elvis watches a special screening of *Jailhouse Rock.*

05 Saturday

Scotty and Bill begin a sixteen-day engagement at the Texas State Fair as

the "Blue Moon Boys." They are booked to do four shows a day for $1,600, with all expenses paid. Just before they leave for Texas, Tom Diskin calls on Elvis' behalf, and they agree to return at $250 a show, starting with upcoming tour dates in California.

07 Monday

The Colonel writes to Lenny Hirshan, the young William Morris agent who has looked after Elvis' interests in Hollywood up till this time, expressing Elvis' desire to do a non-musical movie.

Elvis attends the wrestling matches at Ellis Auditorium, then goes out to eat with Penny Banner, one of the lady wrestlers, whom he takes back to Graceland afterward.

11 Friday

Elvis drives to Madison to confer with Colonel Parker.

12 Saturday

Late in the day Elvis leaves for an approximately ten-day Las Vegas vacation. He stays at the Sahara Hotel, dating exotic dancer Tempest Storm.

17 Thursday

Jailhouse Rock premieres in Memphis, but Elvis does not attend.

26 Saturday

★ *Civic Auditorium, San Francisco, California, at 3:00 and 8:15 P.M.*

October Record Releases

LP: *Elvis' Christmas Album* (#1) (shipped October 15). The deluxe gatefold sleeve offers the Colonel yet another opportunity to charge an extra fee, but right away the album runs into trouble. First, Irving Berlin writes to every major radio station in the country requesting that Elvis' version of "White Christmas" not be played. According to Berlin, who appears unaware that it is almost a direct copy of the Drifters' earlier r & b interpretation, it is a profanation of the spirit of Christmas. Others soon join in the chorus, and radio support suffers. Nonetheless, the album reaches the top of the charts, and though it sells only 200,000 the first Christmas season, over the next ten years sales will top one and a half million.

EP: *Elvis Sings Christmas Songs* (#1 on EP charts) (shipped October 16). According to the by now very well-established pattern, an EP is issued containing a core of cuts from the simultaneously released LP. Although this is a strategy that from today's point of view would seem to make very little sense, it is once again successful, in this instance resulting in sales of over half a million copies.

EP: *Jailhouse Rock* (#1 on EP charts) (shipped October 30). Just two weeks after the Christmas LP and EP are released, RCA puts out yet another EP, with five songs from the movie soundtrack. Sales will reach one million copies.

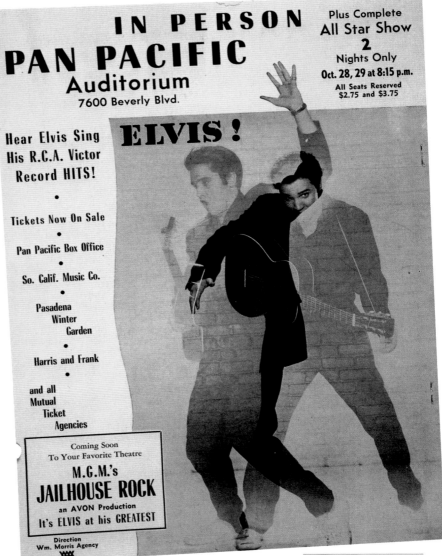

Poster for Pan Pacific shows

Scotty and Bill's first gig under the new contractual arrangement on a tour that appears to have been hastily put together by Lee Gordon after Elvis' new motion picture for Hal Wallis is postponed.

27 Sunday

★ *Oakland Auditorium, Oakland, California*

28 Monday

★ *Pan Pacific Auditorium, Los Angeles, California*

In his first show in his new adoptive hometown, Elvis outrages not only the local and national press but an audience filled with Hollywood celebrities and their children. During the fifty-minute, eighteen-number show he "wiggled, bumped, twisted," and prompted headlines the next day that declared: "Elvis Presley Will Have to Clean Up His Show—Or Go to Jail." The Los Angeles Vice Squad warns Colonel Parker of that same potential consequence, but according to the Colonel, Elvis remains unfazed. "He just said, 'Well, if I don't dance tonight, maybe I don't have to take a shower tonight.'"

29 Tuesday

★ *Pan Pacific Auditorium, Los Angeles*

A far less flamboyant performance passes the scrutiny of the police, who film it just to make sure. At a party in his hotel suite after the show, Elvis meets Ricky Nelson, who has recently had his first hit with Fats Domino's "I'm Walkin'." He tells Ricky that he loves the record and watches *The Adventures of Ozzie and Harriet* all the time, while hosting entertainers Nick Adams, Carol

Arrival in Hawaii, with Colonel Parker and fan

At the Hawaiian Village Hotel

Arrival on the USS *Matsonia*

Channing, Sammy Davis Jr., and Tommy Sands as well.

Booking agent and bandleader Al Dvorin recalls that this was intended to be the last show of the tour until Lee Gordon, who has been booking all of the biggest shows into Australia since the war and has been trying desperately to persuade the Colonel to let him book Elvis there, rolled dice with the Colonel for two Hawaiian dates. From Gordon's point of view, this was like getting Elvis halfway to the goal, and the Colonel continues to talk with Gordon about booking Elvis in Australia until at least 1961, though how serious he is may be judged by the results.

NOVEMBER

05 Tuesday

Elvis sails for Honolulu, Hawaii, on the USS *Matsonia*.

08 Friday

From shipboard Elvis telegrams the *Honolulu Star*, "Aloha, very enjoyable trip. Sunbathing, swimming, tennis, reading."

Jailhouse Rock opens in theaters nationwide. It will appear for three weeks on *Variety*'s National Box Office Survey, peaking at #3, and will be the fourteenth-most-successful film of the year. By 1969 *Variety* will report its U.S. and Canadian earnings to have reached $4,000,000, roughly comparable to those of *The Wizard of Oz*.

09 Saturday

Elvis arrives in Honolulu and, after an onboard press conference, checks into the Hawaiian Village Hotel. Later in the day, the band and the Jordanaires arrive by plane.

10 Sunday

★ *Honolulu Stadium, Honolulu, at 3:00 and 8:15 P.M.*

More than 14,000 fans see the two shows. Undoubtedly part of the Colonel's willingness to bring Elvis to Hawaii is that he himself was stationed here during his army service between 1929 and 1932, and he takes this opportunity to visit with old friends.

11 Monday

★ *Schofield Barracks, Pearl Harbor, Hawaii*

Elvis performs for service personnel and their families as well as the general public. This will be Elvis' last public performance before entering the armed services.

13 Wednesday

Elvis sails for Los Angeles aboard the USS *Lurline*, departing at 4:00 P.M.

18 Monday

Elvis leaves for Las Vegas, where he meets singer Kitty Dolan.

24 Sunday

Back home in Memphis, Elvis has trouble leaving Graceland for the evening when the mechanism that opens the gates jams and he and his friends are forced to climb over the wall.

26 Tuesday

RCA informs Colonel Parker that as of November 1 RCA holds a total of $629,988 in its Presley royalty account, which will be paid out according to the agreed-upon contractual formula.

28 Thursday

Elvis goes to see Pat Boone's new movie, *April Love*, at the Loew's Palace.

DECEMBER

01 Sunday

Elvis donates $1,050 so that all 1,400 Humes High School students

Backstage at the Opry, December 22, 1957, with *(left to right)* Ferlin Huskey, Faron Young, Hawkshaw Hawkins, and Tom Perryman

can go to the annual E. H. Crump Memorial Football Game for the Blind.

06 Friday

The WDIA Goodwill Review this year features Ray Charles, Little Junior Parker, Brook Benton, Bobby "Blue" Bland, the Staple Singers, and the Spirit of Memphis Quartet. Once again Elvis is a warmly greeted backstage visitor, having his picture taken with his heroes, Little Junior Parker and Bobby Bland. The next day he is quoted in the *Memphis Press-Scimitar* as saying that their music, rhythm and blues, is "the real thing. . . . Right from the heart."

In a long letter to Harry Kalcheim, Colonel Parker vigorously defends his decision to stop booking live performances. He reiterates his frequently voiced contention that this kind of overexposure can only harm his client and that all along his goal has been to build Elvis into an artist who will remain at the top of the entertainment field for years to come.

16 Monday

The Memphis Draft Board has let it be known that Elvis will soon receive his draft notice, and every major branch of the military except the Marines makes bids for his services. The navy would create a specially trained "Elvis Presley company"; the air force would have him tour recruiting centers; and the army offers a two-year enlistment with a 120-day deferment to allow him to complete his new movie, which has now been rescheduled for January.

On this same day Elvis purchases the Santa sleigh and eight reindeer still displayed every year on the Graceland lawn for $300 from Bain Sign Company in Memphis.

Meanwhile, Colonel Parker tries to interest MGM in casting Elvis as doomed country music legend Hank Williams in a bio-pic about the first major star to come out of the Louisiana Hayride.

19 Thursday

Elvis receives informal word from Memphis draft board chairman Milton Bowers that his induction notice has been drawn up and is waiting for him.

20 Friday

Elvis stops by Sun Records after picking up his draft notice in person. Later Elvis tells reporters it is a "duty I've got to fill and I'm going to do it."

In the evening Elvis leaves for Nashville to deliver the Colonel's Christmas present, a red Isetta sports car.

21 Saturday

After visiting and conferring with Colonel Parker, Elvis attends the Grand Ole Opry accompanied by Jordanaire Gordon Stoker, who takes him to a clothing store where he purchases a tuxedo for the evening. He spends the night chatting comfortably with performers backstage, making a brief appearance to wave at the audience. Before leaving for Memphis, he changes back into his old clothes and throws the tuxedo in the trash.

24 Tuesday

In a letter to the Memphis Draft Board, Elvis formally requests a deferment for the filming of his new Paramount motion picture "so these folks will not lose so much money, with all they have done so far."

25 Wednesday

Elvis spends Christmas at Graceland with his parents.

26 Thursday

The Draft Board grants a deferment until March 20, 1958.

28 Saturday

Elvis rents out the Rainbow Rollerdrome for the evening.

1 9 5 8

Colonel Parker and Red West on location, *King Creole*, March 1958

JANUARY

01 Wednesday

Hank Snow's son, Jimmie Rodgers Snow, a fellow performer and close friend from the early Jamboree tours, arrives for a visit. Elvis extended the invitation when he ran into Jimmie backstage at the Opry eleven days before.

02 Thursday

Elvis has complained to the Colonel in the past of being bothered by requests for local appearances. He wants his manager to shield him from such harassment, but in a letter today the Colonel takes the opportunity to lecture his young client on the responsibilities of being a star.

03 Friday

The Colonel rejects Bill Bullock's suggestion that RCA produce a classical album utilizing Elvis' repertoire with the observation that it sounds like a "side show medicine pitch," and would be "unfair" to both Elvis and to classical music.

08 Wednesday

Elvis is photographed on the stairs inside Graceland's front door with a March of Dimes poster girl, eight-year-old Mary Kosloski, after keeping her waiting for two hours.

Following his twenty-third-birthday party at Graceland, Elvis asks Alan Fortas to accompany him to California. In a by now familiar scenario, earlier in the week he fired Cliff Gleaves and Lamar Fike after they squabbled over a badminton game. By Friday Cliff will be forgiven, and soon Lamar will be as well.

09 Thursday

Dewey Phillips is fired for real on the fourth night of his new midnight television show, a replacement for the afternoon slot he lost to the syndication of Dick Clark's *American Bandstand*. The firing comes about as a result of the antics of his sidekick, abstract artist Harry Fritzius, who, wearing his customary ape suit, and with Dewey's encouragement, explicitly fondles a life-size cutout of Jayne Mansfield.

10 Friday

Elvis takes the train to Los Angeles with Alan Fortas, Gene Smith, Cliff Gleaves, and Bitsy Mott.

11 Saturday

Great crowds line up at every stop in what appears to be proof almost of extrasensory perception on the part of Elvis' fans but in fact is the result of the Colonel's carefully orchestrated leaks to DJs along the way.

13 Monday

Elvis arrives in California to begin preproduction on his second Paramount picture, which has been adapted from the popular Harold Robbins novel *A Stone for Danny Fisher*. His costars are Dean Jagger, Carolyn Jones, Walter Matthau, and once again Dolores Hart, with veteran director Michael Curtiz (*Casablanca*, *Mildred Pierce*, *Young Man with a Horn*) in charge.

15 Wednesday

Elvis works on the soundtrack at Radio Recorders from 9:00 A.M. to 5:40 P.M. Jerry Leiber and Mike Stoller, who have written several songs for the new picture, are in charge, with the usual Hollywood band (Scotty, Bill, and D.J., augmented by "Tiny" Timbrell and Dudley Brooks) further augmented by bassist Ray Siegel. A four-man horn section is also present to help create a "Dixieland rock" feel, as is only appropriate for a rock 'n' roll film set in New Orleans.

16 Thursday

Recording continues from 9:00 A.M. to 5:30 P.M.

20 Monday

Principal photography begins.

While working on this picture, Elvis will meet one of his idols, Marlon Brando, in the studio commissary.

January 24 1958

Mr. Steve Sholes
Radio Corporation of America
155 East 24th St
New York City, N.Y.

Dear Mr. Sholes :

In regard to the record session set for Saturday February 1st, from 12 noon until 6 p.m. we understand that you have made arrangements for this session for the studio and Thornie Nogar.

Regarding the Jordanaires, they are now at the Hollywood Knickerbocker Hotel, and I have advised them that they would most likely hear from you during the coming week.

We also have discussed with Elvis this session and he said he wants to have Jerry Leiber and Mike Stoller there, as he is able to work out ideas with them, and has confidence working with them.

The Colonel set up this session as this will be the only day Elvis will have to record while he is in Hollywood, due to the pressure of other activities.

Last night following a recording session for the picture Elvis used the studio facilities for about an hour and a half in order to run down two of the songs that he will do on the February 1st session. Therefore, there will be a charge for the studio rental, engineer and the three musicians and the Jordanaires.

If you would like us to make reservations for you at the Beverly Wilshire, will you please advise us. We will be looking for you then on Friday January 31st.

Best wishes,

Sincerely,

TOM DISKIN

Tom Diskin to Steve Sholes, January 24 and 29, 1958

January 29, 1958

Mr. Steve Sholes
RCA Victor Corp.
155 East 24th Street
New York 10, N.Y.

Dear Steve:

The formal greeting of "Dear Mr. Sholes" in my last letter, was purely an error. You know I'm not the formal type, Steve.

I had Elvis read your letter as he specifically was interested in having Leiber and Stoller here. If both of them aren't available he can work with Jerry Leiber, as the boys were very helpful to Elvis on a couple of the songs during the recording session for the picture. They would be there mainly to help Elvis in working out arrangement ideas. If for some reason they will not be available for this coming Saturday, he thought we might postphone the session until such time as either Jerry or both might be available. As you can see he is quite anxious about this.

If nothing can be worked out on this or if the boys will not be available at this time, please let me know immediately so I can get back to Elvis.

The Colonel and I send best wishes.

Sincerely,

Tom Diskin

TD/wp

---

23 Thursday

Elvis re-records Leiber and Stoller's "King Creole," now under very active consideration as the title track of the picture, from 8:00 to 11:00 P.M. The two songwriters are not present, having returned to New York at the conclusion of recording the previous week, thinking their job done. Elvis works on one other movie song and rehearses two songs for an upcoming RCA session.

January Record Release

Single: "Don't" (#1)/"I Beg of You" (#8) (shipped January 7). "One Night" was the original selection for the A-side of this single before it was replaced by the new Leiber-Stoller ballad, "Don't," written with Elvis specifically in mind. Sales reach 1.3 million, considerably lower than sales of previous singles.

With Jan Shepard at birthday party for Shepard (note Elvis' gift tiger) *(courtesy of Jan Shepard)*

24 Friday

Tom Diskin informs Steve Sholes in no uncertain terms that Elvis wants Leiber and Stoller back for the February RCA session, "as he is able to work out ideas with them, and has confidence working with them."

29 Wednesday

In a second letter Diskin reiterates Elvis' strong desire to have Leiber and Stoller present at the next session, even offering to reschedule if necessary.

FEBRUARY

01 Saturday

Elvis begins his last scheduled non-soundtrack recording session prior to induction without either Jerry Leiber or Mike Stoller, whom Steve Sholes has been unable to contact. Elvis works from 10:00 A.M. to 7:00 P.M., but the session is something of a disaster, as he struggles to cut what is intended to be the A-side of his next single, "Wear My Ring Around Your Neck," before moving on to forty-eight desultory takes of the B-side, "Doncha' Think It's Time." He is dissatisfied with both, and Steve Sholes is bitterly disappointed that he has not been able to store up any kind of backlog for the two years that Elvis will be away.

11 Tuesday

Elvis records soundtrack material on Paramount's soundstage from 1:00 to 9:55 P.M., re-recording "Steadfast, Loyal and True" and working on the Ben Weisman song "Danny," which remains under consideration as the film's title song should its name remain *A Stone for Danny Fisher*.

22 Saturday

Dolores Hart gives a birthday party for Jan Shepard, who plays Elvis' sister in the movie, and to everyone's surprise Elvis shows up with a stuffed tiger on his shoulders that he has named Danny Boy, after the song he has often sung on the set. He also gives Shepard a movie camera, with which home movies of the party are shot.

26 Wednesday

There is a brief recording session at Radio Recorders at which Elvis overdubs guitar-slapping and piano on "Wear My Ring Around Your Neck."

MARCH

01 Saturday

Just as cast and crew are about to leave by train for a week of location shooting in New Orleans, Red West, on leave from the Marines, shows up to join the gang. Elvis and his entourage stay on the tenth floor of the Roosevelt Hotel, a block from the French Quarter. Security breaks down when the mayor, against all of the Colonel's advice, proclaims "Elvis Presley Day," and a near riot ensues when Elvis' fans come out to see the star.

03 Monday

Shooting begins in New Orleans' French Quarter. In the course of the

On location for *King Creole* with *(left to right)* Hal Wallis, Michael Curtiz, and Dean Jagger

With Colonel Parker at army induction

week, Cliff Gleaves, whose dreams of show-business success have so far been largely unrequited, makes his movie debut, repeating his single line ("See you next week, baby"—spoken to a prostitute) over and over again, to the guys' amusement. The film company remains in New Orleans until March 11.

12 Wednesday

Back in Hollywood, Elvis attends a cast party thrown by Hal Wallis, and in an interview with columnist Vernon Scott remarks that the army can't be any worse than the merry-go-round he's been on for the past two years.

14 Friday

Elvis and his party get off the train in Dallas, renting a string of Cadillacs for the 500-mile drive to Memphis. Asked by a reporter upon his arrival at Graceland how his parents feel about his going into the service, he concedes that his mother is very upset—but that in this she is no different from any other mother. On the question of whether his popularity will fade during his absence, Elvis responds, "That's the sixty-four-dollar question. I wish I knew."

17 Monday

At Pop Tunes, just around the corner from Lauderdale Courts and his old home on Alabama Street, Elvis buys Dean Martin's "Return to Me," Nat King Cole's "Looking Back," Pat Boone's "Too Soon to Know," Jo Stafford's "Sweet Little Darling," Don Gibson's "I Can't Stop Loving You," and "Maybe" by the Chantels. In preparation for army induction, he gets a haircut at Jim's Barber Shop downtown.

19 Wednesday

Elvis is commissioned as a "Kernel" by popcorn tycoon Jim Blevins on the pretext that his pictures have sold more popcorn than any other films in 1956 and 1957.

20 Thursday

RCA makes an offer to supply Elvis with recording equipment for a home studio. It is their hope that Elvis might do some informal recording while on furlough.

21 Friday

Elvis buys a 1956 Ford for Anita Wood.

22 Saturday

Each night for the past week, Elvis has rented out the Rainbow Roller-drome after its regular closing. During one of the skating parties he meets Red's cousin, Sonny West.

23 Sunday

On the last night before his induction, Elvis, Anita, and various friends go to a drive-in to see Tommy Sands in the leading role of *Sing, Boy, Sing*, adapted from the television vehicle ("The Singing Idol") that was originally written with Elvis in mind. The film costars Nick Adams as the young singer's sidekick, standing in for Elvis' more densely populated entourage. After the movie, everyone goes roller-skating, and Elvis does not go to bed all night. There is no question what is on his mind. "Overnight," he says years later of the feeling of loss that

overcomes him, "it was all gone. It was like a dream."

24 Monday

At 6:35 A.M. Elvis, accompanied by Anita and his parents, reports to the draft board at 198 South Main Street, where he joins twelve other recruits on a bus to Kennedy Veterans Memorial Hospital. He is dressed in black boots, black trousers, a blue shirt, and gray jacket, and carries a small leather bag. Elvis is assigned serial number 53 310 761, and after his physical he is put in charge of the group, which will be taking an army bus to Fort Chaffee, Arkansas. Meanwhile, outside the building his parents wait anxiously to say goodbye, while Colonel Parker hands out *King Creole* balloons to the gathering crowd. During the bus trip he meets Rex Mansfield, from Dresden, Tennessee, who will become one of his closest army friends.

25 Tuesday

The new inductees undergo further processing at Fort Chaffee. Elvis receives the traditional GI haircut before a crowd of fifty-five reporters and photographers. "Hair today, gone tomorrow" is his not-too-original but good-natured comment. By day's end he is assigned to the Second Armored Division, General Patton's "Hell on Wheels" outfit, stationed at Fort Hood, Killeen, Texas.

28 Friday

On the way to Killeen, the army transport bus makes a lunch stop in Hillsboro, Texas, where it takes twenty-five minutes before he is recognized—but then a "small riot" ensues. Upon arrival at Fort Hood at 4:00 P.M., information officer Lieutenant Colonel Marjorie Shulten declares Elvis off-limits to the press from the next day on. Colonel Parker, who has made himself constantly available to reporters at both postings, surrenders meekly to a superior authority. "Well, Colonel," he declares, "you're the boss."

APRIL

02 Wednesday

The Colonel's office has received 5,000 pieces of mail sent to Private Presley at Fort Chaffee during the few days he was stationed there. Mail is by now pouring in from Fort Hood.

16 Wednesday

The Colonel speaks with Elvis on the phone and reports to Hal Wallis that he is finding the army to be a "new adventure," and has enjoyed the "rough and tumble" of the obstacle course.

April Record Release

Single: "Wear My Ring Around Your Neck" (#3)/"Doncha' Think It's Time" (#21) (shipped April 1). Although both sides chart, the record does not measure up to the success of recent singles and points up the difficulty the Colonel and RCA will have in trying to keep Elvis' name alive.

MAY

28 Wedesday

The Colonel arrives in Texas in advance of the furlough that Elvis will get to mark the end of basic training. Private Presley has earned a marksman's medal with a carbine and achieved sharpshooter level with a pistol and has been named acting assistant leader of his squad.

Over the past few weeks Elvis has become more closely acquainted with a Waco businessman named Eddie Fadal, whom he first met during a 1956 Texas tour. During Anita Wood's weekend visits, she and Elvis stay at the Fadal home. There are crude home recordings from these occasions that capture Elvis and Anita singing Hank Williams' "I Can't Help It (If I'm Still in Love with You)" and Anita trying out Connie Francis' brand-new "Who's Sorry Now."

31 Saturday

The Colonel and Anita arrive at the gates of Fort Hood at 6:00 A.M. to pick up Elvis, Rex Mansfield, and fellow Memphian William "Nervous" Norvell. The three soldiers drop the Colonel and Anita off at the Dallas airport before heading for home. Parker returns to Nashville, and Anita is scheduled for a recording session in New York City.

JUNE

01 Sunday

Dressed in full uniform, Elvis takes the time to explain his army insignia to fans at the Graceland gates.

04 Wednesday

Once again Elvis takes up such favorite activities as renting out the Rollerdrome and the Fairgrounds. He takes his parents to see *King Creole,* buys a new red Lincoln, and gets a haircut at Jim's Barber Shop before a family photo session.

10 Tuesday

For two years now Elvis has refused to record again in Nashville, but now with overseas deployment rapidly approaching, the continuous wrangling between Steve Sholes and the Colonel is temporarily resolved, with Elvis agreeing to a single one-night session at RCA's new Studio B. Only D.J. and the Jordanaires are present from the two-year-old RCA lineup, with the rest of the band consisting of such skilled Nashville session players as Hank Garland and Chet Atkins on guitar, Bob

Recording in Nashville, June 10, 1958

Elvis on leave, with Gladys and Vernon at Graceland, June 1958

Moore on bass, drummer Buddy Harman, who works on a second full set of drums and on percussion as well, and Floyd Cramer on piano. The group records five up-tempo numbers between 7:00 P.M. and 5:00 A.M., among

June Record Release

Single: "Hard Headed Woman" (#2)/"Don't Ask Me Why" (#28) (shipped June 10). RCA makes the decision to promote the new movie, *King Creole*, not with its title track but with this triple-speed blues instead. The single performs about as well as the last, but its one million sales represent only about half of what could have been expected the previous year.

them such future hits as "I Need Your Love Tonight" and "A Big Hunk o' Love." Elvis is visibly enthusiastic about the musical versatility and proficiency of the band in general, and in particular the fire with which Hank Garland plays. The Colonel is decidedly less enthusiastic about the band's volume and what he considers the new instrumental focus. This is Elvis' last session for nearly two years.

14 Saturday

Elvis returns to Fort Hood. Every soldier can apply for permission after basic training to live offbase with his dependents (generally his wife and children). Elvis now makes arrangements to bring *his* dependents, his mother and father, down to Killeen.

16 Monday

Elvis begins ten weeks of Advanced Tank Training.

20 Friday

Elvis signs an agreement with Stylemaster Mobile Homes for use of a three-bedroom trailer home in exchange for photographs of himself and his family in the unit. Over the weekend, Gladys, Vernon, Vernon's mother Minnie, and Lamar Fike move into the unit, located near Fort Hood.

23 Monday

Steve Sholes pleads with the Colonel to try to get Elvis back into the studio one more time before he leaves for his overseas assignment.

JULY

01 Tuesday
Very quickly, the group of five adults outgrows their trailer home, and Elvis arranges to lease a house in Killeen (605 Oak Hill Drive) for two months from Judge Chester Crawford at $1,500 a month. Gene and Junior Smith are by now part of the growing household.

02 Wednesday
King Creole opens in theaters nationwide. It appears for four weeks on *Variety*'s National Box Office Survey, peaking at #5.

06 Sunday
Elvis receives a speeding ticket in Fort Worth.

08 Tuesday
The Colonel continues to play the movie studios (20th Century Fox, Paramount, and MGM) off against one another. He even goes so far as to claim an offer of $250,000 plus 50 percent of the profits from a German producer.

09 Wednesday
Dewey Phillips is fired from his job at radio station WHBQ, as his personal disintegration from drugs and drinking continues.

14 Monday
Colonel Parker has been seeking an advertising endorsement for Elvis through the William Morris Agency. Harry Kalcheim reports back that only Revlon is interested and would welcome Elvis' endorsement of their men's hairdressing product, Top Brass, but not for the $100,000 fee the Colonel is demanding.

The Colonel frequently visits throughout the summer to discuss business matters with both Vernon and his son. Elvis continues to express concern that the public will forget him, and the Colonel's ongoing efforts to secure deals and develop new ideas are designed as much to assuage those concerns as to generate new sources of income.

AUGUST

08 Friday
All through the summer Gladys has been feeling ill, with poor color, loss of appetite, and deepening depression. As her condition worsens, Elvis finally insists that she do something about it, putting his parents on a train to Memphis so that she can see her personal physician, Dr. Charles Clarke.

09 Saturday
Responding to an 11:30 A.M. emergency call, an ambulance transports Mrs. Presley from Graceland to Methodist Hospital, where her condition is listed as grave. She appears to be suffering from an undiagnosed liver ailment.

Elvis completes Advanced Tank Training.

11 Monday
Elvis commences his Basic Unit Training.

12 Tuesday
After more effort than it would take for any ordinary soldier, including calls from Gladys' doctor to military personnel in Washington and Elvis' desperate threat to go AWOL, Elvis finally obtains emergency leave, flying from Fort Worth to Memphis with Lamar Fike and going straight to the hospital.

13 Wednesday
Vernon remains at his wife's side throughout the night, while Elvis, after spending the evening at home, returns in the morning and again in the afternoon, not leaving until close to midnight.

14 Thursday
At approximately 3:15 A.M., with her husband at her side, Gladys Love Presley dies. "I knew what it was before I answered," Elvis says of his father's phone call some fifteen minutes later. Both father and son are inconsolable.

In the early afternoon, with hundreds of fans at the gates, Gladys is brought home to Graceland, to be laid out in the music room wearing a baby-blue dress. Elvis wants the funeral to be conducted at the house, but Colonel Parker convinces him that security will not be able to be effectively maintained, and arrangements are made to have the service at the Memphis Funeral Home. Elvis has the Blackwood Brothers, Gladys' favorite quartet, flown in from their concert tour in North Carolina at his expense.

15 Friday
The funeral is held at 3:30 P.M., and several times Elvis and Vernon almost collapse. The Blackwood Brothers are scheduled to perform three or four numbers, but Elvis will not let them stop, and they go on for so long that they have to charter a plane to make it back in time for their next engagement. At the cemetery Elvis leans over the grave, crying out inconsolably, "Goodbye, darling, goodbye. I love you so much. You know how much I lived my whole life just for you." All the funeral arrangements are made by Colonel Parker, with the cost coming to

---

July Record Releases

EP: *King Creole Vol. 1* (#1 on the EP chart) (shipped July 1). Elvis feels strongly there are not enough good songs in the *King Creole* soundtrack to justify an album, so RCA releases two EPs and a single instead (this leaves just one track—the high school alma mater "Steadfast, Loyal and True"—unreleased). The EP-LP distinction—somewhat perplexing by today's standards—continues to work as a commercial strategy at a time when EPs generally outsell LPs. This one sells half a million copies.

EP: *King Creole Vol. 2* (#1 on the EP chart) (shipped July 29). Shipped about a month later, this *King Creole* EP sequel mirrors the success of the first, with sales of another half million.

$20,479.85. When Dixie Locke comes out to see Elvis at Graceland that night at his invitation, he blurts out that he would like to walk away from it all but cannot. "There are too many people that depend on me," he says. "I'm in too far to get out."

16 Saturday

Elvis insists upon attending the funeral for Red West's father, who died the previous day. Services are held once again at the Memphis Funeral Home, and Elvis is once more overcome with emotion, as he practically falls into Red's arms. Later in the afternoon Elvis insists on visiting his mother's grave.

18 Monday

Elvis' seven-day leave is extended for five more days, during which the Memphis Highway Patrol tries to cheer Elvis up by giving him helicopter rides over Graceland and the city.

24 Sunday

Elvis returns to Fort Hood, leaving instructions that nothing is to be altered in his mother's room while he is gone; it is all to be preserved as if she were alive.

28 Thursday

The Colonel reports that Elvis has received more than 100,000 cards and letters, about 500 telegrams, and more than 200 floral arrangements in sympathy over his loss.

SEPTEMBER

02 Tuesday

Colonel Parker makes plans with army personnel to stage another press conference, similar to the one arranged for his induction, to mark Elvis' departure for Germany. "I feel sure that you agree," he writes to William Morris agent Harry Kalcheim of the earlier model, "it left a good taste and no circus flavor."

11 Thursday

Elvis is assigned to the 3rd Armored Division in Germany.

Killeen, Texas, September 18–19, 1958, with *(right to left)* Frances Forbes, Red West, Lamar Fike, Junior Smith, Vernon, Elvis, Eddie Fadal, Earl Greenwood, and Gene Smith with unknown fans.

17 Wednesday

Vernon Presley and Lamar Fike have their passport photographs taken in preparation for going to Germany. Grandma Minnie, too, will be accompanying them, and Red West, just released from the Marines, is a last-minute addition.

18 Thursday

Elvis spends an emotional last night in Killeen with Vernon, Anita, Eddie Fadal, Lamar Fike, Gene and Junior Smith, and Red West, along with several fan club presidents.

19 Friday

Elvis leaves Fort Hood at 7:00 P.M.

September Record Releases

Album: *King Creole* (#2) (shipped September 19). Taking advantage of the publicity surrounding Elvis' departure, RCA puts out the soundtrack album that Elvis at first did not want to see released—but with the Colonel's blessing now. With the exception of "Steadfast, Loyal and True," every track on the album has already been out on one of the EPs or on the single, but the album still sells 250,000 copies.

EP: *Christmas With Elvis* (shipped September 22). A second EP drawn from the popular 1957 Christmas album achieves sales of 80,000 copies.

---

on a troop train bound for the Brooklyn Army Terminal in New York.

20 Saturday

Several friends meet the train at a scheduled refueling in Memphis. These include Alan Fortas and George Klein, who introduces Elvis to a pretty girl from Mississippi named Janie Wilbanks, whom he soon calls from Germany.

21 Sunday

Elvis has received a copy of *Poems That Touch the Heart* from another soldier on the train, and it provides a source of consolation to him on the long ride. Somewhere in Delaware or New Jersey, he meets a pint-size soldier named Charlie Hodge, a native of Decatur, Alabama, and professional quartet singer and entertainer, who later describes himself as having been "bound and determined" to meet Elvis.

22 Monday

The troop train arrives in Brooklyn at 9:00 A.M.

Elvis holds a press conference and once again expresses his hope that the fans won't forget him. Then he walks up the gangplank of the USS *Randall* eight times, toting a borrowed duffel bag, so the assembled photographers and cameramen can

On army troop train

Embarking for Germany

all get a good shot. In a final message to his fans from a brief onboard interview, he expresses his fervent desire that despite the fact that he'll be out of their sight, "I hope I'm not out of their minds. And I'll be looking forward to the time when I can come back and entertain again like I did."

During the crossing Elvis and Charlie Hodge become fast friends. They bunk together at Elvis' request, and Charlie cheers him up with jokes and tales of show business. Together, they are put in charge of a shipboard talent show in which Elvis plays piano in the backup band (at the Colonel's explicit instructions, he does not sing) while Charlie acts as MC.

OCTOBER

01 Wednesday

At 8:46 A.M. the USS *Randall* docks at the German port of Bremerhaven, where it is met by 1,500 fans and a virtual army of press. Elvis' battalion takes a troop train from Bermerhaven to Friedberg, arriving at 7:30 P.M.

02 Thursday

Elvis is assigned to the Ray Kaserne barracks in Friedberg, a row of brick buildings that once housed Hitler's SS troops. After initially being assigned as a jeep driver to the commanding officer of Company D, Elvis is transferred to Company C, a scout platoon frequently on maneuvers. His principal duty will be to drive for Reconnaissance Platoon sergeant Ira Jones. It is hoped that in this capacity Private Presley will be largely out of the public's eye. Before declaring him off-limits to the press, the army schedules a 10:00 A.M. news conference, at which Elvis answers all of the now-familiar questions from reporters, such as: Did he still want to meet Brigitte Bardot now that she was formally engaged?

04 Saturday

Vernon, his mother Minnie, Red West, and Lamar Fike check into the Ritters Park Hotel in Bad Homburg. Elvis joins them for dinner at the hotel while a crowd gathers outside.

05 Sunday

While visiting with his family, Elvis meets sixteen-year-old Margit Buergin, a typist for an electrical supply company in Frankfurt, who arrives with a photographer looking to get a picture of Elvis giving Margit a kiss. Elvis obliges, and they subsequently start to date.

06 Monday

Elvis obtains permission to live off base with his dependents (his father and grandmother), and the whole group moves into Rooms 311, 316, 318, and 319 at the Hilberts Park Hotel in Bad Nauheim. Elvis departs for the base early each morning, either taking a hired taxi or getting a lift from Sergeant Jones. He returns by 6:00 P.M. every evening except Fridays, when barracks and latrines must be cleaned for Saturday inspection.

14 Tuesday

The Colonel writes the first of many long, chatty, and encouraging letters clearly aimed at lifting Elvis' and Vernon's spirits. The army has assured the Colonel that Elvis will not be asked to make any public appear-

With Margit Buergin

ances, but there continue to be efforts to induce him to perform, which the Colonel advises Elvis and Vernon to refuse. The Colonel keeps Elvis informed of his squabbles with Hal Wallis in the most minute detail while reassuring him that everything will come out right in the end. Parker's constant litany, repeated to Elvis over and over both in this letter and others, is that he is doing everything "to keep your name hot over here."

17 Friday

The Colonel makes a deal with RCA, allowing the company to put out a special EP of Elvis' embarkation press conference, to be called *Elvis Sails*, with a $.13 royalty on each record plus an additional $.09 for use of photographs. The company guarantees royalties on 100,000 copies, whether the record sells that many or not.

18 Saturday

Along with his almost daily letter, the Colonel encloses a clipping referring to an East German newspaper's statement that Presley is a key weapon in America's atomic war.

23 Thursday

Elvis attends a Bill Haley performance in Frankfurt and visits Haley backstage, where he meets Swedish rock 'n' roll star Little Gerhard.

27 Monday

Vernon, Grandma, Lamar, and Red, meanwhile, are in the process of moving from the Hilberts Park Hotel into the elegant Hotel Grunewald, a health spa located in Bad Nauheim, about twenty minutes from the base. Charlie Hodge, who is stationed ten miles away, starts coming around on weekends to spend time with Elvis and the guys.

28 Tuesday

Obviously very homesick, Elvis describes himself in a letter to Anita Wood as a "lonely little boy 5000 miles away"—one in fact who would never love anyone in his life as he loved her and who looks forward to their marriage and "a little Elvis."

The Colonel finally succeeds in obtaining a new contract from Hal Wallis, who agrees to pay $175,000 for Elvis' first post-army picture, an increase of $75,000 over *King Creole* and $150,000 more than what Elvis would have been entitled to under the original contract. The agreement includes options for three additional pictures at $125,000, $150,000, and $175,000 against 7½ percent of "gross receipts" after the film has earned out. (The first film made under this agreement is *G.I. Blues*.)

29 Wednesday

Elvis attends another Bill Haley concert, in Stuttgart.

The Colonel follows up on his successful negotiations with Hal Wallis by concluding a revamped deal with 20th Century Fox for one picture at $200,000, an option for a second at $250,000, and a 50-50 division of the profits after all expenses have been recouped. (The pictures made under this contract are *Flaming Star* and *Wild in the Country*.)

October Record Release

Single: "One Night" (#4)/"I Got Stung"(#8) (shipped October 21). It has taken a full year to convince Elvis that his recording of "One Night" is good enough for release, and despite his reservations it's a hit. Competition with the B-side, "I Got Stung," is probably what prevents the record from reaching #1, but sales of 1.5 million make it Elvis' biggest single since "Jailhouse Rock" the year before.

NOVEMBER

02 Sunday

Elvis gives a party at his hotel before going out on maneuvers, singing and playing guitar for Margit Buergin and other friends while a crowd collects in the street below. Around this time he receives a call from Dee Stanley, the wife of an American sergeant stationed in Frank-furt, inviting him to dinner with her family. Elvis sidesteps the invitation, which Vernon will accept while Elvis is on maneuvers.

03 Monday

Company C arrives in Grafen-wöhr, Bavaria, on the Czech border. Here Elvis endures the same field conditions as every other soldier and proves himself adept at reconnaissance maneuvers.

16 Sunday

Elvis writes to Alan Fortas from Grafenwöhr. He appears to be no less homesick but describes his new girlfriend, Margit, as looking "a lot like B.B. [Brigitte Bardot]." He expresses the hope that "a miracle" may occur to get him out of the army earlier than March 1960.

18 Tuesday

The Colonel writes to Vernon and Elvis in great detail about all the hard work he has done and how his multiplicity of promotions will bring in even more income in 1958 than 1957, despite the fact that Elvis will have spent almost the whole year in the service.

19 Wednesday

While Elvis is in Grafenwöhr, Vernon, very likely at the Colonel's instigation, purchases a Grundig tape recorder with a microphone and two reels of tape.

The Memorial Studio in Memphis informs Vernon that the marker for his wife's grave has been completed, and that the Italian statuary has been ordered for her monument. The inscription on the grave reads, "She was the sunshine of our home."

20 Thursday

Elvis and Rex Mansfield, his closest army friend since their induction in Memphis, often attend movies at the post theater in Grafenwöhr. It is here that Elvis meets Elisabeth Stefaniak, the nineteen-year-old German stepdaughter of an American sergeant named McCormick.

"WE COVER THE NATION"

Thomas A. Parker

Exclusive Management

ELVIS PRESLEY

P.O. 417

MADISON, TENN.

Nov 18, 1958

Dear Vernon & Elvis;

Well here is the other news you have been waiting for Have just received the report that 20th Century Fox also is picking up the new deal I worked on the past 8 Months,so this brings the outlook for Elvis in a pretty solid picture for his future,better than it was before he went into the service,I am sure you both will be pleased with this information,this also will prove to Elvis that he is not backsliding in any way,this now brings our picture setup in line with a very healthy setup for the future.And in such a way that now at least I feel that we have what I always wanted to get on the Wallis contract ever since we first started out with them,Elvis knows how I felt about this setup but there was not much I could at that time except get a little more each time we made a picture for Wallis and Hazen. The Facts are now we do not have to call on Wallis everytime with our hat in our hands to ask for a little extra each time.The improvements I have been able to make will run into at least into a couple of hundred Thousand dollars more for the First Wallis and Fox pictures when Elvis comes out plus a percentage. wich we did not have on wither before he went into the service,for a time it even looked pretty bad that we would have to Court on the entire issue,this has all been cleared up.

There is not much news we are currently busy promoting the DeeJay convention for Elvis with records and promotion gimmicks all over the place. We are also getting busy for the regular Xmas promotion with a special card I had made up we will ship you some of them to use over there for your Friends.

Another check came in from MGM on the profits wich we of course mailed on to Bill Fisher this is the Third check so far from MGM on the profit sharing on Jailhouse Rock wich is holding up pretty good .I know this should make Elvis very happy ,with the extra gimmicks on photos and the special RCA Victor gimmicks we were able to include this Year Elvis will do even better this Year than he did last Year even while he is in the service.I did not hear from you regarding the letter I wrote giving you the information what the check was from RCA this Month,I hope you received same okay,also enclosedwas a wire to be send to the WSM on the DeeJay convention Nov 19th or 20th .Write a line with all the news so we at least know what is going on there. Give our best to Grandma and the boys also from Mrs Parker.

Take care of yourselfs

The Colonel .

Colonel Parker to Vernon and Elvis, with outdated mailing address

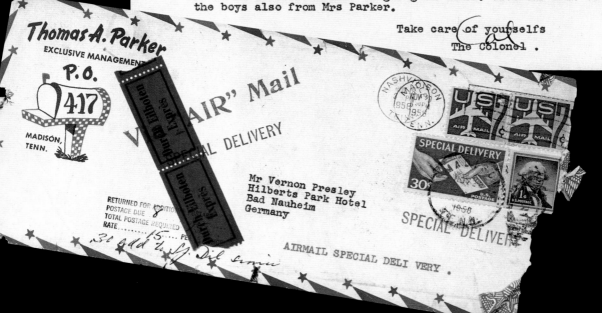

Thomas A. Parker
EXCLUSIVE MANAGEMENT

P.O. 417

MADISON, TENN.

"AIR" Mail

SPECIAL DELIVERY

RETURNED FOR ADDITION
POSTAGE DUE
TOTAL POSTAGE REQUIRED
RATE.........15.....

Mr Vernon Presley
Hilberts Park Hotel
Bad Nauheim
Germany

AIRMAIL SPECIAL DELIVERY

Reading fan mail in Germany

DECEMBER

13 Saturday

Colonel Parker suggests an idea for a movie to Hal Wallis. It would be set in Hawaii, since, the Colonel writes, Hawaiian music looks as though it may be the coming trend, and there is no question that Elvis has the voice for it. The story concerns a gang of unscrupulous promoters who con Elvis into singing with some native Hawaiians while all the while surreptitiously recording him. The Colonel tells Wallis he is also working on a second idea, in which Elvis will play a foundling brought up by a band of gypsies who travel around and sleep outdoors—which will give Elvis a chance to play the kind of rugged character he is good at.

17 Wednesday

The Colonel reports to Elvis that his new single, "One Night," has sold over 1,250,000.

20 Saturday

Elvis returns to Bad Nauheim at the conclusion of maneuvers with a promise from Elisabeth Stefaniak that she will come to work for him as his live-in secretary after the first of the year, helping to answer the stacks of fan mail the Colonel forwards to Germany.

21 Sunday

Elvis leases a white BMW 507 sports car. He has at this point also acquired a black Mercedes sedan, along with a Volkswagen "bug" that Red and Lamar use.

Over Christmas, Elvis and his friends fool around with the new tape recorder that Vernon has purchased. Lamar can be heard pretending to be a radio announcer, while Elvis performs some of his pop favorites, from "Danny Boy" to "Mona Lisa."

24 Wednesday

On Christmas Eve Elvis helps decorate the company's Christmas tree, entertaining fellow soldiers with a moving rendition of "Silent Night."

25 Tuesday

Colonel Parker reports that the news media is full of stories about Elvis. When he comes home, the Colonel says, it will be to "big" movie deals, and with "the respect of many people that he did his service like any other soldier."

Meanwhile, Steve Sholes never lets up in his constant refrain: that the record company needs more material, they are very anxious for Elvis to record in Germany. He offers to pay for Colonel Parker to go to Germany to supervise a session, but the Colonel declines in no uncertain terms, lecturing RCA that it must learn to harvest its resources and space out single releases twenty weeks apart in order to avoid "flooding the market."

27 Thursday

Elvis is promoted to private first class. He drops in unexpectedly for Thanksgiving dinner with Elisabeth Stefaniak and her family.

28 Friday

RCA's Bill Bullock offers to fly Elvis and four of his friends first class to Nashville for three days of recording. This and many other similar offers are turned down unhesitatingly by the Colonel.

November Record Release

EP: *Elvis Sails* (#2 on the EP charts) (shipped November 18). Using every trick in the book to generate income and to keep Elvis' name in front of the public, the Colonel "exploits" this five-and-a-half-minute edit of Elvis' embarkation press conference, together with two contemporaneous interviews, to sales of 60,000 copies—and payment for 100,000.

25 Thursday

The extended Presley family celebrates Christmas at the Hotel Grunewald with a special holiday meal and the gift of an electric guitar to Elvis from Vernon.

The Colonel sends out a Christmas card on behalf of himself and Elvis in which he is dressed in a red Santa suit with Elvis in uniform.

27 Saturday

Elvis attends the Holiday on Ice Show in Frankfurt.

30 Tuesday

The Colonel and RCA are struggling to agree on a selection for Elvis' next single. The Colonel is all for Ivory Joe Hunter's "My Wish Came True"
and "A Big Hunk o' Love," saving Hank Snow's "A Fool Such As I" and "I Need Your Love Tonight," both from the June session, for the next release. He continues to be dead set against the sound of the June session, reiterating frequently in his correspondence that the fans do not want to hear all those other voices and instruments, they just want to hear Elvis. Elvis' opinion is not recorded, but in the end the Colonel is overruled, and the next single is "A Fool Such As I."

In a letter to Elvis and Vernon, the Colonel lets them know that he has run into press reports and questions from reporters and fans about wild parties at the hotel. He cautions them to maintain a low profile.

31 Wednesday

For Christmas Tom Diskin sends Elvis a book by Konstantin Stanislavsky, the father of method acting, pointing out to Elvis that Stanislavsky "believed that truly great acting comes from within, or living the character you play." Much of the book, he says, may not interest Elvis, but in Diskin's view it supports Elvis' instinct that great acting comes from "be[ing] natural."

At the end of 1958, Elvis' accountant reports a total income of $1,001,727.89, with an income tax of approximately $360,000. Vernon has received a salary of $16,138.47.

1959

JANUARY

01 Thursday

In early January Elisabeth Stefaniak moves into the hotel with Elvis and his household, occupying a corner room that has been used for storage of the fan mail she is now in charge of answering, learning quickly from Red and Lamar how to sign Elvis' name.

02 Friday

Elvis calls George Klein in Memphis. He makes regular calls to different friends at home, especially Anita Wood.

04 Sunday

Elvis wakes Colonel Parker with a 5:00 A.M. phone call that turns into an hour-long chat. The Colonel jokes that the call interrupted his dream about Elvis getting an early army release, and now he doesn't know how the dream would have turned out.

08 Thursday

Elvis celebrates his twenty-fourth birthday in Germany, while Dick Clark, with the Colonel's cooperation, produces an *American Bandstand* tribute at home.

09 Friday

Colonel Parker suggests to Elvis in a long letter that he consider making

Donating blood

home tape recordings, featuring voice and piano alone, that will include some of his favorite spirituals, like "Just a Closer Walk With Thee." There would be no need for any further instrumentation, the Colonel explains, because the fans just want to hear his voice. A few days later Parker hints to RCA that he may have a surprise for them, but nothing ever comes of this idea, though Elvis does in fact make three known tapes (two have been found, but a third was catalogued by Vernon) of old favorites, current hits, and new titles supplied by Freddy Bienstock. The quality of the recordings is very rough, but enthusiasm is high.

16 Friday

With other soldiers, Elvis donates blood at the Wartturm Barracks in Friedberg for the German Red Cross.

19 Monday

Probably at his manager's suggestion, Elvis writes to the Colonel,

requesting him to make arrangements with RCA to put out a recorded message to his fans: "I want to be able to thank them not only for buying my records and for their loyalty to me but also for the help they have given me in deciding the kind of songs to sing. . . . I'm deeply grateful to them, and I want them to know it. When I'm out of the army recording again, I will always listen to their ideas, just as I did before. I just wanted to let my fans know how I feel. Sincerely, Elvis." Whatever the impetus, so far as is known, no such message was ever released.

28 Wednesday

In his first extended interview since arriving in Germany, Elvis confesses to Memphis DJ Keith Sherriff that he's still homesick and can't imagine himself doing anything at this point other than show business, "whether it's singing or working as a stagehand. You know, once it gets in your blood, it's hard to stay away from it."

With Vernon and Grandma, at Goethestrasse

Most likely either this week or the next, the Elvis Presley party abandons the cramped quarters and stern atmosphere of the Hotel Grunewald, which caters mostly to elderly guests, and moves to a three-story, five-bedroom, white stucco house at 14 Goethestrasse, nearby. The landlady, Frau Pieper, charges them an exorbitant rent of $800 a month, while continuing to maintain a room in the house both to serve as housekeeper and to oversee her new tenants. She and Grandma soon become fast friends, though they are frequently at odds, each in her own language. Not long after the move, a sign is put up at the gate reading: "Autogramme von 19:30 20:00" (Autographs 7:30-8:00 P.M.).

FEBRUARY

05 Thursday

Elvis learns of the deaths of Buddy Holly, Richie Valens, and the Big Bopper in an airplane crash, and Tom Diskin wires condolences to the families on Elvis' behalf.

07 Saturday

Elvis attends the Holiday on Ice Show in Frankfurt. He has become friendly with a number of the skaters and visits backstage.

08 Sunday

Janie Wilbanks, the girl that Elvis met at the Memphis train station when the troop train passed through, has come to Germany to visit her uncle, an army chaplain, and stays with Elvis for nearly a week at around this time.

On most Sundays, Elvis, Red,

Lamar, Rex, Charlie Hodge, and some of their other friends play touch football on a vacant lot down the street.

11 Wednesday

The representative of a German film company comes to the house to try to persuade Elvis to sing just one song in an upcoming production. Elvis explains that he is hesitant to do anything that might lead to resentment on the part of his fellow soldiers. In passing, he expresses almost equal concern about fan resentment when he is unable to sign autographs.

13 Friday

Elvis creates a traffic jam in Friedberg when he stops to sign autographs.

23 Monday

The Colonel reports to Elvis that since he's been away they have made well over $50,000 in special deals requiring no work on Elvis' part.

February Record Release

LP: *For LP Fans Only* (#19) (shipped February 6). In a continuing commitment to keep Elvis' name alive, and also to reach the growing LP market, RCA releases a compilation of ten previously released songs (including five of the Sun cuts) that have never been on LP before. Despite the paucity of cuts and the familiarity of the material, it sells 200,000 copies.

MARCH

03 Tuesday

Elvis travels to Munich with Red and Lamar to visit Vera Tschechowa, an eighteen-year-old actress whom he met in January while doing publicity shots for the March of Dimes. Elvis buys up all the tickets to the play in which she is performing with a small experimental theater group, sitting through a German-language performance that neither he nor Red nor Lamar can understand. In the evening they go out to dinner with various

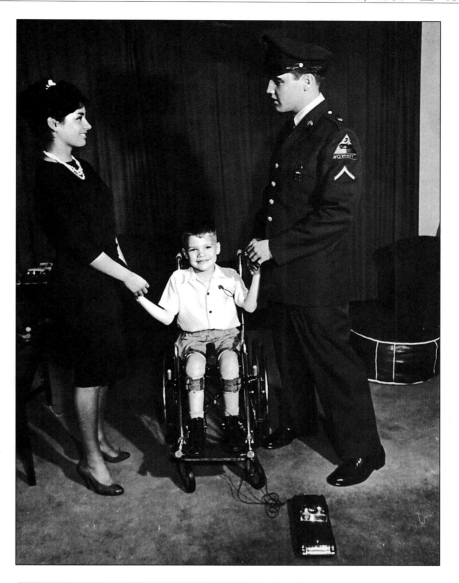

With Vera Tschechowa and March of Dimes poster child, January 1959

theatrical friends of Vera, and then to the Moulin Rouge, a striptease club.

04 Wednesday

Elvis and Vera visit the set of a Viking movie that is being made at the film studios in München-Geiselgasteig, and Elvis, Red, and Lamar return to the Moulin Rouge alone.

The Colonel writes that he has arranged for photographer Don Cravens to come to Germany to portray Elvis in his duties as a "regular soldier." The Colonel hopes that this kind of publicity may help convince the army to let Elvis finish out the

balance of his tour in the States doing recruiting for the army while at the same time building up the supply of photographs "that I must have if we are to maintain our special promotion business."

05 Thursday

Elvis and Vera go for a boat ride at Lake Starnberg, and once again he returns to the Moulin Rouge that evening with just Red and Lamar, to wind up his three-day leave.

06 Friday

The Colonel gets $7,500 from RCA in exchange for pictures for the

With showgirls at the Moulin Rouge in Munich, March 1959

"Over the Hump" party

26 Thursday

Vernon and Elisabeth are in an automobile accident on the Autobahn near Obermorlen, returning from a shopping trip to Frankfurt. Following the incident, rumors spread that Elvis has been killed, although he was not even in the car.

27 Friday

Elvis celebrates the halfway mark of his army stint with an "Over the Hump" party.

APRIL

01 Wednesday

Elvis rents a piano from Music House Kuhlwetter in nearby Giessen and subsequently spends a great deal of time singing and

March Record Release

Single: "A Fool Such As I" (#2)/"I Need Your Love Tonight" (#4) (shipped March 10). With so little new material available, RCA is forced to harvest what it does have very sparingly, and at greater intervals than ever before. This single combines two songs from the June 1958 sessions that the Colonel so disliked because of the way in which he felt the accompaniment overpowered Elvis' voice. Nonetheless, the record proves to be a winner, marking only the second time ("Hound Dog"/"Don't Be Cruel" was the first) that both sides of an Elvis 45 have reached the top five, and selling one million copies in what is generally a declining singles market.

upcoming gatefold LP, *A Date With Elvis.*

18 Wednesday

Elvis hurts his knee when he is thrown from a jeep rounding a corner. He is ordered to rest for three days and requests that no announcement be made to the press.

20 Friday

The bill for Elvis' phone (Bad Nauheim exchange, 2714) shows numerous and lengthy calls to Anita Wood.

At Goethestrasse, early spring 1959

With Vernon at open house at
Ray Kaserne barracks, April 12, 1959

playing. During his last year in
Germany, Elvis continues to
record material with Charlie
Hodge on his home tape recorder,
with a repertoire that includes
gospel numbers that will show
up on 1960's *His Hand In Mine*,
r & b songs like "Such a Night,"
and well-known standards like
"Are You Lonesome Tonight?"
and Tony Martin's "There's No
Tomorrow" (English lyrics set
to the "O Sole Mio" melody

With *(left to right)* Vernon,
Red West, and Lamar Fike at
Goethestrasse, spring 1959

In Paris with Lamar Fike *(back to camera)* and Charlie Hodge *(in profile)*

popularized by Enrico Caruso) that Elvis is considering for future release. Elvis likes the last song so much that he subsequently asks Freddy Bienstock to commission new lyrics, recording the song as "It's Now or Never" once he gets out of the army.

09 Thursday

Steve Sholes has submitted his plan to release "When It Rains, It Really Pours," "Your Cheatin' Heart," or "Tomorrow Night" as the next single. The Colonel strongly demurs, voicing his opinion that none of the songs is strong enough, but, he says, the final decision is up to Elvis. In a separate letter to Elvis he emphasizes this same point, granting that he could be wrong in his judgment but

---

April Record Release

EP: *A Touch of Gold Vol. 1* (shipped April 21). RCA and the Colonel continue to offer old wine in new bottles, the new bottles in this case being primarily different record formats. This EP of three recent "gold hits" plus "Good Rockin' Tonight," his second Sun single, does not chart but sells a respectable 130,000 copies.

---

that it is Elvis' contractual right to pick the single.

12 Sunday

Open house at Elvis' barracks, in celebration of the eighteenth anniversary of the 3rd Armored Division. It is Elvis' job to drive visitors around the camp in a truck.

13 Monday

Elvis is photographed receiving a Salk polio inoculation as part of his continued efforts for the March of Dimes, which publicized his first polio shot in the fall of 1956.

14 Tuesday

Elvis is drafted for another public relations–oriented event when he is sent to Steinfurth as part of a work detail to help erect a memorial statue for veterans of World War I.

Elvis buys a Welchsler stereo and some records in Bad Nauheim.

19 Sunday

Elvis hosts a tea at his home for four German teenagers who have won the visit as part of a newspaper contest. This is one of many such events that the Colonel orchestrates from more than four thousand miles away.

MAY

08 Friday

There is a brief interview with Red West in the *Memphis Press–Scimitar* revealing that he has been home for several days. Elvis tries to recruit Alan Fortas to replace him but fails, because Fortas had already been forewarned by Red of the restrictiveness of life in Germany. Elvis then contacts Cliff Gleaves, who makes plans to depart on the thirteenth.

24 Sunday

This appears to be the Sunday that Elvis first meets Currie Grant, an airman whom Vernon and Lamar have already met in Wiesbaden, where he serves as the producer of a variety show at the Eagle Club, a community center for Air Force families. Grant's introduction to the household coincides with Cliff's belated arrival in Bad Nauheim.

JUNE

01 Monday

Elvis is promoted to Specialist 4th Class, raising his salary to $122.30 per month.

03 Wednesday

Elvis is hospitalized in the 97th General Hospital in Frankfurt with tonsillitis and a high fever. He is discharged six days later.

13 Saturday

The beginning of a fifteen–day furlough, in which Elvis will travel to Munich and Paris with Lamar Fike, Rex Mansfield, and Charlie Hodge. He spends most of his two nights in Munich visiting some of his old acquaintances at the Moulin Rouge, including "Marianne," who has developed a strip routine "wearing nothing but a standard size Presley record."

15 Monday

Elvis and his entourage of three travel to Paris in a private train car.

At home

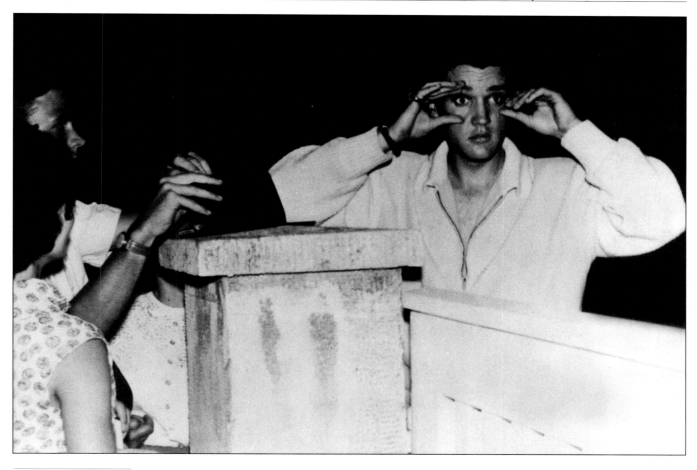

With fans at Goethestrasse

There they are met by Viennese émigrés Jean Aberbach and Freddy Bienstock of Hill and Range, who have arranged reservations at the Prince de Galles (Prince of Wales) Hotel, where they occupy a top-floor suite overlooking the Champs-Élysées.

17 Wednesday

After a brief press conference, Elvis is mobbed sitting at a sidewalk café. Whether because of this experience, or because he has no interest in sightseeing, Elvis spends his days sleeping, his nights at such well-known nightclubs as the Lido, the Moulin Rouge, the Folies Bergère, and the after-hours Le Bantu.

22 Monday

Vernon leaves Germany ostensibly to take care of some business in Memphis, but mainly to pursue Dee Stanley, who has gone home to Virginia with her three sons, leaving her husband (to whom Vernon has yet to confess their affair) in Germany. On June 26, Vernon attends Colonel Parker's fiftieth birthday celebration in Madison.

27 Saturday

In order to be able to stay in Paris right up till the last minute, Elvis hires a limousine to get him back to the barracks.

June Record Release

Single: "A Big Hunk o' Love" (#1)/"My Wish Came True" (#12) (shipped June 23). This is the last single to be released before Elvis' return to the United States, almost nine months away. Its one million sales do little to calm RCA's worries about the future, or to undercut the Colonel's unassailable bargaining position.

JULY

15 Wednesday

It is announced in the press that Elvis will be appearing on television

July Record Release

LP: *A Date With Elvis* (#32) (shipped July 24). Using the same approach as was applied to *For LP Fans Only*, RCA combines five Sun sides, four movie songs, and one cut previously confined to an EP, to create an abbreviated, ten-track album of songs never before heard on LP. The gatefold sleeve, with Don Craven's photographs of GI Elvis on the inside and a calendar marking the date of Elvis' return on the back, is the Colonel's idea—and the basis for the special fee that RCA has to pay. The album sells approximately 175,000 copies.

on the Frank Sinatra show upon his release from the army and that he will be receiving $125,000 for the appearance, more than Frank will get for the whole show.

20 Monday

Perhaps needless to say, RCA has not given up on convincing the Colonel to allow Elvis to record in Germany. Parker's infuriating response is to remind the record company that they have plenty of merchandise to exploit already, what with regular LPs, the Christmas album, and a special golden records package.

27 Monday

Vernon brings Dee Stanley to visit his father, Jessie Presley, in Louisville.

AUGUST

05 Wednesday

On around this date Dick Clark conducts a telephone interview with Elvis, informing him that his new single has just gone gold.

15 Saturday

U.S. Army Captain Paul Beaulieu, his wife, and their three children arrive in Wiesbaden, Germany, from their previous posting at Bergstrom Air Force Base in Austin, Texas.

17 Monday

Filming starts for location shots and background footage of army operations to be used in Elvis' first post-army picture, now entitled

With Hal Wallis in Bad Nauheim

Christmas in Berlin but eventually to become *G.I. Blues.* Hal Wallis, who has spent much of the summer in Europe, visits Elvis in Bad Nauheim, but at the Colonel's explicit instructions Elvis is prohibited from taking any part in the shooting.

27 Thursday

Vernon returns to Germany, followed shortly by Dee, who has left her children in Virginia.

SEPTEMBER

With Mercedes, Goethestrasse

13 Sunday

Currie Grant brings fourteen-year-old Priscilla Beaulieu, whom he has met at the Eagle Club in Wiesbaden, to the house on Goethestrasse to meet Elvis. No one present misses his immediate attraction to the beautiful young girl in the blue and white sailor dress and white socks, and he tells Charlie Hodge not long afterward that Priscilla is "like the woman I've been looking for all my

> ### September Record Release
>
> **EP:** *A Touch of Gold Vol. 2* (shipped September 2). RCA has all but depleted its combination of possible new releases. This EP sells less than Vol. 1, but still manages close to 100,000 copies.

life." From this point on, Priscilla will join the group that gathers at Elvis' house almost every evening during the week and again on weekends, a group that now includes a new army buddy from Chicago, Joe Esposito.

OCTOBER

16 Friday

E. J. Cottrell, the army information officer who has been Colonel Parker's chief liaison in Washington, writes to the Colonel about the visit he has just paid to Elvis in Germany. He reports that Elvis is still homesick but that he is in good shape and is continuing to do a good job.

19 Monday

Elvis' unit goes on maneuvers called the "Big Lift" at the military training area in Wildflecken near the Swiss border.

21 Wednesday

Jessie Presley writes to his son, Vernon, from Louisville, that Joan Crawford has recently visited the Pepsi Cola plant where he works and sought him out to tell him what a fine boy his grandson is.

24 Saturday

Elvis is again hospitalized in the 97th General Hospital in Frankfurt for tonsillitis.

29 Thursday

Elvis is discharged from the hospital and told to remain at home for three more days.

On winter maneuvers, date unknown

With Priscilla Beaulieu

NOVEMBER

27 Friday

Elvis begins weekly herbal skin treatments with a South African self-described doctor named Laurenz Johannes Griessel Landau, whom he contacted after reading a magazine advertisement touting his miraculous method for reducing enlarged pores and acne scars.

DECEMBER

05 Saturday

Elvis' three-day pass begins at 6:00 A.M.

06 Sunday

Elvis starts karate lessons with Jurgen Seydel, known as the "father of German karate." Karate is a discipline with which Elvis has been fasci-

---

November Record Release

LP: *Elvis' Gold Records Vol. 2* (#31) (shipped November 13). Subtitled "50,000,000 Elvis Fans Can't Be Wrong," this ten-track compilation of recent Elvis hit singles takes the RCA re-release policy to extremes. The record sells poorly in comparison to Vol. 1, but over the years it will sell over one million copies, with its cover art of Elvis in his gold lamé suit an instantly recognizable pop classic.

---

nated ever since reading a magazine article about Hank Slamansky, an ex-Marine who pioneered in teaching the sport in the service. He will take lessons from Seydel twice a week until he returns to the States.

24 Thursday

The skin treatments come to an abrupt end when Elvis accuses Griessel Landau of making sexual advances. The doctor responds by threatening to blackmail him about "a sixteen-year-old [*sic*] underage girl" that he knows Elvis has been seeing. After a panicked call to the Colonel the day after Christmas, Elvis goes to the army's Provost Marshal Division, which refers the case to the FBI. An investigation determines Griessel Landau is not a medical doctor, and after receiving a small payment, he flies to London, never to be heard from again.

25 Friday

Elvis arranges to have a French poodle delivered to Anita Wood for Christmas and throws a Christmas party at Goethestrasse for family and friends. Priscilla Beaulieu gives Elvis a set of bongo drums.

31 Thursday

At the Colonel's instigation, and very likely utilizing much of the Colonel's wording, Elvis telegrams his manager: "Please convey my thanks to the various groups in Memphis who have suggested a special homecoming for me when I return to Memphis. However, I wish to return to Memphis the same way that any other serviceman returns to his hometown, without ceremony or fanfare. I served as they served and was proud to do it. Seeing the city of Memphis, my family, friends, and fans, will be the most welcome sight in the world to me. I appreciate their kind gesture. I know they will understand and I am glad you are in agreement with me on this. Best wishes to you and Mrs Parker. From Dad, Grandma and myself."

1960

JANUARY

05 Tuesday

Elvis is granted leave from January 5 through January 17, including permission to travel to Paris.

08 Friday

Dick Clark interviews Elvis on his twenty-fifth birthday for *American Bandstand*, with Elvis speaking in general terms of his upcoming recording session, his appearance on the Frank Sinatra television show, and his new Paramount picture, now titled *G.I. Blues*. A little later in the evening he celebrates at a local recreation center with about two hundred invited guests, including Priscilla Beaulieu. Joe Esposito and the gang present Elvis with a trophy inscribed "Elvis Presley. Most Valuable Player. Bad Nauheim Sunday Afternoon Football Association, 1959."

12 Tuesday

Elvis travels to Paris with Joe, Cliff Gleaves, Lamar Fike, and his karate instructor, Jurgen Seydel. During the visit they attend five karate classes given by Tetsuji

With karate teacher Tetsuji Murakami, Paris, January 1960

Murakami, a Japanese teacher of the shotokan technique. On the advice of their Memphis accountant, Joe Esposito has been charged by Vernon with keeping an account of expenditures on the trip. Joe's accounting at the conclusion of the trip indicates that the group has spent approximately $1,289 apart from hotel and travel expenses during their five-day stay.

During this trip Elvis goes to see the expatriate American gospel group the Golden Gate Quartet, with whose recordings he has long been familiar but to whom he has been reintroduced in Germany by Charlie Hodge. After the show, he sits backstage with the group, happily singing one gospel song after another.

20 Wednesday

Elvis is promoted to acting sergeant three days after reporting back for duty.

24 Sunday

Elvis leaves for "Operation Winter Shield" maneuvers in Grafenwöhr.

FEBRUARY

11 Thursday

Elvis gets his full sergeant's stripes and throws a party to celebrate.

In an interview with Armed Forces Radio around this time, Elvis reflects upon his army experience. "People were expecting me to mess up, to goof up," he says. "They thought I couldn't take it, and I was determined to go to any limits to prove otherwise." Of his return to making records, he com-

ments, "I think it would be a bad mistake if I had somebody else telling me what to record and how to record it, because I work strictly on instinct and impulse. . . . I choose songs with the

public in mind. I try to visualize it as though I'm buying the record myself."

26 Friday

On an army redeployment order document, E. A. Presley is included among soldiers to be transferred to Fort Dix, New Jersey, on March 3, 1960.

Elvis calls Anita Wood as he prepares to resume his old life. Joe Esposito, who has already left for home, has agreed to go to work for him upon his return. So has Elisabeth Stefaniak, who will be

Army leave documents for travel to Paris

Expense account, Paris leave,
probably made out by Joe Esposito

Priscilla at Elvis' departure from Germany

returning to the States with Vernon and Grandma, and Elvis hopes that Rex Mansfield, too, will be part of the team.

29 Monday

As Elvis spends his last days in Germany, *Billboard* reports he has sold eighteen million singles to date, a feat accomplished by no other artist in history.

February Record Release

EP: *A Touch of Gold, Vol. 3* (#17) (shipped February 23). The record's sales of little more than 50,000 make it obvious that RCA is scraping the bottom of the barrel.

MARCH

01 Tuesday

The army holds a press conference just before Elvis' departure from Germany, with over one hundred reporters and photographers in attendance at the enlisted men's club in Friedberg. Elvis' commanding officer presents him with a certificate of merit citing his "cheerfulness and drive and continually outstanding leadership ability." Also present is Marion Keisker from Sun Records, who as army Captain MacInness (her married name) has been serving out her tour of duty in Europe. When Elvis, who has not seen her since her 1957 enlistment, spots her, he reacts excitedly, saying, "I don't know whether to kiss you or salute." "In that order," she says.

In New York the Colonel has worked out new emendations to Elvis' RCA contract retroactive to January 1. Any movie recording can now be used toward the fulfillment of his contractual quota of two LPs and eight single sides annually. In addition, Elvis and the Colonel will receive a three-fourths of 1 percent recoupable royalty on top of the regular 5 percent royalty; the Colonel is granted explicit approval on all advertising, promotion, and publicity material; and, with Elvis' signed assent, his manager will receive an annual payment of $27,000 in exchange for supplying photographs for record covers and, in general, "exploitational" support. RCA also agrees that payments made to musicians, vocalists, and arrangers on recording sessions will no longer be deducted from royalties.

02 Wednesday

Priscilla Beaulieu is held back by military policemen at the Rhine-Main air base as she tries to bid Elvis one last farewell. She is captured by *Life* magazine waving goodbye, with the photo appearing in the March 14 issue and captioned "Girl He Left Behind." The military transport takes off at 5:25 P.M., stopping briefly to refuel in Prestwick, Scotland, before heading for New Jersey.

03 Thursday

Elvis arrives at McGuire Air Force Base near Fort Dix, New Jersey, at 7:42 A.M., in the midst of a snowstorm. After processing their celebrity sergeant through customs, the army holds another full-scale press conference, with a welcoming party that includes Nancy Sinatra, Colonel Parker, Jean Aberbach, and numerous RCA representatives. Elvis spends the next two days at Fort Dix going through the routine discharge procedure.

04 Friday

Tennessee senator Estes Kefauver reads a tribute to Elvis into the *Congressional Record* that includes this passage: "To his great credit this young American became just another G.I. Joe. . . . I for one would like to say to him yours was a job well done, Soldier."

Meanwhile, Vernon has arrived home in Memphis with his mother, Dee Stanley, and Elisabeth Stefaniak.

05 Saturday

Elvis is released from the army at 9:15 A.M. After receiving his mustering-out check of $109.54 and his formal

Certificate of Service

Envelope for official separation
papers, filled out by Elvis (this is
one of the envelopes pictured
in Elvis' left hand)

With Colonel Parker on the train to Memphis

A.M. in the midst of another snow-storm. After greeting fans, Elvis rides out to Graceland in his friend Police Captain Fred Woodward's squad car.

In the afternoon, Elvis holds a press conference in his father's office in a small building just behind Graceland. He tells the gathering of some fifty reporters that he is so happy to be home that "I just can't get it in my mind that I'm here." Anita Wood joins him later in the evening after waiting patiently for her summons at his cousin Patsy's house.

08 Tuesday

Elvis visits the Forest Hill Cemetery to see for the first time the marker and stone angels that have been placed at

A 1966 florist bill for weekly flower delivery to Gladys' grave

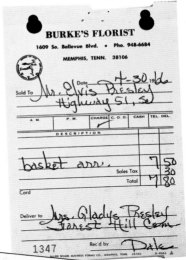

On the train to Memphis, with Tom Diskin and Colonel Parker to Elvis' left, Lamar Fike to his right, and Bitsy Mott seated on the floor

honorable discharge, he and Colonel Parker travel by limousine, "mysteriously vanish[ing]," the press reports, "from a snow-packed and fan-laden highway." Their destination is a Trenton, New Jersey, hotel where they are joined by Lamar Fike and Rex Mansfield. That same evening, the group takes a private railroad car to Washington, D.C.

06 Sunday

In Washington, Elvis and his party board a second private railway car, this time on the "Tennessean," which leaves for Memphis at 8:05 A.M. Throughout the trip, Elvis appears on the observation platform

in his dress blues and waves to the crowds gathered at every station, big and small, along the route.

In Bristol, Tennessee, a young reporter from the *Nashville Tennessean*, David Halberstam, boards the train to cover the story.

07 Monday

Elvis remains awake throughout the night, and in the morning appears still in uniform but with one of the formal lace-fronted shirts given to him by Nancy Sinatra at Fort Dix. The train arrives in Memphis at 7:45

Gladys Presley's grave, Forest Hill Cemetery, Memphis, c. 1960

Arriving in Memphis, March 7, 1960

Invoice for the RCA TV given to Elvis to mark 50 million record sales upon his return home

With Colonel Parker and the RCA award TV in front of Graceland, probably March 7, 1960

his mother's grave. From the time of her burial until her body is moved to Graceland after Elvis' death, there is a standing order at Burke's Florist to deliver fresh flowers once a week to her grave.

09 Wednesday

Elvis takes Elisabeth on a motor-cycle ride to show her Memphis.

10 Thursday

Elvis attends the Holiday on Ice show at Ellis Auditorium, visiting backstage with members of the troupe he first met when they performed in Germany.

Press conference, Vernon's office, Graceland, March 7, 1960

Rehearsal with Frank Sinatra

With Frank Sinatra at taping,
March 26, 1960

11 Friday

Elvis has his hair dyed black, then gives Elisabeth driving lessons in the yellow Lincoln he has bought for her to use. Charlie Hodge and Joe Esposito join Lamar Fike at Graceland, with Red West and Cliff Gleaves coming in from the West Coast not long after.

The Colonel writes to Bill Bullock that trying to oversee Elvis' return to civilian life has been a little bit like "handling the return of Valentino from the grave."

12 Saturday

Elvis throws a party at Graceland, taking time out to greet a group of deaf children who arrive at the gates.

13 Sunday

Returning to Ellis for the ice show's "performance for Negroes," Elvis briefly conducts the seventeen-piece orchestra with a lighted baton.

14 Monday

At Elvis' invitation, the cast of Holiday on Ice visits Graceland during the day. In the evening Elvis rents the Memphian Theater at 11:00 P.M., after the regular showings are done, to screen movies for himself, his family, and friends.

15 Tuesday

Elisabeth Stefaniak leaves, presumably to visit her family in Florida, where her stepfather is now stationed, but actually to meet Rex Mansfield's parents. She and Rex have secretly decided to marry, sending Elvis a telegraphed invitation to their wedding on June 4, but neither one ever sees him again.

19 Saturday

Elvis rents the Rainbow Roller-drome for an evening of roller-skating wars with the guys.

20 Sunday

At noon Elvis, his entourage, Scotty, and D.J. (but not Bill Black, who never plays with Elvis again) take a chartered bus to Nashville for a session at RCA's Studio B, whose recording facilities

have been upgraded with a new three-track machine. There they are joined by all the musicians from the June 1958 session, the Jordanaires, Colonel Parker, various RCA executives, and RCA's new chief studio engineer, Bill Porter. In order to avoid both unwanted publicity and an avalanche of fans, top-secret conditions prevail, with the Nashville musicians told they will be working a Jim Reeves session. Working from 8:00 P.M. to 7:00 A.M., Elvis completes six sides for an urgently needed new single ("Stuck on You"/"Fame and Fortune," which will be pressed and shipped within two days) and toward his upcoming album.

21 Monday

Waiting at the Nashville station in the private railroad car he has reserved for the trip to Miami for the Frank Sinatra show, Elvis tells a reporter from the *Nashville Tennessean* that going back into the recording studio "was sorta strange at first. But after singing a couple of hours it all came natural again." He remains demonstrably worried about the loyalty of his fans, concluding, "If I don't please the audience the money don't mean nothing."

On the train to Miami, Elvis once again greets thousands of fans along a route that takes them through Alabama and Georgia.

22 Tuesday

Elvis checks into the penthouse of Miami's Fontainebleau Hotel with Joe Esposito, Lamar Fike, Gene Smith, and Cliff Gleaves. For the rest of the week he rehearses for the show. Asked if he has changed his mind and set aside his very pronounced views about rock 'n' roll (a music "for cretinous goons"), Sinatra sidesteps the question, responding, "The kid's been away two years, and I get the feeling he really believes in what he's doing."

23 Wednesday

RCA's pressing plant in Indianapolis has worked overtime to produce the new single, and within a little more than forty-eight hours

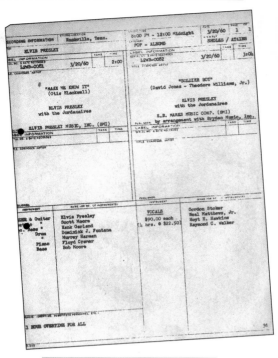

RCA paperwork, first post-army session

of the session, shipment of one million copies has begun, using pre-prepared sleeves that simply announce "Elvis' first new recordings for his 50,000,000 fans all over the world."

26 Saturday

The Sinatra show is taped at 6:15 P.M. for airing on May 12. Elvis performs the two songs that make up his new single and duets with Frank, in a mutual reversal of roles, on both the host's "Witchcraft" and his own "Love Me Tender."

29 Tuesday

Concerned about mounting expenses, the Colonel hires a bus to carry the group back to Memphis.

March Record Release

Single: "Stuck on You" (#1)/"Fame and Fortune" (#17) (shipped March 23). Without waiting for orders, RCA ships more than one million copies directly to the stores, and "Stuck on You" debuts at #84 on *Billboard*'s chart for April 10, reaching the #1 position three weeks later.

APRIL

01 Friday

A fiberglass carport is erected in the process of converting Graceland's three-car garage into an apartment for Vernon and Dee Stanley and her three children.

03 Sunday

Just two weeks after his first post-army recording session, Elvis again boards a chartered bus in Memphis to return to Nashville. The same group of musicians is joined this time by saxophonist Boots Randolph. The plan is to record ten songs over the next few nights, but Elvis puts down twelve of his most diverse and ambitious tracks in one marathon session, from 7:30 P.M. to 7:00 A.M. Some of the songs that he records are "It's Now or Never" (based on the Tony Martin standard "There's No Tomorrow," which in turn was based on "O Sole Mio"); a Peggy Lee–inflected version of Little Willie John's "Fever"; and "Are You Lonesome Tonight?" which Elvis records at the Colonel's urging because it is his wife, Marie's, favorite song. This may be the only time in his career that Elvis will record a song at the explicit suggestion of his manager.

08 Friday

Again RCA has rushed the session tapes to the pressing plant, and just four days after the session the LP, *Elvis Is Back*, is shipped. Its gatefold album of army snapshots has been printed in advance, and the titles of the subsequently recorded songs appear on a sticker.

09 Saturday

Back home in Memphis, Elvis goes on a $4,000 shopping spree, buying his father a watch and purchasing a diamond necklace for Anita, who has dyed her hair black to match his.

Brother Dave Gardner, who is performing at Ellis Auditorium, joins Elvis and his entourage at the Roller-drome and the Memphian.

With Juliet Prowse on the set of *G.I. Blues*

During this period Elvis has begun to date nineteen-year-old Memphian Bonnie Bunkley, whom he met when she came to Graceland with her voice teacher to collect money for a benefit at Whitehaven High School.

17 Sunday

Elvis and Anita attend Easter service at the First Assembly of God Church but are forced to leave when their presence causes a disruption.

18 Monday

The entourage with which Elvis sets out for California to make his first post-army motion picture now includes army buddies Joe Esposito and Charlie Hodge, longtime friend Lamar Fike, Red West's cousin Sonny, and Elvis' cousin Gene Smith. Together with Colonel Parker's staff they occupy two private cars on the Southern Pacific Sunset Limited at a cost of $2,424.41. Old friends Red West and Cliff Gleaves have already returned to Los Angeles to resume their search for show business opportunities.

19 Tuesday

The train is mobbed by fans in El Paso, Texas, en route to Hollywood.

20 Wednesday

To avoid the large crowd gathered for his arrival at Union Station in Los Angeles, Elvis disembarks on a siding just outside the station and takes a cab to the Beverly Wilshire Hotel with Colonel Parker.

21 Thursday

Elvis begins preproduction on *G.I. Blues*, a Hal Wallis production for Paramount. The picture is to be directed by Norman Taurog and costars dancer Juliet Prowse.

Colonel Parker and his wife, Marie, at a party on the set of *G.I. Blues*

In a by now familiar pattern, Cliff Gleaves is fired after a minor dispute, and Vernon quickly telegrams the Colonel: "Mr. Cliff Gleaves is no longer connected with us in any way, and we are in no way responsible for his doings."

22 Friday
Music rehearsals continue, while Elvis spends his evenings at the Crossbow, where he meets Lance LeGault, a white rhythm-and-blues singer from Louisiana who is a friend of Red's. Within days Elvis is introduced to the club owner's fourteen-year-old daughter, Sandy Ferra, who soon becomes a regular date. In later years she will marry Memphis DJ Wink Martindale.

25 Monday
Music rehearsals in the morning are followed by wardrobe tests in the afternoon.

26 Tuesday
Music rehearsals continue.

27 Wednesday
Soundtrack recording for *G.I. Blues* is moved to the RCA studio at 6363 Sunset Boulevard because of a new agreement between RCA and the musicians union. Elvis arrives at the studio at 9:00 A.M. wearing his full dress uniform from the film and works until 8:00 P.M. The band is augmented by guitarist "Tiny" Timbrell and pianist Dudley Brooks, both of whom have played on earlier L.A. sessions. Several songs by Jerry Leiber and Mike Stoller have been set aside for business reasons

April Record Release

Album: *Elvis Is Back* (#2) (shipped April 8). Elvis' best album to date, displaying a wide range of musical tastes and an ambitious expansion of vocal technique. Despite these pluses and its high chart position, however, it is not the 500,000-plus blockbuster that RCA's Bill Bullock and the Colonel are clearly hoping for, with sales of just under 300,000 copies.

(the songwriting duo has refused to accept the same onerous conditions that every other songwriter is forced to submit to), and Elvis is clearly disappointed with the material he is given. The Colonel's somewhat disingenuous comment in a letter to Jean Aberbach on the subject four months earlier: "It is unfair to make different deals for the same service with one party, and not give the same deal to another party giving the same service."

28 Thursday
Recording continues from 12:30 P.M. to 11:03 P.M. The unfamiliar studio, the unsatisfactory songs, and a new, strict enforcement of union rules regarding length of sessions and prescribed breaks create unproductive tensions, and Hal Wallis makes arrangements to complete the session the following week at Radio Recorders, where Elvis has always felt more at home.

29 Friday
Script rehearsals begin. Elvis spends the evening at the Moulin Rouge, paying the bill with a check for $102.35. Elvis often goes to the Moulin Rouge and the Cloister in Hollywood during this time, frequently taking in shows by Bobby Darin and Sammy Davis, Jr.

MAY

02 Monday
Principal photography for *G.I. Blues* begins.

05 Thursday
Elvis has complained to the Colonel that when RCA mastered "It's Now or Never" in New York, the sound was altered, and that, on the test pressing he has received, it no longer sounds like the acetate he got at the session. Bill Bullock responds by suggesting that Elvis' record player probably produces a different sound than the studio equipment, evidently hoping that Elvis' concerns will go away.

06 Friday

Recording for *G.I. Blues* resumes at Radio Recorders, where Elvis works from 1:00 to 10:00 P.M., re-recording several of the songs. He remains dissatisfied, however, with the material, something he emphasizes in a phone call at around this time to Priscilla in Germany. There is nothing he can do to change it, he says. "I'm locked into this thing."

12 Thursday

The Sinatra show is broadcast on the ABC network from 9:30 to 10:30 P.M. EST and attracts 41.5 percent of the viewing audience.

Memphis jeweler Harry Levitch writes to remind Elvis that he has not picked up his new diamond horseshoe ring. Levitch, a stalwart member of the Memphis philanthropical community, originally endeared himself to Elvis because of his kindness to Elvis' friend Red West, whom he helped out in high school.

Elvis attends a kenpo karate demonstration at the Beverly Hills Hotel, where he makes the acquaintance of the instructor, Hawaiian-born Ed Parker, who has developed a new, more flexible, street-fighting karate technique.

28 Saturday

Elvis spends the weekend in Las Vegas, introducing the newer members of his group to his favorite playground. Both Elvis and the entourage have taken to wearing sunglasses and dark continental suits, consciously modeling themselves on Frank Sinatra's "Rat Pack" and before long coming to be referred to as the "Memphis Mafia" in the press. At Elvis' instigation, they will soon start to carry briefcases, although Gene Smith has nothing in his but a hairbrush and a doorknob.

JUNE

04 Saturday

The Colonel arranges for three Scandinavian princesses (Margaretha of Sweden, Astrid of Norway, and Margretha of Denmark) to make a special visit to the set. In the evening Elvis and his entourage go club-hopping, visiting both the Coconut Grove and the Ambassador.

13 Monday

In an interview with Hearst reporter Jean Bosquet, Colonel Parker says of Elvis' films, "They'll never win any Academy Awards. All they're good for is to make money."

17 Friday

Elvis writes to the U.S. Army, requesting that he be placed on standby rather than active reserve, as his work requires him to travel constantly.

Along with Hal Wallis and actress Shirley MacLaine, Elvis attends a birthday party for Dean Martin on the Paramount lot.

21 Tuesday

King Bumiphol and Queen Sirikit of Thailand visit the set.

24 Friday

Principal photography for *G.I. Blues* ends.

With Vernon Presley at the Memphis airport, probably July or November 1960

25 Saturday

Elvis drives to Las Vegas for the weekend, where he reportedly loses $10,000 playing craps and attends shows by Billy Ward and His Dominoes, Della Reese, and Red Skelton.

27 Monday

Having received a test pressing of Elvis' new single, "It's Now or Never," the Colonel lets Bill Bullock know in no uncertain terms that the sound is still unsatisfactory and it must be remastered, forcing RCA to delay the record's release.

29 Wednesday

After three days of publicity stills, Elvis is finally released by the studio and flies to St. Louis with Gene Smith, where he rents a car to drive to Memphis.

30 Thursday

Arriving at around 3:00 P.M., Elvis spends the evening at home with Vernon, Anita, and Gene Smith and his wife, Louise.

Karate certificate

JULY

03 Sunday

Vernon marries Dee Stanley in Huntsville, Alabama. Elvis does not attend but chooses, instead, to go boating on McKellar Lake at Riverside Park in Memphis.

04 Monday

Elvis visits his mother's grave.

06 Wednesday

During an interview with the *Memphis Press-Scimitar*, Elvis says grudgingly of his new stepmother, "She seems pretty nice," then adds: "I only had one mother and that's it. There'll never be another. As long as she understands that, we won't have any trouble." Of his father Elvis says, "He's all I got left in the world. I'll never go against him or stand in his way. He stood by me all these years and sacrificed things he wanted so I could have clothes and lunch money to go to school." The article will not appear until July 17, when Vernon and Dee's marriage is announced in the press.

07 Thursday

Elvis buys a powder-blue sixteen-

July Record Release

Single: "It's Now or Never" (#1)/"A Mess of Blues" (#32) (shipped July 5). Perhaps Elvis' biggest hit worldwide since "Hound Dog," the record will sell over a million not only in the U.S. but in Britain as well, with over $4.5 million in sales worldwide.

foot waterskiing boat with trailer for $3,000. He continues to rent the Rainbow Rollerdrome and the Memphian Theater almost every day.

10 Sunday

The day is spent waterskiing at McKellar Lake.

11 Monday

Elvis rents the Fairgrounds amusement park after hours for himself, Anita, and various friends, family, employees of Graceland, and others. He spends much of the time on his two

Elvis with Charlie Hodge and Gene Smith at McKellar Lake, Memphis, July 1960

With Bobby Darin and George Burns, Las Vegas, end of July 1960

favorite rides, the Dodgems and the Fairgrounds' celebrated Pippin roller coaster.

21 Thursday

Elvis obtains his first-degree black belt in karate and will carry the certificate in his wallet until his death. From anecdotal evidence it appears as if he gets this certificate at an exhibition put on by Hank Slamansky in Memphis and that it is largely ceremonial.

Before his return to Hollywood to film his new picture for 20th Century

Filming *Flaming Star,* August 1960

Fox, currently titled *Flaming Lance,* Elvis goes to Las Vegas, where he is photographed with Bobby Darin and George Burns, for whom Darin is opening.

AUGUST

01 Monday

Elvis reports to 20th Century Fox at 9:00 A.M. for preproduction work on *Flaming Lance,* the working title for a film that will soon evolve into *Black Star* and eventually be released as *Flaming Star.* Produced by David Weisbart (*Love Me Tender*) and directed by Don Siegel (*Invasion of the Body Snatchers*), this otherwise conventional western is intended as a serious look at the life of a young man caught between the worlds of his Indian mother and his white father.

02 Tuesday

Elvis begins horseback-riding lessons each afternoon for the next two weeks in preparation for the role.

04 Thursday

Elvis is fitted with contact lenses to change his blue eyes to brown for his role as a "half-breed," but in the end he keeps his own natural look.

Bill Bullock thanks Colonel Parker for "get[ting] me off the hook on the recording equipment which was planned for Elvis' home." The Colonel has accepted as a poor token of fealty the cost of automobile rental in California and record players for Elvis to use both at the movie studio and in his home. Bullock asks for a "snow letter" for his files, confirming acceptance of the arrangement.

08 Monday

Four songs for the new picture are recorded at Radio Recorders between 8:00 P.M. and 4:00 A.M. Once again Elvis is embarrassed by the material, requesting through the Colonel that two of the numbers not be released on record. Eventually, a third song, "Summer Kisses, Winter Tears," will be dropped from the picture after the audience at a test screening laughs at its inappropriateness, and the title song is re-recorded when the film title is changed.

12 Friday

In the wake of his marriage to Dee Stanley, Vernon signs a quitclaim deed, assigning Elvis sole ownership of Graceland.

16 Tuesday

Principal photography begins at

Staged fight with Red West *(left),* on location, *Flaming Star*

Conejo Movie Ranch in Thousand Oaks, California. Red West, who is working as Elvis' double, suffers a broken elbow during filming of a fight scene.

17 Wednesday

The Colonel orchestrates a steady stream of visitors to the set, ranging from carefully selected media personalities to a high school delegation from Grosse Point, Michigan, on this particular day.

25 Thursday

Don Cravens photographs Elvis at the Beverly Wilshire Hotel for *Life* magazine, following up with an interview the next day on the set. The Colonel has also commissioned Cravens to take some shots for future record sleeves, including covers for the upcoming single "Are You Lonesome Tonight?" and a gospel album that Elvis plans to record in October, to be called *His Hand in Mine.*

SEPTEMBER

01 Thursday

The picture is retitled *Flaming Star.*

03 Saturday

Elvis purchases a black Rolls Royce Silver Cloud II.

08 Thursday

The Colonel requests that should filming on Elvis' next 20th

With Juliet Prowse and new Rolls Royce at the special screening of *G.I. Blues,* September 12, 1960

Century Fox film, *Wild in the Country,* not be completed by December 23, Elvis at least be permitted to spend Christmas at home.

09 Friday

After a number of disruptive incidents at the Beverly Wilshire, which cause the management to take a dim view of his continued presence, Elvis signs a six-month lease on a house located at 525 Perugia Way in Bel Air, a part of Beverly Hills. The house is owned by Ali Kahn, rent is $1,400 per month, and Elvis will remain here off and on for the next five years.

12 Monday

Elvis and costar Juliet Prowse attend a special theater owners' screening of *G.I. Blues* that Hal Wallis' assistant, Paul Nathan, describes as a "howling success." Also present is gossip columnist Hedda Hopper and the film's choreographer Charlie O'Curran, with his wife, Patti Page.

19 Monday

Once again Elvis complains to the Colonel that RCA has "remixed" (in fact, remastered) the sound on another one of his songs. This time it is the upcoming single "Are You Lonesome Tonight?" on which he feels his voice has been brought up unnecessarily at the expense of the background vocals. He threatens to go back into the studio and re-record the song if they can't get it right.

29 Thursday

Reporter Vernon Scott has a luncheon interview with Elvis on the set. Also visiting today are Vernon Presley and his friends, Mr. and Mrs. Carl Nichols from Memphis, along with twenty-seven-year-old Gary Pepper, a multiple sclerosis victim whom Elvis has befriended and who, as head of the Tankers fan club (formed when Elvis was in the tanker corps), remains in Elvis' circle of Memphis friends until his death.

OCTOBER

04 Tuesday

Principal photography for *Flaming Star* ends, with dubbing completed on Thursday.

07 Friday

Elvis records the new title song, "Flaming Star," at Radio Recorders in an 8:00 to 11:00 P.M. session.

08 Saturday

The group stops off in Las Vegas for a time before returning to Memphis.

16 Sunday

Elvis breaks his finger playing touch football at Graceland. Shortly afterward (you can still see the bandaging on his finger in photographs of the occasion) he is inducted into

Colonel Parker's office at the 20th Century Fox Studios

With Tau Kappa Epsilon fraternity members

Arkansas State College's Tau Kappa Epsilon fraternity in a ceremony at Graceland. Although he originally conceived of it as a publicity stunt, and something of a goof, fraternity president Rick Husky is surprised at how moved Elvis is by the ceremony and convinced of his sincerity when he confides to Husky that he wishes he could have attended college himself. After the presentation Elvis takes the group out to see his new Rolls Royce while also downplaying its significance by telling them the maid had called it "some old black car."

25 Tuesday

Elvis purchases a monkey at Katz Drug Store for $123.55, adding to a menagerie that has included poodles, Pyrenees, peacocks, mynah birds, chickens, pigs, and spider monkeys (going back to Audubon Drive in 1956).

29 Saturday

Freddy Bienstock arrives to go over songs for the upcoming recording session in Nashville, which has been set up to produce Elvis' first full gospel album as well as a single for early 1961 release. For the single Freddy has commissioned songwriters Doc Pomus and Mort Shuman ("A Mess of

Blues") to come up with new lyrics for another classic Neopolitan ballad, "Torna a Surriento," much in the manner of "It's Now or Never."

30 Sunday

After traveling to Nashville by bus, Elvis joins all the regular Nashville musicians and backup singers, along with Charlie Hodge to provide harmony, in RCA's Studio B. Working from 6:30 P.M. to 8:00 A.M. with intense concentration, Elvis completes both the album *His Hand*

Arriving for the RCA recording session in Nashville with security, fans, Joe Esposito *(between couple on right)*, and Charlie Hodge *(far right)*

in Mine and the A-side of his next single, "Surrender" ("Torna a Surriento"). His version of "Crying in the Chapel," originally intended for the album, will not be released for five years because Elvis, who has always loved the Orioles' r & b take on the song, is dissatisfied with his interpretation and feels he can do better.

October Record Release

LP: *G.I. Blues* (#1). This soundtrack album of material for which Elvis has little liking sets a new record for album sales, selling 700,000 copies within just a few months and far surpassing *Elvis Is Back*.

NOVEMBER

01 Tuesday

Forty-six-year-old Memphis police inspector Fred Woodward, who has provided personal security and friendship to Elvis since the beginning of his rise to fame, suffers a fatal heart attack while supervising schoolchildren at an afternoon Memphis Symphony youth concert at Ellis Auditorium. Elvis rushes to St. Joseph's Hospital as soon as he hears the news and, oblivious to the presence of reporters, attempts to comfort the widow. "He was a great guy, a good friend," he says, obviously distraught. "[He] was supposed to come out to my house tonight."

With police captain Fred Woodward in 1956

02 Wednesday

The Colonel reaches an agreement with the Mirisch Brothers production company and United Artists to pay $500,000 plus 50 percent of the profits on each of the pictures in a two-picture deal. (The films will be *Follow That Dream* and *Kid Galahad*.) Hal Wallis has the right to preempt the offer by matching it, but on November 14 he declines, as the Colonel knew he would, because of the expense.

06 Sunday

Elvis has finally persuaded Alan Fortas to rejoin the group, and they all fly to Los Angeles for preproduction on 20th Century Fox's *Wild in the Country*. The new film has a script by playwright Clifford Odets based on the well-received J. R. Salamanca novel *The Lost Country*. It is to be produced by Jerry Wald, directed by Philip Dunne (screenwriter for *How Green Was My Valley* and *The Ghost and Mrs. Muir*), and costars Hope Lange, Tuesday Weld, and Millie Perkins. Although the original idea was to shoot the picture without any music, the plan now is to find five songs that can fit into the dramatic arc of the film.

07 Monday

Elvis reports to Radio Recorders for soundtrack recording at 8:00 P.M., working until 2:30 A.M.

With Tuesday Weld *(left)* and Brenda Lee during the filming of *Wild in the Country*

November Record Releases

Single: "Are You Lonesome Tonight?" (#1)/ "I Gotta Know" (#20) (shipped November 1). As a follow-up to the enormously successful "It's Now or Never," "Are You Lonesome Tonight?" establishes a trend, confirming Elvis as the kind of all-ages performer the Colonel is anxious to convert him into. The single sells over two million copies.

Album: *His Hand in Mine* (#13). The solid success of 1957's *Peace in the Valley*, an EP of spiritual material, is secondary to Elvis' long-standing ambition to make a full album that will stand as a tribute to his faith, serve as a memorial to his mother, and express his love for the music that first motivated him and which he will always love most. The material on this record honors the Blackwood Brothers and the Statesmen in particular, while paying more than a nod to the jubilee style of the Golden Gate Quartet as well.

With Colonel Parker as Santa and costar Hope Lange on the set of *Wild in the Country*

08 Tuesday

Elvis completes the soundtrack in a session between 9:00 and 11:45 A.M. He cuts two different versions of "I Slipped, I Stumbled, I Fell," at the time planned as a single release, each in a different key.

09 Wednesday

Principal photography for *Wild in the Country* begins on location in Napa, California, where the film company stays at the Casa Bellvue-al Motel.

10 Thursday

The Legion of Decency, which scrutinizes films for "questionable" content, reports that *G.I. Blues* is "highly objectionable in its theme and treatment." Like so many humanistic works, in their view it condones and glamorizes "immoral behavior."

15 Tuesday

A special showing of *G.I. Blues* is held in Hollywood as a benefit for the Hemophilia Foundation, but Elvis does not attend.

19 Saturday

Members of the entourage begin to take notice of Elvis' frequent mood swings and occasional eruptions of temper during the shooting of *Wild in the Country*. On a weekend excursion to San Francisco, Elvis pulls a gun on a group of guys in another automobile who he feels have insulted him. His performance in the film seems to betray the amphetamine use that began in the army.

22 Tuesday

Filming of *Wild in the Country* moves to the 20th Century Ranch, fifteen miles north of Santa Monica.

23 Wednesday

G.I. Blues opens across the country. By the following week it will be #2 on *Variety*'s National Box Office Survey and will be the fourteenth-highest-grossing film of the year. Just to give a somewhat comparative perspective on its success, in 1969 *Variety* will report that this somewhat less than $2 million film has grossed $4.3 million in domestic rentals, roughly the equivalent of *The African Queen*.

26 Saturday

Elvis flies to Las Vegas for the weekend with Charlie Hodge, Joe Esposito, Red West, and Alan Fortas.

DECEMBER

04 Sunday

Colonel Parker reads a newspaper article about an attempt to raise funds for a memorial to the USS *Arizona*, which was sunk in the Japanese attack on Pearl Harbor with 1,177 aboard. Seizing upon this as an inspiration, the Colonel immediately begins plans for a benefit concert in Hawaii, which will coincide with the filming of Elvis' next picture, *Blue Hawaii*.

20 Tuesday

The Colonel is in Memphis to announce that Elvis will perform at the Memphis Charity Show on February 25, 1961. Even Elvis will have to buy a ticket to get into Ellis Auditorium's North Hall, according to the Colonel, and, he adds, he will pay the $1,000 fee for celebrated toastmaster George Jessel to appear as master of ceremonies. "I wanted someone who could tell you people in Memphis what Hollywood and the show world think of Elvis," he explains.

22 Thursday

Flaming Star opens across the country. It will appear for only one week, at #12, on the National Box Office Survey.

23 Friday

This is Elvis' last day on the set before flying home for the week off that the Colonel has arranged.

25 Sunday

Elvis spends his first Christmas at Graceland since the death of his mother. This year's card from Elvis and the Colonel, taken on the movie set, shows the Colonel dressed as Santa Claus with Elvis on his lap.

Onstage, Memphis Charity show,
Ellis Auditorium, February 25, 1961,
with D.J. Fontana *(drums left)*,
Bob Moore *(bass)*, and
Buddy Harmon *(drums)*

1961

JANUARY

02 Monday

Elvis flies back to Los Angeles with Sonny, Charlie, Alan, and Gene Smith.

04 Wednesday

Filming resumes on *Wild in the Country*.

06 Friday

There is a birthday party for Elvis on the set. Cast and crew present him with a plaque saying, "Happy Birthday, King Karate."

Hal Wallis agrees to amend Elvis' October 1958 contract, turning it into a five-picture deal, with payments of $175,000 apiece for the first three, $200,000 each for the last two. (The pictures made under this contract are *Blue Hawaii*, *Girls! Girls! Girls!*, *Fun in Acapulco*, *Roustabout*, and *Paradise Hawaiian Style*.)

11 Wednesday

After completing negotiations, the Colonel holds a press conference at the Hawaiian Village Hotel in Honolulu to announce details of Elvis' charity concert. Everyone will pay his own way, including Elvis and the Colonel. "You know, Elvis is twenty-six," he told the assembled press, "and that's about the average age of those boys entombed in the *Arizona*. I think it's appropriate that he should be doing this."

20 Friday

Elvis is released by the studio, principal shooting having been completed three days earlier.

After a week of negotiations, the Colonel reaches agreement with MGM for a four-picture deal at a salary of $400,000 plus $75,000 for expenses and $25,000 for musical expenses per picture. Furthermore, Elvis will receive 50 percent of the

Elvis' birthday cake, with Colonel Parker and the guys, *(left to right)* Lamar Fike, Alan Fortas, Gene Smith, Sonny West, and Joe Esposito, with what appears to be a cardboard cutout of Elvis

profits (and all of Elvis' pictures to date have made a profit) after the first $500,000 is recouped. (Pictures made under this agreement are *It Happened at the World's Fair*, *Viva Las Vegas*, *Kissin' Cousins*, and *Girl Happy*.)

30 Monday

Elvis flies home to Memphis by way of Chicago.

With Sam Phillips at press conference, Hotel Claridge, February 25, 1961

Hal Wallis writes to the Colonel with some serious concerns about Elvis' appearance in the upcoming Hawaiian picture. He wants to make sure that Elvis will "look very much like he did for *G.I. Blues* except he should have a good overall coat of tan on his body as well as his face." Wallis goes on to recommend a particular brand of ultraviolet tanning lamp ("the Hanovia"), then urges the Colonel to make sure to talk to Elvis about his weight and overall physical condition.

FEBRUARY

01 Wednesday

Elvis takes Joe Esposito and Anita Wood to Tupelo to show them his hometown. In the field behind his birthplace they find that the sign declaring this to be the future site of the Elvis Presley Youth Center has fallen down, and no work has been done toward construction of either the building or the swimming pool for which Elvis donated $14,000 from his 1957 Tupelo performance.

04 Saturday

Elvis' cousin, Junior Smith, who has not been right since suffering shell shock in the Korean War, dies of alcohol poisoning in their uncle Travis' home. Elvis' friend from Waco, Eddie Fadal, accompanies Elvis to the house. "He just kept saying, 'It's all over, Junior. It's all over.'"

06 Monday

Elvis cannot attend Junior Smith's funeral because he has been called back to Hollywood to reshoot the ending of *Wild in the Country*. Preview audiences have reacted badly to the suicide of Hope Lange's character.

According to an amendment of Elvis' RCA contract, Elvis will now receive an annual guaranteed payment of $300,000 against royalties, while the Colonel will get $100,000, as called for by their 75-25 split. This is in addition to the $1,000 a week Elvis is still getting according to the terms of his 1956 contract, with the Colonel realizing $4,333.33 quarterly (or $17,333 per year). It probably goes without saying that there is no time when Elvis' royalty advances are not almost astronomically outstripped by sales.

08 Wednesday
Elvis stops at the Skyrider Hotel in Phoenix en route to Los Angeles.

24 Friday
With filming once again completed, Elvis has returned to Memphis, where he holds a rehearsal with Scotty, D.J., the Nashville session players, and the Jordanaires at Graceland for his Memphis charity show.

25 Saturday
Tennessee governor Buford Ellington

February Record Releases

Single: "Surrender"(#1)/"Lonely Man" (#32) (shipped February 7). Elvis' latest adaptation of an Italian standard (from his October session) is coupled with a studio version of a song from *Wild in the Country*. With sales of only 750,000, there is a falling-off of one million from the last single, "Are You Lonesome Tonight?"

EP: *Elvis By Request—Flaming Star* (#14). Spurred by radio broadcast of a bootleg recording of the songs from the movie, RCA creates an aptly named "request" EP. Both Elvis and the Colonel feel the soundtrack material is unsuitable for record release but swallow a healthy dose of reality, agreeing to put out the two best songs from the soundtrack sessions, "Flaming Star" and "Summer Kisses, Winter Tears" with 1960's two smash hits, "It's Now or Never" and "Are You Lonesome Tonight?"

Addressing the Tennessee State Legislature *(courtesy of Joe Tunzi)*

and Memphis mayor Henry Loeb both declare "Elvis Presley Day." At a special luncheon at the Hotel Claridge, Elvis is presented by RCA with a diamond-studded watch to honor record sales of more than 75 million. At the 1:45 P.M. press conference, Sam Phillips asks why Sun Records gets so little recognition for Elvis' success, reminding everyone that "RCA wouldn't have him if it wasn't for Phillips."

★ *Memphis Charity Show, Ellis Auditorium, Memphis, at 3:00 and 8:30 p.m.*

Attendance at the matinee is 3,860, with 6,540 at the second show. Comedian George Jessel introduces Elvis in the evening as "one of the greatest singer-actors of this century," while the *Memphis Commercial Appeal* describes the show as combining elements "from Negro cotton field harmony, camp meeting fervor, Hollywood showmanship, beatnik nonchalance, and some of the manipulations of mass psychology." Overall $51,612 is raised, with $47,823 distributed among twenty-six Memphis charities and $3,789 earmarked for the Elvis Presley Youth Center in Tupelo. After the evening show Elvis holds a party at Graceland.

MARCH

08 Wednesday
Elvis drives his Rolls to Nashville, to be honored by the Tennessee legislature, thanking the lawmakers for the "finest honor [I've] ever received." He adds, to cheers, that he will never abandon his home in Memphis to move to Hollywood.

Accompanied by the governor's daughter, Ann, Elvis gets a private tour of the governor's mansion. On the way back to Memphis, he stops at the Tennessee State Prison to visit Johnny Bragg, lead singer for the Prisonaires, the group that Sam Phillips first recorded at Sun in 1953.

10 Friday
Long before he met Elvis, the Colonel was promoting the idea of a movie on the life of Hank Williams. Now he and MGM are discussing seriously the possibility of Elvis starring in such a film, and the studio agrees to Elvis' getting publishing on any non-Williams songs he might perform. Most likely the Colonel withdraws Elvis' name from consideration when he comes to the belated recognition that

At *Blue Hawaii* recording session with Dudley Brooks
(left) and Charlie O'Curran

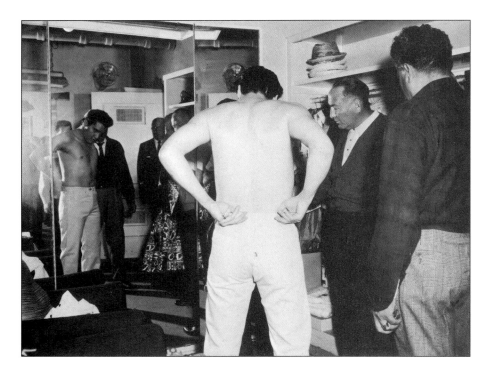

Trying on costumes for *Blue Hawaii*, with Hal
Wallis to Elvis' immediate right

there is no money to be made on the Williams songs at the heart of the picture. Eventually, the film is made as *Your Cheatin' Heart* in 1964, starring one of the Colonel's protégés, George Hamilton, and utilizing both the Colonel's sales plan and the Colonel himself for promotion.

11 Saturday

Back in Memphis Elvis goes for a ride in a Piper Comanche airplane, circling over Graceland and even briefly taking the controls.

12 Sunday

Elvis travels by bus to RCA's Studio B in Nashville, where, in just over eleven hours (6:00 P.M. to 5:15 A.M.), he records eleven songs for an album and one song, Chuck Willis' "I Feel So Bad," for a new single. While the material is less striking on the whole than last year's *Elvis Is Back*, the pop sound that Elvis is aiming for is perfectly realized by the band, and Elvis' voice is at its peak as an interpretive instrument, particularly on Don Robertson's beautiful ballads.

14 Tuesday

RCA's Bill Bullock writes to tell Elvis how pleased he is with the recent recording session and reintroduces the idea of building a studio for Elvis at Graceland, in hopes no doubt of coaxing more product from a star who, on his manager's advice, is increasingly reluctant to enter the recording studio save for soundtrack sessions. Once again the project fails to materialize.

18 Saturday

On a layover in Chicago on the way to Los Angeles, Elvis stays at the O'Hare Inn near the airport.

20 Monday

Elvis reports to the Paramount studio to begin work on *Blue Hawaii*. The director of the new Hal Wallis picture will be *G.I. Blues* director Norman Taurog, and it will costar thirty-five-year-

Bloch Arena, Honolulu, March 25, 1961
(courtesy of Joe Tunzi)

23 Thursday

Soundtrack recording at Radio Recorders runs from 1:00 to 5:22 P.M.

25 Saturday

Elvis flies to Honolulu, arriving at 12:15 P.M. with country comedian Minnie Pearl, a longtime Opry stalwart, who is booked to appear on the benefit show. After watching the way in which Elvis is mobbed, a frightened Minnie Pearl tells him: "Those women could kill you," but Elvis expresses confidence that "they're not going to hurt me." There is a press conference at 3:30 P.M. in the Carousel Room at the Hawaiian Village Hotel at which not just the two Honolulu dailies but twenty-seven Oahu high schools and middle schools

old Angela Lansbury as Elvis' mother. After preproduction meetings, Elvis goes to Radio Recorders to rehearse with the band.

21 Tuesday

Blue Hawaii soundtrack recording begins at Radio Recorders from 1:00 to 11:50 P.M. In three days fifteen songs will be completed, including the classic "Can't Help Falling in Love." One song, "Steppin' Out of Line," will be cut from the film, although it will be released the following year on the album *Pot Luck*. The usual Nashville and Los Angeles session players are joined this time by percussionist Hal Blaine, as well as steel guitar and ukuleles to help create a Hawaiian sound.

22 Wednesday

Soundtrack recording at Radio Recorders continues from 1:00 to 10:20 P.M.

With Snowmen on the set of *Blue Hawaii*, spring 1961, *(left to right)* Colonel Parker, Joe Esposito, Gene Smith, Charlie Hodge, Cliff Gleaves, Red West, and Richard Davis are represented. "Elvis answered questions with a matter-of-fact mumble," the *Sunday Advertiser* reported. "Colonel Tom Parker, his manager, supplied the punch lines that brought laughter and applause from the students."

★ *Bloch Arena, Honolulu*

The show raises over $62,000 toward building a memorial for the entombed sailors of the USS *Arizona*. Crude recordings of the show reveal a joyfully uninhibited Elvis, energized by both his performance and that of the band (the Nashville session players and the Jordanaires), which has now had the opportunity to work with him consistently for a full month, both live and in the studio, and clearly benefits from the experience.

27 Monday

Principal photography for *Blue Hawaii* begins on location in Hawaii and continues for three weeks.

The Colonel remains an imperturbable contributor to high jinks on the set, hypnotizing the guys one day for Hal Wallis, halting shooting on another when he insists on extra payment from Wallis because of a provision in Elvis' contract guaranteeing $10,000 if the star supplies his own wardrobe. When Wallis expresses confusion as to what wardrobe Elvis can have supplied (since he is wearing nothing but a bathing suit), the Colonel points to his wristwatch.

The Colonel is always on the lookout for new recruits to his own phantom organization, the Snowmen's League of America, dedicated to the fine art of "snowing," or putting the other person on (*con brio*), an organization that costs nothing to get into and $10,000 to get out of. The Colonel promotes even his mock promotions in elaborate and resourceful ways.

APRIL

05 Wednesday

While Elvis is away, extensive renovations are completed at Graceland on the living room, dining room,

kitchen, and Elvis' bedroom, with upstairs and basement stairways fitted with mirrors and Elvis' dressing room decked out with padded walls and gold carpeting. Total cost comes to $5,340.66.

17 Monday

Location shooting in Hawaii ends.

20 Thursday

Cast and crew return to Hollywood, where filming continues at Paramount.

22 Saturday

After the completion of their two highly publicized fund-raising events, the Colonel writes to newly inaugurated vice president Lyndon Johnson announcing his and Elvis' availability for future patriotic projects, whether "to use our talents or help load the trucks." On May 6 Johnson sends a congratulatory return note, thanking Elvis and the Colonel for the fine work they did raising money for the USS *Arizona* memorial.

MAY

01 Monday

Sometime during May or June, Colonel Parker's older brother, Ad, visits from Holland, staying in the Colonel's apartment for seventeen days. His trip has been financed by the Dutch magazine *Rosita*, where the Colonel's family had recognized a picture of their long-lost brother the previous spring. Parker introduces a number of his colleagues to Ad; to some he even mentions that he has a brother visiting him. But none gets even a hint of the Colonel's Dutch background, and Ad is smart enough to keep his mouth shut. Ad's visit is the basis for a series of articles in *Rosita* revealing much of the Colonel's true origins, but for some reason this story is not picked up in the States for twenty years, though it is common knowledge among Elvis' Dutch fans.

05 Friday

Colonel Parker and RCA maintain their long-standing dispute over what songs should go on Elvis' next single and when the record should be released. In this case, the Colonel wants to pair the title song of *Wild in the Country* with another soundtrack item, "I Slipped, I Stumbled, I Fell." Bill Bullock holds out for a non-soundtrack number as the B-side, and Elvis resolves the issue by picking "I Feel So Bad" from the last (non-soundtrack) Nashville session. The Colonel is philosophical about the outcome. "I don't pick the tunes," he says. "Elvis does."

23 Tuesday

Principal photography for *Blue Hawaii* ends, and publicity stills are shot as well, with dubbing scheduled for the next two days.

May Record Release

Single: "I Feel So Bad"(#5)/"Wild in the Country" (#26) (shipped May 2). What was originally intended as the B-side becomes the hit, with the single selling more than 600,000 copies.

JUNE

01 Thursday

Elvis flies home to Memphis.

08 Thursday

Elvis buys a twenty-one-foot Coronado waterskiing boat powered with a 325-horsepower Cadillac Crusader engine and a boat trailer for $9,205.

15 Thursday

Wild in the Country premieres in Memphis, but Elvis does not attend.

22 Thursday

Wild in the Country opens across the country.

25 Sunday

Elvis arrives at RCA's Studio B in Nashville to cut new singles material. The session starts, however, with

With Vernon on location, *Follow That Dream*

three songs that will end up on 1962's *Pot Luck* album, including the first song to which Elvis has ever intentionally put his name as author. "That's Someone You Never Forget" is actually written by Red West from a title suggestion by Elvis that carries a good deal of emotional weight, though the someone is never named. Two Doc Pomus–Mort Shuman songs, "(Marie's the Name) His Latest Flame" and "Little Sister," round out the session in the early-morning hours and will be released as the next single in a little more than a month.

30 Friday

Elvis throws a party the night before Red West's marriage to Elvis' secretary, Pat Boyd.

June Record Release

LP: *Something for Everybody* (#1). Once again, with sales of 300,000 copies, a nonsoundtrack album does not achieve anywhere near the sales of what the *G.I. Blues* soundtrack has already sold or what *Blue Hawaii* will.

JULY

01 Saturday

Elvis is so late to Red West's wedding that Joe Esposito has to replace

him as best man. In the early-morning hours after the reception, the group heads out to the Fairgrounds to ride the Pippin and crash into each other on the Dodgems.

02 Sunday

Elvis travels to Nashville to record six songs for the soundtrack for his upcoming Mirisch Bothers movie, currently called *Pioneer, Go Home* but soon to be retitled *Follow That Dream*. One of the songs, "A Whistling Tune," will be dropped from the picture and re-recorded for the next; another, "Sound Advice," is left off the soundtrack EP because Elvis has so little liking for it. After the session is over, Elvis checks into the Anchor Hotel in Nashville before returning to Memphis.

06 Thursday

Elvis arrives in a chartered bus at

On location, *Follow That Dream*, summer 1961

the Port Paradise Hotel in Crystal River, Florida, for the start of filming. The new movie will be produced by *Love Me Tender* producer David Weisbart and directed by Gordon Douglas. Elvis' nineteen-year-old cousin, Billy Smith, accompanies him for the first time on the road, as does the usual entourage and new group member Ray "Chief" Sitton. Alan Fortas and Lamar Fike follow the bus in Elvis' Cadillac limousine, towing his new waterskiing boat behind them.

11 Tuesday

Principal photography for *Follow That Dream* begins.

30 Sunday

In what might well be deemed an extension of Snowmen's League business, the Colonel arranges for a special ceremony honoring Elvis for his achievements in show business at an event in Weeki Wachee Springs, Florida, where the newly convened Elvis Presley Underwater Fan Club puts on a show for the assembled multitudes.

AUGUST

11 Friday

Location filming in Florida for *Follow That Dream* ends.

12 Saturday

Elvis flies from Tampa to Los Angeles.

14 Monday

Filming resumes in Hollywood.

23 Wednesday

Elvis is offered $250,000 for two days' work as the voice (speaking and

---

August Record Release

Single: "(Marie's the Name) His Latest Flame"(#4)/"Little Sister"(#5) (shipped August 8). Sales of 700,000 are a considerable improvement over the May single release, as are the songs.

---

singing) of John Tom, a tomcat in an animated feature tentatively titled *Gay Purr-ee*. After a typically contentious exchange with Hal Wallis' partner, Joe Hazen, about whether Elvis is contractually permitted to appear in a cartoon without Paramount's permission, the Colonel heeds what has undoubtedly been his inclination all along and turns down the offer.

28 Monday

Principal photography for *Follow That Dream* is completed.

SEPTEMBER

01 Friday

Elvis spends much of September in Las Vegas catching lounge acts like Fats Domino, Della Reese, Jackie Wilson, the Dominoes, and the Four Aces.

19 Tuesday

Elvis is back home in Memphis and signs for a new Schimmel piano and organ from Jack Marshall Pianos and Organs. On September 26 a new Allen organette with mandolin repeat is delivered to Graceland from the same firm and is signed for by Vernon with the note "This is with the understanding that Elvis has endorsed purchase."

26 Tuesday

Hank Snow sues his erstwhile partner, Colonel Tom Parker, for his part of Elvis' earnings. For reasons that remain unexplained, the suit never goes anywhere.

OCTOBER

15 Sunday

After several weeks in Las Vegas, Elvis has returned to Memphis before traveling to Nashville to record five songs at RCA's Studio B between 6:00 P.M. and 4:00 A.M. Guitarist Hank Garland has been seriously injured in a car accident in September and is replaced by Jerry Kennedy on guitar. The focus once again is to produce a new single, this time "Good Luck Charm" and "Anything That's Part of You."

---

21 Saturday

Elvis flies to Los Angeles with Joe Esposito, Charlie Hodge, and Billy Smith, while Ray Sitton and several other of the guys drive the cars out. Just before leaving, Elvis hires old friend Marty Lacker, who originally came into the circle through George Klein.

Another new addition is Scatter, a chimpanzee Elvis has obtained from Memphis TV personality Captain Bill Killebrew. The monkey has been trained to "drive a car"—or at least give that appearance—and Alan Fortas takes him under his wing. Elvis and the guys are captivated by Scatter's escapades, though some of the girls whom Scatter assaults and Samuel Goldwyn, whose office Scatter tears apart, are not. Scatter is actually on consignment until his formal purchase on November 28. Eventually he has to be boarded with a veterinarian and then returned to Graceland, where it is rumored that he is poisoned some time later by a maid after a finger-biting episode.

23 Monday

Elvis reports to United Artists for preproduction of his second Mirisch Brothers film, *Kid Galahad*, meeting with producer David Weisbart and director Phil Karlson. After appointments with wardrobe and makeup, Elvis has his cast insurance medical exam and then starts workouts with former world welterweight champion Mushy Callahan, for his boxer role in a film costarring Charles Bronson.

24 Tuesday

Elvis attends a music meeting, then is introduced to the fighters who will appear in the film so that one can be selected as Elvis' double.

October Record Release

LP: *Blue Hawaii* (#1). Elvis' biggest album seller during his lifetime, with two million copies in the first twelve months alone.

25 Wednesday

Elvis completes dubbing for *Follow That Dream* and in the afternoon attends another music meeting for *Kid Galahad*.

26 Thursday

Elvis begins recording the six songs for the *Kid Galahad* soundtrack at Radio Recorders, working from 6:00 P.M. to 4:25 A.M.

27 Friday

Recording at Radio Recorders continues from 4:00 to 8:00 P.M.

NOVEMBER

02 Thursday

Elvis has a script meeting for *Kid Galahad* on location at Hidden Lodge in Idyllwild, California.

04 Saturday

Principal photography begins.

21 Tuesday

A snowstorm causes filming to be moved back to the Hollywood lot.

22 Wednesday

Elvis moves out of the Perugia Way house to a new rental just around the corner at 10539 Bellagio Road. The entourage is currently made up of Joe Esposito, Gene Smith, Lamar Fike, Ray "Chief" Sitton, Marty Lacker, and Sonny West, who is working as a stuntman on the film. Both Charlie Hodge and Red West are still part of the picture, but Charlie has gone to work for country singer Jimmy Wakely and Red is continuing to seek outside work and establish his own independence in Hollywood.

Blue Hawaii opens nationally. The picture appears on *Variety*'s National Box Office Survey for four weeks, peaking at #2, and will be the eighteenth-highest-grossing picture of 1961, easily recouping its $2 million cost. It will be the fourteenth-highest-grossing picture of 1962 as well, and by 1969 domestic rentals will reach $4.7 million, roughly equal to those of *Gunfight at the O.K. Corral.*

November Record Release

Single: "Can't Help Falling in Love"(#2)/ "Rock-A-Hula Baby"(#23) (shipped November 21). These two songs from the *Blue Hawaii* soundtrack come out as a single one month after the album. This represents a substantial concession on the part of the Colonel, who firmly believes that all singles should be released four to six weeks prior to album release. In deference to the Colonel's views, RCA agrees to guarantee Elvis and the Colonel royalties on one million copies, regardless of actual sales —though, as it turns out, sales will surpass a million.

DECEMBER

02 Saturday

Elvis' automobile insurance form for this date gives a good idea of his all-terrain mobility. It includes a 1962 Chrysler New Yorker station wagon; the 1955 Cadillac 60 four-door sedan (this is the pink Cadillac); the 1950 Chevy one-ton truck in which Elvis likes to drive anonymously around Memphis; a 1958 Harley-Davidson; a 1960 Jeep; the 1960 Cadillac four-door sedan; the 1956 Lincoln two-door and 1960 Rolls Royce; and a 1962 Mercury Comet four-door station wagon.

20 Wednesday

Principal photography on *Kid Galahad* is completed.

22 Friday

With no particular desire to return to Graceland while his father is still residing there with his new wife and her three boys (Vernon has just bought a house on Hermitage, around the corner), Elvis travels to Las Vegas, staying at the Sahara through the holidays.

28 Thursday

Vernon and his family move into their new home at 3650 Hermitage Drive.

Elvis' 1961 income consists of $902,610 from movies and $775,078 from music publishing and recording.

1962

JANUARY

03 Wednesday

The Colonel has worked out a new contract with RCA permitting the company to release either two singles or two EPs from previously released material in addition to their regular four singles and two LPs per year. RCA at this point pays off the remainder of the $1,000-per-week guarantee spelled out in 1956 for the duration of the contract (Elvis receives a lump sum of $259,995, the Colonel $86,665), substituting new non-returnable payments adding up to $150,000 and $50,000 annually. This appears to be in addition to the $400,000 combined annual payments contracted for the previous year (these are not designated "nonreturnable"). For the first time the RCA contract spells out a new arrangement between Elvis and the Colonel in which payments for all special side deals (that is, deals outside the 5 percent royalty paid for everything released by regular contractual arrangement) will be split 50-50 between the star and his manager. Elvis formally acknowledges his acceptance of this new arrangement with his signature on a line marked "Accepted and Agreed To," evidently embracing the Colonel's argument that they are engaged in what amounts to a "joint venture" on these specially arranged deals. In addition, RCA increases the three-fourths of 1 percent royalty that has been going to the Colonel for "exploitation" to a full 1 percent, to be split 50-50 between Elvis and his manager. The contract period extends through 1966.

08 Monday

Elvis celebrates his twenty-seventh birthday at the Sahara in Las Vegas, with a cake supplied by Milton Prell, the casino's owner and a friend of Colonel Parker's.

Elvis' twenty-seventh birthday, in Las Vegas, with Sahara owner Milton Prell, January 8, 1962

10 Wednesday

The IRS has begun to look into Elvis' 1955–1960 tax returns, questioning how the law applies to Elvis' various contracts with RCA, the movie companies, Sun Records, the Louisiana Hayride, etc., but assuring Elvis' accountants that they see no evidence of intentional avoidance of tax payments. Perhaps the largest issue raised has to do with the designation of large, unaccounted-for sums as "expenses" rather than salary in most of the movie contracts. Various plans are contemplated to deal with other potential problems, but ultimately the matter is resolved with few serious consequences other than the eventual elimination of $50,000–$150,000 "expense" designations in the studio contracts.

29 Monday

From Las Vegas Elvis travels to Lake Tahoe, staying one night at Del Webb's Sahara Tahoe before returning to Los Angeles.

30 Tuesday

Elvis flies home to Memphis through Chicago.

FEBRUARY

14 Wednesday

While home, Elvis frequently screens motion pictures, both current and historic, in Graceland's basement TV room on a 16mm projector supplied by RCA. Prints of films ordered this week by mail include *God Is My Co-Pilot*, *High Noon*, *The Inspector General*, *Las Vegas Shakedown*, Don Siegel's 1954 *Riot in Cellblock Eleven*, and *The Wayward Wife*.

February Record Release

Single: "Good Luck Charm" (#1)/"Anything That's Part of You" (#31) (shipped February 27). The A-side reinstates Elvis at the top of the singles charts for the first time since "Surrender" one year before. But sales of less than a million represent a drop from the 1.2 million copies sold on the last single, "Can't Help Falling in Love."

MARCH

03 Saturday

On this day, the next, and all through the following week, Elvis makes trips to Lansky's (Lansky Brothers' Men's Shop) on

---

Beale, where he has bought clothes since he was in high school. In a similar demonstration of unchanging loyalties, he frequently eats at Chenault's Drive-In or orders take-out food from the modest restaurant that he has been patronizing for almost as long.

12 Monday

Elvis purchases a 1962 Dodge House Car complete with double bed, two bunks, air-conditioning, and full kitchen for $10,541.21. This is the way he plans to drive back and forth to California from now on.

With Scatter on the set of *Girls! Girls! Girls!*, spring 1962

14 Wednesday

From jeweler Harry Levitch Elvis purchases various items, including a handmade fourteen-karat yellow gold diamond tie tack.

18 Sunday

Elvis records seven sides at RCA's Studio B in Nashville from 7:30 P.M. to 6:30 A.M. for the album *Pot Luck*. Guitarists Grady Martin and Harold Bradley replace Jerry Kennedy in the studio band. Elvis also records "You'll Be Gone," another song he has cowritten with Red West, which was originally set to the melody of Cole Porter's "Begin the Beguine." When Porter's publisher refuses to grant them permission, they enlist Charlie Hodge to come up with a simple Spanish-tinged melody line.

19 Monday

Elvis stays over at the Anchor Hotel in Nashville, then records four more songs between 7:30 P.M. and 2:00 A.M., including the A-side of his upcoming single, the beautiful ballad "She's Not You."

20 Tuesday

Elvis leaves for Los Angeles in his new Dodge motor home, which he plans to have customized by George Barris, Los Angeles' "Customizer to the Stars," who has already provided the same service for Elvis' 1960 Cadillac limousine. The drive to California takes the group west on Route 40 through Little Rock, Oklahoma City, Amarillo, Albuquerque, Flagstaff, and into southern California, where they pick up Route 10 into Los Angeles.

22 Thursday

The Colonel informs Bill Bullock at RCA that according to established practice Elvis will select the twelve songs for his next album. The Colonel also reiterates his standard policy that no credits are to appear on the record, despite pressure from some of the Nashville musicians. He feels that to do so would invite the naming of the entire entourage, the engineers, the janitors, the police detail outside the studio, and even "Krystal Castle" for supplying the take-out hamburgers. He concludes that there would be no room for himself or Tom Diskin—or even for Elvis, who, the Colonel declares, is the real producer.

26 Monday

Elvis reports to Paramount for pre-production of the new Hal Wallis picture, *Girls! Girls! Girls!* The success of *Blue Hawaii* has underscored Wallis' determination to promote Elvis the entertainer over Elvis the rebel actor, and to showcase him in pictures that provide wholesome, all-ages fun and good times. Toward that end, *Blue Hawaii* director Norman Taurog is once again put in charge.

Soundtrack recording sessions begin at Radio Recorders and run from 11:00 A.M. until after midnight. Over three days, fifteen songs are recorded, including Otis Blackwell's "Return to Sender." This song was not written for the film, but as soon as the Colonel hears it, he promises Blackwell to get it in the picture because it is so well suited to Elvis' style.

27 Tuesday

Elvis is examined by the studio doctor in the morning for cast insurance, then works on the soundtrack at Radio Recorders from 1:00 P.M. to 12:30 A.M.

28 Wednesday

Elvis continues recording from 1:00 P.M. to 1:40 A.M.

Arriving in Hawaii with Colonel Parker to film *Girls! Girls! Girls!*, April 7, 1962

APRIL

03 Tuesday

To accommodate Elvis' insistence on traveling to Hawaii not by plane but by ship, the scheduled start of the picture is delayed. At the last minute Elvis is forced to fly because of a strike but uses the intervening time to drive to Las Vegas, where he stays at the Sahara.

06 Friday

Elvis returns to Los Angeles.

07 Saturday

At 9:00 A.M. Elvis, Joe Esposito, Ray "Chief" Sitton, Gene Smith, Alan Fortas, and Red West, along with Vernon and Dee Presley, board Pan Am flight #817 to Honolulu. The Colonel, already in Hawaii, has arranged for Elvis to take a helicopter from airport to hotel, where

On location, *Girls! Girls! Girls!*, April 1962

With Colonel Parker and *(left to right)* Tom Diskin, Billy Smith, Joe Esposito, Ray "Chief" Sitton, Alan Fortas, and Gene Smith on the set of *Girls! Girls! Girls!*, spring 1962

With cameraman on the set of *Girls! Girls! Girls!*, spring 1962

27 Sunday

Many Sundays in Hollywood, Elvis and the guys play football at De Neve Park, near his home, with actors Ty Hardin and Bob Conrad, musicians Ricky Nelson and Pat Boone, Gary Crosby, and Max Baer Jr., among others. Elvis' team is suspiciously invincible.

JUNE

01 Friday

The Colonel informs Hal Wallis that he has some reluctance about taking Elvis to Mexico for filming because of the false rumor that first surfaced in 1958 that Elvis has a disparaging view of Mexican women.

"the snow jobs will be set up." Eight thousand screaming fans are on hand to greet the star, and he loses his yachting cap, his diamond ring, and his jeweled tie clasp in the one-hundred-yard walk from the helicopter to the door of the Hawaiian Village Hotel, where he stays on the fourteenth floor.

09 Monday

Principal photography for *Girls! Girls! Girls!* begins. Each morning Elvis' wardrobe is brought to the hotel before he is driven to the set for makeup. During filming Elvis practices karate in his hotel suite, breaking as many as forty boards a night, until finally Hal Wallis puts a stop to the practice for fear his star will break his hand.

April Record Release

EP: *Follow That Dream* (#15). Although the EP market is starting to fade, this soundtrack EP sells half a million copies.

---

26 Thursday

Location filming in Hawaii is completed.

MAY

01 Tuesday

Filming for *Girls! Girls! Girls!* resumes at Paramount Studio on Stage 5.

Hal Wallis begins developing the story idea for his next film with Elvis. Inspired by a travel magazine article about the cliff divers of Acapulco, Mexico, Wallis, together with writer Allan Weiss, dreams up a scenario in which Elvis will play an entertainer or boat captain befriended by a native boy, who takes him up and manages him in the manner of a very junior Colonel Parker.

23 Wednesday

Follow That Dream opens nationally, appearing on *Variety*'s National Box Office Survey for two weeks and peaking at #5.

03 Sunday

Elvis donates a second wallaby given to him by Australian fans to the Memphis Zoo (the first was presented in 1957).

06 Wednesday

The William Morris Agency informs Hal Wallis that Elvis' name has been used without authorization in an advertisement for Coppertone suntan lotion placed in the June issue of the *Ladies' Home Journal* in connection with the film *Girls! Girls! Girls!* The Colonel forces Wallis to put a stop to the advertising campaign.

08 Friday

Principal photography for *Girls! Girls! Girls!* is completed.

11 Monday

Elvis finishes looping for the film. Sometime this week Lamar leaves the group after a blowup with Elvis. He briefly becomes road manager for Brenda Lee, a classmate of Sandy Ferra at the Hollywood Professional School, but before long moves to Nashville, where he secures a position with song publisher Hill and Range through Elvis' intervention.

12 Tuesday

Elvis poses for publicity stills for the picture. The Colonel refuses extra payment for the two days the film has run over schedule, because, he says, Elvis is at fault for his initial refusal to fly to Hawaii. A payment check is issued by the studio but never cashed.

17 Sunday

Priscilla Beaulieu arrives from Germany on the weekend for a two-week visit. After lengthy negotiations Elvis has convinced her parents to allow her to fly to Los Angeles, where he assures them she will be well chaperoned in the Griffith Park home of Kustom King George Barris and his wife.

19 Tuesday

After a very brief visit with the Barrises, Priscilla has moved into 10539 Bellagio Road for approximately one day before Elvis decides to show her Las Vegas. They travel with the guys in the newly customized motor home and stay at the Sahara for the next twelve days.

June Record Release

Album: *Pot Luck* (#4) (shipped June 5). Because there are not enough songs in the movie *Follow That Dream* to fill an album, the Colonel suggests taking material from the March sessions in Nashville and combining it with four cuts recorded the previous year, along with "Steppin' Out of Line," an unreleased song from *Blue Hawaii*. The aptly named *Pot Luck* sells approximately 300,000 units, about the same as *Elvis Is Back* and *Something For Everybody*.

JULY

01 Sunday

After checking out of the Sahara, Elvis and Priscilla return to Los Angeles, where she takes a tearful flight

back to Germany while Elvis prepares to drive home to Memphis.

10 Tuesday

Elvis arrives at Graceland.

12 Thursday

Elvis borrows $134,000, using Graceland as collateral, in order to purchase the land directly across Highway 51 from the Graceland Christian Church next to his home, where Elvis' airplane, the *Lisa Marie*, and the parking lot for visitors are currently located.

13 Friday

Marty Lacker leaves Elvis to begin a job at Memphis radio station WHBQ.

15 Sunday

Elvis rents out the Fairgrounds for family and friends.

19 Thursday

Elvis is at the Fairgrounds once again and will continue to return there at least three or four nights a week the entire time he is at home. The bill for the night at the Albert D. Parker Cosy Dog concession stand includes 212 "Cosy Dogs" and 403 Cokes.

20 Friday

According to the British fan magazine *Elvis Monthly*, another typical day in Memphis consists of touch football ending at 8:00 P.M., a meatball sandwich at an Italian sub shop, and a screening of *West Side Story* that Elvis attends at the Memphian Theater in a royal-blue suit, with the night coming to an end in the dawn hours at the Fairgrounds.

July Record Release

Single: "She's Not You"(#5)/"Just Tell Her Jim Said Hello" (#55) (shipped July 17). Hill and Range representative Freddy Bienstock is convinced that "Just Tell Her Jim Said Hello" is the hit, but the figures prove him wrong, as he cheerfully admits. Despite diminished chart placement, the record does almost as well as "Good Luck Charm," with sales of 800,000.

---

22 Sunday

According to another contemporaneous fan account, Elvis has the Memphian projectionist replay his favorite scene from *West Side Story*, in which the Jets and the Sharks confront one other in a dance sequence to the song "Cool."

AUGUST

06 Monday

Anita Wood announces in the *Memphis Press-Scimitar* that she and Elvis have broken up. She has moved out of Graceland and returned home to Jackson, Tennessee, because, she says, it is evident that Elvis is not yet ready to settle down.

28 Tuesday

Returning to Hollywood, Elvis reports for preproduction on *It Happened at the World's Fair*, the first movie in his new four-picture deal with MGM. MGM producer Ted Richmond conscientiously pursues the same formula as Hal Wallis, selecting a colorful location (the Seattle World's Fair) and even employing Elvis' favorite director, Norman Taurog.

29 Wednesday

Kid Galahad opens across the country. It appears for one week on *Variety*'s Box Office chart at #9 and will be ranked #37 for the year, grossing $1.75 million.

30 Thursday

Because Elvis has caught a cold, there is a considerable amount of concern at MGM that the start of shooting will be delayed. Soundtrack recording begins at 7:00 P.M. at Radio Recorders but is canceled after only a

---

August Record Release

EP: *Kid Galahad* (#30 on the singles chart) (shipped August 28). A special six-song movie soundtrack EP, the record sells 400,000 copies, a hundred thousand less than the *Follow That Dream* EP.

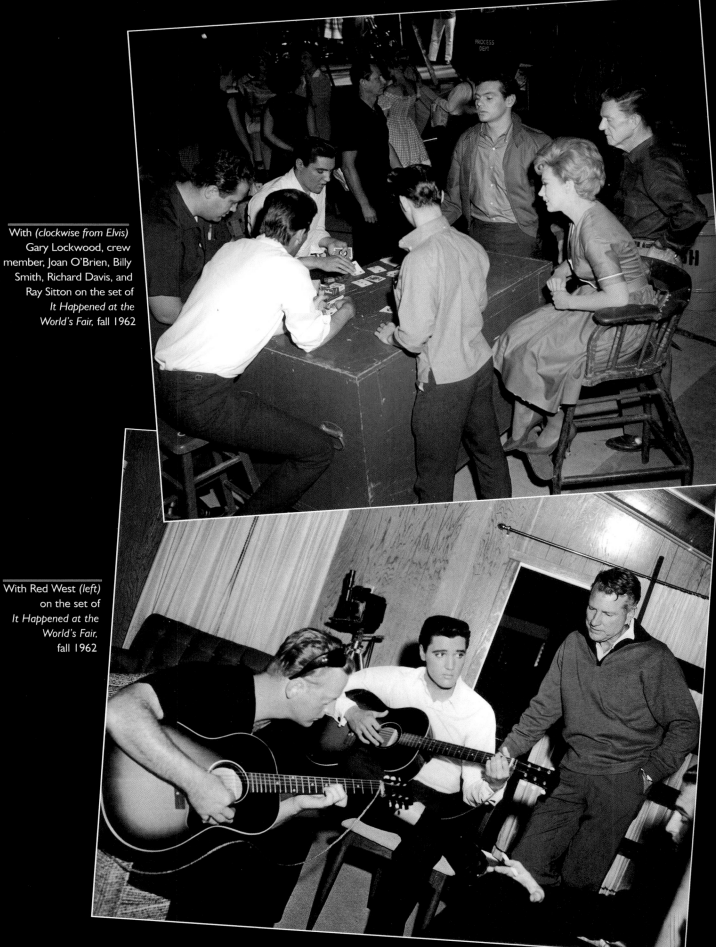

With *(clockwise from Elvis)* Gary Lockwood, crew member, Joan O'Brien, Billy Smith, Richard Davis, and Ray Sitton on the set of *It Happened at the World's Fair*, fall 1962

With Red West *(left)* on the set of *It Happened at the World's Fair*, fall 1962

few hours when it becomes evident that Elvis is having difficulty singing.

The Colonel renegotiates amendments to an RCA contract that has already been substantially upgraded in January. In two special deals, which by definition are split 50-50 between Elvis and the Colonel, the two principals will have their extra nonrecoupable 1 percent royalty on all domestic sales increased to 2 percent (above the regular recoupable 5 percent). In addition, RCA will now make a special bonus payment of $100,000 per year for three years, also not to be charged against royalties. Beginning in 1965, the bonus payment will be reduced to $75,000 per year. The contract period is extended to December 31, 1969, with an option for two additional years.

31 Friday

Elvis reports to wardrobe fitting at MGM. In an AP interview two weeks later, Hollywood couturier Sy Devore reports that Elvis' wardrobe for the movie costs $9,300 and includes ten suits, two cashmere coats, and fifty-five ties, but no underwear because "Elvis, I discovered, doesn't wear any."

SEPTEMBER

04 Tuesday

Elvis arrives in Seattle for location shooting, checking into a fourteenth-floor suite at the Doric New Washington Hotel. He is accompanied by Gene and Billy Smith, Alan Fortas, Red West, Ray Sitton, and Joe Esposito. Memphis friends Richard Davis and Jimmy Kingsley, who showed up at Bellagio the previous day while on vacation from their Memphis jobs, are invited to come along as extra "security" and by the end of their stay are regular members of the group.

05 Wednesday

Principal photography begins at the Monorail terminal of the Seattle World's Fair. In one scene in this pic-

Colonel Parker works on layout, fall 1962

ture a child actor named Kurt Russell comes up to Elvis and kicks him in the shin.

13 Thursday

On the final day of location filming, Elvis presents a ceremonial gift of two Tennessee hams from Tennessee governor Buford Ellington to Washington governor Albert Rosellini and the head of the World's Fair, before the troupe returns to Hollywood.

Once the group is back in L.A., cots and bedding are rented for Richard Davis and Jimmy Kingsley so they can move into Elvis' Bellagio home.

17 Monday

Filming resumes at MGM Studios in Hollywood.

In a lengthy interview with Lloyd Shearer on the set some time over the next few weeks, Elvis speaks of the friends with whom he has chosen to associate, saying that it's "important to surround yourself with people who can give you a little happiness." He also speaks of his interest in studying philosophy and mentions that he would have liked to become a doctor and often reads medical texts. He says that he is hesitant to make any major changes in his career ("If I can entertain people with things I'm doing—well, I'd be a fool to tamper with it"), but at the same time expresses an interest in exploring new directions.

22 Saturday

Elvis is at Radio Recorders from 11:30 A.M. to 11:00 P.M. to complete soundtrack recording for It Happened at the World's Fair. Songwriter Don Robertson, the author of some of Elvis' best and most eloquent ballads, is invited to play at the session, alternating on piano and organ.

With the guys in uniform on the set of *It Happened at the World's Fair, (left to right)* Jimmy Kingsley, Gene Smith, Billy Smith, Alan Fortas, and Joe Esposito

OCTOBER

Elvis continues filming of *It Happened at the World's Fair* through the month.

October Record Release

Single: "Return to Sender"(#2)/"Where Do You Come From"(#99) (shipped October 2). Spearheading the *Girls! Girls! Girls!* movie and movie soundtrack release, Otis Blackwell's catchy "Return to Sender" sells well over a million copies, rivaling "Are You Lonesome Tonight?" as Elvis' top seller of the 1960s.

NOVEMBER

08 Thursday

Vernon Presley accompanies Memphis mayor Loeb to the set, where the mayor officially accepts Elvis' donation of $50,000 to combined Memphis charities.

09 Friday

Elvis concludes work on *It Happened at the World's Fair* with publicity stills, then travels to Las Vegas, where he catches Johnnie Ray at the Hacienda, among many other favorite acts.

21 Wednesday

Girls! Girls! Girls! opens nationwide, appearing for three weeks on *Variety*'s National Box Office Survey, where it peaks at #6. *Variety* ranks it #31 for 1962 with a domestic gross of $2.6 million, but by the beginning of 1964 profits will have reached only $30,000.

November Record Release

LP: *Girls! Girls! Girls!* (#3) (shipped November 9). After the enormous success of the *Blue Hawaii* soundtrack, this new thirteen-song Hal Wallis movie album is somewhat of a disappointment, with sales of less than 600,000 copies.

For the year 1962 Elvis will have three of the fifty top-grossing films. The others are *Blue Hawaii* at #14 and *Kid Galahad* at #37.

29 Thursday

Back in Memphis Elvis has more than a month off, owing to a change in personal appearance plans. In combination with RCA, the Colonel has been working on a giant forty-three-city tour, which he bills as "The Biggest Tour Ever" and for which RCA, as promoter, will guarantee Elvis more than $1 million. RCA, however, gets cold feet, proposing that the tour be scaled back to eleven dates, and the Colonel, who believes firmly in the grand gesture, declines.

DECEMBER

09 Sunday

A day for touch football with friends.

Christmas at Graceland, early 1960s

19 Wednesday

Vernon and Dee fly to Idlewild Airport in New York to meet Priscilla Beaulieu, who is arriving on a flight from Germany. They will accompany her to Memphis, with her ticket reserved in the name of Priscilla Fisher. Elvis picks her up at his father's home on Hermitage Road so that he can show her Graceland for the first time himself, driving her past the annual Christmas display on the lawn, including the life-size Nativity scene that is still in use today.

20 Thursday

Priscilla misses her first two days in Memphis because of the pills Elvis has given her to help her sleep on the first night. The rest of her vacation is spent seeing the places where Elvis grew up, roller-skating, attending movies at the Memphian, and dining out at Chenault's Drive-In.

25 Tuesday

Elvis and Priscilla have a private party for thirty friends, and he gives her a toy poodle she names Honey. Priscilla gives Elvis a wooden ciga- rette box that plays his 1961 hit "Surrender."

31 Monday

There is a fireworks display at Graceland, followed by a party at the Manhattan Club for over two hun- dred friends, family, and fans.

Elvis' accountants report that in 1962 his personal income is $902,000 from movies and $775,000 from music and record- ing. He pays more than $800,000 in income taxes.

1963

Cliff diving in *Fun in Acapulco*

JANUARY

07 Monday

The Colonel turns down a nonpaying television guest spot for Elvis to promote Paramount's new picture, *Fun in Acapulco*. He has declined all television offers to date, he informs Hal Wallis, including numerous high-paying guest appearances, in order to avoid the kind of overexposure that would cut into movie profits.

11 Friday

Despite Elvis' efforts to convince her parents to allow her to stay in Memphis, Priscilla flies home on schedule to Frankfurt, Germany.

18 Friday

Elvis takes the train to Kansas City, then boards the Super Chief to Los Angeles, where he will be moving back into the original Perugia Way rental.

21 Monday

Production on the new Hal Wallis picture, *Fun in Acapulco*, begins, with *Jailhouse Rock* director Richard Thorpe at the helm.

22 Tuesday

Soundtrack recording starts at 1:00 P.M. and runs for just over twelve hours at Radio Recorders. To highlight the film's Mexican setting, brass arrangements echo the currently popular sound of Herb Alpert and the Tijuana Brass. Everyone expects that "Bossa Nova Baby," a Leiber and Stoller song originally recorded by Tibby and the Clovers, will be the hit.

23 Wednesday

Soundtrack recording continues from 1:00 P.M. till 3:50 A.M., concluding two marathon sessions of more than twenty-four hours in two days.

24 Thursday

The Colonel, maintaining that he alone controls RCA's use of movie soundtrack material, declares that the record company will not be getting an album from *Fun in Acapulco*. This very likely ties in with a letter he writes to Bill Bullock five days later, fulminating against RCA's continuing pressure to be allowed to include Elvis' recordings in the RCA Record Club. The Colonel leaves no doubt whatsoever about who is in control.

25 Friday

The Paramount makeup department requests that when Elvis reports at 1:30 P.M. he bring his favorite hair dye.

28 Monday

Principal photography on *Fun in Acapulco* begins at Paramount Studios. All of Elvis' scenes are filmed in

Hollywood, with background material shot in Acapulco.

FEBRUARY

08 Friday

Elvis films the "Bossa Nova Baby" sequence of the movie.

20 Wednesday

The Colonel is pushing MGM, meanwhile, to schedule Elvis' next picture or release him to pursue television and/or live performance opportunities.

27 Wednesday

Elvis overdubs vocals in Spanish for the song "Guadalajara" at Radio Recorders. He also has two dental crowns applied at a cost of $170.

MARCH

01 Friday

While filming the performance of the song "Marguerita," Elvis complains of feeling self-conscious in an untucked, short-sleeved shirt, explaining that he would never wear such clothing in real life. The outfit cannot be changed because a shot of his double leaving the bandstand has already been filmed.

02 Saturday

Sometime before filming is completed, Priscilla arrives in Los Angeles with her father, Captain Paul Beaulieu, to meet with Elvis and conclude arrangements permitting Priscilla to live in Memphis with Vernon and Dee and complete her senior year at Immaculate Conception High School. His father and stepmother will take good care of her, Elvis assures Captain Beaulieu, and she will get a good education at the Catholic parochial school.

13 Wednesday

Principal photography on *Fun in Acapulco* is completed, and the Colonel throws a special party for cast and crew at which he distributes promotional packages containing an LP and souvenir photograph of Elvis.

14 Thursday

Publicity stills are taken in the morning, and Hal Wallis approves a request from Elvis to keep two of the black silk shirts and the flamenco outfit that he wore in the movie.

18 Monday

Elvis completes dubbing on *Fun in Acapulco.*

22 Friday

Elvis is released after Hal Wallis views and approves the film Thursday evening, leaving almost immediately for Memphis, where Priscilla is waiting.

APRIL

01 Monday

Shortly after his return to Memphis, Elvis buys Priscilla a red Corvair so that she can drive herself to school instead of being chauffeured every day by Vernon.

02 Tuesday

Elvis is spotted with Priscilla in the Chenault's parking lot by a *Memphis Press-Scimitar* reporter. He tells the reporter that Priscilla is the daughter of an army officer who "sent her ahead because she wanted to graduate on time." Her family, he suggests, is not far behind and was, as has already been reported in the *Commercial Appeal,* friendly with his family in Germany. On the subject of movies he tells the reporter that he has seen both *Lawrence of Arabia* and *To Kill a Mockingbird* since returning home and expects the former will win an Oscar "because more money was spent on it, but I think *Mockingbird* was really better—that's a wonderful movie."

04 Thursday

On this and at least five other days in the next two weeks Elvis purchases a total of $1,388.69 worth of women's clothing at Laclede's on Union Avenue.

10 Wednesday

It Happened at the World's Fair opens nationwide. At the end of the year *Variety* will report that it ranks #55 among 1963's top-grossing films, with box-office receipts of $2.25 million.

15 Monday

From his office on Graceland's grounds Vernon takes care of all of Elvis' financial concerns and oversees the running and maintenance of the estate. Eighteen trees are planted on the grounds today. In Elvis' absence Vernon has had new front and back porches constructed, heavy burglarproof window screens installed, and the house painted. The work has been done by Vernon and Gladys' friend Carl Nichols, who accompanied the Presleys to Hollywood with his wife during the filming of *Loving You.*

17 Wednesday

For a party at Graceland Elvis orders 80 Tasty Dogs and 115 Cokes.

Performing with bullfighter's cape, *Fun in Acapulco*, winter 1963

Cast party, *Fun in Acapulco*, with *(left to right)* Billy Smith, Jimmy Kingsley, and the Colonel

Wearing the *Fun in Acapulco* outfit he asked to keep

24 Wednesday

Elvis has the following books picked up at the Readin' & Ritin' Shop for a total order of $126: *Eyewitness History of World War II, First 100 Days of the Kennedy Administration, Exploring the Earth, Giants of Medicine, Underwater, All About Our Fifty States, Giants of Science, Strange People, World Philosophy, Transport to Disaster, I Take This Land, East of Eden, Host's Handbook,* Hedda Hopper's *The Whole Truth, Joke Dictionary, World Atlas, Trail Guide, Jokes for the John, Guns, Antique Guns, Right to Privacy, Lonely Life, Vocabulary Builder, I O Russia $1200* by Bob Hope, *Good Night Mrs. Calabash, If I Knew Then, Picture History of World War II.*

MAY

06 Monday

The Colonel continues to pressure Wallis to make up his mind about what Elvis' next film will be. At the moment the producer is leaning toward a ski picture but wants to hold off, in case something better should come along.

13 Monday

Elvis screens movies at the Memphian virtually every night through June 23, viewing many recent releases, including *The Nutty Professor* (three times), *Village of the Damned, The List of Adrian Messenger,* and *Harold Lloyd's World of Comedy.*

26 Sunday

Elvis goes in to RCA's Studio B in Nashville, working from 6:30 P.M. till 5:30 A.M. on what will eventually turn out to be fourteen recorded masters. The songs are intended to make up an album and a single, with "(You're the) Devil in Disguise" selected as the A-side of the single. The album, however, is never released, with the material parceled out over the next few years as singles or soundtrack album "bonus selections."

27 Monday

Recording continues from 7:00 P.M. to 4:00 A.M.

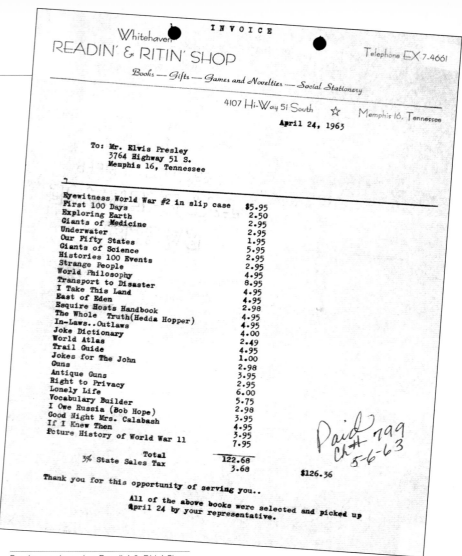

INVOICE

Whitehaven
READIN' & RITIN' SHOP

Telephone EX 7-4661

Books — Gifts — Games and Novelties — Social Stationery

4107 Hi-Way 51 South   ☆   Memphis 16, Tennessee

April 24, 1963

To: Mr. Elvis Presley
3764 Highway 51 S.
Memphis 16, Tennessee

Eyewitness World War #2 in slip case	$5.95
First 100 Days	2.50
Exploring Earth	2.95
Giants of Medicine	2.95
Underwater	1.95
Our Fifty States	5.95
Giants of Science	2.95
Histories 100 Events	2.95
Strange People	4.95
World Philosophy	8.95
Transport to Disaster	4.95
I Take This Land	4.95
East of Eden	2.98
Esquire Hosts Handbook	4.95
The Whole Truth(Hedda Hopper)	4.95
In-Laws..Outlaws	4.00
Joke Dictionary	2.49
World Atlas	4.95
Trail Guide	1.00
Jokes for The John	2.98
Guns	3.95
Antique Guns	2.95
Right to Privacy	6.00
Lonely Life	5.75
Vocabulary Builder	2.98
I Owe Russia (Bob Hope)	3.95
Good Night Mrs. Calabash	4.95
If I Knew Then	3.95
Picture History of World War 11	7.95
Total	122.68
3% State Sales Tax	3.68
	$126.36

Paid Ch# 799
5-6-63

Thank you for this opportunity of serving us..

All of the above books were selected and picked up
April 24 by your representative.

Books purchased at Readin' & Ritin' Shop

29 Wednesday

Priscilla graduates from Immaculate Conception High School, but Elvis does not attend after Priscilla expresses concern that his presence will cause too much of a disruption. He waits outside in his car before taking her home for the graduation party that he has planned. They will spend the next month together at Graceland.

JUNE

June Record Release

Single: "(You're the) Devil in Disguise" (#3)/"Please Don't Drag That String Around." This newly recorded studio single sells close to 700,000 copies and will remain #1 in Denmark for thirteen weeks, inspiring at least one Danish enthusiast to a misguided adulthood.

JULY

04 Thursday

Elvis and the guys stage their annual fireworks show and fight at Graceland. Within the next day or two Elvis returns to Hollywood.

09 Tuesday

Elvis reports to MGM for preproduction on *Viva Las Vegas,* which is to be both produced and directed by George Sidney, veteran of such lavish MGM productions as *Annie Get Your Gun, Show Boat,* and *Kiss Me Kate.* Sidney has just completed work on *Bye Bye Birdie,* the splashy vehicle that introduces Elvis' new costar, Ann-Margret.

Soundtrack recording for *Viva Las Vegas* begins at Radio Recorders at 7:00 P.M. and runs till 4:15 A.M. The three-day session features the largest group of musicians Elvis has ever worked with, combining the usual Nashville and L.A. players with a brass section, organist, and additional percussionist. Elvis and Ann-Margret perform three duets, but only one, "The Lady Loves Me," will actually appear in the movie, and none are released on record. Songwriters Doc Pomus and Mort Shuman deliver the hit song "Viva Las Vegas," a witty movie theme that will become a camp-and-kitsch favorite in various interpretations over the years.

10 Wednesday
Soundtrack recording continues from 7:00 P.M. to 3:30 A.M.

11 Thursday
Soundtrack recording concludes, running from 3:00 P.M. to 12:40 A.M.

14 Sunday
The film's cast and crew travel to Las Vegas, where they stay at the Sahara Hotel.

15 Monday
Principal photography for *Viva Las Vegas* begins, with shooting continuing six days a week while on location.

23 Tuesday
Today's filming takes place in the parking lot of the Sahara Hotel.

24 Wednesday
Elvis begins three days of filming at the Lake Mead Marina.

26 Friday
Location shooting for *Viva Las Vegas* ends.

27 Saturday
Over the weekend cast and crew return to Los Angeles. By now Elvis and Ann-Margret are the subject of much on-set gossip and will soon become a prominent item in all the gossip columns. "They hold hands. They disappear into his dressing room between shots. They lunch together in

With Ann-Margret on location, *Viva Las Vegas*, summer 1963

seclusion," writes Bob Thomas in an AP dispatch ten days later.

29 Monday

Shooting resumes at MGM Studios. The Colonel, concerned that the director is focusing too much on Ann-Margret, cuts her on-screen duets with Elvis to just one song.

AUGUST

06 Tuesday

Back in Memphis, Priscilla starts reading press reports of the romance between Elvis and Ann-Margret.

15 Thursday

Although the Colonel tries desperately to prevent it, the cost of *Viva Las Vegas* soars well over budget, threatening a loss of profit participation (a given in every Elvis picture). In this atmosphere the Colonel finalizes a deal with another MGM producer, Sam Katzman, that virtually guarantees profits by promising a radical diminution of shooting time and tight control of all costs. Katzman, who produced the first rock 'n' roll film, *Rock Around the Clock*, for $300,000 in 1956, is known as the "King of the Quickies" for good reason.

22 Thursday

Hal Wallis commissions the script that will eventually become *Roustabout* for his next Presley picture. It is to be based on the story of a traveling circus.

August Record Release

LP: *Elvis Golden Records Vol. 3* (#3). Substantially lower sales of studio albums in comparison to movie soundtracks leads to the scrapping of the Nashville album recorded in May in favor of yet another *Golden Records* package. With huge sellers like "It's Now or Never" and "Are You Lonesome Tonight?" (which have never before been on LP), it quickly sells 600,000 copies and becomes a standard backlist item.

Rehearsing with Ann-Margret, *Viva Las Vegas*

30 Friday

MGM decides to add another up-tempo song to *Viva Las Vegas*, and Elvis records Ray Charles' "What'd I Say?" at Radio Recorders.

SEPTEMBER

04 Wednesday

Rehearsals and filming for the last-minute dance sequence begin today and run through Friday. The setting is a Vegas nightclub, where Elvis and Ann-Margret dance to a black quartet's version of Leiber and Stoller's "The Climb" (the soundtrack recording is actually by the Jordanaires) before Elvis gets up on stage himself and launches into "What'd I Say?"

06 Friday

Hal Wallis contacts Mae West about playing the part of the crusty circus owner in the upcoming *Roustabout*. She quickly turns the offer down, calling the part too "downbeat" for her.

10 Tuesday

Elvis reports for the shooting of publicity stills.

11 Wednesday

Elvis completes stills and dubbing for *Viva Las Vegas* before returning to Memphis.

16 Monday

In Memphis Elvis receives song suggestions for his next film, Sam Katzman's *Kissin' Cousins*. The songs have been picked out by Gene Nelson, a former dancer and actor, with the help of music director Fred Karger.

23 Monday

While home, Elvis attends shows at the Memphian almost every night. This month he screens films ranging from Roger Corman's *The Terror*, with Boris Karloff and Jack Nicholson, to *The Sky Above, The Mud Below*,

Elvis and Elvis, *Kissin' Cousins*, fall 1963

13 Sunday

Cast and crew travel about a hundred miles east of Los Angeles to the town of Big Bear in the San Bernardino Mountains.

14 Monday

Location shooting for *Kissin' Cousins* begins.

At some point during the filming Elvis confesses to Gene Nelson how excited he was, at the age of seventeen when Nelson came to Memphis with his costar, Virginia Mayo, to promote their new picture, *She's Working Her Way Through College.* "You know, I really love the stuff you do," he tells Nelson, who will always appreciate the extent to which Elvis goes out of his way to show respect.

17 Thursday

This is the date of Elvis' second-degree black belt, an "honorary [award] in the Chito style of karate for outstanding work, enthusiasm and support of karate." Elvis kept this card in the wallet he carried at the time of his death.

Second-degree black belt, October 17, 1963

an Oscar-winning French documentary about primitive tribes in New Guinea, to *Hootenanny Hoot*, a musical comedy by *Kissin' Cousins* director Gene Nelson. He also watches *All the Way Home*, based on James Agee's autobiographical novel about his Tennessee childhood and his father's death.

29 Sunday

Soundtrack recordings for *Kissin' Cousins* begin at RCA's Studio B in Nashville and run from 7:00 P.M. to 3:30 A.M. With *Viva Las Vegas* over budget, the Colonel is determined to protect Elvis' profit margin at every turn, including cutting the soundtrack more cheaply and conveniently in Nashville. A cold prevents Elvis from recording his vocals, although he does stop by the studio to meet the film's director, Gene Nelson, who plays congas with the band.

30 Monday

Recording continues from 7:00 P.M. to 3:30 A.M.

OCTOBER

07 Monday

Elvis reports to MGM in Hollywood for preproduction on *Kissin' Cousins.* During the week he has script and choreography rehearsals as well as wig fittings for his role as the blond twin (he also plays the black-haired twin) in the picture. Lance LeGault, who has doubled for Elvis in previous pictures, stands in for one twin in scenes that require both to appear.

10 Thursday

At MGM's soundstage Elvis records his vocals for the *Kissin' Cousins* backing tracks that were recorded in Nashville.

October Record Release

Single: "Bossa Nova Baby"(#8)/"Witchcraft"(#32) (shipped October 1). RCA's original plan was to release "Bossa Nova Baby" with Chuck Berry's "Memphis, Tennessee," recorded at the May session. Elvis, however, is so attached to the Berry number that he wants to have a chance to re-record it, taking it further in the driving pop direction he has already begun. His decision leads to its replacement by another r & b number from the session, "Witchcraft," originally by the Spiders. The record sells somewhat less than 700,000 copies.

With Marie Parker, Priscilla, Colonel Parker, and Sam Katzman at MGM Studios, c. November 7, 1963

NOVEMBER

05 Tuesday
Location filming of *Kissin' Cousins* is completed, and cast and crew return to Los Angeles.

06 Wednesday
Filming begins at the MGM Studios. Priscilla joins Elvis in Hollywood after reading press reports that he and Ann-Margret have been seen motorcycle riding together.

08 Friday
The Colonel completes an agreement with Allied Artists for one picture. Elvis will receive $600,000 plus $150,000 in expenses and 50 percent of the profits. The Colonel insists that the contract include a ceiling of $1,500,000 on costs (in other words, Elvis' salary will equal exactly one half of the budget). The picture that is eventually made under this agreement is *Tickle Me.*

Meanwhile, Ann-Margret is quoted in a nationally syndicated UPI report from London, where she is attending the royal premiere of *Bye Bye Birdie*, that she is in love with Elvis but doesn't know if they will marry. With the story's publication, the Colonel advises Elvis to send Priscilla back to Memphis immediately in order to avoid press inquiries into *their* relationship.

Principal photography on *Kissin' Cousins* concludes.

14 Thursday
Elvis is released by MGM after publicity stills for the picture have been shot.

22 Friday
With Ann-Margret back in Los Angeles, she and Elvis watch the news of President Kennedy's assassination together at Elvis' Perugia Way home.

November Record Release

LP: *Fun in Acapulco* (#3). After some inconclusive palaver with Hal Wallis on the Colonel's part earlier in the year about whether a soundtrack album is even merited in the present, downsized market, the soundtrack comes out right on time, with two "bonus" tracks from the Nashville sessions in May. In spite of the bonus tracks and significantly improved sound quality, sales more or less match the Colonel's artificially gloomy prognostications.

27 Wednesday

Fun in Acapulco opens nationwide. It appears on *Variety*'s National Box Office Survey for three weeks, peaking at #5, but at a cost of close to $3 million it is still in the red at the end of the year. In another year-end survey, Elvis will be listed as the seventh-biggest-moneymaking star in Hollywood.

DECEMBER

10 Tuesday

After a private screening of *Viva Las Vegas*, Hal Wallis sends a long letter to the Colonel expressing his concern over Elvis' appearance in the MGM film. Wallis feels he no longer has a "lean, handsome, rugged look" but is soft, fat, and jowly with a hairdo that makes him look as if he is wearing a wig that is painted too black. "I will appreciate it," Wallis writes his sometime adversary, "if you will have a talk with Elvis, as this is a very serious concern both for us and for him, as it could have a very detrimental effect on his entire career." He wants to be sure that Elvis will be in shape to play the tough, hard-hitting character that he is slated to portray in Wallis' upcoming production, *Roustabout*. The upshot of this and similar follow-up communications is that Elvis will be told he cannot bring his own hairdresser to the set, a decision with which the Colonel entirely concurs. "You must strongly impress on your people in production," Colonel Parker advises Wallis in a letter some weeks later, "that they should only convey your desires . . . because if Elvis is not sure what someone is supposed to do and they ask him how he likes it, he naturally is going to tell them what he likes, regardless of the picture."

17 Tuesday

Back home in Memphis, Elvis is photographed in the mayor's office, presenting a check for $55,000 for fifty-eight Memphis charities.

RCA exercises its option to extend Elvis' recording contract two additional years, to December 31, 1971.

19 Thursday

The Legion of Decency objects to some of the dance sequences in *Viva Las Vegas*, and the Colonel expresses his concern about releasing such a picture at Easter time.

25 Wednesday

Elvis spends Christmas with Priscilla at Graceland.

Elvis' accountants report that in 1963 Elvis made $1,253,000 from films and $546,000 from music and recording. He pays over $800,000 in income taxes.

1964

JANUARY

03 Friday

Elvis goes shopping for clothes at Lansky's.

08 Wednesday

Elvis celebrates his twenty-ninth birthday quietly at home.

12 Sunday

Elvis arrives on his motorcycle at RCA's Studio B in Nashville at 6:30 P.M., starting off the five-hour session by sending out for a take-out order for all. He re-records both "Ask Me" and "Memphis, Tennessee" from the May session, then delivers a moving performance of "It Hurts Me," a ballad that will remain a personal favorite for several years.

13 Monday

On the eve of the Beatles' arrival in New York Elvis sends what appears to be a "canned" telegram to his manager. "Regarding the Beatles. I feel the same way as you feel about them. I just hope the fans over here are as good to them as the fans in England are to me. Sincerely yours, Elvis Presley."

The Colonel informs RCA that Elvis wants to delay the release of "Memphis" once again, this time, apparently,

With Danny Thomas at the press conference to announce the presentation of the USS *Potomac* to St. Jude's Hospital, February 14, 1964

because he feels the timing is not right. Instead, the newly recorded "It Hurts Me" becomes the B-side of "Kissin' Cousins."

30 Thursday

The Colonel purchases Franklin D. Roosevelt's retired yacht, the *Potomac*, in Elvis' name for $55,000. Apart from tax considerations, his eleemosynary aim is to generate publicity by donating the boat to one of Elvis' favorite charities, the March of Dimes, but when the gift is refused, the Colonel scrambles to find another suitable recipient.

Elvis around this time arrives in Las Vegas for an extended vacation with an entourage including foreman Joe Esposito, Alan Fortas, Richard Davis, Jimmy Kingsley, Billy Smith, and the newly returned Marty Lacker. While in Vegas, the group attends shows by Fats Domino, Della Reese, the Clara Ward Singers, Don Rickles, and Tony Martin.

FEBRUARY

09 Sunday

For the Beatles' first appearance on *The Ed Sullivan Show*, Elvis and the Colonel send a telegram to be read on the air. "Congratulations on your appearance on the *Ed Sullivan Show* and your visit to America STOP We hope your engagement will be successful and your visit pleasant STOP Sincerely Elvis and the Colonel."

14 Friday

Elvis interrupts his Vegas stay to travel to Long Beach, California, for presentation of the *Potomac* to Danny Thomas on behalf of St. Jude's Hos-

With the Clara Ward Singers in Las Vegas, February 1964; inscribed "To the Wonderful Mr. Elvis Presley 'Clara Ward' and Singers"; Clara Ward is to Elvis' immediate right

pital in Memphis, a research hospital "dedicated to finding cures for catastrophic diseases of children" that has been a special interest of Thomas' since its inception.

17 Monday

The Colonel's close involvement in the development of Elvis' next picture, *Roustabout*, has extended to offering insider tips on carnival life, providing suggestions on casting and locations, and stressing that the film should not denigrate those who work in the circus world. His detailed responses to the script include the addition of a scene in which a child discovers a worm in his candied apple. "No charge for the

meat, son" is the line the Colonel provides for Elvis' character to deliver. For his "technical advice," Wallis will pay the Colonel $25,000.

20 Thursday

Throughout Elvis' career, Vernon, who experienced a Depression-era education, has anxiously overseen his son's finances, living in constant fear of financial ruin. Elvis has always cavalierly dismissed his father's concerns, but Vernon keeps meticulous track of every penny he pays out, maintaining careful financial records. Today he writes at length to Joe Esposito in California, reprimanding him for sloppy

bookkeeping and warning of the consequences.

26 Wednesday

Elvis reports to Paramount for preproduction on *Roustabout*. The movie costars Leif Erickson as a sentimental heavy and Barbara Stan-

---

February Record Release

Single: "Kissin' Cousins" (#12)/"It Hurts Me" (#29). "It Hurts Me" charts substantially higher than any recent B-side and the record sells 700,000, about the same as "Bossa Nova Baby."

Dueling cigars, on the set of *Roustabout*, spring 1964

wyck in the role turned down by Mae West. The film will be directed by John Rich, whose television directing credits include *Our Miss Brooks*, *Gunsmoke*, *Bonanza*, and *The Dick Van Dyke Show*.

MARCH

02 Monday

Elvis begins recording sessions for his new Paramount film at Radio Recorders. He completes four songs, working from 1:00 to 11:35 P.M.

03 Tuesday

On the second day of sessions, working from 12:30 P.M. till midnight, Elvis records seven more songs, including a title song by Otis Blackwell and Winfield Scott that ultimately is not used.

05 Thursday

Elvis reports to the Paramount makeup department for a haircut by the studio barber, followed by a 1:00 P.M. music meeting.

06 Friday

Principal photography for *Roustabout* begins at the Hidden Valley Ranch north of Los Angeles. Throughout the filming Elvis will work at various locations around the city.

Kissin' Cousins opens nationwide. It will appear at #11 for one week on the *Variety* National Box Office Survey and be ranked #26 for the year.

11 Wednesday

Elvis begs *Roustabout* director John Rich to let him do his own fight scene, promising to take full responsibility if there is an accident. There is, and Elvis

is mortified, the director reluctant to face Wallis. In the end Rich comes up with an ingenious solution to explain the stitches required to sew up the cut above the star's eye: it is the result of his motorcycle being run off the road (already a story point), and Elvis will simply wear a Band-Aid from the next scene on. Wallis, Elvis, and the public all buy it, and no shooting days are lost.

APRIL

15 Wednesday

The Colonel continues to complain to MGM about budget overruns on *Viva Las Vegas*, expressing his profound objection to the fact that advertising for the picture is aimed at promoting Ann-Margret as much as Elvis. He doesn't go for any of MGM's rationalizations about generating "more drawing power [than the] normal Presley audience." He objects to ads that refer to Ann-Margret's previous films and says he's never asked to include a phrase like Elvis Presley, "the *Fun in Acapulco* boy," or "the *Jailhouse Rock* boy." He tells the studio, "If someone else should ride on our back then we should get a better saddle."

20 Monday

The end of principal photography for *Roustabout*.

An article appears in the *Las Vegas Desert News and Telegram*, headlined "Elvis Helps in Success of Burton-O'Toole Movie." The gist of the article, which centers around an interview with Hal Wallis, is that it is the profits from Elvis Presley pictures that enable Wallis to finance a classy vehicle like *Becket*, starring Richard Burton and Peter O'Toole. "In order to do the artistic pictures," Wallis declares, "it is necessary to make the commercially successful Presley pictures. But that doesn't mean a Presley picture can't have quality too." Elvis is deeply hurt by the remarks, referring to them obliquely in private to the end of his life.

On the set of *Roustabout*
just after completing his
own stunt, March 11, 1964

With Barbara Stanwyck,
sporting a Band-Aid
over his cut

22 Wednesday

Publicity stills are shot.

29 Wednesday

Elvis is absent when the backing track for a new title song for *Roustabout* is recorded at Radio Recorders. He will overdub his vocal on May 14.

30 Thursday

At 4:00 P.M. Larry Geller arrives at the Perugia Way house as a replacement for Elvis' regular hairdresser, Sal Orifice. During a lengthy conversation, Larry speaks of his dedication to spiritual studies, and Elvis confesses his own long-standing fascination with such matters. "What you're talking about," he says to Larry, "is what I secretly think about *all the time*. . . . I've always known that there had to be a purpose for my life. I mean, there's got to be a reason . . . why I was chosen to be Elvis Presley." Elvis will not let Larry go before he promises to quit his job at Jay Sebring's hair salon and go to work for Elvis—and bring some of the books they have been talking about to the studio the next morning.

This marks the beginning of one

With Colonel Parker and Larry Geller in 1966

April Record Releases

LP: *Kissin' Cousins* (#6). Two "bonus" songs from the May 1963 session are added to the ten movie songs. Sales of 300,000 are pretty much the equivalent of the last two soundtrack albums.

Single: "Kiss Me Quick" (#34)/"Suspicion" (shipped April 14). Both songs are taken from the 1963 *Pot Luck* album and are released in response to Elvis soundalike Terry Stafford's cover version of "Suspicion." It is too late to compete with Stafford's #3 hit, however, and at just over 200,000 copies, this is Elvis' worst-performing single to date.

Single: "What'd I Say" (#21)/"Viva Las Vegas" (#29) (shipped April 28). Following on the previous single's release by just two weeks, this record fights it out with its predecessor for airplay. Sales of just half a million, a new low for a single that offers previously unreleased material, reflect the poor state of marketing affairs.

---

of Elvis' most significant long-term relationships outside his immediate circle of Memphis and show-business acquaintances.

MAY

01 Friday

Elvis reports to Paramount for publicity stills and, as promised, is met there by Larry Geller with copies of several of the books that they have discussed. One, *The Impersonal Life*, first published in 1917, promulgates the view that each person's divinity lies within himself, that God is in fact "the divine I." Elvis' response to this slim volume is instantaneous, and he will continue to read and reread it over the years, passing out annotated copies to friends and acquaintances up until the time of his death. For the next month

Elvis will devote himself almost exclusively to the study of the books Larry brings him at Perugia Way.

14 Thursday

Elvis completes his work on *Roustabout* with more publicity stills, followed by a brief recording session at Radio Recorders to overdub the new title song.

May Record Release

EP: *Viva Las Vegas* (#92 on the singles chart). The movie soundtrack contains twelve songs. Two have already been released on the April single and, now, four more on this EP. One of the three duets recorded with Ann-Margret, "Today, Tomorrow and Forever," appears here in a solo version by Elvis. The EP sells 150,000 copies.

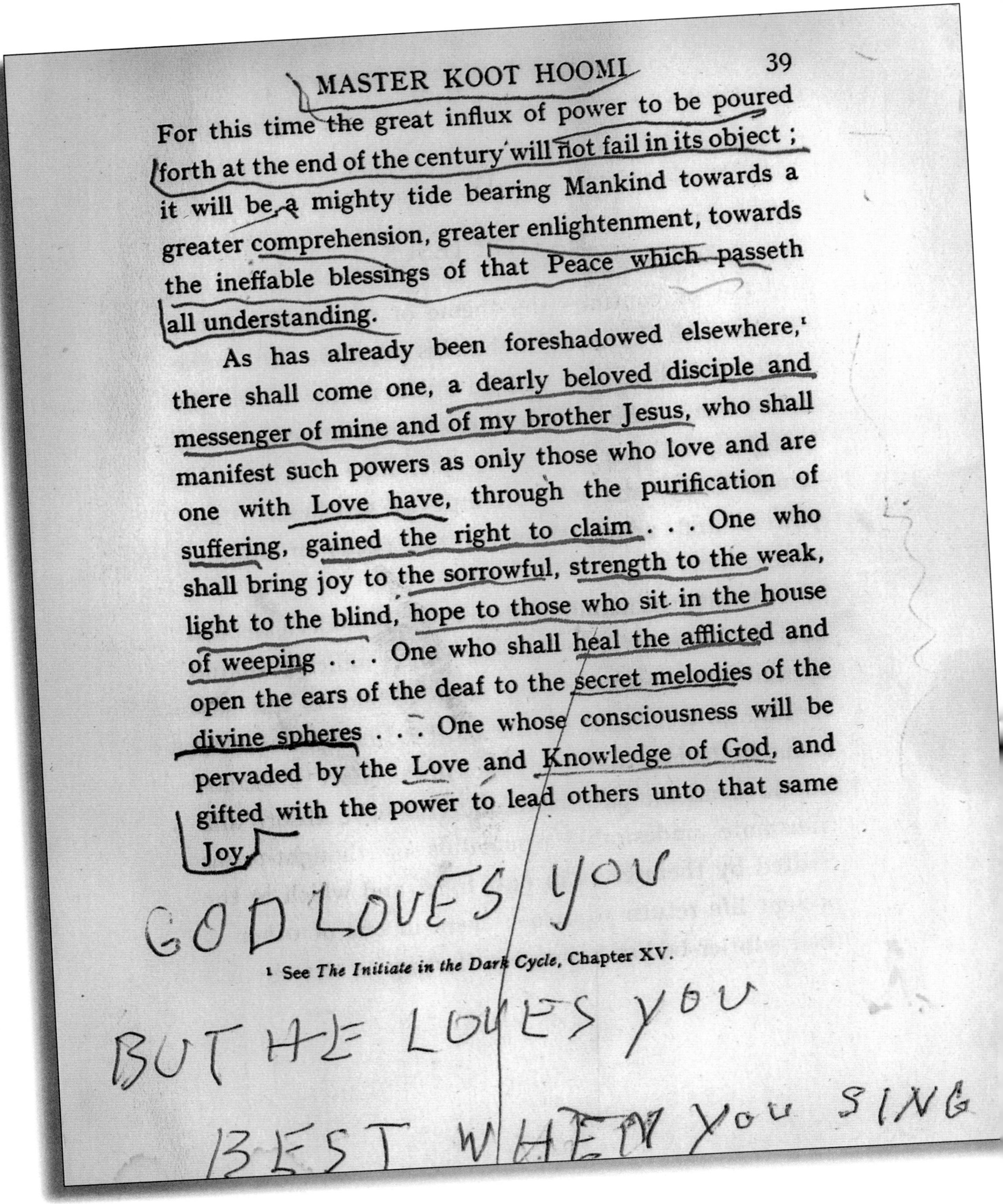

For this time the great influx of power to be poured forth at the end of the century will not fail in its object; it will be a mighty tide bearing Mankind towards a greater comprehension, greater enlightenment, towards the ineffable blessings of that Peace which passeth all understanding.

As has already been foreshadowed elsewhere,[1] there shall come one, a dearly beloved disciple and messenger of mine and of my brother Jesus, who shall manifest such powers as only those who love and are one with Love have, through the purification of suffering, gained the right to claim . . . One who shall bring joy to the sorrowful, strength to the weak, light to the blind, hope to those who sit in the house of weeping . . . One who shall heal the afflicted and open the ears of the deaf to the secret melodies of the divine spheres . . . One whose consciousness will be pervaded by the Love and Knowledge of God, and gifted with the power to lead others unto that same Joy.

GOD LOVES YOU

[1] See *The Initiate in the Dark Cycle*, Chapter XV.

BUT HE LOVES YOU

BEST WHEN YOU SING

A page from *Through the Eyes of the Masters: Meditations and Portraits,* annotated by Elvis at unknown date (the book is by David Anrias, pseud. [London: Routledge & Kegan Paul, 1936])

JUNE

09 Tuesday

Elvis reports to a music meeting at MGM for his new picture, *Girl Happy*, a Joe Pasternak production to be directed by Boris Sagal. Elvis will receive $500,000 and 50 percent of the profits on this story about college students on spring break in Fort Lauderdale by the producer who back in 1957 had wanted to star Elvis in the first "beach movie," *Gidget*.

10 Wednesday

Elvis reports to Radio Recorders at 7:00 P.M. to begin soundtrack recordings for *Girl Happy*, working until 3:00 A.M.

11 Thursday

Soundtrack recording continues from 7:00 P.M. to 5:00 A.M. Disheartened by the quality of the material, and unhappy with his own performance, Elvis leaves the sessions after thirty-four exhausting takes of "Do Not Disturb." The band continues to record instrumental tracks.

With Lynda Bird Johnson on another occasion, on the set of *Spinout*, 1966

12 Friday

Elvis does not report at the arranged session time of 7:00 P.M., and the band is dismissed at 10:40 P.M. after completing several more backing tracks.

The Colonel conducts discussions about a possible television series to be based on *Kissin' Cousins*.

15 Monday

Elvis returns to Radio Recorders from 2:00 to 6:00 P.M. to complete vocal tracks for *Girl Happy*. It will be another eight months before he sets foot in a recording studio again.

17 Wednesday

Viva Las Vegas opens nationwide, appearing for two weeks on *Variety*'s National Box Office Survey, where it peaks at #14. At the end of the year it is reported as the eleventh-highest-grossing film of 1964 (outranking the Beatles' *A Hard Day's Night*), with box office receipts of $4,675,000. This is the highest standing any Presley picture achieves in the year of its release. By 1969 it will have become Elvis' highest-grossing film ever, with revenues of $5.5 million.

22 Monday

Principal photography begins on *Girl Happy*.

During filming Elvis is visited on the set by President Johnson's daughter, Lynda Bird, with her boyfriend, actor George Hamilton, a protégé of the Colonel's, who has recently completed filming of *Your Cheatin' Heart*, in which he plays the role of Hank Williams.

23 Tuesday

Colonel Parker's fifty-fifth birthday is celebrated three days early, with various friends and acquaintances (including the actor, Nick Adams, in whose career the Colonel has continued to take an interest) in attendance on the set.

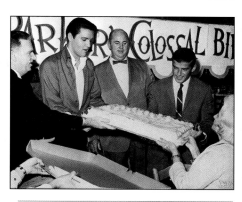

Colonel Parker's Colossal Birthday party, *Girl Happy*, June 23, 1964, with Tom Diskin, the Colonel, William Morris agent Irving Schecter, and Marie Parker

JULY

July Record Release

Single: "Such a Night" (#16)/"Never Ending" (shipped July 14). Elvis' fourth single release in six months, despite the fact that he has scarcely set foot in the studio for any non-soundtrack recordings during this time. "Such a Night" is pulled from 1960's *Elvis Is Back* album in an attempt to capitalize on the Conway Twitty version that is currently on the charts. It is coupled with one of the weaker May 1963 recordings but does surprisingly well, reaching #16 and selling more than 300,000 copies.

AUGUST

03 Monday

Principal photography on *Girl Happy* concludes, but Elvis is not released from the picture until Wednesday, August 12.

17 Monday

According to Larry Geller's memoir, *"If I Can Dream": Elvis' Own Story*, Elvis meets privately with Colonel Parker at the MGM lot, while Larry and some of the guys wait impatiently to leave for Memphis. Elvis emerges enraged from the meeting, declaring that the Colonel has accused him of being on a "religious kick. . . . He doesn't know anything about me," Elvis insists. "My life is not a kick. It's real."

Tensions are mounting among Elvis' entourage as well. Almost to a man, they are deeply resentful of Larry's growing influence on Elvis and his constant presence around him. Some of the tension comes out when Elvis fires Joe Esposito in Amarillo over what amounts to little more than a minor misunderstanding, replacing him with Marty Lacker.

21 Friday

Elvis' next picture will be *Tickle Me*, to be produced for Allied Artists by Ben Schwalb and directed by Norman Taurog. Elvis will receive $750,000, more than half the total budget, and 50 percent of the profits. Because Allied is in financial trouble, not to mention the increasing difficulty of getting Elvis into the recording studio, the Colonel comes up with a new scheme for the soundtrack. In a letter to Elvis of this date the Colonel suggests "the idea of using in this picture ten or twelve songs that you have already recorded and have been released on albums in the past but never have been released on either singles or 45s." The beauty of the scheme, the Colonel explains, is that it saves both time and money; all Elvis has to do is to indicate his assent as soon as possible. Elvis' sparsely worded reply a month later reads simply: "Arrangements with records okay. Elvis."

24 Monday

Elvis continues his spiritual studies with Larry Geller in Memphis, even flying in Larry's wife and two young children to stay at the Howard Johnson's motel just down the road. None of the usual Memphis pursuits are abandoned, however, with the Fairgrounds or the Memphian rented out nearly every night—and sometimes both. During this visit Elvis will screen *Dr. Strangelove*, one of his all-time favorite pictures, starring Peter Sellers, one of his favorite actors, five times. Other films run the gamut from biblical epics (*King of Kings* and

The Robe) to Peter Sellers comedies (*A Shot in the Dark*) to classic action pictures (*The Great Escape*) to Alfred Hitchcock's *Marnie* and MGM's *Big Parade of Comedy*.

SEPTEMBER

21 Monday

Up till now an "Honorary Chief Deputy Sheriff" of Shelby County (the seat of one of Memphis' two city governments), Elvis is now appointed "Special Deputy Sheriff" and photographed and fingerprinted for his badge. He had "always been interested in law enforcement," he tells Sheriff Bill Morris, and in fact even "applied for a job as a Memphis policeman" at age nineteen. Whether or not this is actually true, he is clearly drawn to the uniform and the badge.

22 Tuesday

Not feeling well, Elvis calls Dr. Charles Clarke, the physician who attended his mother at her death. Clarke comes out to Graceland to see him and submits a bill of $10 for the house call.

23 Wednesday

Elvis has a chest X ray and blood work and for the second night in a row does not attend the movies. His

---

September Record Release

Single: "Ask Me"(#12)/"Ain't That Loving You Baby"(#16) (shipped September 22). Johnny Rivers' hit version of "Memphis" has eliminated the Chuck Berry song as a single release; hence, "Ask Me" from the January session. With very little left in the RCA vault, the B-side is a number from the June 1958 session, which has never been released because there was no satisfactory master. At this point, evidently, take four is judged to be satisfactory enough, and in fact represents a refreshing return to bluesily rocking form as the single registers a significant upturn in sales, at 700,000 copies.

---

scheduled departure for Los Angeles is delayed.

25 Friday

On his final night at home, Elvis screens *Dr. Strangelove* at the Memphian once again. He has just hired Memphian Mike Keaton to accompany the group to California, and now, in the early-morning hours, asks twenty-two-year-old Memphis State student Jerry Schilling if he would like to go. Schilling, whose brother Billy Ray grew up with Red West and is a Memphis policeman, has been around the group since 1954, when at the age of twelve he started playing football with Elvis and his friends in Guthrie Park.

26 Saturday

The caravan sets out for Hollywood.

OCTOBER

06 Tuesday

Elvis reports to Allied Artists for preproduction of *Tickle Me* (original title *Isle of Paradise*).

12 Monday

Principal photography begins.

23 Friday

Vernon Presley moves from his house on Hermitage to a new home at 1266 Dolan, just behind Graceland.

October Record Release

LP: *Roustabout* (#1). Concern over the lackluster quality of material originally led to replacement of the title song and then to RCA's decision not to release a single from the picture. Nonetheless, the soundtrack album does manage one week at the top of the charts (January 2, 1965), preceded by *The Beach Boys In Concert* and followed by *Beatles '65*. With sales of 450,000 copies, the album sells 150,000 more than any of the last three soundtracks.

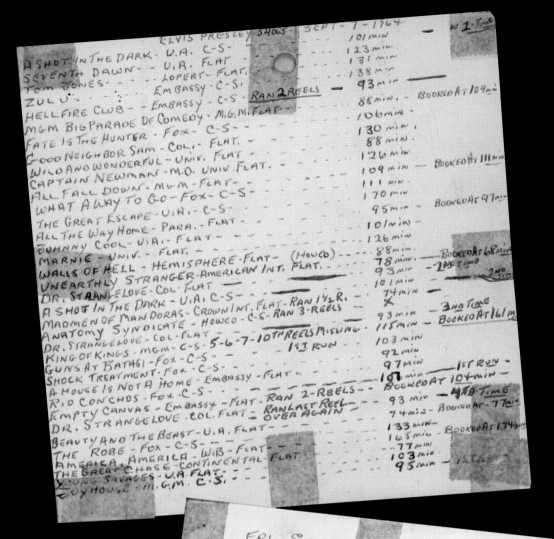

ELVIS PRESLEY SHOWS - SEPT. 1 - 1964 - #1 Time
A SHOT IN THE DARK - U.A. C-S - - - - - 101 MIN
SEVENTH DAWN - - - U.A. FLAT - - - - - - 123 MIN
TOM JONES - - - - LOPERT - FLAT - - - - - 131 MIN
ZULU - - - - - EMBASSY C-S - - - - - - 138 MIN
HELLFIRE CLUB - - EMBASSY - C-S - RAN 2 REELS - 93 MIN
MGM BIG PARADE OF COMEDY - M.G.M. FLAT - 88 MIN. - BOOKED AT 109 MIN
FATE IS THE HUNTER - FOX - C-S - - - - 106 MIN
GOOD NEIGHBOR SAM - COL. FLAT - - - - 130 MIN
WILD AND WONDERFUL - UNIV. FLAT - - - 88 MIN.
CAPTAIN NEWMAN - M.D. UNIV. FLAT - - - 126 MIN
ALL FALL DOWN - MGM - FLAT - - - - 109 MIN - BOOKED AT 111 MIN
WHAT A WAY TO GO - FOX - C-S - - - 111 MIN
THE GREAT ESCAPE - U.A. - C-S - - - 170 MIN
ALL THE WAY HOME - PARA. - FLAT - 95 MIN - BOOKED AT 97 MIN
JOHNNY COOL - U.A. - FLAT - - 101 MIN
MARNIE - UNIV. - FLAT. - - 126 MIN
WALLS OF HELL - HEMISPHERE - FLAT - (HOWCO) - 88 MIN - BOOKED AT 68 MIN
UNEARTHLY STRANGER - AMERICAN INT. FLAT. - 78 MIN - 2ND TIME
DR. STRANGELOVE - COL. FLAT - 93 MIN - 2ND TIME
A SHOT IN THE DARK - U.A. C-S - 101 MIN
MAD MEN OF MAN DORAS - CROWN INT. FLAT - RAN 1½ R. - 74 MIN
ANATOMY SYNDICATE - HOWCO - C-S - RAN 3-REELS X - 3RD TIME
DR. STRANGELOVE - COL. FLAT - 93 MIN - BOOKED AT 161 MIN
KING OF KINGS - MGM - C-S - 5-6-7-10TH REELS MISSING - 115 MIN
GUNS AT BATASI - FOX - C-S - 1ST RUN 103 MIN
SHOCK TREATMENT - FOX - C-S - 92 MIN
A HOUSE IS NOT A HOME - EMBASSY - FLAT - 97 MIN - 1ST RUN
RIO CONCHOS - FOX - C-S - 107 MIN - BOOKED AT 104 MIN
EMPTY CANVAS - EMBASSY - FLAT - RAN 2-REELS - 93 MIN - 4TH TIME
DR. STRANGELOVE - COL. FLAT - RAN LAST REEL OVER AGAIN 74 MIN - BOOKED AT 77 MIN
BEAUTY AND THE BEAST - U.A. FLAT - 133 MIN - BOOKED AT 174 MIN
THE ROBE - FOX - C-S - 165 MIN
AMERICA, AMERICA - WB - FLAT - 77 MIN
THE GREAT CHASE - CONTINENTAL - FLAT - 103 MIN
YOUNG SAVAGES - U.A. FLAT - 95 MIN - 1ST RUN
TOY HOUSE - M.G.M. C-S -

Movies screened at the
Memphian Theater,
September 1964

FRI. SEPT. 25 - 1964
PARIS WHEN IT SIZZLES - PARA - FLAT - 110 MIN
5½ R. FEATURE - - - RAN 4½ REELS - 5½ FEATURE
THE ORGANIZERS - CONTINENTAL - FLAT - 126 MIN
7-R-FEATURE - - - RAN ONLY 8 MIN OF SHOW -
KINGS OF THE SUN - U.A. - C-S - - 108 MIN
7-R-FEATURE - - - RAN 4 8 MIN OF SHOW -
DR. STRANGELOVE - COL - FLAT - 93 MIN.
5TH TIME -

ELVIS WAS ALWAYS ONE HR. TO THREE HRS. LATE

NOVEMBER

11 Wednesday

Roustabout opens nationwide, appearing for two weeks on *Variety's* Box Office Survey and peaking at #8. It is 1965's #28 film, with a gross of $3 million. In 1964 Elvis will be ranked as the sixth-biggest-money-making movie star.

14 Saturday

Hal Wallis begins preparations for Elvis' next film, saying that he is looking for a character with a chip on his shoulder who does something about it. This, Wallis concludes, is what Elvis' audiences want.

18 Wednesday

In a memo to Hal Wallis, Wallis associate Paul Nathan describes a conversation with Beatles press officer Brian Somerville about the British group appearing in the finale of Elvis' next Paramount picture. He learns that the Beatles "are crazy about Elvis" and would be very interested in working with him if the right contractual arrangements can be made.

24 Tuesday

Production of *Tickle Me* ends, and Elvis drives home to Memphis.

November Record Release

Single: "Blue Christmas"/"Wooden Heart" (shipped November 3). To generate holiday sales, RCA couples a song from the 1957 Christmas album with the German children's song from *G.I. Blues.* The single does reach #1—but only on the special Christmas sales charts.

DECEMBER

03 Thursday

Elvis is at the Memphian nearly every night of the month.

14 Monday

Elvis again donates $55,000 to Memphis charities.

On set of *Tickle Me,* fall 1964

16 Wednesday

The Colonel completes a deal with United Artists for two pictures at $650,000 each. (The pictures will be *Frankie and Johnny* and *Clambake.*)

22 Tuesday

The Colonel negotiates a new deal with MGM, to go into effect on January 4, 1965, for three motion pictures. (They will be *Harum Scarum, Spinout,* and *Double Trouble.*) Elvis will receive $1,000,000 for the first picture, $250,000 of which will be paid in $1,000-a-week installments over the course of the next five years. For the two following films he will receive $750,000 each, with 40 percent of the profits on all three. Perhaps needless to say, one of the key elements of the deal is that the Colonel has finally achieved his benchmark figure of $1 million.

24 Thursday

Elvis signs another one-year lease on the Perugia Way house to run through the following year.

25 Friday

At Marty Lacker's behest, the guys' Christmas present to Elvis is a special Bible with a "tree of life" motif drawn on the front page. On each of the branches is the name of one of the dozen or so guys, and at the bottom is one of Elvis' favorite quotations: "And ye shall know the truth, and the truth shall set you free," written in English, Hebrew, and Latin. Elvis notices that Larry's name has been omitted and refuses to accept the gift until the slight has been corrected. It is during this same time period that Elvis, who may or may not know that his mother's maternal grandmother, Martha Tackett, was Jewish, begins to wear a Jewish "chai" around his neck (he is, he says, just hedging his bets) and adds a Jewish star to Gladys' grave marker.

31 Thursday

Elvis rents out the Memphian for New Year's Eve.

Elvis' accountants report that in 1964 his personal income is $1,508,000 from movies and $506,000 from music and recording. Income tax is $784,000.

1965

JANUARY

08 Friday

Numerous newspaper and magazine articles note the passing of an era with the arrival of Elvis' thirtieth birthday, but Elvis celebrates quietly at home. It is only two months later that some of his reflections on growing older find their way into print in an extended interview with James Kingsley of the *Memphis Commercial Appeal*. "I can never forget the longing to be someone," he says in the March 7 newspaper story. "I guess if you are poor you always think bigger and want more than those who have everything."

FEBRUARY

24 Wednesday

A soundtrack session for Elvis' new MGM film, *Harum Scarum*, once again to be produced by Sam Katzman, is set up at the last minute in Nashville. Because of the hurried manner in which the session has been scheduled, Elvis' regular accompanists are unavailable, and their places are taken by Charlie McCoy on guitar, Henry Strzelecki on bass, and Kenny Buttrey on drums. They are joined by Rufus Long and Ralph Strobel on flute and oboe in order to lend a Middle Eastern touch to the soundtrack.

Signing publicity photographs in the dressing room, *Harum Scarum*, spring 1965

This is Elvis' first time in a recording studio in eight months, and the other participants note his distraction and disaffection with the material. He breaks off at 3:30 A.M. on the first night after working for only four hours and doing thirty-eight dreary takes of "Shake That Tambourine."

25 Thursday

Recording continues from 10:15 P.M. to 3:30 A.M.

26 Friday

Elvis records two songs, while the band lays down three additional tracks.

Meanwhile, the Colonel, recognizing the lethargy and general lack of interest that Elvis has been showing lately toward his Hollywood career, has been sending anxious letters of encouragement to new foreman Marty Lacker, dubbing him the "caravan superintendent" and warning him to leave plenty of time for the

February Record Release

Single: "Do the Clam" (#21)/"You'll Be Gone" (shipped February 9). "Do the Clam" does little for the soon-to-be-released *Girl Happy*, from which it is taken. Sales are approximately 350,000, and little is made of the B-side, one of Elvis' two legitimate composer credits, recorded in March 1962.

cross-country trip and to be on the lookout for bad weather.

27 Saturday

To accommodate Elvis' desire to put off his departure as long as possible, the Colonel arranges for his cast insurance medical examination to be conducted in Memphis. At the same time, one would imagine, the Colonel is looking for some kind of quid pro quo from his increasingly recalcitrant client.

MARCH

01 Monday

This appears to be the approximate date of the thoughtful interview with James Kingsley, in which Elvis muses at length about how far he has come and what it all means. "I know what it is to scratch and fight for what you want," he declares in a story that appears in the rotogravure section the following Sunday with some of the first pictures ever officially permitted inside Graceland. "I certainly haven't lost my respect for my fans," he says. "I withdraw not from my fans but from myself."

05 Friday

In the course of the trip to Los Angeles Elvis confides to Larry Geller his disappointment that, after all of his study and meditation, he has had no "experience of God." It is shortly after this conversation that Elvis stops the motor home in the middle of the desert as he sees a cloud formation that resembles the face of Joseph Stalin, then turns into the face of Jesus.

09 Tuesday

Elvis reports to MGM for preproduction on *Harum Scarum* with the *Kissin' Cousins* team of "quickie king" producer Sam Katzman and director Gene Nelson. After wardrobe tests Elvis records vocal tracks for the instrumental backups that were made in Nashville.

15 Monday

Principal photography begins on *Harum Scarum*. Joe Esposito, whom

Elvis fired on the ride home to Memphis in August 1964 after the completion of *Girl Happy*, returns to the group to become "coforeman" with Marty Lacker.

It is during the filming of *Harum Scarum* that Elvis becomes involved with the Self-Realization Fellowship. Founded in 1920 by Paramahansa Yogananda, an Indian holy man who came to this country in 1920 at the invitation of the International Congress of Religious Liberals, the Fellowship is an ecumenical movement teaching broad-based religious principles by which the seeker of any persuasion can find spiritual solace. Elvis begins to spend a good deal of time at the group's Lake Shrine retreat in Pacific Palisades, then meets Sri Daya Mata, a disciple of Yogananda and the group's spiritual leader since 1955, at Fellowship headquarters in Pasadena. Elvis' relationship with Daya Mata remains central to his spiritual quest for the rest of his life.

March Record Release

LP: *Girl Happy* (#8). Weak songs combined with a flat sound quality quickly wipe out any sense of progress created by the success of the *Roustabout* LP the previous October. Peaking at #8, the new soundtrack album sells 50,000 fewer copies than the last.

APRIL

04 Sunday

During the filming of *Harum Scarum*, Jerry Schilling buys a Triumph 650 motorcycle and Elvis is inspired to purchase a fleet of cycles, one for each of the guys. When Bel Air residents complain about the noise, Elvis simply transports the bikes by trailer to and from the entrance of the gated community.

07 Wednesday

Girl Happy opens nationwide and will be the twenty-fifth-top-grossing film of the year.

19 Monday

Just one month after he began it, Elvis completes work on *Harum Scarum*.

April Record Release

Single: "Crying in the Chapel" (#3)/"I Believe in the Man in the Sky" (shipped April 6). In January the Colonel got RCA to pay an extra $10,000 for this special single to be released at Easter time. It combines "Crying in the Chapel," an unreleased cut left over from the 1960 session that produced *His Hand in Mine*, with a track from that album. The record storms up the charts on both sides of the Atlantic, reaching #3 in the United States and #1 in Great Britain. The single is Elvis' first Top 10 hit since "Bossa Nova Baby" in October 1963. One million–plus sales are recorded both at home and abroad, and the unexpected success of a previously rejected recording reinforces the Colonel's belief that a combination of marketing and timing can produce miracles.

MAY

9 Sunday

The Colonel arranges and pays for a special Mother's Day radio show broadcast on stations across the country aimed at showcasing "Crying in the Chapel" and *His Hand in Mine*.

11 Tuesday

Elvis begins preproduction at the Samuel Goldwyn Studios on the United Artists picture *Frankie and Johnny*. It is to be produced by Edward Small and directed by Fred De Cordova, whose credits include *Leave It to Beaver* and *The Jack Benny Show* on television and who will go on to produce Johnny Carson's *Tonight Show*.

12 Wednesday

Soundtrack sessions for *Frankie and Johnny* begin at Radio Recorders from 7:00 P.M. to 4:00 A.M. According to Alan Fortas, Elvis was meant to lay down his vocals live, but "he threw a

In costume, *Harum Scarum*

temper tantrum and [said] that he wasn't in any mood to record," so the band simply cuts instrumental tracks. The group consists mainly of the usual Nashville musicians, including Charlie McCoy (now a regular on guitar, bass, and harmonica), with the addition of Tiny Timbrell and transplanted Memphian Larry Muhoberac, who appeared on the 1961 Memphis charity concert bill as Larry Owens and will join Elvis' band briefly in Las Vegas, in 1969, on piano.

13 Thursday

The sessions at Radio Recorders recommence at 5:00 P.M., with Elvis overdubbing lead vocals on tracks recorded the day before. After doing two additional songs, he leaves the band once again to its own devices.

14 Friday

At Radio Recorders Elvis returns for overdubs from 5:00 to 7:30 P.M., with the band working on tracks until 4:30 A.M.

18 Tuesday

Elvis has script rehearsals at the studio throughout the week.

19 Wednesday

Elvis records his final vocal for the *Frankie and Johnny* soundtrack at the Goldwyn Studios.

Meanwhile, the Colonel is using every trick in his capacious book to promote *Tickle Me*. He has persuaded

With gold Cadillac in 1966

RCA to purchase Elvis' gold Cadillac and ship it around the country as a kind of stand-in for the star himself at local premieres. This is the black 1960 Cadillac limousine that George Barris customized for Elvis with two telephones, a complete entertainment console, a refreshment bar, and an electric shoe buffer, all gold-plated with a golden guitar insignia, while the outside is finished in a white-gold Murano pearl with gold-plated trim. Today it helps bring in fans to the Atlanta opening, but it does little to alleviate the Colonel's increasing concern over his inability to deliver his star.

24 Monday

Principal photography begins on *Frankie and Johnny*. The film is a remake of a 1938 picture starring Helen Morgan.

JUNE

18 Friday

A viewing of *Harum Scarum* challenges even the Colonel's belief. For one of the few times in his professional association with Elvis, he gives free rein to his critical faculties, blasting the film's incoherence and seemingly doubting even his own judgment in agreeing to so hurried a production schedule. It would take "a fifty-fifth cousin to P. T. Barnum" to sell this picture, he declares, and maybe the best thing to do would be to "book it fast, get the money, then try again." He even comes up with a suggestion a month later to add a talking camel as narrator so that the ridiculousness of the presentation might at least seem intentional.

23 Wednesday

At the completion of principal photography Elvis gives away dozens of the wristwatches that he has specially designed and had executed by Memphis jeweler Harry Levitch. Alternating a cross with a Jewish star on their face, they stand for Elvis as a symbol of universal brotherhood and are given to cast and crew.

24 Thursday

Elvis completes publicity stills and is recognized at a special ceremony on the set at which Barbara Stanwyck, Frank Sinatra, Bud Abbott, and other luminaries represent the film community in expressing their thanks to Elvis for contributing $50,000 to the Motion Picture Relief Fund.

26 Saturday

The Colonel receives an electric golf cart from Elvis on his birthday.

May Record Release

Single: "(Such An) Easy Question"(#11)/"It Feels So Right"(#55) (shipped May 28). Two weeks before "Crying in the Chapel" peaks on the singles charts, RCA ships yet another 45, made up of two songs from the recycled *Tickle Me* soundtrack. The A-side originally appeared on 1962's *Pot Luck* LP, while "It Feels So Right" is plucked from 1960's *Elvis Is Back*. The record sells half a million copies, once again bearing out the Colonel's faith in indiscriminate "exploitation."

June Record Release

EP: *Tickle Me* (shipped June 15). This soundtrack EP contains five previously released cuts, but unlike the previous month's single it enjoys little success, never charting and selling only 100,000 copies.

JULY

07 Wednesday

Tickle Me opens nationwide. Though it never appears on the top box-office charts, the film quickly earns back its cost, saving Allied Artists in the process.

12 Monday

Tony Curtis' dressing room at

Frankie and Johnny, with Billy Smith on Colonel Parker's knee, spring 1965

Paramount is prepared for Elvis' arrival.

26 Monday

Citing illness, Elvis fails to report to Paramount for the start of his next Hal Wallis picture, and recording sessions at Radio Recorders begin without him. Titles under consideration for the film are *Hawaiian Paradise*, *Song of Hawaii*, *Polynesian Paradise*, and *Hula Heaven*. The picture eventually becomes *Paradise Hawaiian Style*, and Elvis receives a salary of $200,000 as well as a specially negotiated $90,000 bonus, to be split equally with the Colonel.

27 Tuesday

Again, Elvis is expected to report to Paramount. The Colonel calls the studio to say he will be there within an hour, but Elvis fails to appear either at the studio or at the sched-

uled evening recording sessions at Radio Recorders.

At some point during the summer Elvis urges everyone in the group to read Timothy Leary's 1964 *Psychedelic Experience* and Aldous Huxley's *The Doors of Perception* while also encouraging Red and Sonny West and Alan Fortas to try LSD under his supervision. Later in the summer Elvis serves the group marijuana brownies, obviously fascinated by the psychedelic experience.

AUGUST

02 Monday

A week late, Elvis arrives at Paramount for preproduction on *Paradise Hawaiian Style* and meetings with Hal Wallis and director Mickey Moore, assistant director to Norman

Taurog on three previous pictures in addition to serving in the same capacity on *Roustabout* and *King Creole*. After a cast insurance medical exam and wardrobe fittings, Elvis reports to Radio Recorders at 2:00 P.M. to do vocals over previously recorded instrumental tracks. He sings one additional tune, "Sand Castles," before winding up at 2:30 A.M.

03 Tuesday

Elvis continues overdubbing at Radio Recorders between 3:00 and 10:00 P.M.

04 Wednesday

Working from 7:00 to 10:30 P.M., Elvis completes the soundtrack.

05 Thursday

Accompanied by Jerry Schilling, Mike Keaton, Larry Geller, Richard Davis, Red and Sonny West, Ray Sitton, Billy Smith, as well as his father and stepmother, Elvis flies to Hawaii for location shooting.

07 Saturday

Principal photography for *Paradise Hawaiian Style* begins.

13 Friday

The day is spent filming authentic Hawaiian dances at the Polynesian Culture Center.

15 Sunday

Elvis, Vernon, and Colonel Parker visit the USS *Arizona* memorial to lay a bell-shaped wreath designed by Colonel Parker and containing 1,177 carnations, one for each serviceman killed aboard the ship.

16 Monday

Elvis receives a telegram from the president of Capitol Records inviting him to a cocktail party in Los Angeles on August 24 to meet the Beatles.

18 Wednesday

Elvis attends a windup party at the Polynesian Culture Center before returning to the mainland the following day.

He is also interviewed by Peter

Noone of Herman's Hermits, whom he rather cavalierly puts on. Asked who is his favorite group after the Beatles, he names first the Boston Pops, then the Boston Symphony.

With Peter Noone of Herman's Hermits, *Paradise Hawaiian Style,* August 18, 1965

August Record Releases

Single: "I'm Yours" (#11)/"(It's a) Long Lonely Highway" (shipped August 10). More songs from the *Tickle Me* "soundtrack." "I'm Yours" is originally from the album *Pot Luck,* and "(It's a) Long Lonely Highway" appeared as one of the bonus songs on the *Kissin' Cousins* album. Like the first single from the movie, this one sells half a million copies, and each outperforms the poorly received EP.

LP: *Elvis For Everyone* (#10). The original title for this album was *Today Only,* but then it was announced that it was an anniversary album (with no explanation as to what occasion it marked) and the title was changed. Although it is the first LP since *Pot Luck* to include unreleased, nonmovie songs, the songs, of course, are from old sessions. Whether meaning to or not, the cover art appears to reveal something of the album's intent, with a painting of a cash register and the RCA trademark dog, Nipper. The back displays reproductions of the covers of fifteen of Elvis' twenty-two albums, with the income that each has generated printed above. This album does not live up to most of its predecessors in that regard, however, with sales of only 250,000 copies.

With wreath designed by Colonel Parker, USS *Arizona* memorial, August 15, 1965

27 Friday

In the midst of elaborate security arrangements, carried out with great élan by the Colonel, the Beatles arrive at 10:00 P.M. for a visit at Elvis' Perugia Way home. Despite the security precautions, or perhaps because of them, hundreds of fans gather at the Bel Air gates, but the visit itself is something of an anticlimax. Elvis is sitting in front of a soundless TV on the long L-shaped white couch in the den when his guests arrive. After a while he picks up a bass and starts playing along with Charlie Rich's "Mohair Sam," which is on the jukebox. Over the next few hours what conversation takes place is desultory, and the Beatles go home disappointed, but John Lennon tells Jerry Schilling several days later that the evening really meant a lot to him and asks Jerry to tell Elvis that "if it hadn't been for him we would have been nothing."

SEPTEMBER

08 Wednesday

Paradise Hawaiian Style is the eighth and last picture to be made under the revised 1961 Hal Wallis contract. During filming the Colonel initiates lengthy and complex negotiations with Wallis for a new deal. He wants $500,000 for his client, plus 20 percent of the profits, and a role in which Elvis does not sing. A deal will be struck on several occasions, only to be delayed as the Colonel comes up with additional changes. It will not be finalized until April 1966, and needless to say Elvis sings in the pic-

Paradise Hawaiian Style, summer 1965

OCTOBER

01 Friday
Elvis completes dubbing on *Paradise Hawaiian Style* and soon after leaves for Memphis.

04 Monday
Elvis and the entourage make the usual stop at the Holiday Inn on Route 66 in Albuquerque.

07 Thursday
Elvis arrives at Graceland at 11:00 P.M., driving the Dodge Motor Home himself while followed by a caravan of five cars.

08 Friday
Marty Lacker telegrams the Colonel to announce in cryptic fashion that the "ponies" have arrived home safely.

While Elvis has been away, construction has begun on the Meditation Garden located just beyond the swimming pool. It has been designed with the Self-Realization Park in Pacific Palisades in mind, with stained-glass panels, Italian marble statues, and a fountain with fourteen different sprays and underwater light forma-

ture that is made in the fall of that year, *Easy Come, Easy Go*.

11 Saturday
In a *Saturday Evening Post* article the Colonel appears to show some of his frustration at Elvis' increasingly erratic behavior when he tells reporter C. Robert Jennings that he might be retiring. "Sooner or later someone else is going to have to take the reins."

30 Thursday
Principal photography on *Paradise Hawaiian Style* is completed. Just before the picture closes, Tom Jones—who has recently topped the charts with "What's New Pussy Cat?"—visits the set and meets Elvis for the first time. To Jones' surprise, Elvis starts singing his hit as publicity photos are shot.

With Tom Jones *(center)* in Hollywood, *Paradise Hawaiian Style*, September 1965

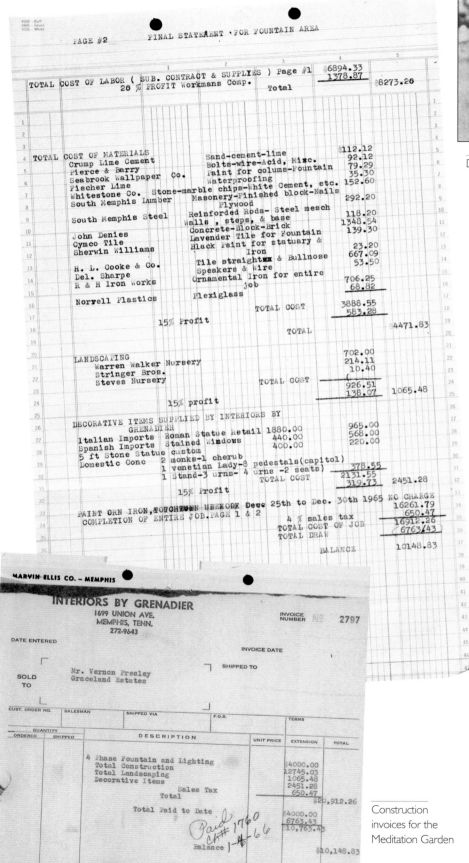

Construction invoices for the Meditation Garden

Driving a go-cart at Graceland, late 1960s

tions designed and commissioned by Marty Lacker's sister and brother-in-law, Ann and Bernie Grenadier. Work will not be fully completed on the Garden until the end of the year, at a cost of $21,000.

09 Saturday

At home for the first time in seven months, Elvis purchases a 1966 Olds Toronado and three days later buys a 1966 Electric Glide Harley-Davidson for $1,941.25 from Taylor Harley-Davidson Sales. He is frequently spotted whizzing around the Graceland grounds during this time on his new motorcycle and on a low-slung go-cart.

12 Tuesday

Priscilla's white Honda motorcycle arrives C.O.D. from California.

21 Thursday

Thirty-nine-year-old Bill Black, Elvis' original bass player, dies of a brain tumor at 7:15 A.M. at Baptist Hospital in Memphis. Elvis is quoted in the *Commercial Appeal* as saying that Bill "was a great man and a person that everyone loved. This comes as such a shock to me that I can hardly explain how much I loved Bill." While Vernon and Dee attend the funeral, Elvis does not, expressing fear of causing a disruption.

In 1965 Elvis sells 40 percent fewer records than he did in 1960, but even so, the Colonel is able once again to renegotiate Elvis' RCA contract on substantially improved terms. The new agreement adds one additional year, extending the contract through

With Priscilla, Sandy Kawelo, and Jerry Schilling in the Meditation Garden, c. 1966

1972 with a two-year option. The guaranteed annual nonrefundable payment against the regular 5 percent royalty is raised from $200,000 to $300,000, with 75 percent going to Elvis and 25 percent to the Colonel. In addition, Elvis and the Colonel will receive nonrecoupable bonuses of $150,000 apiece and an additional $25,000 each in January of 1966. The already existing extra royalties (2 percent domestic, 1 percent foreign) continue to be split equally between Elvis and the Colonel. Finally, the Colonel's annual payment for photographs and consulting goes from $27,000 to $30,000.

22 Friday

Just about every other evening is spent watching films at the Memphian. Tonight Elvis screens *Dr. Strangelove* once again, while other films include *King Rat, A Patch of Blue, The Pawnbroker, Cleopatra, Johnny Nobody, The Spy Who Came in from the Cold, Thunderball,* and *Dr. No.*

23 Saturday

Returning home from the Memphian around 4:00 A.M., Elvis gets a speeding ticket near Graceland.

NOVEMBER

24 Wednesday

Harum Scarum opens nationwide and is #11 on the following week's *Variety* Box Office Survey. It is the fortieth-highest-grossing film for 1965, with domestic sales of $2 million.

29 Monday

Elvis buys a Greyhound bus, a retired D'Elegance coach that he plans to refurbish and use to drive to and from California.

DECEMBER

17 Friday

Elvis makes his annual donation of approximately $50,000 to a variety of Memphis charities.

24 Friday

Elvis' last-minute gift purchases from Harry Levitch include gold wristwatches, one with the initials "GK" (for George Klein), one with "EP," diamond rings, bracelets and charms, and a butterfly pin.

25 Saturday

This year the entourage gives Elvis a statue of Jesus, which they have commissioned for $500 from a local artist (the statue is still in the Meditation Garden). Picking up on Elvis' latest enthusiasm, Priscilla gives him a home slot-car racing set, purchased at the Robert E. Lee Raceway in Whitehaven, where they have been spending much of their recreational time since returning to Memphis. Elvis was introduced to slot-car racing in California, and like all of his enthusiasms he approaches it with a passion that borders on monomania for a time.

October Record Releases

Single: "Puppet on a String" (#14)/"Wooden Heart." A full five years after its original release on the *G.I. Blues* soundtrack, "Wooden Heart" appears as the B-side on a second single within twelve months so that RCA can recoup the money already paid out for permission for international single release of the song. Normally this would be the appropriate time to release as an A-side a song from the upcoming film, *Harum Scarum,* but neither Elvis nor the Colonel feels there is a suitable single. Instead, they select a song from *Girl Happy* that, with sales of 500,000, ends up doing better than the movie's first single, "Do the Clam."

Single: "Santa Claus Is Back in Town"/"Blue Christmas" (shipped October 26). Just one year after the release of "Blue Christmas" as the A-side of a single, RCA releases it as a B-side. Both of these sides originally appeared on *Elvis' Christmas Album* back in 1957. The record never charts but eventually will earn Presley a gold record and go on to near-platinum sales.

November Record Release

LP: *Harum Scarum* (#8). With no prospect for a single, the *Harum Scarum* soundtrack is released with two "bonus" songs that were dropped from the film. Sales stall at 300,000 copies.

December Record Release

Single: "Tell Me Why" (#33)/"Blue River" (#95) (shipped December 14). The year to date has seen the release of six singles, one EP, and three albums, and this seventh single underscores RCA's and the Colonel's willingness to cash in on anything that might sell. Here there is very little radio airplay, probably because "Tell Me Why" is an eight-year-old unreleased cut with a recognizably dated sound. Still, without any particular effort, the label is able to sell more than 400,000 copies.

26 Sunday

Elvis has a small party at Grace-land with food provided by Monty's Catering for $52.52.

Sometime over this Christmas season Elvis finally tries LSD under carefully controlled conditions. He has read about it for more than a year now and, according to Larry Geller, like everything else Elvis did, "he tripped Elvis-style. . . . Several hours after we had started we watched a science fiction movie, *The Time Machine*, and sent out for pizza." Later, Elvis, Larry, Priscilla, and Jerry Schilling walk out behind Graceland and talk about "how lucky we were to have such good friends and about how much we cared about one another." So far as anyone knows, this is the only time Elvis took LSD.

31 Friday

Elvis holds a New Year's Eve party at the Manhattan Club once again for friends, family, and fans. Among the groups and singers that entertain are a local rock group, the Guillotines, the Willie Mitchell Band with Don Bryant on vocals, local soul singer Vaneese Williams (who performs "Hound Dog"), and songwriter ("Hold On, I'm Comin'") David Porter.

Post-summit correspondence between
Brian Epstein and the Colonel

Hille House 9 Stafford Street London W1 telephone Mayfair 5248 cables Nemsta

4th September, 1965.

There are many things for which I must thank you. Above all, for the trouble and consideration you took towards making the meeting of the boys and myself with Mr. Presley such a wonderfully relaxing and happy evening. I cannot say how much we all enjoyed ourselves.

Now that I am safely back in London, I have unpacked your most beautiful gift which I will really cherish for many years. Thank you too for the box of records which I shall also enjoy.

Finally, let me say what a pleasure it was to see you again and that I look forward to renewing our association (and also a trip to Vegas) when next on the West Coast.

With best wishes to you and Mr. Presley.

September 10, 1965

Mr. Brian Epstein
Hille House
9 Stafford Street
London W1, England

Dear Colonel Epstein:

Thank you for your nice letter. It was good of you to write. You owe me no thanks for friends don't have to thank each other.

Chris Hutchins will relay to you the following. He said you had asked what we would like to have from the boys and yourself. Not being selfish and to make it easy I suggested a couple of midget ponies, but they must be real small. I figured this assignment would throw anyone but you. I wish I could have given Chris a tougher assignment relay. We mean live ponies of course, about 26 inches high, but not over 30, so we can carry them in our trunk and perhaps to Las Vegas to play roulette to keep the dealer looking at the ponies while we pick up the chips.

Regards from all of us.

Sincerely,

The Colonel

1966

JANUARY

05 Wednesday

Elvis' upcoming MGM film is now to be called *Never Say Yes*. When producer Joe Pasternak asks Colonel Parker to suggest a better title, the Colonel comes up with several ideas, including *Jim Dandy* and *Clambake*. Eventually the film will be called *Spinout*, and the Colonel reserves *Clambake* for a later picture.

08 Saturday

Elvis celebrates his thirty-first birthday by attending *It's a Mad, Mad, Mad, Mad World* at the Memphian. He will continue to screen films approximately every other night while he is at home, with fare varying from *The Virgin Spring* to *Die, Monster, Die!*

Elvis receives a ceremonial telegram from ninety RCA executives, declaring, in what seems like more a statement of hope than of history: "Your

On location, *Spinout*, with Joe Esposito and Larry Geller to Elvis' right and Jerry Schilling on motorcycle to his left, spring 1966

understanding and cooperation made 1965 the biggest of all the ten years you have been with us."

13 Thursday

With only a single picture (*Harum Scarum*) completed under his December 1964 three-picture deal with MGM, the studio extends the original deal for four more pictures at a uniform rate of $850,000, with profit participation upgraded to 50 percent. (The four pictures will be *Speedway*, *Stay Away, Joe*, *Live a Little, Love a Little*, and *The Trouble with Girls*.)

14 Friday

With his enthusiasm for slot-car racing having already outpaced the capacity of Priscilla's Christmas gift, Elvis orders a professional slot-car racetrack called "Highspeed Raceway Road America" for $4,990 and has Bernie Grenadier draw up plans for an addition specifically designed for the track. This addition, off the pool patio, is known as the "trophy room" today. By the end of the month all of the guys have their own personal cars, and fights soon break out over the conduct and outcome of hotly contested races.

18 Tuesday

In the wake of new contracts with RCA, MGM, and Paramount, the Colonel, in a letter, supplies Elvis with various business details, joking about stories that have appeared recently in the press with regard to the likelihood of his selling Elvis' contract.

22 Saturday

After an unusual four-inch snowfall, Elvis and the guys are observed having a snowball fight and building a snowman in front of Graceland.

26 Wednesday

In anticipation of Elvis' departure for California, the Colonel sends Marty Lacker a wire, addressing him as "Colonel, Jr." and warning him to allow plenty of time in case of bad weather.

28 Friday

Rumors of the Colonel selling Elvis' contract continue to appear. Today columnist Dorothy Manners writes: "You could have knocked Elvis Presley over with a beetle when he read in his Memphis newspaper a rumor out of London that Brian Epstein, manager of the Beatles, is buying up his contract as well as Colonel Parker's interest in it. Elvis got the Colonel long distance as fast as possible. 'No,' drawled the good Colonel Tom. 'Not unless they want to pay us enough so we can retire and not have to work any more. If

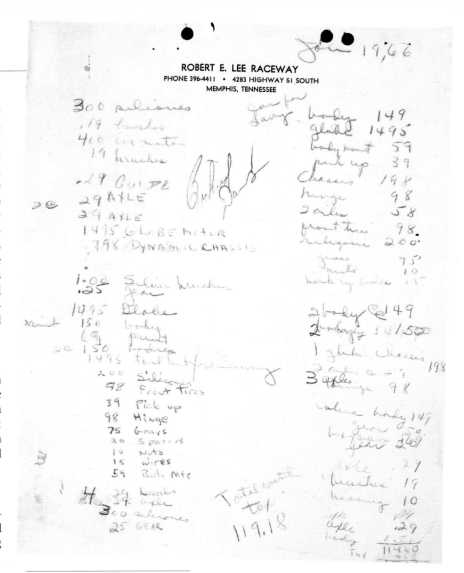

Invoice for slot-car track accessorizing

they want us under those conditions I strongly suggest our selling.'"

30 Sunday

At 10:00 A.M. Elvis leaves Memphis for Los Angeles in the Dodge motor home, heading out on Highway 40 West.

FEBRUARY

01 Tuesday

In Clines Corners, New Mexico, the caravan of cars and motor home stops to purchase 75.8 gallons of fuel.

03 Thursday

Elvis arrives in Los Angeles and settles into his new home at 10550 Rocca Place, Bel Air, which, like the Bellagio house, is rented from Mrs. Reginald Owen. The new ranch-style house is meant to offer more privacy for Elvis and Priscilla. Marty Lacker, who oversees its interior decoration, will reside there, along with Charlie Hodge, who is no longer traveling with singer Jimmy Wakely. Joe Esposito, Red West, and some of the others by now have their own homes. Red has been busy making demos of his song compositions and paying a soon-to-be-famous Glen Campbell $20 a song to accompany him on guitar.

On the day he returns, Elvis purchases a lens for his new Sony video camera and recorder. The product, which has just been introduced for home use, is hard to obtain, but in an impulsive burst of generosity he will give his away to director Norman Taurog within the next few weeks on the *Spinout* set, leaving it to Marty to locate a replacement.

Script reading, *Spinout*

11 Friday

Elvis reports to MGM for preproduction on *Spinout*.

14 Monday

Elvis attends a music meeting to select songs for the soundtrack.

16 Wednesday

Elvis begins two days of soundtrack recording at Radio Recorders, starting at 3:00 P.M. and working till midnight. The core of the Nashville studio band has been flown in and is joined by "Tiny" Timbrell and guitarist Tommy Tedesco.

17 Thursday

Elvis continues recording from 7:00 P.M. to midnight.

The recently purchased Greyhound bus is presently being customized by George Barris in North Hollywood and is nearing completion. Impulsively, at the conclusion of recording, Elvis decides to take it for a trial spin to Las Vegas for the weekend.

21 Monday

Principal photography begins on *Spinout*.

During filming Elvis tells journalist May Mann that he will always keep Graceland as his home because of his mother. He also speaks of working on songs for a new religious album that will be his first nonsoundtrack record in two and a half years.

As a further indication of his renewed musical interest, Elvis has been fooling around with Red and Charlie on a diverse assortment of songs, singing and playing almost constantly at home. Today an amplifier, twelve-string guitar, and harmonica are purchased from Western Musical Instruments. Elvis' favorite listening during this period, in addition to the gospel records he will never abandon, consists of such unlikely "folk" material as *Peter, Paul and Mary in Concert* plus the group's latest, *See What Tomorrow Brings*, albums by Ian and Sylvia, and *Odetta Sings Dylan*. He is clearly almost as interested in Bob Dylan's compositions at this point (though almost

always filtered through a less abrasive vocal interpretation) as he is by Jimmy Jones, the brilliant bass singer for the Harmonizing Four, a black gospel quartet that he envisions backing him on his upcoming session.

MARCH

19 Saturday

Elvis flies to Las Vegas for the weekend.

30 Wednesday

Frankie and Johnny opens nationwide. The film will be ranked #48 in 1966, according to *Variety*'s National Box Office Survey, grossing $2 million.

March Record Releases

Single: "Frankie and Johnny" (#25)/"Please Don't Stop Loving Me" (#45) (shipped March 1). The new movie single performs as well as can be expected, selling about 400,000 copies.

LP: *Frankie and Johnny* (#20). The album follows the same pattern as the single, with sales of 250,000.

APRIL

02 Saturday

The last contract with Wallis is finally completed, after the Colonel has finished combating Wallis on virtually every point. Elvis will receive $500,000 for one picture, along with 20 percent of the profits. There are no options, and not altogether surprisingly, Wallis will never attempt to do another picture with Elvis Presley or the Colonel after *Easy Come, Easy Go*.

05 Tuesday

Elvis' continuing interest in spiritual studies is reflected in his purchases from Gilbert's Book Shop on Hollywood and Vine, which include *The Changing Condition of Your World* by J.W. of Jupiter and *Billy Graham Presents Man in the 5th Dimension*.

08 Friday

Principal photography for *Spinout*

February Record Releases

Two singles: "Joshua Fit the Battle"/"Known Only to Him" and "Milky White Way"/"Swing Down Sweet Chariot" (shipped February 15). Encouraged by the great success of the 1965 Easter single, "Crying in the Chapel," RCA releases not one but two singles from *His Hand in Mine*, this time unfortunately with little commercial success.

is completed, and by the end of the following week Elvis winds up his work on the film.

16 Saturday

Elvis is at the wheel of his new customized Greyhound bus as the group leaves Los Angeles this weekend, followed by the usual convoy of cars. As always, Elvis does most of the driving, listening to tapes that Charlie and Red have made of potential material for the upcoming recording session.

20 Wednesday

The group stays over in Albuquerque, following the usual pattern of traveling by night, sleeping by day.

23 Saturday

Elvis pulls into Graceland at about 9:00 P.M. and is welcomed by about fifty fans, many carrying signs and balloons.

28 Thursday

During this stay at home, movies are screened at the Crosstown Theater almost every night. Tonight the group is joined by local friends to watch Lana Turner in *Madame X*.

Earlier in the day the Memphis fan club appeals without success to the Memphis Coliseum board to reconsider its rejection of a plan to rename the facility after Elvis Presley.

MAY

07 Saturday

Soul Brother #1 James Brown appears at the Coliseum and, after getting Elvis' number from George Klein, attempts to reach him by phone during the day. Every time he calls, however, he is told, undoubtedly accurately, that Elvis is asleep.

In the evening Elvis watches *Plague of the Zombies* and *The Magnif-*

Clowning with Colonel Parker on the set of *Spinout*, spring 1966

FAIRGROUNDS AMUSEMENT PARK

EAST PARKWAY SOUTH / MEMPHIS, TENNESSEE 38104

Mr. Elvis Presley
Graceland
Highway 51 South
Memphis, Tenn.

INVOICE

Elvis Presley Party

May 19, 1966

201 Cokes @ .15 each	$30.15
78 Pronto Pups @ .25 each	19.50
2 Bags of Peanuts @ .10 each	.20
16 Candy Bars @ .10 each	1.60
58 Cups of Coffee @ .10 each	5.80
31 Ice Cream Sandwiches @ .15 each	4.65
5 Dill Pickles @ .10 each	.50
16 Potato Chips @ .10 each	1.60
12 Devil Food Cakes @ .10 each	1.20

Total $65.20
35.85
$101.05

Please mail check to:

Henry Meyer
553 Valleybrook Drive
Memphis, Tenn.

Paid Ck# 2098 6-6-66

FAIRGROUNDS AMUSEMENT PARK

EAST PARKWAY SOUTH / MEMPHIS, TENNESSEE 38104

Mr. Elvis Presley
Graceland
Highway 51 South
Memphis, Tenn.

INVOICE

Charter on rides May 14, 1966
12:30 A. M. - 5:30 A. M.
5 hours

Pippin
Dodgem 4 hrs. @ $30.00 per hr. 120.00 $ 40.00
$160.00 $160.00

Charter on rides May 16, 1966
12:15 A. M. - 9:45 A. M.
9½ hrs. less 1½ hrs. due to rain
8 hours

Pippin
Dodgem 7 hours @ $30.00 per hr. 210.00 $ 40.00
$250.00 $250.00

Charter on rides May 19, 1966
12:00 Midnight - 7:30 A. M.
7 hours

Pippin
Dodgem 6 hrs. @ $30.00 per hr. 180.00 $ 40.00
$220.00 $220.00

Total $630.00

Please mail check to:

Fairgrounds Amusement Park
E. Parkway S.
Memphis, Tenn.

Paid Ck# 2097 6-6-66

icent *Seven* at the Crosstown, while a number of the guys go to Brown's concert. Other movies Elvis will see during his time at home include *Cat Ballou, The Ten Commandments, Duel at Diablo, Night of the Grizzly, Let's Kill Uncle, A Fine Madness,* and *Rasputin—The Mad Monk.*

08 Sunday
The Colonel has once again arranged a Mother's Day program of Elvis' recordings on radio stations across the country, both as a promotion and in memory of Elvis' mother, Gladys.

13 Friday
As on many other nights, Elvis rents out the Fairgrounds after the movies.

18 Wednesday
From midnight to 7:00 A.M. Thursday morning the group consumes 201 Cokes, seven Pronto Pops, two bags of peanuts, sixteen candy bars, fifty-eight cups of coffee, thirty-one ice-cream sandwiches, five dill pickles, sixteen bags of potato chips, and twelve devil's food cakes, for a total of $101.05 billed by Fairgrounds Amusements.

22 Sunday
On many Sundays Elvis plays touch football at Whitehaven High School, near Graceland.

25 Wednesday
At 1:00 A.M. Elvis leaves for Nashville on a chartered Greyhound equipped with fifteen extra pillows.

At Studio B Elvis meets his new producer, thirty-year-old Felton Jarvis. Chet Atkins, never a night owl, has brought in Felton, who has recently joined the RCA staff, because he thinks Felton has a temperament better suited to Elvis' and to staying up for all-night sessions. Felton, a huge fan of Elvis', recorded an Elvis tribute/imitation, "Don't Knock Elvis," before going on to

Invoices, Memphis Fairgrounds, May 1966

a career as an r & b producer in his native Atlanta. This will be Elvis' first time in the studio for nonsoundtrack recording in two and a half years, and his task, as spelled out by RCA under the terms of the new contract, is to deliver two singles, a Christmas single, and a religious album. Working from 10:00 P.M. to 7:00 A.M. on the first night and continuing through the four-day session, Elvis will show a greater degree of musical focus than he has in years, concentrating primarily on the gospel numbers that will make up the album, *How Great Thou Art*, but also completing a handful of pop tunes, including Bob Dylan's "Tomorrow Is a Long Time," learned from the *Odetta Sings Dylan* album.

With Jordanaires Neal Matthews, Gordon Stoker, Hoyt Hawkins, and Ray Walker at RCA studio, Nashville, May 1966

26 Thursday

Tonight's session runs from 6:30 P.M. until 7:00 A.M. One of the highlights of the first three days of the session is the presence of the Imperials, formed as an all-star gospel quartet by one of Elvis' singing idols, Jake Hess, the previous year. The Imperials are a last-minute suggestion from Chet Atkins' secretary, Mary B. Lynch, via Tom Diskin when Diskin is unable to locate Jimmy Jones of the Harmonizing Four. Elvis could not be more happy with their presence, however, attempting in several instances to give Hess the vocal lead. These religious recordings are one of the highlights of Elvis' latter-day recording career, and one of the achievements of which he is most proud.

An interesting sidelight: Tonight's session marks the debut of David Briggs, a young piano player recently arrived from Muscle Shoals, Alabama, who is booked for the first session, beginning at 6:30 P.M. (at which generally nothing is recorded), because regular pianist Floyd Cramer is working elsewhere until 9:00 P.M. To everyone's surprise Elvis shows up on time and ready to work, and

Briggs accompanies him on a cover of Ketty Lester's r & b–tinged ballad "Love Letters," remaining in his chair even after Cramer arrives because Elvis has grown used to his sound. Briggs will become an integral part of Elvis' recording band in the early seventies, then of his touring band a few years later.

27 Friday

Recording runs from 7:00 P.M. to 5:00 A.M.

28 Saturday

Felton extends the session in hopes of fulfilling RCA's requirements, but with the Imperials gone (they had a prior booking in Canada), material running out, and Elvis' spirits flagging, just two songs are completed between 7:00 and 10:00 P.M. As a result, a second session is scheduled two weeks later in hopes of getting material more suitable for singles.

JUNE

10 Friday

Elvis is back in Nashville but holes up at the Albert Pick Motel complaining of a bad cold. He sends Red West to the studio in his place to lay down

reference vocals against the instrumental tracks.

11 Saturday

Elvis remains at the motel, still refusing to go to the studio for reasons that are unclear to the entourage. He listens to the recordings that Red has done of "Indescribably Blue," "I'll Remember You," and Red's own composition, "If Every Day Was Like Christmas," on all of which Elvis' stand-in sounds remarkably like the star himself, singing with sensitivity and feeling.

12 Sunday

Elvis finally reports to the studio, spending just thirty minutes on vocals for the three songs, every one of which obviously has personal meaning for him despite the brevity of the session.

14 Tuesday

Back in Memphis, before resuming his routine of filmgoing followed by excursions to the Fairgrounds, Elvis dictates a note to Felton: "Dear Felton, Please convey how much I deeply appreciate the cooperation and consideration shown to me and my associates during my last two trips to Nashville. I would like to thank you, the engineers, musicians, singers and everyone connected with the sessions. Please see that every one of them know my feelings. And as General MacArthur once said, 'I shall return.' Gratefully, Elvis Presley."

26 Sunday

Elvis flies back to Los Angeles with Red West, Jerry Schilling, Marty Lacker, and Charlie Hodge, because his bus needs a new engine. Joe Esposito, Alan Fortas, Richard Davis, Mike Keaton, Ray Sitton, Sonny West, and Billy Smith have left a few days earlier, driving Elvis' new black Cadillac Eldorado convertible and several other cars plus a trailer full of motorcycles.

27 Monday

Elvis reports to MGM for a music meeting and wardrobe fittings for *Double Trouble*, which is for the time being called *You're Killing Me*. Norman Taurog will once again direct, with Judd Bernard and Irwin Winkler producing.

28 Tuesday

Elvis works on the new soundtrack from 7:00 P.M. to 2:45 A.M. at Radio Recorders with a complete contingent of musicians from Nashville.

Tracy Smith, Gladys' retarded younger brother, who has lived on and off with the family since childhood, dies after a brief illness. Elvis has always been kind to his uncle Tracy, whose favorite saying was "I got my nerves in the dirt."

29 Wednesday

After a 7:00 P.M. cast insurance medical exam, Elvis resumes soundtrack recording at the MGM recording stage. It is indicative of both his growing disenchantment with Radio Recorders and his utter disdain for the soundtrack material that he acquiesces to MGM's desire to cut costs by recording at the studio. Work ends at 3:00 A.M.

30 Thursday

From 7:00 P.M. until midnight, once again on MGM's recording stage, Elvis overdubs vocals for three more songs.

Soul singer Jackie Wilson opens an eleven-day engagement at The Trip on Sunset Boulevard, and George Klein, taking his summer vacation in Hollywood to coincide with the filming of Elvis' latest picture, organizes an expedition to the club, most likely on the second weekend of the booking. Elvis has been a huge admirer of Wilson's ever since seeing him perform in Las Vegas in November of 1956 as lead singer for Billy Ward's Dominoes, and brings most of the entourage with him for the show. Meeting Wilson for the first time, Elvis takes the opportunity not only to tell him how much he admires his singing but to invite him to visit the *Double Trouble* set. Also in the audience on the night that Elvis attends is singer James Brown, whose performance Elvis so much admired in the 1964 concert film *The T.A.M.I. Show*. Klein, who has had both Jackie Wilson and James Brown on his Memphis television show a number of times, brings Elvis over to Brown's table, where, after the usual exchange of compliments, Brown says of his unsuccessful attempts to reach Elvis on the phone, "Man, Elvis, you sure do sleep a lot." According to Klein, "Elvis almost fell on the floor laughing. He said, 'Aw, James, you know how it is, being a night person . . .' And James said, 'I know, brother,' and slapped Elvis' hand."

Elvis will maintain friendships with both Brown and Wilson until his death.

June Record Releases

Single: "Love Letters" (#19) /"Come What May" (shipped June 8). "Love Letters" is the sole cut from the May sessions with any hope of success on the singles charts—and even then, for all of its feeling, it is scarcely in the pop mainstream. With sales of 400,000, it barely outsells "Frankie and Johnny."

LP: *Paradise Hawaiian Style* (#15). This soundtrack charts higher than the last (*Frankie and Johnny*) but sells 25,000 less.

JULY

01 Friday

Elvis begins a week of rehearsals for *Double Trouble* at MGM.

06 Wednesday

Paradise Hawaiian Style opens nationwide and will rank #40 for the year, grossing half a million dollars beyond its $2 million cost.

11 Monday

Principal photography begins on *Double Trouble*. Either this week or, possibly, the previous one, during rehearsals, Jackie Wilson visits Elvis on the set. Wilson will carry around an autographed print of the picture taken on the set until stricken with illness eight years later.

12 Tuesday

The Colonel turns down a movie offer from Japan with word that Mr. Presley is booked through 1969.

30 Saturday

After considering titles like *A Girl in Every Port* and *Easy Does It*, Hal Wallis decides that Elvis' next Paramount picture, in which he will play a Navy SEAL scuba diver, will be titled *Easy Come, Easy Go*.

Double Trouble, summer 1966

With Jackie Wilson at MGM studio, July 1966

AUGUST

06 Saturday

During filming of *Double Trouble*, Elvis will spend most weekends in either Las Vegas or Palm Springs, where the Colonel now has a home loaned to him cost-free by the William Morris Agency.

16 Tuesday

The Colonel makes an agreement with RCA for the release of Elvis' recordings on eight-track tape at an advance against royalties of $100,000, which, as a side deal, will be split 50-50 between Elvis and the Colonel.

22 Monday

Joe Esposito returns to Memphis in order to drive the bus with its new engine back to California. The Colonel arranges to give the Dodge motor home to the children's charity TEACH.

30 Tuesday

Elvis completes principal photography on *Double Trouble*.

RCA decides not to wait until late 1967 to pick up its option on Elvis' contract, informing him that they are extending it as of now through December of 1974.

Throughout the summer the press has been reporting rumors of marriage between Elvis and Priscilla. In a letter that appears in *Elvis Monthly*, Vernon writes to the official British fan magazine to quash the story but adds that he wouldn't object to his son marrying Priscilla or anyone else he might choose.

SEPTEMBER

02 Friday

Elvis completes his work on *Double Trouble*.

06 Tuesday

In preparation for *Easy Come, Easy Go*, Hal Wallis writes a long letter to the Colonel, once again expressing concern about Elvis' appearance, which he feels has deteriorated significantly since *Roustabout*. He refers to responses from exhibitors and fans who say something must be "radically wrong" with the star. According to Wallis, Elvis' hair is too

As a navy frogman, *Easy Come, Easy Go*, fall 1966

fluffed up, too black, and looks too much like a wig, but the bottom line is that he doesn't look like a Navy frogman.

14 Wednesday

The Colonel informs Hal Wallis of Elvis' continuing disenchantment with Radio Recorders and his willingness to do the soundtrack for *Easy Come, Easy Go* on the soundstage.

21 Wednesday

Elvis signs a one-year lease on an ultramodern home in Palm Springs at 1350 Ladera Circle.

27 Tuesday

Elvis reports to Paramount for preproduction for *Easy Come, Easy Go*, attending a music meeting with Hal Wallis and director John Rich, who also directed Elvis in *Roustabout*.

28 Wednesday

Elvis arrives late for a noon wardrobe fitting, then takes lunch in his dressing room. As a consequence, he is also late to the recording session, as is noted with annoyance in internal Paramount production notes.

29 Thursday

Despite a 3:00 P.M. appointment to get his hair cut at Paramount, Elvis has it cut at home, arriving at the studio at 4:25 P.M., an hour after the scheduled start of his recording session. By midnight he has completed several songs, including "She's a Machine." After he leaves, the band cuts instrumental tracks for a Ray Charles tune, "Leave My Woman Alone," and a new number called "You Gotta Stop." When Elvis subsequently expresses his preference for "You Gotta Stop," it is substituted for "She's a Machine" in the film.

September Record Release

Single: "Spinout" (#40)/"All That I Am" (#41) (shipped September 13). The title song for the about-to-be-released film sells the by-now-predictable 400,000 but never rises above #40, a new all-time low for a nonseasonal single A-side.

OCTOBER

03 Monday
Principal photography begins on *Easy Come, Easy Go*, Elvis' last picture for Hal Wallis and Paramount.

10 Monday
Elvis films on location at the Long Beach Naval Station.

October Record Release

LP: *Spinout* (#18). The Colonel has pushed for more up-tempo songs on this soundtrack, and as a result the album is more "peppy" than some of Elvis' recent releases. The best songs, however, do not come from the film at all but are the three bonus cuts from the May Nashville sessions, including a raunchy, foot-stomping cover of the Clovers' 1953 "Down in the Alley" and the Dylan number "Tomorrow Is a Long Time." Sales of 300,000 are a slight improvement over the last two soundtrack albums.

NOVEMBER

07 Monday
Principal photography of *Easy Come, Easy Go* is completed.

22 Tuesday
Perhaps out of sheer exasperation, or maybe just to get a measure of revenge, Hal Wallis delays releasing Elvis from *Easy Come, Easy Go* until today, despite the fact that shooting concluded two weeks ago.

Elvis spends most of the two-week interval at his new Palm Springs home.

23 Wednesday
Spinout opens nationwide, and will be ranked #57 for the year, grossing only $1.77 million. Nonetheless, Elvis remains the tenth-highest-paid star in 1966, down just four places from 1965.

24 Thursday
After spending Thanksgiving with

Yoga class, *Easy Come, Easy Go*

Colonel Parker in Palm Springs, Elvis heads for home in his rebuilt bus.

29 Tuesday
Just outside of Little Rock, Elvis hears George Klein play Tom Jones' "Green Green Grass of Home" on his radio show and calls again and again to request George to keep playing it, much to the annoyance of Red West, who brought Elvis the song the year before and was told it was far too country for Elvis to even consider recording. Elvis will eventually record

November Record Release

Single: "If Every Day Was Like Christmas"/"How Would You Like to Be" (shipped November 15). The new Christmas single that both the Colonel and RCA were so anxious for Elvis to record never charts and sells only 200,000 copies. This can only be a disappointment for Red West, who wrote and first recorded "If Every Day Was Like Christmas," but it will be a long-term seller in many subsequent releases.

the country weeper in 1975—but by then its hit potential has passed.

At Graceland Elvis' bedroom has been redecorated by Bernie and Ann Grenadier, with a black-and-red Spanish motif on the walls and the ceiling covered with green Naugahyde into which two television sets have been embedded at an angle so that Elvis (like President Johnson) can have a full range of viewing activities in bed. With minor changes, this decor will remain substantially the same until Elvis' death.

DECEMBER

02 Friday
The movies at the Memphian this evening are *Fantastic Voyage* and *Dead Heat on a Merry-Go-Round*. Elvis screens movies almost every other night in December, including *Stagecoach* with Ann-Margret, *The Professionals*, *Funeral in Berlin*, *Who's Afraid of Virginia Woolf?*, *Seconds*, and (several times) *After the Fox*, starring one of his all-time favorites, Peter Sellers.

05 Monday

Elvis begins to take a serious interest in horseback riding, purchasing three pairs of boots, five jackets, and various other elements of riding costume and equipment from Ben Howell and Son Saddlery in Whitehaven.

12 Monday

Elvis donates checks totaling $105,000 to combined local charities.

15 Thursday

Elvis gives George Klein a yellow Cadillac convertible.

19 Monday

This week Elvis is interviewed by the *Memphis Commercial Appeal* and reminisces about Christmases past and present. "Everything is so dreamy when you are young," he says. "After you grow up it kind of becomes—just real."

20 Tuesday

Elvis buys two bay horses, one of which is his Christmas gift to Priscilla.

As part of this new gentleman-farmer phase, he also purchases a horse for Jerry Schilling's fiancée, Sandy Kawelo, so that Priscilla will have someone with whom to ride.

24 Saturday

Just before Christmas, Elvis proposes to Priscilla, presenting her with a ring he has purchased from jeweler Harry Levitch some time before.

25 Sunday

Elvis spends Christmas at Graceland with Priscilla and his family. Christmas dinner is catered by Monte's Catering Service.

28 Wednesday

Just how involved Elvis has become in his equestrian activities is evident by the rapid increase in his purchases. Today he returns one of the bay horses and buys a registered sorrel horse and a yellow horse.

29 Thursday

Elvis buys a chestnut sorrel horse named Whirlaway.

30 Friday

Today's purchase is a registered quarter horse gelding, along with a great deal of riding equipment.

31 Saturday

Further additions to the stable are a sorrel horse named Spurt, a bay horse named Guy, and one chestnut horse.

Elvis holds his annual New Year's Eve party at the Manhattan Club but does not attend because he cannot find a parking place outside. His guests enjoy catering by Monte's and music from Willie Mitchell and his band.

Elvis' accountants report that in 1966 Elvis' personal income from motion pictures is $2,500,000 plus $644,000 from music and recording. Personal income tax comes to more than $1,100,000.

Date 1967	Firm	Amt Paid	Check No	Inv'd and Explanation
1-4	Cecil Stallings			
1-9	Ben Howell & Son Saddlery	250 00	2573	1 Saddle horse
1-5	Morris White	49 71	2567	Bal. Due account
1-5	G. R. Hunter	1,000 00	2577	1 Horse Trailer
1-6	Graceland Farm - W.N. Spence	3,000 00	2579	1 Quarter Horse
1-9	W. W. Tabler, Jr.	171 40	2589	Horse feed 135 Bales hay
1-9	W. N. Spence	250 00	2599	1 Black quarter horse
1-9	David E. Spence	78 00	2603	1 Buckskin mare 10 weeks
1-11	The American Quarter Horse Assn.	1,000 00	2604	1 sorrell horse (Cutter Bill)
1-11	National Palomino Breeders Assn.	5 00	2608	for Transfering Registration
1-13	W.N. Spence, Graceland Farm	5 00	2609	for Transfering Registration
13	Bill J. Spence	900 00	2612	1 Registered Gelding horse (Brown)
13	Horse Services	1,000 00	2617	1 Horse (Midnight Sun)
13	Van Swearengen	1,199 75	2618	Services and Supplies
20	Cecil Stallings	200 00	2620	1 Saddle, pr. chaps
20	J. L. Mason	200 00	2626	1 Bay Mare
25	W.N. Spence - Graceland Farm	250 00	2627	1 Buckskin mare
26	Cecil Stallings, Jr.	750 00	2633	1 Soda Horse (Reno)
30	Horse Services - Bill J. Spence	235 00	2636	1 Bay Mare, 1 Black saddle horse
31	L. W. Turner	2,113 46	2646	Horse Service and Equip
2-6	DLL Farms	750 00	2653	1 Registered horse (Colaghunt)
6	Ben Howell & Son Saddlery	5 00	2669	50 lbs Minerals @ 10¢ lb
6	Lem Couch	534 76	2670	Inv. 1967-1968-1972-1993
6	John McWhirter (M.)	191 00	2676	Shoeing Horses
2	Mrs. Alfred Page	300 00	2698	White Buckskin for Scotty
6	J. H. Ellis	5,000 00	2699	Am. Bred saddle horse
6	Raines Road Animal Clinic	1490 00	2714	one Reg. Quarter Horse
9	George Hutson	180 00	2719	Horses & Dog Treatment
10	Bill J. Spence, Horse Service	42 70	2727	Shoeing Horses
14	George Hutson	761 77	2729	Service and Equipment
20	Walter Stevens	17 50	2735	Shoeing Pal. three Twin Feet
20	Walter Stevens			one 1 Grey Horse
20	Orma L. Senders, Jr.	350 00	2750	One Red Chestnut Gelding
		550 00	2751	Alan Factor, Pal. Mare

Equine expenses, Circle G ledger book

1 9 6 7

Riding at Graceland, c. 1967

JANUARY

02 Monday

This is the date of Elvis' new agreement with Colonel Parker, which for the first time explicitly recognizes that they are engaged in what amounts to a partnership, or joint venture. According to the terms of this contract, Colonel Parker will continue to collect a 25 percent commission on all of Elvis' movie salaries and contractually guaranteed record company advances, but the Colonel will now receive 50 percent of any profits or royalties beyond basic payments from the film and record contracts, as well as 50 percent of all "special," or side, deals.

03 Tuesday

Just how popular horseback riding has become with Elvis and the gang is evidenced by the fact that they rent out the Memphian for movies only four times this month. Almost everything now revolves around horses: buying them, riding them, purchasing equipment for both the horses and their riders. During the next two weeks Elvis will purchase not only his own favorite horse, a registered palomino called Midget's Vandy that he rechristens Rising Sun, but a horse for his father, Midnight Sun, and a Tennessee walker named Traveler.

06 Friday

The barn behind Graceland is being renovated to accommodate its many new residents. Soon it will come to be referred to, in typical Elvis wordplay, as "The House of the Rising Sun."

08 Sunday

Elvis' thirty-second birthday is spent at Graceland, with Gordon Stoker of the Jordanaires paying him a visit.

09 Monday

Today Elvis buys three more horses: a black gelding, a buckskin mare, and a sorrel horse named Cutter's Bill.

15 Sunday

Elvis arranges for the funeral of his uncle-by-marriage Pat Biggs, the husband of Vernon's sister Delta, inviting the widow to live with her mother, Minnie, at Graceland, where she will remain until her death on June 29, 1993. Pat Biggs, a gambler and nightclub owner, had always encouraged Elvis to believe in himself and had been a favorite of his nephew.

17 Tuesday

Elvis has the area behind Graceland cleared and bulldozed to create a riding ring while work continues on the barn.

20 Friday

Elvis buys a bay mare and a buckskin mare.

24 Tuesday

The Colonel renegotiates Elvis' contract with RCA through 1974, with an extension to run through 1980. The annual guarantee (a nonrefundable advance against royalties) will remain at $300,000 per year through 1970 but will be reduced to $200,000 per year for the five years after that and then will pay no advance at all other than a $50,000 payment to both Elvis and the Colonel on or before January 1, 1976. It probably should be noted that this reduction of guaranteed payments works to the Colonel's advantage, in that his 50-50 deal kicks in all the sooner according to the terms of his new agreement with Elvis. In the wake of the RCA extension Elvis sends the Colonel a telegram: "Dear Colonel. The greatest snowman on earth has caused another storm. Looking forward to another great forecast from you. Respectfully, Elvis."

25 Wednesday

Elvis buys a horse for Red West named Keno.

26 Thursday

Elvis buys a bay mare.

31 Tuesday

Today's acquisition is a registered horse named Pokey Dunit.

January Record Release

Single: "Indescribably Blue" (#33) /"Fools Fall in Love" (shipped January 10). The third single to come out of the 1966 Nashville sessions performs even more poorly than the last regular single, selling 300,000 copies.

New partnership agreement between Elvis and the Colonel

January 2, 1967

Mr. Elvis Presley
3764 Highway 51 South
Memphis, Tennessee

Dear Elvis:

As per our understanding on the telephone a few weeks ago here is the amended agreement pertaining to our existing management agreement. The following will be effective as of this date, January 2, 1967:

The regular 25% management commission on existing contracts, their renewals, and new contracts that may be negotiated and completed, will remain the same on all the flat payments.

As of this date on all existing contracts except the music firms contracts, all overages on royalties other than the guaranteed payments now in effect, and profit participations on any contracts now in existance and their renewals, will be 50% to Elvis Presley and 50% to All Star Shows on all overages and profits. All expense payments will be 50% to Elvis Presley and 50% to All Star Shows.

If any agency commissions are to be paid on any contracts this commission will be deducted before division of royalties and profits is made.

The merchandising agreement will remain the same as now in existance.

Regular music firms payments will remain the same as in the past.

Page No. 2

It is understood of course that all promotion, advertising, and office expenses made by All Star Shows will be paid for by All Star Shows under our regular merchandising agreement and unless otherwise agreed to in writing none of these expenses will be charged to any of your percentages with the exception of course of the regular agency commissions as stated above.

Sincerely,

Colonel Thomas A Parker
Col. Thomas A. Parker

Agreed to and accepted:

Elvis A Presley
Elvis A. Presley

FEBRUARY

02 Thursday

Elvis pays $5,000 for an American-bred saddle horse.

04 Saturday

In order to enlarge the riding area behind Graceland, several small buildings, including the house where Billy Smith once lived, are bulldozed, with Elvis gleefully taking part in the work.

06 Monday

Elvis buys a white buckskin horse and a quarter horse named Conchita's Gold, as well as a Case tractor and two El Camino pickup trucks.

08 Wednesday

During a horse-buying expedition in Mississippi, Elvis comes across Twinkletown Farm, a 160-acre cattle ranch marked by a lighted sixty-five-foot-high white cross, near Walls, Mississippi, about ten miles south of Graceland. The property is for sale, and Elvis decides almost immediately to buy it, making a $5,000 down payment toward a $437,000 purchase price on this date. Renamed the Circle G (for Graceland), the ranch will immediately become a new home for Elvis' growing herd of horses, and over the next few weeks Elvis and the guys will adopt the communal cowboy life, as Elvis undertakes extensive and rapid-fire improvements to the property.

10 Friday

Over the next three weeks Elvis purchases more than two dozen pickups and other vehicles for use on the ranch.

14 Tuesday

From Harry Levitch Elvis buys a man's white gold horseshoe ring for $475, a lady's horseshoe pin for $475, and a special Valentine's charm.

15 Wednesday

The main ranch house on the property is too small for the whole group, so Elvis starts buying house trailers and initiates extensive repairs on the septic system.

17 Friday

Elvis continues to buy pickup trucks for the guys, his relatives, and others who work on the property. Today's purchases include one 1967 Chevy custom El Camino, two Dodges, and five Fords, as well as two more house trailers.

20 Monday

Elvis buys a red chestnut gelding and a palomino mare.

21 Tuesday

This is the day Elvis was supposed to report to United Artists in Hollywood for the start of production on *Clambake*. Realizing the impossibility of luring Elvis away from the ranch, the Colonel has arranged for the cast insurance exam to take place at 5:30 P.M. at RCA's Studio B in Nashville, where soundtrack recording is now scheduled to take place. Elvis arrives in a rented Learjet and, after discussing song selection for the film, records until 6:00 A.M. the following morning. It is obvious to all present, however, that he has little interest in the movie songs, focusing instead on the Eddy Arnold standard "You Don't Know Me," on which he expends twenty-one takes but is still not satisfied with the result, re-recording the song at a later date.

22 Wednesday

Recording of backing tracks continues from 7:00 P.M. to 5:00 A.M.—but without Elvis, who remains at his hotel.

23 Thursday

Elvis returns to the studio, wearing a cowboy outfit complete with chaps, to overdub vocals on the pre-recorded instrumental tracks. Some are completed on this date, but several will have to wait until his return to Hollywood. The start of filming has now been pushed back to March 3.

While Elvis is in Nashville, work continues at the ranch, with the delivery of a prefabricated guard-house and storage shed and the installation of a quarter mile of temporary plywood fencing.

25 Saturday

After flying back to Memphis in the early evening, Elvis has the Learjet circle over the ranch.

26 Sunday

Elvis delays his departure to Los Angeles once again, complaining of painful saddle sores. On the recommendation of George Klein's girlfriend, Barbara Little, he calls on Dr. George Nichopoulos to come out to the ranch to examine him. The doctor prescribes an ointment and agrees to call the Colonel to explain the severity of the problem, although he recognizes that the postponement stems more from patient preference than medical emergency. He and Elvis, however, hit it off almost from the start, and this is the beginning of a long-standing relationship, both personal and professional.

28 Tuesday

The Colonel, furious that he has been unable even to get Elvis on the phone, issues a stern warning to Marty Lacker, whose job it is to keep lines of communication open. "We have spent hundreds of dollars in at least three weeks on telephone calls and have accrued practically no information whatsoever and this must stop," he writes, adding that things may soon "come to a head, where we will have some proper assignment, whether it be you or someone else where we have a definite immediate contact at all times."

February Record Release

LP: *How Great Thou Art* (#18). The sincerity and accomplishment of Elvis' performance on the new religious album receives high critical praise but initially finds only 200,000 buyers. The album rewards RCA's and the Colonel's confidence that it will become a strong backlist item, however, and there is understandable pride all around when it becomes Elvis' first Grammy-winning record, receiving the 1967 award for "Best Sacred Performance."

MARCH

03 Friday

The Colonel, embarrassed and frustrated by Elvis' continuing delays, has managed to get a second postponement from United Artists, and Elvis is informed that he is expected to appear without fail on Monday, March 6.

Back on the ranch Elvis continues his spending spree, purchasing a Ford pickup, a Ranger, and eleven Rancheros, as well as another mobile home.

05 Sunday

Elvis finally boards a plane for California with Charlie Hodge, Ray Sitton, Marty Lacker, Red West, Billy Smith, and Larry Geller, as well as a new addition to the group, Gee Gee Gambill, who is married to Elvis' cousin Patsy. Alan Fortas remains at the ranch as foreman, nominally in charge of maintenance and livestock.

06 Monday

Elvis reports to United Artists to meet with Arnold Laven, Arthur Gardner, and Jules Levy, the producers of *Clambake*, and Arthur Nadel, its director. In the evening Elvis records vocal overdubs at the Annex Studios.

At Graceland the money spent on the ranch continues to add up. Today Vernon receives bills for one black Welch pony and for $8,500 worth of fencing.

08 Wednesday

The Colonel is hard at work trying to encourage MGM to come up with a good hard-hitting story for Elvis' next picture. He wants to do away, he says, with the same old scenarios focusing on girls in bikinis and nightclub scenes "which have been in the last fifteen pictures. . . . I sincerely hope that you are looking in some crystal ball with your people to come up with some good, strong, rugged stories."

09 Thursday

Sometime late Wednesday night or

Clambake set, spring 1967

early Thursday morning Elvis falls in the bathroom at Rocca Place. The Colonel arrives, and a doctor is called, returning on Friday with a portable X-ray machine which indicates that Elvis has not sustained a fracture. This unforeseen event, which causes yet another delay in the start of production, gives the Colonel the opportunity he has been long waiting for, and he upbraids Elvis for actions that could jeopardize his entire career, then calls a meeting of all the guys in which he reprimands each and every one—but Larry Geller most of all. There are going to have to be some changes made, the Colonel thunders; economies are going to have to go into effect; and some people had better start looking for new jobs.

12 Sunday

After learning of the accident, Vernon and Priscilla fly out immediately from Memphis. The Colonel has by now dismissed Marty Lacker as coforeman, leaving Joe Esposito in sole charge. Larry Geller is essentially banished, forbidden by the Colonel's edict to spend any time alone with

Elvis. There are to be no more religious discussions and no more books. "Some of you," the Colonel declares, "think maybe [Elvis] is Jesus Christ who should wear robes and walk down the street helping people. But that's not who he is."

15 Wednesday

Jerry Schilling marries his long-time fiancée, Sandy Kawelo, in a ceremony in Las Vegas not attended by Elvis because he is in Palm Springs recuperating from his fall. At about this time the Colonel, who has very strongly encouraged Jerry and Sandy to wed, begins planning for Elvis' wedding.

20 Monday

After eleven days off, Elvis finally returns to the studio to begin rehearsals for *Clambake*.

In Nashville, producer Felton Jarvis overdubs an instrumental track for a home recording made by Elvis late last year with Charlie Hodge accompanying him on piano. The song, "Suppose," a romantic ballad, is one that Elvis continues to be drawn to and will re-record in June.

22 Wednesday

Principal photography for *Clambake* finally begins, with Elvis seemingly restored both to health and to his old Hollywood state of mind. Costar Bill Bixby recalls many high jinks on the set, but he also remembers an album that Elvis plays for him on numerous occasions, a series of recitations by French actor Charles Boyer called *Where Does Love Go?* Elvis listens to one song in particular again and again, a melancholy composition called "Softly As I Leave You," which Elvis explains are the words of a dying man to his wife.

Easy Come, Easy Go opens nationwide just before Easter. Poor box office reports from the start provide Hal Wallis with all the proof he needs that Presley is no longer the attraction he once was. By year's end the picture has grossed less than $2 million and ranks #50 in box-office receipts.

March Record Release

EP: *Easy Come, Easy Go.* This six-song soundtrack bears the distinction of being the least successful recording of Elvis' career as well as his last EP release, as the format is finally phased out. It never enters the charts and sells a paltry 30,000.

APRIL

05 Wednesday

Double Trouble opens nationwide, just weeks after *Easy Come, Easy Go*—but Hal Wallis does not even bother to object. This picture will rank eight places lower at the box office than the Wallis film and take in just $1.6 million.

12 Wednesday

Vernon oversees the installation of the ironwork over the windows that can be seen at Graceland today, replacing burglarproof screens that were installed in 1963.

27 Thursday

Elvis completes work on *Clambake*.

28 Friday

Rumors of Elvis' imminent marriage appear in the press just as members of the wedding party begin to assemble in Palm Springs. Security is so tight that not even Alan Fortas and Lamar Fike, in Memphis and Nashville respectively, receive invitations, with George Klein and jeweler Harry Levitch the only non–family members to fly out from Memphis. Larry Geller first learns of the wedding from a supermarket tabloid.

April Record Release

Single: "Long Legged Girl (With the Short Dress On)"(#63)/"That's Someone You Never Forget"(#92) (shipped April 28). Three weeks after the release of *Double Trouble*, RCA comes out with a single containing one song from the soundtrack backed by a cut from the 1962 *Pot Luck* album. Sales barely approach 200,000 copies.

MAY

01 Monday

After midnight, on Monday morning, the wedding party (consisting of family, George Klein, Harry Levitch, and those members of the entourage already in California) leaves for Las Vegas in two leased jets, and at 3:30 A.M. Elvis and Priscilla obtain a $15 marriage license at the Clark County Courthouse. The ceremony is held at approximately 11:45 A.M. at the Aladdin Hotel in the second-floor suite of the Colonel's friend, owner Milton Prell, with Nevada Supreme Court Justice David Zenoff presiding and the Colonel in charge. Out of the entire entourage and their wives, only Joe Esposito and Marty Lacker, Elvis' two best men, are present, with everyone else told at the last minute by Colonel Parker's direction that there is no room for them at the ceremony. A press conference is held in the Aladdin Room immediately after the ceremony, with reporters peppering the wedding party with questions. "Our little girl is going to be a good wife," says Priscilla's father,

Colonel Beaulieu. "I guess it was about time," declares Elvis, then turns to his father. "Hey, Daddy, help me," he says. "I can't reach you, son," declares Vernon, smiling. "You just slipped through my fingers." "Remember," says the Colonel, "you can't end bachelorhood without getting married."

At the reception afterward all members of the entourage are present with the exception of Red West, who is so furious at his and his wife Pat's exclusion from the ceremony that he will be estranged from Elvis for the next two years.

04 Thursday

After two days in Palm Springs, the newly married couple fly to Memphis, arriving at about 6:00 A.M.

05 Friday

Elvis and Priscilla visit the ranch but return in the evening to see *Casino Royale* at the newly refurbished Memphian Theater. Throughout the summer Elvis' interest in the ranch wanes, and he begins to spend more and more time in Memphis, screening movies at least four times a week.

According to Priscilla, it is during this time period that she persuades Elvis to burn the books the Colonel has banned. One night at Graceland they dump a large box filled with books and magazines into an abandoned well, pour gasoline over the pile, and "kiss the past goodbye."

08 Monday

Ann-Margret marries the actor Roger Smith in Las Vegas.

16 Tuesday

Elvis sees *A Shot in the Dark* and *After the Fox*, a Peter Sellers double bill, at the Memphian.

24 Wednesday

For Priscilla's twenty-fourth birthday, Elvis buys her a special "Happy Birthday" charm with rubies and sapphires from Harry Levitch.

29 Monday

Dressed in their wedding attire, Elvis and Priscilla hold a reception at

Wedding group, May 1, 1967, *(left to right)* Joe Esposito, Marty Lacker, George Klein, Billy Smith, Marvin "Gee Gee" Gambill *(courtesy of Jerry Schilling)*

Graceland for friends, relatives, and employees. The room just off the pool patio that held the recently dismantled slot-car track has been decorated in green and white for the 8:30 P.M. affair, with a buffet and wedding cake provided by Monte's Catering Service and accordion music from Tony Barrasso. Elvis screens *War Wagon* at the Memphian later in the evening and returns to the theater almost every night until going back to California.

31 Wednesday

Elvis holds a bowling party at the Whitehaven Plaza from midnight to 4:00 A.M.

JUNE

03 Saturday

Harry Levitch makes a special handmade wedding band for Elvis.

05 Monday

Elvis rents the Memphis Fairgrounds from 12:30 to 3:30 A.M.

07 Wednesday

For Ann-Margret's opening in Vegas, Elvis sends a guitar-shaped flower arrangement, something he will do for every one of her Vegas openings until his death.

09 Friday

Just before leaving for California, Priscilla learns that she is pregnant.

10 Saturday

A somewhat larger caravan than usual sets out for California. For the first and only time wives are included, and the trip out is something like an extended family vacation, with conventional tourist excursions and home movies taken by Joe Esposito. Included are the Espositos, the Billy Smiths, the Schillings, the Gambills, the Lackers, and Charlie Hodge, with Elvis at the wheel of the Greyhound and a trail of cars behind.

Wedding press conference

13 Tuesday

The group stays over two nights in Flagstaff, Arizona, while visiting the Grand Canyon.

19 Monday

Elvis reports to MGM for preproduction of *Speedway*, beginning with a 10:00 A.M. music meeting and a 2:00 P.M. wardrobe fitting. Douglas Laurence will produce the eighth Elvis film to be directed by Norman Taurog. Elvis presents costar Nancy Sinatra with a car that has "Speedway" painted on one door and "Starring Nancy and Elvis" on the other.

20 Tuesday

From 7:00 P.M. to 4:00 A.M. Elvis records the soundtrack for *Speedway* at the MGM studio in Culver City. At the end of the session Elvis cuts two new versions of "Suppose," the song that Felton overdubbed in Nashville in March. Charlie Hodge again provides piano accompaniment, this time backed by a full complement of studio musicians.

21 Wednesday

The Colonel requests that Elvis'

dressing room at MGM be painted and made "more homelike."

Elvis completes soundtrack recording and is visited by Vernon and Dee and the three Stanley boys. They all meet New York governor Nelson Rockefeller while he is at the MGM studio between 7:00 and 11:00 P.M.

26 Monday

Principal photography on *Speedway* begins.

June Record Release

LP: *Double Trouble* (#47). The nine-song soundtrack is supplemented by three cuts from the May 1963 recording session, only one previously unreleased. Sales are less than 200,000 copies.

JULY

01 Saturday

Elvis, Vernon, and various members of the entourage travel to Las Vegas to see Ann-Margret's show.

12 Wednesday

Back on the movie set, Elvis announces that Priscilla is pregnant, and tells reporters, "This is the greatest thing that has ever happened to me."

16 Sunday

Elvis is in Las Vegas once again for the weekend. During the filming of *Speedway* he spends most weekends either in Las Vegas or Palm Springs.

AUGUST

07 Monday

In a special arrangement above and beyond the terms of the regular RCA recording contract, Elvis and the Colonel receive $25,000 for the *Clambake* LP and $35,000 for the Colonel's new promotional scheme for the 1957 Christmas album. This promotion will include a Christmas radio show broadcast on more than 2,400 stations, and the $60,000 appears to be

With Nancy Sinatra, *Speedway*, summer 1967

equally split between Elvis and the Colonel.

08 Tuesday

With Elvis' interest in the ranch having waned almost to the point of nonexistence, Vernon begins to sell off pickup trucks, mobile homes, and cattle.

18 Friday

Principal photography for *Speedway* is completed. Sometime during the filming, Marty Lacker returns to Memphis to join Alan Fortas on the ranch. This is just one of a number of personnel changes essentially precipitated by the *Clambake* crisis. Larry Geller, of course, has long since decamped, and Jerry Schilling has decided to strike out on his own, even-

tually settling on apprenticeship as a film editor. Red and Sonny West are no longer around, and the social circle is shrinking in conjunction with plans to seek a new house that will encourage a more intimate family atmosphere.

21 Monday

In the morning Elvis completes looping on *Speedway* and after lunch has makeup tests for his next picture, *Stay Away, Joe*.

22 Tuesday

Released from *Speedway*, Elvis is scheduled to begin two nights of recording at RCA's Studio A on Sunset Boulevard for a nonsoundtrack release. The decision was made in June not to return to Nashville but to record in Los Angeles with "more

At MGM Studio, *Speedway* recording session, June 21, 1967, with *(left to right)* Nancy Sinatra, Nelson Rockefeller, Vernon and Dee Presley, and Ricky, David, and Billy Stanley

sophisticated" musicians, and although Felton Jarvis will continue to produce, it is veteran session guitarist Billy Strange (an alumnus of several Elvis soundtrack sessions and one of the principal architects of Nancy Sinatra's recent success) who will serve as arranger and contractor for the session. Plans are radically altered at the last minute when Richard Davis accidentally runs over and kills a gardener who steps out from behind a hedge on a curve screened from view near Elvis' Bel Air home. The Colonel, fearing bad publicity,

sends Elvis and Priscilla off to Las Vegas accompanied by Joe, Charlie, Billy, and Gee Gee.

26 Saturday

Elvis and Priscilla arrive home in Memphis at 8:20 A.M.

27 Sunday

Elvis continues to spend some time at the ranch, but instead of horseback riding he has taken up a new hobby, target shooting, and purchases rifles, clay targets, ear protectors, and other supplies. By the

end of September he decides to put the ranch up for sale.

August Record Release

Single: "There's Always Me"(#56)/"Judy" (#78) (shipped August 8). With virtually nothing left in the can, there is no new material available for release, and RCA selects two songs from 1961's *Something for Everybody* album for single release. This single will do marginally better than April's "Long Legged Girl."

With costars Burgess Meredith and Katy Jurado, on location, *Stay Away, Joe,* fall 1967

With Felton Jarvis, Nashville sessions,
September 10–11, 1967 *(courtesy of Mary Jarvis)*

SEPTEMBER

10 Sunday

The abrupt cancellation of the Los Angeles session has led to its rescheduling in Nashville during the brief hiatus that Elvis has between films. The aim is still to record material for new singles as well as "bonus" songs to fill out the *Clambake* soundtrack album. One of the songs Elvis has focused on recently is "Guitar Man," a minor hit that summer for its writer, Jerry Reed. As they fool around with the song in the studio, the musicians find it difficult to replicate Reed's guitar sound with the exactitude that Elvis demands, so eventually Chet Atkins' secretary, Mary Lynch, tracks Reed down for the session. The resulting song is a triumph of artistry and feeling, and Reed backs up Elvis with great effectiveness on the classic blues "Big Boss Man" as well—but the good feeling is dissipated when Freddy Bienstock gets into a publishing dispute with Reed and the songwriter storms out. Recording continues until 5:30 A.M., but the heart has gone out of the session.

11 Monday

Recording continues from 6:00 P.M. to 3:30 A.M., with Elvis taking over the piano bench for Rodgers and Hammerstein's inspirational "You'll Never Walk Alone" (a big hit for Roy Hamilton, one of Elvis' r & b idols, in 1954).

29 Friday

Memphis mayor William Ingram and Governor Buford Ellington each declares "Elvis Presley Day" in recognition of the star's many charitable contributions.

OCTOBER

01 Sunday

Elvis returns to Nashville's Studio B to record three songs for the soundtrack of his next film, *Stay Away, Joe.* He has not even been involved in song selection and is so discouraged by the quality of the movie material that he makes Felton Jarvis swear that he will never release one of its songs on record, "Dominick," a song sung to a bull.

04 Wednesday

Elvis flies to Los Angeles with Sonny West, Joe Esposito, Billy Smith, Gee Gee Gambill, and Charlie Hodge.

05 Thursday

Elvis holes up in Las Vegas for a few days before traveling to the Arizona location shoot for his new picture, to be produced by Douglas Laurence and directed by Peter Tewksbury, the director of such television comedies as *Father Knows Best* and *My Three Sons.*

08 Sunday

Elvis reports for shooting in Sedona, Arizona.

09 Monday

Principal photography on *Stay Away, Joe* begins.

26 Thursday

Priscilla and several other wives and girlfriends leave Memphis to travel to Sedona.

On the set Elvis tells a reporter from *Cosmopolitan* magazine that he still has a lot to learn about acting. Much of his progress, he says, comes from just "hanging out with real good professionals, and there isn't a day that goes by that I don't pick up on something from the other actors."

September Record Release

Single: "Big Boss Man" (#38)/"You Don't Know Me" (#44) (shipped September 26). The Nashville session provides both the A-side and the re-recording of Eddy Arnold's "You Don't Know Me." Sales do not exceed 350,000, but this is a big leap forward in terms of both quality and commitment—although it might have been a bigger leap if the dispute over "Guitar Man" had been resolved in time for it to be the A-side.

October Record Release

LP: *Clambake* (#40). Although the two best songs from the soundtrack recording session, "How Can You Lose What You Never Had" and "The Girl I Never Loved," have been dropped from the film, they appear here as "bonus" tracks. Also included are both sides of the current single, along with "Guitar Man," on which a deal has finally been worked out and which will subsequently appear as a single. Another "bonus" included in the album's first pressing of 300,000 is a twelve-by-twelve color wedding shot of Elvis and Priscilla. Even that, however, fails to save the album from lower sales than the poorly received *Double Trouble* soundtrack.

NOVEMBER

04 Saturday

There is an auction of equipment and other items at the Circle G that brings in $108,000.

Sometime during this month Elvis and Priscilla purchase their first Los Angeles home, at 1174 Hillcrest Road in the Trousdale section of Beverly Hills, for approximately $400,000.

06 Monday

The Colonel has been busy trying to line up work for Elvis, now that his movie contracts have run out. He makes a deal with National General Pictures at around this time for one film (*Charro!*) that will pay Elvis $850,000 plus 50 percent of the profits, and he continues negotiations, begun in October, with NBC West Coast vice president Tom Sarnoff for a Christmas show to be televised in 1968.

22 Wednesday

Elvis completes location shooting for *Stay Away, Joe*.

Clambake opens nationwide. It will appear at #15 for one week on *Variety*'s National Box Office Survey.

27 Monday

Elvis arranges for a catered lunch for the cast and crew on the set at the conclusion of filming of *Stay Away, Joe*.

28 Tuesday

Elvis completes looping and is released from *Stay Away, Joe*.

30 Thursday

An architect has been hired to draw up plans for a nursery and other renovations on the second floor at Graceland.

DECEMBER

01 Friday

Elvis has pledged a total of $10,500 to the Memphis Jewish Community Center Building Fund and pays a $2,500 installment on this date.

On location, *Stay Away, Joe*

07 Thursday

Since the completion of *Stay Away, Joe*, Elvis, Joe Esposito, Charlie Hodge, and Gee Gee Gambill have been staying at the Aladdin Hotel in Las Vegas, and they return to Memphis today.

10 Sunday

Elvis flies to San Francisco with Priscilla to visit her family, now stationed at Travis Air Force Base, near Sacramento.

16 Saturday

Elvis and Priscilla return to Memphis.

20 Wednesday

Elvis buys the Colonel an eighteen-karat gold Accutron calendar wristwatch for $595 and a second watch for Tom Diskin. He also purchases a new grand piano for Graceland.

22 Friday

Priscilla buys a gentleman's watch for $1,500 from Harry Levitch.

24 Sunday

Chairs, champagne flutes, tablecloths, and other party supplies are rented from Dixie Rents for the Graceland Christmas party. The grounds are decorated with the usual life-size Nativity scene and eight lighted garland trees that have always been rented but are now owned by Graceland.

25 Monday

Christmas at Graceland.

By the end of the year the ranch operation has been shut down and the remaining horses moved back to Graceland, where Elvis and everyone else continue to ride in the fields behind the mansion.

31 Sunday

Elvis' New Year's Eve party is held for the first time at the Thunderbird Lounge on Adams Street and catered by Monte's, with music by Flash and the Board of Directors, Stax recording artists the Bar Kays, Vaneese Starks, and Sun Records rockabilly singer Billy Lee Riley. Elvis dances several times with Priscilla, including once to his request of "Summertime."

Elvis' accountants report that in 1967 Elvis' personal income is $2,700,000 from motion pictures and $817,000 from recording. His taxes are $1,400,000.

1968

JANUARY

03 Wednesday

Elvis complains to RCA about the mastering of his new single, "Guitar Man," which sounds to him as if it has been altered from the sound he achieved in the studio, where his voice was more integrated with the band.

08 Monday

Elvis celebrates his thirty-third birthday at Graceland, attending the movies at the Memphian later in the evening.

12 Friday

NBC vice president Tom Sarnoff announces that a deal has been struck for Elvis' first television appearance since 1960. The agreement, which includes a feature film as part of the deal, will pay Elvis $250,000 for the Christmas special, $850,000 for the film, and $25,000 for the film's music. Thus the Colonel can say that he has once again exceeded his benchmark figure of $1,000,000.

15 Monday

Elvis flies to Nashville to record two new tracks for *Stay Away, Joe*, as well as some additional material for RCA. He is accompanied by all the Nashville regulars, along with Jerry

With Priscilla and Lisa Marie at Graceland, February 1968

Reed once again on guitar, in a session that runs until 5:00 A.M. Elvis' opener is a rousing Jerry Reed–driven version of Chuck Berry's "Too Much Monkey Business," but the movie song that he takes up next drains all the energy out of the session, as Elvis struggles through thirty takes of "Goin' Home" before quitting and going home himself, in his rented Lincoln, to the Jack Spencer Motor Hotel.

16 Tuesday

Work resumes at 10:00 P.M., continuing until 5:00 A.M. once again. Elvis turns immediately to the second movie song, "Stay Away," a variation on the "Greensleeves" melody. This marks the end of the soundtrack part of the session, and with no good material in sight Elvis finally settles on a new Jerry Reed tune, "U.S. Male," which is suggested by guitarist Chip Young. Although one of the cardinal rules of an Elvis session is that There Shall Be No Pitching of Outside Songs, Freddy Bienstock offers no demurral, because Elvis has already rejected all of the songs that have been officially pitched. With Reed's typically offbeat accompaniment, "U.S. Male" is a fitting complement to "Guitar Man" and the only sensible choice for the next single, whatever the publishing arrangements.

January Record Releases

Single: "Guitar Man" (#43)/"Hi-Heel Sneakers" (shipped January 9). A great single with disappointing sales of less than 300,000.

LP: *Elvis Gold Records Vol. 4* (#33). This fourth collection of "million sellers" contains the lesser hits but sells 350,000 copies over the course of the year, and like the other Gold Records collections will go on to become a reliable backlist item.

FEBRUARY

01 Thursday

Priscilla gives birth to a baby girl at Baptist Hospital in Memphis at 5:01 P.M. while Elvis and other members of the entourage wait in a doctor's lounge specially set aside for their use. Elvis is so nervous before leaving the house that his grandmother reminds him that it is Priscilla, not he, who is having the baby. A special detail of Memphis police, paid for by Elvis, will stand by at the hospital over the next four days.

05 Monday

Elvis brings Priscilla and the baby, Lisa Marie, home from the hospital.

06 Tuesday

Elvis' friend, actor Nick Adams, dies.

Elvis grants power of attorney to his father, putting him in official charge of all of his business activities from Vernon's office in a converted outbuilding a few steps from Graceland's back door.

14 Wednesday

Elvis and Priscilla leave a wreath of flowers on Gladys' grave with a card from "Elvis—Priscilla—Lisa Marie" and special orders that the card is to

With Billy Strange, *Live a Little, Love a Little*, March 7, 1968 *(courtesy of Billy Strange)*

be burned along with the flowers when they wilt.

25 Sunday

Elvis flies to Los Angeles to Priscilla's and his new home at 1174 Hillcrest Drive. This smaller, four-bedroom house offers the young family a greater degree of privacy than before, with only Charlie Hodge and Patsy and Gee Gee Gambill residing with the Presleys.

28 Wednesday

Priscilla arrives in California with Lisa Marie and Joanie Esposito and her two daughters.

February Record Release

Single: "U.S. Male" (#28) /"Stay Away" (#67) (shipped February 27). The Colonel fulfills his promise to MGM to support the release of the new film by including a track from the score as one side of the new single. "U.S. Male" is the song that garners all the attention, however, Elvis' third strong single release in a row and the one that puts him back in the top thirty for the first time since the summer of 1966. Sales of just under half a million are the best since "I'm Yours" in 1965.

MARCH

04 Monday

Elvis reports to MGM for preproduction of his new film, whose working title, *Kiss My Firm But Pliant Lips*, is the same as that of the comic novel by Dan Greenburg on which it is based, but which will soon be retitled *Live a Little, Love a Little*. It will be produced by Douglas Laurence and directed, once again, by Norman Taurog.

05 Tuesday

As Elvis begins script readings and rehearsals for his new film, Bob Finkel is selected as producer for the NBC television special.

07 Thursday

Script rehearsals continue in the morning; then Elvis goes to Western Recorders, at 6000 Sunset Boulevard, where Billy Strange, the arranger/contractor for the canceled L.A. session the previous summer, is firmly in charge. He has assembled the same band that he planned to use on the earlier session, L.A. musicians who for the most part are unfamiliar to Elvis but who work sessions for everyone from Sinatra to Sonny and Cher. Elvis works on the soundtrack from 7:00 P.M. to 3:00 A.M., with songwriter Mac Davis, a

At Marineland, *Live a Little, Love a Little*, spring 1968

recent discovery of Billy Strange's, in attendance for Elvis' rendition of his "A Little Less Conversation."

08 Friday
Script rehearsals continue at MGM.

Stay Away, Joe opens nationwide. *Variety* ranks it #65 in 1968, with a gross of only $1.5 million.

11 Monday
Elvis returns to Western Recorders to cut the vocal for "Almost in Love."

13 Wednesday
Principal photography for *Live a Little, Love a Little* begins.

15 Friday
Elvis films scenes for *Live a Little, Love a Little* at Marineland.

The Presleys hire Bernard and Rene Sinclair as butler and cook for their new Hillcrest home.

March Record Release

Single: "You'll Never Walk Alone" (#90)/"We Call on Him" (shipped March 26). A religious release to celebrate Easter, this marks the fourth single in six months to be drawn from the two recent Nashville sessions. The Colonel pushes RCA to conduct a full-scale Easter exploitation, but whether or not RCA fully satisfies his campaign directives, the single sells only 50,000 copies. Nonetheless it will be nominated for a Grammy for Best Sacred Performance, losing out to "Beautiful Isle of Somewhere" by Elvis' gospel idol, Jake Hess.

---

28 Thursday
Tom Sarnoff suggests that Elvis do a brief walk-on on another NBC show while shooting his own in June. The Colonel responds that a walk-on and a wave will cost NBC $250,000, as Sarnoff himself will understand, since neither he nor the Colonel would want to undervalue their product.

APRIL

04 Thursday
Martin Luther King is assassinated in Memphis, an event which Elvis takes just as hard as John F. Kennedy's assassination five years earlier—but more personally because it happened in his hometown. Dr. King's "I Have a Dream" speech is one of Elvis' favorite rhetorical pieces, something he recites often over the years, but no more often than Douglas MacArthur's "Farewell Address."

06 Saturday
Elvis and Priscilla go to Las Vegas, where they catch Tom Jones' midnight show at the Flamingo.

08 Monday
To ensure a greater degree of privacy as Lisa Marie grows older, Elvis has an electric gate installed at the Hillcrest house.

09 Tuesday
A new Lincoln Continental Mark II, black with a black vinyl top, is delivered to Graceland, and Vernon drives the car out to California for Elvis. While there, he has a small nonspeaking part in *Live a Little, Love a Little*.

14 Sunday
Elvis and Priscilla spend Easter in Palm Springs at their new rental house on Camino del Norte.

MAY

01 Wednesday
For Elvis and Priscilla's first wedding anniversary the Deli Restaurant

Elvis in his role as photographer takes a picture of Vernon in his role as a hotel guest, *Live a Little, Love a Little*, spring 1968

on La Cienega caters a party at the house, and Elvis sends flowers to Priscilla from *Sadie's Flowers* in Culver City with a card saying "Love, Elvis."

Principal photography on *Live a Little, Love a Little* ends, with Elvis released from the picture one week later.

The Colonel holds a meeting at his office at MGM with representatives from NBC and executives from the Singer Sewing Machine Company, the special's sole sponsor. Producer Bob Finkel persuades the Colonel at this point to allow him to expand the concept of the show from strictly a Christmas special to an *Elvis* special, with material taken from his entire career. The Colonel agrees, as long as Elvis controls

With Priscilla and Tom Jones in Las Vegas, April 6–7, 1968 *(courtesy of Joe Tunzi)*

the publishing, and concedes creative control to Finkel, subject to Singer's final approval.

14 Tuesday

As a follow-up to the network-and-sponsor meeting, producer Bob Finkel meets with Elvis, who volunteers, according to Finkel's contemporaneous memo, that he would like the "show to depart completely from the pattern of his motion pictures and from everything else he has done." Elvis, reports Finkel, "wants everyone to know what he really can do."

16 Thursday

Now that Elvis has expressed his willingness to venture out into previously uncharted territory, Finkel hires a young director, Steve Binder, who will also take on a large part of the production role. Binder, who has received critical accolades for a splashy, "mod" Petula Clark special, also directed *The T.A.M.I. Show*, a 1964 concert film with arresting performances by Chuck Berry, Marvin Gaye, James Brown, and the Rolling Stones, among others. It is a show with which Elvis is very familiar and whose James Brown segment in particular knocks him out. Binder's partner, Bones Howe, worked as an assistant engineer at Radio Recorders when Elvis first started recording there in 1956 and will, in essence, produce the music for the special.

17 Friday

Before they are officially okayed as

May Record Releases

Single: "Your Time Hasn't Come Yet Baby" (#71)/"Let Yourself Go" (shipped May 21). The new single features material from the upcoming soundtrack for *Speedway*. Definitely a step back, it attracts little radio play and 150,000 less sales than "U.S. Male."

LP: *Speedway* (#82). The album contains two "bonus" tracks cut from the film, a solo from costar Nancy Sinatra and her duet with Elvis. To complete the twelve-track compilation, three songs from earlier sessions are added.

---

the creative team, Binder and Howe must first pass muster with Colonel Parker and have a 7:00 A.M. breakfast meeting at his MGM Studios office. Later in the day Elvis comes to their offices at 8833 Sunset Boulevard to discuss the show. Binder and Howe explain that they want to give Elvis the opportunity to show the world who he really is and what he's all about and to do it through his music. It is agreed that while Elvis vacations in Hawaii they will have a preliminary script prepared.

18 Saturday

Elvis, Priscilla, and Lisa Marie, with Charlie Hodge, the Gambills, and the Espositos, fly to Hawaii.

21 Tuesday

The Colonel gets NBC's agreement to turn over to RCA, free of charge, all audiotapes of recordings made for the television show for exclusive release by RCA if they so choose. This becomes a sore point later when Binder and Howe seek to augment their meager salaries with production points on a record which up until virtually the day of its release the Colonel denies even contemplating. There is no provision in the Binder-Howe contract for participation, by way of either compensation or credit, so they are left with the Colonel's original admonition that "you guys are going to have a million-dollar experience."

25 Saturday

In Hawaii Elvis and Priscilla attend Ed Parker's championship karate tournament, put on at the Honolulu International Center, where Elvis is reintroduced to Parker, whom he first met in 1961, and the couple meets former international light-contact champion Mike Stone.

JUNE

02 Sunday

Elvis, Priscilla, and their party return from Hawaii to Los Angeles.

03 Monday

Elvis, looking tan and fit, reports

to the Binder-Howe offices on Sunset at 1:00 P.M. for the start of two weeks of informal rehearsals. Writers Chris Beard and Allan Blye have created a show with the same thematic link as Belgian playwright Maurice Maeterlinck's 1909 theater staple *The Blue Bird*, in which a young man sets out from home searching for happiness, travels halfway around the world, and returns home again only to find that happiness has resided all along in his own backyard. The show will use Elvis' music to carry out this theme, with very little actual dialogue—and with the song "Guitar Man" serving as a kind of autobiographical link, tying the various sequences together. The show will end with a Christmas song, after which Elvis will simply say goodnight. Asked his opinion of this approach, Elvis says he likes it, and when Binder and Howe ask for additional input, he simply says, "I like it all."

06 Thursday

Robert Kennedy dies after being shot in San Francisco on Wednesday night. Elvis' heartfelt reaction to yet another assassination is one of the principal elements that ultimately impels Steve Binder to ask songwriter Earl Brown to compose a closing number that will capture something of his unexpectedly idealistic sentiments. "I wanted to let the world know," Binder later says, "that here was a guy who was not prejudiced, who was raised in the heart of prejudice, but who was really above all that."

10 Monday

Rehearsals at Binder-Howe Productions offices continue through this week and the weekend.

11 Tuesday

Elvis meets with costume designer Bill Belew to discuss his ideas for the show, readily accepting Belew's suggestions of high "Napoleonic" collars and a black leather suit, balking only at a reprise of the gold suit the Colonel gave him in 1957 but finally agreeing on a gold jacket with black tuxedo pants.

12 Wednesday

Speedway opens across the country. The film reaches #40 on *Variety*'s 1968 charts but barely recovers production costs.

17 Monday

Elvis reports to rehearsals at the NBC studios in Burbank, California, at 1:00 P.M. for a meeting with Billy Goldenberg, Steve Binder's musical arranger. For most of the past two weeks Billy Strange, too, has served as musical director—*Elvis'* musical director—but this has proved to be a duplication with little practical application, and by this time Billy Goldenberg, who, like nearly every other member of the crew, has worked with Binder on several previous productions, is in sole charge. From 3:00 to 5:00 P.M. there is a dance rehearsal with choreographer Jaime Rogers. Also present is Lance LeGault, who will help Elvis with his dance sequences and production numbers, as he has on many of the movies, as well as providing personal encouragement and all-around support. Elvis ends the day with a 5:00 P.M. music and dialogue rehearsal. This schedule will be repeated on both Tuesday and Wednesday.

NBC announces to the press that Elvis Presley will star in his first television special, to be aired at Christmas.

18 Tuesday

Tickets are made available for taping of the arena segments of the show.

19 Wednesday

At some point during the week Steve Binder comes up with the inspiration that the show should replicate the altogether charming, totally informal atmosphere of Elvis' dressing-room rehearsals rather than follow the stiff, somewhat arch "informal" segment specified in the script. For a very short time he thinks of actually shooting the dressing-room jams with Elvis and his buddies—but then, after talking to Elvis, he settles on the idea of flying in original guitarist Scotty Moore and drummer D. J. Fontana and shooting the segment in the small boxing ring

At Western Recorders, June 20–23, 1968 *(courtesy of Joe Tunzi)*

of a stage that has been designed for the more formal live concert at the heart of the show.

20 Thursday

On this day and the next Elvis has wardrobe fittings at his home.

On the day that music for the show's production numbers is to be prerecorded, the Colonel reminds song publisher Freddy Bienstock to stay out of the way once a song has been recorded because song selection and production are strictly up to Elvis and the producers. "If the Colonel can't stick his nose in, the other people are self-explanatory."

At 8:00 P.M. Elvis reports to Studio One at Western Recorders for prere-cording, with Bones Howe in charge of production. The band is made up of many of the same musicians who worked the Billy Strange sessions for *Live a Little, Love a Little*, with gospel-laced vocal backups by the Blossoms (featuring well-known Phil Spector favorite Darlene Love), who also appear in several of the production numbers. The first number recorded is the long, complicated "Guitar Man" medley, and by the time Elvis finishes with this, everyone knows that they are home free.

21 Friday

Prerecording continues at Western Recorders for three more days, with Elvis reporting at 2:00 P.M. each afternoon. On either Thursday or Friday Steve Binder, moved by the intensity

With Steve Binder on the set for the opening of the 1968 special *(courtesy of Joe Tunzi)*

With *(left to right)* Alan Fortas, Colonel Parker, Lamar Fike, Joe Esposito, and Charlie Hodge on the set of the 1968 special

that Elvis brings to the recording process and by the person he feels he has gotten to know over the last few weeks, charges vocal arranger Earl Brown with writing a song that embodies the idealism he feels the show should project. To end with "I'll Be Home for Christmas," Binder feels, would at this point be sacrilege. Brown writes the song overnight, a hopeful message of sincere, if broadly generalized, idealism called "If I Can Dream," and brings it to Binder, who prevails upon all the powers that be (Colonel, Singer, NBC) to let Elvis end the show on this note. Elvis embraces the idea wholeheartedly, and everyone else falls in line, even the Colonel, who merely insists that there must be a Christmas song *somewhere* in the show.

22 Saturday

Scotty Moore and D. J. Fontana arrive from Nashville on the weekend, immediately reestablishing the same musical and personal rapport they have always had with Elvis.

23 Sunday

Elvis records the Earl Brown composition "If I Can Dream" in several impassioned takes, and the band completes an instrumental track of "Memories," a new Mac Davis composition on which Elvis will overdub studio vocals the following day for the LP version while singing it live to the backing track on the show.

24 Monday

Elvis rehearses at the NBC studio from 11:00 A.M. to 4:00 P.M., then begins work on the informal sequence with Scotty and D.J.

In the late afternoon Elvis returns to Western Recorders, where he lays down vocals for "Memories." Bones

Press conference with Steve Binder *(left)* and Bob Finkel, June 25, 1968

Howe has spent the day mixing the recordings that will be used as the soundtrack for the production numbers in the show.

25 Tuesday

From 10:00 A.M. to 1:00 P.M. Elvis again rehearses for the informal segment, then spends two hours with the dancers and the Blossoms practicing the gospel medley. From 3:00 to 5:00 P.M. the entire ensemble rehearse the "Guitar Man" segment, and then Elvis holds a 6:15 P.M. press conference. Asked why he is finally doing a television special now, he says, "We figured it was about time. Besides, I figured I'd better do it before I got too old." The day ends for Elvis with a meeting with Steve Binder and the two writers.

26 Wednesday

There is a complete run-through of the show between 10:00 A.M. and 5:00 P.M.

At an on-set birthday party for the Colonel, Elvis sings lyrics specially written to depict some of his manager's more calculatedly crass peccadillos, set to the melody of "It Hurts Me." "It hurts me," the parody by scriptwriters Chris Beard and Allan Blye declares, "to see the budget climb up to the sky," and then has the Colonel go on to express comical frustration at "the way Finkel spends my dough" and the manner in which he has been inveigled into listening to "Binder's same old lies." The song concludes with the Colonel's familiar plaint: "Is it too much to ask for one lousy, tired ol' Christmas song?"

27 Thursday

At 9:00 A.M. Elvis rehearses the gospel medley, with taping of the amusement-park scene beginning at 1:00 P.M. In this segment Elvis lip-synchs "Guitar Man," "Big Boss Man," and "It Hurts Me" to a prerecorded tape. Six P.M. marks the beginning of the first of the two one-hour "informal" sets in front of a live audience, with just Scotty on guitar, D.J. beating sticks on an upside-down guitar case, Charlie Hodge on rhythm guitar and harmony vocals, Alan Fortas banging on the back of a guitar, and Lance LeGault shaking a tambourine as accompaniment to Elvis' own singing and guitar playing. As he is about to go on, Elvis panics, and Steve Binder and Joe Esposito momentarily wonder if he will go on at all. What if he freezes up? Elvis demands of Binder. "Then you go out, sit down, look at everyone, get up, and walk off," says Binder. "But you *are* going out there." His performance on this night marks a high-water point that is still riveting today; the fear that he has expressed translates into a degree of engagement rarely revealed on stage. Costume designer Bill Belew recalls that after the first show Elvis was so drenched in perspiration that he practically had to be cut out of his leather suit, which then had to be cleaned and reshaped between shows.

28 Friday

Work begins again at 9:00 A.M. with the taping of the gospel medley, which is performed to prerecorded tracks, as is the bordello scene featuring "Let Yourself Go." Meanwhile choreographer Claude Thompson is rehearsing the Elvis "look-alikes,"

Singing a special version of "It Hurts Me" for the Colonel's birthday on the set of the 1968 special, June 26, 1968

With Scotty Moore, sit-down show, 1968 special

while the studio vocal will be used for the single, but each of the three full performances is electric, impassioned, and heartfelt. The rest of the day is spent on various sequences, with some portions presenting Elvis singing live to the prerecorded track, others mixing in the prerecorded vocal.

JULY

01 Monday
Elvis spends a week resting in Palm Springs.

04 Thursday
Elvis' 1964 Rolls Royce is auctioned in Hollywood to benefit SHARE, a children's charity. The car, with a left-hand steering wheel and customized interior of walnut paneling, has been driven 17,000 miles.

08 Monday
Elvis reports to National General for preproduction of his new film, whose title is in a state of flux, somewhere between *Jack Valentine*, *Johnny Hang*, *Come Hell or Come Sundown*, and its final nomenclature, *Charro!* It is to be produced by Harry Caplan, with a script by its director, Charles Marquis Warren, creator of the television westerns *Gunsmoke*, *Rawhide*, and *The Virginian*.

20 Saturday
Elvis' uncle, Johnny Smith, who with his father's brother, Vester, helped encourage his love for music when he was a child, dies of Bright's disease, a kidney ailment, at the age of forty-six.

22 Monday
Principal photography for *Charro!* begins on location in Apache Junction, Arizona, at the Apacheland Movie

Tickets for the sit-down and stand-up shows, 1968 special

who will be featured in the giant "Guitar Man" frame that makes up the opening shot.

29 Saturday
More rehearsals starting at 9:00 A.M.

At 6:00 P.M. and again at 8:00 P.M., Elvis tapes the two "stand-up" segments, where he appears alone once again on the same small, boxing-ring stage, surrounded this time not just by a live audience but by a full orchestra conducted by Billy Goldenberg, which runs through abbreviated arrangements of his hits.

30 Sunday
The production has fallen behind schedule, and an extra day is needed to complete the taping. The day begins with repair work on parts of the "Guitar Man" road medley, and then Elvis, dressed in the Edwardian-style white suit that Bill Belew has designed as if presenting the star as a southern gentleman of unassailable purity, pours his heart once again into four live vocal tracks (three of them complete) of the climactic number "If I Can Dream." The final take (officially the fifth, since an incomplete rehearsal is counted as the first) will be used for the broadcast,

"If I Can Dream," 1968 special *(courtesy of Joe Tunzi)*

"Trouble," 1968 special

Stand-up show, 1968 special

On the set of *Charro!*, summer 1968

Ranch. Elvis and the guys (Joe, Charlie, Gee Gee, and Alan) occupy rooms on the second floor of the Superstition Inn outside of Phoenix, with a dining room of their own. Elvis arrives bearded for a movie that he hopes will offer a raw depiction of the early West but soon discovers that the production is in as much a state of confusion as its wandering title.

23 Tuesday

Gossip columnist Rona Barrett announces, erroneously, that Elvis and Priscilla have separated. In an on-set interview at around this time Elvis speaks of touring again, saying, "I miss the personal contact with audiences."

24 Wednesday

Because Elvis has already fulfilled his contractual obligations for the year to RCA with the release of four singles and two albums, the Colonel extracts an additional $10,000 before permitting the release of two more singles from *Live a Little, Love a Little*. Eventually one of these will be replaced by "If I Can Dream" from the television spe-

cial. The Colonel also finally acknowledges what everyone has known for months, that there *will* be an album from the special, in exchange for another $10,000 payment to be shared and a $50,000 promotional fee to be paid to the Colonel alone. None of these payments will be charged against royalties. In addition, RCA agrees to pay for the printing of 250,000 eight-by-ten photographs, to be used as part of the Colonel's promotion.

AUGUST

20 Tuesday

After seeing a screening of a rough cut of the special at NBC, the Colonel expresses his outrage to Tom Sarnoff that not a single Christmas song has been included. In a two-page memo, which includes sharp criticism of the selection of live cuts and the pointlessness of some of the production numbers, he expresses astonishment that after all the talks, after all his concessions, the one thing he had been assured would never happen has hap-

pened, against all promises and binding contractual agreements. The Christmas number had to be put back in the show, "or we will all lose a tremendous amount of promotion not only from my company, All Star Shows, but through many other mediums and the following of Presley fans." If the number is not restored, the Colonel declares, the show should be put on ice until the following summer and NBC should "do a complete Christmas show for this fall as per our contract." The song is restored in the form of a throwaway version of "Blue Christmas" from the informal concert.

27 Tuesday

Elvis throws a buffet dinner for cast and crew at 6:00 P.M. at the Goldwyn Studios, then travels to Las Vegas for a brief stay at the Aladdin Hotel.

28 Wednesday

Elvis completes looping and is released from *Charro!*

SEPTEMBER

02 Monday

Elvis spends most of the month in Palm Springs.

11 Wednesday

Variety announces that the bordello scene has been cut from the TV

Colonel Parker on location, *Charro!*, Apache Junction, Arizona, summer 1968, in a photograph he had made up as a card to send to friends

Colonel Parker wirh Lisa Marie, probably Palm Springs, 1968

special. The NBC censors have passed it, but the sponsor, Singer, requests that it be removed.

13 Friday

Billy Smith's older brother, Bobby, dies at the age of twenty-seven after drinking rat poison. Billy and Bobby are Gladys' brother Travis' sons.

25 Wednesday

Elvis flies home, arriving in Memphis about 6:00 A.M.

26 Thursday

Elvis goes to the Memphian with Priscilla, Sonny, Gee Gee, Charlie, and Lamar to see *The Thomas Crown Affair* with Steve McQueen, and Clint East-

wood in *Hang 'Em High*. He will go to the movies almost every night during his two-and-a-half-week stay at home.

28 Saturday

Wildman Memphis DJ Dewey Phillips, the first to play Elvis' records on the air, dies at the age of forty-two. Elvis tells a local reporter, "I am awfully hurt and feel very sorry about Dewey's death. We were very good friends, and I have always appreciated everything he did for me in helping me in my career in the early days."

OCTOBER

01 Tuesday

Elvis attends Dewey's funeral at the Memphis Funeral Home, where ten years earlier services for his mother were conducted. He offers Dewey's widow condolences and help, saying, "Mrs. Dorothy, Dewey was my friend."

04 Friday

Elvis screens *Gone with the Wind* at the Crosstown Theater.

13 Sunday

Elvis flies back to Los Angeles with Priscilla and Lisa Marie.

15 Tuesday

The intention all along has been for *Charro!* to present Elvis in a straight dramatic role, but MGM now calls upon him to record a Mac Davis title song, along with one other number which in the end does not make it into the finished film. He works on these two songs at the Samuel Goldwyn Studios soundstage from 7:00 P.M. until midnight, with arranger-producer Hugo Montenegro (whose "The Good, the Bad, and the Ugly," from the spaghetti Western of the same name, peaked at #2 on the pop charts earlier in the year) conducting.

19 Saturday

Elvis spends the weekend in Palm Springs.

22 Tuesday

Elvis begins preproduction for his new (and final) MGM feature film, presently called *Chautauqua*, with rehearsals starting at 11:00 A.M. The film is to be produced by Lester Welch and directed by *Stay Away, Joe* director Peter Tewksbury. The Colonel expresses concern that the title will be difficult to advertise properly, and the name is eventually changed to *The Trouble with Girls (And How to Get Into It)*.

23 Wednesday

Live a Little, Love a Little opens nationwide and does as poorly as *Speedway* in June.

From 7:00 P.M. to 3:15 A.M. Elvis works on the soundtrack for *The Trouble with Girls* at United Artists Recorders at 6050 Sunset Boulevard, with Billy Strange as producer. Later Felton Jarvis will overdub and remix the tracks in Nashville.

26 Saturday

Elvis spends every weekend during filming in Palm Springs.

29 Tuesday

Principal photography begins.

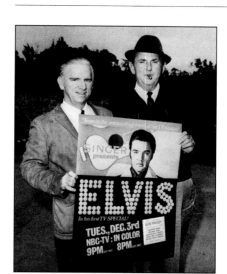

Tom Diskin and Colonel Parker promote the television show on the set of *The Trouble with Girls*, fall 1968

NOVEMBER

14 Thursday

Elvis has a day off from filming and flies to Reno for the day.

November Record Releases

Single: "If I Can Dream" (#12)/"Edge of Reality" (shipped November 5). "If I Can Dream" is released just a month in advance of the NBC television special's airing on December 3. With the show's broadcast, sales climb dramatically, cresting at something like 800,000 units and setting the stage for even greater triumphs.

LP: *Elvis* (#8) (shipped November 22). The album from the special is rushed into release and, with the single, marks the beginning of a new Presley era. More than just a soundtrack of the show, it stands as testimony to Elvis' continued vitality as an artist and sells more than 500,000 in its original chart run.

DECEMBER

03 Tuesday

"Elvis" (in the ad it says "SINGER presents ELVIS") airs in a sixty-minute version at 9:00 P.M. EST and is seen by 42 percent of the viewing audience, making it the number-one show for the season and giving NBC its biggest ratings victory of the year. It is greeted by critical hosannas (this is the Elvis who "performed existential acts to liberate an entire generation," proclaims the *Boston Phoenix*; "Rock Star's Vintage Blues Have Explosive Quality," opines the *New York Times*) as well as some doubters ("He still can't sing," declares *Variety*; "I don't think many viewers care to see singers sweat on TV," sniffs the *Los Angeles Times*)—but there is no question: Elvis is back.

10 Tuesday

The Colonel informs Abe Lastfogel at William Morris that Elvis will consider an engagement in Las Vegas if he can have Mondays off, play one show a night on weeknights (at 11:30 P.M.) with two shows a night on the weekend, and receive compensation of $500,000 for four weeks, or $300,000 for two weeks.

At the same time, the Colonel has convinced RCA to pay him a flat fee of $100,000 for the promotional effort he will provide in 1969. This is in addition to the regular merchandising arrangement between RCA and the Colonel.

As Bonnie and Clyde with costar Marlyn Mason on the set of *The Trouble with Girls*, fall 1968

12 Thursday

Abe Lastfogel is swamped with requests for more TV appearances, but the Colonel tells him to simply respond that Elvis is not available.

14 Saturday

Elvis spends the weekend in Palm Springs.

18 Wednesday

The Trouble with Girls is completed, and Elvis is released by the studio.

19 Thursday

The Colonel accepts a deal for Elvis to perform at Kirk Kerkorian's yet-to-be-built International Hotel, but turns down the opportunity to open the projected two-thousand-seat showroom (the largest in Vegas) in July, since the Colonel feels someone else should have the opportunity to iron out the bugs. The arrangement is for four weeks, seven nights a week, and the standard two shows a night, although the contract stipulates that should any other performer get a less demanding schedule within a year of Elvis' engagement, the hotel will pay a $50,000 penalty. Salary is $100,000 a week, out of which Elvis will pay for his band and backup singers.

20 Friday

Elvis flies home to Memphis, arriving early in the morning.

In the evening he is at the movies seeing John Wayne's *Hellfighters* and Richard Burton, Marlon Brando, and an all-star cameo cast in *Candy*. He will attend the movies almost every night during the month he is at home.

23 Monday

Joe Esposito purchases gift certificates from Goldsmith's Department Store in amounts between $100 and $200 to be used by Elvis as Christmas presents.

25 Wednesday

Elvis and Priscilla spend Christmas at Graceland. For Lisa Marie's first Christmas Vernon dresses up as Santa.

31 Tuesday

Elvis' New Year's Eve party is at the Thunderbird Lounge again this year. Performers are the Short Cuts, Vaneese Starks, Flash and the Board of Directors, Billy Lee Riley, and B. J. Thomas.

Elvis' accountants report that in 1968 Elvis' personal income from motion pictures is $2,600,000, with $532,000 from music and recording and $350,000 from television. His income tax comes to $1,422,000.

1969

JANUARY

06 Monday

Early in the New Year Felton Jarvis meets with Elvis at Graceland to make plans for a recording session scheduled for Nashville later in the month. At the prompting of George Klein and Marty Lacker, the idea of recording at Chips Moman's American Studio at 827 Thomas Street in a run-down section of North Memphis is considered. Moman, one of the founders of Stax Records, has had a string of something like 164 hit records come out of his little studio in the past eighteen months. Not only do Klein and Lacker have connections with American (the latter has actually gone to work there recently), Red West has written and recorded there as well. Elvis can easily see the convenience of recording just a few miles from home, Felton thinks it might give Elvis a fresh sound, and the decision is made.

08 Wednesday

Elvis celebrates his thirty-fourth birthday at Graceland.

09 Thursday

Elvis takes an American Airlines flight to Dallas with two of the guys for a couple of days.

With Chips Moman, American Studio, c. January 22, 1969

11 Saturday

Elvis returns to Memphis, where he will remain until January 24.

13 Monday

Elvis reports to American and is greeted somewhat skeptically by a band that includes virtuoso guitarist Reggie Young, bassists Tommy Cogbill and Mike Leech, Gene Chrisman on drums, and Bobby Wood and Bobby Emmons on keyboards. These musicians always come to work, and they are not so sure that Elvis has—but with the first song, a country ballad called "Long Black Limousine" which Elvis turns into an impassioned soul shout, they are convinced. They go until five o'clock in the morning, despite the fact that Elvis has a bad cold, completing three songs, two

of which ("Wearin' That Loved On Look" is the other) are among the strongest, most gut-wrenching examples of Elvis' art in recent years.

14 Tuesday

Recording continues from 7:00 P.M. to 8:30 A.M. with several more successful sides, but Elvis' cold gets worse and vocal tracks on Hank Snow's "I'm Movin' On" and John Hartford's "Gentle On My Mind" will have to be redone. Elvis in fact does not return to the studio until the following Monday, with the band continuing to lay down new tracks on Wednesday and Thursday nights and on Sunday doing instrumental overdubs (including horn parts) on some of the songs already recorded.

At American, c. January 22, 1969, with *(left to right)* Bobby Wood, Mike Leech, Tommy Cogbill, Gene Chrisman, Bobby Emmons, Reggie Young, Ed Kollis, and songwriter Dan Penn *(courtesy of Knox Phillips)*

20 Monday

Elvis returns to American at 9:00 P.M. with the firm determination to record Mac Davis' "In the Ghetto," a kind of "protest song" about which he had some reservations to begin with. In the end he is won over by Davis' songwriting artistry and the compassionate view he articulates (the song's subtitle is "The Vicious Circle")—and by the fact that Elvis has come to believe the song can be a hit. His twenty-three focused takes occupy most of the evening, and he leaves at 4:00 A.M. with only one other throwaway number complete.

21 Tuesday

Working another long night from 8:00 P.M. to 4:00 A.M., Elvis records the Beatles' "Hey Jude" and one of his father's country favorites, "From a Jack to a King," but spends most of the night overdubbing vocal parts with the female singers.

22 Wednesday

Elvis comes into the studio early specifically to meet thirty-nine-year-old Roy Hamilton, one of his earliest r & b heroes, who has been working on a new album for Chips' AGP (American Group Productions) label. Accompanied by George Klein, Elvis is mesmerized by Hamilton's compelling presence and vocal style, a combination of r & b, gospel, and controlled near-operatic virtuosity. In a typical moment of

With Priscilla and Lisa Marie

spontaneous generosity, Elvis offers the older singer one of the new songs he has been planning to record, "Angelica." After spending several hours with Hamilton, Elvis resumes his own recording at 12:30 A.M., concluding this first set of American sessions with some of his most inspired singing on such gospel-inflected numbers as "Without Love" and "I'll Hold You in My Heart," a smooth Eddy Arnold ballad which he utterly transforms. The session ends with the song that Chips has had in mind for Elvis all along, "Suspicious Minds," a number by one of his staff writers, Mark James, that he is convinced will be a smash. Elvis needs only four full takes to get it right, and everyone says their goodbyes at 4:00 A.M., with Chips quoted in the *Memphis Commercial Appeal* later that day as finding Elvis to be "one of the hardest-working artists I have ever been associated with." "We have some hits, don't we, Chips?" Elvis puts in with disarming plaintiveness. "Maybe some of your biggest" is the reply.

24 Friday

Elvis, Priscilla, and Lisa Marie fly to Aspen, Colorado, with several of

the entourage for a ski-and-snow-mobile vacation.

FEBRUARY

01 Saturday

In Aspen the group celebrates Lisa Marie's first birthday.

By this time it has already been determined that there will be a follow-up session at American, a logical enough conclusion given the success of the first session but not an inescapable one if you take into account the politics involved. There had been a huge fight in the studio over the publishing of "Suspicious Minds," which was wholly owned by Chips, and while the dispute was eventually resolved in the studio owner's favor, feelings have definitely lingered. In addition, a growing division has sprung up between Chips and Felton Jarvis, who appears to have begun to realize during the sessions that his artist is being taken away from him. Nonetheless, all differences are for the time being smoothed over, and by January 29 correspondence about a second session has begun, with all

business arrangements worked out over the next few days.

17 Monday

Elvis reports back to American at 8:00 P.M., working until 4:00 A.M. An impromptu jam on an early Chips Moman composition, "This Time," starts the session off with a kind of musical joke on Elvis' part. The evening moves on to a soulful "True Love Travels on a Gravel Road" and a powerful reworking of the Percy Mayfield blues "Stranger in My Own Home Town," which Elvis sings as if it were written with him in mind.

18 Tuesday

Recording continues from 7:30 P.M. to 5:30 A.M. with the completion of three more songs, including a radical revamping of the Eddy Arnold ballad "After Loving You" (already reworked by Della Reese in an r & b vein several years earlier).

19 Wednesday

Recording once again runs all night, with material running the gamut from Eddie Rabbitt's surefire hit in a contemporary country mode, "Kentucky Rain," to a cover of soul singer Jerry Butler's just-released "Only the Strong Survive," which like so many other songs on the American sessions Elvis clearly feels and makes his own.

20 Thursday

Another all-night session, with Johnny Tillotson's 1962 country hit "It Keeps Right on A'Hurtin'" and Chuck Jackson's "Any Day Now," an r & b hit from the same year, the clear standouts.

Earlier in the day, probably at the suggestion of the Colonel, Elvis buys a microfilm reader from Eastman Kodak and subsequently has more than 4,000 personal items microfilmed.

21 Friday

Everyone is clearly beginning to run out of steam—or at least material—as just one song and an instrumental track are completed between 7:30 and 10:30 P.M.

22 Saturday

This is the last night in the studio, and, with no good new additional material in sight, Elvis records only "Who Am I?" a gospel number previously recorded by keyboardist Bobby Wood, whose "If I'm a Fool (For Loving You)" he has cut two nights before. The session, and the American experience, ends at midnight.

23 Sunday

Elvis returns to Los Angeles.

24 Monday

After shopping for clothes in Beverly Hills, Elvis flies to Las Vegas.

26 Wednesday

Together Elvis and the Colonel provide a photo opportunity to publicize his upcoming engagement at the International. On a roughed-in stage at the casino construction site Elvis signs his "contract," though the actual document will not be signed until April 15.

February Record Release

Single: "Memories" (#35)/"Charro!" (shipped February 25). Just prior to the movie's premiere, the title track is released as the B-side to "Memories" from the television special. Despite the strength of "Memories," and its long-term appeal to Elvis fans, the single sells only 300,000 copies initially.

MARCH

05 Wednesday

Back in Los Angeles, Elvis begins what will be his last feature film, *Change of Habit.* This is the movie element of the NBC deal and is being coproduced by NBC with Universal Pictures. Elvis plays an idealistic doctor working with ghetto youth and assisted by nuns in civilian disguise, headed by Mary Tyler Moore. On this and the following night Elvis records

With Mary Tyler Moore, *Change of Habit,* spring 1969

the movie soundtrack at the Decca Universal Studio, working each evening from 7:00 P.M. to 2:00 A.M.

08 Saturday

On this and most other weekends during filming Elvis relaxes in Palm Springs.

10 Monday

Elvis reports to Universal for preproduction on *Change of Habit.* Produced by Joe Connelly and directed by Billy Graham, perhaps its most notable aspect is the participation at Elvis' request of Billy Goldenberg, musical director for the television special,

March Record Releases

Single: "His Hand in Mine"/"How Great Thou Art" (shipped March 25). This year's Easter release brings together "His Hand in Mine" from the 1960 gospel album and "How Great Thou Art," the title song of the 1967 gospel album. It sells 25,000 copies but is intended, really, more as a seasonal message and statement of faith than a commercial blockbuster.

Budget LP on RCA's Camden Label: *Elvis Sings Flaming Star* (#96) (shipped March 28). RCA puts out its own regular retail release of the album on which Singer had a three-month exclusive. This is the first Elvis album to be released on RCA's budget Camden line, and it sells half a million copies.

whom Elvis asks to accompany him to Las Vegas as his arranger/musical director. Because of his own ambitions in film and theater, Goldenberg declines.

12 Wednesday

Principal photography begins. Filming takes place primarily at the studio but includes some locations around Los Angeles.

13 Thursday

Charro! opens in theaters nationwide.

27 Thursday

In preparation for his upcoming Las Vegas engagement, Elvis begins to think about material and, in Red's continued absence, to work with Charlie Hodge on plans for the show. Today Joe Esposito purchases a new tape recorder, speakers, and other audio equipment, as well as a drum set for ongoing musical experimentation.

APRIL

09 Wednesday

Elvis complains of a sore throat and, after an examination by studio doctors, is given the rest of the week off. He will spend it in Palm Springs.

15 Tuesday

Elvis signs the official contract for his appearance at the Las Vegas Inter-

With Mahalia Jackson on Change of Habit *set, spring 1969*

national Hotel in August. It includes a clause permitting filming of a concert documentary as well as an option for a second appearance and complimentary suites at the International for the Colonel and himself.

29 Tuesday
Elvis reports to the studio and, after completing looping, is dismissed from *Change of Habit.*

April Record Release

Single: "In the Ghetto" (#3)/"Any Day Now" (shipped April 14). The first release from the American sessions lives up to every expectation by virtue of chart position, sales (1.2 million copies), and critical raves. The first two weeks that the single appears on the charts Felton Jarvis is listed in *Billboard* as producer; the following two weeks, at Marty Lacker's instigation, Chips Moman's name replaces Felton's; and there is no producer's credit thereafter per order of the Colonel.

MAY

02 Friday
Elvis spends the weekend in Palm Springs.

04 Sunday
Elvis, Priscilla, and Lisa Marie, booked as the Carpenters (the name of Elvis' *Change of Habit* character is Dr. John Carpenter), fly to Hawaii with the Gambills, the Fikes, Charlie Hodge, and the Espositos. They spend the first and last weeks at the Ilikai Hotel, with the intervening weekend at the Coco Palms Hotel.

18 Sunday
The group returns to Los Angeles.

20 Tuesday
The Circle G Ranch in Mississippi is sold for $440,000 to the North Mississippi Gun Club, though eventually the property will revert to Elvis when the purchaser defaults on the payments.

23 Friday
Elvis flies to Palm Springs for the weekend.

27 Tuesday
Elvis flies home to Memphis, where, except for a brief trip to Las Vegas and Los Angeles, he remains until July 5.

28 Wednesday
After sleeping most of the day, Elvis takes a swim in the late afternoon before going horseback riding on the grounds. He ends up down at the gates talking with the fans and signing autographs, a pattern that is repeated throughout his time at home in what appears to be a conscious strategy to renew his roots before going out in public again to perform. Later in the evening Elvis screens *Goodbye, Columbus, Winning* (a racing film with Paul Newman), and *Death of a Gunfighter* at the Memphian. He continues to screen movies almost every night while he is home.

JUNE

08 Sunday
Elvis is down at the Graceland gates again, signing autographs and talking with, and singing to, the fans. According to his uncle Vester, the Colonel doesn't like him doing this, but he feels that he needs "to get used to the crowds again."

June Record Releases

Single: "Clean Up Your Own Backyard" (#35)/"The Fair Is Moving On" (shipped June 17). The time for movie songs is clearly past, but the Colonel feels certain nonetheless that "Clean Up Your Own Backyard" from *The Trouble with Girls (And How to Get Into It)* will succeed, because kids like "provocative titles." It doesn't, they don't, and sales remain stuck at the 300,000 level.

LP: *From Elvis in Memphis* (#13). There might have been an element of disappointment in the chart position and sales (half a million copies) of this first LP from the Memphis sessions, but the album remains an enduring classic that effectively completes the job the "Comeback Special" has begun: to restore Elvis to a state of popularity and artistic respectability and to validate his work to a new generation. "The new album is great," declares *Rolling Stone* in its lead review on August 23, "flatly and unequivocally the equal of anything he has ever done."

10 Tuesday

International owner Kirk Kerkorian arranges an 8:00 P.M. flight for Elvis, Charlie, Gee Gee, and Lamar from Memphis to Las Vegas to view construction of the new two-thousand-seat showroom. Elvis continues on to Los Angeles for wardrobe fittings of NBC special designer Bill Belew's costumes for the Vegas opening.

13 Friday

Elvis flies down to Palm Springs for the weekend.

16 Monday

Elvis stops off in Vegas on his way back to Memphis.

21 Saturday

Elvis returns to Memphis.

JULY

05 Saturday

Elvis flies to Los Angeles to prepare for his Las Vegas opening.

07 Monday

With the help of Charlie Hodge in particular, Elvis continues to work up material for Vegas, while Joe Esposito shuttles song titles to the Colonel's office so that publishing rights can be cleared.

10 Thursday

The Graceland Christian Church, whose property abuts Graceland, grants Elvis an easement allowing him to use the church driveway to drive to and from the highway, thus avoiding the fans at the gates. In return Elvis agrees to pay a nominal fee of $10 as well as the cost of paving the driveway, promising not to use any motor vehicles on the easement during Sunday church services "unless absolutely necessary."

14 Monday

During this period Elvis speaks with virtually every musician he knows about accompanying him to Las Vegas, finally putting together a band led by guitarist James Burton, a native of Shreveport, Louisiana, whose

stabbing blues-inflected leads he has been familiar with since Burton's weekly appearances in 1957 on the *Ozzie and Harriet Show* as the leader of Ricky Nelson's band. Burton has gone on to become a top L.A. session musician as well as a member in the mid-sixties of the band that appeared every week on the popular musical series *Shindig!* Burton brings in piano player Larry Muhoberac (formerly Larry Owens of Memphis, whose band appeared on the bill of Elvis' 1961 Memphis charity concert), who in turn suggests a drummer fresh out of Dallas, Ronnie Tutt. Burton also contacts studio bass player Jerry Scheff and rhythm guitarist John Wilkinson, who has just signed an RCA recording contract as a solo artist. On his own Elvis gets in touch with the Imperials to provide the kind of male gospel-quartet backup that he has always prized (the Imperials, with Jake Hess as their then-leader, sang on Elvis' *How Great Thou Art* session). He also hires the Sweet Inspirations, a black female quartet that has backed Aretha Franklin and had a big soul hit of their own with "Sweet Inspiration" in 1967. Elvis has never met the Sweet Inspirations but admires their work. His articulated idea for the show is that it will encompass *all* of the diverse strands of the American vernacular tradition, black and white, sacred and secular, bringing together on one stage all the music that has influenced him.

18 Friday

Rehearsals begin, without either of the backup groups or the International orchestra, at the RCA studio on Sunset where Elvis began recording the soundtrack for *G.I. Blues* in 1960. In James Burton's recollection, "Right off the bat we probably learned 150 songs" over six nights of work. The upcoming engagement will be the first time that Elvis has ever presented a full-hour set. With Charlie Hodge he works on the pacing of the show, going back and forth over the playlist, adding and subtracting songs right up to the last minute. Charlie establishes his role as a serious musical collaborator and onstage gofer almost from the start.

24 Thursday

Rehearsals continue in Las Vegas in either a rehearsal room or one of the ballrooms, while Barbra Streisand finishes her opening stand at the new International showroom. The backup groups join in here for the first time, and Felton Jarvis flies in from a three-day honeymoon with his new bride, Chet Atkins' assistant, Mary Lynch. According to Myrna Smith, who functions as Sweet Inspirations spokesperson and manager (gospel singer Cissy Houston, whose daughter, Whitney, will become a pop superstar two decades later, is the lead voice for this engagement): "Rehearsals were always great. Elvis went through the whole thing, just as though he were on stage. He just let us experiment." He did, however, know "exactly what he wanted to hear. He added our group because he wanted the spice of soul, but he didn't want it to be overbearing."

25 Friday

Rehearsals run each day until the Streisand show closes on Monday night, the twenty-eighth. At Streisand's invitation Elvis and some of the guys attend at least one of her performances, and, looking at the singer alone on a bare stage, Elvis remarks to Charlie that it looks like a "helluva big stage to fill." This is not the way it is going to be for him, he says. He will be surrounded by his band and backup singers. He will not be alone.

29 Tuesday

There are two days of rehearsals in the showroom with the thirty-piece International orchestra, led by Bobby Morris. The Colonel, meanwhile, is coordinating an advertising blitz that includes posters, banners, balloons, pictures, calendars, catalogues, taxi mini-marquees, and a blanketing assault of radio and television ads. As the Colonel says to Elvis, even "the gophers in the desert will know you're here, everyone in town will know Elvis Presley is coming. But you're the only one that can bring them in."

31 Thursday

The final full-dress rehearsal con-

Onstage, Las Vegas, August 1969

Press conference following opening night, Las Vegas, August 1, 1969

sists of two complete run-throughs of the show with full orchestra accompaniment and Elvis dressed in one of Bill Belew's karate-style "Cossack suits" with dangling macramé belt.

★ *Showroom, International Hotel, Las Vegas*

At 8:15 P.M. the Sweet Inspirations open the single opening-night show, while backstage Elvis copes with another near panic attack of stage fright that does not let up until he steps out on stage at 10:15 P.M., following comedian Sammy Shore's set. Appearing from the side with almost no fanfare, he hesitates for a moment, then rocks the house with an all-out rendition of "Blue Suede Shoes." This invitation-only gala attracts celebrities from Cary Grant to Carol Channing, Pat Boone, Fats Domino, and Phil Ochs, as well as a large contingent of press, many of whom the Colonel has had flown in on International owner Kirk Kerkorian's private jet. Also in attendance at Elvis' invitation is Sam Phillips of Sun Records. The response to Elvis' performance is practically cataclysmic, as Elvis is bursting with energy, falling to his knees, sliding across the stage, even doing somersaults. The celebrity audience is on its feet for almost the entire show, and rave reviews come in from all over— from the trades, the dailies, and such representatives of the cultural establishment *and* counterestablishment as *The New Yorker, The Village Voice,* and *The New York Times.* Perhaps never before in his career has Elvis enjoyed such near-universal acclaim.

In the hotel coffeeshop after the show, the Colonel outlines terms for a new contract on the stained pink tablecloth that serves as an impromptu negotiating site for himself and International president Alex Shoofey. The new contract will be formalized over the next four days and will raise Elvis' salary to $125,000 a week while extending the International's option to include two engagements a year for the next

Onstage, Las Vegas, August 1969

Backstage, Las Vegas, August 1969

five years (the only thing the Colonel doesn't get from the "tablecloth contract" is a $50,000 bonus on top of the $100,000 additional that Elvis receives to bring his current salary up to par). Thus Elvis will be guaranteed $1 million a year for just eight weeks' work annually through 1974, though he will have to pay all of his show expenses out of this before he and his manager divide the net.

AUGUST

01 Friday

Elvis holds a 12:30 A.M. Friday-morning press conference following the show, during which he confesses he was "a little nervous for the first three songs, but then I thought, 'What the heck, get with it, man, or you might be out of a job tomorrow.'"

This evening the show takes on the normal routine of two shows a night, at 8:15 P.M. and midnight.

14 Thursday

Colonel Parker completes a deal for Elvis to appear at the Houston Livestock Show and Rodeo at the Astrodome February 27–March 1, 1970, for a $150,000 fee.

It is in the early stages of this engagement in Las Vegas that reporters first begin to comment on the Colonel's frequent appearance at the roulette table.

Early in the engagement Elvis tells Ray Connolly of the *London Evening Standard*, "I've always wanted to perform on the stage again for the last nine years, and it's been building inside of me since 1965 until the strain became intolerable."

15 Friday

Throughout the engagement Elvis entertains friends and celebrities in his suite after the late show. He sings with the Imperials as often as he can, and with friends like Tom Jones. One night he conducts a karate demonstration with Ed Parker, who has

come to see him about a business proposition to market Parker's kenpo system of karate. Elvis has already begun to include karate moves in his performance.

21 Thursday

Felton Jarvis tests recording equipment during both an afternoon rehearsal and the dinner show for taping of the midnight show. These will be the first recordings of Elvis performing with his new stage band.

22 Friday

RCA again records Elvis' performance, taping both shows tonight and continuing each night through Tuesday, August 26.

By now Elvis appears almost wholly at ease onstage, engaging in informal, sometimes close to stream-of-conscious bantering with the audience. In the Colonel's view, he may have grown *too* relaxed, as he writes to Elvis in the aftermath of his performance on this night: "Before I left I talked to Joe, as the pressure is getting a little heavy regarding the off-color material. I am of course speaking mostly in regard to the dinner show when there are a great many children. I can only relate this to

August Record Release

Single: "Suspicious Minds" (#1)/"You'll Think of Me" (shipped August 26). This is Elvis' first #1 single since "Good Luck Charm" in 1962—and, as it turns out, the last he will ever have. But it is not as it was recorded at the American studio. Instead, it incorporates the way Elvis has come to perform it onstage, with a kind of false ending in which the volume fades down, then comes back up again, with the same three lines repeated over and over and the International horns riffing strongly in the background. Felton takes the horns into the Las Vegas studio of Bill Porter, RCA's chief engineer in Nashville in the early sixties, where they replicate the live sound with a four-and-a-half-minute coda that cements the rift between Chips and Felton but helps the record sell 1,250,000 copies.

you. You are the only one who can change it," the Colonel calculatedly declares, voicing his concern that Elvis not "undo all the good that we have created during the first part of our engagement."

26 Tuesday

As RCA continues taping, Elvis cannot stop laughing during (and after) Cissy Houston's soprano obbligato on "Are You Lonesome Tonight?" at the midnight show. This perplexing performance becomes an underground legend among Elvis fans until its official release on *Elvis Aron Presley*, an eight-LP set, in 1980.

28 Thursday

Elvis completes his record-breaking Las Vegas engagement, with total attendance of 101,500 and gross receipts of $1,522,635. By comparison, Dean Martin has drawn 50,000 to the smaller Riviera in a three-week engagement earlier in the summer.

International vice president Alex Shoofey conveys his congratulations on the success of the show, presenting Elvis with an all-expense-paid trip to Hawaii for himself plus eight.

29 Friday

With the Colonel, the Colonel's staff, and all of the guys, their wives and girlfriends, Elvis and Priscilla attend Nancy Sinatra's opening at the International. After the show they go to a party hosted by Nancy's father, Frank.

SEPTEMBER

01 Monday

Elvis is back in Los Angeles, and for the first time in almost ten years has no movie to make, no recording session to attend, in fact nothing on his calendar until January 1970, when he is scheduled to return to Las Vegas. Over the next few months he will spend time doing little but traveling back and forth between his various homes and his favorite vacation spots, restlessly seeking a place to alight.

03 Wednesday

The Trouble with Girls (And How to Get Into It) opens nationwide.

10 Wednesday

Elvis flies to Las Vegas.

12 Friday

He returns to Los Angeles before flying to Palm Springs for a week.

22 Monday

Elvis flies home to Memphis, arriving early Tuesday morning. Except for brief trips to Nashville and Dallas, he will remain at home until October 5.

25 Thursday

Elvis flies to Nashville with Charlie Hodge to add vocal overdubs and make repairs on several songs.

27 Saturday

Elvis returns to Memphis.

29 Monday

Tonight *Butch Cassidy and the Sundance Kid* is on the bill at the Memphian.

30 Tuesday

Elvis is at the movies once again, screening *Midnight Cowboy*. It should be noted that while he remains faithful in his movie attendance, he does not appear often at the Graceland gates to greet the fans during this stay.

OCTOBER

01 Wednesday

Elvis flies to Dallas, returning the following day.

05 Sunday

Elvis flies to Los Angeles, then continues on to Hawaii accompanied by Priscilla, Vernon and Dee, the Espositos, the Gambills, and the Schillings, in a trip largely financed by the International Hotel.

12 Sunday

The group returns to Los Angeles with plans formulated in Hawaii to continue their vacation in Europe. The European contingent consists of Elvis and Priscilla, Jerry and Sandy Schilling, Joe and Joanie Esposito, and Patsy and Gee Gee Gambill, and everyone who does not already have one gets a passport on an accelerated basis. The idea is dropped almost immediately, however, when the Colonel argues vociferously that Elvis' European fans will be insulted if he travels there as a tourist before performing either in England or on the continent. Although Elvis puts up a brave front at first, plans are quickly switched to go to the Bahamas, where the Colonel has contacts and, he says, they will enjoy the gambling.

22 Wednesday

The four couples who were planning to go to Europe together fly to Miami and then on to Nassau, where they stay at the Paradise Island Hotel. Their stay is marred by rain and hurricane winds, and they return home earlier than intended one week later.

30 Thursday

Elvis flies to Las Vegas, where he is spotted by gossip columnist Rona Barrett at the blackjack tables with a woman on each arm. On November 6 Barrett writes: "Everybody is commenting on how good Elvis Presley looks these days while he's having fun at the International. . . . Elvis' answer in response to such compliments: 'That's what a bad marriage does for you!'"

31 Friday

The Colonel signs a deal with RCA in which the record company pays $20,000 total for two extra singles ("Suspicious Minds" and the not-yet-released "Don't Cry Daddy") and the just-released special double album, *From Vegas to Memphis/From Memphis to Vegas*. As with all side and special deals, the money is to be split 50-50 between the Colonel and Elvis.

NOVEMBER

02 Sunday

Elvis flies to Palm Springs.

07 Friday

Elvis returns to Las Vegas, where he consults a doctor and receives an antibiotic treatment.

He will spend the next five weeks flying back and forth between Las Vegas, Palm Springs, and Los Angeles. While in Los Angeles he takes karate lessons from Ed Parker, who awards him certificates of advancement in his kenpo institute based largely on his contributions to the sport.

10 Monday

Change of Habit is released nationwide. The film will appear on *Variety*'s Box Office Survey for four weeks, peaking at #17.

28 Friday

Elvis flies to Palm Springs for the weekend.

October Record Release

LP: *From Memphis to Vegas/From Vegas to Memphis* (#12) (shipped October 14). This double album, following on the heels of *From Elvis in Memphis*, combines one LP of live recordings entitled *Elvis in Person at the International Hotel* with another ten-cut selection from the American sessions called *Back in Memphis*. Thirteen months later these LPs will be split up and packaged individually, but this special "collector's set" sells 300,000 copies, even without either the current ("Suspicious Minds") or upcoming ("Don't Cry Daddy") hit single on it. The live album does include a nearly eight-minute version of the former, however.

November Record Release

Single: "Don't Cry Daddy" (#6)/"Rubberneckin'" (shipped November 11). This third single from the American sessions, the second from the pen of writer Mac Davis, is another big seller, with sales of 1,200,000, as well as being a personal favorite of Elvis' for a sentimental message with which he strongly identifies.

DECEMBER

12 Friday

The Colonel makes a special agreement with RCA for four Elvis Presley albums to be released on RCA's Camden budget label, three in 1970, one in 1971. Since it is a special agreement, Elvis and Colonel Parker will split the advance against royalties of $300,000 50-50, with the full amount due between January 1 and January 10, 1970.

18 Thursday

Elvis returns somewhat belatedly to Memphis for the Christmas season. He will spend almost every night at the Memphian until his return to Los Angeles on January 6, 1970.

25 Thursday

For Christmas Vernon again dresses up as Santa, and Elvis gives Priscilla a black fox coat while she gives him a velvet suit and shirts and slacks designed for his personal use by Bill Belew.

30 Tuesday

A total of $612.41 worth of fireworks are delivered to Graceland for the New Year's Eve display.

31 Wednesday

Elvis' New Year's Eve party is held at T.J.'s, a popular new Memphis club where Alan Fortas is now working. Entertainment is provided by Ronnie Milsap (the house act at T.J.'s), Flash and the Board of Directors, and Vaneese Starks, with songwriter Mark James performing his song "Suspicious Minds."

Elvis' accountants report that in 1969 his personal income is $1,096,000 from motion pictures, $794,000 from music and recording, and $150,000 from television. Personal appearances bring in another $401,000. His income taxes are $1,126,000.

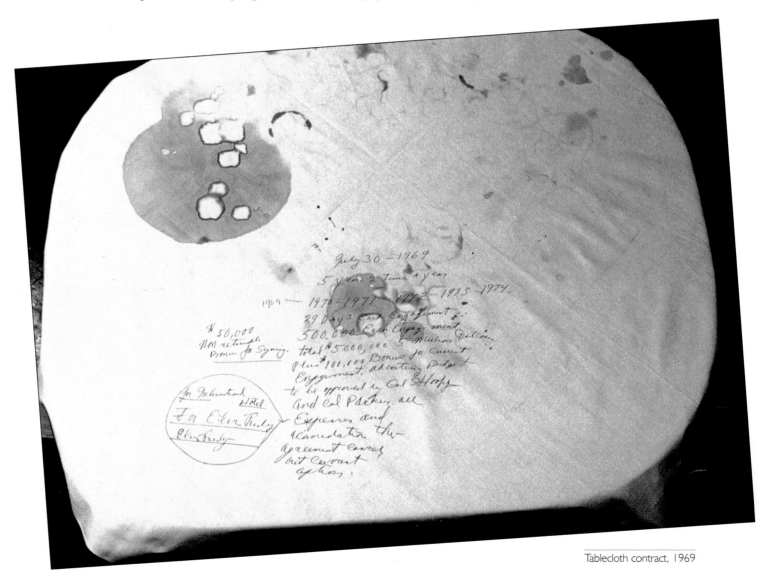

Tablecloth contract, 1969

1970

JANUARY

01 Thursday

Every night until he leaves for Los Angeles, Elvis goes to the Memphian. It is during this period that he sees the movie *Patton*, with George C. Scott's Academy Award–winning performance, for the first time. This film makes an enormous impression on him, and he memorizes the dramatic speech at its beginning as he once memorized General Mac-Arthur's "Farewell Address." He sees the movie many times over the years, and it is almost certainly the impetus for his seeking out retired World War II general Omar Bradley, a Beverly Hills neighbor, later in the year.

03 Saturday

Elvis spends approximately $3,900 to remodel two rooms and a bathroom in the basement of Graceland to be used as an apartment for Charlie Hodge and to install a replacement bar and new cabinets in the basement rec room.

06 Tuesday

Elvis flies to Los Angeles with Priscilla and Lisa Marie to prepare

Las Vegas, January–February 1970

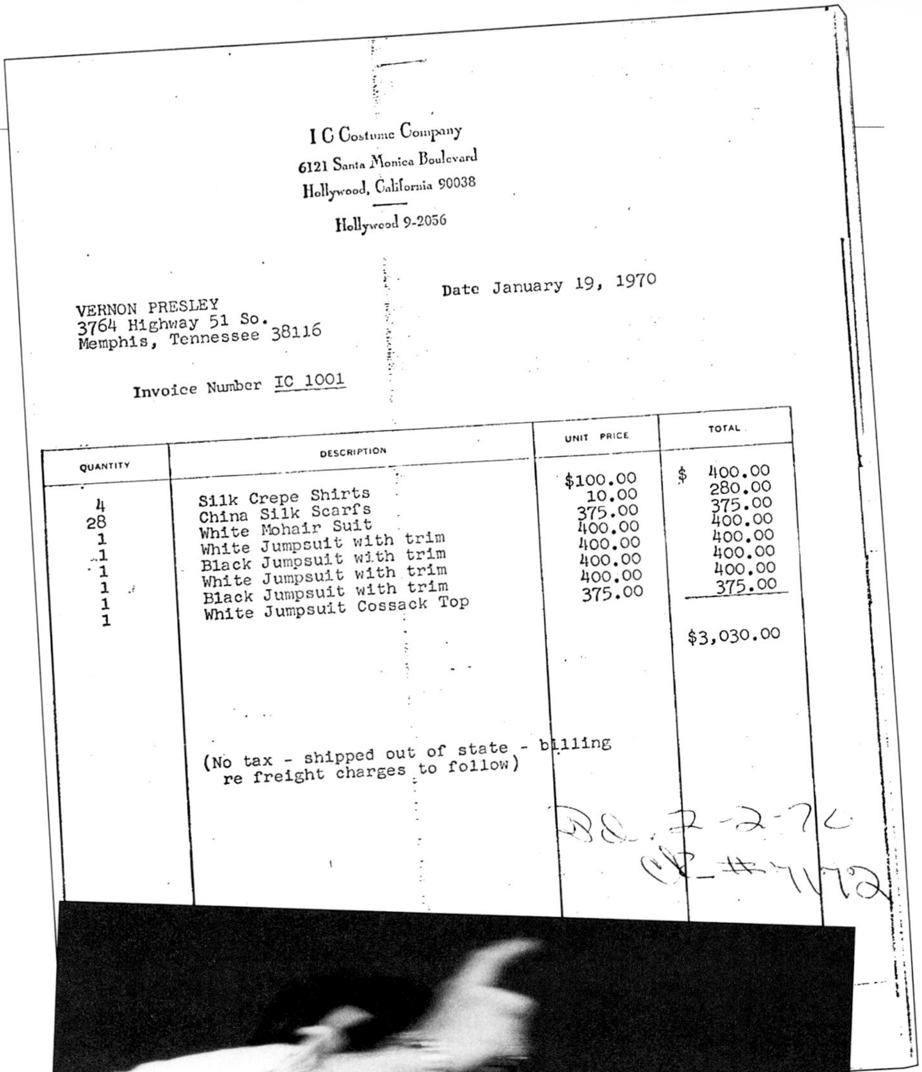

Invoice from IC Costume Company for
Elvis' first jumpsuits

for his upcoming Las Vegas engagement.

10 Saturday

Rehearsals begin at the RCA studio on Sunset. Because Ronnie Tutt has been unable to reach an agreement on salary, he has been replaced on drums by Bob Lanning. Pianist Larry Muhoberac, too, drops out, and James Burton recruits his friend, Glen D. Hardin, a native of Lubbock, Texas, who played with Buddy Holly's backing group, the Crickets. Sweet Inspiration Cissy Houston, too, has departed, to be replaced for a time by Ann Williams.

Elvis wants to change the repertoire from his first Vegas appearance, partly because another live album is scheduled to be recorded but also to better reflect his evolving taste in contemporary music. He adds Creedence Clearwater Revival's "Proud Mary," Tony Joe White's "Polk Salad Annie," Joe South's "Walk a Mile in My Shoes," and Neil Diamond's "Sweet Caroline," among others, along with a number of examples of his own recently recorded work.

12 Monday

After taking Sunday off, Elvis rehearses for the next five nights, generally arriving at the studio about 7:00 P.M. and working for five or six hours.

19 Monday

Rehearsals begin in Conference Room C at the International Hotel in Las Vegas and run through Friday, January 23. The Sweet Inspirations and the Imperials are scheduled at 2:00 P.M. each day and join Elvis and the band at 7:00 P.M. each evening.

24 Saturday

Rehearsals move into the showroom, commencing at 1:00 P.M. each day. Because of his dissatisfaction with the

Las Vegas, January–February 1970

I C Costume Company
6121 Santa Monica Boulevard
Hollywood, California 90038

Hollywood 9-2056

VERNON PRESLEY
3764 Highway 51 So.
Memphis, Tennessee 38116

Date January 19, 1970

Invoice Number IC 1001

QUANTITY	DESCRIPTION	UNIT PRICE	TOTAL
4	Silk Crepe Shirts	$100.00	$ 400.00
28	China Silk Scarfs	10.00	280.00
1	White Mohair Suit	375.00	375.00
1	White Jumpsuit with trim	400.00	400.00
1	Black Jumpsuit with trim	400.00	400.00
1	White Jumpsuit with trim	400.00	400.00
1	Black Jumpsuit with trim	400.00	400.00
1	White Jumpsuit Cossack Top	375.00	375.00
			$3,030.00

(No tax - shipped out of state - billing
re freight charges to follow)

showroom's sound in August, Elvis has hired engineer Bill Porter to help Felton run the sound board during the show.

26 Monday

★ *Showroom, International Hotel, Las Vegas*

Elvis opens his four-week engagement with a single invitation-only show, attended by everyone from Fats Domino to Zsa Zsa Gabor, that generally draws rave reviews. The *Los Angeles Herald-Examiner* declares, "The new decade will belong to him," though future biographer Albert Goldman points out in *Life* that much of the show revolves around a series of studied poses: "Elvis as the Discus Hurler, Elvis as Sagittarius, Elvis as the Dying Gaul." Many of the poses derive from karate stances, and karate plays more and more of a part in the act. This is the first time that one-piece jumpsuits, allowing for greater freedom of movement, make an appearance, and Bill Belew has supplied an array of these—in either all black or all white—for the engagement. They are made by IC (Ice Capades) Costumes in Los Angeles.

28 Wednesday

Priscilla and party fly in from Los Angeles.

January Record Release

Single: "Kentucky Rain" (#16)/"My Little Friend" (shipped January 29). Hot on the heels of "Don't Cry Daddy," the fourth single from the Memphis sessions performs well, but, with sales of 600,000, only half as well as the previous single.

FEBRUARY

01 Sunday

Lisa Marie joins her mother at the dinner show to celebrate her second birthday.

04 Wednesday

Elvis performs on both this and the following night with a bad case of the flu.

16 Monday

Felton Jarvis supervises the recording of selected songs from both the dinner and midnight shows which will serve as the backbone for Elvis' upcoming *On Stage* album. It is clear from the recordings that Tony Joe White's swamp rocker "Polk Salad Annie," complete with karate moves, is the new showstopper.

17 Tuesday

RCA continues to record selectively at both evening shows.

18 Wednesday

An afternoon rehearsal is called to work out arrangements for three additional songs, since there is not enough satisfactory new material in the show to fill out an album. The three songs are the 1959 Ray Peterson ballad "The Wonder of You," Ray Price's country classic "Release Me," and the blues standard "See See Rider," which Elvis probably knew best from Chuck Willis' 1957 hit version. Recording continues during both shows on this and the following night.

22 Sunday

Persistent difficulties with the showroom sound system lead the Colonel to threaten that Elvis will not perform his last two nights if the problem isn't fixed. It is.

Backstage, Las Vegas, January–February 1970

23 Monday

Elvis closes his engagement with a midnight show that runs until 3:00 A.M., giving what many consider to be one of his finest performances. He plays the piano on an impromptu medley of "Lawdy, Miss Clawdy" and "Blueberry Hill," and toward the end of the evening introduces the Colonel to the audience, saying "He's not only my manager, but I love him very much."

Meanwhile, the Colonel, never one to encourage anyone to take his act for granted, informs newly named International president Alex Shoofey that Elvis may not be appearing again at the hotel for some time. Plans for an

Las Vegas, January–February 1970

Las Vegas or the Houston Astrodome, early 1970

extended personal appearance tour as well as unspecified documentary and feature film projects may well prevent him from working in Vegas for the next year, according to the Colonel. Since Elvis ultimately will keep all of his regularly scheduled Vegas commitments for the next five years, one can only surmise that this is just one more element in the Colonel's carefully orchestrated philosophy of "always keep them on their toes" and "always look to improve your position."

25 Wednesday

Elvis flies to Houston for his engagement at the Houston Livestock Show and Rodeo in Kirk Kerkorian's private jet. The Colonel has done all he can to get Elvis to limit the size of his entourage ("It should be strongly considered to travel on your own steam," he writes to Joe Esposito, "so we will not be obliged to look after people when we get there, as we will not have time to do this. Also, from the undercurrent I've received, there is a great possibility that if there is any junket of that sort we would lose our complete privacy, which we always guard so carefully for Elvis' sake"), but his success can be measured by the manifest, which includes Joe, Red and Sonny West, Charlie Hodge, Gee Gee Gambill, Cliff Gleaves, and Vernon Presley, but no wives. Elvis holds a brief press conference at the airport before checking into the Astroworld Hotel for his first performance outside Las Vegas since 1961.

26 Thursday

Elvis becomes aware from the first moments of rehearsal that the sound system is hopeless and the band will be unable to hear itself. "Don't fight it," he says to pianist/arranger Glen D. Hardin. "Just go ahead and play."

27 Friday

Elvis holds a noon press conference at the Astroworld Hotel and talks about his musical roots, the current music scene, and how his Sun records sound "funny" to him today.

★ *Annual Texas Livestock Show, Houston Astrodome, Houston, Texas, at 2:00 and 7:45 P.M.*

Elvis makes a dramatic entrance, circling the arena in an open jeep, but he is discouraged both during and after the first show because of the poor acoustics and what he judges to be an indifferent response from a less-than-capacity crowd. "I guess I just can't bring it in like I used to," he says mournfully to Gee Gee Gambill in between shows. But then his spirits are lifted at the evening show by the tumultuous response from a crowd of 36,299 (10,000 more than the previous record), and his performance, according to Robert Hilburn in the *Los Angeles Times*, is "masterful."

28 Saturday

★ *Annual Texas Livestock Show, Houston Astrodome, at 2:00 and 7:45 P.M.*

The evening crowd of 43,614 sets a record for indoor rodeo performances in any arena. Priscilla flies in to attend the next day's show as rumors appear in the Houston papers about a possible breakup of her marriage.

MARCH

01 Sunday

★ *Annual Texas Livestock Show, Houston Astrodome, at 2:00 and 7:45 P.M.*

Elvis holds another press conference, after the final show, at which he is presented with gold records for five of his 1969 releases: "Don't Cry Daddy," "In the Ghetto," "Suspicious Minds," and the two LPs, *From Elvis in Memphis* and *From Memphis to Vegas/From Vegas to Memphis*. He also receives gifts of a Stetson hat, a limited-edition (number 343) Rolex "King Midas" watch, and a gold deputy's badge. The Colonel, not to be left out, demands a badge for himself from Houston sheriff Buster Kern and gets it.

Between the Vegas and Houston appearances, Elvis grosses $653,354.75 for less than five weeks' work. His expenses (talent, musical arrangements, promotion, etc.) come to $133,354.75, leaving a net income of $520,000, of which 25 percent ($130,000) goes to the Colonel, 10 percent of the remainder ($39,000) to William Morris, and the remaining $351,000 to Elvis.

---

02 Monday

Elvis returns to Los Angeles.

03 Tuesday

Elvis and Priscilla fly to Palm Springs to stay for two weeks at their rented Camino del Norte home while looking for a house to buy.

17 Tuesday

The Colonel has conceived of an idea for a pay-per-view, closed-circuit, theatrical showing of a special Elvis concert, a formula that up till now has been used only for sporting events. Elvis would receive a $1,100,000 fee, representing, according to the Colonel, the largest payment to a single performer for one show in entertainment history. On this date a nonrefundable advance of $110,000 (representing 10 percent) is paid to Elvis and the Colonel by the production company, Filmways.

19 Thursday

Robert Hilburn reports in the *Los Angeles Times* that Elvis has agreed to the pay-per-view deal and that the film will be shown in more than two hundred theaters on August 8.

23 Monday

Elvis returns to Los Angeles and the next evening flies on to Memphis.

25 Wednesday

Elvis arrives home in Memphis for a couple of days and learns that the Colonel has called off the closed-circuit concert. He had told the promoters that the deal would be canceled if word leaked to the press, and while the source of the leak is unclear, he now makes good on his word. He will subsequently try to revive the idea with

Press conference, Houston, March 1, 1970

With gold records,
Houston, March 1, 1970
(courtesy of Joe Tunzi)

new partners in various forms, but ultimately the concept is retired for the time being and replaced by a concert film to be shot in Vegas by MGM and given a conventional theatrical release. The deal is made on April 7 with Kirk Kerkorian, the new owner of MGM, for $500,000, roughly half the sum originally sought.

27 Friday

Elvis flies back to Los Angeles and spends the next weeks jetting back and forth between there, Palm Springs, and Las Vegas, never spending more than a few days in any location.

APRIL

02 Thursday

Elvis and Priscilla make a down payment of $13,187.83 on a house at 845 Chino Canyon in Palm Springs, signing a mortgage for $85,000.

06 Monday

Elvis buys a six-door 1969 Mercedes limo.

07 Tuesday

The Colonel concludes the MGM deal in Vegas. The film will be produced by Herbert Soklow and directed by Dennis Sanders, and will eventually be called *That's the Way It Is.*

22 Wednesday

Furniture that has been stored in Los Angeles is moved to the new Palm Springs home. The house is in the process of being remodeled, including the addition of a swimming pool.

23 Thursday

Elvis arrives in Palm Springs, remaining at his new home until April 28.

April Record Releases

Single: "The Wonder of You" (#9) /"Mama Liked the Roses" (shipped April 20). Recorded live in Las Vegas at the previous engagement, "The Wonder of You" sells close to one million copies.

Budget LP: *Let's Be Friends* (#105). The first of the Camden budget releases under the December 1969 deal, *Let's Be Friends* consists mostly of previously unreleased movie and studio cuts and bears out the Colonel's faith in the free-market economy, selling almost 400,000 copies. The reason it does not achieve a higher position on the charts is that album charts are based on dollar volume, not sales figures.

MAY

02 Saturday

Elvis spends most of the next three weeks in his new Palm Springs home. During this time he watches rented 16mm prints of *The Magus, No Way to Treat a Lady, The World in My Pocket, Where Eagles Dare, Guns of St. Sebastian, Citizen Kane,* and *Compulsion,* among others.

21 Thursday

Elvis and Priscilla return to Memphis, remaining until July 5 except for brief trips to Dallas by Elvis.

22 Friday

The group sees *Tick . . . Tick . . . Tick* and *M*A*S*H* at the Memphian, continuing to attend the movies every night that Elvis is at home.

24 Sunday

Elvis holds a surprise twenty-fifth-birthday party for Priscilla at Graceland.

29 Friday

Elvis flies to Dallas as John Carpenter with Charlie Hodge, Richard Davis, and Joe Esposito. They stay at the Royal Coach Motor Hotel through June 2.

Nashville session band, early-morning hours, June 9, 1970: *(top, left to right)* David Briggs, Norbert Putnam, Elvis, Al Pachucki, Jerry Carrigan; *(bottom, left to right)* Felton Jarvis, Chip Young, Charlie McCoy, James Burton

JUNE

01 Monday

A new guardhouse is completed at the Graceland gates for $1,950.

In Nashville Felton Jarvis quits his job as staff producer for RCA in order to work directly for Elvis not only in the recording studio but in Las Vegas and on the road. With respect to RCA, he will operate as an independent contractor, receiving $750 for every master cut of Elvis' that he delivers, with a 2 percent royalty override. The catch is that he is required by contract to deliver between fifteen and twenty sides from the first session, which is scheduled to begin in just three days. That number of recordings has not come out of any recent non-soundtrack sessions except the American ones—and Felton is not going back to American.

03 Wednesday

Elvis returns to Memphis from Dallas.

04 Thursday

Elvis begins five days of recording at RCA's Studio B in Nashville, reporting each evening at 6:00 P.M. and working until the dawn hours. During the thirty months that have elapsed since Elvis' last Nashville session, the studio has been upgraded from a simple four-track system to (briefly) an eight-track and now to a sixteen-track board. While this allows for greater ease of overdubbing, it also requires a greater degree of technical facility to access the advances, and Felton's main strength has never been technology. Nonetheless, he goes into the sessions with a great sense of optimism, sure of both his artist and the musicians who will be backing him—for Felton has finally reconstituted the studio band. Gone are Scotty Moore and D. J. Fontana, Elvis' original accompanists, as well as pianist Floyd Cramer, bassist Bobby Moore, drummer Buddy Harman, and the Jordanaires. In their place, working with Elvis for the first time are Norbert Putnam on bass and Jerry Carrigan on drums, along with multi-instrumentalist Charlie McCoy, pianist David Briggs, and guitarist Chip Young, who have appeared on various sessions since the mid-sixties. James Burton, the guitarist in Elvis' show band, takes over lead guitar in an ensemble that Felton believes will provide the kind of energy and expertise that the American session players were able to offer. The first night runs more than ten hours and proves highly productive, with eight songs completed, spanning every style from gospel to bluegrass jams to contemporary pop (an example of the latter would be the grandiloquently realized "I've Lost You," soon to become Elvis' next single).

05 Friday

Maintaining the same level of energy and commitment that he showed on the previous night, Elvis completes another seven masters, including a raucous jam on a combination of Muddy Waters' "Got My Mojo Working" and Jay McShann and Priscilla Bowman's "Hands Off," as well as a beautifully sung cover of Simon and Garfunkel's gospel-inflected "Bridge Over Troubled Water."

06 Saturday

Among the songs recorded tonight is an intricately arranged remake of Dusty Springfield's "You Don't Have to Say You Love Me," but the session runs down as Hill and Range song pluggers Freddy Bienstock and Lamar Fike run out of new material with which to tempt the singer.

07 Sunday

Starting at 6:00 P.M. and not quitting until 4:30 A.M., Elvis seizes on older country-and-western material

such as Ernest Tubb's "Tomorrow Never Comes," Bob Wills' "Faded Love," and Eddy Arnold's "I Really Don't Want to Know." The almost accidental result is a collection of songs that forms the basis for a "concept album," *Elvis Country*.

08 Monday

With a total of thirty-five masters completed in five nights, Felton Jarvis can feel confident both of his job and of his artist-employer. In terms of sheer numbers, this is the most productive recording session Elvis will ever have, and the quality of the material rivals—though it does not equal—that of the American sessions of the previous year. At this point the future must look bright ahead.

09 Tuesday

Elvis flies home to Memphis.

22 Monday

Elvis buys three Jetstar snowmobiles from W. H. Godwin Camper Broker in Memphis at $900 apiece. The snowmobiles come equipped with treads that allow them to be driven on the Graceland grass.

23 Tuesday

Elvis attends movies at the Memphian, then flies to Nashville, perhaps to review and make repairs on some of the recordings.

25 Thursday

Elvis flies on to Dallas, where he stays again at the Royal Coach Motor Hotel.

June Record Release

LP: *On Stage* (#13). Despite the three new songs added to the stage repertoire at the last minute, there is still a dearth of good new live material, so two tracks are included from the August 1969 recordings, and the new single, a live version of "The Wonder of You," is included among eight 1970 cuts. Reviewers express disappointment at this weak follow-up to the two American sessions albums, but the record sells well over half a million copies nonetheless.

---

27 Saturday

"John Carpenter," Richard Davis, and Charlie Hodge fly home to Memphis from Dallas.

29 Monday

There is a screening at the Memphian tonight and every night until Elvis returns to California.

JULY

05 Sunday

Elvis flies to the West Coast by way of Chicago, where he checks into the Marriott during his layover.

09 Thursday

From Los Angeles Elvis flies in a chartered jet to Las Vegas, checking into the International before going on to Palm Springs.

13 Monday

Elvis returns to Los Angeles.

14 Tuesday

Rehearsals for the upcoming show in Las Vegas are held at MGM's studio in Culver City and are filmed for use in the documentary that will be titled *That's the Way It Is*.

15 Wednesday

Rehearsing and filming continue at MGM.

16 Thursday

Rehearsal very likely continues.

17 Friday

Elvis flies to Palm Springs for a five-day break.

20 Monday

Elvis buys patio furniture in Palm Springs as a gift to the Colonel for his birthday the previous month.

22 Wednesday

Elvis returns to Los Angeles.

23 Thursday

Rehearsals move to the RCA studio on Sunset. Working from 7:00 P.M. to 1:00 A.M., Elvis runs through more than sixty songs, including twenty from the June recording session. Drummer Ronnie Tutt has returned, and Glen D. Hardin and David Briggs in Nashville continue to write new arrangements and orchestrations.

24 Friday

Elvis continues rehearsals at RCA.

28 Tuesday

Most likely rehearsals continue at RCA.

29 Wednesday

Elvis returns to MGM in Culver City for more filming on *That's the Way It Is.*

31 Friday

Elvis flies to Las Vegas on a chartered jet.

July Record Release

Single: "I've Lost You" (#32)/"The Next Step Is Love" (shipped July 14). Despite its chart position, this first single from the June Nashville sessions sells slightly more than 500,000 copies.

AUGUST

01 Saturday

The Colonel has launched yet another lavish promotional campaign in preparation for what he has dubbed "The Elvis Presley Summer Festival." This campaign includes 100,000 specially printed menus, 50,000 eight-by-ten photos, 100,000 special postcards, 60,000 four-color catalogues, 20,000 souvenir photo albums, and 25 gross of imitation straw hats for hotel employees.

04 Tuesday

Three days of rehearsals at the International's Convention Center begin today, with the singers scheduled at 1:00 P.M. and the entire group at 7:00 P.M. Filming for *That's the Way It Is* takes place today and on Friday in the showroom.

07 Friday

Rehearsals for the entire show

Filmed rehearsal for Las Vegas show, July 1970

move to the main stage of the showroom, with Joe Guercio, the new musical director of the International, leading the orchestra and working with Elvis for the first time. Despite his initial dismay over the disorganized state of Elvis' written musical arrangements and what he deems to be an "amateurish" approach to the whole show, he is bowled over by the star. "You talk to a lot of people who'll say that discipline makes a star," he will say in later years, looking back on the experience in some wonderment. "Horseshit! Charisma makes a star. Elvis Presley was a happening. He could walk across the stage and not even have to open his mouth." Rehearsals continue through Monday, the day of the opening, and continue to be filmed by the MGM crew.

10 Monday

★ *Showroom, International Hotel, Las Vegas*

Elvis opens the engagement, as usual, with a single dinner show. The reviews this time are exemplified by *Cashbox*'s rather offhand remark that "Elvis' show lacked the excitement of previous years." The impact on the audience is unchanged, however, and Elvis' sense of confidence is very much in evidence, as he spends much of his time talking, free-associating, and pursuing practical jokes in between songs. He regularly wears a white bell-bottomed jumpsuit with extra-long fringes and turns his habit of handing out scarves to fans into one of the central elements of the show. He orders the red and blue scarves by the dozen from IC Costumes in Los Angeles and soon from Mr. Guy in Las Vegas as well. MGM will continue to film through Thursday of this week, employing as many as five large Panavision cameras, which sometimes seem to hinder Elvis' spontaneity.

14 Friday

A paternity suit is filed against Elvis by a Los Angeles woman, Patricia Ann Parker, who claims that Elvis fathered the child she is carrying during his January–February Las Vegas engagement. Ed Hookstratten, Elvis' Los Angeles attorney, hires John O'Grady, a private investigator who was formerly head of the LAPD Hollywood Narcotics Detail, to investigate the charges. Elvis comments on the paternity suit from the stage.

17 Monday

Soprano Kathy Westmoreland replaces Millie Kirkham, who has in essence taken over some of departed

Stage rehearsal, convention room, Las Vegas, August 4, 1970

Stage rehearsal with full band, Las Vegas, August 7, 1970

Sweet Inspiration Cissy Houston's solo duties solely for the filming. Kirkham, who is busy with session work and her family in Nashville, cannot extend her commitment through the engagement, and Westmoreland signs on initially just for the remaining three weeks—but stays for the next seven years.

21 Friday

Elvis' grandmother, Minnie Presley, and his aunt, Delta Biggs, fly in with Dr. George Nichopoulos and attend the dinner show.

26 Wednesday

At 2:55 P.M. a telephone caller tells the hotel's security office that Elvis will be kidnapped tonight, and extra security is added at the hotel.

28 Friday

An early-morning caller to Joe Esposito's home in Los Angeles demands $50,000 in small bills to reveal the name of an individual who plans to kill Elvis during his Saturday-night show. With this second threat, Ed Hookstratten calls in the FBI and arranges for John O'Grady to fly in to oversee private security arrangements in Las Vegas. Meanwhile, the Colonel writes Elvis a letter in which he advises him to be sure his boys are with him at all times when he moves through the hotel and when he is in his dressing room. Elvis places calls to Ed Parker, Jerry Schilling, and Red West, requesting them to fly in to Las Vegas at his expense to join the other bodyguards and security men, all of whom will be armed and all of whom will take up positions around the stage during the show. Even Elvis is "packing" during the show, with a pistol stuck in each boot. Also standing by backstage is one of Elvis' Las Vegas doctors, Dr. Thomas "Flash" Newman, along with the Mercy Ambulance Service. These preparations evidently accomplish the aim of any good security system: neither potential kidnapper nor assassin is ever heard from again.

29 Saturday

Elvis' visitors include MGM head Jim Aubrey and his date, Barbara Leigh. Also present are Ricky Nelson and his wife, Kris. Senate Armed Services Committee staff member Joyce Bova, whom Elvis met the previous year in Vegas, is Elvis' guest at the show.

August Record Release

Four-LP Set: *Worldwide 50 Gold Award Hits Vol. 1* (#45). Encouraged by the success of the budget-price Camden release, RCA and the Colonel come up with yet another special package (and special deal) to recycle the Presley repertoire. This four-album set containing most of Elvis' hit songs sells 150,000 units, which, like any other multiple-record package, represents a proportionally higher net and chart position because of the higher retail price and, like every other special deal, falls under Elvis and the Colonel's 50-50 arrangement.

SEPTEMBER

05 Saturday

In the aftermath of the assassination threat and the reassembling of the old gang, Elvis has gold ID bracelets made up for all the guys, with each one's nickname on the back. The cost of twelve "Gents" bracelets and four "ladies chains and pendants," all in fourteen-karat gold, comes to $1,486.50, from Sol Schwartz and Lee Ableser's jewelry store in Beverly Hills.

07 Monday

On Elvis' final night there is an additional 3:30 A.M. show for which the Colonel negotiates an additional $12,500 in pay. In the wake of this third record-setting engagement, the International Hotel presents Elvis with a wide gold belt, similar to a boxing championship belt. It has the hotel logo on it, with stars set with diamonds around the words: "World's Championship/Attendance Record/Las Vegas Nevada/International Hotel." The belt is reported to be worth $10,000, and Elvis wears it, from this point on, proudly and often.

09 Wednesday

Elvis flies to Phoenix to begin a six-city "pilot" tour arranged by the Colonel during the Las Vegas engagement. The tour is a kind of piecemeal affair, with RCA promoting the first date, the Colonel taking responsibility for the Tampa shows four days later, and the four remaining dates taken care of by a newly formed concert promotion company called Management III. The group consists of Jerry Weintraub, a former talent agent who has just become manager of the still-unknown singer/songwriter John Denver; Tom Hulett, who with his company Concerts West has pioneered in establishing the guidelines for the contemporary rock tour with Jimi Hendrix and Led Zeppelin, among others; and Terry Bassett, a Dallas entrepreneur who financed a good deal of Concerts West's start-up costs and provided a good deal of their working capital as well. Management III pays the Colonel a guarantee of $240,000 for its four dates, but the Colonel retains control over all advertising and promotion. The tickets for almost all dates sell out within hours of going on sale.

★ *Coliseum, Phoenix, Arizona*

MGM films portions of this performance, which includes all the musicians from the Vegas show except the Imperials, who explain that they were not given sufficient notice to get out of a prior booking. They are replaced by an impromptu quartet formed by ex-Jordanaire Hugh Jarrett. Joe Guercio continues to direct the orchestra, though with the exception of a single trumpet player it is a band picked up and rehearsed in each of the cities in which Elvis is booked, an unsatisfactory arrangement for all concerned.

10 Thursday

★ *Kiel Auditorium, St. Louis, Missouri*

This is the first show produced by Management III, and Tom Hulett hires Clair Brothers to provide an up-to-date sound system with onstage monitors that allow Elvis to really

Presentation of gold belt, inscribed "World's Championship Attendance Record," by International president Alex Shoofey, on behalf of the hotel, September 7, 1970

Arrival in Phoenix, September 9, 1970, with Vernon Presley and Colonel Parker *(in profile)*

hear himself for the first time. Until this show Elvis has always relied on the PA system provided by the room or auditorium, and after initial objections by Tom Diskin (the Colonel has specified exactly the same stage setup as in Vegas, and Diskin worries that the changes will upset Elvis) it is an ear-opening experience.

11 Friday
★ *Olympia Arena, Detroit, Michigan*
Charlie Hodge remains in his role of stage manager and general assistant to Elvis, providing water and scarves. Lamar Fike takes care of lighting, and Sonny West is security chief, while Richard Davis is in charge of wardrobe, Dr. Nichopoulos is tour doctor, and Joe Esposito remains in overall command. The Colonel advances the tour, arriving in each city before Elvis and then flying on to oversee the setup of the next day's concert either that night or early the next morning.

12 Saturday
★ *Miami Beach Convention Center, Miami Beach, Florida, at 3:00 and 8:30 P.M.*

13 Sunday
★ *Curtis Hixon Convention Center, Tampa, Florida, at 3:00 and 8:30 P.M.*

14 Monday
★ *Municipal Auditorium, Mobile, Alabama*

In Mobile the group stays at the Admiral Semmes Hotel. When Elvis last played Mobile in October of 1955, the Admiral Semmes was the city's premier hotel, but now it has fallen on hard times. Elvis complains bitterly that in its present state it is "the dump of dumps," but when Joe tries to book other accommodations, he is told there isn't a room available, doesn't he know "Elvis Presley's in town?"

Before the tour breaks up Elvis gives out generous bonuses to each of the guys. Elvis will realize $174,212.53 from this six-day trial run, after all expenses (including the Colonel's share) are deducted, but clearly it is accounted more than just a monetary success, and just as clearly there will soon be another one.

15 Tuesday
Elvis leaves Mobile at 3:00 P.M., flying home to Memphis so that he can complete a scheduled two-day recording session in Nashville before returning to the West Coast on September 24.

21 Monday
Sheriff Roy C. Nixon makes Elvis an honorary deputy sheriff of Shelby County, the Tennessee county in which Memphis is located.

22 Tuesday
Elvis arrives at RCA's Studio B in Nashville at 7:00 P.M. a day late and in a bad mood. Throughout the evening he impatiently pushes Felton to speed things up. In six hours they record both sides of a single, "Where Did They Go, Lord" and "Rags to Riches," as well as the two songs needed to complete the country album, with Eddie Hinton replacing James Burton on lead guitar because Burton is unavailable.

23 Wednesday
Elvis returns to Memphis, screening a movie at the Crosstown before flying to Los Angeles the following day.

24 Thursday
The Colonel, meanwhile, draws up

a biting three-page memo for MGM president Jim Aubrey after watching a rough cut of *That's the Way It Is*. In his opinion the movie as it stands fails to show Elvis' act to advantage by having "too many cut-ins on the songs . . . which tend to distort the real-life performance"; it is condescending to the fans and needlessly insults other performers, like Frank Sinatra and Dean Martin. "Every artist," the Colonel reminds Aubrey, "has a right to be big in his own way. . . . We must all stand on our own feet." Finally, in trashing Elvis' own past work, the filmmakers do a disservice to all. "The slurs on *Blue Hawaii* and *G.I. Blues* should be removed, as these were two of the most successful films ever made by Elvis, and they do not deserve to be mentioned as just trash in such a way." If the Colonel is to be able to effectively promote the film, is the strong implication, fundamental changes must be made.

26 Saturday
Elvis spends the weekend in Palm Springs.

OCTOBER

08 Thursday
After the success of the first tour, there is no question that there will be another, and the Colonel sets up a full-scale eight-day tour with Concerts West at this time, requiring a deposit of $1 million against, most likely, 65 percent of the gate, as a test not just of the promoters' good faith but of their solvency. Jerry Weintraub and Tom Hulett manage to come up with the money and in turn are given a piece of the concessions, but the main thing is, the Elvis Presley road show is back in business.

09 Friday
Elvis buys a black 1971 Stutz Blackhawk from Jules Meyers Pontiac in Los Angeles and turns it over to George Barris for customizing. According to Barris, the car, the first of its kind to arrive in Los Angeles,

SOL SCHWARTZ
LEE ABLESER

FINE JEWELRY — DIAMONDS

Phones: 274-3088   247 No. Beverly Dr.
      271-6477   Beverly Hills, Calif.

Bill for the first TCB pendants

was earmarked for Frank Sinatra, but Elvis uses his persuasive powers to drive it off the lot.

10 Saturday

Elvis flies to Memphis, where he will spend the next week before returning to Los Angeles. One of the principal reasons for the trip appears to be the private ceremony at which he receives his official deputy sheriff's badge from Shelby County Sheriff Roy Nixon. This new badge replaces his recently received honorary one and permits Elvis to carry a pistol. His long-held interest in police work and firearms appears to have been heightened by the recent threats in Las Vegas.

12 Monday

Elvis most likely flies to Las Vegas, where his new car is delivered to the International by Barris' Kustom Industries and received by Sonny West.

15 Thursday

Back in Memphis, Elvis goes shopping and purchases a shoulder holster, in the evening attending the Gospel Quartet Convention at Ellis Auditorium, where he is introduced to the crowd by Blackwood Brothers leader James Blackwood.

17 Saturday

Elvis returns to the Quartet Convention, where he forms an impromptu quartet with James Blackwood, Statesmen founder Hovie Lister, and bass singer J. D. Sumner while having his picture taken backstage.

18 Sunday

Elvis flies to Los Angeles.

19 Monday

The woman who has instituted the paternity suit against Elvis, Patricia Parker, gives birth to a son whom she names Jason Peter Presley.

In Beverly Hills, Elvis picks up twelve pendants specially ordered at a cost of $90 each from Sol Schwartz

Backstage at the Gospel Quartet Convention, October 17, 1970, with *(left to right)* James Blackwood, Hovie Lister, and J. D. Sumner *(courtesy of James Blackwood)*

October Record Releases

Single: "You Don't Have to Say You Love Me" (#11)/"Patch It Up" (shipped October 6). The Dusty Springfield song, one of the highlights of the June Nashville session, places higher than the last single, selling a very respectable 800,000 units.
Budget LP: *Almost In Love* (#65) Unlike the last low-priced Camden release, *Let's Be Friends*, this one contains nothing but previously released material but achieves a chart position forty points higher and sales of about 400,000 copies.

Record Re-Releases

Two LPs: *Elvis in Person at the International Hotel* and *Back in Memphis*. Originally released in 1969 as the double album *From Vegas to Memphis/From Memphis to Vegas*, the two records that made up the set are now released separately, with each achieving immediate sales of 100,000.

and Lee Ableser, owners of Schwartz and Ableser, Fine Diamonds and Jewelry. These are the original TCBs made to order from a design sketched out by Priscilla and Elvis and purchased as gifts for each current member of the entourage. The fourteen-karat gold charm consists of the letters TCB over a zigzag lightning bolt. Over the years Elvis will give various explanations for the provenance of the lightning-bolt symbol (one is the Captain Marvel comic books that Elvis loved as a child), but its meaning, embroidering upon the Aretha Franklin declaration in her recording of "Respect," is "Taking care of business—in a flash."

20 Tuesday

At the Schwartz and Ableser establishment Elvis signs personally for two diamond rings and will pick up ten more TCBs with chains and one without a chain the following day.

22 Thursday

Elvis flies to Palm Springs for the weekend.

31 Saturday

Elvis is in Palm Springs once again for the weekend, purchasing ammunition, holsters, and a grip for a Colt Cobra at Tiny's Gun Shop.

NOVEMBER

01 Sunday

Elvis spends a final weekend in Palm Springs before going out on the November tour.

02 Monday

Elvis returns to Los Angeles, where he picks up six pairs of customized prescription "goggles" and two pairs of nonprescription glasses at the Optique Boutique in Beverly Hills.

04 Wednesday

Elvis orders gold handles from Schwartz and Ableser jewelers for his new Colt and Berretta pistols.

09 Monday

Elvis purchases four more TCBs on the same day that he puts down a deposit on a new home at 144 Monovale Drive in the Holmby Hills section of Beverly Hills.

10 Tuesday

★ *Coliseum, Oakland, California*

The tour opens in Oakland. In general Elvis will sing more ballads on this tour and for the first time will introduce the gospel number "How Great Thou Art" as one of the highlights of the show, with the Imperials returned to contribute backing vocals.

11 Wednesday

★ *Memorial Coliseum, Portland, Oregon*

The documentary film *That's the Way It Is* opens nationwide.

12 Thursday

★ *Coliseum, Seattle, Washington*

13 Friday

★ *Cow Palace, San Francisco, California*

14 Saturday

★ *Inglewood Forum, Los Angeles, California, at 3:00 and 8:30 P.M.*

Total attendance for these two shows is a record-breaking 37,398, with a gross of over $300,000, more than a 1969 appearance at the Forum by the Rolling Stones. At the hotel,

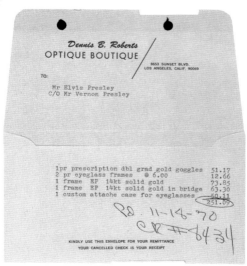

Bill for customized glasses, Optique Boutique

between shows, a process server posing as a fan presents Elvis with papers for the ongoing paternity suit. During the second show a nettled Elvis reminds fans that he has fifty-six gold singles and fourteen gold albums and has outsold the Beatles, the Stones, and Tom Jones, "all of them put together."

15 Sunday

★ *International Sports Arena, San Diego, California*

16 Monday

★ *State Fair Grounds Arena, Oklahoma City, Oklahoma*

Inglewood Forum, Los Angeles, afternoon show, November 14, 1970

17 Tuesday

★ *Coliseum, Denver, Colorado*

In Denver, Elvis chats more with the off-duty policemen assigned to protect him than he does with the guys, making friends with detectives Ron Pietrafeso and Jerry Kennedy in particular. He shows them his collection of police badges and is disappointed when they can only come up with an honorary badge in exchange. He makes plans to come back to Denver to collect a real badge soon, however, and invites the Denver policemen to come out to see him the next time he plays Las Vegas.

With fringe, Inglewood
Forum, Los Angeles,
evening show,
November 14, 1970

18 Wednesday

Elvis flies back to Los Angeles, arriving at 5:45 P.M.

In Los Angeles at around this time Elvis meets voice-over specialist Paul Frees through John O'Grady. O'Grady prods Frees to show Elvis the Federal Bureau of Narcotics and Dangerous Drugs (BNDD) badge he has received in recognition of his extensive undercover work for the agency, and Elvis, increasingly fixated on the acquisition of badges as he is, determines to get this prize badge for himself.

21 Saturday

During one of his weekends in Palm Springs at around this time, Elvis seeks out Vice President Spiro Agnew, a regular visitor to the desert resort, and attempts to give him a commemorative gun as a present. As an elected official, Agnew is forced to refuse the gift but is impressed with the patriotic sentiments that Elvis articulates.

23 Monday

Elvis flies to Memphis, arriving early

November Record Releases

Budget LP: *Elvis' Christmas Album.* This third low-priced Camden album of the year is the original 1957 Christmas album minus its four gospel cuts and with "Mama Liked the Roses" added to make a total of nine songs. Despite these shortcomings, it will sell more than one million copies over the next three holiday seasons, eventually selling over six million records in the U.S. alone and becoming Elvis' all-time best-selling album.

LP: *That's the Way It Is* (#21). Released in conjunction with the documentary, this is not a soundtrack album by any stretch of the imagination. It features four songs from the actual shows and none from the rehearsals, filling out the album with eight cuts from the Nashville sessions in June. This is the eighth album to be released in 1970, which can be compared to 1956 alone in marketing profligacy. It sells more than 500,000 copies, about the same level as other albums of original material put out during this "comeback" period.

George Klein's wedding, December 5, 1970, *(back, left to right)* Richard Davis, Bill Morris, Dick Grob, Red West; *(front, left to right)* Charlie Hodge, Marty Lacker, Lamar Fike, Elvis, George Klein, Joe Esposito, Sonny West, Jerry Schilling, Alan Fortas, Vernon Presley, and Dr. George Nichopoulos *(courtesy of Jerry Schilling)*

the following morning. During his brief two-day stay he posts a $2,000 bond for a gun permit for his father.

25 Wednesday

Elvis returns to Los Angeles.

DECEMBER

01 Tuesday

Elvis purchases a pair of silver "goggles with reverse fade" and gold prescription glasses, with the initials "EP" and a TCB lightning bolt molded to the frame, at the Optique Boutique.

03 Thursday

Elvis donates $7,000 to the Los Angeles Police community relations program, requesting that news of the gift not be made public. This is the largest single donation made to the program to date. Soon after, Elvis receives a gold commissioner's badge from Chief Davis.

On the same date he begins what amounts to a three-night $20,000-plus gun-buying binge at Kerr's Sporting Goods, where it takes four salesmen to keep up with him as he makes purchases for himself, his friends, and customers who have just wandered in off the street.

04 Friday

Elvis and Priscilla complete their purchase of the new home at 144 Monovale for $339,000. This house is considerably larger than the one on Hillcrest, providing additional bedrooms for members of the entourage and their wives, while its grounds offer a greater degree of privacy.

Elvis buys seven more TCB pendants as well as other jewelry at Schwartz and Ableser.

05 Saturday

Elvis arranges for everyone, including his father and stepmother, to fly to Las Vegas for the wedding of

With President Richard Nixon, Sonny West *(left),* and Jerry Schilling, December 21, 1970 *(courtesy of National Archives and Records Service)*

With President Nixon, December 21, 1970 *(courtesy of National Archives and Records Service)*

Hotel Washington bill for Jon Burrows, December 22, 1970

George Klein and Barbara Little in his International Hotel suite.

06 Sunday

Elvis makes a number of purchases from the Gun Shop in Las Vegas.

08 Tuesday

Elvis buys a house for Joe Esposito and his wife in west Los Angeles, and Mercedeses for himself, Jerry Schilling, and Barbara Leigh.

09 Wednesday

The Colonel writes to Elvis in exasperation at not being able to reach him on the phone. He reminds

Elvis with a degree of self-amusement how hard he has been working for him, expresses his frustration at Elvis' obvious avoidance of him in somewhat sarcastic terms, and concludes, "Remember, your slogan TCB . . . only works if you use it."

On the same day the Colonel completes an agreement with RCA to extend his annual $100,000 consultant's fee through 1975.

10 Thursday

Elvis and Priscilla take out a construction permit for renovations on the Monovale house.

11 Friday

Elvis hosts another wedding, this time in Palm Springs, where Palm Springs policeman Dick Grob is married in Elvis' home. Grob, a weapons training specialist, originally met Elvis while working security details at the house. Elvis' wedding gift is a new Cadillac, and Grob will eventually join the entourage on a full-time basis.

14 Monday

Elvis returns to Los Angeles.

16 Wednesday

Elvis rents the projection room at MGM to screen *That's the Way It Is*.

He also countersues Patricia Parker, the litigant in the paternity suit.

17 Thursday

Elvis flies to Memphis, where he will be headquartered until January 9, 1971.

18 Friday

Evidently in hopes of placating his father, who has expressed increasing concern over Elvis' expenditures in the last few weeks, Elvis buys him a Mercedes.

19 Saturday

Vernon and Priscilla attempt to confront Elvis over his spending habits. In a fury, Elvis leaves Graceland, drives to the airport, and boards a flight to Washington, D.C., where he briefly checks into the Hotel Washington and attempts to get in touch with Joyce Bova before flying on to Los Angeles via Dallas. Elvis calls his new limousine driver, Gerald Peters, and Jerry Schilling from Dallas, arranging for them to meet his TWA flight but warning them to tell no one where he is.

20 Sunday

Upon arrival at 2:17 A.M., Elvis sees a doctor about a rash he has developed on his face and neck, most likely caused by an allergic reaction to the medication he is taking for an eye infection, aggravated by chocolate he ate on the plane. In the afternoon he explains to Jerry that he wants to return to Washington.

The entourage with badges, December 28, 1970, *(standing, left to right)* Billy Smith, former sheriff Bill Morris, Lamar Fike, Jerry Schilling, Sheriff Roy Nixon, Vernon Presley, Charlie Hodge, Sonny West, George Klein, Marty Lacker; *(front, left to right)* Dr. George Nichopoulos, Elvis, Red West

When Jerry protests that he has to be back in California for work this week, Elvis allows him to call Sonny West and have him meet them in Washington, giving Sonny permission to tell Priscilla and Vernon that he is safe but not where he is. On the flight a full-fledged plan seems to formulate only after he runs into California senator George Murphy, whom he speaks to about getting the BNDD badge and at whose suggestion he begins a letter in longhand to President Nixon offering his services in the government's efforts to combat illicit drug use.

21 Monday

Picked up at the airport by the same Liberty Limousine Service driver who had piloted him around the capital the first time, Elvis drops off his letter to the president at approximately 6:30 A.M. After registering once again at the Hotel Washington, Elvis proceeds to BNDD headquarters to try to meet with Bureau director John Ingersoll, whom Senator Murphy has promised to contact for him. If President Nixon telephones while he is out, he says, Jerry should simply call him at the Bureau. He is unsuccessful in his attempts to meet

with Ingersoll or to persuade Deputy Director John Finlator to give him a badge—but President Nixon's deputy counsel, Egil Krogh, does call while he is out to inquire if Elvis can meet with him in about forty-five minutes at the Old Executive Office Building on the White House grounds. Elvis returns immediately to the hotel, where he picks up Jerry and Sonny (who has just arrived) and meets with Krogh and then President Nixon. To everyone's surprise perhaps but Elvis', he persuades the President of his sincerity, patriotism, and goodwill—in fact, in a strange way they really hit it off. After an exchange of gifts, the President is convinced to have Ingersoll give him a badge, and Elvis leaves Washington the following day with what he came for—though he never does get to meet FBI director J. Edgar Hoover, to whom Senator Murphy has also promised to drop a note of introduction. He does, however, get to see Joyce Bova, whom he will visit again nine days later.

22 Tuesday

Elvis returns to Graceland with gifts for Priscilla and Lisa Marie and many stories to tell.

24 Thursday

Elvis presents Mercedeses to Sonny West (who is about to get married, in the third wedding ceremony of the season that Elvis will sponsor), Dr. Nick, and Bill Morris, the ex–Shelby County sheriff who has helped Elvis to obtain his deputy sheriff's badge and has sponsored him for the JCC (Junior Chamber of Commerce) Award as one of the nation's Ten Outstanding Young Men of the Year that he will receive in January. In the early-morning hours of Christmas day, he visits Memphis Police headquarters "to say hello," reports the *Memphis Commercial Appeal*, "to the men and women who had to work on Christmas."

25 Friday

After all of his exertions, Elvis celebrates Christmas quietly at home with Priscilla and Lisa Marie, then goes to see *Little Fauss and Big Halsy*, with Robert Redford, at the Memphian.

26 Saturday

Elvis purchases more firearms and supplies from Taylor's Gun Shop and in the evening screens *That's the Way It Is* again at the Memphian.

28 Monday

Elvis is best man, Priscilla matron of honor at Sonny West's wedding. Elvis arrives dressed in a "fur cloth," black bell-bottomed suit that is a Christmas gift from Priscilla, along with a white tie, a belt with gold eagles and chains, a second belt adorned with the gold belt buckle set off by a large sheriff's star and his own official deputy number (six) that Sheriff Nixon has just presented to him, two guns in a shoulder holster, two pearl-handled pistols in the waist of his pants, a derringer in his boot, and a fifteen-inch police flashlight. Then, after a church reception, he hosts a second reception at Graceland, where a picture is taken with Elvis and all the guys displaying the badges they, too, have just received from Sheriff Nixon.

29 Tuesday

Elvis drives to Tupelo to collect yet another badge, this one from Tupelo sheriff Bill Mitchell, whom Elvis has known from the time Mitchell played fiddle in the band led by Mississippi Slim on radio station WELO when Elvis was a child.

30 Wednesday

Elvis returns to Washington, D.C.,

December Record Release

Single: "I Really Don't Want to Know" (#21)/"There Goes My Everything" (shipped December 8). The movie soundtrack album, *That's the Way It Is*, has been in stores less than a month when RCA releases Elvis' fifth single of the year as a forerunner to the forthcoming *Elvis Country* album. The A-side, an Eddy Arnold (and Solomon Burke) classic, does not chart particularly well but sells close to 700,000 copies.

---

with eight friends, including ex-sheriff Bill Morris, for a visit to the headquarters of the National Sheriffs Association, where Elvis takes out memberships for everyone so that they will all be eligible for automatic life insurance policies. Morris has also promised to arrange for an appointment with J. Edgar Hoover, but once again this falls through, though the group does visit FBI headquarters the following day for a special tour.

31 Thursday

Elvis expresses his admiration for J. Edgar Hoover to the FBI agent conducting the tour, remarking "in private comments" after the tour, as recorded in the agent's memo, "that he, Presley, is the 'living proof that America is the land of opportunity' since he rose from truck driver to prominent entertainer almost overnight." Elvis offers to serve in an undercover capacity in any way he can. On the agent's recommendation Director Hoover sends Elvis a note on January 4, indicating that "your generous comments concerning the Bureau and me are appreciated, and you may be sure we will keep in mind your offer to be of assistance."

The group flies home to Memphis in a leased jet in time for the annual New Year's Eve party at TJ's, with entertainment provided by TJ's artist-in-residence Ronnie Milsap.

Elvis' accountants report that in 1970 his personal income from motion pictures is $730,000. Music and recording come to $1,325,000, and personal appearances $2,042,000. He will pay $1,728,000 in income tax.

Family portrait, December 10, 1970

1971

January

04 Monday

Elvis flies to Dallas with Charlie Hodge, Sonny West, Richard Davis, and Bill Morris, where he registers at the Royal Coach Motor Hotel under the name of Jon Burrows, long one of his favorite pseudonyms and the name under which he registered at the Hotel Washington the previous month.

05 Tuesday

Elvis returns from Dallas to Memphis.

08 Friday

Perhaps as a birthday gift to himself, Elvis has a police radio installed in his Mercedes and buys an array of police equipment, including revolving blue lights, shoulder holsters, chemical weapons, and handcuffs. Over the next few days he will purchase a number of Smith & Wesson pistols as well as additional police equipment.

09 Saturday

The Junior Chamber of Commerce of America announces that Elvis has been selected as one of the nation's Ten Outstanding Young Men of the Year for 1970. The Jaycee awards have been given out since 1939 and have been awarded to distinguished men in all

With fellow JCC award winner Boston City Councillor Tom Atkins

fields (including Leonard Bernstein, Orson Welles, the Reverend Jesse Jackson, and Ralph Nader), with one common denominator: they must all be thirty-five or younger. Elvis has been nominated by former sheriff Bill Morris and joins other winners, who this year include Ronald Reagan's press secretary,

Ron Ziegler, Tom Atkins, a civil rights activist from Boston, and a medical researcher from Harvard University.

Elvis flies to Los Angeles and then to Palm Springs for the weekend, where he purchases another $3,520 worth of guns and gun-related equipment.

With Priscilla at the JCC prayer breakfast, January 16, 1971; Charlie Hodge to Elvis' right, Sonny West visible between Elvis and Priscilla, Red West and Joan Esposito to Priscilla's left, Sandy Schilling behind Red, and Jerry Schilling at far right

13 Wednesday

Back in Los Angeles, Elvis obtains more firearms as well as twenty-two additional TCB pendants.

15 Friday

After arriving in Memphis with Priscilla at 11:30 P.M., Elvis spends several hours in the study next to his bedroom working on his acceptance speech for the JCC awards dinner.

16 Saturday

Elvis and Priscilla attend the JCC prayer breakfast at the Memphis Holiday Inn Rivermont. At the press conference Elvis responds to a question about the effect of music on today's youth. "I don't go along with music advocating drugs and desecration of the flag. I think an entertainer is for entertaining and to make people happy."

United Nations ambassador-appointee George Bush is the keynote speaker at the JCC luncheon, which is attended by Marion Keisker, formerly Sam Phillips' assistant at Sun Records, among others.

At 5:00 P.M. Elvis holds a reception at Graceland for award winners and Jaycee officials, during which he conducts informal tours of the house. An hour later Elvis and Priscilla host a formal dinner for one hundred guests at the Four Flames Restaurant, where place cards have been embossed with the TCB logo and signed by the star. An elegant "Chateaubriand dinner" is served at a cost of $1,907.51, with entertainment provided by singer and accordionist Tony Barrasso and two violins.

During the 8:00 P.M. awards ceremony at Ellis Auditorium Elvis proudly accepts an honor that clearly means as much to him as any public recognition he has ever received. "When I was a child, ladies and gentlemen," he declares in a halt-

WILLIAMS COSTUME RENTAL

226 N. Third St. — Phone 384-1384

LAS VEGAS, NEVADA
OPEN 10 A.M. — 6 P.M. MONDAY — SATURDAY

NAME OF LESSEE ~~SETH~~ JOE ESPOSITO

ADDRESS INT. HOTEL RM 3000

PHONE _____ CITY Show Elvis

ITEMS RENTED / Gorilla Head

Rent	$7.50
Overt	4.00
Tax	.41
Total	11.91
Deposit	10.00
Total	21.91

Hats ✓
Jewelry
Wigs
Gloves
Props
Hose
Tie

RENTAL DATE 1/26   RETURN DATE 1/29/71   TIME 10-10 PM

CONTRACT TERMS

Lessee agrees to pay in full value for any and all items not returned. Deposit will not be refunded if costumes are returned late. Cleaning, damage, and loss charges will be deducted from deposit. No article may be altered without consent of **WILLIAMS COSTUME RENTAL.** Lessee shall not sublet any leased article. All rent is payable in advance. In case where no deposit has been posted Lessee agrees to pay in full value all loss, damage, cleaning, and late charges. **No** CANCELLATION OR EXCHANGE ▬▬▬

SIGNED FOR THE LESSEE BY _____   DATE 1/26/71

WILLIAMS COSTUME RENTAL BY _____

NOTE:
No refunds against check payments will be made before the lapse of seven (7) days from date of deposit to permit checks to clear.

Invoice for stage prop, Las Vegas show

---

ing voice, "I was a dreamer. I read comic books, and I was the hero of the comic book. I saw movies, and I was the hero in the movie. So every dream that I ever dreamed has come true a hundred times." He concludes with a quote that he first learned from a Roy Hamilton record: "'Without a song the day would never end / Without a song a man ain't got a friend / Without a song the road would never bend / Without a song . . .'

January Record Release

LP: *Elvis Country* (#12). This album of country material is critically well received and offers a puzzling "album concept," as snippets of the Golden Gate Quartet's "I Was Born 10,000 Years Ago" are interspersed between the cuts—but neither critical acceptance nor theme nor performance pushes the record beyond the customary half-million copies.

So I keep singing a song." The trophy he receives becomes one of his most treasured possessions, one that will subsequently accompany him at all times on his travels.

17 Sunday

Elvis most likely returns to Los Angeles for band rehearsals, arriving in Las Vegas by at least the following Sunday.

26 Tuesday

★ *Showroom, International Hotel, Las Vegas, Nevada*

Elvis opens the engagement, as usual, with a single 8:00 P.M. dinner show, continuing with two shows nightly. The new program emphasizes ballads and inspirational numbers, with "How Great Thou Art" and "The Impossible Dream" (the show-stopping number from *Man of La Mancha* with which Jack Jones had a big 1966 hit) particular favorites.

27 Wednesday

Sol Schwartz sends Elvis' order of four TLC (Tender Loving Care) pendants to Las Vegas. This is a female variation that Elvis has come up with on the TCB theme.

FEBRUARY

01 Monday

Lisa Marie is in attendance at the dinner show for her third birthday. A number of Elvis' friends from the Denver police force are present as well, at Elvis' invitation.

12 Friday

Despite flu and a fever, Elvis continues to perform all his shows.

19 Friday

Elvis accidentally knocks himself in the mouth with the microphone when a fan rushes the stage, chipping his tooth in the process.

23 Tuesday

Elvis concludes his Las Vegas engagement with a show that ranges from an uninhibited "Mystery Train"/"Tiger Man" medley to a sadly bittersweet "Help Me Make It Through the Night." As on almost every other final night, there is also a water fight.

Wearing the JCC award medallion

24 Wednesday

Elvis and Priscilla remain in Las Vegas to attend Ann-Margret's opening at the International.

26 Friday

Elvis and Priscilla see the Irish Royal Show Band at the Stardust.

February Record Release

Single: "Rags to Riches" (#33)/"Where Did They Go, Lord" (shipped February 23). The old Tony Bennett standard proves to be the wrong choice for a single, selling approximately 400,000 copies.

MARCH

01 Monday

A surveillance system is installed at Graceland, with cameras placed at the gates and in several rooms of the house. These are hooked up to four monitors, which Elvis will come to see as a diversification of his television viewing at times—and which in future occasionally serve as a substitute for human contact.

02 Tuesday

Elvis leaves Las Vegas and flies to Los Angeles.

03 Wednesday

Elvis and his family, as Dr. and Mrs. John Carpenter and Lisa Carpenter, fly home to Memphis by way of Dallas, along with Elvis' stepbrother, Ricky Stanley, and Charlie Hodge.

08 Monday

Elvis and Priscilla attend the closed-circuit broadcast of the first Ali-Frazier fight at Ellis Auditorium. Elvis arrives wearing his gold "championship" belt from the International, accompanied by a large group of guys and former sheriff Bill Morris. Later in the evening Elvis goes to the Memphian for the first time since his return home and will subsequently attend the movies for the next four nights.

15 Monday

Elvis arrives in Nashville for a session at RCA's Studio B, while Priscilla flies to California to supervise the redecorating of the new house. It is the hope of the Colonel and RCA, not to mention Felton Jarvis, that Elvis will repeat his recording success of the previous year, but there are problems from the start. The record company wants to see several singles, a pop album, a gospel album, and, most important, a new Christmas album come out of the session, but Elvis seems to have his mind on something else. He starts off with Scottish folksinger Ewan McColl's "The First Time Ever I Saw Your Face," a song he knows from Peter, Paul and Mary's 1965 version, next embarks upon "Amazing Grace," a recent Top 20 hit for folksinger Judy Collins, and goes on to two Gordon Lightfoot songs also familiar from Peter, Paul and Mary versions. Before he can complete an "Elvis Presley, Folksinger" concept album, however, he calls off the session at approximately 1:30 A.M., after experiencing increasing discomfort in his eye.

16 Tuesday

Dr. Nick flies in from Memphis with Dr. David Meyer, an ophthalmologist, who treats Elvis at his hotel before admitting him to Nashville's Baptist Hospital, where a diagnosis of iritis and secondary glaucoma is confirmed. Actress Barbara Leigh flies in from California to join Elvis in the hospital, and while he is hospitalized he is visited by Tennessee governor Winfield Dunn.

At the studio Felton Jarvis resumes work, overdubbing background vocals in anticipation of Elvis' return.

17 Wednesday

With Elvis still hospitalized, the remainder of the paid-up studio time is given over to guitarist James Burton, who uses the session band to record a solo album for A & M Records.

19 Friday

Upon Elvis' discharge from the hospital, Barbara Leigh flies back to California, while Joyce Bova arrives from Washington to accompany Elvis to Memphis.

22 Monday

In Memphis Elvis has an appointment at Memphis Eye and Ear Hospital.

23 Tuesday

Elvis buys twenty-five watches at $75 each from Memphis jeweler Harry Levitch.

26 Friday

Another Memphis jeweler and friend of Dr. Nick's, Lowell Hays, sends Elvis a bill for an American flag pin he had ordered while in the hospital.

29 Monday

While in Memphis, Elvis contacts Korean-born karate instructor Kang Rhee, whom Ed Parker has recommended for his expertise in tae kwon do. Elvis visits Master Rhee's studio on Poplar Avenue, across from Overton Park, and the two of them immediately hit it off, with Elvis receiving his fourth-degree black belt on this date.

30 Tuesday

Elvis purchases a Colt Python from a gun shop in Mississippi.

31 Wednesday

Colonel Parker sets up a new deal with RCA to release three albums in 1972 on the Camden label for which Elvis and the Colonel will each receive an advance of $90,000 and improved royalties. The Colonel also arranges a special deal for a second volume of *Gold Award Hits* that will guarantee payment of $525,000 (to be split 50-50) against 150,000 sales, at $3.50 per unit, with all regular royalties waived.

March Record Release

Budget LP: *You'll Never Walk Alone* (#69). This is a collection of religious material, all previously issued with the exception of one cut, "Who Am I?" from the 1969 American sessions. As with the two previous gospel albums, sales start slow (approximately 200,000), but over the years this Camden budget release will sell nearly two million copies.

RECEIPT No. 14962

Self-Realization Fellowship
3880 SAN RAFAEL AVENUE
LOS ANGELES, CALIFORNIA 90065 U.S.A.

DATE: December 17, 1970
ORDER NO.

RECEIVED FROM:
E. A. Presley

ST	S		REC. ENC.	BY
SRF LESSONS Through	19	@	Enrollment Fee per month	

____ New ____ Renew ____ Year(s)
Gift Subscription(s)

SELF-REALIZATION MAGAZINE

DONATIONS: General ☒   Building   India
                          Welfare   Misc. $2,000.00
PY Mem.

BOOKS AND MISCELLANEOUS

Order Enc.:
☐ CASH ☑ CHECK ☐ M.O. ☐ FOREIGN BANK ☐ OTHER   TOTAL RECEIVED $ *2000.00*

Thank You

Receipt for a donation to the Self-Realization Center

APRIL

10 Saturday
Elvis flies to Los Angeles in time for Easter. Priscilla and Joanie Esposito organize an Easter egg hunt for the children the following day at the Palm Springs house on Camino del Norte.

19 Monday
Elvis is in Los Angeles for most of the month. He and Priscilla may have flown to Mount Holly, New Jersey, on this date to visit for two days with Priscilla's brother, Don, on leave from Vietnam.

April Record Release

Single: "Life" (#53)/"Only Believe" (shipped April 27). Just two months after the release of "Rags to Riches," the year's second single is shipped for Easter airplay. As is common with this kind of seasonal release, sales are a flat 275,000 copies.

It is during this time period that Priscilla begins to take karate classes from Ed Parker, and on April 13 Elvis buys such martial arts supplies as two black karate ghis, sweatbands, headbands, a rubber knife, and skin toughener.

23 Friday
Elvis purchases a Sony tape recorder, some speakers, and a bass guitar at Bel Air Camera and Hi Fi.

30 Friday
Elvis flies to Palm Springs for the weekend.

MAY

01 Saturday
Elvis most likely spends his fourth wedding anniversary in Palm Springs.

03 Monday
Elvis is seen as an outpatient at the Palm Springs hospital.

07 Friday
After returning to Los Angeles, Elvis flies to Las Vegas with Joe Esposito, Charlie Hodge, James Caughley (Richard Davis' replacement in the entourage), Red West, and Mike Keaton, while limousine driver Gerald Peters ("Sir Gerald") drives so as to be available for chauffeur duty for the length of Elvis' stay.

10 Monday
Late in the evening Elvis flies back to Los Angeles.

12 Wednesday
Sir Gerald takes Elvis to the Self-Realization Center overlooking Pasadena. It should be noted that while Larry Geller has long since been banished and Elvis burned many of his religious texts shortly after his marriage to Priscilla four years before, he has never abandoned his spiritual search, and there are numerous indications over the years of his sustained spiritual commitment. His renewed contact with Sri Daya Mata is remarked upon in a somewhat confused way in a Rona Barrett column in September.

15 Saturday
Elvis returns to Nashville under pressure from RCA, who have already announced the upcoming release of a new Christmas album and who are, as always, looking for new singles material. To establish the right kind of mood, Felton sets up a decorated Christmas tree, complete with gaily wrapped packages (all empty), and Lamar even appears dressed as Santa Claus. Elvis grudgingly accepts the task at hand, but only when the group jams on the Charles Brown blues classic "Merry Christmas Baby" does he show any real engagement. He is still able to complete about half the album tonight before breaking off at 4:00 A.M.

16 Sunday
Drummer Jerry Carrigan fails to show up for the second day of recording, and his place is taken by Kenny Buttrey. The highlight of the evening

comes during a break between "Winter Wonderland" and "O Come, All Ye Faithful," when Elvis and the band jam on an eleven-minute version of Bob Dylan's "Don't Think Twice, It's All Right," after which Elvis, showing a distinct lack of enthusiasm for the Christmas material, hangs it up for the night and the band lays down three instrumental tracks.

17 Monday

On the third night Elvis' attention returns at first to the folk-rock material from the March session. He begins with Kris Kristofferson's "Help Me Make It Through the Night," next turns to Cree Indian folksinger Buffy Sainte-Marie's "Until It's Time for You to Go," and finally gives himself over to the gospel album that was one of the original reasons for the session, completing one track, the classic "Lead Me, Guide Me." The mood is broken not long afterward when Elvis, demonstrating how to disarm a gunman with a karate kick, kicks the gun out of either Charlie or Red's hand (memories differ) through Chip Young's handcrafted Conde-Hermanos guitar, which puts a definite damper on the session.

18 Tuesday

Three more gospel sides are recorded, including "He Touched Me," which will become the title of the album.

19 Wednesday

After completing two more spiritual numbers, Elvis unwinds at the piano in the early hours of the morning accompanied only by Norbert Putnam on bass, singing two compositions by one of his old favorites, Ivory Joe Hunter—"I Will Be True" and "It's Still Here"—as well as another song recorded by Hunter and half remembered from childhood, "I'll Take You Home Again Kathleen." These will be overdubbed later, but taken by themselves they are probably the highlight of the session.

20 Thursday

Elvis focuses on pop repertoire, recording "I'm Leavin'," "We Can Make the Morning," and "It's Only Love," all of which will be released as singles over the next nine months.

21 Friday

Joyce Bova is Elvis' guest at the studio on this last day of the session. After singing a single pop song, he records his vocals for the Christmas tracks, having completed thirty masters in a marathon, weeklong session but still clearly needing additional material to complete his contractual requirements.

22 Saturday

Early in the morning Elvis awakens in his Nashville hotel room in pain, returning directly to Memphis with Joyce and going directly to Dr. Nichopoulos' house from the airport.

23 Sunday

Elvis flies to Los Angeles, where he remains for two weeks.

JUNE

01 Tuesday

Elvis' birthplace in Tupelo is opened to the public in a prettified state.

08 Tuesday

Elvis returns to Nashville, registering at the Quality Court Motel and working at the RCA studio until about 2:00 A.M. Before tackling more gospel material, he insists on redoing the Buffy Sainte-Marie tune from the last session, "Until It's Time for You to Go."

09 Wednesday

Elvis records four songs to complete the gospel album about 4:30 A.M.

While Elvis is in Nashville, Priscilla begins lessons at Kang Rhee's karate studio in Memphis.

10 Thursday

Returning to the studio for a final night, Elvis throws himself into a triumphantly dramatic version of Frank Sinatra's "My Way" as well as redoing "I'll Be Home on Christmas Day." But the session ends on a sour note at 4:30 A.M. when Elvis storms out of the studio in apparent frustration at the inattention of the backup singers.

12 Saturday

Elvis is back home in Memphis, where he spends time at Kang Rhee's studio and is seen riding around Graceland on a go-cart.

26 Saturday

Hilton Hotels has taken over the International in Las Vegas, and the new vice president, Henri Lewin, throws a surprise sixty-second birthday party for Colonel Parker. Although Elvis' contract with the International allows him to leave should any ownership change occur, the Colonel has already made it clear that he and Elvis will continue under the new ownership on the same terms.

28 Monday

Elvis visits the Memphian for the first time this trip but will henceforth be at the movies either here or at the Crosstown almost all of his remaining nights in town.

June Record Releases

Single: "I'm Leavin'" (#36)/"Heart of Rome" (shipped June 22). "I'm Leavin'" is a fine dramatic performance which everyone, including Elvis, believes will be a big hit, but it does little better than its predecessor.

LP: *Love Letters from Elvis* (#33). For reasons that to this day remain somewhat baffling, RCA, instead of using the newly recorded (and in many cases very effective) material it has been clamoring for, cobbles together an album of unreleased material from the June 1970 sessions. One reviewer declares accurately, with no idea of the truth of the statement, that the songs sound like a bunch of "leftovers." That response seems to be shared by the public, who buy less than 300,000 copies. This figure probably represents the hardcore fan base, who will buy almost any Elvis release. Overall, the year's falling sales figures have failed to be checked by the release of any of Elvis' records to date.

29 Tuesday

The Memphis City Council votes to change the name of Highway 51 South, from South Parkway to the Mississippi state line, to Elvis Presley Boulevard. (Graceland's official address will change from 3764 Highway South to 3764 Elvis Presley Boule-

vard.) The formal renaming ceremony will occur in January 1972.

JULY

03 Saturday

A generous order of fireworks is delivered to Graceland, and the group repairs once again to the Memphian.

04 Sunday

After the usual Fourth of July fireworks display, Elvis and the gang go to the Crosstown for *Willard* and *The Cat o' Nine Tails*, an Italian horror film starring James Franciscus.

05 Monday

Elvis returns to Los Angeles to begin rehearsals for his first engagement at Del Webb's Sahara Tahoe at Lake Tahoe in Stateline, Nevada. He will receive $300,000 for two weeks, $25,000 more per week than he is currently getting in Las Vegas.

06 Tuesday

Rehearsals are held on this and probably three of the next five nights at the RCA studio on Sunset.

14 Wednesday

Elvis is in Tahoe in preparation for the opening.

15 Thursday

Elvis rehearses in the showroom of the Sahara Tahoe.

20 Tuesday

★ *High Sierra Room, Sahara Tahoe, Stateline, Nevada*
Elvis opens the engagement to sellout crowds. Comedian Nipsey Russell replaces Sammy Shore; Shore will not return.

With Kang Rhee,
c. 1973
*(courtesy of
Kang Rhee)*

Elvis receives NARAS's Bing Crosby Award in his dressing room, Las Vegas, August 28, 1971; with NARAS representatives Gene Merlino and Bill Cole *(left and right)* of the Mello Men and Bing Crosby's son Chris *(courtesy of Joe Tunzi)*

Orchestra leader Joe Guercio institutionalizes the opening that he and Elvis fooled around with during the last Vegas engagement, an adaptation of Richard Strauss' *Also Sprach Zarathustra* that is best known through the enormous popularity of Stanley Kubrick's *2001: A Space Odyssey.* Elvis' entrance, previously relatively low-key, now becomes one of the dramatic highlights of the show. For the first time since he began to work with Elvis, Felton Jarvis is not able to be present, as he is suffering from kidney failure.

July Record Release

Budget LP: *C'mon Everybody* (#70). This new low-priced Camden album of movie songs not previously released on albums sells about 100,000 copies.

AUGUST

02 Monday
Elvis closes an engagement that has broken attendance records at the Sahara Tahoe and, after expenses and commissions, takes home $142,062.50.

03 Tuesday
Elvis travels to Las Vegas to the newly renamed Las Vegas Hilton.

05 Thursday
Renovations of the Monovale house are now complete, and the Hillcrest home is put up for sale with an asking price of $550,000.

07 Saturday
Because the entire troupe has come directly from performing in Tahoe, rehearsals are held for just three days at the Hilton showroom, beginning today. The comedian for this engagement is Bob Melvin.

09 Monday
★ *Showroom, Las Vegas Hilton, Las Vegas*

The second annual "Elvis Summer Festival" opens to a poor review from the *Hollywood Reporter*, which calls the show "sloppy, hurriedly rehearsed, mundanely lit, poorly amplified, occasionally monotonous, often silly, and haphazardly coordinated. . . . [Elvis] looked drawn, tired, and noticeably heavier." The audience, the paper reports, "couldn't have cared less. . . . They absolutely loved, honored, and obeyed his every whim."

13 Friday
Joyce Bova visits Elvis.

14 Saturday
On stage Elvis complains that he is coming down with the flu.

15 Sunday
The show lasts less than thirty minutes because of Elvis' illness.

22 Sunday
Although Elvis is beginning to feel better, his continuing throat problems cause him to call in ENT specialist Dr. Sidney Boyer, who remains a trusted medical adviser for the rest of his Las Vegas engagements. Under Dr. Boyer's ministrations, Elvis is able to carry on, though he continues to experience some throat problems.

28 Saturday
In his dressing room Elvis receives a lifetime achievement award from the National Academy of Recording Arts

With Joyce Bova, Las Vegas, August 1971 *(courtesy of Joyce Bova)*

and Sciences (NARAS). There have been only five previous recipients of the award: Bing Crosby (for whom it has just been renamed), Frank Sinatra, Duke Ellington, Ella Fitzgerald, and Irving Berlin. This is one of the few legitimate forms of recognition that Elvis gets from the recording industry during his lifetime— but it is a highly significant one.

August Record Release

Four-LP Set: *The Other Sides—Elvis World-wide Gold Award Hits Vol. 2* (#120). RCA and the Colonel continue to pursue their policy of releasing albums in the same format until that format fails. The first four-album set in *this* format, *Worldwide Gold Award Hits Vol. 1*, came out in 1970 and consisted mainly of A-sides; this new set, made up primarily of B-sides, sells 100,000 less but still moves 50,000 units, with a special advance of $350,000 against royalties (as if RCA were anticipating 100,000 sales at a flat rate of $3.50 per copy) for Elvis and the Colonel to divide.

SEPTEMBER

01 Wednesday

The Colonel writes to Management III to complain about lax management and "some unpleasant experiences" on the last tour. After expressing some underlying skepticism about their ongoing association ("The reflection upon this operation will be thoroughly scrutinized for any future business for 1972"), he does eventually relent and allow the promoting team to put up a $1 million guarantee against twelve dates for the next tour, which will begin in November.

Furniture and personal belongings in storage are moved into the new Mono-vale house, but Elvis will continue to live at Hillcrest, when in L.A., for the rest of the month.

06 Monday

Elvis completes his Las Vegas engagement, closing the final show with a cape as part of his costume for the first time. After expenses, he

Las Vegas, August–September 1971

and the Colonel realize $351,000 for four weeks' work. Numerous reports in the press refer to Elvis' illness during this engagement and the daily attendance of doctors, and, in a factually muddled September 9 column, Rona Barrett offers his involvement with the Self-Realization Fellowship and Sri Daya Mata as explanations for his occasionally unorthodox behavior.

08 Wednesday

Elvis purchases a second custom-made Stutz Blackhawk to fill in for the first, which was badly damaged in an accident on July 1 and will not be repaired until 1974.

09 Thursday

Elvis travels to Los Angeles.

15 Wednesday

In the aftermath of Elvis' elevation in salary in Tahoe, and having already proved his ongoing loyalty to the

International Hilton, the Colonel pushes for a similar increase in Vegas money. He prepares a chart that shows Elvis selling more seats in Vegas than any other performer, with an average daily attendance of 3,840 compared to 3,000 for Tom Jones and 2,600 for Barbra Streisand.

16 Thursday

In Los Angeles Elvis purchases two guns from Kerr's Sports Shop.

21 Tuesday

Elvis arrives in Memphis and takes in movies every night that he is home at either the Memphian or the Crosstown.

23 Thursday

The *Los Angeles Citizen News* runs a story headlined "ELVIS PRESLEY TO DUMP PARKER?" in the midst of an increasing spate of rumors that the Colonel may be selling his management contract. The British music weekly *New Musical*

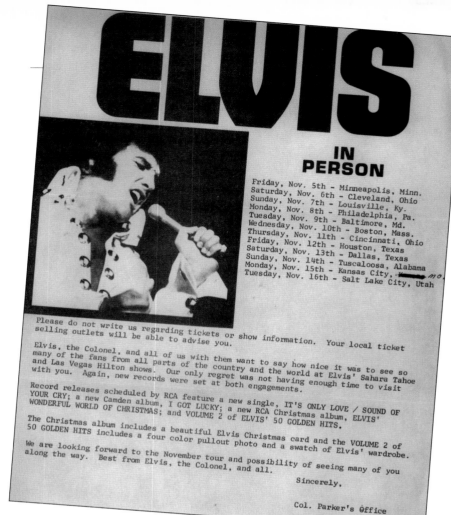

ELVIS

IN PERSON

Friday, Nov. 5th - Minneapolis, Minn.
Saturday, Nov. 6th - Cleveland, Ohio
Sunday, Nov. 7th - Louisville, Ky.
Monday, Nov. 8th - Philadelphia, Pa.
Tuesday, Nov. 9th - Baltimore, Md.
Wednesday, Nov. 10th - Boston, Mass.
Thursday, Nov. 11th - Cincinnati, Ohio
Friday, Nov. 12th - Houston, Texas
Saturday, Nov. 13th - Dallas, Texas
Sunday, Nov. 14th - Tuscaloosa, Alabama
Monday, Nov. 15th - Kansas City, mo.
Tuesday, Nov. 16th - Salt Lake City, Utah

Please do not write us regarding tickets or show information. Your local ticket selling outlets will be able to advise you.

Elvis, the Colonel, and all of us with them want to say how nice it was to see so many of the fans from all parts of the country and the world at Elvis' Sahara Tahoe and Las Vegas Hilton shows. Our only regret was not having enough time to visit with you. Again, new records were set at both engagements.

Record releases scheduled by RCA feature a new single, IT'S ONLY LOVE / SOUND OF YOUR CRY; a new Camden album, I GOT LUCKY; a new RCA Christmas album, ELVIS' WONDERFUL WORLD OF CHRISTMAS; and VOLUME 2 of ELVIS' 50 GOLDEN HITS.

The Christmas album includes a beautiful Elvis Christmas card and the VOLUME 2 of 50 GOLDEN HITS includes a four color pullout photo and a swatch of Elvis' wardrobe.

We are looking forward to the November tour and possibility of seeing many of you along the way. Best from Elvis, the Colonel, and all.

Sincerely,

Col. Parker's Office

Colonel Parker's letter to fans about the November 1971 tour

Express runs an article to this effect at around this time, suggesting that Parker has entered into talks with Tom Jones' flamboyant manager, Gordon Mills, and there *is* an odd exchange of correspondence between Mills and the Colonel's camp all through the fall, in which the Colonel and Tom Diskin appear to deny any such discussions in language that suggests such talks may indeed have taken place.

There are also reports in the press that Elvis and Priscilla are estranged.

28 Tuesday

Elvis returns to Los Angeles, traveling the next day to Palm Springs.

September Record Release

Single: "It's Only Love" (#51)/"The Sound of Your Cry" (shipped September 21). The second single from the May Nashville sessions sells less than 150,000 copies initially.

OCTOBER

02 Saturday

At the Palm Springs Frontier Gun Shop Elvis purchases six guns and a pair of derringers, along with ammunition.

06 Wednesday

Elvis returns to Los Angeles and for the first time stays at the Monovale house. In addition to Priscilla and Lisa Marie, Sonny and Judy West and Charlie Hodge are permanent residents, and the house is big enough to accommodate others as well.

16 Saturday

Elvis is in Palm Springs for the weekend.

22 Friday

Elvis most likely flies back to Palm Springs, where he remains until at least Tuesday.

29 Friday

Elvis is back in Los Angeles.

October Record Releases

Budget LP: *I Got Lucky* (#104). Like July's budget release, *C'mon Everybody*, this Camden release once again contains movie songs not released on albums. Like the earlier record, this one sells about 100,000 copies.

LP: *Elvis Sings the Wonderful World of Christmas.* The Christmas album that RCA and the Colonel considered such a high priority never charts, but over the next two years the album will sell close to 400,000 units, eventually reaching a multiplatinum level.

NOVEMBER

01 Monday

Elvis flies to Washington, D.C., to visit Joyce Bova. He is accompanied by Sonny West and James Caughley, checking into the Hotel Washington as Jon Burrows.

02 Tuesday

Elvis flies back to Memphis in a chartered jet in time to make final preparations for his upcoming tour.

05 Friday

★ *Metropolitan Sports Center, Minneapolis, Minnesota*

Due to scheduling conflicts, or perhaps because of the Colonel's unwillingness to accommodate their desire for higher pay, the Imperials are not on this tour and soon discover that they have been permanently replaced. In their stead Elvis hires J. D. Sumner, whom he has known since the bass singer first joined the Blackwood Brothers in the summer of 1954, and Sumner's new group, the Stamps, while Jackie Kahane, until recently Wayne Newton's opener, fills the comic's role on a permanent basis. It is on this tour that Elvis first starts to close each show with his arms flung wide, his silk-lined cape spread out, as if in benediction. This grand gesture frequently heightens dramatic renditions of songs like "How Great Thou Art,"

"The Impossible Dream," and "Bridge Over Troubled Water" as well.

06 Saturday
★ *Cleveland Public Hall Auditorium, Cleveland, Ohio, at 2:30 and 8:30 P.M.*

This would appear to be the first time that Al Dvorin, formerly band-leader, talent supplier, occasional security man, and longtime concessionaire, takes over as announcer, a role in which he will institutionalize the famous phrase "Elvis has left the building" at the conclusion of each show.

07 Sunday
★ *Freedom Hall, State Fair and Expo Center, Louisville, Kentucky*

From the stage Elvis introduces his grandfather, Jessie Presley.

08 Monday
★ *Spectrum, Philadelphia, Pennsylvania*

09 Tuesday
★ *Civic Center, Baltimore, Maryland*

10 Wednesday
★ *Boston Garden, Boston, Massachusetts*

11 Thursday
★ *Cincinnati Gardens, Cincinnati, Ohio*

12 Friday
★ *Hofheinz Pavilion, Houston, Texas*

13 Saturday
★ *Memorial Auditorium, Dallas, Texas, at 2:30 and 8:30 P.M.*

14 Sunday
★ *University of Alabama Field House, Tuscaloosa, Alabama*

15 Monday
★ *Municipal Auditorium, Kansas City, Missouri*

16 Tuesday
★ *Salt Palace, Salt Lake City, Utah*

After all expenses have been paid, Elvis and the Colonel net $804,000

Probably Houston, Texas, November 12, 1971

from the tour, which they divide according to a new two-thirds/one-third formula that they have agreed upon but which will not be formalized until the following February.

17 Wednesday
Elvis flies home to Memphis and takes in several movies at the Crosstown.

November Record Release

Single: "Merry Christmas Baby"/"O Come, All Ye Faithful" (shipped November 9). The best cut from the Christmas sessions fails as a single when RCA sells only 30,000 of 100,000 shipped initially but will sell another 50,000 copies the following Christmas.

---

18 Thursday
Elvis flies to Los Angeles, spending the weekend in Palm Springs.

21 Sunday
While Elvis is in Palm Springs, Billy Stanley, one of Elvis' stepbrothers, is married in Memphis.

22 Monday
Elvis spends the week in Los Angeles.

24 Wednesday
The results of blood tests in the ongoing paternity suit indicate that Elvis cannot have fathered Patricia Parker's child.

26 Friday
Elvis returns to Palm Springs, where he remains until December 3.

DECEMBER

03 Friday

Elvis returns to Los Angeles from Palm Springs and within a few days flies to Dallas.

10 Friday

Elvis arrives back in Memphis, attending a show at the Memphian which, instead of being open to the usual large circle of friends, fans, acquaintances, and employees, is closed to all but the inner circle.

11 Saturday

Joyce Bova is in town and goes to the movies with Elvis at the Crosstown.

12 Sunday

Elvis and Joyce fly to Washington, staying at the Washington Hilton.

14 Tuesday

Elvis returns to Memphis, flying as Jon Burrows, along with Charlie Hodge, Sonny West, and James Caughley, who travel under their real names.

18 Saturday

Priscilla and Lisa Marie arrive in Memphis, and Elvis receives a bill for the installation of a basketball court at his Palm Springs home.

21 Tuesday

Elvis sees *Dirty Harry* and *Straw Dogs* at the Memphian. He will screen *Shampoo* and *Soul Soldier* on Thursday.

24 Friday

Elvis purchases an $1,100 watch, a $500 ring, and a $1,200 chain from Lowell Hays, a transaction that according to Hays' recollection takes place in the Memphian's men's room.

25 Saturday

Christmas at Graceland. When it comes time to hand out gifts, Elvis jokingly distributes gift certificates to MacDonald's before revealing his real presents. Although everything seems normal, in retrospect many of the guys will say that Priscilla and Elvis appeared distant over the Christmas holidays.

28 Tuesday

Elvis continues to screen movies at the Memphian and the Crosstown, seeing *The Hunting Party* with Candice Bergen and *The Night Visitor* tonight, *Shaft* and *Let's Scare Jessica to Death* on Wednesday.

30 Thursday

Priscilla and Lisa Marie fly back to Los Angeles. Following their departure, Elvis announces to everyone that Priscilla is leaving him. She hasn't told him why, he says, simply that she no longer loves him.

Elvis hosts a small New Year's Eve party at Graceland, not at a local club as he has in the past.

Elvis' accountants report that in 1971 his personal income from motion pictures is $114,000, while music and recording bring in $1,200,000 and personal appearances $2,700,000. He will pay $1,300,000 in income taxes.

Trying on costumes, Las Vegas,
January–February 1972

1972

Elvis Now booth, Hilton, Las Vegas, January–February 1972

JANUARY

01 Saturday

There are movies at the Memphian and the Crosstown almost every night in the New Year, but they remain closed to all but the inner circle.

08 Saturday

Joyce Bova comes to Memphis for Elvis' birthday.

12 Wednesday

Elvis flies to Los Angeles.

13 Thursday

Rehearsals for the upcoming Las Vegas engagement begin at RCA Studio C on Sunset at 7:00 P.M. Elvis works with the rhythm section for six hours on both this and the following night and for three hours each on Saturday and Sunday.

18 Tuesday

Elvis arrives in Las Vegas.

19 Wednesday

Rehearsals begin at the Las Vegas Hilton.

As has happened each time before, several new songs are included in early rehearsals but are dropped as showtime approaches. Among them are Gordon Lightfoot's "The Last Time I Saw Her Face," Joe Cocker's "Delta Lady," Don and Dewey's "I'm Leavin' It Up to You," and the Walker Brothers' "The Sun Ain't Gonna Shine Anymore."

For the opening the Colonel has ordered 50,000 catalogues of Elvis' records with a Las Vegas Hilton imprint, 75,000 calendars, 10,000 vinyl bags, and 5,000 buttons for hotel employees.

26 Wednesday

★ *Showroom, Las Vegas Hilton, Las Vegas*

Elvis opens with the single dinner show, with reviews citing his slimmer appearance and less talkative manner. The cape has become a permanent fixture of the show, and Elvis does feature a number of new ballads, including Marty Robbins' "You Gave Me a Mountain," "It's Over," and "It's Impossible." All are songs of lost love, all are sung with a feeling that seems to suggest autobiographical association, as Priscilla flies in for the opening but is otherwise not seen until the end of the engagement. Elvis also introduces "American Trilogy," songwriter Mickey Newbury's dramatic melding of "Dixie," "The Battle Hymn of the Republic," and the black spiritual "All My Trials."

On this day there is a court ruling that Elvis is not the father of Patricia Parker's child, and the case is for all intents and purposes closed.

28 Friday

The Colonel, still dissatisfied with Management III's attention to detail, has persuaded RCA to set up its own concert promotion company, RCA Record Tours, which the Colonel will in effect control. The Colonel's All Star Shows today signs a joint agreement with Management III and RCA Record Tours to promote a thirteen-day tour in April.

January Record Release

Single: "Until It's Time for You to Go" (#40)/"We Can Make the Morning" (shipped January 4). The Buffy Sainte-Marie cover sells 275,000 copies, considerably more than the last single, but its chart position remains problematic.

FEBRUARY

04 Friday

Elvis and the Colonel formalize the change in their personal management contract that was informally embraced on the last tour. From this point on, all income received from live performances will be split two-thirds/one-third between Elvis and Colonel Parker.

14 Monday

RCA tapes both dinner and midnight shows primarily for the purpose of recording newly introduced songs. Felton Jarvis supervises the taping, but his health problems have worsened, and he requires dialysis treatment several times a week. The intended live album never actually materializes, but the recordings will show up in dribs and drabs on various subsequent releases.

February 4, 1972

Mr. Elvis Presley
3764 Elvis Presley Highway
Memphis, Tennessee

Dear Elvis:

The following constitutes our agreement, between you and Col. Tom Parker, All Star Shows, P.O. Box 220 Madison, Tenn. with respect to personal appearance tours of the Elvis Presley Show, concert dates as selected by Col. Parker exclusively.

In consideration for the rendition of our complete organizing of tours, handling all transportation, reservations, talent, tour, tour supervision, packaging, show security setup, chartering of aircraft, etc., with Mr. Diskin and his staff, it is understood that after deduction of all show related expenses including agency commissions, any bonuses that you may decide to distribute at the close of the tours (similar but not limited to what has been done in the past), all charter transportation for booking and handling of tours and the tours themselves as needed, including charges for your transportation, talent costs, personnel and office expenses, telephone and show related expenses from opening until closing, but not including any personal expenses, promotion and advertising, from the total gross receipts received by All Star Shows or by Elvis Presley, the remaining balance shall be divided:

        2/3 to Elvis Presley

        1/3 to All Star Shows

If the above meets with your approval kindly so indicate by signing in the space below.

Approved and accepted:

Elvis Presley
Elvis Presley

Col. Tom Parker
Col. Tom Parker, All Star Shows

Agreement between Elvis and the Colonel on new division of profits from tours, February 4, 1972

16 Wednesday

Recording has continued each night and will conclude tomorrow. With the exception of one song ("It's Over"), all masters that are eventually released will stem from tonight's midnight show.

23 Wednesday

Priscilla flies in for the end of Elvis'

February Record Releases

Single: "He Touched Me" /"Bosom of Abraham" (shipped February 29). Another of the Colonel's traditional Easter releases is taken from the upcoming *He Touched Me* gospel album, with initial sales of just over 50,000 copies.

LP: *Elvis Now* (#43). If the title is intended to suggest a contemporary musical statement by Elvis, it is hardly accurate, as the album includes two 1970 recordings and one from 1969, along with the latest single and a hodgepodge of five other recordings. It sells just over 400,000 copies.

---

engagement and informs him that she is involved with karate champion Mike Stone.

Elvis is awarded a fifth-degree black belt from Ed Parker's International Kenpo Karate Association.

MARCH

04 Saturday

Elvis returns to Los Angeles, moving back into the unsold Hillcrest house while Priscilla remains at the Monovale address.

08 Wednesday

The Colonel and Freddy Bienstock begin discussions of forming their own publishing company in the wake of the Aberbach brothers' decision to dissolve Hill and Range for business and personal reasons. Many variations will be considered over the next year and a half, including at one point the purchase of Hill and Range.

"Always on My Mind," March 30, 1972
(Red West *foreground*, J. D. Sumner *background*) (*courtesy of Joe Tunzi*)

17 Friday

Elvis flies to Las Vegas for several days.

22 Wednesday

Elvis returns to Los Angeles for a recording session at RCA's Hollywood studio scheduled just prior to rehearsals for the upcoming April tour. This will also tie in with a second documentary concert film (this one of Elvis on tour rather than Elvis in Las Vegas) that the Colonel seems to have hurriedly put together with MGM in a deal that may not have been fully worked out at this point.

27 Monday

Although Elvis has been rehearsing for his Vegas openings at the RCA studio since 1969, he has not recorded here since his not-very-happy experience at the outset of the *G.I. Blues* sessions in April 1960. This will also be the first time that Elvis records with J. D. Sumner and the Stamps and with his live band, all of whom are present except for Jerry Scheff, who is replaced on bass by

Nashville session player Emory Gordy. The first night's session begins at 7:00 P.M., ending in the early-morning hours. Elvis' mood is similar to the one prevalent during his recent Las Vegas engagement, as he focuses on bittersweet songs of loss and regret like "Where Do I Go From Here," Kris Kristofferson's "For the Good Times," and the song with which he begins the evening, Red West's "Separate Ways," which could have been (and essentially was) written for and about him.

28 Tuesday

After a good deal of effort, Felton finally persuades Elvis to try a rocker that he has gotten from his friend, Nashville publisher Bob Beckham. Both Beckham and Felton are convinced that songwriter Dennis Linde's "Burning Love" can be a big hit for Elvis, just the kind of thing he needs to jump-start his career at this point, and while Elvis never fully gets in the mood he does allow himself to be persuaded to try something upbeat in the midst of all the downers.

29 Wednesday

The last night of recording begins with yet another melancholy declaration, "Always on My Mind," concluding at 1:00 A.M. with a total output of seven masters achieved over the three nights.

In what would appear in retrospect to have been a negotiating ploy, the Colonel informs the Las Vegas Hilton that Elvis will most likely be unavailable for the remainder of 1972 in order to complete the filming of the concert documentary that is about to begin (and in fact will conclude before the end of the April tour). If this *is* a negotiating ploy, it succeeds in less than a month, resulting in a revised contract with the Hilton by April 20.

30 Thursday

Filming of the MGM documentary, tentatively titled *Standing Room Only* but eventually to be released as *On Tour*, begins with a simulated recording session (it could, conceivably, be regarded as a studio rehearsal session) of the just-completed songs. The movie is to be produced and directed by the team of Bob Abel and Pierre Adidge, two young filmmakers fresh from the success of *Mad Dogs and Englishmen*, a dizzying documentary of the 1970 Joe Cocker all-star and all-experience tour.

31 Friday

Filming continues, as Elvis and the musicians work through the tour repertoire. The night ends with Elvis, Charlie Hodge, James Burton, and J. D. Sumner and the Stamps gathered around the piano for an impromptu gospel sing. Before leaving the studio Elvis gives a brief informal interview that focuses on his lifelong love of gospel music and performing. Asked how it is that there is such a special feeling among all the members of the group, Elvis replies, "I think it's because we constantly enjoy this music. You know, we do two shows a night for [four] weeks, but we never let it get old. Every time is like we do it for the first time—and that's one of the secrets."

APRIL

05 Wednesday
★ *Memorial Auditorium, Buffalo, New York*

Filmmaker Bob Abel shoots this performance with a small Sony videotape camera to create a visual and audio record to be used as a concert blueprint for the full camera crew, which will begin work on Sunday in Hampton Roads, Virginia.

06 Thursday
★ *Olympia Stadium, Detroit, Michigan*

07 Friday
★ *University of Dayton Arena, Dayton, Ohio*

08 Saturday
★ *Stokely Athletic Center, University of Tennessee, Knoxville, Tennessee, at 2:30 and 8:30 P.M.*

Elvis' performances here have long since been scheduled to be recorded by RCA in order to complete the live album begun in Las Vegas. However, a malfunction in the power supply fries the recording equipment, and the whole idea of the album is abandoned shortly thereafter, first in favor of a soundtrack album from the film (which also never comes about), then as a result of the Colonel's inspiration to record an album live at Madison Square Garden in New York City a couple of months later.

09 Sunday
★ *Coliseum, Hampton Roads, Virginia, at 2:30 and 8:00 P.M.*

Abel and Adidge's film crew shoots the evening show while RCA records.

10 Monday
★ *Coliseum, Richmond, Virginia*

This show is also recorded and filmed.

11 Tuesday
★ *Civic Center, Roanoke, Virginia*

12 Wednesday
★ *Fair Grounds Coliseum, Indianapolis, Indiana*

13 Thursday
★ *Coliseum, Charlotte, North Carolina*

14 Friday
★ *Coliseum, Greensboro, North Carolina*

This show is filmed and recorded.

15 Saturday
★ *Coliseum, Macon, Georgia, at 2:30 and 8:30 P.M.*

April Record Releases

Single: "An American Trilogy" (#66)/"The First Time Ever I Saw Your Face" (shipped April 4). Because of the reception that it got in Las Vegas, and his belief in the song, Elvis insists that this live version of Mickey Newbury's vision of national reconciliation be released as the A-side, with Ewan Mac-Coll's tender ballad, recorded in Nashville the previous March, as the B. Despite Elvis' personal investment in both songs, the single sells only 100,000 copies, with a dismal chart performance to match.

LP: *He Touched Me* (#79). Although the new gospel album sells less than 200,000 to begin with, it will follow the pattern of its 1967 predecessor, *How Great Thou Art*, both in terms of public recognition (it will receive a Grammy award in 1973) and in long-term sales.

Greensboro, North Carolina, April 14, 1972

Jacksonville, Florida, afternoon show, April 16, 1972 (a virtually identical image was originally to be used as the cover for the never-released *Standing Room Only* but found a place as the cover for the Madison Square Garden album instead)

16 Sunday

★ *Veterans Memorial Coliseum, Jacksonville, Florida, at 2:30 and 8:30 P.M.*

17 Monday

★ *T. H. Barton Coliseum, Little Rock, Arkansas*

18 Tuesday

★ *Convention Center Arena, San Antonio, Texas*

This concert is filmed and recorded.

19 Wednesday

★ *Tingley Coliseum, Albuquerque, New Mexico*

Following this show, Elvis flies home to Memphis.

The cost of the jumpsuits designed by Bill Belew and made by I.C. Costume for this tour comes to $11,088.

---

20 Thursday

In response not just to the Colonel's suggestion that Elvis might be tied up with movie work all year but to broad hints (in the form of denials) that he might jump in a year or two to Kirk Kerkorian's presently-under-construction MGM Grand, the Hilton agrees to pay $130,000 a week for the next two engagements and $150,000 a week for the three engagements after that. Colonel Parker will also receive $50,000 a year for the next three years as a consultant to the hotel chain.

22 Saturday

Elvis is back in California, spending the weekend in Palm Springs.

26 Wednesday

Elvis flies home to Memphis. He will be at the movies most nights, but again the theater will be closed to all but the inner circle and other specially selected guests.

MAY

07 Sunday

With a ticket issued in the name of Dr. John Carpenter, Elvis flies to Los Angeles before leaving the next day for a Hawaiian vacation at the Coco Palms Hotel with Vernon and Dee and some of the guys.

19 Friday

Elvis returns to Los Angeles.

24 Wednesday

Elvis flies to Las Vegas and on Sunday night attends Glen Campbell's show at the Hilton.

30 Tuesday

Elvis returns to Los Angeles before flying home to Memphis the following night.

JUNE

04 Sunday

Elvis is spotted horseback riding at Graceland.

05 Monday

Elvis returns to Los Angeles.

06 Tuesday

There are rehearsals with the band on both this and the next night at the RCA studio on Sunset.

08 Thursday

Elvis flies to New York City, arriving at the Hilton Hotel for the first stop on his new tour.

The troupe by now is made up of some seventy to eighty people (including tech people, equipment handlers, musicians, stagehands, and concessionaires), traveling in three leased airplanes while ground crews transport two complete stage setups from city to city on the twelve-day tour. The Colonel will continue to do the advance work, traveling ahead of the show to set up in the next city, sometimes just after Elvis has arrived in the last.

09 Friday

Elvis has never performed in New York City before save for his 1956 and 1957 appearances on the Dorsey brothers, Steve Allen, and Ed Sullivan television shows. This was a not unintended consequence of the Colonel's plan to protect his boy from the intense media scrutiny that so condescendingly dismissed him at the start of his career. But it is just as conscious a decision now to allow Elvis to win over those same media, grown older and, the Colonel believes, wiser, too. A poised and confident Elvis, taking a break from rehearsals with the band, bears out his manager's faith in him at a clamorous 4:00 P.M. press conference at the Hilton. Asked about his image as a shy, humble country boy, Elvis responds, "I don't know what makes them say that," then stands to reveal the International Hotel gold belt under his jacket, with his father proudly beaming beside him.

★ *Madison Square Garden, New York*

10 Saturday

★ *Madison Square Garden, New York, at 2:30 and 8:30 P.M.*

RCA records both shows in preparation for releasing a live album just eight days after the final New York City date. The intent, according to the Colonel, is to foil bootleggers, but he is surely not oblivious to the sales and publicity advantages of drawing attention to the continuing preeminence of his single client in this manner. The album is drawn from the evening show exclusively and will be titled *Elvis As Recorded Live at Madison Square Garden.*

11 Sunday

★ *Madison Square Garden, New York at 2:30 P.M.*

This show is added when tickets to the first three original shows are sold out almost immediately, thus making Elvis the first entertainer to sell out four consecutive shows in the Garden, with a box-office gross of $730,000. The *New York Times* headlines one of its three stories on the phenomenon "Like a Prince from Another Planet," characterizing Elvis as "a special champion [like] a Joe Louis, a José Capablanca, a Joe DiMaggio, someone in whose hands the way a thing is done becomes more important than the thing itself. . . ."

Press conference, June 9, 1972
(bottom photograph © David Gahr)

Friday night at Madison Square Garden, Elvis was like that. He stood there at the end, his arms stretched out, the great gold cloak giving him wings . . . the only one in his class."

12 Monday
★ *Memorial Coliseum, Fort Wayne, Indiana*

13 Tuesday
★ *Roberts Municipal Coliseum, Evansville, Indiana*

14 Wednesday
★ *Milwaukee Auditorium Arena, Milwaukee, Wisconsin*

15 Thursday
★ *Milwaukee Auditorium Arena, Milwaukee*

16 Friday
★ *Chicago Stadium, Chicago, Illinois*

17 Saturday
★ *Chicago Stadium, Chicago, at 2:30 and 8:30 P.M.*

18 Sunday
★ *Tarrant County Convention Center, Fort Worth, Texas*

19 Monday
★ *Henry Levitt Arena, Wichita, Kansas*

20 Tuesday
★ *Civic Assembly Center, Tulsa, Oklahoma*

June Record Releases

Budget LP: *Elvis Sings Hits from His Movies* (#87). The album contains movie songs, certainly, but not, by any stretch of the imagination, hits. It sells 130,000 copies.
LP: *Elvis As Recorded Live at Madison Square Garden* (#11) (shipped June 18). Released just eight days after the Madison Square Garden shows, this is Elvis' most successful album in nine years, going gold (over 500,000 sales) within two months and over the years reaching triple-platinum sales of more than three million.

21 Wednesday
The fourteen shows gross a total of $1,200,000. After expenses Elvis' share comes to $610,000, the Colonel's $305,000. As is rapidly becoming evident, this is a better way of making money than even the movies.

Elvis flies home to Memphis, resuming film attendance at the Memphian immediately.

JULY

06 Thursday
Through George Klein, Elvis is introduced to the present Miss Tennessee, a twenty-two-year-old Memphis State student named Linda Thompson, at the Memphian. He sees her again the following night and is captivated by her beauty and sense of humor, but is prevented for the time being from following up when she goes off on a three-week family vacation. Later in the month Elvis will briefly date another Memphis beauty queen, actress Cybill Shepherd.

08 Saturday
The Colonel announces that there will be a worldwide satellite broadcast of an Elvis concert from Hawaii in October or November. "It is the intention of Elvis to please all of his fans throughout the world," the Colonel is quoted in the *Memphis Commercial Appeal*, and "since it is impossible for us to play in every major city," this, by implication, is the next best thing.

Elvis flies to Los Angeles, then on to Palm Springs for a few days.

12 Wednesday
Elvis is back in Los Angeles, where he remains until returning to Memphis on the evening of the twentieth.

20 Thursday
It is possible that this is the date that Elvis records an audio-only interview for the documentary *Elvis*

On Tour, in his old MGM dressing room, though it is somewhat more likely that he does so upon his return to Los Angeles the following week. In the interview he speaks candidly on a number of subjects, expounding upon his musical background with a specificity that he has rarely taken the opportunity to volunteer. He also speaks of his movie career. "I cared so much," he says, "until I became physically ill. . . . I don't think anyone was consciously trying to harm me. It was just Hollywood's image of me was wrong. . . . I was never indifferent. I was so concerned until that's all I talked about . . . but it did not change, it did not change, and so I became very discouraged. They couldn't have paid me no amount of money in the world to make me feel self-satisfaction inside." Segments from this forty-minute interview will be interspersed in voice-overs throughout the film.

21 Friday
Elvis arrives in Memphis.

24 Monday
Elvis goes to Baptist Memorial Hospital with an ankle injury and is fitted with an ankle corset.

26 Wednesday
Elvis flies out of Memphis at 5:45 P.M., arriving in Los Angeles in time to take a limousine to the RCA studio for a 9:00 P.M. rehearsal for his upcoming Las Vegas engagement.

Elvis is legally separated from Priscilla on this date, and by the end of the month the press will report authoritatively that a "black belt karate man" (Mike Stone) has split up the Presley marriage.

27 Thursday
Rehearsals are held at RCA Studio C, beginning at 7:00 P.M. both tonight and tomorrow.

29 Saturday
A leased minivan picks up Elvis' belongings at both the Hillcrest and Monovale homes and drives with them

Probably Tulsa, Oklahoma,

to Las Vegas, as it does at the beginning and end of each engagement.

31 Monday

Rehearsals are held on this and the following day at the Las Vegas Hilton, with just the backup singers at 2:00 P.M. and the whole show, including Elvis, at 7:00.

At some point in this three-day period Elvis goes to Los Angeles to meet Linda Thompson, whom he has persuaded to fly in from Memphis. Together they travel back to Las Vegas, where Linda stays for most of the engagement (Cybill Shepherd is a visitor at one point during Linda's absence).

AUGUST

02 Wednesday

Noon rehearsals for all continue in the showroom through opening day.

04 Friday

★ *Showroom, Las Vegas Hilton, Las Vegas*

Opening night of the "Elvis Summer Festival," with one show at 8:00 P.M. Reviewers note an improvement over his last Vegas appearance, but fans express concern over the fact that Elvis seems more subdued and

spends less time fooling around with the audience in between songs.

14 Monday

Under pressure from MGM, which is concerned about the October/November opening of the movie, the Colonel agrees to postpone the satellite broadcast of the Hawaiian show until early next year. Probably this appeals to his sense of drama anyway, since the satellite broadcast now goes from the televising of just another concert, however ambitious, to a stand-alone, one-of-a-kind event.

15 Tuesday

As part of the formal separation agreement with Priscilla, Elvis relinquishes half ownership in the Hillcrest home, and on September 10 will do the same with the Monovale house.

August Record Release

Single: "Burning Love" (#2)/"It's a Matter of Time" (shipped August 1). The success of the live Madison Square Garden album and the accompanying resurgence in Elvis' popularity undoubtedly helps "Burning Love" sales. Within a few weeks of its release, the song that Felton had to practically beg Elvis to record sells over a million copies.

---

18 Friday

The Colonel conducts a meeting with Jean and Julian Aberbach to discuss the liquidation of the Elvis and Gladys Music firms.

The press reports that a divorce action has been entered in Santa Monica Superior Court. The unreported settlement that has been agreed upon gives Priscilla a lump sum of $100,000, plus $1,000-a-month spousal and $500 child support.

SEPTEMBER

02 Saturday

Elvis performs a special 3:00 A.M. show on the Labor Day weekend, for which he receives an additional $27,500.

04 Monday

The Colonel stages a press conference between the dinner and midnight shows, with Elvis and RCA president Rocco Laginestra both present, to announce the January 14 worldwide satellite broadcast of *Aloha from Hawaii.* Reporters are told that an estimated 1.4 billion viewers will watch the first entertainment special to be broadcast live around the world. (This is not, strictly speaking, true, since a good part of the world, including both Europe and

Probably Las Vegas,
August–September 1972

Las Vegas, August 1972

Elvis closes his Las Vegas engagement, taking home $266,000 for his efforts, while the Colonel's share is $133,000.

12 Tuesday

The Colonel signs an agreement with RCA Record Tours, making this somewhat self-generated paper corporation the exclusive sponsor of Elvis' tours from November of 1972 through the end of 1973. RCA will put up a $4 million advance against 65 percent of the gate, with an additional $250,000 going to All Star Shows for "professional services and supervision" on all dates.

16 Saturday

Elvis leaves Las Vegas, returning to Los Angeles, where he will remain for almost two weeks.

28 Thursday

Elvis flies to Palm Springs, accompanied by Linda Thompson, for a long weekend.

OCTOBER

03 Tuesday

Elvis and Linda return to Los Angeles, then fly home to Memphis the following evening.

America, will view it on a delayed basis, with America not getting the show for several months.) RCA Record Tours will be the sole producer of the show, displacing Management III and receiving $100,000 of the $1 million fee that NBC will pay for its efforts. RCA will also release a record of the event, "the first time in the history of the record industry," according to the press announcement, that an album will be released simultaneously on a global basis. This is clearly an event after the Colonel's heart, and Elvis is left a little speechless. "It's very hard to comprehend," he says several times in the course of the press conference, but "it's my favorite part of the business, a live concert."

Press conference at the Hilton, Las Vegas, September 4, 1972, to announce the *Aloha from Hawaii* concert with RCA president Rocco Laginestra

With Linda Thompson, Hawaii, November 1972

08 Sunday

Between now and the end of the month, Elvis will screen movies almost every night at the Memphian or the Crosstown.

23 Monday

Elvis buys a $3,456 gentleman's diamond and ruby ring from Lowell Hays.

NOVEMBER

01 Wednesday

Elvis and Linda return to Los Angeles.

The concert documentary *Elvis On* *Tour* opens, appearing on *Variety*'s Box Office Survey for two weeks, where it peaks at #13. The film will go on to be named cowinner of a Golden Globe Award as Best Documentary of 1972. There is no soundtrack album from the film, however, because most of the songs have appeared either on the Madison Square Garden album or will be included on the *Aloha from Hawaii* album to be released in January.

08 Wednesday

Elvis flies to Lubbock, Texas, to begin an eight-day tour, his third of the year.

★ *Municipal Coliseum, Lubbock, Texas*

09 Thursday

★ *Community Center Arena, Tucson, Arizona*

10 Friday

★ *Coliseum, El Paso, Texas*

11 Saturday

★ *Oakland Coliseum, Oakland, California*

An integral part of every Elvis show continues to be the dispensing of scarves and kisses to the fans. Today he orders 115 scarves in assorted colors from Mr. Guy in Las Vegas.

12 Sunday

★ *Swing Auditorium, San Bernardino, California, at 5:00 P.M.*

13 Monday

★ *Swing Auditorium, San Bernardino*

November Record Releases

Single: "Separate Ways" (#20)/"Always on My Mind" (shipped October 31). The follow-up to "Burning Love" comes from the same March sessions, but this combination of two mournful tales of separation, which clearly mirrors Elvis' own mood and experience, does not fare as well, with sales of only half a million.

Budget album: *Burning Love and Hits From His Movies* (#22). Advertising this release as a somewhat dubious industry first ("the first time that a current hit single has been included in an album on a budget label"), RCA releases a collection burdened with some of the poorest and most deservedly neglected of movie soundtrack songs. It undoubtedly *is* a first. Under pressure from RCA, the Colonel apparently agrees to the record company's use of Elvis' huge hit as bait because he does not want to lose the very tidy up-front income (split 50-50 with Elvis) generated by the budget albums. Recent Camden sales have been a disaster, and the record company correctly suspects that a hit song can make all the difference. Sales of more than 700,000 bear this theory out but also suggest that for the first time Elvis the artist has been abandoned not just by his record label but by his manager as well.

Probably Honolulu, afternoon show, November 18, 1972

14 Tuesday
★ *Arena, Long Beach, California*

15 Wednesday
★ *Arena, Long Beach*

16 Thursday
Elvis, Linda, and Lisa Marie fly from Los Angeles to Honolulu with a large group, including James Caughley, Joe Esposito, Dick Grob, Gee Gee Gambill, Charlie Hodge, Dr. Nichopoulos, Sonny West, Red West, and the three Stanley brothers, Ricky, David, and Billy.

17 Friday
★ *Honolulu International Center, Honolulu, Hawaii*

Either this or the next night's is the show that was originally planned as the worldwide satellite broadcast.

18 Saturday
★ *Honolulu International Center, Honolulu, at 2:30 and 8:30 P.M.*

20 Monday
Elvis holds a press conference at the Hawaiian Village Hotel to announce the satellite show once again. It will be broadcast live to the Far East at 12:30 A.M. Hawaiian Time on the morning of January 14, 1973, with a concert dress rehearsal for a live audience the night before. Since the Las Vegas press conference it has been turned into a charity concert at the instigation of *Honolulu Advertiser* columnist Eddie Sherman, who suggested that it should benefit the Kui Lee Cancer Fund. Both the Colonel and Elvis seize upon this suggestion to honor a musician whom Elvis much admires (Kui Lee is the author of his concert staple "I'll Remember You") and make the first contribution with a $1,000 check, which is matched by Rocco Laginestra on behalf of RCA.

25 Saturday
Elvis and the group return to Los Angeles.

28 Tuesday
Elvis goes to Las Vegas.

DECEMBER

04 Monday
Elvis is back in Memphis and at the Memphian almost every night into the New Year.

08 Friday

A bill from IC Costume, typical for this time, lists: one white jumpsuit with cape and embroidered Aquarius design—$1,400; one light

December Record Release

Budget LP: *Separate Ways* (#46). This album follows the model of *Burning Love* but includes another current, but less successful, single to go with a strange mélange of ballads going back to 1956. The results are lower chart placement and, at 300,000 copies, less than half the sales.

blue jumpsuit with cape, embroidered with sun design—$1,400; one black jumpsuit with cape, embroidered with Mexican tile design—$1,600; one white jumpsuit embroidered with thunderbird design—$1,800; five silk shirts at $125 each; five custom-made corduroy suits at $450 each; also, repairs to eight jumpsuits.

10 Sunday

Elvis is out of town, possibly in Dallas, for two days.

21 Thursday

The *Memphis Press-Scimitar* reports that Elvis has once again given generously to local charities.

25 Monday

For Christmas Elvis presents Linda Thompson with a mink coat that he has purchased from King Furs in Memphis.

Elvis' accountants report that in 1972 Elvis' personal income from motion pictures is $356,000, with $1,100,000 from music and recordings, and $4,300,000 from personal appearances. His income tax is $1,800,000.

Aloha show, with Charlie Hodge

1973

JANUARY

01 Monday

Elvis spends the first three evenings of the New Year at the Memphian.

04 Thursday

Elvis appears to be in the best of spirits as he flies to Los Angeles on the way to Hawaii. *Aloha* producer-director Marty Pasetta, whom he first met at the Long Beach show in November, had told Elvis he had to lose weight, and he and Sonny have each lost twenty-five pounds on a crash diet that Elvis has picked up in Las Vegas.

09 Tuesday

After arriving at the Honolulu airport, Elvis is airlifted to the Hilton Hawaiian Village Hotel by helicopter and has his first rehearsal with the band and backup singers, who have already arrived.

10 Wednesday

The full orchestra is present, and rehearsals continue with Felton Jarvis on hand to lend encouragement, though he is still weak from the kidney transplant that Elvis helped to arrange and pay for in October.

11 Thursday

Elvis is planning to wear an American-eagle jumpsuit and cape

Arrival in Hawaii, January 9, 1973

specially designed for the occasion at his suggestion by Bill Belew. Either on the previous night, or the night before, he gives the matching, ruby-encrusted belt to the wife of his friend Jack Lord, star of the popular television show *Hawaii Five-O*. Joe Esposito places a frantic call to Belew to reproduce the belt, and it is flown in on this date by Belew's assistant.

12 Friday

Elvis attends an extra rehearsal at the International Convention Center Arena to iron out some technical difficulties. He will perform on a stage, specially designed by Marty Pasetta, with a long runway extending out

into the audience and a giant flashing figure of Elvis as the backdrop.

★ *International Convention Center Arena, Honolulu, Hawaii, at 8:30 P.M.*

This first performance with an audience is billed as a dress rehearsal and taped in case there are problems with satellite transmission the next night. Thus the repertoire for each show is identical. No admission is charged, but contributions are expected, and a goal of $25,000 to be contributed to the Kui Lee Cancer Fund has been announced.

13–14 Saturday–Sunday

★ *International Convention Center Arena, Honolulu*

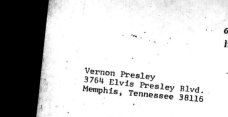

I G Costume Company
6121 Santa Monica Boulevard
Hollywood, California 90038

Hollywood 9-2056

Vernon Presley
3764 Elvis Presley Blvd.
Memphis, Tennessee 38116

Date January 17, 1973

Invoice Number   00329

Job No. 6057 - Hawaiian Show

QUANTITY	DESCRIPTION	UNIT PRICE	TOTAL
1	custom-tailored white jumpsuit w/long cape w/embroidered Eagle Design ... matching belt w/emb. Eagle Design		$2,300.00
1	custom-tailored white jumpsuit w/cape w/embroidered Eagle Design... w/matching belt w/emb. Eagle Design		2,050.00
7 dz.	silk scarves..asstd. colors	$120.00	840.00
1	blue custom-tailored suede suit		N/C
2	custom-made silk shirts		N/C
			$5,190.00

Aloha from Hawaii

Just after midnight on Saturday night, Elvis' performance is broadcast live via satellite to most countries in the Far East, including Japan, Korea, and Hong Kong, where Elvis is known in Chinese as "King Cat." Japan registers the highest ratings ever with a 37.8 percent share in a highly competitive market, while twenty-eight European countries linked by EuroVision will see the show on a delayed basis later in the day. The show more than triples its announced goal of $25,000, and at the conclusion of his performance Elvis flings both his newly replaced belt and his jewel-encrusted American eagle cape into the audience, where the latter is caught by local sportswriter Bruce Spinks. This was, according to the *Los Angeles Times*, "the highlight of the night." The cape is now at Graceland.

RCA records the concert and plans to mix it in the recently developed quadraphonic format (a double stereo that never really catches on) for worldwide release within a month.

As soon as the audience has left the auditorium, and with the live broadcast complete, Elvis and the band perform "Early Morning Rain" plus four additional songs from *Blue Hawaii* that are to be added to the U.S. version of the show, which will be broadcast in April.

At 3:00 A.M. Sunday morning the Colonel writes an unusually emotional letter to Elvis in which he states that they have no need for hugging because they can tell "from seeing each other on stage and from the floor by the stage" how they feel and then goes on to declare, "I always know that when I do my part, you always do yours in your own way and in your feeling in how to do it best. That is why you and I are never at each other when we are doing our work in our own best way possible at all times." He concludes with the kind of explicit, generous praise that is rare in their relationship: "You above all make all of it work by being the leader and the talent. Without your

dedication to your following it couldn't have been done."

15 Monday
Elvis returns to Los Angeles.

18 Thursday
Elvis flies to Las Vegas to prepare for his almost immediately upcoming engagement at the Hilton.

24 Wednesday
Rehearsals begin at the Hilton Showroom for the whole group at noon, continuing for the next two days.

26 Friday
★ *Showroom, Las Vegas Hilton, Las Vegas*
Elvis opens his eighth Las Vegas engagement with the usual opening-night show at 8:00 P.M.

28 Sunday
In New York, *Elvis On Tour* co-wins a Golden Globe Award with *Walls of Fire* as best feature documentary of 1972.

Elvis is ill almost from the start of the engagement, something remarked upon by both fans and the press. The *Hollywood Reporter* attributes his evident "lack of energy and interest" to the effects of illness, but some of the fans and the guys around him are worried about a deeper spiritual malaise.

FEBRUARY

01 Thursday
Lisa Marie is present at the 8:00 P.M. show for her fifth birthday.

02 Friday
At some point during the first two weeks of the engagement, Elvis presents Muhammad Ali, training for his February 14 title defense in Vegas against Joe Bugner, with a robe emblazoned "The People's Champion." Ali's fond recollection of Elvis is that "I felt sorry for [him] because he didn't enjoy life the way he should.

He stayed indoors all the time. I told him he should go out and see people." At some point Ali presents his boxing gloves to Elvis with the inscription "You're the greatest" on the left glove and "To Elvis, my main man, from Muhammad Ali" on the right.

06 Tuesday
On this and the following night, Elvis misses the midnight show because of illness.

13 Tuesday
The Colonel writes to Elvis to remind him that they are in the process of forming new music publishing firms and Elvis must be sure to avoid making any commitments until these publishing arrangements are complete. "This is to protect you," the Colonel advises his client, "from becoming involved with recording a great many tunes in the coming year when you would receive a tremendous amount of pats on your back for being a great guy but no royalty checks. . . . Now that you are aware of the situation and have the proper information, I would appreciate it if you would be good enough in your very well-known, intelligent way to tell anyone discussing any future music or songs that you do not plan to record for a while. Until the Colonel negotiates a new music deal there is no need to discuss anything. This will place you in a very intelligent position, where someone just can't snow you by putting their arms around your shoulders and telling you how great you are."

Elvis continues to be ill, and his doctors recommend that he cancel both shows. He goes ahead with the dinner show but follows the doctors' advice by canceling the midnight shows both on this night and the next.

14 Wednesday
The Hilton releases this announcement before the dinner show: "Ladies and Gentlemen, Elvis because of illness was unable to do his late show

Sparring with Muhammad Ali, Las Vegas, c. February 1973 (Ali is wearing the robe presented to him by Elvis)

last night. He did, however, do the dinner show last night against doctors' advice. Again, tonight, he was asked by his doctors not to do a show, but he wants to do the best he can. He does not want to disappoint the people who came to see him. There will be no late show tonight. Thank you."

15 Thursday

Elvis walks off stage during the dinner show. When he returns, he announces, "I'm sorry, ladies and gentlemen, but I have a touch of the flu, and my voice suddenly disappeared." He finishes the show, but again the midnight show is canceled.

Barron Hilton informs Colonel Parker that Elvis will be paid in full despite the missed performances, and the Colonel responds that he intends to make up for the lost shows at a later engagement. "This letter," the Colonel declares, "is not intended to match your generosity and understanding, but it is intended [to show] that we think the same way along these lines. We will never, and never have intended to, shuck our obligations."

18 Sunday

Four men jump on stage toward the end of Elvis' performance at the midnight show. Several members of the entourage rush to defend Elvis, and Elvis himself knocks one of his presumed assailants back into the audience. When order is finally restored, Elvis tells the audience, "I'm sorry, ladies and gentlemen. I'm sorry I didn't break his goddamned neck is what I'm sorry about."

19 Monday

Although by now it is clear to everyone that the four attackers were nothing more than overstimulated fans, Elvis remains convinced that there is something more to it, eventually coming to believe in the early hours of the morning that they have been sent by Priscilla's boyfriend, Mike Stone. Raging to all the guys, Elvis is sedated several times throughout the day in the midst of accusations that it was Stone who broke up his marriage and is now trying to take his daughter away from him. The upshot of all this is that in the heat of the moment he resolves to have Stone killed, an

idea which all are relieved to see him abandon when he finally calms down several days later.

20 Tuesday

Variety reports that Elvis has been offered half a million dollars for six London concerts at the Earl's Court Stadium in London. This is just one of numerous offers that are made to the Colonel by British, European, and Japanese promoters—but the Colonel turns them all down summarily.

February Record Release

Double LP: *Aloha from Hawaii Via Satellite* (#1). The concert soundtrack is released semi-simultaneously throughout the world, with sleeves printed in advance and titles stickered on the album, some two months before the American show airs. In just four weeks this two-record set will sell half a million copies and shoot to the top of the LP charts, a spot Elvis last occupied with the *Roustabout* soundtrack in 1965.

```
                    I C Costume Company
                    6121 Santa Monica Boulevard
                    Hollywood, California 90038

                        Hollywood 9-2056

                                        Date   April 3, 1973
    Vernon Presley
    3764 Elvis Presley Blvd.
    Memphis, Tenn. 38116
                        0345

      Invoice Number
```

Job No. 6012			
QUANTITY	DESCRIPTION	UNIT PRICE	TOTAL
1	Eagle design cape w/heavy jewelled emb.		$ 785.00
2	Embroidered belts	$45.00	90.00
1	Custom-tailored white suit		550.00
1	White jumpsuit w/matching cape w/heavy jewelled embroidery w/matching belt		1,950.00
13	Jumpsuits w/capes - repaired/refurbished	50.00	650.00
	Cleaning as per Malone Studio Bill #2651 dtd. 3/20/73 - copy attached		255.00
			$4,280.00
	Tax		168.75
			$4,448.75

*PD. 4-16-73
ck # 286
E. A. Presley
Acct*

Invoice from IC Costume Company

23 Friday

Ann-Margret, booked next into the showroom, is in the audience on Elvis' closing night. To Lamar, operating the spotlight, Elvis declares, "Leave the light on her, man. I just want to look at her."

24 Saturday

Elvis and Linda attend Ann-Margret's opening, then remain in Las Vegas, along with Elvis' Memphis karate instructor, Kang Rhee, who conducts karate classes in the suite.

MARCH

01 Thursday

In an agreement first suggested by RCA the previous fall and worked out in its details over the next few weeks with a March 1 date affixed, Colonel Parker arranges for the sale of Elvis' back catalogue to RCA Records. The idea for the sale originally came from RCA executive Mel Ilberman, who saw it as a way for the record company to gain control over the Presley material so as to be able to have it for

March Record Release

Single: "Steamroller Blues" (#17)/"Fool" (shipped March 4). Release of a somewhat overwrought live version of the James Taylor blues spoof "Steamroller Blues," taken from *Aloha from Hawaii*, is timed to stimulate interest in the first U.S. broadcast of the show on April 4. The record sells about 400,000 copies.

various uses (including the RCA Record Club and repackaging) that were consistently blocked, or thwarted, by the Colonel. RCA, of course, has exclusive rights to all of Elvis' material but has been thoroughly stymied by the Colonel's hands-on management of what can and cannot be released (and in what format) from the start. With a single, one-time payment of $5.4 million, RCA now purchases the rights to all material recorded before 1973 in perpetuity, with Elvis and the Colonel forfeiting all further royalties and control.

At the same time Elvis enters into a new management agreement with the Colonel, whereby all income deriving from recording (in other words, not simply the proliferating side deals) will be split 50-50 from here on in, though touring will remain on a two-thirds/one-third basis.

Elvis enters into a new seven-year contract with the record company as well, entailing a yearly obligation of two albums and four singles for a guaranteed annual payment against royalties of at least $500,000, which, of course, is subject to the 50-50 agreement. In all, something like $10.5 million worth of business is done, with the Colonel making various special deals of his own (all signed off on by Elvis) for promotion of the records and tours, and for "assisting" RCA in the "development of merchandising and promo concepts." Of the $10.5 million changing hands, the Colonel will receive approximately $6 million and Elvis $4.5 million.

05 Monday

Elvis buys $2,600 worth of jewelry in Vegas.

08 Thursday

Elvis leaves Las Vegas and flies to Los Angeles, where, except for occasional weekends in Palm Springs, he remains until the beginning of his April tour.

19 Monday

Jessie Presley, Elvis' grandfather, dies of a heart attack in Louisville. Elvis does not attend the funeral.

APRIL

02 Monday

Ed Parker promotes Elvis to sixth-degree black belt in his International Kenpo Karate Association.

04 Wednesday

Elvis: Aloha from Hawaii is broadcast on NBC at 8:30 P.M. Fifty-seven percent of the television audience watches the show, as does Elvis, who is at home in Los Angeles.

08 Sunday

Elvis, along with Linda, Joe Esposito, Charlie Hodge, Gee Gee and Patsy Gambill, Jerry Schilling, James Caughley, new recruit Kenny Hicks, and Kang Rhee, flies to San Francisco to attend Ed Parker's California Karate Championships, but when he discovers the unauthorized use of his name both in the promotion and on the marquee, he leaves the hotel, the Del Webb Town House, and flies back to Los Angeles, disappointed at what he sees as exploitation by friends.

09 Monday

To assuage some of Elvis' disappointment, Kang Rhee awards Elvis a seventh-degree black belt in his Pasaryu school of karate.

17 Tuesday

Elvis spends three days rehearsing at RCA's Studio C.

21 Saturday

Elvis flies to Phoenix to begin a new tour. Emory Gordy, who recorded with Elvis in Hollywood in March of 1972, replaces Jerry Scheff on bass, but otherwise all personnel are the same.

22 Sunday

★ *Veterans Memorial Coliseum, Phoenix, Arizona, at 3:00 P.M.*

After the show Elvis returns to his home in L.A., driving the next evening to Anaheim, where he stays at the Anaheim Royal Inn.

23 Monday

★ *Anaheim Convention Center, Anaheim, California*

24 Tuesday

★ *Anaheim Convention Center, Anaheim*

Lisa Marie is in the audience for this show.

25 Wednesday

★ *Selland Arena, Fresno, California, at 4:30 and 8:30 P.M.*

26 Thursday

★ *International Sports Arena, San Diego, California*

27 Friday

★ *Memorial Coliseum, Portland, Oregon*

28 Saturday

★ *Coliseum, Spokane, Washington, at 3:00 and 8:00 P.M.*

29 Sunday

★ *Center Arena, Seattle, Washington, at 3:00 and 8:00 P.M.*

30 Monday

★ *Denver Coliseum, Denver, Colorado*

After the show Elvis goes directly to the Sahara Tahoe Hotel.

MAY

02 Wednesday

Priscilla retains a lawyer to reopen her divorce in order to obtain what she has come to feel is a more equitable settlement for herself and Lisa Marie.

04 Friday

★ *High Sierra Theater, Sahara Tahoe, Stateline, Nevada*

Elvis opens a seventeen-day engagement at Del Webb's Sahara Tahoe, for which he is to receive $300,000 (his fee for the usual two-week booking) while the Colonel is to be paid $100,000 for his contributions. *Variety* reports that Elvis is "some thirty pounds overweight, puffy, white-faced, and blinking against the light." His voice is "weak, delivery is flabby," according to the same review. He is accompanied by former Palm Springs policeman Dick Grob, Red West, Sonny West, Jerry Schilling, Lamar Fike, Ed Parker, and Parker's karate associate, Dave Hebler, like Grob a recent security addition and full-fledged member of the entourage. Also on hand is Memphis hairdresser Homer Gilliland, who is frequently flown in during this period to take care of Elvis' hair.

13 Sunday

Elvis performs a special Mother's Day show at 3:00 P.M. at the Sahara Tahoe to benefit a local hospital.

17 Thursday

Illness causes Elvis to cancel both shows.

18 Friday

Elvis is taken to a local hospital for chest X rays, and as fans wait in line, they are told that both tonight's and the weekend shows will have to be canceled. Elvis and Linda fly home to Memphis, and the Colonel returns his $100,000 payment to the hotel.

19 Saturday

In the wake of the Tahoe debacle, there has for the first time been somewhat open discussion among family and friends about Elvis' abuse of prescription medication. Prompted by the concerns of the Colonel and Vernon Presley in particular, Los Angeles attorney Ed Hookstratten opens an investigation into who is providing Elvis with his seemingly unending supply of drugs. Using John O'Grady as his primary investigator over the next few weeks and months, Hookstratten uncovers the three physicians and one dentist whom he takes to be the principal suppliers. There are various attempts to threaten the doctors and interdict the supplies, but in the absence of any cooperation from the principal victim they all come to naught.

JUNE

04 Monday

Elvis attends screenings at either the Memphian or the Crosstown almost every night for the month he is at home until going out again on tour on the twentieth.

RCA Records | 6363 Sunset Boulevard | Hollywood, CA 90028 | Telephone (213) 461-9171

RECEIVED

JUL 11 1973

JOAN DEARY

RESERV.

JUL 5 1973

P. M. LAGINESTRA

George L. Parkhill
Division Vice President
Professional Artist Programs

RCA

June 29, 1973

MR. ELVIS PRESLEY

Dear Elvis:

In order to have the merchandise available for our summer release, we are planning a recording session in the middle of July.

We need the following products to enable our Sales Department to plan these merchandising campaigns:

1 - A new RCA album (10 songs)

2 - Two new single records (4 sides)

3 - A new religious RCA album (10 songs)

I will appreciate you letting me know as soon as possible where you would like to record, either Tennessee or California, and we will make arrangements for this.

The important product first is the new RCA album on the new catalog contract and the two singles. The religious album could be done at the end of the recording session. All of these songs must be songs not previously recorded by you, in keeping with the new contract signed by you March 1, 1973.

Best regards,

GEORGE L. PARKHILL

GLP/lm

cc: Mr. Rocco Laginestra, Colonel Tom Parker
Mr. Freddy Bienstock, Mr. Tom Diskin

RCA to Elvis re the upcoming session

29 Friday

★ *Omni, Atlanta, Georgia*

RCA writes to Elvis requesting him to schedule a recording session and laying out what product will be expected: one new album, two new singles, and a new album of religious music. "In order to have the merchandise available," writes George Parkhill with uncharacteristic peremptoriness, "we are planning a recording session in the middle of July." He gives Elvis a choice of where that session can be, but there is no question that it will take place.

30 Saturday

★ *Omni, Atlanta, at 3:00 and 8:30 P.M.*

JULY

01 Sunday

★ *Municipal Auditorium, Nashville, Tennessee, at 3:00 and 8:30 P.M.*

02 Monday

★ *Myriad Center Arena, Oklahoma City, Oklahoma*

03 Tuesday

★ *Omni, Atlanta, Georgia*

04 Wednesday

Upon completion of the tour Elvis returns to Memphis, where he remains at home for the most part, attending the movies infrequently.

17 Tuesday

In papers presented to the court Priscilla's new attorney formally seeks to set aside the original divorce settlement.

On this same date, or thereabouts, Elvis buys Linda Thompson's brother, Sam, a house at 1317 Favel Drive in Memphis for $37,500.

20 Friday

Knowing that Elvis has little motivation to leave Memphis, especially

---

19 Tuesday

Late at night, Elvis has minor surgery on his foot at a podiatrist's office in Memphis.

20 Wednesday

★ *Mobile Municipal Auditorium, Mobile, Alabama*

21 Thursday

★ *Omni, Atlanta, Georgia*

Initial demand for the original June 29 and 30 Atlanta dates has been so great that shows are added both here, at the front end of the tour, and on July 3.

22 Friday

★ *Nassau County Veterans Memorial Coliseum, Uniondale, New York (just outside New York City)*

23 Saturday

★ *Nassau County Veterans Memorial Coliseum, Uniondale, at 3:00 and 8:30 P.M.*

24 Sunday

★ *Nassau County Veterans Memorial Coliseum at 3:00 P.M.*

25 Monday

★ *Civic Center Arena, Pittsburgh, Pennsylvania*

26 Tuesday

★ *Civic Center Arena, Pittsburgh*

27 Wednesday

★ *Cincinnati Gardens, Cincinnati, Ohio*

28 Thursday

★ *Kiel Auditorium, St. Louis, Missouri*

with Lisa Marie in town for her summer visit, Marty Lacker has suggested recording at the Stax studio, located just minutes from Graceland, on MacLemore Avenue a few doors down from the old Assembly of God church that Elvis and Dixie Locke once attended. Lacker, who was instrumental in bringing Elvis to American, has just begun working for Stax, Memphis' predominant r & b label. Perhaps taking his cue from these parallel circumstances, producer Felton Jarvis contacts some of the same musicians who worked the 1969 American sessions, now based in Nashville, to join James Burton and Ronnie Tutt from the show band. As indicated by Parkhill's letter to Elvis and various other RCA communications, this is clearly an important session, and one that Felton feels must be productive if he is to keep his job. Unfortunately, Elvis fails to show up at all on this first scheduled

With Governor and Mrs. Jimmy Carter, backstage at the Omni, probably June 29, 1973

night of recording and arrives late on the second night dressed in a white suit, black cape, and Superfly-style Borsalino slouch hat, accompanied by Linda Thompson and Lisa Marie.

21 Saturday

The studio musicians, most of whom have not seen him in some time, are shocked at Elvis' attitude and appearance. "It was the first time I ever saw him fat," says Nashville drummer Jerry Carrigan, substituting for Gene Chrisman in the basic American lineup. "His speech was slurred. It just seemed like he was miserable." When the session breaks off at 3:00 A.M., three complete masters have been recorded but little of note has been accomplished save for a

Probably summer 1973, wearing the suit he wore on the cover of the *Today* album

stumbling karate exhibition with Kang Rhee in the studio.

22 Sunday

Working another perfunctory studio shift from 11:00 P.M. until 3:00 A.M., Elvis does manage to record three more songs, including one noticeably improved piece of material that Felton has picked up in Nashville from his friend, song publisher Bob Beckham—the Tony Joe

July Record Release

LP: *Elvis (Fool)* (#52). After the catalogue buyout and the end of "special deals," RCA's new management team is determined to limit Elvis releases according to a more conventionally thought-out game plan, but the enormous success of *Aloha from Hawaii* is the spur for a summer album, despite the clear lack of enough good material to justify one. Not even waiting for the Stax sessions to take place, the label digs out what little it has in the vaults and pieces together a record that consists mostly of leftover takes from Elvis' studio recordings, the last of which took place in March of 1972. The result sells less than 200,000 copies.

White composition, "I've Got a Thing About You, Baby."

23 Monday

Another perfunctory night, with just two songs completed between 11:00 P.M. and 3:30 A.M. The tunes, Mark James' "Raised on Rock" and "For Ol' Times Sake," another number from Tony Joe White, will make up the next single.

24 Tuesday

Elvis is frustrated by the sound and walks out when he learns from engineer Al Pachucki that his personal vocal mike has been stolen from the studio. Only one song has been recorded, and this is, in essence, the end of the session, though Felton keeps recording backing tracks the following night in the vain hope that Elvis may return.

25 Wednesday

Barely half of what the record company has set out for the goals of the session has been completed, but Elvis takes in a movie at the Crosstown.

29 Sunday

Elvis flies from Memphis to Los Angeles.

31 Tuesday

At 9:00 P.M. Elvis begins three days of band rehearsals for Vegas at the RCA studio on Sunset. A handful of older titles like "She's Not You," "I Feel So Bad," and "A Mess of Blues" are tried, but only "Trouble" and the extended "Rock 'n' Roll" medley that Elvis has been performing frequently on tour make it into the regular show. Two unrecorded songs, "The Twelfth of Never" and "Are You Sincere?" (the latter of which Elvis will record in Palm Springs in September), are rehearsed but later dropped from the Vegas show, and the just-recorded A-side of his next single, "Raised on Rock," is dropped as well after opening night. In fact, the only new song that will be included as a regular part of the show is a cover version of actor Richard Harris' 1971 divorce weeper, "My Boy."

AUGUST

03 Friday

Elvis flies to Vegas to begin rehearsals at the Hilton.

06 Monday

★ *Showroom, Las Vegas Hilton, Las Vegas*

Elvis opens his latest "Summer Festival" with the usual single dinner show. A special "jazz" arrangement of the *2001* theme is used for this one performance, which is attended by Petula Clark, Liza Minnelli, and Joan Rivers, among others. The *Hollywood Reporter* gives a dismaying description of opening night. "It's Elvis at his most indifferent, uninterested, and unappealing," declares the trade paper. "The Living Legend was fat and ludicrously aping his former self. . . . His personality was lost in one of the most ill-prepared, unsteady, and most disheartening performances of his Las Vegas career. . . . It is a tragedy, disheartening and absolutely depressing to see Elvis in such diminishing stature."

17 Friday

Travis Smith, Gladys' brother, dies.

19 Sunday

While demonstrating a karate hold in his suite after the show, Elvis accidentally breaks the ankle of one of his guests, Beverly Albrecq. Dr. Elias Ghanem arranges for her care, and Elvis continues to pay all her medical bills and travel expenses to and from Las Vegas for physical therapy over the next several years. She will bring a lawsuit against Elvis in 1975, which will be settled for $5,000 on May 27, 1977.

31 Friday

The Hillcrest house is sold for $450,000.

SEPTEMBER

02 Sunday

Elvis appears "by popular demand" in a special 3:00 A.M. show.

03 Monday

Elvis concludes the engagement, arriving on stage for the final show on Lamar's back with a toy monkey attached to his neck. He delights the crowd by singing "What Now My Love" while tossing back and forth on a bed that Sonny West has pushed out on stage. He upsets the Colonel, however, when he rips into the Hilton Hotel organization for what he feels is their poor treatment of a favorite employee. At the end of the show he

Colonel Parker's office, Las Vegas Hilton

seems to be trying to make amends as he declares, "I know we kid a lot and have fun and everything—but we really love to sing, play music, and entertain people. As long as I can do that, I'll be a happy old sonofabitch."

The Colonel, however, is not to be mollified. He comes storming into the dressing room, determined to straighten Elvis out about his "unprofessional" behavior toward the very people who are paying them and have treated them so well over the years. It seems as if all the resentment that has been building over the last few years now explodes, and he and Elvis get into a public shouting match in front of shocked members of the entourage. This ends with Elvis firing the Colonel later in the evening up in his suite, with the Colonel countering that he quits and merely wants to be paid all that he is owed. He then retires to *his* suite to draw up the bill.

Elvis receives $610,000 for the four-week engagement, with expenses coming to approximately $168,000 and Elvis and the Colonel dividing $438,000 between them with a small reserve retained, $292,000 to Elvis, $146,000 to his manager.

---

04 Tuesday

Over the next week and a half, Elvis and the Colonel trade accusations and barbs via intermediaries, with Elvis uncertain whom to turn to if he should actually leave the only real manager he has ever had and his father increasingly concerned over how they will ever pay the Colonel all the money that they owe him according to his meticulously detailed bill. The Colonel, meanwhile, continues to carry on as if he were conducting business as usual.

In the meantime, Elvis has flown in a gospel quartet from Nashville that includes recently departed Stamp Donnie Sumner (J. D. Sumner's nephew) and ex-Imperial Sherrill Nielsen. His original idea was to present them to Tom Jones, who has

been having difficulties with his backup group, and he has them perform for Jones and singer Bobbie Gentry ("Ode to Billy Joe") at the wrap party the previous night. Things don't work out with Jones, but Elvis likes their singing so much he draws up a contract hiring them for $100,000 a year as his personal backup group, subject to his beck and call, and they remain in Las Vegas to sing with him for the next week. He names them Voice after the single-issue spiritual journal *New Age Voice*, which Larry Geller has put out and given to Elvis when he came to Las Vegas with Johnny Rivers not long before to see the show.

07 Friday

An altercation just outside the Hilton suite leads to accusations that Red West and two other members of the entourage attacked and beat up one of Elvis' guests, Kaijo Peter Pajarinen. A lawsuit is filed against Elvis, Red, and other unnamed bodyguards on May 29, 1975, with the case unresolved until after Elvis' death, when charges will ultimately be dismissed.

08 Saturday

Elvis and Linda attend Tom Jones' show at Caesar's Palace, with Elvis appearing briefly on stage to wild cheers from the audience.

11 Tuesday

Elvis remains in Las Vegas, breaking up the furniture in karate workouts with Kang Rhee and singing with Voice. At one point he breaks a finger on his left hand.

16 Sunday

Just before leaving for Palm Springs Elvis finally has Sonny West call the Colonel, and while Sonny does not overhear the conversation between Elvis and his manager, one way or another the dispute is resolved.

17 Monday

Palm Springs Music delivers a Sterling Clark piano costing $1,695, with special ebony finish and silver

trim, to Elvis' Chino Canyon home.

18 Tuesday

Elvis visits a Palm Springs ophthalmologist.

19 Wednesday

The injury he sustained in Las Vegas the week before continues to bother him, and he sees an orthopedist, who X-rays and casts the finger.

21 Friday

Lisa Marie flies into Palm Springs, along with Elvis' Los Angeles dentist, Max Shapiro.

22 Saturday

Because the Stax sessions generated so few masters, RCA has insisted that Elvis complete vocals for at least four of the instrumental tracks that Felton recorded. With the Colonel's complicit approval, the record company sends a mobile recording truck to Elvis' Palm Springs home, but even now Elvis is more interested in cutting demos on his new group, Voice, with the idea of getting them a recording contract (he has signed them to his new song publishing company, which the Colonel has finally set up), than he is in making records himself. After spending four hours producing two demos on Voice, Elvis completes the overdubbing of one of his own songs, "Sweet Angeline," at 3:00 A.M.

23 Sunday

Recording continues from 7:00 P.M. to 3:15 A.M., with Elvis completing two more songs, "Are You Sincere?", which he rehearsed in Los Angeles earlier in the summer, and Voice leader Donnie Sumner's "I Miss You." This provides RCA with just enough

---

September Record Release

Single: "Raised on Rock" (#41)/"For Ol' Times Sake" (shipped September 21). The first single from the Stax sessions sells just 250,000 copies.

Leaving the Santa Monica courthouse, October 9, 1973 *(courtesy of Michael Ochs Archives)*

cuts for one album. The ragtag band on the newly recorded tracks includes Charlie Hodge on acoustic guitar, Donnie Sumner on piano, and Voice's bass player, Tommy Hensley, with James Burton, present to overdub his guitar on the prerecorded tracks, contributing lead guitar.

24 Monday

Elvis flies to Los Angeles, where he remains at home and is visited by several of his doctors.

OCTOBER

09 Tuesday

The divorce decree is finalized at the Los Angeles County Superior Court-house in Santa Monica. The agreed-upon settlement calls for shared custody of Lisa Marie and will give Priscilla an outright cash payment of $725,000, $4,200 a month in spousal

---

October Record Release

LP: *Raised on Rock/For Ol' Times Sake* (#50). Nearly everything about this album seems ill-fated, from the cover art, which replicates the design of the just-released single of the same name, to the unhappy conditions of its recent recording in Memphis and Palm Springs. The public's desire for such shoddily assembled product seems to be diminishing, as sales are less than 200,000.

---

support for a year plus $6,000 a month for ten years, plus $4,000 a month in child support, 5 percent of the new publishing companies, and half of the sale of the Hillcrest house. After the brief twenty-minute hearing Elvis and Priscilla walk out of court hand in hand.

11 Thursday

Elvis experiences some difficulty breathing just before flying to Memphis with Linda.

12 Friday

Upon arrival at Graceland, Linda calls Dr. Nichopoulos, who arranges for his office nurse, Tish Henley, to care for Elvis at home.

14 Sunday

Elvis feels well enough to attend a show at the Memphian.

15 Monday

Elvis' continuing breathing difficulties force Dr. Nichopoulos to admit his patient to Memphis' Baptist Memorial Hospital, where he undergoes extensive testing to determine the cause of his condition. Congestive heart failure is almost immediately ruled out, and the team of doctors put together by Dr. Nichopoulos is puzzled until Dr. Nick ascertains that Elvis' almost daily "acupuncture" treatments in California have included injections with a syringe filled with Demerol. Subsequent treatment focuses on what amounts to an addiction to Demerol, and Elvis remains in the hospital with Linda at his side for two weeks.

NOVEMBER

01 Thursday

Elvis is released from Baptist Memorial Hospital.

During this week Elvis spends an evening at Linda and Sam Thompson's parents' house, relaxing and singing blues numbers and other old favorites like "I'm So Lonesome I

Could Cry" and "Spanish Eyes," as well as a duet with Linda on her college sorority song, in a performance that Sam Thompson tapes.

09 Friday

Elvis flies to Los Angeles, and then on to Palm Springs, without Linda, who will spend the next week in Puerto Rico with Vernon's wife, Dee.

15 Thursday

Elvis flies back to Los Angeles, returning to Memphis on Monday.

20 Tuesday

Elvis attends a show at the Memphian tonight and again on Thursday, the twenty-ninth.

It is very likely during this period that Elvis is introduced to racquetball as a form of therapeutic exercise by Dr. Nick, an accomplished player, and they play frequently in the early morning hours at the local Y and at Memphis State.

DECEMBER

10 Monday

Elvis returns to Stax for a weeklong session. To overcome some of the technical problems that plagued the session in July, RCA sends its recording truck, along with four engineers. Each night things get under way at 9:00 P.M., with a band composed of TCB band stalwarts James Burton and Ronnie Tutt together with Norbert Putnam

and David Briggs from Nashville, Memphian Johnny Christopher on rhythm guitar, and Swedish-born Per-Erik "Pete" Hallin (who now plays piano for Voice) doubling with Briggs on keyboards. The number of backup vocalists reaches an almost unmanageable total of eleven, including Voice. Tonight's session goes until 4:30 A.M., and although they come out of it with only two finished masters, Elvis' attitude is entirely different from what it was during the summer, and one of the songs, Dennis Linde's "I Got a Feeling in My Body," is a real high point among recent recordings.

11 Tuesday

By the time the session knocks off at 2:00 A.M. two more songs have been recorded, including Red West's "If You Talk in Your Sleep," a future hit single.

12 Wednesday

Working hard until 5:00 A.M., Elvis focuses exclusively on four songs either written or brought to him by Voice.

13 Thursday

Another productive session, with three masters achieved by 4:00 A.M., including Tom Jans' "Loving Arms."

14 Friday

Elvis calls a halt to the session at 3:00 A.M. when he discovers no one has ordered food for the group. Only one song, Jerry Reed's rousing "Talk About the Good Times," is cut.

15 Saturday

The session picks up again, running from 9:00 P.M. to 6:00 A.M. and including a rocking version of Chuck Berry's "Promised Land."

16 Sunday

After a final night that goes until 5:00 A.M., Felton has eighteen masters to deliver to RCA, many of a quality that reflects Elvis' healthier and happier state.

24 Monday

Elvis has been spending most of his evenings at the movies, but tonight he has surgery to remove an ingrown toenail at a podiatrist's office in Memphis.

25 Tuesday

Christmas at Graceland. Among the gifts that Elvis gives are a three-quarter-length mink coat and a $2,000 fox suede coat with a red fox purse, both purchased from King Furs in Memphis.

30 Sunday

The podiatrist makes a house call at Graceland.

Elvis' accountants report that in 1973 his income from motion pictures is $143,000, from personal appearances $3,860,000, and from music and recording $4,214,000. His income tax is $2,959,000.

1974

JANUARY

03 Thursday
A toothache sends Elvis to the dentist.

07 Monday
Mel Ilberman of RCA informs the Colonel that while RCA Record Tours will continue to play a substantial financial role in booking Elvis' tours, Management III has been brought back to do most of the work.

08 Tuesday
The two mayors of Memphis, city and county, declare Elvis' thirty-ninth birthday to be Elvis Presley Day,' and both march in a parade down Elvis Presley Boulevard to Graceland. In Georgia governor Jimmy Carter issues a similar proclamation, in deference to Elvis' five Atlanta performances in 1973.

11 Friday
On both this day and the next Elvis spends time at the podiatrist's and the dentist's offices.

12 Saturday
Elvis flies to Los Angeles.

With Colonel Parker and friend, Las Vegas, January–February 1974

15 Tuesday

Elvis is picked up at 7:45 P.M. at his Monovale home and driven to the RCA studio on Sunset to rehearse for his upcoming Vegas opening. He returns home at 1:45 A.M., maintaining a similar schedule for the next three nights. Among the new numbers that Elvis rehearses are some of the recordings from his most recent Stax session, as well as "The Twelfth of Never," "Born to Lose," and "I'm Leavin' It Up to You." In the end, however, the only new material that is introduced into the show on a consistent basis are Olivia Newton-John's "Let Me Be There," Kris Kristofferson's "Why Me Lord," and

---

January Record Releases

Single: "I've Got a Thing About You Baby" (#39)/"Take Good Care of Her" (shipped January 11). Top 40 disc jockeys seem to have lost interest in Elvis, but the single's half-million sales are obviously helped by its #4 position (Elvis' highest since 1958) on the country charts.

LP: *Elvis: A Legendary Performer, Vol. 1* (#43). One direct result of RCA's buyout of all of Elvis' pre-1973 recordings is the freedom to repackage his old material any way they choose, with no interference from the Colonel and no royalties to pay. The "Legendary Performer" series has long been producer Joan Deary's dream, and while the Colonel does throw up enough initial roadblocks to delay the album's release by a couple of months, in the end the package that Deary puts together is a previously inconceivable combination of Sun outtakes, interview snippets, numbers that were left out of the '68 Special, and such commonplace items as "Heartbreak Hotel" and "Don't Be Cruel." The Colonel is eventually allowed some participation in the package, mostly via an elegant twelve-page, memorabilia-filled booklet that would have been just as inconceivable prior to the '73 buyout, and while this is not Elvis' most successful album, its sales of over 750,000 copies (beating out all three Stax session albums combined) bear out the Colonel's worst fears about the past obliterating the present.

Larry Gatlin's "Help Me," which Elvis picked up through Voice.

19 Saturday

Elvis pays $350 for a screening at MGM of *The Exorcist*.

21 Monday

Early in the evening Elvis flies to Las Vegas.

24 Thursday

Rehearsals are held in the Las Vegas Hilton showroom for three days, beginning at noon each day.

25 Friday

In Las Vegas Elvis receives emergency dental treatment.

26 Saturday

★ *Showroom, Las Vegas Hilton, Las Vegas*

At Dr. Nick's urging, Elvis' Las Vegas engagement has been reduced from four weeks to two. Because it is a Saturday night, Elvis plays two shows this evening, with the official invitational "opening" (originally scheduled for Friday but put off so as not to conflict with Frank Sinatra's "comeback" at Caesars Palace) postponed until the following night. Duke Bardwell replaces Emory Gordy on bass, and Voice makes its first appearance on stage with Elvis. For the first time in three years Elvis appears without the usual cape.

27 Sunday

Elvis is reported by the press to look well and to be in good humor at his "opening." Special guests include George Burns, Lorne Green, Ernest Borgnine, and Danny Thomas.

FEBRUARY

01 Friday

Because Lisa Marie is ill, she is forced to miss her usual birthday visit to Las Vegas.

09 Saturday

Elvis closes out what has been a

---

generally good engagement, in which he has been described as being "in good humor" and "at the top of his form." At the same time he has continued to exhibit the kind of erratic personal behavior that has shown up increasingly over the past year, shooting out a chandelier and several television sets during this engagement alone.

19 Tuesday

Elvis is back in Los Angeles and with Lisa Marie when she has a tonsillectomy.

28 Thursday

Just before leaving to go out on tour, Elvis sees a Dr. Kantor in Beverly Hills about throat problems.

MARCH

01 Friday

★ *Mabee Special Events Center, Oral Roberts University, Tulsa, Oklahoma*

02 Saturday

★ *Mabee Special Events Center, Oral Roberts University, Tulsa, at 1:30 P.M.*

03 Sunday

★ *Astrodome, Houston, Texas, at 2:00 and 7:00 P.M.*

Toward the end of Elvis' performance of "Fever," the Colonel appears on stage, riding a small donkey led by Elvis' father, Vernon. As Elvis goes into "Let Me Be There," Vernon mounts the donkey and the Colonel slaps it and leads it off stage.

04 Monday

★ *Civic Center, Monroe, Louisiana*

Because of ongoing internal disputes within Voice, Sherrill Nielsen leaves the tour after this date and is replaced by the group's piano player, Per-Erik Hallin.

05 Tuesday

★ *Memorial Coliseum, Auburn University, Monroe, Alabama*

Entering the Houston Astrodome, with Sonny West, Vernon Presley, and Red West, March 3, 1974

15 Friday
★ *Stokely Athletic Center, University of Tennessee, Knoxville, Tennessee, at 2:30 and 8:30 P.M.*

16 Saturday
★ *Mid-South Coliseum, Memphis, Tennessee, at 2:30 and 8:30 P.M.*

This is Elvis' first appearance in his hometown since February 1961, and the four shows that are initially booked sell out immediately, prompting the Colonel to add a fifth, which he determines will be the perfect occasion for a live homecoming album and also the perfect way to avoid having to coax Elvis back into the studio.

06 Wednesday
★ *Garrett Coliseum, Montgomery, Alabama*

The show is attended by Governor George Wallace.

07 Thursday
★ *Civic Center, Monroe, Louisiana*

08 Friday
★ *Civic Center, Monroe*

09 Saturday
★ *Coliseum, Charlotte, North Carolina, at 2:30 and 11:00 P.M.*

10 Sunday
★ *Civic Center, Roanoke, Virginia*

11 Monday
★ *Coliseum, Hampton Roads, Virginia*

12 Tuesday
★ *Coliseum, Richmond, Virginia*

13 Wednesday
★ *Coliseum, Greensboro, North Carolina*

14 Thursday
★ *Middle Tennessee State University Athletic Center, Murfreesboro, Tennessee*

With Alabama governor George Wallace and *(back left)* Sonny West and Dick Grob, March 6, 1974

Probably Hampton Roads, Virginia, March 11, 1974

The four weekend shows draw 49,000 fans, who convincingly refute any thought that "Memphis and Mid-South fans might not turn out to see one of their own." Elvis seems both happy and mildly amused to be here, as he declares, "Hello, Memphis. It's good to be home."

17 Sunday

★ Mid-South Coliseum, Memphis, at 2:30 and 8:30 P.M.

March Record Release

LP: *Good Times* (#90). Sales of 200,000 only reinforce the impression that the public at large prefers the young Elvis Presley, as exemplified by Joan Deary's royalty-free *Elvis: A Legendary Performer*—though Elvis once again makes a strong showing (#5) on the country charts.

18 Monday

★ Coliseum, Richmond, Virginia

19 Tuesday

★ Middle Tennessee State University Athletic Center, Murfreesboro, Tennessee

20 Wednesday

★ Mid-South Coliseum, Memphis, Tennessee

With no particular preparations with regard to either repertoire or plans for backup recording, RCA has its mobile recording truck on hand to record this final show of the tour. The *Memphis Press-Scimitar*'s review of Sunday night's show could very well stand for this one: upon the completion of the overture, "like a streak of white lightning, Presley darts on stage. He is dramatically clad in all-white which sparkles with jewels and nailheads." This and the unfurling of the American flag

for "An American Trilogy" at the end are seen as the high points of the show.

The tour grosses $2,310,553.50, and after expenses Elvis takes home $789,021.72, the Colonel $394,510.86.

26 Tuesday

Elvis flies to California and most likely remains in Los Angeles and Palm Springs for the next two and a half weeks.

28 Thursday

Arthur "Big Boy" Crudup, the author and originator of Elvis' first Sun record, "That's All Right," as well as such later RCA recordings as "My Baby Left Me" and "So Glad You're Mine," dies in Nassawadox, Virginia, at the age of sixty-eight. Elvis vividly described the influence Crudup had on

Probably May–June 1974 tour

his music in a 1956 interview that must have provided more than a moment of puzzlement for the reporter from the *Charlotte* [North Carolina] *Observer*: "Down in Tupelo, Mississippi, I used to hear old Arthur Crudup bang his box the way I do now, and I said if I ever got to the place where I could feel all old Arthur felt, I'd be a music man like nobody ever saw."

APRIL

12 Friday

Elvis returns to Memphis, where he will remain until the start of his May tour, frequently playing racquetball with Dr. Nick and attending the movies almost every night.

MAY

06 Monday

Elvis flies to Los Angeles to get ready for a brief Cali-fornia tour, to be followed by another Tahoe engagement.

10 Friday

★ *Swing Auditorium, San Bernardino, California*

11 Saturday

★ *Forum, Inglewood, California, at 2:30 and 8:30 P.M.*

12 Sunday

★ *Selland Arena, Fresno, California, at 3:00 P.M.*

13 Monday

★ *Swing Auditorium, San Bernardino, California*

14 Tuesday

Elvis flies from Los Angeles to Lake Tahoe to begin rehearsals with orchestra leader Joe Guercio and the rhythm section for the upcoming show. He is accompanied by Joe Esposito, Sonny West, Charlie Hodge, Lamar Fike, Jerry Schilling, new enlistee Al Strada (who has joined up after working as a security guard at the Monovale house), and David and Ricky Stanley.

Show statement for the May 10–13 tour

```
ELVIS   PRESLEY   SHOW

Memphis, Tennessee


SHOW STATEMENT


INCOME:

From Management III/RCATours representing
earnings of the Elvis Presley Show based
upon 65% of the gross box office receipts
as per attached statement forshow performances
May 10-11-12-13, 1974. . . . . . . . . . . . . . . . .$309,853.00


EXPENSES:

TALENT SALARY AND EXPENSES............$16,250.00
BACK-UP BAND . . . . . . . . . . . . . . .$ 7,303.75
TRANSPORTATION . . . . . . . . . . . . . . .$   621.37
EQUIPMENT HANDLING AND CARTAGE .......$ 1,650.00
TECHNICAL ASSISTANTS . . . . . . . . .......$ 6,100.00
MISC ELLANEOUS. . . . . . . . . . . . .......$ 1,100.00
ALL STAR SEOWS . . . . . . . . . . .......$15,000.00
WM. MORRIS AGENCY . . . . . .: . . .......$10,000.00

TOTAL OF EXPENSES . . . . . . . . . . . $ 58,025.00
RESERVE HELD FOR ADDITIONAL EXPENSES. $   577.88

TOTAL. . . . . . . . . . . . . . . . . $58,603.00  $ 58,603.00


BALANCE FOR DISTRIBUTION. . . . . . . . . . . . .  $251,250.00

DISTRIBUTED TO:   ELVIS PRESLEY (2/3) ..$167,500.00
                  COLONEL PARKER (1/3) ..$ 83,750.00
```

15 Wednesday

Rehearsals are held at noon both today and tomorrow. Tenor Sherrill Nielsen has rejoined the show, still singing with Voice but no longer an official member of the group.

16 Thursday

★ *High Sierra Room, Sahara Tahoe Hotel, Stateline, Nevada*

Elvis opens at Del Webb's Sahara Tahoe, playing two cocktail shows each evening. Twice during the engagement he misses shows because of the flu. The *San Francisco Examiner* reviews the opening as "listless, uninspired and downright tired."

20 Monday

Edward L. Ashley, a land developer from Grass Valley, California, claims that he is beaten by several of the bodyguards (with Elvis looking on) while awaiting admittance to Elvis' suite after the evening's final show. The claim leads to an October 11 lawsuit for over $6 million, which will not be settled for a number of years.

23 Thursday

There is a party in celebration of Linda Thompson's twenty-fourth birthday after the show.

26 Sunday

Elvis ends his engagement with an added performance at 3:00 A.M. Monday morning.

27 Monday

The Jackson Five open their show at the Sahara. This would appear to be the time that a five-year-old Lisa Marie first meets Michael Jackson, when Jerry Schilling and Myrna Smith take her to see the show.

JUNE

01 Saturday

Elvis flies to Los Angeles, then on to Palm Springs for a week, accompanied by Voice.

11 Tuesday

Vernon has separated from Dee and buys a house at 1293 Old Hickory Road, also in the neighborhood behind Graceland, which he moves into with Sandy Miller, a nurse he met in Denver, and her two children.

13 Thursday

Elvis flies into Memphis before taking off on his third tour of 1974.

15 Saturday

★ *Tarrant County Convention Center, Fort Worth, Texas, at 3:00 and 8:30 P.M.*

16 Sunday

★ *Tarrant County Convention Center, Fort Worth, at 3:00 and 8:30 P.M.*

17 Monday

★ *Louisiana State University Assembly Center, Baton Rouge, Louisiana*

18 Tuesday

★ *Louisiana State University Assembly Center, Baton Rouge*

19 Wednesday

★ *Civic Center Auditorium, Amarillo, Texas*

20 Thursday

★ *Veterans Memorial Auditorium, Des Moines, Iowa*

21 Friday

★ *Convention Center Public Hall, Cleveland, Ohio*

22 Saturday

★ *Civic Center Auditorium, Providence, Rhode Island, at 3:00 and 8:30 P.M.*

23 Sunday

★ *Spectrum, Philadelphia, Pennsylvania, at 3:00 and 8:30 P.M.*

24 Monday

★ *International Convention Center, Niagara Falls, New York, at 3:00 and 8:30 P.M.*

25 Tuesday

★ *St. John Arena, Columbus, Ohio*

26 Wednesday

Under some duress, the entire troupe gathers on the tarmac at the Louisville airport to sing "Happy Birthday" to the Colonel as Elvis' plane arrives and the Colonel's is about to take off. It is Colonel Parker's sixty-fifth birthday.

★ *Fair and Expo Center's Freedom Hall, Louisville, Kentucky*

27 Thursday

★ *Indiana University Assembly Hall, Bloomington, Indiana*

28 Friday

★ *Arena, Milwaukee, Wisconsin*

29 Saturday

★ *Municipal Auditorium, Kansas City, Missouri, at 2:30 and 8:30 P.M.*

30 Sunday

★ *Auditorium Arena, Omaha, Nebraska, at 2:30 and 8:30 P.M.*

JULY

01 Monday

★ *Auditorium Arena, Omaha*

02 Tuesday

★ *Salt Palace, Salt Lake City, Utah*

The eighteen-day tour grosses almost $3 million, leaving Elvis and the Colonel almost $2 million as their 65 percent share. Out of

---

May Record Release

Single: "If You Talk in Your Sleep" (#17)/ "Help Me." In hopes of gaining more radio airplay, RCA devotes a considerable amount of time and money to promotion of the new single. As a result, it charts far better than the last but sells 150,000 fewer copies, thus illustrating how misleading the equation of airplay and sales figures, which is used to make up the chart positions, can be.

With Ed Parker, Tennessee Karate Institute, July 4, 1974

this, of course, all expenses must be paid before divvying up what remains, but the sheer numbers should serve as an illustration of the rewards of touring versus Las Vegas, where $600,000 is the outer limit for four weeks' work.

04 Thursday

Back in Memphis, Elvis puts on a ninety-minute karate lecture/demonstration with Ed Parker at the Tennessee Karate Institute, a new school he has established, which will be run by Red West and Elvis' cousin

Jungle room, Graceland

Bobbi Wren (née Mann). National kumite (sparring/kickboxing) karate champion Bill "Superfoot" Wallace, who had run a school for Kang Rhee while getting his master's from Memphis State, has been hired as the principal instructor.

This marks the beginning of Elvis' strongest and longest-lasting commitment to karate. Probably just prior to this time Elvis has gotten it into his mind that he will make a film celebrating karate as both a sport and a philosophical discipline. Ideas about the film continue to shift back and forth, with Elvis occasionally seeing it as an opportunity to return to acting via the medium of the Bruce Lee type of action film and just as often returning to the idea of a straight documentary that will film some of Ed Parker's tournaments in California, then send a karate team to compete in Europe in the fall. In the end, the latter idea wins out, and Elvis comes to see himself as providing a narration that will give the film focus and possibly performing demonstrations along the lines of this Memphis appearance.

05 Friday

Elvis will remain in Memphis for the most part until the middle of the following month, screening occasional movies, shopping at Lansky's, and attending the opening game of the World Football League's Memphis

With Linda Thompson, 1974

Southmen (subsequently renamed the Grizzlies), with the usual spur-of-the-moment excursion to Las Vegas or Palm Springs. During this time Graceland is being extensively refurbished under Linda's supervision. A total of $51,504.66 will be paid to Engle's Interiors by year's end, and $11,386 to Fortner Furniture Company; Donald Furniture Company will supply both the ornate Polynesian-style decor in what has come to be known as the "Jungle Room" and the high-backed red dining room chairs and vivid red living room furniture as well. In the fall the chandeliers and Tiffany shades that can be seen at Graceland today will be installed as well as the stained glass panels with peacocks in the living room and the panels with a rose design in the front foyer. Elvis moves

An artist's rendering of the showroom at the Las Vegas Hilton

into the Howard Johnson's Motel down the street for a short time during these renovations.

AUGUST

05 Monday

Elvis responds to a request for donations to help r & b singer-songwriter Ivory Joe Hunter, best known for "Since I Met You Baby" (and author of several of Elvis' songs, including "My Wish Came True"), who is hospitalized with cancer. Elvis sends a check for $1,000 to the Ivory Joe Hunter Fund in Memphis with a note saying, "I am very sorry to hear of Joe's illness. I have been a long-time admirer of Ivory Joe and his talent. Please tell Joe for me that I wish him a speedy recovery. Joe is a great talent and has been an inspiration to many artists that have come along. It hurts me deeply to hear of his condition. I sincerely hope that this check will be of some help. Thank you for letting me know about Joe. Sincerely, Elvis Presley."

10 Saturday

Elvis trades his Baldwin Grand for the Story and Clark piano that is presently at Graceland.

12 Monday

Elvis flies to Los Angeles.

14 Wednesday

Elvis holds three days of rehearsals at RCA's Sunset Boulevard studio, running tonight from 7:00 P.M. until 1:20 A.M. and continuing on the next two nights from 9:00 P.M. till midnight.

19 Monday

★ *Showroom, Las Vegas Hilton,*
   Las Vegas

Elvis opens the annual "Elvis Summer Festival" at the Las Vegas Hilton with an entirely new program. Gone is the *2001* introduction and the medley of past hits. Blues like "Big Boss Man," "My Baby Left Me," and "Down in the Alley" replace some of the more sentimental numbers, although two songs by Olivia Newton-John more than make up for these omissions. Elvis seems invigorated simply to be reinventing the show, as evidenced by the *Hollywood Reporter*'s panegyric to "the best show . . . in at least three years. [Presley] looks great, is singing better than he has in years, and was so comfortable with his show—almost all new songs—the packed Hilton showroom gave him several standing ovations."

Linda Thompson is present, as usual, on opening night, but Elvis' new girlfriend, Sheila Ryan, takes her

place for most of the rest of the engagement.

20 Tuesday

Despite the reviews, by the second night almost all the new material is gone, the *2001* theme is back, and the show returns to its old format. Perhaps it was the fan reaction, which according to one British fan report (and contrary to the *Hollywood Reporter*), was more reserved than usual on opening night. But it may be nothing more than a bad case of nerves.

Tom Jones is frequently in the audience during this time.

24 Saturday

After the midnight show Elvis paints one of the decorative eighteenth-century, court-of-Louis–XIV ladies on the showroom wall black, with the

---

August Record Release

LP: *Having Fun with Elvis On Stage* (Boxcar label). This recording consists solely of snippets from Elvis' onstage monologues circa 1969–1972, caught when the shows were being taped for live albums. By the Colonel's interpretation of the contract, RCA has no right to spoken-word recordings, and so the Colonel releases it on a limited basis on his own label, an outgrowth of the new merchandising corporation (his first such formal incorporation) that he has established earlier in the year not only to market Elvis product but to work with newly signed artists like Kathy Westmoreland. The deal to which RCA somewhat inexplicably agrees commits the record company to manufacturing the album through its Custom Record division, paying Elvis a fifty-cent royalty per album on all concert sales with a commitment to distribute the album worldwide at some point in the near future *and* to pay a guaranteed advance of $100,000 against royalties. The Colonel sells the record at all the shows, where it excites largely negative comment because, if it is a joke, the joke appears to be on Elvis.

Onstage at Tom Jones' show, Las Vegas, September 3, 1974

help of Jerry and Red. Elvis proudly points to his handiwork in nearly all of the succeeding shows, comparing himself jokingly to Michelangelo painting the ceiling of the Sistine Chapel.

26 Monday

Tonight's performances are canceled either because Elvis has stomach flu or because he is exhausted from his labors. Comedian Bill Cosby fills in.

29 Thursday

Karate has been taking up more and more time during the act, but tonight, during the dinner show, Elvis puts on a full-scale demonstration with Red West, something that the Colonel advises strongly against in future. Although there are no more exhibitions, most likely in the next couple of nights Elvis awards certificates to those

band members and singers who have been studying with him in his suite and presents orchestra leader Joe Guercio, a notable skeptic on the subject, with a tenth-degree black belt baton.

SEPTEMBER

02 Monday

On his final night in Las Vegas Elvis launches into a long, digressive, and embarrassing monologue that focuses somewhat incoherently on a number of personal subjects, including his relationship with Priscilla, who is in the audience with Lisa Marie.

03 Tuesday

With Sheila, Elvis goes to Tom Jones' show at Caesars Palace and then the following night attends his

doctor, Elias Ghanem's, fiancée Vikki Carr's opening at the Tropicana before flying out on Thursday evening.

06 Friday

Elvis purchases his third Stutz Blackhawk, a 1973 model which is presently on exhibit in the car museum at Graceland.

09 Monday

Elvis and Sheila spend five days in Palm Springs before Elvis goes on to Memphis on Saturday.

16 Monday

With Linda, Elvis appears at the Tennessee Karate Institute, putting on an exhibition with Red and Bill Wallace and Ed Parker associate Dave Hebler as the cameras roll. He announces to reporters that he is

With Red West, karate exhibition, September 16, 1974

"preparing to produce his first motion picture. 'I want to have the top karate instructors and their specific specialty in the art of self defense,' said Elvis, while filming part of the documentary," reports the *Memphis Commercial Appeal*.

17 Tuesday

Elvis begins a ten-day buying spree, in the course of which he purchases more than a dozen vehicles for friends, family, strangers, and staff.

He also buys his cousin Billy Smith a 1975 Woodcrest double trailer with three bedrooms for $19,495, so that Billy and his family can live in comfort on the grounds of Graceland. His relationship with Billy, always strong, becomes more and more central from this point on,

right up until the time of his death.

19 Thursday

Linda Thompson's brother Sam's wife, Louise, gives birth to a daughter at Methodist Hospital, and Elvis insists not only on seeing Louise and her newborn baby girl but on visiting the labor room with Linda, where he is recognized, despite a surgical mask. "Oh my God, you look like Elvis Presley," says one mother-to-be, obviously thinking she is hallucinating. "Honey, I *am* Elvis Presley," he declares.

21 Saturday

Probably while he is still in Memphis, with Linda's help Elvis draws up detailed plans for his karate movie, to be called *The New Gladiators*. It will feature "the best men and women in

karate," and promote Elvis' philosophy that karate is a way of "helping a person help himself." He envisions an idealized world in which good conquers evil, and the strong help "the weak and oppressed of all classes, regardless of color, creed, or religion"; the theme of universality will be underlined at the end with a scene in which Elvis stands on a solitary hill "in fighting stance [and], with what looks like every karateka in the world doing the moves with him [he] does the Lord's Prayer *in Indian sign language* as a soft wind gently blows around him. The picture ends with *The Beginning* written across the screen."

26 Thursday

Elvis flies out of Memphis to begin the year's fourth tour.

27 Friday

★ *University of Maryland Cole Fieldhouse, College Park, Maryland*

Tony Brown, the new keyboard player for Voice, witnesses Elvis fall to his knees as he gets out of the limousine, then practically sleepwalk through the show. Newspaper accounts as well as fans express puzzlement and regret about his performance throughout the tour.

28 Saturday

★ *University of Maryland Cole Fieldhouse, College Park*

29 Sunday

★ *Olympia Stadium, Detroit, Michigan, at 2:30 P.M.*

Elvis performs for only thirty minutes, reportedly because of illness.

September Record Release

Single: "Promised Land" (#14) /"It's Midnight" (shipped September 27). "Promised Land," a notable performance from the December Stax session, sells only 320,000 copies but is the highest-ranking single on the charts since "Burning Love," probably a result of stepped-up RCA radio promotion on the record.

30 Monday
★ *University of Notre Dame's Athletic and Convention Center, South Bend, Indiana*

OCTOBER

01 Tuesday
★ *University of Notre Dame's Athletic and Convention Center, South Bend, Indiana*

02 Wednesday
★ *Civic Center, St. Paul, Minnesota*

03 Thursday
★ *Civic Center, St. Paul*

04 Friday
★ *Olympia Stadium, Detroit, Michigan*

05 Saturday
★ *Expo Convention Center, Indianapolis, Indiana, at 2:30 and 8:30 P.M.*

06 Sunday
★ *University of Dayton Arena, Dayton, Ohio, at 2:30 and 8:30 P.M.*

07 Monday
★ *Henry Levitt Arena, Wichita State University, Wichita, Kansas*

08 Tuesday
★ *Convention Center, San Antonio, Texas*

09 Wednesday
★ *Expo Center, Abilene, Kansas*
After the show Elvis flies to Lake Tahoe.

The fifteen-day tour leaves Elvis and the Colonel with $960,000 to divide.

---

11 Friday
★ *High Sierra Room, Sahara Tahoe Hotel, Stateline, Nevada*
Elvis performs eight shows at the Sahara Tahoe in four days to make up for his canceled appearances in May.

15 Tuesday
Sometime during this week, following his October 14 closing, Elvis

Las Vegas, August–September 1974 or fall tour 1974

travels to Las Vegas with Sheila Ryan, putting himself under the care of Dr. Elias Ghanem, one of the physicians who has attended him during his engagements at least since 1972.

21 Monday
Dr. Ghanem orders a series of tests to determine the cause of Elvis' intestinal problems. These turn up a "nonpenetrating ulcer crater," along with "edematous mucosal folds." Elvis remains in a wing of Dr. Ghanem's home specially added on for celebrity patients, undergoing a new "sleep diet," consisting of liquid nourishment and sedated rest, which Dr. Ghanem recommends.

October Record Release

LP: *Having Fun with Elvis On Stage* (#130). RCA wastes no time in putting out the Colonel's collection of "humorous" stage moments. The record sells 130,000 copies at a time when studio albums are generally selling not a great deal more, which would seem to indicate that, on the one hand, there is a predictable group of hardcore fans who will buy virtually anything by Elvis, but, on the other, that it may be difficult to attract anyone *but* these hardcore fans, no matter what product is put out on the market.

NOVEMBER

04 Monday

Full-scale production of the karate movie is finally gearing up after shoots in California and Europe. Jerry Schilling, now officially installed as executive producer, wants to set up an office and hire editors to put together a preliminary cut of the film to attract investors. It is probably during this week that he comes to Las Vegas to confer with Elvis and get Elvis' financial commitment to go ahead. On Friday he has his first meeting with principal editor Bert Lovitt, and the following Wednesday (November 14) Lovitt sets up the editing rooms and office that Jerry has rented on the corner of Hollywood and Vine.

As something more than a footnote, Elvis also arranges to buy Jerry a house from their mutual friend, Rick Husky, while Jerry is in Vegas. "Jerry, you know why I bought you this home?" he says the following month at the official housewarming party. "I know I drove all those other guys crazy buying you this house, but your mother died when you were a year old, and you never had a home, and I wanted to be the one to give it to you."

11 Monday

Elvis leaves Las Vegas in an aircraft leased from the Jet Fleet Corporation to return to Memphis.

19 Tuesday

The *National Enquirer*, in anticipation of Elvis' upcoming fortieth birthday, runs a front-page headline: "Elvis at 40—Paunchy, Depressed and Living in Fear."

20 Wednesday

The Colonel drafts a memo essentially absolving himself of all responsibility for the karate film if Elvis does not follow the attached business plan exactly as he has laid it out. He has disapproved of the project from the start, had even gotten Elvis to promise that under no circumstances would he invest his own money in it, but now, with more than $100,000 of that money committed, he appears to be doing his best to protect Elvis' interests—or at least to try to protect Elvis from himself.

Elvis is back in Palm Springs with Linda, flying Voice out on a whim during Thanksgiving week but finding little use for them once they are there.

DECEMBER

03 Tuesday

Elvis returns to Dr. Ghanem's home probably during this week to undergo a second "sleep diet," accompanied this time by Linda Thompson and Charlie Hodge.

04 Wednesday

The *Nashville Banner* reports that Elvis has a "tummy" ulcer and planned recording sessions have been postponed.

23 Monday

Elvis flies back to Memphis through Amarillo, Texas, with Linda and Lisa Marie.

24 Tuesday

For no known reason other than Elvis' evident loss of interest, the karate movie office is shut down and the project abandoned. There has been a reasonably successful screening of the synched-up footage for potential investors just the previous Friday, and things are closed up in such a hurry that nobody is paid for the last two weeks. The official explanation is Elvis' "health problems."

25 Wednesday

Elvis spends Christmas at Graceland, flying Voice in and out at various points during the holiday season.

29 Sunday

The Colonel has been hearing from different members of the entourage about Elvis' health problems and increasingly erratic behavior over the past few months. With a phone call to Elvis today he confirms that the reports are true and makes the decision that Elvis will not be able to fulfill his January commitment in Las Vegas.

30 Monday

The Colonel informs the Las Vegas Hilton of his determination: "I see no way that this artist can be ready to perform at the Hilton Jan 26, 1975," he writes, and goes on to explain that it would be "an inconsiderate solution for us to pursue the possibility and persuade Elvis to perform for this engagement. I know that you and myself are not ones to be party to such an endeavor. May I suggest that you contact Dr. Ghanem personally for the proper interpretation for the appropriate press release for the postponement of this engagement so it will be a release with the proper and correct interpretation."

In the meantime, at the Colonel's direction, Elvis telegrams his manager: "Dear Colonel. I appreciate your signing any papers necessary for me while I am recuperating. The best from all the boys and myself. Happy New Year. Elvis"

During 1974 Elvis' tours have netted approximately $4 million, to be divided two-thirds/one-third with the Colonel. Income from Las Vegas and Tahoe comes to $650,000–$700,000 (also split two-thirds/one-third), with an additional $750,000 income from RCA split 50-50.

1975

Possibly Huntsville, Alabama, June 1, 1975

JANUARY

08 Wednesday

Elvis celebrates his fortieth birthday "in self-imposed seclusion" at Graceland, writes the *Memphis Commercial Appeal*. His uncle Vester, who, the story notes, "has worked as a security guard at Graceland since 1957, has not seen his nephew since Christmas."

09 Thursday

The Colonel reads reports of a tornado in McComb, Mississippi, that has killed ten people, left hundreds homeless, and caused millions of dollars in property damage. Seeking a way to galvanize Elvis and get him back on the road,

---

January Record Releases

Single: "My Boy" (#20)/"Thinkin' About You" (shipped January 3). Inspired by the unexpected success in England of "My Boy" from the *Good Times* album, RCA releases this song from the December 1973 Stax session as a single, and while it fails to sell 200,000 copies, it becomes Elvis' third Top 20 hit in a row.

LP: *Promised Land* (#47). Put together from what is left of the 1973 Stax material, but with two Top 20 singles included, the album achieves sales of approximately 300,000 copies, somewhat better than the two previous Stax albums.

Colonel Parker flies to Memphis with promoter Tom Hulett the following day and persuades Elvis to do a benefit for the tornado victims as part of a tour that he authorizes his manager to set up.

13 Monday

A special benefit concert for the McComb, Mississippi, tornado victims, to be held on May 5, 1975, is announced by Mississippi governor Bill Waller, who has met with the Colonel and his staff, including Tom Hulett, over the weekend. The concert will come toward the conclusion of a two-week April–May tour which the Colonel has nailed down by the following Tuesday, to begin three weeks after the now-rescheduled Las Vegas engagement ends.

20 Monday

Elvis puts down a deposit of $75,000 on an impounded Boeing 707 previously owned by exiled financier Robert Vesco. With Memphis entertainers Jerry Lee Lewis and Charlie Rich having recently obtained private Learjets, Elvis obviously sees it as time to acquire a plane of his own.

29 Wednesday

Elvis is admitted to Baptist Memorial Hospital in Memphis after Linda awakens to find him struggling for breath. Publicly Elvis is said to be undergoing tests for a "liver problem," but in fact Dr. Nick is once again attempting to get Elvis' use of prescription medication under control. Linda stays with him in the hospital, and the two of them spend time watching the newborns in the nursery over the hospital's closed-circuit television system.

FEBRUARY

05 Wednesday

Vernon Presley has a heart attack at his home and is admitted to the hospital, where he recuperates in a room next to Elvis'.

14 Friday

In order to avoid crowds of fans Elvis is discharged from the hospital between midnight and 1:00 A.M., returning to Graceland to recuperate. Dr. Nick has hopes of regulating Elvis' medication and diet and establishes a routine by which either he or his office nurse, Tish Henley, will stop by Graceland each day to dispense the allotted prescriptions. Dr. Nick also encourages his patient to exercise, playing racquetball with him as often as he can and spending a good deal of time in discussion with Elvis as well. Elvis gets "laugh therapy" from his constant viewing of old *Monty Python* episodes, which he can by now recite by heart.

MARCH

03 Monday

Elvis flies to California for the recording session originally planned for the fall and in preparation for his Vegas opening.

10 Monday

The session begins at RCA's Sunset Boulevard studios at 9:00 P.M. when Elvis arrives with Sheila Ryan and Lisa Marie in tow. RCA is particularly anxious to get enough product from this session for at least one new single and album, because, without a single session by Elvis in 1974, there is virtually nothing left in the can. Working with only his own vocal group, Voice, for backup, Elvis manages to put down four masters by 7:00 A.M., including the Pointer Sisters' "Fairy Tale" (suggested to him by Linda) and Don McLean's "And I Love You So," which he sings to Sheila in the studio.

11 Tuesday

Working pretty much the same hours as the previous night, Elvis once again gets four masters, including a Jerry Lee Lewis–styled "T-R-O-U-B-L-E" and an old r & b favorite, Faye Adams' "Shake a Hand," which Elvis has known since its original 1953 version but which Felton introduces into the session via a Delbert McClinton album.

12 Wednesday

Elvis concludes the session with two more masters before breaking off at 3:30 A.M. The ten songs recorded are barely enough for a brief album but obviously don't offer anything in the way of additional singles material.

13 Thursday

Elvis returns to the RCA studio for rehearsals for the Las Vegas show, working from 9:00 P.M. to 3:00 A.M.

15 Saturday

Elvis travels to Las Vegas by charter jet, while the luggage van delivers his belongings to the Las Vegas Hilton.

16 Sunday

Three days of rehearsals are held, beginning each day at noon. As has happened in advance of every other opening, Elvis tries out many songs that will never be performed on stage, as well as numbers (like Roy Hamilton's "You Can Have Her" and "Suzie Q," the Dale Hawkins song with which James Burton made his mark) that will be played only once or twice during the engagement.

18 Tuesday

★ Showroom, Las Vegas Hilton, Las Vegas

The usual "invitation only" show is postponed until the final night in order to coincide with the opening of the Hilton's new thirty-story addition. Both press and fans describe this first night as revealing a more relaxed, physically fit Elvis, though the singer does make fun of his weight and does not show off his usual karate moves. The one new recording that he incorporates from his recent session is the Perry Como–styled "And I Love You So," though the repertoire does include such recent additions as Olivia Newton-John's "Let Me Be There" and "If You Love Me (Let Me Know)," "My Boy," and "It's Midnight." The one leftover from 1974's revisionist r & b declaration is the Jimmy Reed blues "Big Boss Man."

28 Friday

Barbra Streisand attends the midnight show and, with her boyfriend,

With Sheila Ryan, Las Vegas, March 1975 *(courtesy of Sheila Ryan Caan)*

Warner Brothers, makes its formal offer for Elvis' services, which includes a $500,000 salary and 10 percent of the profits but no participation in either music or recording rights. Elvis and the Colonel, however, are offered the opportunity to produce the two live concerts at the heart of the picture and to profit from them.

14 Monday

The Colonel's response to Streisand's offer comes ten days later via the William Morris Agency. If Elvis is to make this picture, he will have to be paid $1 million in salary, plus $100,000 in expenses and 50 percent of the profits from the first dollar, along with approval of any songs that he is to perform and a separate deal to be negotiated later on soundtrack rights. As the Colonel stresses in his letter to William Morris lawyer Roger Davis, "Mr Presley has indicated that he would like to make this movie, [but] I advised him not to allow this to become a part of making a cheap deal." By the end of the month, there is little worry in this regard, as Elvis' interest has waned and First Artists never seems to come up with a suitable counteroffer.

17 Thursday

With dreams of a fleet, Elvis buys a Convair 880 jet, taken out of service by Delta, for $250,000. The purchase will be announced on June 11, and the plane will be named the *Lisa Marie*, with the subsequent cost of its customized refurbishment in Fort Worth, Texas, coming to an additional half-million dollars. Amenities will include a queen-size bed, gold plumbing fixtures, and a videotape system, and the tail will sport the TCB logo.

18 Friday

Elvis okays the mix for his new album, *Today*.

21 Monday

Elvis returns to Memphis. On this date he buys a house for Linda Thompson in her name at 1254 Old Hickory, near Graceland.

hairdresser Jon Peters, meets backstage with Elvis afterward. The purpose of her visit is to offer him the costarring role in her upcoming remake of the classic Hollywood story of success and failure, *A Star Is Born*. Elvis shows enormous enthusiasm for the project, which is scarcely dampened when the Colonel weighs in over the next few days with such business concerns as who would

control the publishing, what the payment would be, and above all what the alliance with Peters (who is scheduled to produce and direct the picture, despite an utter lack of previous experience) would mean to the way in which Elvis would be served and presented.

APRIL

01 Tuesday

Elvis' final night in Las Vegas begins with the postponed "invitation only" dinner show, followed by the regular midnight show, during which a wild water fight breaks out among singers and musicians. The revelry climaxes when both the Colonel and Lamar appear on stage dressed as Santa Claus.

04 Friday

Elvis leaves Las Vegas and flies to Los Angeles.

Streisand's production company, First Artists, in combination with

March Record Release

Mid-price Album: *Pure Gold.* This ten-track compilation of hits from '56 to '72 once again bears out the Colonel's worst suspicions about the catalogue deal. At the time of its release, albums not sold at full price are not included on the charts, but in later years the album will sell more than 2.5 million copies and continue to demonstrate the extent to which RCA can now exploit Elvis' back catalogue with profit and impunity.

23 Wednesday

Elvis flies to Macon, Georgia, to begin a tour that will come to a conclusion with the benefit in Jackson, Mississippi, for victims of the McComb tornado, followed by two dates in Murfreesboro, Tennessee.

24 Thursday

★ *Coliseum, Macon, Georgia*

Jerry Scheff returns for the first time in two years on bass and notes how much the pace of the show, and Elvis' own physical well-being, have flagged. Reviewers throughout the tour remark upon much the same thing.

25 Friday

★ *Veterans Memorial Coliseum, Jacksonville, Florida*

26 Saturday

★ *Curtis-Hixon Auditorium, Tampa, Florida, at 2:30 and 8:30 P.M.*

27 Sunday

★ *Civic Center Arena, Lakeland, Florida, at 2:30 and 8:30 P.M.*

28 Monday

★ *Civic Center Arena, Lakeland*

29 Tuesday

★ *Middle Tennessee State University Athletic Center, Murfreesboro, Tennessee*

30 Wednesday

★ *Omni, Atlanta, Georgia*

April Record Release

Single: "T-R-O-U-B-L-E" (#35)/"Mr. Songman" (shipped April 22). Despite the infectiousness of its writing and performance, and Elvis' eventual inclusion of the song in his show, "T-R-O-U-B-L-E" fails to ignite the pop music–buying public's interest, bringing Elvis' string of three Top 20 singles in a row to a halt. Sales are flat at 200,000 copies, but the song does achieve a #11 position on the country charts.

MAY

01 Thursday

★ *Omni, Atlanta, Georgia*

02 Friday

★ *Omni, Atlanta*

03 Saturday

★ *Civic Center, Monroe, Louisiana, at 2:30 and 8:30 P.M.*

04 Sunday

★ *Civic Center, Lake Charles, Louisiana, at 2:30 and 8:30 P.M.*

05 Monday

★ *Mississippi State Fair Coliseum, Jackson, Mississippi*

Once again a benefit performance conceived by Colonel Parker creates headlines as Elvis presents Mississippi governor Bill Waller with a check for more than $100,000.

06 Tuesday

★ *Middle Tennessee State University Athletic Center, Murfreesboro, Tennessee*

07 Wednesday

★ *Middle Tennessee State University Athletic Center, Murfreesboro*

At the end of the two-week tour Elvis and the Colonel have more than $700,000 to divide.

---

09 Friday

Although the Colonel has succeeded in prompting Elvis to return to the road, each continues to have his own reasons to be concerned about money, with Elvis in no hurry to curb his spending habits and the Colonel equally unable to curb his gambling losses. In keeping with his characteristic aversion to any corporate money-wasting that will cut into profits, Colonel Parker today writes to RCA Record Tour's Pat Kelleher about the need to keep tour expenses down. "There must be a closer check on the expenditures for hotels, buses, trucks, limousines," he concludes, "so there won't be double expenses."

Back home Elvis screens films at the General Cinema in Whitehaven both tonight and tomorrow night, seeing *Day of the Locust* and *The Four Musketeers.*

29 Thursday

A complaint is filed against Elvis, Red West, and other unnamed bodyguards by Kaijo Peter Pajarinen for a beating he claims to have received outside Elvis' Las Vegas suite on September 7, 1973.

30 Friday

Elvis travels to Huntsville to begin his second 1975 tour.

★ *Von Braun Civic Center, Huntsville, Alabama*

31 Saturday

★ *Von Braun Civic Center, Huntsville, at 2:30 and 8:30 P.M.*

On this tour Elvis uncharacteristically goes out of his way to promote the new single, "T-R-O-U-B-L-E," and presents a show that is in general more upbeat, bringing back such numbers as "Burning Love." He also appears more fit, wearing jumpsuits that he could not fit into earlier in the year.

May Record Release

LP: *Today* (#57). The album is made up entirely of the ten songs from the March session, including "T-R-O-U-B-L-E," and sells between 300,000 and 400,000 copies, while reaching #4 on the country charts.

JUNE

01 Sunday

★ *Von Braun Civic Center, Huntsville, Alabama, at 2:30 and 8:30 P.M.*

Performance, May–June 1975

02 Monday
★ *Municipal Auditorium, Mobile, Alabama, at 4:30 and 8:30 P.M.*

03 Tuesday
★ *University of Alabama Memorial Coliseum, Tuscaloosa, Alabama*

04 Wednesday
★ *Hofheinz Pavilion, Houston, Texas*

05 Thursday
★ *Hofheinz Pavilion, Houston*

06 Friday
★ *Convention Center's Memorial Auditorium, Dallas, Texas*

07 Saturday
★ *Hirsch Coliseum, Shreveport, Louisiana, at 2:30 and 8:30 P.M.*

08 Sunday
★ *State Fair Coliseum, Jackson, Mississippi, at 2:30 and 8:30 P.M.*

09 Monday
★ *State Fair Coliseum, Jackson*

10 Tuesday
★ *Mid-South Coliseum, Memphis, Tennessee*

Recordings made by the sound engineer on this tour appear on the 1980 release *Elvis Aron Presley (The Silver Box),* edited together to simulate a complete show.

The twelve-day tour nets Elvis and the Colonel $811,000.

14 Saturday
At home in Memphis, Elvis sets up occasional screenings at the General Cinema in Whitehaven.

15 Sunday
Elvis is admitted to the Mid-South Hospital for two days for what the press reports as "an extensive eye examination" but what is in fact cosmetic surgery around his eyes. Both Dr. Nick and the plastic surgeon, Dr. Asghan Koleyni, try to talk him out of it, but he insists, threatening to have another doctor perform the procedure if they won't.

17 Tuesday
Elvis is released from the hospital.

18 Wednesday
The 144 Monovale Drive house in Los Angeles is sold for $625,000 to Telly Savalas.

Sometime soon after this Elvis leases an apartment for Linda on Holman Avenue in West L.A.

29 Sunday
Between 11:00 P.M. Sunday and 1:15 A.M. Monday morning Elvis has surgery at a podiatrist's office in Memphis.

JULY

08 Tuesday
Elvis flies to Oklahoma City to begin his third tour of the year, a seventeen-day one this time. Despite all of his efforts, he is unable to persuade Sheila Ryan to join him, and by the end of the tour he recognizes that their relationship is over. Sheila goes on to marry actor James Caan soon after.

★ *Myriad Convention Center Arena, Oklahoma City, Oklahoma*

09 Wednesday
★ *Hulman Civic Center, Terre Haute, Indiana*

10 Thursday
★ *Cleveland Coliseum, Richfield, Ohio*

11 Friday
★ *Civic Center, Charleston, West Virginia*

12 Saturday
★ *Civic Center, Charleston, at 2:30 and 8:30 P.M.*

13 Sunday

★ *International Convention Center, Niagara Falls, New York, at 2:30 and 8:30 P.M.*

14 Monday

★ *Civic Center, Springfield, Massachusetts*

Seemingly unable to keep his emotions in check, Elvis tosses his guitar into the crowd, declaring, "Whoever got the guitar can keep the damned thing—I don't need it anymore."

15 Tuesday

★ *Civic Center, Springfield*

16 Wednesday

★ *Veterans Memorial Coliseum, New Haven, Connecticut*

17 Thursday

★ *Veterans Memorial Coliseum, New Haven*

18 Friday

★ *Cleveland Coliseum, Richfield, Ohio*

Vernon hires an architect to design and oversee construction of a separate building behind Graceland to house a racquetball court and lounge. Scheduled completion date is Christmas 1975.

19 Saturday

★ *Nassau County Veterans Memorial Coliseum, Uniondale, New York, at 2:30 and 8:30 P.M.*

The high point of the evening show is a wrenching performance of "You'll Never Walk Alone" (inspired by Roy Hamilton's 1954 gospel-laced version of the Rodgers and Hammerstein song), with Elvis seated alone at the piano.

20 Sunday

★ *Scope, Norfolk, Virginia, at 2:30 and 8:30 P.M.*

Onstage tensions between Elvis and soprano Kathy Westmoreland, his sometime companion, have been mounting since the last tour. Both in Cleveland and in Uniondale he has introduced her by saying under his breath, "She will take affection from anybody, any place, any time," and

Possibly Asheville, North Carolina, July 23, 1975 (note Band-Aids on Elvis' fingers to prevent his rings from being pulled off by fans)

she has complained about this to Tom Diskin. Elvis' reaction to the complaint is predictable enough, and at this evening's concert, after further remarks on his part, not only Kathy but two of the Sweet Inspirations walk off, leaving Myrna Smith as the sole female backup singer onstage.

21 Monday
★ *Veterans Memorial Coliseum, Greensboro, North Carolina*

After gifts (Lowell Hays, Elvis' personal jeweler, is along on the tour) and an emotional round of apologies, the Sweet Inspirations return, but Kathy does not.

22 Tuesday
★ *Civic Center, Asheville, North Carolina*

Felton Jarvis arranges to fly in soprano Millie Kirkham to take Kathy's place on the last three dates of the tour, but she only gets to watch the show as Kathy at last returns. In a by now all-too-familiar gesture Elvis continues to attempt to mend broken feelings by giving expensive gifts, purchasing what jeweler Lowell Hays will later describe as "practically a whole jewelry store." Six separate invoices show that Elvis spent $85,680 in this week alone.

Jewelry bill for purchases, July 1975 tour

On this day or the next, Elvis becomes angry at Dr. Nick for attempting to limit his intake of medications and waves his Beretta pistol around in front of his father and the physician in his hotel suite. The gun goes off, with the bullet ricocheting off a chair and hitting Dr. Nick in the chest, though it does not injure him.

23 Wednesday
★ *Civic Center, Asheville*

24 Thursday
★ *Civic Center, Asheville*

Frustrated by what he feels is a lack of response from the audience, Elvis serially loses his temper, solicits requests from the crowd, gives away a $6,500 ring to a fan, and throws his guitar into the audience. On checking out of the Roadway Inn, he is presented with an invoice for $367.68, the value of the RCA television set he has shot out in his room, and he subsequently writes a check for that amount.

26 Saturday
Upon completion of the tour, Elvis presents the Colonel with a Grumman Gulfstream G-1 airplane. The Colonel's response, upon hearing the news from a reporter, is less than wholeheartedly enthusiastic. "You've got to be kidding," he says, then turns the gift down on the grounds that he doesn't need it and can't afford it.

27 Sunday
Back in Memphis, on a visit to Madison Cadillac Elvis spends $140,000 for fourteen Cadillacs that he gives away as gifts. One goes to Myrna Smith in appreciation for her loyalty on tour, another to a black bank teller named Mennie Person who has been window-shopping with her family at the dealership when Elvis shows up.

29 Tuesday
Elvis loans Dr. Nick $200,000, interest-free and with no schedule of repayment, for construction of his new home.

AUGUST

02 Saturday
Elvis attends the Memphis Grizzlies opening football game, transporting a busload of friends to Memphis Memorial Stadium in a rented Greyhound. Later in the evening he watches movies at the General Cinema in Whitehaven, where he will continue to screen films for the next three nights.

03 Sunday
Elvis leases a Fairchild F-27 aircraft for one year, putting down a $26,000 deposit against $13,000 a month rental.

06 Wednesday
Elvis gives his dentist, Dr. Lester Hofman, a new Cadillac Seville.

07 Thursday
Arrangements are made for Linda and her friend, Jeannie LeMay, to fly with Elvis' chow, Get Lo, to Boston, so that the dog can receive treatment for a kidney ailment. When the dog is too ill to travel on to the West Boylston veterinary hospital where it is scheduled to be treated, the whole party remains at the Ritz for two days before continuing.

09 Saturday
Elvis attends the Grizzlies' second game, watching as usual from the stadium press box. After the game he invites Grizzlies hostess Jo Cathy Brownlee, whom he has been dating, to fly with him to Meacham Field in Fort Worth to check up on the progress on his new plane, and when she turns him down he gets another girl who is at the game to take her place. He and his party fly on from Fort Worth to Palm Springs, where they remain for three days.

15 Friday
Elvis cancels his lease on the Fairchild F-27 and buys an Aero Jet Commander in its place at a cost of $508,000.

Linda Thompson with Get Lo at Graceland, undated

Late in the evening Elvis leaves Memphis for Las Vegas, very likely in the Jet Commander, but the plane is forced to make an unscheduled stop in Dallas when Elvis has difficulty breathing. After resting for several hours in a motel, he recovers sufficiently to continue on the trip.

16 Saturday

Noon rehearsals are held each day for three days in preparation for the Vegas opening.

18 Monday

★ *Showroom, Las Vegas Hilton, Las Vegas*

Elvis opens with the usual 8:00 P.M. "invitation only" show, and fans and critics alike report that he is overweight, appears tired, and has to sit down for much of the performance. "It is difficult for him to sustain creditable vocal lines or lyric commitments," reads the *Variety* review, "and his dogging of main intent and purpose . . . is very noticeable."

19 Tuesday

Elvis continues the practice that he began in North Carolina of collecting requests from the audience (here Charlie Hodge takes the requests in a champagne bucket) and then doing his best to fulfill them. In this way, such rarely performed songs as "Loving You," "Trouble," and "Crying in the Chapel" turn up in the show, and he regularly duets with Sherrill Nielsen on "Softly As I Leave You," the melancholy song to which he has been drawn ever since first hearing it on the Charles Boyer album *Where Does Love Go?* in 1966. During the dinner show he lies down onstage at one point to sing.

20 Wednesday

Pleading illness, Elvis at the last minute wants to cancel his two evening shows, but the Colonel insists that he perform because no prior notice has been given. Throughout the evening Elvis glances repeatedly at his watch, and by the next morning all traces of his presence are gone—every banner and photograph has been removed, and there is a small sign in the lobby declaring that "the remainder of the Elvis Presley engagement has been canceled due to illness."

21 Thursday

Elvis leaves the Hilton at 6:00 A.M. accompanied by Dr. Nick and flies back to Memphis, where he is admitted to the Baptist Memorial Hospital. An announcement is issued by the Hilton to the effect that "Mr. Elvis Presley was asked by his physician to cancel the remainder of his present engagement. This decision was prompted by a fatigue state which developed in recent weeks. Mr. Presley is to be hospitalized in Memphis for further tests and rest. His physicians do not believe there is any reason for alarm but are doing this for conservation reasons." It is signed by Dr. Elias Ghanem and Dr. George Nichopoulos.

Elvis receives $53,571.45 from the Hilton for his five performances, out of which the Colonel pays the singers and musicians in full for the scheduled two-week engagement. He reassures Elvis that through his extensive contacts and negotiations with "the hotel, ad agency, radio, newspapers and others" he has limited his and Elvis' loss to $39,010.47, immediately contributing his one-third share.

27 Wednesday

Elvis enters into an agreement with Omni Aircraft Sales, an airplane broker, who will sell the Colonel's airplane and the Jet Commander that Elvis purchased just two weeks earlier. In five days, on September 2, Elvis will purchase a 1960 Lockheed JetStar aircraft for $899,702.60.

30 Saturday

While in the hospital Elvis receives get-well calls from both President Nixon (on this date) and Frank Sinatra.

SEPTEMBER

05 Friday

Elvis has been hospitalized not so much for fatigue as for the increasingly depressed state that Dr. Nick has observed, as well as for continuing concerns about his chronic intestinal and bowel problems, a "fatty liver," and a high cholesterol count. Upon his release today, Marion Cocke, the nurse who has attended him during this and his last hospitalization, agrees to alternate shifts with another nurse from the hospital, Kathy Seamon, and Dr. Nick's nurse, Tish Henley, to give Elvis around-the-clock care. To signal his appreciation for Mrs. Cocke's special attention, Elvis arranges for a Pontiac Grand Prix to be delivered to her at the hospital during his stay.

10 Wednesday

Elvis is out on the highway in one of the three-wheeled motorcycles that he bought just before leaving for Las Vegas in August and is ticketed by a policeman.

15 Monday

Out riding his three-wheeler once again, while dressed in a windbreaker and sunglasses and puffing on a cigar, Elvis tells a UPI reporter that he's feeling fine.

September Record Release

Single: "Bringing It Back" (#65) /"Pieces of My Life" (shipped September 30). Elvis' only 1975 recordings have been used up in the ten-track LP *Today,* which was issued in May with the April single ("T-R-O-U-B-L-E") included. To come up with a new single, two more songs have to be lifted from the album, a policy to which the Colonel was always opposed because he felt the fans would legitimately feel they were not getting their money's worth. There is no alternative now, however, and no material with which to follow up when the new single sells only 60,000 copies.

29 Monday

Singer Jackie Wilson suffers a stroke while performing at a nightclub in Cherry Hill, New Jersey. Upon hearing of Wilson's circumstances through George Klein, Elvis immediately sends a check to help defray hospital expenses and medical bills.

OCTOBER

06 Monday

Elvis pays over $30,000 in decorating bills for the house he has bought for Linda Thompson.

Meanwhile, Linda, exhausted from the demands of taking care of Elvis and the ambivalence of his commitment to her, has started spending more time in California to pursue an acting career.

On three-wheeler, Elvis Presley Boulevard

08 Wednesday

Milo High, Elvis' personal pilot, takes Elvis and five others for a brief one-hour flight in Elvis' newly purchased Lockheed JetStar aircraft.

09 Thursday

Milo High flies Elvis and eight others to Dallas and back.

14 Tuesday

Construction on the new racquetball court at Graceland, originally conceived of in July, begins.

21 Tuesday

The Colonel has suggested various schemes to RCA to fulfill Elvis' contractual commitment to the record company. One is a collection of movie title tracks, another an album bringing together all of the songs Elvis has recorded that would be suitable for children, with a special, yet-to-be-recorded version of "Happy Birthday" at the end. RCA has not responded with enthusiasm to any of his sug-

gestions, and today he comes armed with a telegram from Elvis in language that sounds suspiciously as if it may have been dictated. "I would like to work on an album for early '76 release," Elvis declares, "where I would do a combination, part conventional and [part] live from Las Vegas during my Dec. 2–15 engagement. This would give a much better flavor with all the new material. Best regards, Elvis." Nothing more comes of this suggestion than of any of the other schemes.

Milo High flies Elvis' aunt, Delta Biggs, and Mike McGregor to Boston to pick up Elvis' chow, Get Lo, who has been recuperating at the New England Institute for Comparative Medicine veterinary hospital in West Boylston for almost three months.

27 Monday

Tonight and almost every night until November 16 Elvis screens movies at the Crosstown Theater.

NOVEMBER

10 Monday

The *Lisa Marie* is delivered to Memphis, joining the 1960 JetStar and a 1966 Dessault-Falcon, which Elvis has bought for an investment.

18 Tuesday

Elvis telegrams the Colonel to thank him for arranging a special (and highly remunerative) New Year's Eve show at the new Silverdome stadium in Pontiac, Michigan. "We're looking forward to having the best show ever for this event," he concludes.

25 Tuesday

Clearly in need of cash as a result of his recent purchases of airplanes, cars, racquetball courts, and jewelry, as well as a sizable payroll that includes nearly every one of his relatives, increasing medical bills, expensive upkeep on his various houses, and unchecked gifts to friends, family, and casual acquaintances, Elvis borrows $350,000 from the National Bank of Commerce in Memphis, putting up Graceland as collateral. The loan is to be repaid in two equal installments in November of 1976 and 1977.

27 Thursday

With his newly hired personal pilot, Milo High, Elvis takes his first real flight in the *Lisa Marie*, traveling with Linda Thompson to Las Vegas for the start of a two-week engagement that will make up for the abbreviated August stay.

30 Sunday

Rehearsals are held at noon each day for the next three days in the showroom of the Las Vegas Hilton.

By Dr. Nick's orders, Elvis is scheduled to work just one show a night except for Saturdays.

DECEMBER

02 Tuesday

★ *Showroom, Las Vegas Hilton, Las Vegas*

Elvis opens his "Pre-Holiday Jubilee" in better apparent health and spirits than he has been in some time. Not only is the room full every night, but the hotel enjoys 100 percent occupancy at a time of year when 50 percent is the norm.

Voice, a focal point for internal dissension for some time, has left the show, although Sherrill Nielsen remains as a dramatic second voice and featured tenor, while J. D. Sumner and the Stamps take over the opening spot.

13 Saturday

Two soundboard recordings from this evening's performance, "Softly As I Leave You" and "America the Beautiful," will be released posthumously as B-sides of different singles.

15 Monday

Elvis closes his two-week-long Las Vegas engagement. The hotel pays him $263,142.85, leaving $180,000 after expenses to be split two-thirds/one-third with the Colonel.

17 Wednesday

Elvis takes the *Lisa Marie* back to Memphis.

24 Wednesday

In Memphis Marion Cocke has resumed her duties as night nurse at Graceland. According to her recollection, Elvis awakens on Christmas Eve from a dream in which he has gone broke and finds himself deserted by all his friends. The dream was so real, according to Cocke, that Elvis awoke "in a rage," and he doesn't go downstairs until all the people who have been waiting for him have gone home.

25 Thursday

In the evening Elvis takes everyone up in the *Lisa Marie* and gives out jewelry that he has personally selected for each individual from Lowell Hays' collection. The evening ends in somewhat of a debacle, as Elvis' aunt Delta gets drunk and curses out his friends.

30 Tuesday

Around midnight Elvis leaves for Pontiac, Michigan.

31 Wednesday

★ *Silverdome, Pontiac, Michigan*

In another one of the Colonel's almost obligatory "firsts," Elvis' New Year's Eve performance grosses over $800,000, the largest sum ever brought in by a single artist in a one-night appearance. Elvis and the Colonel divide more than $300,000 after expenses, but the show itself is somewhat less of a triumph, with frigid weather and poor sound contributing to the musicians' discomfort and a performance by Elvis (which begins with his ripping his pants) that everyone agrees is not one of his best. Immediately after the show, Elvis flies back to Memphis with his entourage, which includes Vernon, country singer T. G. Sheppard and his wife, Lisa Marie, and Linda, to celebrate the New Year in his bedroom, watching tapes of old *Monty Python* shows.

In Denver police uniform with *(standing, right)* Denver police chief Art Dill and *(kneeling, left to right)* officers Bob Cantwell and Ron Pietrafeso, January 1976

1976

JANUARY

04 Sunday

On the spur of the moment Elvis decides to fly to Colorado for a vacation with Linda and a party of seventeen. After checking into a Denver hotel, Elvis dispatches Joe Esposito and Denver police officers Jerry Kennedy and Ron Pietrafeso to Vail to find enough rental houses and condos for the group.

08 Thursday

Elvis spends the evening of his forty-first birthday in a rental home on the slopes of Vail with Jerry Schilling and Myrna Smith, who have been living together for more than a year and will eventually marry. There has been a good deal of tension on this vacation, largely stemming from Elvis' fluctuations of mood, and Elvis is in a subdued state until Myrna reveals that she has not seen one of his favorite recent films, *Across 110th Street*, starring Yaphet Kotto and Anthony Quinn. This is the catalyst for him to recite, in character, every line of dialogue from the picture.

Many of the guys and their wives and girlfriends have been taking skiing lessons, but Elvis only appears on the slopes at night in a rented skimobile, causing eighteen-year-old Susan

From the roof of the racquetball-court building, showing the back of Graceland, the carport, and the buildings that include Vernon's office on the far right, 1976–77

Ford, daughter of the president, to protest his violation of local regulations and the *National Enquirer* to run a headline, "It's Elvis, the Nightstalker," complete with suitably lunary illustration, in its February 10 edition.

10 Saturday

Dr. Nick and his family fly out to Denver at Elvis' invitation, returning to Memphis the following day. Dr. Nick will return to Colorado on Thursday, January 15, while his son, Dean, remains as one of the regular retinue.

14 Wednesday

As a thank-you gesture to his friends on the force, Elvis purchases two Lincolns and a Cadillac for Jerry Kennedy, Ron Pietrafeso, and police surgeon Gerald Starkey, along with Cadillacs for Linda and Joe's girlfriend, Shirley Dieu. In all, the bill comes to more than $70,000.

16 Friday

Construction on the racquetball court at Graceland is completed.

20 Tuesday

In reporting the story of Elvis' generosity to his police friends, Denver television newsman Don Kinney jokes on the air that he'd like a car, too. Elvis buys him a Seville.

The vacation, meanwhile, has degenerated into festering outbreaks of internal dissension, in the course of which Jerry Schilling quits for good, telling Elvis that "friendship is more important than the job."

22 Thursday

An agreement of this date between Elvis and the Colonel calls for a new 50-50 split on all live appearances: "It is hereby understood by both parties that these [tours] are a joint venture and that Elvis Presley is responsible for the presentation of his stage performance and Colonel Tom Parker and his representatives [for the] advertising and promotion of the show. . . . This authorization and agreement will run for seven years from [January 22, 1976]."

23 Friday

Elvis has returned to Memphis by now to prepare for a special recording session to be held at Graceland. Because neither Felton Jarvis nor the Colonel has been able to lure Elvis into the recording studio since March, Jarvis has arranged for RCA to bring the studio to Elvis via its big red recording truck. Once all the Polynesian-style furniture has been removed, cables are run into the room behind the

The RCA recording truck parked at Graceland, January–February 1976

kitchen that has come to be known as the "Jungle Room."

28 Wednesday

It would appear that the session is scheduled to begin around this date, but it has to be postponed when Elvis is called out of town for the funeral of Denver police officer Eugene Kennedy, Captain Jerry Kennedy's brother. Elvis arranges for J. D. Sumner and the Stamps to sing at the service and wears a specially tailored Denver police captain's uniform to the service.

FEBRUARY

02 Monday

The recording session begins at Graceland amid high hopes that Elvis will be able to deliver in this relaxed domestic setting, but though the band is made up of musicians from the stage show, it doesn't work out that way. Elvis appears on the first night in his Denver police uniform,

and it is evident to all concerned that his mind is not on the session, and even when it is he focuses almost exclusively on downbeat material. Three masters are completed between 8:00 P.M. and 9:30 A.M.

03 Tuesday

This session runs from 9:00 P.M. to 10:30 A.M., but only one song, Neil Sedaka's "Solitaire," is recorded, as Elvis remains distracted and occasionally (when he retreats to his bedroom to plot with Red and Sonny West the violent rubout of all the drug dealers in Memphis) on the verge of delusionary paranoia.

04 Wednesday

Work continues in the same vein with just two more songs completed, including a future single, the new Mark James song "Moody Blue."

05 Thursday

From 9:00 P.M. Thursday evening to 2:00 P.M. Friday afternoon, the session is once again punctuated by

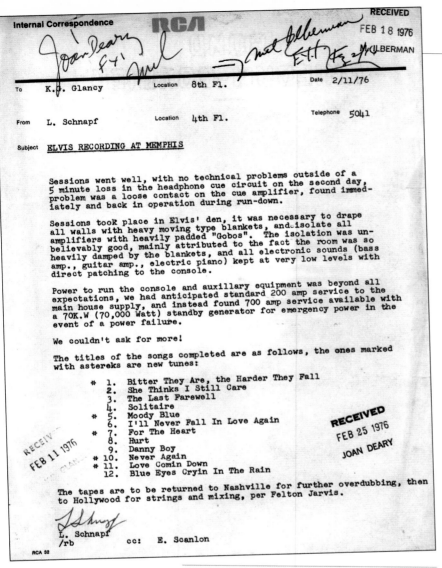

Internal Correspondence **RCA**

RECEIVED FEB 18 1976 M. KULBERMAN

To   K.D. Glancy   Location 8th Fl.   Date 2/11/76

From   L. Schnapf   Location 4th Fl.   Telephone 5041

Subject   ELVIS RECORDING AT MEMPHIS

Sessions went well, with no technical problems outside of a 5 minute loss in the headphone cue circuit on the second day, problem was a loose contact on the cue amplifier, found immediately and back in operation during run-down.

Sessions took place in Elvis' den, it was necessary to drape all walls with heavy moving type blankets, and isolate all amplifiers with heavily padded "Gobos". The isolation was unbelievably good, mainly attributed to the fact the room was so heavily damped by the blankets, and all electronic sounds (bass amp., guitar amp., electric piano) kept at very low levels with direct patching to the console.

Power to run the console and auxillary equipment was beyond all expectations, we had anticipated standard 200 amp service to the main house supply, and instead found 700 amp service available with a 70K.W (70,000 Watt) standby generator for emergency power in the event of a power failure.

We couldn't ask for more!

The titles of the songs completed are as follows, the ones marked with astereks are new tunes:

```
  * 1.  Bitter They Are, the Harder They Fall
    2.  She Thinks I Still Care
    3.  The Last Farewell
    4.  Solitaire
  * 5.  Moody Blue
    6.  I'll Never Fall In Love Again
  * 7.  For The Heart
    8.  Hurt
    9.  Danny Boy
 * 10.  Never Again
 * 11.  Love Comin Down
   12.  Blue Eyes Cryin In The Rain
```

RECEIVED FEB 25 1976 JOAN DEARY

RECEIVED FEB 11 1976

The tapes are to be returned to Nashville for further overdubbing, then to Hollywood for strings and mixing, per Felton Jarvis.

L. Schnapf
/rb   cc: E. Scanlon

RCA 32

RCA report re recording at Graceland, February 11, 1976

many starts and stops. There is no question, however, that Elvis is at last engaged when he cuts a new Dennis Linde song, "For the Heart," and performs a truly heartfelt version of "Hurt," inspired by the 1954 Roy Hamilton original.

06 Friday

Because Thursday night's session ran until early afternoon, tonight's session does not begin until midnight, with two songs completed in eight hours.

07 Saturday

Band members James Burton, Glen D. Hardin, and Jerry Scheff all have to leave due to prior commitments, which would not have interfered had it not been for the session's original postponement. They are replaced by Nashville players Billy Sanford, Bobby Emmons, and Norbert Putnam. The session tonight begins at midnight but achieves little, with a studio version of "America the Beautiful," which will become a staple of the live show in this bicentennial year, scrapped, and just one master recording achieved, Willie Nelson's 1975 hit, "Blue Eyes Crying in the Rain."

08 Sunday

The musicians arrive and wait, but Elvis fails even to put in an appearance and this marks the end of Elvis' first official home recording session. Although it has been a difficult week for all, Felton Jarvis is at least able to deliver to RCA twelve masters, which will provide the basis for one ten-track album, a standalone single, and a second single that is drawn from the album.

10 Tuesday

Elvis is made a captain in the Memphis Police Reserve.

13 Friday

On this day an agreement is drawn up between Elvis and real estate developer T. Michael McMahon, Joe Esposito, and Dr. Nick for the creation of a chain of racquetball courts around the country to be called Presley Center Courts. Elvis enters into the deal evidently believing that he will receive his 25 percent of the company simply for lending his name to the enterprise, which will begin with facilities in Memphis and Nashville.

18 Wednesday

Elvis has returned to Colorado with the idea of buying a vacation home but returns to Memphis almost immediately after his Denver police friends attempt to talk to him about his increasingly erratic behavior.

MARCH

17 Wednesday

The first tour of the year starts amid some confusion. Piano player Glen D. Hardin has handed in his resignation and will be replaced by Nashville session player Shane Keister. Guitarist James Burton and drummer Ronnie Tutt indicate that they, too, intend to leave, and Tutt is replaced by Nashville drummer Larrie Londin, but at the last minute Burton returns.

★ *Freedom Hall Civic Center, Johnson City, Tennessee*

18 Thursday

★ *Freedom Hall Civic Center, Johnson City*

19 Friday

★ *Freedom Hall Civic Center, Johnson City*

Three nights in Johnson City, Tennessee, may be indicative of the

Colonel's disinclination to expose Elvis to the scrutiny of big-city audiences and critics at this stage.

20 Saturday

★ *Coliseum, Charlotte, North Carolina, at 2:30 and 8:30 P.M.*

The highlights of the show generally come in the "big" numbers—"Hurt," "How Great Thou Art," "You Gave Me a Mountain," "America the Beautiful," and, occasionally, "You'll Never Walk Alone." The everyday numbers, however, are done with a singular lack of interest, and Elvis appears "confused" to both fans and reporters, frequently forgetting lyrics to familiar songs.

21 Sunday

★ *Riverfront Coliseum, Cincinnati, Ohio, at 2:30 and 8:30 P.M.*

Onstage with fan, fall 1976

22 Monday

★ *Kiel Auditorium, St. Louis, Missouri*
Despite their new "joint venture" agreement, the Colonel continues to take his old one-third commission with the explicit understanding that Elvis will pay him back when he is not quite so strapped for cash.

26 Friday

In the evening Elvis comes across an accident scene on I-240 and, carrying out his official police function, helps the victims after first displaying his badge.

27 Saturday

Elvis takes his three-wheeled Supercycle for a spin on the Graceland grounds with Linda.

At accident scene, Memphis, March 26, 1976

March Record Releases

Single: "Hurt" (#28)/"For the Heart" (shipped March 12). "Hurt" is one of the recently recorded songs that means the most to Elvis, and "For the Heart" is one of the best, but the record sells only 250,000 copies.

LP: *The Sun Sessions* (#76). Encouraged by sales of the Legendary Performer series, RCA rushes out a compilation originally produced in England. Although it does not do as well as the earlier packages, it sells 300,000 copies initially and, in various forms, will become a cornerstone of the Elvis catalogue.

APRIL

03 Saturday
Elvis flies out of Memphis, most likely for a brief visit to Las Vegas or Palm Springs.

07 Wednesday
Elvis returns to Memphis for two weeks, until the start of the next tour.

21 Wednesday
★ Kemper Arena, Kansas City, Missouri

Elvis begins a hastily scheduled six-day tour that will serve as a lead-in to his Tahoe engagement. Drummer Ronnie Tutt has returned to the band and observes that "there were nights he was so tired or so down I felt like I had to physically hit the drums much, much harder than I had before."

A picture appears in the *Memphis Press-Scimitar* showing Joe Esposito, Dr. Nick, and Mike McMahon ceremonially breaking ground at Mendenhall and Mt. Moriah in Memphis, the site of one of the first two racquetball facilities to be developed under the auspices of Presley Center Courts, Inc. According to the photo caption, the Memphis facility will open in September and is Elvis' "first business venture outside the entertainment world."

22 Thursday
★ City Auditorium Arena, Omaha, Nebraska

23 Friday
★ McNichols Arena, Denver, Colorado

24 Saturday
★ Sports Arena, San Diego, California

25 Sunday
★ Arena, Long Beach, California, at 2:30 and 8:30 P.M.

According to the *Long Beach Press-Telegram*, "An eerie silence filled the concert hall when he sang, 'And now the end is near,' the opening line of the Frank Sinatra favorite 'My Way.' It was like witnessing a chilling prophecy."

26 Monday
★ Coliseum, Seattle, Washington

27 Tuesday
★ Coliseum, Spokane, Washington

After this evening's show Elvis flies to Lake Tahoe.

30 Friday
★ High Sierra Theater, Sahara Tahoe, Stateline, Nevada

Elvis opens an eleven-day stand that will pay $315,000 for one 10:00 P.M. show on weeknights, two shows a night on Fridays and Saturdays. Private investigator John O'Grady, with whom Elvis has been associated since 1970, visits during the gig and later describes his reaction. "I felt so strongly for him I cried. He was fat. He had locomotive attacks where he couldn't walk. . . . I really thought he was going to die." In the aftermath of this experience, O'Grady and Elvis'

April Record Release

LP: *From Elvis Presley Boulevard, Memphis, Tennessee* (#41). Although it is a good hook to exploit, and RCA and the Colonel do their best to exploit it, the Graceland recordings ignite little out-of-the-ordinary interest in the pop market, but it *is* a #1 country album for four weeks.

Los Angeles attorney, Ed Hookstratten, will talk about trying to get Elvis committed to the drug-treatment program at the Scripps Clinic in San Diego, but nothing ever comes of this.

MAY

09 Sunday
Elvis closes out the Tahoe engagement and flies home to Memphis.

21 Friday
Elvis executes a quitclaim deed permitting the City of Memphis to widen Elvis Presley Boulevard in front of Graceland.

27 Thursday
★ Athletic Center, Bloomington, Indiana

Elvis begins another short tour of eleven days, and reviews continue to report on his deteriorating condition.

28 Friday
★ James W. Hilton Coliseum, University of Iowa, Ames, Iowa

29 Saturday
★ Myriad Center Arena, Oklahoma City, Oklahoma

30 Sunday
★ Ector County Coliseum, Odessa, Texas, at 2:30 and 8:30 P.M.

Elvis last played Odessa in 1955, when he appeared on four separate occasions before screaming audiences of 750 to 2,000. This time total attendance comes to 16,000.

31 Monday
★ Municipal Coliseum, Lubbock, Texas

JUNE

01 Tuesday
★ Community Center Arena, Tucson, Arizona

02 Wednesday
★ Civic Center Coliseum, El Paso, Texas

03 Thursday
★ *Tarrant County Convention Center, Fort Worth, Texas*

04 Friday
★ *Omni, Atlanta, Georgia*

05 Saturday
★ *Omni, Atlanta, at 2:30 and 8:30 P.M.*

06 Sunday
★ *Omni, Atlanta*

On this tour Elvis and the Colonel take in $800,000, which they continue to divide according to the old two-thirds/one-third split.

---

07 Monday
Elvis returns to Memphis in the early afternoon and for the next few weeks remains mostly in his room, rarely seeing anyone except his cousin Billy and Billy's wife, Jo, as well as Lisa Marie, who visits for ten days.

16 Wednesday
It has become increasingly difficult for the Colonel to get in touch with Elvis, and he now writes to him with more than a hint of desperation. "As I told Vernon today, I have not heard from anyone since I got back, neither from Sonny or from any other member of your staff. I just wanted you to know in the event you feel that they are in contact with me but they are not." Joe Esposito is living in California. Lamar Fike works and lives in Nashville. Jerry Schilling is gone. And Elvis' relationship with Sonny and Red West is strained, in part because of the various lawsuits brought against Elvis for his bodyguards' actions, but more because of the general air of suspicion and mistrust that now permeates the group.

25 Friday
★ *Memorial Auditorium, Buffalo, New York*

26 Saturday
★ *Civic Center, Providence, Rhode Island, at 2:30 and 8:30 P.M.*

Bicentennial suit, March–September 1976

27 Sunday
★ *Capital Center Arena, Landover, Maryland, at 2:30 and 8:30 P.M.*
Singer Elton John visits Elvis backstage after the evening show, recalling later that "he had dozens of people around him, supposedly looking after him, but he already seemed like a corpse."

28 Monday
★ *Spectrum, Philadelphia, Pennsylvania*

29 Tuesday
★ *Coliseum, Richmond, Virginia*

30 Wednesday
★ *Coliseum, Greensboro, North Carolina*

JULY

01 Thursday
★ *Hirsch Coliseum, Shreveport, Louisiana*

02 Friday
★ *Louisiana State University Assembly Center, Baton Rouge*

03 Saturday
★ *Tarrant County Convention Center, Fort Worth, Texas*
Elvis and Sonny West have a blowup over Vernon's cancellation of plane tickets for Sonny's wife and son to come join him in Fort Worth. It is just the latest in a series of

increasingly unpleasant confrontations within the group.

04 Sunday
★ *Mabee Center, Oral Roberts University, Tulsa, Oklahoma, at 2:30 P.M.*

05 Monday
★ *Mid-South Coliseum, Memphis, Tennessee*

Elvis wears his red-white-and-blue bicentennial jumpsuit, as he has for much of the tour. "America the Beautiful" is the highlight of the show, but his spirits are far from festive, and the fireworks display and party that have been scheduled for after the show are canceled.

06 Tuesday
Elvis gives J. D. Sumner a check for $25,000 with which to purchase a new touring bus for the Stamps.

07 Wednesday
Elvis leaves in the early hours of the morning for Los Angeles, then flies on to Palm Springs.

13 Tuesday
In the morning a series of phone calls goes out from Vernon's office, first to Sonny West in Memphis, then to Red in California and karate expert Dave Hebler. Each is to be terminated with one week's pay, because, Vernon says with a certain amount of disingenuousness, it has been a difficult year and now it is belt-tightening time. The underlying causes have far more to do with the friction within the group and Vernon's never-far-from-the-surface suspicion that his son is somehow being taken advantage of. Each of the three men is deeply offended not just to be let go so unceremoniously but to be let go without Elvis even taking the trouble to deliver the message himself. Red's is, understandably, the most emotional reaction, since his ties with Elvis go back to Humes High.

On this same day Elvis trades the Dessault-Falcon airplane, which he purchased in late 1975 as an investment, for a second Lockheed JetStar. The first JetStar aircraft will become the center of a long, drawn-out FBI investigation into what appears to be a sophisticated swindle perpetrated on Elvis and Vernon involving the leasing and refurbishing of the aircraft. The case is not concluded until after Elvis' death.

14 Wednesday
Elvis travels on to Las Vegas with Linda, where he once again puts himself under Dr. Ghanem's care.

23 Friday
★ *Freedom Hall, Louisville, Kentucky*

Elvis begins his fifth tour of the year, with review after review criticizing what appear to be little more than perfunctory performances and Elvis himself in a sad state of disrepair.

24 Saturday
★ *Civic Center, Charleston, West Virginia, at 2:30 and 8:30 P.M.*

25 Sunday
★ *Onondaga War Memorial Auditorium, Syracuse, New York*

26 Monday
★ *Community War Memorial Auditorium, Rochester, New York*

27 Tuesday
★ *Onondaga War Memorial Auditorium, Syracuse, New York*

28 Wednesday
★ *Civic Center, Hartford, Connecticut*

The Colonel confronts Elvis about the show, and Elvis is so shaken by the criticism that he seeks out promoter Tom Hulett for reassurance. Hulett tells Elvis, "You are the biggest entertainer there is, and everybody loves you," but Hulett is also aware of how far Elvis has fallen.

29 Thursday
★ *Civic Center, Springfield, Massachusetts*

30 Friday
★ *Veterans Memorial Coliseum, New Haven, Connecticut*

31 Saturday
★ *Hampton Coliseum, Hampton Roads, Virginia*

AUGUST

01 Sunday
★ *Hampton Coliseum, Hampton Roads, Virginia, at 2:30 P.M.*

Newport News Times-Herald reporter Cheryl Tucker describes a desultory performance which is still greeted with uncritical adulation by Elvis' loyal fans. "Judging by his performance," she writes with discernment, "they were screaming for what he was, what he symbolizes, rather than what he is."

02 Monday
★ *Civic Center, Roanoke, Virginia*

03 Tuesday
★ *Cumberland County Memorial Auditorium, Fayetteville, North Carolina*

04 Wednesday
★ *Cumberland County Memorial Auditorium, Fayetteville*

05 Thursday
★ *Cumberland County Memorial Auditorium, Fayetteville*

06 Friday
In the evening Elvis returns to Memphis.

10 Tuesday
Through his attorney Elvis withdraws precipitately from the racquetball agreement. He wants his name taken off the project because, he says, contrary to his initial understanding, he has come to realize that he is expected to contribute a considerable amount of money to uphold his end of the partnership. More consequential than the legal entanglement that ensues is his anger at Joe Esposito and Dr. Nick for getting him into the deal in the first place. He mutters about firing Joe, and in a late-night phone call to Dr. Nick a few days later from Palm

Springs, to which he decamps on this day, he announces that he is going to take another doctor out on the next tour.

27 Friday

★ *Convention Center Arena, San Antonio, Texas*

Elvis begins his sixth tour with a rousing performance, momentarily raising the band's hopes.

Dr. Ghanem has replaced Dr. Nick, although Dr. Nick's nurse, Tish Henley, who moved into one of the trailers behind Graceland earlier in the year, remains with the tour. Linda Thompson's brother, Sam, who quit the Memphis Sheriff's Department with just one day's notice to go out on the last tour, is now officially cohead of security with Dick Grob, the former Palm Springs policeman, in Red and Sonny's place. Larry Geller also joins this tour, part of the entourage for the first time since his expulsion in 1967. He has spent more and more time with Elvis in recent months, after renewing his acquaintance in Las Vegas several years earlier. All opposition to Larry has faded by now; even the Colonel's perspective is at this point a pragmatic one. If Larry's presence, and Elvis' renewed interest in spiritual studies, keep Elvis happy, so much the better for the show.

28 Saturday

★ *The Summit, Houston, Texas, at 2:30 P.M.*

Bob Claypool of the *Houston Post* describes the show with dismay the next day as a "depressingly incoherent, amateurish mess served up by a bloated, stumbling and mumbling figure who didn't act like 'The King' of anything, least of all rock 'n' roll." The critic's lead: "Elvis Presley has been breaking hearts for more than 20 years now, and Saturday afternoon in the Summit—in a completely new and unexpected way—he broke mine."

The Colonel's reaction is one close to panic. If reporters can see it, then the fans can see it. And he is devastated to realize that the off-duty Houston policemen who augment the security force are talking about it too. He fixes things with the police through his old friend, Houston Livestock Show chairman Bill Williams, and he tries to fix things with Elvis by calling on Dr. Nick to return, which Elvis' regular physician does the following day.

29 Sunday

★ *Municipal Auditorium, Mobile, Alabama, at 2:30 and 8:30 P.M.*

30 Monday

★ *University of Alabama Memorial Coliseum, Tuscaloosa, Alabama*

31 Tuesday

★ *Coliseum, Macon, Georgia*

SEPTEMBER

01 Wednesday

★ *Coliseum, Jacksonville, Florida*

02 Thursday

★ *Curtis Hixon Hall, Tampa, Florida*

Bitsy Mott, the Colonel's brother-in-law who has worked with Elvis off and on from 1956 to 1970, is shocked by his first view of the show in some years, leaving with his wife before it is over.

03 Friday

★ *Bayfront Center, St. Petersburg, Florida*

04 Saturday

★ *Civic Center, Lakeland, Florida, at 2:30 and 8:30 P.M.*

05 Sunday

★ *Mississippi State Fair Civic Center, Jackson, Mississippi*

06 Monday

★ *Von Braun Civic Center, Huntsville, Alabama, at 2:30 and 8:30 P.M.*

This is the last road date on which Elvis performs two shows.

07 Tuesday

★ *Convention Center, Pine Bluff, Arkansas*

08 Wednesday

★ *Convention Center, Pine Bluff*

This tour's profits total nearly one million dollars.

11 Saturday

Back in Memphis, Elvis is seen out riding his motorcycle.

By now rumors are spreading that Red, Sonny, and Dave Hebler are writing a book that will reveal the truth about their life with Elvis. In fact, after first approaching Rick Husky and former *Los Angeles Herald-Examiner* writer Frank Lieberman, the three are in the midst of forming a collaboration with Steve Dunleavy of *The Star* to produce just such an exposé. Elvis' feelings on the matter run from grim resignation to bursts of anger directed against his former employees and old friends.

19 Sunday

Elvis flies to Palm Springs, returning on Sunday the twenty-sixth.

OCTOBER

04 Monday

Before leaving to join Linda at her new, larger apartment, just down the street from her old one in West L.A., Elvis is spotted once again out riding his motorcycle.

05 Tuesday

Elvis flies to Los Angeles and stays with Linda at her new apartment for about a week, picking up a new Ferrari that he has ordered in Hollywood. He also meets with private detective John O'Grady, who has been trying to talk Elvis into taking a more proactive role in keeping the bodyguards' book from being published. Elvis authorizes O'Grady to approach the three men with a cash offer, and O'Grady reports back to Elvis at Linda's apartment on the failure of the plan. He has offered each man payment of $50,000 along with an "education allowance" to prepare him for a new line of work, but they have turned him down flat.

O'Grady wants to ratchet up the pressure, but Elvis is noncommittal.

11 Monday

Elvis returns to Memphis with Linda, arriving home at about 4:00 A.M. When Red West calls from California later in the day, Charlie Hodge tells him Elvis is asleep, although Red suspects he is listening in on the upstairs line.

12 Tuesday

Elvis returns Red's call, and the two have an extended conversation for the first time since the abrupt firing. On the tape that Red secretly makes, Elvis sounds confused and incoherent, with the overall tone regret on both sides. Elvis is never quite able to bring himself to confront Red directly, simply saying, "If you need me for anything, I would be more than happy to help out," and adding, "You do whatever you have to do. I just want you and Pat [Red's wife] to know I'm still here."

14 Thursday

★ *Chicago Stadium, Chicago, Illinois*
Elvis begins his seventh tour of the year.

15 Friday

★ *Chicago Stadium, Chicago*

16 Saturday

★ *Duluth Arena, Duluth, Minnesota*

17 Sunday

★ *Metropolitan Sports Center, Minneapolis, Minnesota*

18 Monday

★ *Arena, Sioux Falls, South Dakota*

19 Tuesday

★ *Dane County Coliseum, Madison, Wisconsin*

20 Wednesday

★ *Notre Dame University Athletic and Convention Center, South Bend, Indiana*

21 Thursday

★ *Wings Stadium, Kalamazoo, Michigan*

22 Friday

★ *University of Illinois Assembly Hall, Champaign, Illinois*

23 Saturday

★ *Coliseum, Richfield, Ohio*

24 Sunday

★ *Roberts Stadium, Evansville, Indiana*

25 Monday

★ *Memorial Coliseum, Fort Wayne, Indiana*

26 Tuesday

★ *University of Ohio, Dayton, Ohio*
The Star publishes an article by Red and Sonny's collaborator, Steve Dunleavy, that includes portions of the surreptitiously taped conversation between Elvis and Red. Headlined "ELVIS' DRAMATIC PLEA TO HIS EX-BODYGUARDS: DON'T WRITE THAT BOOK ABOUT ME," it is a devastating wake-up call for Elvis, proving that what he has considered till now to be in part just another private quarrel between friends has now spun wholly out of control.

27 Wednesday

★ *Southern Illinois University Arena, Carbondale, Illinois*

This tour brings in $1,005,000.09 in profits, which is still being divided two-thirds/one-third with the Colonel.

28 Thursday

The RCA recording truck is parked behind Graceland upon Elvis' return to Memphis.

29 Friday

A makeshift studio is set up once again in the "Jungle Room," with the first night's session running from 9:00 P.M. to 8:00 A.M. Three songs are recorded, including the next single A-side, "Way Down." As at the last home recording session, Elvis once again spends much of the evening in his bedroom, occasionally inviting some of the sixteen singers and musicians to join him. He even gives

away some of his old clothes, outfitting J. D. Sumner and the Stamps in Superfly–style outfits.

30 Saturday

On the second night the musicians record instrumental tracks while waiting for Elvis to come downstairs. Not long after he at last appears, the session is interrupted by the delivery of a shipment of new Harley-Davidson motorcycles, which Elvis insists on taking for trial runs, up and down the driveway and to Linda's house around the corner. Later Elvis reappears from upstairs, brandishing a Thompson submachine gun. Finally, toward morning, he offers a rare apology to the assembled group, admitting that he is not in the mood for recording. Felton cancels the remainder of the session, and the night ends with Elvis calling up the *Lisa Marie* for the West Coast–based singers and musicians and the JetStar for the Nashville players and then making sure each musician has special arrangements for his ride home. He even goes so far as to make a gift of his white Lincoln limousine to J. D. Sumner, so that J.D. and the Stamps can ride back to Nashville in style.

NOVEMBER

01 Monday

Elvis spends much of the next three weeks flying back and forth between Memphis, Denver, Palm Springs, and Dallas.

16 Tuesday

Elvis has had his new Ferrari delivered to Memphis in a Ryder rental truck.

19 Friday

George Klein brings Terry Alden, the present Miss Tennessee, out to Graceland with her two sisters, Rosemary and Ginger. Ginger, nineteen, is the current Miss Mid-South Fair and former Miss Traffic Safety, and while George thought it was Terry to whom he would be attracted, Elvis is immediately drawn to the youngest sister.

20 Saturday

Elvis' Saturday-night date with Ginger starts as a flight to view the Memphis skyline but ends with a trip to Vegas, chaperoned by his cousin Patsy and her husband, Gee Gee Gambill. Ginger calls her mother for permission, and the group flies back the next day.

23 Tuesday

Jerry Lee Lewis appears at the gates of Graceland in the early hours of the morning, waving a gun and demanding to see Elvis. According to the *Memphis Press-Scimitar*, "Witnesses were quoted as saying [he] was screaming and cursing . . . and police reported the singer was sitting in his car with a loaded .38 caliber derringer resting on his knee when they arrived." This is the second night in a row that Lewis has shown up, telling Elvis' cousin Harold Loyd that he and Elvis have been trying to get together for a long time. Elvis watches the whole drama on closed-circuit monitors.

24 Wednesday

★ *Centennial Coliseum, Reno, Nevada*
Elvis begins his eighth tour of 1976, accompanied by Linda Thompson.

25 Thursday

★ *University of Oregon McArthur Court, Eugene, Oregon*

26 Friday

★ *Memorial Coliseum, Portland, Oregon*

27 Saturday

★ *University of Oregon McArthur Court, Eugene, Oregon*

28 Sunday

★ *Cow Palace, San Francisco, California*
Elvis calls up Ginger Alden and invites her to join the tour, sending the JetStar to bring her out to California while suggesting to Linda that she looks a little worn out and might like to take a little time for herself in Memphis.

29 Monday

★ *Cow Palace, San Francisco*
Ginger arrives but is confined to her room because Elvis has been unable to persuade Linda to leave. When Linda finally does depart, it is for the last time, as she soon takes up a relationship with keyboard player David Briggs that has begun several months earlier. Although she speaks to Elvis a number of times on the phone, she never sees him again.

30 Tuesday

★ *Convention Center, Anaheim, California*
Ginger attends this show, and many detect a noticeable improvement in Elvis' performance. He will later tell Larry Geller that he was inspired by Ginger's presence.

November Record Release

Single: "Moody Blue" (#31)/"She Thinks I Still Care" (shipped November 29). With nothing from the most recent session ready to be used for a single (every cut requires extensive overdubbing), RCA brings out the last of the unreleased material from the February sessions. The record peaks three places below the last single, "Hurt," but sells 50,000 more copies and is a #1 country hit.

DECEMBER

02 Thursday

★ *Showroom, Las Vegas Hilton, Las Vegas*
Elvis goes directly to Las Vegas with Ginger accompanying him, opening his "Pre-Holiday Jubilee" with a single dinner show. He will continue to perform one show a night except for Fridays and Saturdays. The entire two-week run is, as always, sold out.

05 Sunday

Elvis has started out with strong performances but falls just before tonight's show, suffering an ankle injury that will plague him for days. Reviews and fan reports paint a mixed picture of a performer who is not in the best physical condition,

who seems "tired" and "sad," but who continues always to make an effort to connect with his audience.

06 Monday

Elvis cuts this show short because of pain from his ankle injury.

07 Tuesday

Vernon, who is in the audience for tonight's show, is later taken to the hospital with what appears to be another heart attack. Evidently it is a false alarm, because by Thursday he will be released—but it is equally evident that he is a very sick man.

10 Friday

Ginger has been with Elvis for almost two weeks now. When she tells him a few days into the Hilton engagement that she has to go home to see her family, at first he enlists Dr. Ghanem to persuade her to stay, then flies her mother and father, her brother and his wife, and her two sisters to Las Vegas on this date. Today's *Memphis Commercial Appeal* runs a story in which Ginger's mother confirms that Elvis has recently given her daughter a Lincoln Continental, although she says "she doesn't think it was an engagement gift" and is unaware of any definite plans for an impending marriage.

During the late show this evening, the fatigue that Elvis has increasingly shown throughout the week seems to come to a head as he announces casually, "I hate Las Vegas," to bewildered applause from the crowd. At the conclusion of the next song he picks up the mike from the stand and asks, "Does anyone want this tinny sonofabitch?" He goes on to suggest that he may not continue, "because these damn microphones are [so] cheap. I ain't gonna do it, you know. 'Cause this is my living, folks, my life." He finishes the show, but not without a number of other conversation-stopping asides.

12 Sunday

Memphis Press-Scimitar reporter Bill Burk writes of Elvis' closing

Performing, October–December 1976

performance tonight: "One walks away wondering how much longer it can be before the end comes" and speculates as to "why the King of rock 'n' roll would subject himself to possible ridicule by going onstage so ill-prepared."

In his dressing room after the show, Elvis seeks religious counsel from tele-vangelist Rex Humbard, speaking despairingly of the life that he is lead-ing and its lack of meaning. "I took both his hands in mine," Humbard later recounts, "[and] said, 'Elvis, right now I want to pray for you.' He said, 'Please do,' and started weeping."

13 Monday

Elvis returns to Memphis for a two-week rest before hitting the road again on a brief five-day tour.

27 Monday

★ *Wichita State University, Henry Levitt Arena, Wichita, Kansas*

28 Tuesday

★ *Memorial Auditorium, Dallas, Texas*

29 Wednesday

★ *Birmingham-Jefferson County Coliseum, Birmingham, Alabama*

30 Thursday

★ *Omni, Atlanta, Georgia*

31 Friday

★ *Civic Center Arena, Pittsburgh, Pennsylvania*

This is a very different occa-sion from the previous New Year's Eve, showing Elvis at his best in a ninety-minute perfor-mance that is undoubtedly spurred on by Ginger's presence.

After the concert Vernon informs Elvis of his cousin Bobbi Mann's death at thirty-eight after taking an overdose of pills several days earlier. The whole party returns to Memphis at 6:30 A.M.

Onstage singing with lyric sheet, probably Pittsburgh, Pennsylvania, December 31, 1976

With Ginger Alden, Hawaii, March 1977

1977

With comedian Jackie Kahane, 1976–77

JANUARY

03 Monday

Elvis flies Ginger and her family to Harrison, Arkansas, to attend the funeral of Ginger's grandfather.

04 Tuesday

Elvis, Ginger, and Ginger's sister, Rosemary, fly to Palm Springs to celebrate Elvis' forty-second birthday on January 8.

09 Sunday

Very likely on this date Elvis urges his dentist, Max Shapiro, to marry his fiancée in Palm Springs, then gets Larry Geller to perform the ceremony on the spot, with Elvis supplying the rings and Ginger as maid of honor. He takes the occasion to muse out loud about the possibility of his marrying Ginger in the near future.

14 Friday

Elvis, Ginger, and Rosemary return to Memphis.

20 Thursday

Felton Jarvis has arranged for Elvis to record at Buzz Cason's new up-to-date Nashville studio, Creative Workshop, where many of the musicians have worked before and Felton is confident Elvis will feel at home. The band is, simply, Elvis' own, plus Chip Young on guitar and Randy Cullers on percussion. But just hours before the scheduled start Joe Esposito calls to say Elvis has not yet left Memphis.

21 Friday

Elvis finally arrives in Nashville, but without Ginger. The delay seems to have been brought about by his futile attempts to persuade her to accompany him, and his mood definitely reflects her absence. After registering at the Sheraton South Hotel, Elvis stays in his room complaining of a sore throat while the musicians wait in the studio.

22 Saturday

Elvis returns to Memphis without ever setting foot in the studio, leaving Felton Jarvis to complete overdubs on the material recorded at Graceland in October before canceling the remainder of the session.

26 Wednesday

Elvis calls jeweler Lowell Hays in the early hours of the morning to order an engagement ring for Ginger, which he wishes to present to her in the evening. Hays tells him there simply isn't time to obtain another stone as big as the eleven-and-a-half-carat center diamond in his TCB ring that Elvis wants it to match, and eventually Elvis is persuaded to allow Hays to remove the diamond from Elvis' own ring. Late in the evening Elvis gets down on one knee to propose to Ginger, who is seated in his reading chair in the bathroom.

28 Friday

The *Nashville Banner* publishes a story by Bill Hance in his column, "Wax Fax," about Elvis' aborted recording session. Not only is it revealing of Elvis' distraught emotional state, it suggests deep fissures in the inner circle, as Hance quotes "friends" and "aides" to the effect that Elvis is "paranoid and . . . afraid to record." Colonel Parker, according to the column, told Elvis to "get off your tail [and] fulfill your commitment, or there will be no more tours." Many Presley aides, Hance writes, "contend the singer's new girlfriend, Ginger Alden, 20, is 'absolutely running him ragged.'"

FEBRUARY

01 Tuesday

At 2:30 A.M. Elvis and Ginger leave for Las Vegas with Billy and Jo Smith, then travel on to Los Angeles to celebrate Lisa Marie's ninth birthday, after which they return to Memphis.

12 Saturday

★ *Sportatorium, Hollywood, Florida*

Elvis insists that Ginger accompany him on this first tour of the year. The highlights of the show for the most part remain the great dramatic displays, "Unchained Melody," "Hurt," and "How Great Thou Art." This is David Briggs' last tour. He has come out at Elvis' insistence, not knowing whether, or how much, Elvis is aware of his relationship with Linda, but he finds out when Elvis pulls the plug on his electronic keyboard toward the end of the tour.

13 Sunday

★ *Auditorium, West Palm Beach, Florida*

14 Monday

★ *Bayfront Center, St. Petersburg, Florida*

15 Tuesday

★ *Sports Stadium, Orlando, Florida*

16 Wednesday

★ *Garrett Coliseum, Montgomery, Alabama*

17 Thursday

★ *Civic Center, Savannah, Georgia*

18 Friday

★ *Carolina Coliseum, Columbia, South Carolina*

19 Saturday

★ *Civic Center Freedom Hall, Johnson City, Tennessee*

Because Ginger misses her family, Elvis flies them in for the final days of the tour.

20 Sunday

★ *Coliseum, Charlotte, North Carolina*

Much to Ginger's sister, Terry's, embarrassment, Elvis calls Terry up on stage to play a short selection of classical music on the piano.

21 Monday

★ *Coliseum, Charlotte*

After the show Elvis returns to Memphis.

MARCH

03 Thursday

Elvis has planned a vacation in Hawaii in order to show the islands to Ginger. Before leaving, he takes care of several business matters, including a loan to Dr. Nick for an additional $55,000 at 7 percent interest with a repayment schedule of twenty-five years (this is on top of an earlier, previously unsecured and interest-free loan of $200,000). Also, at his father's urging, in the early hours of the morning he has finally signed his will, which designates Vernon as executor and trustee, entrusting to him total responsibility for the "health education, comfortable maintenance and welfare" of himself, Grandma, and Lisa Marie, the sole heir. Witnesses to the will are Ginger, Charlie Hodge, and Beecher Smith's wife, Ann.

04 Friday

Elvis and his party of thirty arrive in Hawaii, checking into the Hilton Rainbow Tower. After two days Elvis and the Alden sisters and a couple of the guys move to a beach house at Kailua on the west side of Oahu.

12 Saturday

A visit to the USS *Arizona* memorial is canceled as Elvis prepares for an abruptly scheduled return to Memphis. He has gotten sand in his eye, and Dr. Nick, concerned that he may have scratched his cornea, suggests that he recuperate at home for a week or so before going out on tour again. He returns home—most likely on the following day—and confides to Larry Geller afterward that while the trip may have cost him $100,000, "What profiteth it to gain the world if you couldn't share your good fortune with your friends?"

22 Tuesday

Late in the evening Billy Smith is

Grandma, Lisa Marie, and Aunt Delta, Graceland, date unknown

The disappointing recording sessions at Graceland in October and the canceled Nashville sessions in January represent a major problem for producer Felton Jarvis. Needing to deliver a new album to RCA, he rents an eight-track machine and begins to record Elvis on tour. Because almost all of Elvis' show repertoire has by now been repeatedly released on records, Felton actually suggests titles for Elvis to sing but still gets only a handful of unfamiliar songs over the course of the tour. Ginger's absence seems to markedly affect Elvis' mood as the tour continues.

27 Sunday

★ *Taylor County Coliseum, Abilene, Texas*

Felton records "Trying to Get to You," "That's All Right," "My Way," and "Lawdy, Miss Clawdy" at this show.

28 Monday

★ *Municipal Auditorium, Austin, Texas*

29 Tuesday

★ *Rapides Parish Coliseum, Alexandria, Louisiana*

30 Wednesday

★ *Rapides Parish Coliseum, Alexandria*

Felton continues to record at this show. Both shows in Alexandria are very brief, and Elvis appears markedly tired as he stumbles through the lyrics of some of his most familiar songs. The lyric change on his closing number, "Can't Help Falling in Love," seems somewhat more than accidental, as he sings, "Wise men know/When it's time to go. . . ."

March Record Release

LP: *Welcome to My World* (#44). With no new recordings available, RCA puts out a compilation of previously released country material, which charts about as well as Elvis' recent newly recorded albums. In the aftermath of Elvis' death this album will soar to platinum status, obscuring any doubts about its worth or provenance.

barely able to rouse Elvis and get him on the plane to depart for his second tour of the year, and Dr. Nick is forced to put him on an IV. Ginger's absence seems to be the determining psychological factor.

23 Wednesday

★ *Arizona State University Activities Center, Tempe, Arizona*

Just before stepping out on stage, Elvis whispers to his cousin, "You didn't think I'd make it, did you?"—then puts on what Billy calls "a hell of a show."

24 Thursday

★ *Civic Center, Amarillo, Texas*

On this tour Elvis' stage wardrobe is limited to two jumpsuits that he can fit into: the white Aztec calendar design and a suit with a jeweled gold-and-blue spade motif.

25 Friday

★ *University of Oklahoma Lloyd Noble Center, Oklahoma City, Oklahoma*

26 Saturday

★ *University of Oklahoma Lloyd Noble Center, Oklahoma City*

31 Thursday

★ *Louisiana State University Assembly Center, Baton Rouge, Louisiana*

Elvis is unable to go on, and the last three days of the tour—sold-out shows in Mobile, Alabama; Macon, Georgia; and Jacksonville, Florida—are canceled as well. The tour up till now has grossed $994,881.42, with profits of $375,000 to be split two-thirds/one-third between Elvis and the Colonel, and the Colonel makes plans to add the canceled dates onto the first tour after the next one scheduled.

APRIL

01 Friday

Elvis returns to Memphis in the early-morning hours, going to Graceland before checking into the Memphis Baptist Hospital at 6:45 A.M.

04 Monday

The Colonel adds the canceled dates to the end of the fourth tour scheduled for 1977.

05 Tuesday

With his patient champing at the bit to go home (and hospitalization necessitated as much for show insurance purposes as by health concerns), Dr. Nick discharges him from the hospital. Elvis returns to Graceland at 5:00 A.M., and later in the day Priscilla and Lisa Marie fly in.

13 Wednesday

Elvis flies to Las Vegas with Alicia Kerwin, a twenty-year-old bank teller he has recently met, and his near-constant companions Billy and Jo Smith. They continue on to Palm Springs, where he buys Alicia a car but also experiences another episode of labored breathing that necessitates a call to Dr. Elias Ghanem, who flies in from Las Vegas to attend to his patient.

18 Monday

Elvis returns home.

21 Thursday

★ *Coliseum, Greensboro, North Carolina*

Elvis begins his third tour of 1977, this time accompanied by Ginger. In both fan and reviewer accounts of this tour Elvis is described as "seeming not to care," with a Detroit columnist simply writing, "He stunk the joint out."

22 Friday

★ *Olympia Stadium, Detroit, Michigan*

23 Saturday

★ *University of Toledo Centennial Hall, Toledo, Ohio*

Felton Jarvis continues the recording he started on the last tour.

24 Sunday

★ *Crisler Arena, Ann Arbor, Michigan*

Felton records "Unchained Melody" and "Little Darlin'," both of which will appear on the upcoming *Moody Blue* album.

25 Monday

★ *Civic Center, Saginaw, Michigan*

Felton records "If You Love Me," also for the upcoming *Moody Blue* album.

26 Tuesday

★ *Wings Stadium, Kalamazoo, Michigan*

The *National Enquirer* runs a grotesque cover picture of Elvis over the headline "Elvis' Bizarre Behavior and Secret Face Lift." The story itself rehashes an April 12 story in *The Star* headlined "Elvis, 42, Fears He's Losing His Sex Appeal." It is as if at this point Elvis is open season for the tabloids.

27 Wednesday

★ *Auditorium Arena, Milwaukee, Wisconsin*

Felton records selectively once again both on this night and each night through the end of the tour.

Elvis pays $5,000 on this date to settle the suit that Beverly Albrecq originally brought in 1973 when she suffered a broken ankle in a karate demonstration in Elvis' suite.

28 Thursday

★ *Brown County Veterans Memorial Coliseum, Green Bay, Wisconsin*

29 Friday

★ *Arena, Duluth, Minnesota*

To keep Ginger with him on the tour, Elvis flies in her mother and sister Rosemary.

The story breaks in the *Nashville Banner* that the Colonel is selling Elvis' management contract. "Authoritative" sources in Nashville, Memphis, and Los Angeles are cited, and the reason given is the Colonel's gambling debts. From St. Paul, where he is advancing the tour, the Colonel's reaction is instantaneous. "I'm here," he declares, "I'm working with Elvis, I'm in good health, and I don't have any debts—at least none that I can't pay." Nothing further ever comes of this, but one suspects that premature exposure of the Colonel's plan may have had as much to do with the lack of follow-through on it as any change of heart on the Colonel's part.

In order to guarantee Priscilla the $494,024.49 still owed her on the divorce settlement, a deed of trust to Graceland is issued to her for this amount.

30 Saturday

★ *Civic Center, St. Paul, Minnesota*

MAY

01 Sunday

★ *Chicago Stadium, Chicago, Illinois*

02 Monday

A lawsuit is filed on the part of Mike McMahon, current president of Center Courts, Inc. (formerly Presley Center Courts) because of Elvis' "failure to follow through with initial commitments which included loaning the corporation money." Joe Esposito and Dr. Nick appear to be plaintiffs in the original filing but very quickly remove themselves from the suit, which is resolved just two months later with what appears to be a loan by Elvis of a little less than $50,000.

★ *Chicago Stadium, Chicago*

TOM HULETT

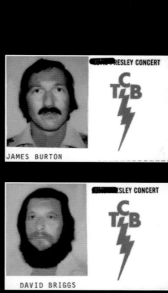

JAMES BURTON

KATHY WESTMORELAND

AL DVORIN

DAVID BRIGGS

MYRNA SMITH

DR. NICK

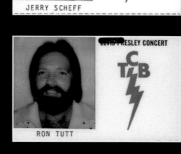

JERRY SCHEFF

ESTELLE BROWN

SAM THOMPSON

RON TUTT

SYLVIA SHEMWELL

JOE ESPOSITO

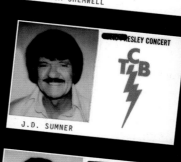

FELTON JARVIS

J.D. SUMNER

LAMAR FIKE

JACK KAHANE

Tour security badges, 1977

May–June 1977,
wearing the
Mexican
sundial suit

03 Tuesday

★ *Saginaw Center, Saginaw, Michigan*
After the show Elvis flies home to Memphis.

06 Friday

According to reports, Elvis shoots out his bedroom window. He spends most of the next two and a half weeks upstairs at Graceland, occasionally taking motorcycle rides on the Graceland grounds.

20 Friday

★ *University of Tennessee Stokely Athletic Center, Knoxville, Tennessee*
Another tour, the fourth of the year. Throughout the entire thirteen days he wears the same white jumpsuit with a gold Aztec calendar design. A doctor seeing him backstage reports that "he was pale, swollen—he had no stamina."

21 Saturday

★ *Freedom Hall, Louisville, Kentucky*

22 Sunday

★ *Capital Center Arena, Landover, Maryland*
During the show Elvis tosses two microphones to the ground and leaves the stage for what he refers to as "nature's call."

23 Monday

★ *Civic Center, Providence, Rhode Island*

24 Tuesday

★ *Civic Center, Augusta, Maine*

25 Wednesday

★ *Community War Memorial, Rochester, New York*

26 Thursday

★ *Broome County Veterans Memorial Arena, Binghamton, New York*
Ginger leaves the tour, and Elvis' mood, bad to begin with, appears, if anything, to steadily worsen.

27 Friday

★ *Broome County Veterans Memorial Arena, Binghamton*

28 Saturday
★ *Spectrum, Philadelphia, Pennsylvania*

29 Sunday
★ *Civic Center, Baltimore, Maryland*

Again, Elvis leaves the show in the middle of his performance, for thirty minutes this time, while the backup singers do their best to carry on. A building spokesman attributes his "murmuring, swearing, and unscheduled hiatus to the reported intestinal problems that had kayoed him" earlier, but according to *Variety*, "at the finale there was no ovation, and patrons exited shaking their heads and speculating on what was wrong with him."

30 Monday
★ *Coliseum, Jacksonville, Florida*

31 Tuesday
★ *Louisiana State University Assembly Center, Baton Rouge, Louisiana*

Newspapers in England and Australia begin to serialize Red and Sonny West's collaboration with Dave Hebler, *Elvis: What Happened?*, and fans around the world begin to exchange shocked phone calls about its contents.

JUNE

01 Wednesday
★ *Coliseum, Macon, Georgia*

The press announces that Elvis has signed a contract with CBS for a one-hour special in the fall. No further details are announced immediately, but the special is to be filmed at concerts on Elvis' next tour. The fee is $750,000, which will be split 50-50 between Elvis and the Colonel after $10,000 has been assigned to All Star Shows for promotional expenses. This is the first time the partnership deal dated January 22, 1976, is actually employed.

02 Thursday
★ *Municipal Auditorium, Mobile, Alabama*

Elvis returns to Memphis at the conclusion of the show.

This fourth tour grosses $2,309,841.60. Elvis' two-thirds of the profit comes to $798,762.75, but for the first time it is clearly stipulated that this division of money is only temporary and that all accounts will be settled by year's end, with the Colonel repaid all past and present moneys owed at that time.

04 Saturday
In Memphis Elvis presents both Kathy Westmoreland and Larry Geller with Lincoln Mark Vs as rewards for their continued loyalty.

13 Monday
Elvis puts in a call to President Jimmy Carter to try to help out his friend George Klein in a federal court case.

14 Tuesday
President Carter returns the call at 5:18 P.M. but reluctantly gives up after about ten minutes when he cannot understand Elvis' rambling, incoherent conversation. Elvis places another call Wednesday morning, but the president chooses not to take it.

17 Friday
★ *Southwest Missouri State University Hammons Center, Springfield, Missouri*

Elvis begins his fifth tour of the year, which will turn out to be his last. Ginger remains behind at the outset to watch her sister relinquish her Miss Tennessee crown, then joins him in Kansas City.

18 Saturday
★ *Kemper Arena, Kansas City, Missouri*

Elvis appears tired but announces to the crowd, "In spite of what you may hear or you may read, we're here, and we're healthy, and we're doing what we enjoy doing."

19 Sunday
★ *Civic Auditorium Arena, Omaha, Nebraska*

This concert is filmed and recorded for the CBS-TV special that will be

called *Elvis in Concert* and provide the basis for an RCA album of the same name. Just three songs from this evening's show will appear in the film, as it is one of the poorest shows Elvis has given to date, a sad and incoherent performance for the most part.

20 Monday
★ *Pershing Municipal Auditorium, Lincoln, Nebraska*

21 Tuesday
★ *Rushmore Plaza Civic Center, Rapid City, South Dakota*

This is the second show to be filmed for *Elvis in Concert* and is far better than the first. Perhaps the highlight of the show (although it is neither easy viewing nor listening) is Elvis' version of Roy Hamilton's "Unchained Melody," which will not be included in the television broadcast, though Elvis performs it in bravura fashion, alone at the piano, toward the end of the show.

22 Wednesday
★ *Arena, Sioux Falls, South Dakota*

23 Thursday
★ *Veterans Memorial Auditorium, Des Moines, Iowa*

Drummer Ronnie Tutt leaves the tour after tonight's show, citing a family crisis. He is replaced for one night by Sweet Inspirations drummer Jerome "Stump" Monroe, then by Larrie Londin on the final two nights of the tour.

24 Friday
★ *Dane County Coliseum, Madison, Wisconsin*

On the way to his hotel at 1:00 A.M., after flying in from Des Moines, Elvis has the limo driver stop the car so he can get out to assist a gas station attendant who is being set upon by two youths. "He was willing to fight," officer Thomas McCarthy is quoted in wire-service reports, "that's the bad part." All three participants, however, almost immediately subside into stunned silence when they recognize who the intervenor is, and Elvis subsequently poses with them for pictures.

Toward the end, with Charlie Hodge holding microphone, probably singing "Unchained Melody"

25 Saturday

★ *Riverfront Coliseum, Cincinnati, Ohio*
When the air-conditioning in his hotel fails, Elvis sets off down the street with his security detail trailing behind to look for a new hotel. After an energetic performance, he flies home to Memphis to get a good night's rest.

26 Sunday

★ *Market Square Arena, Indianapolis, Indiana*
On the Colonel's sixty-eighth birthday, Elvis gives what many remember as his finest performance in months,

---

June Record Release

Single: "Way Down" (#18) /"Pledging My Love" (shipped June 6). The last Elvis Presley single to be released during his lifetime would probably have placed about #30 on the charts and sold a respectable 300,000 copies, but his death will eventually push sales close to 900,000.

---

remaining on stage for approximately eighty minutes and ending with strong versions of "Hurt" and "Bridge Over Troubled Water." Upon arrival in Indianapolis he is presented with a plaque commemorating the pressing of the two billionth record at RCA's Indianapolis pressing plant, which comes during the manufacture of Elvis' new album, *Moody Blue*. After the show he and Ginger and a large party that includes friends and family return to Memphis.

JULY

01 Friday

Elvis is officially released from the racquetball court agreement. Most of this month will be spent upstairs at Graceland, where almost his only visitors are Billy and Jo Smith and Charlie Hodge. Dr. Nick is in attendance, and Ginger Alden comes and goes, but there are few others whom he sees on anything like a regular basis.

13 Wednesday

Elvis gives Ginger a Triumph sports car.

31 Sunday

Dick Grob brings Lisa Marie from Los Angeles for a two-week visit, which is scheduled to end just before the beginning of the next tour.

July Record Release

LP: *Moody Blue* (#3). Felton Jarvis pieces together this album from cuts from the Graceland sessions and songs recorded on the spring tour, having to add in the previously released "Let Me Be There" to make up a minimum ten-track selection. Elvis' death will make this album Elvis' most successful since the 1973 release of *Aloha from Hawaii*, and it will eventually sell more than two million copies.

AUGUST

04 Thursday

Elvis: What Happened? is published.

08 Monday

Elvis rents Libertyland, the renamed Fairgrounds, in the early-morning hours as a special treat for Lisa Marie, Ginger's niece, Amber, and a host of friends.

10 Wednesday

Elvis screens a number of films at the General Cinema in Whitehaven, including the James Bond picture *The Spy Who Loved Me.*

14 Sunday

Elvis and Ginger go motorcycling with Billy and Jo.

15 Monday

This is the day before Elvis is planning to leave to begin a tour scheduled to start in Portland, Maine, on the seventeenth. He awakens at about 4:00 P.M. and commissions Ricky Stanley to try to arrange a screening of *MacArthur*, starring Gregory Peck, but when a print cannot be found, he watches television instead until it is time for a 10:30 P.M. dentist appointment with Dr. Lester Hofman. Dressed in a black DEA (Drug Enforcement Agency) sweatsuit with two .45s stuck in the waistband of his pants, he leaves with Ginger to have his teeth cleaned and a couple of small cavities filled.

16 Tuesday

Elvis and Ginger return to Graceland soon after midnight. At about 2:15 A.M. Elvis calls Dr. Nick to request some painkillers because the fillings he has just had are bothering him, and his stepbrother, Ricky Stanley, is sent to the hospital pharmacy with a prescription for six Dilaudid tablets. A couple of hours later Elvis awakens Billy and Jo with a phone call to see if they will play racquetball. The game between Elvis and Billy is short-lived, but before leaving the racquetball building Elvis sits down at the piano and sings a couple of

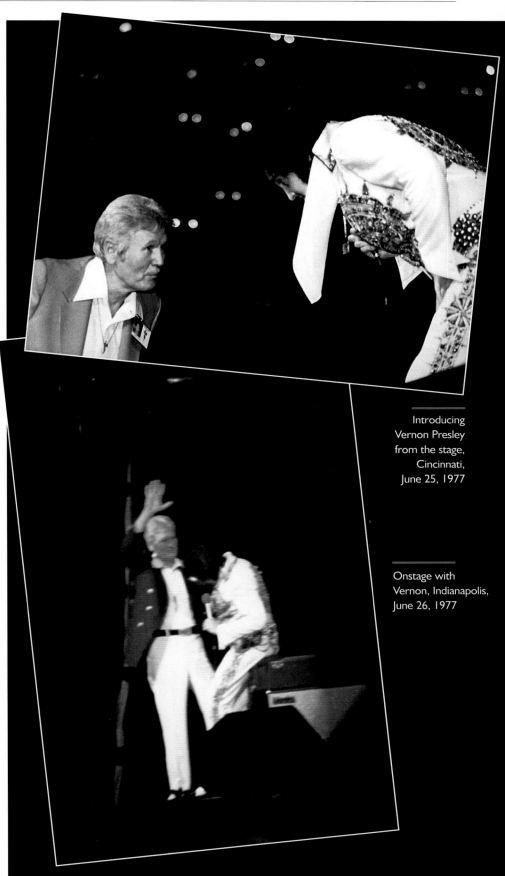

Introducing Vernon Presley from the stage, Cincinnati, June 25, 1977

Onstage with Vernon, Indianapolis, June 26, 1977

Leaving the stage with Joe Esposito and Ed Parker *(rear)*

Vernon at Elvis' grave, Graceland

gospel numbers and the old country song recently popularized by Willie Nelson, "Blue Eyes Crying in the Rain."

Back in his bedroom Elvis takes the first of three packets of sleeping pills, depressants, and placebos prescribed for him nightly by Dr. Nick, and a few hours later takes the second. In the morning he calls for a third, and when his aunt Delta brings it to him, Elvis tells her he plans to get up at around 7:00 P.M. When Ginger awakens at about 1:30 P.M., Elvis is not in bed, and she discovers him shortly thereafter lying facedown in a pool of vomit on the bathroom floor. An ambulance rushes him to Baptist Memorial Hospital, where all efforts to revive him fail and his death is recorded at 3:30 P.M. An autopsy will begin at 7:00 P.M., but long before it is completed, the press is informed that Elvis has died of "cardiac arrhythmia due to undetermined heartbeat." Because the results of the autopsy will remain private, a debate over the real causes of Elvis' death will rage for years, right up to the present day, but the two principal lab reports filed two months later will argue convincingly that the underlying cause of his death was polypharmacy, and the Bio-Science Laboratory report, under-

taken under a false name as a "blind" study, indicates the detection of fourteen drugs in Elvis' system, ten in significant quantity.

17 Wednesday

At Vernon's request Larry Geller and Charlie Hodge fix Elvis' hair at the Memphis Funeral Home. Vernon has also insisted that there will be a viewing at Graceland for the fans, who have been gathering outside since news of Elvis' death and by now have swelled to an estimated 50,000. At 3:00 P.M. the mourners begin filing in, from every location and every walk of life, passing by the open copper casket that lies in the front hallway in a steady, tearful stream. Because the number is so large, viewing is extended from 5:00 to 6:30 P.M., after which the coffin is moved into the living room for a private viewing by family and close friends. Sam Thompson and then Dick Grob remain by the body throughout the night.

18 Thursday

The 2:00 P.M. service is held in the living room of Graceland, led by the Reverend C. W. Bradley of the Wooddale Church of Christ, who barely knew Elvis but has been asked by Ver-

non to preside because he was Vernon's ex-wife Dee's pastor. Televangelist Rex Humbard offers a guest sermon, and comedian Jackie Kahane delivers an informal eulogy composed on the plane. J. D. Sumner and the Stamps, the Statesmen, Jake Hess, James Blackwood, and Kathy Westmoreland all perform some of Elvis' favorite hymns in a ceremony that extends far beyond the half hour allotted. The body is carried in a white hearse, followed by seventeen white limousines, to the Forest Hill cemetery, where, after a brief service in the mausoleum chapel, Elvis is interred in a crypt a few hundred yards from his mother's grave.

OCTOBER

02 Sunday

The bodies of both Elvis and Gladys Presley are moved under Sam Thompson's supervision to the Meditation Garden behind Graceland.

03 Monday

The CBS special shot in June airs. In the sobering words of Sweet Inspiration Myrna Smith, "The night of the show I told Jerry Schilling [on the phone], 'It really went great.' He said, 'Well, how did Elvis look?' I said, 'He really looks good. He's lost a little weight.' But afterwards, when I watched it, I just burst out crying. We were all wearing blinders."

October Record Release

Double Album: *Elvis in Concert* (#5). The soundtrack to the special is released in the wake of unparalleled demand for new Elvis material and quickly achieves platinum status, selling 1.5 million copies.

September 8, 1954
(© Opal Walker)

INDEX

Page numbers in italics indicate illustrations.

reaction to erratic behavior, 207, 209, 227–28, 343
and record contract acquisition, 31, 32–33, 35, 41, 43–44, 53–54
in record contracts and agreements, 54, 86, 110, 145, 173, 180, 210–11, 226, 251, 263, 264, 285, 292, 321, 323
and recording session schedule, 98, 121, 122, 129, 130, 140, 175
and record releases, 84, 137, 154, 172, 173, 183, 204, 215, 249, 323, 332
relationship with Elvis, 105, 199–200, 268, 321, 328
representation agreements of, 44, 45, 50, 64
and satellite television broadcast, 310, 312
and song selection, 130, 137, 152, 168–69, 175, 249
spoken-word record release of, 339
on stage behavior, 44–45, 54–55, 56, 61, 70, 110, 262
and television bookings, 34, 56, 103, 104–5, 106, 108, 183, 236, 239
and Tommy Sands, 27, 33
and tour advance, 279, 308
and tour bookings, 31, 40, 41, 43, 50, 71, 262, 277, 279, 298, 322, 333
and variety show format, 72
and wedding of Elvis and Priscilla, 228
Parker (M.B.) Company, 12, 14
Pasetta, Marty, 319
Pasternak, Joe, 199, 213
"Patch It Up," 280
Patton, 265
Payne, Leon, 41
"Peace in the Valley," 95
Peace in the Valley, 103, 159
Pearl, Minnie, 167
Penn, Dan, 254
Pepper, Gary, 157
Perkins, Carl, 21, 53, 56, 61, 66, 67, 73
in "Million Dollar Quartet" session, 92, 93
Perryman, Tom, 24, 46, 115
Person, Mennie, 351
Peter, Paul and Mary, 215, 292
Peters, Gerald, 293
Peters, Jon, 347
Peterson, Ray, 267
Phillips, Dewey, 31, 64, 80, 83, 89, 94, 102, 111
airing of "That's All Right," 18–19
in California, 105
death of, 250
fired from WHBQ, 117, 123
Hippodrome anniversary show of, 21
radio show of, 8, 70
Phillips, Sam, 8, 12, 13, 17, 18, 19, 26, 27, 30, 31, 40, 49, 52, 99, 102, 164, 165, 259
"Pieces of My Life," 353
Pierce, Webb, 22, 39, 44, 59
Pietrafeso, Ron, 281, 356, 357
"Playing For Keeps," 96
"Please Don't Drag That String Around," 186
"Please Don't Stop Loving Me," 215
"Pledging My Love," 376
Poems That Touch the Heart, 124
Pointer Sisters, 346
"Polk Salad Annie," 266, 267
Pomus, Doc, 158, 169, 187
"Poor Boy," 83, 91

Popsie (William S. Randolph), 44
Porter, Bill, 151, 262
Porter, Cole, 175
Porter, David, 212
Post, Leon, 28
Pot Luck, 167, 169, 197, 206, 208
production, 175
release, 178
Potomac, USS, purchase and donation of, 193–94, 193
Precision Tool, 12, 14, 15
Prell, Milton, 173, 229
Presley, Dee Stanley (stepmother), 127, 139, 140, 145, 152, 182, 184, 210, 263, 308, 330
marriage to Vernon, 155
on movie set, 232, 233
separation from Vernon, 336
Presley, Elvis Aron
on acting, 235
and African Americans, 76, 93, 109
airplanes of, 178, 346, 347, 351, 353, 354, 355, 363
amphetamine use by, 161
animal menagerie of, 158, 171, 177
and Ann-Margret, 187–88, 187, 188, 191, 230
army service of
in basic training, 121
departure for Germany, 124, 125, 126, 126
discharge from, 145, 146, 147
and draft notice, 116
and draft status, 95
in Germany, 8, 126–45
homecoming from, 141, 147, 148
at induction, 120–21, 120
Munich furlough during, 133, 134, 137
offbase housing during, 122–23, 126, 127, 130, 132, 132, 136, 138, 139
Paris furlough during, 137, 137, 139, 143–44
promotions during, 129, 137, 144
assassination/kidnapping threats against, 277
automobiles of. See Automobiles/vehicles
awards and honors
Grammy, 227, 306, 338
Jaycee, 287, 289–91, 289, 290, 291
lifetime achievement (NARAS), 197, 297–98
and Beatles, 193, 202, 207, 208, 212
birth of, 1, 236
birth of Lisa Marie, 238
birthday celebrations, 8, 59, 95, 131, 143, 173, 193, 203, 213, 225, 237, 331, 369
book selections of, 186, 215
on career goals, 180
charitable donations of, 93, 99, 102, 105, 109, 112, 115–16, 161, 164, 193–94, 193, 202, 206, 211, 221, 223, 235, 245, 283, 317, 339
in charity shows, 161, 162, 163, 165, 167–68, 167, 316, 319, 345–46
childhood and youth, 1, 3, 9, 12
guitar playing in, 4–5, 7

moving during, 1, 2–3, 4, 5, 6, 7, 8, 9, 10, 11–12
musical talent of, 2, 4–5, 6, 8, 12
in school, 3, 5–6, 6, 7, 8, 9, 12
and Christmas gift exchanges, 130, 141, 182, 202, 211, 223, 236, 252, 264, 287, 317, 330, 355
cosmetic surgery of, 349
costumes and dress, 9, 13, 14, 37, 50, 69, 72, 86, 99, 100, 101, 102, 180, 184, 185, 241, 245, 267, 275, 287, 298, 302, 308, 317, 319, 320, 321, 323, 363
criticism of physical appearance, 164, 192, 221
death of, 377, 379
death of mother, 123–24
dental treatment of, 86, 88, 104, 105, 184, 324, 331, 332, 377
deterioration of appearance and performances, 324, 326, 327, 360, 361, 363, 366–67, 371–72, 374
dog of, 351, 352, 354
employees of. See Entourage; specific names
employment of, 9, 10, 12, 14, 15, 19
erratic behavior of, 207, 209, 227–28, 332, 339–40, 343, 351, 359, 365, 366
eye problems of, 292, 370
and F.B.I., 287, 363
financial problems of, 354–55
first LP of, 67
first single of, 18–19
and folk music, 215
funeral of, 379
gold "championship" belt of, 277, 278, 292, 308
and gospel music, 13, 14, 80, 104, 110, 144, 159, 215, 218, 258, 305
grave of, 379, 379
guitars of, 4–5, 21, 23, 42, 130, 215
guns of, 80, 277, 280, 281, 283, 285, 287, 289, 290, 292, 298, 299, 365
in Hawaii, 114–15, 176–77, 207, 241, 257, 262, 263, 308, 316, 319, 321, 370
health of, 137, 200, 293, 295, 297, 298, 310, 321–22, 324, 328, 329, 332, 342, 343, 346, 353, 372
homes of. See Graceland; Homes
income of, 9, 12, 14, 19, 30, 49, 71, 105, 130, 172, 182, 192, 202, 223, 236, 252, 264, 269, 287, 301, 317, 330, 343
injuries to, 135, 157, 228, 366
Jewish background of, 202
and karate, 141, 143–44, 143, 156, 189, 241, 262, 263, 267, 292, 295, 296, 323, 324, 326, 327, 328, 337–38, 337, 340–41, 341
karate movie plan of, 341, 343
in Las Vegas. See Las Vegas (Nevada); Las Vegas Hilton (International Hotel)
LSD use by, 207, 212
management contracts
with Bob Neal, 26, 27
with Colonel Parker, 67, 214, 225, 226, 298–99, 304, 304, 323, 358, 360, 372

with Scotty Moore, 17, 19
and Martin Luther King assassination, 239
on meaning of success, 204
on movie career, 310
negative publicity about performances, 73, 75, 77, 80, 102, 113
in New York, 60–61, 62, 65–67, 308, 309, 310
and Nixon, 284, 286–87
paternity suit against, 275, 280, 281, 285, 300, 304
police badges of, 200, 280, 281, 282, 283, 286–87, 286, 360
police equipment of, 289
police friends of, 147, 159, 159, 281, 356, 357, 358
prescription drug abuse by, 324, 329, 346
on pressures of success, 103, 105, 124
and Priscilla Beaulieu, 178, 182, 183, 184, 186, 191, 192, 211, 212, 214, 223
breakdown of marriage, 263, 269, 299, 301, 310, 322
divorce settlement with, 312, 324, 325, 329, 329, 372
engagement of, 223
first meeting with, 140
in Germany, 140, 141, 141, 142, 143, 145
rumors of marriage, 221
wedding of, 228, 229–30, 230, 231
pseudonyms of
Burrows, John, 299, 301
Carpenter, John, 257, 271, 273, 308
Reno, Clint, 84
in racquetball venture, 359, 361, 363, 372
recreation and hobbies. See Recreational activities
relationship with Colonel Parker, 105, 199–200, 268, 321, 328
relationship with father, 155
relationship with Larry Geller, 197, 200
relationship with mother, 2, 5
in seclusion at Graceland, 345, 362, 374
skin treatments of, 141
sound system of, 267, 277, 279
spiritual studies of, 197, 198, 202, 204, 215, 228, 229, 293, 298
with Starlite Wranglers, 17–18, 19
tax payments of, 173–74
on teenage fans, 72, 77, 80, 89
weight of, 297, 319, 324, 326
will of, 370
See also Motion pictures; Recording sessions; Television; Tour dates
Presley, Gladys Love Smith (mother), 1, 3, 18, 24, 40, 41, 42, 48, 50, 79, 80, 120, 217
at Audubon Drive, 65, 78, 94
Cadillac of, 64
at contract signings, 19, 23, 54, 54
death of, 123
employment and income of, 1, 7, 9, 11
funeral of, 123–24
at gospel shows, 14
at Graceland, 98–99, 105, 108, 122
grave of, 127, 147, 147, 149, 202, 238, 379